S0-BOM-660

WORD BIBLICAL COMMENTARY

WORD BIBLICAL COMMENTARY

VOLUME 50

Jude, 2 Peter

RICHARD J. BAUCKHAM

WORD BOOKS, PUBLISHER • WACO, TEXAS

Word Biblical Commentary:
JUDE, 2 PETER

Library of Congress Cataloging in Publication Data
Main entry under title:

Word biblical commentary.

Includes bibliographies.
1. Bible—Commentaries—Collected works.
BS491.2.W67 220.7′7 81–71768
ISBN 0–8499–0249–5 (v. 50) AACR2

Printed in the United States of America

89801239 AGF 987654

To My Mother
and in Memory of My Father

Contents

Editorial Preface

The launching of the *Word Biblical Commentary* brings to fulfillment an enterprise of several years' planning. The publishers and the members of the editorial board met in 1977 to explore the possibility of a new commentary on the books of the Bible that would incorporate several distinctive features. Prospective readers of these volumes are entitled to know what such features were intended to be; whether the aims of the commentary have been fully achieved time alone will tell.

First, we have tried to cast a wide net to include as contributors a number of scholars from around the world who not only share our aims, but are in the main engaged in the ministry of teaching in university, college, and seminary. They represent a rich diversity of denominational allegiance. The broad stance of our contributors can rightly be called evangelical, and this term is to be understood in its positive, historic sense of a commitment to scripture as divine revelation, and to the truth and power of the Christian gospel.

Then, the commentaries in our series are all commissioned and written for the purpose of inclusion in the *Word Biblical Commentary.* Unlike several of our distinguished counterparts in the field of commentary writing, there are no translated works, originally written in a non-English language. Also, our commentators were asked to prepare their own rendering of the original biblical text and to use those languages as the basis of their own comments and exegesis. What may be claimed as distinctive with this series is that it is based on the biblical languages, yet it seeks to make the technical and scholarly approach to a theological understanding of scripture understandable by—and useful to—the fledgling student, the working minister as well as to colleagues in the guild of professional scholars and teachers.

Finally, a word must be said about the format of the series. The layout in clearly defined sections has been consciously devised to assist readers at different levels. Those wishing to learn about the textual witnesses on which the translation is offered are invited to consult the section headed "Notes." If the readers' concern is with the state of modern scholarship on any given portion of scripture, then they should turn to the sections on "Bibliography" and "Form/Structure/Setting." For a clear exposition of the passage's meaning and its relevance to the ongoing biblical revelation, the "Comment" and concluding "Explanation" are designed expressly to meet that need. There is therefore something for everyone who may pick up and use these volumes.

If these aims come anywhere near realization, the intention of the editors will have been met, and the labor of our team of contributors rewarded.

General Editors: *David A. Hubbard*
Glenn W. Barker †
Old Testament: *John D. W. Watts*
New Testament: *Ralph P. Martin*

Author's Preface

No NT books have been more neglected by scholars than Jude and 2 Peter. Most of the conventional scholarly opinions about them derive from a past era of NT scholarship. This commentary is therefore an attempt to drag the study of these two books into the 1980s. Although I am deeply indebted to a few important recent contributions to the understanding of Jude and 2 Peter (such as those of Fornberg, Neyrey and Ellis), for the most part I have been unable to draw on the mass of recent research in articles and monographs which is available to commentators on most other NT books. Consequently I regard this commentary as in many respects an exploratory work, opening up lines of thought and investigation which I hope others will discuss and pursue further, whethei or not they confirm my conclusions.

The general scholarly neglect of these books probably reflects the conventional judgments that they are late in date and of little theological value. Yet, even if these judgments were correct, Jude and 2 Peter would still be valuable evidence of the early history of Christianity. Any Christian document from the first century and a half of Christian history is relevant to the investigation of Christian origins and deserves the closest study for that reason alone. If my conclusions about the background and character of the two works are correct, then their historical interest is considerable: Jude offers a rare glimpse into those original Palestinian Christian circles in which Jesus' own blood-relations were leaders, and 2 Peter documents the way in which one form of early Christianity managed the difficult transition from the apostolic to the postapostolic generation. I hope this commentary also shows that these two books do not deserve the contempt with which scholars have all too often regarded them. Of course they do not have the central theological importance of the Gospels or the Pauline letters, but when a serious and patient attempt is made to understand them in their own terms, they can be seen to be worthy of their place in the canon of Scripture and to make their own distinctive contributions to the message of the Word of God even today. The moral imperative of the Gospel still needs to be urged in opposition to ethical libertinism, and the Christian eschatological hope still needs to be sustained in the face of shallow skepticism.

Among those who have given me generous assistance, in various ways, during the preparation of this commentary, I should like to thank Dr. Loveday Alexander, Dr. Philip Alexander, Mr. Malcolm Harrison, Dr. John Kane, Professor C. F. D. Moule, Miss Gillian Shepherd, Dr. Terry Smith, and Dr. David Wenham.

University of Manchester,
November 1981

RICHARD BAUCKHAM

Note: The author has written his commentary using the sequence of books Jude–2 Peter, thereby departing from the order in modern editions of the NT. The reason for this change lies in his argument that Jude was in fact written first, and that 2 Peter shows signs of literary dependence on the earlier work. This explains the sequence followed in the subsequent pages.

All references to the LXX are to A. Rahlfs ed. *Septuaginta: Id est Vetus Testamentum graece iuxta LXX interpretes.* 2 vols. 8th ed. Stuttgart: Wurttembergische Bibelanstalt, 1965.

Biblical and other translations are the author's own unless otherwise indicated.

Abbreviations

Ancient literature

ʾAbot R. Nat.	*ʾAbot de Rabbi Nathan*
Acts John	*Acts of John*
Acts Paul	*Acts of Paul*
PH	Hamburg Papyrus of the *Acts of Paul*
Acts Paul & Thecla	*Acts of Paul and Thecla*
Acts Pet.	*Acts of Peter*
Acts Thom.	*Acts of Thomas*
Act. Verc.	*Actus Vercellenses* (Latin version of the *Acts of Peter*)
Adam and Eve	*Vita Adae et Evae*
Andr. Caes.	Andreas Caesariensis (Andrew of Caesarea)
Ap. John	*Apocryphon of John*
Apoc. Abr.	*Apocalypse of Abraham*
2 Apoc. Bar.	Syriac *Apocalypse of Baruch*
3 Apoc. Bar.	Greek *Apocalypse of Baruch*
Apoc. El.	Coptic *Apocalypse of Elijah*
Apoc. Paul	*Apocalypse of Paul*
Apoc. Pet.	*Apocalypse of Peter*
Apoc. Pet. A	*Apocalypse of Peter:* Greek fragment from Akhmim
Apoc. Pet. B	*Apocalypse of Peter:* Bodleian fragment
Apoc. Pet. E	*Apocalypse of Peter:* Ethiopic version
Apoc. Pet. R	*Apocalypse of Peter:* Rainer fragment
Apoc. Thom.	*Apocalypse of Thomas*
Asc. Isa.	*Ascension of Isaiah*
As. Mos.	*Assumption of Moses*
b. ʿAbod. Zar.	Babylonian Talmud tractate *ʿAboda Zara*
Bar	Baruch (1 Baruch)
Barn.	*Epistle of Barnabas*
b. B. Bat.	Babylonian Talmud tractate *Baba Batra*
b. B. Meṣ.	Babylonian Talmud tractate *Baba Meṣiʿa*
BG	Berlin Gnostic Codex
b. Ḥag.	Babylonian Talmud tractate *Ḥagiga*
Bib. Ant.	Pseudo-Philo, *Liber Antiquitatum Biblicarum*
b. Ketub.	Babylonian Talmud tractate *Ketubot*
b. Menaḥ	Babylonian Talmud tractate *Menaḥot*
b. Qidd.	Babylonian Talmud tractate *Qiddušin*
b. Šabb.	Babylonian Talmud tractate *Šabbat*
b. Sanh.	Babylonian Talmud tractate *Sanhedrin*
b. Yoma	Babylonian Talmud tractate *Yoma*
Cant	Canticles (Song of Songs)
Cant. Rab.	*Midraš Rabbah* on Canticles

CG	Nag Hammadi Gnostic Codices
1 Chr	1 Chronicles
2 Chr	2 Chronicles
1 Clem.	*1 Clement*
2 Clem.	*2 Clement*
Clem. Alex.	Clement of Alexandria
Clem. Hom.	Pseudo-Clementine *Homilies*
Clem. Rec.	Pseudo-Clementine *Recognitions*
Col	Colossians
1 Cor	1 Corinthians
2 Cor	2 Corinthians
"3 Cor."	Apocryphal correspondence of Paul and the Corinthians
Corp. Herm.	*Corpus Hermeticum*
Dan	Daniel
Deut	Deuteronomy
Diogn.	*Epistle to Diognetus*
Eccl	Ecclesiastes
Eccl. Rab.	*Midraš Rabbah* on Ecclesiastes
1 Enoch	*Apocalypse of Enoch* (Ethiopic + Greek and Aramaic fragments)
2 Enoch	Slavonic *Apocalypse of Enoch*
Ep. Apost.	*Epistle of the Apostles*
Ep. Arist.	*Epistle of Aristeas*
Ep. Pet. Phil.	*Epistle of Peter to Philip* (CG 8,2)
Eph	Ephesians
Ep Jer	Epistle of Jeremiah
1 Esdr	1 Esdras (LXX)
Esth	Esther
Exod	Exodus
Ezek	Ezekiel
Frg. Tg.	*Fragmentary Targum*
Gal	Galatians
Gen	Genesis
Gen. Rab.	*Midraš Rabbah* on Genesis
Gnostic *Apoc. Pet.*	*Apocalypse of Peter* (CG 7,3)
Gos. Eb.	*Gospel of the Ebionites*
Gos. Eg.	*Gospel of the Egyptians* (CG 3,2 and 4,2)
Gos. Heb.	*Gospel of the Hebrews*
Gos. Pet.	*Gospel of Peter*
Gos. Phil.	*Gospel of Philip* (CG 2,3)
Gos. Thom.	*Gospel of Thomas* (CG 2,2)
Gos. Truth	*Gospel of Truth* (CG 1,3 and 12,2)
Hab	Habakkuk
Hag	Haggai
Heb	Hebrews
Herm. *Mand.*	Hermas, *The Shepherd: Mandates*
Herm. *Sim.*	Hermas, *The Shepherd: Similitudes*
Herm. *Vis.*	Hermas, *The Shepherd: Visions*
Hos	Hosea
Ign. *Eph.*	Ignatius, *Letter to the Ephesians*
Ign. *Magn.*	Ignatius, *Letter to the Magnesians*
Ign. *Phld.*	Ignatius, *Letter to the Philadelphians*
Ign. *Pol.*	Ignatius, *Letter to Polycarp*
Ign. *Rom.*	Ignatius, *Letter to the Romans*
Ign. *Smyrn.*	Ignatius, *Letter to the Smyrnaeans*
Isa	Isaiah
Jas	James
Jdt	Judith
Jer	Jeremiah
Josephus, *Ant.*	Josephus, *Antiquitates Judaicae*
Josephus, *BJ*	Josephus, *Bellum Judaicum*

Josephus, *C. Apion.*	Josephus, *Contra Apionem*
Josephus, *Vit.*	Josephus, *Vita*
Josh	Joshua
Judg	Judges
Ker. Pet.	*Kerygma Petrou*
1 Kgdms	1 Kingdoms (LXX = 1 Sam)
2 Kgdms	2 Kingdoms (LXX = 2 Sam)
3 Kgdms	3 Kingdoms (LXX = 1 Kgs)
4 Kgdms	4 Kingdoms (LXX = 2 Kgs)
1 Kgs	1 Kings
2 Kgs	2 Kings
Lam	Lamentations
Lev	Leviticus
Lev. Rab.	*Midraš Rabbah* on Leviticus
LXX	Septuagint
1 Macc	1 Maccabees
2 Macc	2 Maccabees
3 Macc	3 Maccabees
4 Macc	4 Maccabees
Mal	Malachi
Mart. Pol.	*Martyrdom of Polycarp* (Letter of the Smyrnaeans)
Matt	Matthew
Mek.	*Mekilta*
Mic	Micah
Midr. Ps.	*Midraš on Psalms*
m. Sanh.	Mishna tractate *Sanhedrin*
m. Soṭa	Mishna tractate *Soṭa*
MT	Masoretic text
Nah	Nahum
Neh	Nehemiah
NT	New Testament
Num	Numbers
Num. Rab.	*Midraš Rabbah* on Numbers
Obad	Obadiah
Odes Sol.	*Odes of Solomon*
OT	Old Testament
Pap. Oxy.	Oxyrhynchus Papyrus
Paral. Jer.	*Paraleipomena Jeremiou*
Pesiq. R.	*Pesiqta Rabbati*

1 Pet	1 Peter
2 Pet	2 Peter
Phil	Philippians
Philo, *Abr.*	Philo, *De Abrahamo*
Philo, *Agr.*	Philo, *De Agricultura*
Philo, *Cher.*	Philo, *De Cherubim*
Philo, *Conf.*	Philo, *De Confusione Linguarum*
Philo, *Decal.*	Philo, *De Decalogo*
Philo, *Det.*	Philo, *Quod Deterius Potiori insidiari soleat*
Philo, *Ebr.*	Philo, *De Ebrietate*
Philo, *Gig.*	Philo, *De Gigantibus*
Philo, *Leg. All.*	Philo, *Legum Allegoriarum*
Philo, *Mig.*	Philo, *De Migratione Abrahami*
Philo, *Mos.*	Philo, *De Vita Mosis*
Philo, *Mut.*	Philo, *De Mutatione Nominum*
Philo, *Plant.*	Philo, *De Plantatione*
Philo, *Post.*	Philo, *De Posteritati Caini*
Philo, *Praem.*	Philo, *De Praemiis et Poenis*
Philo, *Quaest. Gen.*	Philo, *Quaestiones et Solutiones in Genesin*
Philo, *Quaest. Exod.*	Philo, *Quaestiones et Solutiones in Exodum*
Philo, *Quis Her.*	Philo, *Quis rerum divinarum Heres sit*
Philo, *Sob.*	Philo, *De Sobrietate*
Philo, *Som.*	Philo, *De Somniis*
Philo, *Spec. Leg.*	Philo, *De Specialibus Legibus*
Philem	Philemon
Pirqe ʾAboṯ	Sayings of the (Jewish) Fathers (in the Mishna)
Pirqe R. El.	*Pirqe Rabbi Eliezer*

Pol. *Phil.*	Polycarp, *Letter to the Philippians*
Pr Man	Prayer of Manasseh
Prot. Jas.	*Protevangelium of James*
Prov	Proverbs
Pr. Thanks.	*Prayer of Thanksgiving* (CG 6,7)
Ps, Pss	Psalm, Psalms
Pss. Sol.	*Psalms of Solomon*
4Q 176, 177, 182, 183	Texts from Qumran Cave 4
4Q *ʿAmram*	*Testament of Amram* (*Visions of ʿAmram*) from Qumran Cave 4
1QapGen	*Genesis Apocryphon* from Qumran Cave 1
4QDibHam	*Words of the Heavenly Lights* from Qumran Cave 4
4QEn	Aramaic fragments of *1 Enoch* from Qumran Cave 4
4QFlor	*Florilegium* from Qumran Cave 4
1QH	*Hodayot* (*Thanksgiving Hymns*) from Qumran Cave 1
1QM	*Milḥamah* (*War Scroll*) from Qumran Cave 1
11QMelch	*Melchizedek* text from Qumran Cave 11
1QpHab	*Pesher on Habakkuk* from Qumran Cave 1
4QpIsa[a,b,c]	*Pesharim on Isaiah* from Qumran Cave 4
4QpNah	*Pesher on Nahum* from Qumran Cave 4
11QpPs[a]Zion	*Hymn to Zion* in the Psalms Scroll from Qumran Cave 11
1QS	*Serek hayyaḥad* (*Community Rule*) from Qumran Cave 1
4QTestim	*Testimonia* text from Qumran Cave 4
Rev	Revelation
Rom	Romans
1 Sam	1 Samuel
2 Sam	2 Samuel
Sib. Or.	*Sibylline Oracles*
Sir	Ben Sira (Ecclesiasticus)
T. Abr.	*Testament of Abraham*
T. Asher	*Testament of Asher*
T. Benj.	*Testament of Benjamin*
T. Dan	*Testament of Dan*
Testim. Truth	*Testimony of Truth* (CG 9, 3)
Tg., Tgs.	Targum, Targums
T. Gad	*Testament of Gad*
Tg. Neof.	*Targum Neofiti 1*
Tg. Ps.-J.	*Targum Pseudo-Jonathan*
1 Thess	1 Thessalonians
2 Thess	2 Thessalonians
Thom. Cont.	*Book of Thomas the Contender* (CG 2,7)
T. Iss.	*Testament of Issachar*
T. Job	*Testament of Job*
T. Jos.	*Testament of Joseph*
T. Jud.	*Testament of Judah*
T. Levi	*Testament of Levi*
T. Mos.	*Testament of Moses* (often called *Assumption of Moses*)

T. Napht. — *Testament of Naphtali*
Tob — Tobit
T. 12 Patr. — *Testaments of the Twelve Patriarchs*
Treat. Seth — *Second Treatise of the Great Seth* (CG 7,2)
T. Reub. — *Testament of Reuben*
T. Sim. — *Testament of Simeon*
t. Soṭa — Tosephta tractate *Sota*
T. Zeb. — *Testament of Zebulun*
Wis — Wisdom of Solomon
Yal. Rub. — *Yalquṭ Rubeni*
Yal. Šimʿoni — *Yalquṭ Šimʿoni*
y. Sanh. — Jerusalem Talmud tractate *Sanhedrin*
y. Taʿan. — Jerusalem Talmud tractate *Taʿanit*
Zech — Zechariah
Zeph — Zephaniah
θ — Theodotion's version

Modern serials, journals, reference works, Bible versions

AnBib — Analecta biblica
APOT — R. H. Charles ed., *Apocrypha and Pseudepigrapha of the Old Testament*
ATANT — Abhandlungen zur Theologie des Alten und Neuen Testaments
AV — Authorized (King James) Version
BAG — W. Bauer, W. F. Arndt, and F. W. Gingrich, *Greek-English Lexicon of the NT*
BaL — Bampton Lectures
BDF — F. Blass, A. Debrunner, and R. W. Funk, *A Greek Grammar of the NT*
BFCT — Beiträge zur Förderung christlicher Theologie
BHT — Beiträge zur historischen Theologie
Bib — *Biblica*
BNTC — Black's New Testament Commentaries
BOS — Bonner Orientalistischen Studien
BTN — Bibliotheca Theologica Norvegica
BZ — *Biblische Zeitschrift*
BZAW — Beihefte zur *ZAW*
BZNW — Beihefte zur *ZNW*
BZRGG — Beihefte zur *Zeitschrift für Religions- und Geistesgeschichte*
CACat — Collezione "Amici delle Catacombe"
CBC — Cambridge Bible Commentary
CBQ — *Catholic Biblical Quarterly*
CBQMS — Catholic Biblical Quarterly-Monograph Series
CBSC — Cambridge Bible for Schools and Colleges
CDios — *Ciudad de Dios*
CGTSC — Cambridge Greek Testament for Schools and Colleges
ConB. NT — Coniectanea biblica. NT Series
ConNT — *Coniectanea neotestamentica*
CThM — Calwer theologische Monographien
DAC — J. Hastings ed., *Dictionary of the Apostolic Church*
DB(H) — J. Hastings ed., *Dictionary of the Bible*
DBSup — L. Pirot, H. Cazelles, and A. Feuillet ed., *Supplément au Dictionnaire de la Bible*
DB(V) — F. Vigoroux and L. Pirot ed., *Dictionnaire de la Bible*
DMOA — Documenta et Monumenta Orientis Antiqui
EBib — Etudes bibliques
EE — *Estudios ecclesiásticos*
EvQ — *Evangelical Quarterly*
Exp — *The Expositor*
ExpB — Expositor's Bible

ExpTim	*Expository Times*
FRLANT	Forschungen zur Religion und Literatur des Alten und Neuen Testaments
GCS	Griechische christliche Schriftsteller
GNB	Good News Bible
GRBS	*Greek, Roman, and Byzantine Studies*
HKNT	Handkommentar zum Neuen Testament
HNT	Handbuch zum Neuen Testament
HTKNT	Herders theologischer Kommentar zum Neuen Testament
HTR	*Harvard Theological Review*
HUCA	*Hebrew Union College Annual*
ICC	International Critical Commentary
JB	Jerusalem Bible
JBL	*Journal of Biblical Literature*
JJS	*Journal of Jewish Studies*
JNES	*Journal of Near Eastern Studies*
JP	*Journal of Philology*
JSJ	*Journal for the Study of Judaism in the Persian, Hellenistic and Roman Period*
JTS	*Journal of Theological Studies*
LBC	Layman's Bible Commentaries
LPGL	G. W. H. Lampe, *Patristic Greek Lexicon*
MBTh	Münsterische Beiträge zur Theologie
MeyerK	H. A. W. Meyer, Kritisch-exegetischer Kommentar über das Neue Testament
MFOB	*Mélanges de la faculté orientale de l'université Saint Joseph* (Beyrouth)
MNTC	Moffatt New Testament Commentary
MSGVK	*Mitteilungen der schlesischen Gesellschaft für Volkskunde* (Breslau)
Mus	*Le Muséon*
NCB	New Century Bible
NEB	New English Bible
NedTTs	*Nederlands Theologisch Tijdscrift*
Neot	*Neotestamentica*
NGWG.PH	Nachrichten der Gesellschaft der Wissenschaften in Göttingen. Philologisch-historische Klasse
NHS	Nag Hammadi Studies
NIV	New International Version
NovT	*Novum Testamentum*
NovTSup	Supplements to *Novum Testamentum*
NTAbh	Neutestamentliche Abhandlungen
NTApoc.	E. Hennecke, W. Schneemelcher, and R. McL. Wilson ed., *New Testament Apocrypha*
NTD	Das Neue Testament Deutsch
NTM	New Testament Message
NTS	*New Testament Studies*
NTSR	New Testament for Spiritual Reading
OBO	Orbis Biblicus et Orientalis
PC	Proclamation Commentaries
PG	J. P. Migne, *Patrologia graeca*
PGMT	Pelican Guide to Modern Theology
PL	J. P. Migne, *Patrologia latina*
RB	*Revue biblique*
RechBib	Recherches bibliques
RESl	*Revue des études slaves*
RestQ	*Restoration Quarterly*
RevQ	*Revue de Qumran*
RHR	*Revue de l'histoire des religions*
RivB	*Rivista biblica*
RNT	Regensburger Neues Testament
RSR	*Revue des sciences religiueses*
RSV	Revised Standard Version
RTP	*Revue de théologie et de philosophie*
RV	Revised Version
SB	Sources bibliques
SBLDS	Society of Biblical Literature Dissertation Series
SBLSCS	Society of Biblical Literature Septuagint and Cognate Studies
SBS	Stuttgarter Bibelstudien
SBT	Studies in Biblical Theology
SC	Sources chrétiennes

SCHNT	Studia ad Corpus Hellenisticum Novi Testamenti
Scr	*Scripture*
ScrHie	*Scripta Hierosolymitana*
SD	Studies and Documents
SE	Studia Evangelica
Sem	*Semitica*
SJLA	Studies in Judaism in Late Antiquity
SNTSMS	Society for New Testament Studies Monograph Series
SPAW.PH	Sitzungsberichte der preussischen Akademie der Wissenschaften (Berlin). Philosophisch-historische Klasse.
SPB	Studia postbiblica
ST	*Studia theologica*
STAT	Suomalaisen tiedeakatemian toimituksia. Annales academiae scientiarum Fennicae.
Str-B	H. Strack and P. Billerbeck, *Kommentar zum Neuen Testament aus Talmud und Midrasch*
SUNT	Studien zur Umwelt des Neuen Testament
SVTP	Studia in Veteris Testamenti pseudepigrapha
SVTQ	*St. Vladimir's Theological Quarterly*
TBC	Torch Bible Commentaries
TDNT	G. Kittel ed., *Theological Dictionary of the New Testament*
TEV	Today's English Version
TextsS	Texts and Studies
THKNT	Theologischer Handkommentar zum Neuen Testament
TNTC	Tyndale New Testament Commentaries
TS	*Theological Studies*
TU	Texte und Untersuchungen
TynB	*Tyndale Bulletin*
TynNTL	Tyndale New Testament Lecture
TZ	*Theologische Zeitschrift*
UNT	Untersuchungen zum Neuen Testament
UUÅ	Uppsala universitetsårsskrift
VC	*Vigiliae christianae*
VT	*Vetus Testamentum*
WC	Westminster Commentaries
WUNT	Wissenschaftliche Untersuchungen zum Neuen Testament
ZAW	*Zeitschrift für die alttestamentliche Wissenschaft*
ZNW	*Zeitschrift für die neutestamentliche Wissenschaft*
ZTK	*Zeitschrift für Theologie und Kirche*
ZWT	*Zeitschrift für wissenschaftliche Theologie*

Miscellaneous

al	and other MSS
ap.	*apud* (quoted in)
bis	twice
ed.	edition, edited by, editor
EVV	English versions
fragm.	fragment
lit.	literally
MS, MSS	manuscript, manuscripts
par.	parallel to, and parallels
s.	under
sc.	understand
s. v.	under the word
tr.	translator, translated by
v. l.	variant reading

The Letter of Jude

Introduction

Most introductory issues can really only be settled as a result of detailed exegesis. This Introduction is therefore dependent on the discussions of particular verses and passages throughout the commentary and gathers together some of their results. Thus wherever its statements are supported by reference to verses of Jude, the interpretation of those verses argued in the commentary is presupposed.

Form and Structure

The letter of Jude is a real letter. Formally, this is shown by the letter-opening (vv 1–2) which conforms to the style of the ancient Jewish letter. It was the letter-opening which was the really essential formal constituent of the ancient letter. Jude then states the occasion and theme of his message in a passage which corresponds formally to the "body-opening" of the ancient letter form (vv 3–4). The body of the letter, however, is more like a homily than a letter: it consists of a midrash on a series of scriptural references and texts (vv 5–19) and a paraenetic section (vv 20–23). The work closes with a doxology (vv 24–25), a conclusion more appropriate to a homily than to a letter.

We might therefore regard the work as an "epistolary sermon," i.e. a work whose main content could have been delivered as a homily if Jude and his readers had been able to meet, but which has been cast in letter form so that it can be communicated to readers whom Jude could not visit in person. This practice of delivering a sermon at a distance by writing it within an epistolary framework was a natural extension of the genre of the letter, and was probably already in use before Jude's time. The letter from Baruch to the exiles in *2 Apoc. Bar.* 78–86 is a fictional example of the genre, but the fiction presupposes that this form of letter could be written in fact. It must therefore have existed in Judaism as well as in primitive Christianity. NT letters vary in the extent to which they resemble private letters, and in several cases are really written homilies or theological treatises with very little epistolary framework (Hebrews, James, 1 John). In Jude's case the formal characteristics of the letter are quite sufficient to establish its right to belong to the genre of the letter.

Jude is also a genuine letter in the sense that it was written for and sent to specific addressees. The content of the work makes it clear that it is not a tract against heresy in general (as Wisse, "Jude," argues), but a message for a specific situation in which a specific group of false teachers were troubling a specific church or group of churches. There is therefore no need to regard the occasion for the letter (v 3) as fictional, and, despite the generality of the address (v 1), we should not see it as a "catholic letter" addressed to all Christians, but as a work written with a specific, localized audience in mind.

The statement of the theme of the letter (vv 3–4) contains two parts: an appeal to Jude's readers ("to carry on the fight for the faith") and the background to this appeal (v 4: the false teachers, their character and their judgment). The two parts of the body of the letter correspond to this division. The midrash (vv 5–19) is devoted to the background of the appeal: it establishes, by exegesis of types and prophecies, that the false teachers are people whose behavior is condemned and whose judgment is prophesied in OT types and in prophecy from the time of Enoch to the time of the apostles. Its purpose is to demonstrate that the false teachers constitute a serious danger to the church(es). It therefore prepares the way for the real purpose of the letter, which is Jude's appeal to his readers to fight for the faith. This appeal, stated as the theme of the letter in v 3, is spelled out in detail in vv 20–23.

Commentators have usually been misled by the length and central position of the midrash (vv 5–19) into regarding it as the main content of the letter, but this is a serious mistake. The structure of the letter indicates that the midrash, though important, is important only as necessary background to the appeal (vv 20–23), which is Jude's main purpose in writing. The appeal occupies the position it does toward the end of the letter, not because it is a kind of postscript or "closing exhortation," but because it is the climax of the letter to which all the rest leads up. Recognizing this is a vital key to the understanding of the work as a whole.

That the section vv 5–19 is in the form of a midrash has been shown by Ellis (*Prophecy and Hermeneutic*), though his detailed analysis will be somewhat modified in this commentary. (The word "midrash" is used here in the general sense of an exegesis of Scripture which applies it to the contemporary situation, not with the implication that Jude's midrash bears any close resemblance to the forms of later rabbinic midrashim.) In order to demonstrate the statement in v 4, that the character and judgment of the false teachers has been prophesied, Jude cites a series of "texts" (vv 5–7, 11, 14–15, 17–18), though his "texts" are not always actual quotations. The first two "texts" are summary references to two sets of three OT types (vv 5–7, 11); he then quotes a prophecy of Enoch (vv 14–15) and a prophecy of the apostles (vv 17–18). Each "text" (indented in the translation in this commentary) is followed by a passage of interpretation (vv 8–10, 12–13, 16, 19) which, by pointing to the character and behavior of the false teachers, identifies them as those to whom the type or prophecy applies. In one case, a secondary text (v 9) is introduced in the course of a passage of interpretation (vv 8–10); there are also less explicit allusions to other texts in other passages of interpretation (vv 12–13, 16).

Two main stylistic features mark the alternation of "text" and interpretation in the midrash. The past tenses (vv 5–6, 9), prophetic aorists (vv 11, 14), and future tenses (v 18) of the citations, representing historical types and prophecies, are matched by present tenses in all the interpretations, where Jude explains the fulfillment of the prophecies in the present. Secondly, although the "texts" are introduced in no consistent way, the passages of interpretation are consistently introduced by the words *οὗτοι* ("these people") or *οὗτοί εἰσιν* ("these people are"), a formula which resembles one sometimes used in exegesis at Qumran (see *Form/Structure/Setting* section in the commentary on vv 5–10). A further general stylistic characteristic of Jude's midrashic method is his considerable use of catchwords to link the exposition to the "text": catchwords in the "text" are picked up in the interpretation both before and after the citation of the "text," and sometimes also link the "texts" together. Catchwords are not entirely limited to the midrashic section, but they are most prominent there.

Principal examples are *ἀσεβής/ἀσεβεῖν/ἀσέβεια* (vv 4, 15, 18), *σάρξ* (vv 7–8, 23), *βλασφημεῖν/βλασφημία* (vv 8–10), *πλάνη/πλανήτης* (vv 11, 13), *λαλεῖν* (vv 15–16), *κατὰ τὰς ἐπιθυμίας πορευόμενοι* (vv 16, 18), *ζόφος . . . τηρεῖν* (vv 6, 13), *τηρεῖν* (vv 1, 6, 13, 21).

Jude's midrashic method bears some comparison with the pesher exegesis of Qumran. There is the same conviction that the ancient texts are eschatological prophecy which the interpreter applies to the events of his own time, understood as the time of eschatological fulfillment. Whereas the main Qumran pesharim are commentaries on whole passages or whole books of the OT ("continuous pesharim"), there are also "thematic pesharim" (4QFlor, 11QMelch, 4Q 176, 177, 182, 183) which are commentaries on a collection of texts on one theme, in this resembling Jude's midrash. (The terms "pesher continu" and "pesher thématique" are those of J. Carmignac, "Le document de Qumran sur Melkisédeq," *RevQ* 7 [1969–71] 360–61.) But there are also differences between Jude and Qumran. The Qumran pesharim offer no analogies for Jude's quotations from apocryphal books (vv 9, 14–15) or from oral Christian prophecy (vv 17–18, perhaps v. 11), or for his use of summaries of scriptural material instead of an actual quotation from the OT (vv 5–7, 11). Moreover, Jude's use of *typology* (vv 5–7, 11) is not really to be found in the Qumran pesharim, which are concerned only to interpret the texts as prophecy. Jude applies Scripture to the last days not only as prophecy, but also as typology, in which the events of redemptive history are seen to foreshadow the eschatological events: this perspective he shares with Jewish apocalyptic and with the primitive Church generally.

OUTLINE OF STRUCTURE

1–2	Address and Greeting
3–4	Occasion and Theme of the Letter
3	A. The Appeal
4	B. The Background to the Appeal
5–19	B. The Background to the Appeal: A Midrash on the Prophecies of the Doom of the Ungodly
5–7	(1) Three OT Types
8–10	*plus* interpretation
9	(1a) Michael and the Devil
11	(2) Three More OT Types
12–13	*plus* interpretation

14–15 (3) The Prophecy of Enoch
16 *plus* interpretation
17–18 (4) The Prophecy of the Apostles
19 *plus* interpretation
20–23 A. The Appeal
24–25 Closing Doxology

Language

Jude's command of the Greek language is best shown in his wide and effectively used vocabulary. Considering its brevity, the letter includes a high number of NT *hapax legomena.* There are fourteen words not found elsewhere in the NT (*ἀποδιορίζειν*, v 19; *ἄπταιστος*, v 24; *γογγυστής*, v 16; *δεῖγμα*, v 7; *ἐπαγωνίζεσθαι*, v 3; *ἐπαφρίζειν*, v 13; *μεμψίμοιρος*, v 16; *παρεισδύνειν*, v 4; *σπιλάς*, v 12; *φθινοπωρινός*, v 12; *φυσικῶς*, v 10; *ἐκπορνεύειν*, v 7; *πλανήτης*, v 13; *ὑπέχειν*, v 7), and of these only four occur in the LXX (*ἄπταιστος*, v 24; 3 Macc 6:39; *ἐκπορνεύειν*, v 7; *πλανήτης*, v 13; Hos 9:17; *ὑπέχειν*, v 7). Moreover, there are three more words which occur elsewhere in the NT only in 2 Peter, which borrowed them from Jude (*ἐμπαίκτης*, v 18; 2 Pet 3:3; *συνευωχεῖσθαι*, v 12; 2 Pet 2:13; *ὑπερογκος*, v 16; 2 Pet 2:18). Of course, some discrimination is needed in assessing the significance of this list: some words (*δεῖγμα*, *φυσικῶς*, *ὑπέχειν*) are relatively common words which other NT writers happen not to use; some (*σπιλάς*, *φθινοπωρινός*, *πλανήτης*) are rather specialized words which Jude's subject matter requires; some (*γογγυστής*, *ἐμπαίκτης*) are cognate with words (*γογγύζειν*, *γογγυσμός*, *ἐμπαίζω*, *ἐμπαιγμός*) which are found elsewhere in the NT and are characteristic of biblical Greek; some (*ἀποδιορίζειν*, *ἐπαφρίζειν*) are rare. More important than the statistic is Jude's evident ability to vary his vocabulary and choose effective and appropriate words (cf., e.g., vv 12–13; *γογγυσταί μεμψίμοιροι*, v 16) and expressions from good literary, even poetic, Greek (*ὑπὸ ζόφον*, v 6; *κύματα ἄγρια*, v 13). His command of good Greek idiom is also noticeable (*πᾶσαν σπουδὴν ποιούμενος*, v 3; *πρόκειται δεῖγμα*, *δίκην ὑπέχουσαι*, v 7; *κρίσιν ἐπενεγκεῖν*, v 9; *τὰ ἄλογα ζῷα*, v 10).

If the vocabulary is rich and varied, the sentence construction is relatively simple, though parataxis is largely avoided (but cf. v 11). But sentence construction is handled with considerable rhetorical effect.

Semitisms can be found, but are not very prominent, probably less common than in most Jewish Greek. (Those in vv 14–15 result from direct translation from the Aramaic.) Examples are: *ἐκ γῆς Αἰγύπτου*, v 5; *οὐαὶ αὐτοῖς*, v 11; *ἐν τῇ ὁδῷ τοῦ Καιν ἐπορεύθησαν*, v 11; *θαυμάζοντες πρόσωπα*, v 16; *ὀπίσω* with the genitive, v 7; perhaps omission of the article before *κρίσιν*, v 6, and *ἀγάπῃ*, v 21, through the influence of the construct state. Also to be noticed are the "prophetic" aorists in vv 11, 14, the use of synonymous parallelism (v 6) and antithetical parallelism (v 10), the chiasmus in v 1a and perhaps in the structure of the whole letter (see the outline on pages 5 and 6). The author's fondness for triple expressions is a marked stylistic trait, evident throughout the letter, but is not necessarily Jewish (cf. E. von Dobschütz, "Zwei- und dreigliedrige Formeln," *JBL* 50 [1931] 117–47): used to this extent, it must be an individual stylistic preference.

The style is lively and vigorous, and the whole work gives evidence of careful composition. Close exegesis soon reveals great economy of expression. Single words, phrases, and images are chosen for the associations they carry, and scriptural allusions and catchword connections increase the depth of meaning. The section vv 11–13 is perhaps especially effective in its use of carefully chosen vocabulary, a series of vivid images suggested with almost poetic economy of words, scriptural allusions, catchword connections, and the use of climax. The modern reader requires study in order to appreciate it. The much praised doxology (vv 24–25) is more readily accessible to modern appreciation.

Sources

Despite his competence in Greek, the author's real intellectual background is in the literature of Palestinian Judaism.

It is usually assumed that Jude, like many NT authors, habitually used the OT in its Greek version, the LXX, but this assumption is mistaken. Of course, Jude shows himself familiar with the usual Greek renderings of certain OT Hebrew expressions, used both in the LXX and in later Jewish Greek literature (note especially: *ἐνυπνιάζεσθαι*, "to dream" v 8; *θαυμάζειν πρόσωπα*, "to show partiality" v 16; and cf. *γογγυστής*, "grumbler" v 16), but this is unremarkable. Much more significant is the fact that at no point where he alludes to specific verses of the OT does he echo the language of the LXX. In two of these cases he must depend on the Hebrew text because the Septuagint does not give even the meaning he adopts (v 12: Prov 25:14; v 13: Isa 57:20), while in three other cases his vocabulary notably fails to correspond to that of the LXX (v 11: Num 26:9; v 12: Ezek 34:2; v 23: Amos 4:11; Zech 3:3). This evidence shows conclusively that it was the Hebrew Bible with which Jude was really familiar. When he wished to allude to it he did not stop to find the Septuagint translation, but made his own translation, in terms appropriate to the context and style of his work.

His use of Jewish apocryphal works is at least as extensive as his use of the OT. He has a close familiarity with *1 Enoch* (vv 6, 12–16), from which he takes his only formal quotation from a written source (vv 14–15). It seems to be the Aramaic text that he uses (vv 6, 14), though he probably knew the Greek text (v 15). As for his knowledge of the various parts of our *1 Enoch,* he certainly knew chaps 1–36 (vv 6, 12–13, 14–16, cf. v 8), probably chap 80 (vv 12–13), perhaps chaps 83–90 (v 13), but there is no conclusive evidence that he knew chaps 37–71, the Parables (cf. vv 4, 14) or chaps 91–107 (perhaps cf. vv 8, 11, 16). The other Jewish apocryphal work which he used is the *Testament of Moses* (hereafter *T. Mos.*), both its extant text (probably, v 16; cf. v 3) and its ending, which is no longer extant (v 9).

In addition to these written sources, Jude was familiar with Jewish paraenetic and haggadic traditions which cannot be pinned down to any particular written source (vv 5–7, 11). These had probably already been adopted into Jewish Christian instruction.

There is no convincing case of allusion to a written Christian source, though of course Jude is familiar with traditional catechetical (vv 20–23) and liturgical (vv 24–25) material, while the purpose of his midrashic section (vv 5–19) is explicitly to remind his readers of instruction which they received, in substance at least, from the apostles at the time of the founding of their church(es). In v 18 he gives a quotation from the apostles which is probably a summary in his own words of the kind of apocalyptic warning which all the early Christian missionaries included in their instruction to new converts. It is possible that v 11 is a quotation from an oracle of a Christian prophet. There seems to be no allusion to gospel traditions, but, given the brevity of the letter, this hardly distinguishes Jude from most other NT letters.

Most commentators repeat the now well-established scholarly tradition that Jude is indebted to the ideas and terminology of Paul. But this assertion does not stand up well to detailed investigation. It depends on the too ready assumption that ideas and terminology which Paul uses are distinctively Pauline, so that other writers who use them must be dependent on Paul or "Paulinism." In fact, of course, as Pauline scholarship has shown and as should in any case be expected, Paul took over a great deal from the common traditions of primitive Christianity, and great care is needed in distinguishing ideas and terminology which are so distinctively Pauline that they must derive from Paul. No alleged case of "Paulinism" in Jude can really be substantiated. The contacts with Pauline language all belong to the common vocabulary of the early church (see commentary on "called," "loved," v 2; "saints," v 3; "grace," v 4; ψυχικοί, "people who follow natural instincts," v 19; "build yourselves up," "pray in the Holy Spirit," v 20; and the doxology, vv 24–25).

The relationship between Jude and 2 Peter is discussed in the Introduction to 2 Peter, where the judgment of most modern scholars, that 2 Peter is dependent on Jude, not *vice versa,* is accepted.

Allusions to classical Greek literature, which have sometimes been suggested (vv 6, 13), are most unlikely.

Character of the Letter

Is it "Early Catholic" or Apocalyptic Jewish Christian?

Where should the letter of Jude be placed on the map of early Christianity? The usual answer to this question is that Jude, along with the Pastoral Epistles, Luke-Acts, 2 Peter and perhaps other NT books, should be seen as a product of the developing "early Catholicism" of the postapostolic generation of Christians.

The whole concept of "early Catholicism" as NT scholars have used it to illuminate the history of first-century Christianity is ripe for radical reexamination. It has undoubtedly promoted too simple a picture of the development of Christianity. Martin Hengel has recently stated: "If we want to, we can find 'early catholic traits' even in Jesus and Paul: the phenomena thus denoted are almost entirely a legacy of Judaism" (*Acts and the History of Early Christianity* [London: SCM Press, 1979] 122). But even if the usual theory of early Catholicism is accepted, Jude's right to be included in the category must be seriously questioned.

A recent discussion of early Catholicism in the NT (J. D. G. Dunn, *Unity and Diversity in the New Testament* [London: SCM Press, 1977] chap. XIV) distinguishes three main features: (1) the fading of the Parousia hope, (2) increasing institutionalization, (3) crystallization of the faith into set forms. None of these three features is evident in Jude: (1) The Parousia hope is lively and pervades the letter (vv 1, 14, 21, 24). The whole argument of the midrash section (vv 5–19) hinges on the belief that the false teachers are to be judged by the Lord at his coming (vv 14–15) and therefore presupposes an imminent Parousia. (2) There is no mention of ecclesiastical officials in Jude (see commentary on vv 8, 11, 16), and no hint of a tendency to emphasize office and order in reaction to the dangers represented by the false teachers. The false teachers themselves were itinerant charismatics who claimed prophetic revelations (v 8), and they were evidently accepted as prophets in the church(es) to which Jude writes (v 12). Jude denies their claim to be men of the Spirit (v 19), but he does not respond by asserting that charismatic activity must be subject to properly constituted officials or by stressing that it is the officials who are endowed with the Spirit. He does not address himself to elders or bishops who have a special responsibility for guarding the faith against heretical deviations. Instead he addresses the whole community, who all enjoy the inspiration of the Spirit in charismatic prayer (v 20) and are all responsible for upholding the gospel (v 3). His response to the threat from the false teachers is quite different from that of Ignatius, with his assertion of episcopal authority, or even from that of the Pastorals, with their emphasis on office. (3) The case for classifying Jude as "early Catholic" usually rests largely on v 3, understood to refer to a fixed body of orthodox doctrine, passed down from the apostles, which only has to be asserted against heresy (D. J. Harrington, "The 'Early Catholic' Writings of the New Testament," in R. J. Clifford and G. W. MacRae [eds.], *The Word in the World: Essays in Honor of Frederick L. Moriarty* [Cambridge, Mass.: Weston College Press, 1973] 107; Schelkle, "Spätapostolische Briefe," 226). But this is a misinterpretation of v 3, which refers simply to the gospel itself, not to any formalized and unalterable "rule of faith," and which, in opposition to deviant teaching, urges its readers to remain faithful to the gospel which they received at their conversion. This is exactly the tactic which Paul used against false teaching (Gal 1:6–9; Rom 16:17). The "early Catholic" interpretation of v 3 is peculiarly inappropriate since the dispute between Jude and his opponents was not concerned with orthodoxy and heresy in belief, but with the relationship between the gospel and moral obligation. Whether or not a set form of Christian belief existed in Jude's churches, he had no occasion to refer to it, since his concern was with the moral implications of the gospel, which certainly featured in Christian catechesis from the beginning.

Since the development of "early Catholicism," with its growing insistence on institutional order and on creedal orthodoxy, is usually attributed in large part to the fading of the imminent eschatology and to the struggle with heresy, it is clear that Jude does not belong to this development at all. The primitive eschatological perspective remains dominant, and the response to false teaching is quite different from the "early Catholic" response. So there is not just a lack of evidence for Jude's "early Catholicism," there is compelling evidence against it.

Is there a more appropriate category in which Jude can be placed? Most recent commentators have recognized the strongly Jewish character of Jude's Christianity, but the category of Jewish Christianity is a large and flexible one. There are two or three features of the letter which perhaps enable us to be a little more specific:

(1) Jude's attitude to the law of Moses can be gathered at all only by

reading between the lines. Against its rejection by the false teachers, he seems to imply that it remains a moral authority for Christians (vv 8–9), but he does not stress the law of Moses in his response to antinomianism. He refers rather to the moral authority of Christ (vv 4, 8) and the holiness of Christian life on the basis of the gospel (v 20, cf. v 24). No doubt he saw the Law fulfilled in the gospel. Perhaps it would be safe to say that his attitude to the Law, while perhaps more conservative than Paul's, was not the hard-line position of the right wing of the Jerusalem church.

(2) As we have already noticed, Jude's brief letter is remarkably full of allusions to the apocryphal books *1 Enoch* and the *T. Mos.* This is one feature which sets Jude rather apart from most first-century Christian literature, and although *1 Enoch* seems to have become more popular in second-century Christianity, the *T. Mos.* was never widely used in Christian circles. *1 Enoch* and the *T. Mos.* are Jewish apocalyptic works, and Jude's evidently high respect for them, along with other aspects of his letter, places him definitely within those early Christian circles whose Christianity was of a strongly apocalyptic kind. Their Jewish apocalyptic outlook was now reinterpreted and focused on Jesus, and it was not unnatural that some of them should have interpreted the Jewish apocalypses in the light of Jesus, just as they did the OT. Jude's letter gives us a rare glimpse of those circles which did this.

(3) Another indication of the character of Jude is to be found in his argument about the false teachers. We have seen that he does not respond to them in an "early Catholic" way, insisting on the authority of ecclesiastical office. A common complaint of the commentators is that he indulges in "mere denunciation" (V. Taylor, "The Message of the Epistles: Second Peter and Jude," *ExpTim* 45 [1933–34] 439; cf. Kelly, 223: "Jude's almost unrelievedly denunciatory tone"), but this rests on a failure to enter Jude's apocalyptic world of thought. Jude does not merely denounce, he engages in a serious argument which, though strange to modern readers, carried conviction in its own context. His midrash (vv 5–19) demonstrates that the false teachers' behavior incurs divine judgment, by the exposition of eschatological typology and apocalyptic prophecy. Its hermeneutical principle is the apocalyptic principle that inspired Scripture speaks of the last days in which the interpreter is living. The same principle enabled the Qumran community to see its enemies portrayed in Habakkuk and Isaiah. In the NT it is widespread, but the exegetical work is often below the surface, presupposed rather than explicit. Jude offers us a sustained example of this kind of exegesis.

Apocalyptic was a very considerable influence on the whole Christian movement from the very beginning, and its influence was still strong in second-century Christianity in, for example, Asia Minor. To say that Jude belongs to apocalyptic Jewish Christianity is not a very precise statement, but the dominance of the apocalyptic outlook in Jude and his use of the Jewish apocalypses at any rate locates him in circles where apocalyptic was not just one influence, but the dominant vehicle through which faith in Jesus found expression.

Rowston (*NTS* 21 [1974–75] 561–62; and *Setting,* 100–19) argues that Jude used apocalyptic in a deliberate attempt to counter a developing antinomian Gnosticism. Gnosticism developed out of Paulinism and apocalyptic, but away from the apocalyptic sources of Paul's theology. Jude attempted to reverse this trend, to revive the apocalypticism of Paul and the apostolic church against the postapostolic drift toward Gnosticism. But this is too subtle a view of Jude's strategy. He does not assert apocalyptic eschatology against denials of it (as Paul in 1 Cor 15 does, and as 2 Pet 3 does). Jude's apocalyptic is not at all self-conscious. It is the world-view within which he naturally thinks and which he takes it for granted his readers accept.

The Opponents

Jude's opponents are a group of itinerant charismatics who have arrived in the church(es) to which he writes. Everything else Jude tells us about them is related to their antinomianism, which is the target of his attack. They reject all moral authority, whether that of the law of Moses (vv 8–10) or that of Christ himself (vv 4, 8), even though they claim to be followers of Christ. Evidently they understand the grace of God in Christ (v 4) as a deliverance from all external moral constraint, so that the man who possesses the Spirit (v 19) becomes the only judge of his own actions (cf. v 9), subject to no other authority. When accused of sin by the standard of the law of Moses or of the moral order of creation, they speak disparagingly of the angels who gave the Law and administer the moral order of the world, alleging that they are motivated by ill will toward men and women (vv 8–10). This tactic enables them to detach accepted moral standards from the will of God himself, attributing them only to malicious angels, but Jude sees their contempt for the commandments as presumptuousness in relation to God himself, rooted in resistance to his will: so their complaints about the commandments and their arrogant, insolent words are directed against God (v 16), and their characteristic attitude is irreverence (v 12). It is a plausible, but not certain, deduction, that they denied the reality of future judgment (this depends on the mention of Cain in v 11)—or perhaps they denied that as men of the Spirit they themselves would be subject to the judgment.

In line with their rejection of moral authority, they indulge in immoral behavior, especially sexual misconduct (vv 6–8, 10); in this they may be deliberately flouting accepted standards of Jewish morality and conforming to the permissiveness of pagan society. For their authority to behave in this way they appeal to their charismatic inspiration, manifested in prophetic visions (v 8), in which perhaps they receive revelations of the heavenly world and of their own exalted status above the angels of the Law. Such visions and similar ecstatic phenomena are probably for them the mark of possession of the Spirit (cf. v 19), and so they gather their own group of followers in the congregation whose enjoyment of ecstatic experience gives them the status of spiritual people, to which more conventional Christians have not yet attained (v 19).

It is clear that Jude's opponents are not simply members of the church, but teachers (vv 11–13). They are present at the church's fellowship meals (v 12), where no doubt they impart their prophecies and teachings to the rest of the community. Like other itinerant teachers in the early church, they are dependent on the hospitality and support of the churches, and Jude accuses them of being motivated by greed for the material gain they receive from the church or from their particular followers (vv 11–12). Their lax moral teaching helps them to ingratiate themselves with their followers, Jude implies (v 16).

Most of these characteristics can be paralleled from other early Christian literature. Itinerant charismatics were frequently a source of trouble in the churches (Matt 7:15; 2 Cor 10–11; 1 John 4:1; 2 John 10; *Did.* 11–12), and their reliance on the support of the churches was easily abused (Rom 16:18; 1 Tim 6:5; Tit 1:11; *Did.* 11:5–6, 12). Their claim to possess the Spirit in ecstatic experience and the élitist implications of this have parallels in 1 Corinthians, and the appeal to the authority of private visionary experience is also found elsewhere (2 Cor 12:1–3; Col 2:18; cf. Rev 2:24). Again, their antinomianism resembles the attitude of the Corinthians (1 Cor 5:1–6; 6:12–20; 10:23) and the prophetic teaching of "Jezebel" and her followers (Rev 2:14, 20–22). Only the blaspheming of angels seems to have no parallel.

There are some reasons, though not conclusive ones, for thinking that Pauline teaching may have had some influence on the false teachers. Not only did Paul recognize and oppose the danger of an antinomian distortion of his teaching on Christian freedom (Rom 3:8; 6:1, 15; Gal 5:13), but also the otherwise unparalleled feature of blaspheming angels is not too distant from some of Paul's teaching about the angels of the Law and "the elemental spirits of the world" (*τὰ στοιχεῖα τοῦ κόσμου*) (Gal 3:20; 4:3, 8–9; Col 2:8–23; Rom 8:33–39).

If the exegesis supporting the above sketch of the false teachers is sound they cannot be called Gnostics. What is missing from their teaching is the cosmological dualism of true Gnosticism. Even though their sense of moral autonomy and spiritual status and their attitude to the angels of the Law resemble the views of many later Gnostics, Jude provides no evidence that they saw these hostile angels as creators and lords of the material world, thereby detaching not only morality but also all other features of this material cosmos from the will of the supreme God. Nor do we know that their indulgence in sins of the flesh was linked to a disparagement of the body as material. In the absence of cosmological dualism, it is misleading even to call their teaching "incipient Gnosticism." It is better to see their antinomianism as simply one of the streams that flowed into later Gnosticism, but which at this stage is not distinctively gnostic.

Many commentators have detected truly gnostic doctrines as the target of some of Jude's attacks: a docetic Christology (v 4), doctrines of the demiurge and the archons which deny the unity of God (vv 4, 8, 25), and the gnostic division of mankind into pneumatics and psychics (v 19). On these grounds they have dated Jude as late as the second century, when such developed Gnosticism first appeared (so, most recently, Sidebottom). But such teachings have to be read into Jude's words. It is unlikely that Jude should oppose such serious and extensive deviation from common Christian belief with the merest hints of disapproval. If his polemic is really aimed against Gnosticism it is singularly inept. Of course, it is always possible that Jude was ill-informed about the full extent of his opponents' heretical teaching, but in that case the modern scholar has no means of knowing it. The strength of the view of Jude's opponents argued in this commentary is that it both provides a coherent picture of the false teachers themselves and accounts for the kind of argument which Jude uses against them.

Date

Questions relevant to the date of the letter have already been discussed in previous sections. Jude is not dependent on "Paulinism," nor does the letter display features of the "early Catholicism" of postapostolic Christianity. The opponents confronted in the letter are not second-century Gnostics. Jude belongs to the milieu of apocalyptic Jewish Christianity and combats teachers of antinomian libertinism, who *may* have been influenced by Pauline teaching. These features make it unlikely that the letter could be later than the end of the first century A.D., but they do not really place it more precisely than in the second half of the first century. Comparable antinomianism can be found in Corinth in the 50s, but also (if the book of Revelation is rightly dated in the reign of Domitian) in Asia in the 90s. Apocalyptic Jewish Christianity remained a strong influence in the church throughout the first century. All the same, once one has cast off the spell of the early Catholic and anti-gnostic reading of Jude, the letter does give a general impression of primitiveness. Its character is such that it might very plausibly be dated in the 50s, and nothing requires a later date.

The relationship to 2 Peter is relevant to the date, but if Jude is prior and 2 Peter is not written by the apostle himself (the position argued in the commentary on 2 Peter) it gives no very firm indication of the date of Jude. All that can be said is that if 2 Peter belongs to the later first century, it favors an earlier rather than a later date for Jude.

The tendency of modern scholars to prefer a date at the end of the first century or the beginning of the second has resulted not only from the early Catholic reading of v 3 and the gnostic interpretation of the false teachers, but also from the usual interpretation of v. 17, in which Jude is thought to be looking back on the apostolic age as an era now past. This is a misunderstanding. In v 17, as in vv 3, 5, Jude is recalling his readers to the instruction they received at their conversion, from the apostles who founded their church(es). It is not the apostles themselves, but their missionary activity in founding these particular churches, which belongs to the past. Jude's statement is exactly parallel to many of Paul's in which he refers his readers back to the teaching he gave them when he founded their church (1 Cor 15:1–3; Gal 1:9; 1 Thess 4:1–2), with the one difference that, since Jude was evidently not one of the founding missionaries of the church(es) to which he writes, he speaks of the apostles' teaching rather than his own (but cf. Rom 6:7; 16:17). In fact vv 17–18 put not a lower but an upper limit on the date, for "they said to you" (*ἔλεγον ὑμῖν*, v 18) implies that most of the original converts are still living.

Only one other issue has an important bearing on the date: the authorship (see next section). If the letter is pseudonymous it must have been written after the death of Jude the Lord's brother, if authentic before his death. We shall argue for the second alternative, but unfortunately we do not know when Jude died. It could have been as late as A.D. 90 (see next section). J. A. T. Robinson (*Redating,* 197) argues that if James (v 1) were dead he would probably be given some epithet such as μακάριος ("blessed"), ἀγαθός ("good"), or δίκαιος ("just": his usual epithet: Hegesippus, *ap.* Eusebius, *Hist. Eccl.* 2.23.4; *Gos. Thom.* 21), and so Jude must be dated before James's martyrdom in A.D. 62. But this cannot be regarded as a very conclusive argument.

Authorship

The Jude (Judas) named in v 1 is almost certainly Judas the brother of Jesus, and his brother James is James "the Just," leader of the Jerusalem church. (Other suggestions are discussed and this conclusion argued in the commentary on v 1.) Most modern commentators agree on this, but disagree as to whether the real author was Jude himself or someone who used Jude's name as a pseudonym. The pseudepigraphal hypothesis has prevailed in most recent commentaries (Barnett, Schelkle, Reicke, Sidebottom, Kelly, Grundmann; also Rowston, *Setting*), but largely because the arguments for a late date have been held to place the letter outside Jude's probable lifetime. These arguments have already been shown to have no force.

Against the pseudepigraphal hypothesis, it has often been asked why anyone should adopt as a pseudonym the name of so obscure a figure as Jude. This objection does not hold if Jude comes from the milieu of Palestinian Jewish Christianity, that "dynastic Christianity" (Rowston) in which the family of Jesus was revered and Jude would be a figure of authority. In that case, however, it is inexplicable that the letter does not call Jude "the brother of the Lord," the title by which he was always known in such circles and by which his authority was indicated. The description of Jude as "brother of James" only (v 1) is much more easily explicable on the hypothesis of authenticity than on that of pseudepigraphy (see commentary on v 1).

We know little about Jude the brother of Jesus. One of four brothers of Jesus, probably younger than James (Matt 13:55; Mark 6:3), he was presumably, like the other brothers, not a follower of Jesus during his ministry (Mark 3:21, 31; John 7:5), but became a believer after the resurrection (Acts 1:14). According to 1 Cor 9:5, the brothers of the Lord were traveling missionaries; Jude is very likely included here, especially as James probably is not. His missionary labors were no doubt among Jews, but not necessarily in Palestine only: he could have gone to the Diaspora. Julius Africanus (*ap.* Eusebius, *Hist. Eccl.* 1.7.14) says that the relatives of Jesus, οἱ δεσπόσυνοι, spread the gospel throughout Palestine, starting from Nazareth and Cochaba (in Transjordan). According to the *Acts of Paul* (*NT Apoc.* 2, 388), Judas the Lord's brother befriended Paul in Damascus, but this is no doubt based only on identifying the Judas of Acts 9:11 with the brother of the Lord.

Hegesippus (*ap.* Eusebius, *Hist. Eccl.* 3.19.1–20.8) has a story about the grandsons of Jude (whose names are given in another fragment as Zoker [i.e. Zechariah] and James: C. de Boor, *Neue Fragmente des Papias, Hegesippus und Pierius* [TU 5/2; Leipzig: J. C. Hinrichs, 1889] 169). They were brought before Domitian as belonging to the royal family of David and therefore politically dangerous. But when they explained that they were only poor farmers, supporting themselves by their own labor, and that the kingdom of Christ they expected was eschatological and heavenly, the Emperor dismissed them as harmless and ordered the persecution of the church to stop. Hegesippus adds that they became leaders of the churches and survived till the reign of Trajan.

It is remarkable how uncritically most scholars writing on Jude have accepted this story from Hegesippus, whose legendary account of the martyrdom of James does not inspire confidence in his historical accuracy. The story of the grandsons of Jude has clear apologetic features, and historical improbabilities (the investigation before Domitian himself; the cessation of persecution as a result). Although there is no doubt some historical fact behind it, it would not be wise to put too much trust in the *chronological* implication which commentators on Jude have usually drawn—that Jude had grandsons who were adult in the reign of Domitian, when Jude himself was dead. There is even some question whether Hegesippus referred to *grandsons* of Jude, as in the text in Eusebius, or to *sons* of Jude (H. J. Lawlor, *Eusebiana* [Oxford: Oxford University Press, 1912] 44–45).

Even if we can trust Hegesippus' story, it does not tell us how long Jude lived. It probably implies that Jude himself was dead when the incident occurred, but he need have died only recently. As Mayor calculated (cxlviii), if Jude, as one of the youngest of Jesus' brothers, was born in A.D. 10, he could have had grandsons aged thirty in A.D. 90, when he himself was eighty. This enables commentators such as Mayor who hold the letter to be authentic, still to date it as late as C. A.D. 80 (cf. also Zahn, *Introduction,* 255). But in any case we have already seen that the letter itself contains no evidence which requires so late a date.

The one real difficulty in the way of attributing the letter to the brother of Jesus is the language. Although the author was certainly a Semitic speaker, who habitually used the OT in Hebrew and probably the book of Enoch in Aramaic (see third section), he also had a considerable command of good literary Greek. It is true that many recent studies have shown that both the Greek language and Hellenistic culture had penetrated Jewish Palestine to a much greater extent than used to be supposed, but it is still surprising that a Galilean villager should show such a high degree of competence in the Greek language. On the other hand, it must be admitted that our knowledge is insufficient to set limits on the competence which the brother of Jesus could have acquired. He was probably still a very young man when he became a Christian missionary, and if his missionary travels took him among strongly Hellenized Jews there is no reason why he should not have deliberately improved his command of Greek to increase his effectiveness as a preacher. A wide vocabulary, which Jude has, is easier to acquire than a skill in literary style, where Jude's competence is less remarkable. The kinds of skills he shows are the rhetorical skills which a Jewish preacher in Greek would need. Moreover, the features of good literary Greek, both vocabulary and idiom, with which he shows himself familiar, need not have been acquired directly from the reading of secular Greek literature; familiarity with Hellenistic Jewish literature and much listening to Jewish and Christian sermons would be sufficient to account for them. Since there are no other reasons for denying the authenticity of the letter, it would be unwise to consider this extremely uncertain question of language an insuperable obstacle.

Finally, we should notice that the general character of the letter, its Jewishness, its debt to Palestinian Jewish literature and haggadic traditions, its apocalyptic perspective and exegetical methods, its concern for ethical practice more than for doctrinal belief, are all entirely consistent with authorship by Jude the brother of Jesus.

Destination

Attempts to determine the locality of the church(es) which Jude addresses are largely guesswork. Since Jude recalls his readers to the teaching which they received from the apostles at their conversion, but not to his own teaching, it is probable that he himself was not one of the missionaries who founded those churches, though he may have visited them at a later date. It is natural to think of predominantly Jewish Christian churches, both because they evidently come within the area of Jude's pastoral concern and responsibility, and also because of the high degree of familiarity with Jewish literature and traditions which Jude's allusions presuppose. The latter is not necessarily a decisive argument, since such Jewish material was no doubt used in the instruction of Gentile converts and since a writer does not always tailor his allusions to the knowledge of his readers. It is usually said that the antinomianism of the false teachers argues a Gentile background, but it should be noticed that the false teachers are itinerant teachers who have arrived in the church(es) from elsewhere (v 4), and also that antinomianism was not unknown even in first-century Judaism (Vermes, "Decalogue"; and cf. perhaps Matt 7:21–23, for Jewish Christianity). Nevertheless the antinomian problem finds its most plausible context in a church in a Gentile environment (as in Paul's Corinth, and the churches of the book of Revelation). A predominantly, but not exclusively, Jewish Christian community in a Gentile society seems to account best for what little we can gather about the recipients of Jude's letter.

A destination in Syria has often been suggested and would be appropriate, except for the fact that this was the one area of the later church which did not accept Jude as canonical (see Chaine, 266–67, for details). Asia Minor, with its large Jewish communities, the influence of Paul, and antinomian movements attested by Rev 2:14, 20, is a strong possibility, and the contacts between Jude and the *Martyrdom of Polycarp* (hereafter *Mart. Pol.*) (vv 2, 25; *Mart. Pol.* inscr., 20:2) could point in this direction. Another possibility is Egypt, where Jude was accepted as canonical by the time of Clement of Alexandria, and from its use by Clement and Origen seems to have been a popular work.

Attestation

Passages from the *Didache, 1 Clement,* the *Epistle of Barnabas,* Polycarp, the *Mart. Pol.,* Justin, Athenagoras, and Theophilus have often been cited (e.g., Bigg, 307–308; Chaine, 261–62) as showing the influence of Jude, but none is a really convincing case of dependence. The only clear early witness is 2 Peter, if the priority of Jude to 2 Peter is accepted. But that such a brief work should not have left unambiguous marks on the Christian literature of the second century is not surprising. More remarkable is the evidence that by the end of the second century Jude was widely accepted as canonical: by Tertullian in North Africa, Clement and Origen in Alexandria, the Muratorian Canon in Italy (for the detailed evidence see Chaine, 263–67). It was only subsequent to this general acceptance that doubts about the book, attested by Origen, Eusebius, Didymus, and Jerome, arose because of its use of the apocryphal books *1 Enoch* and the *Assumption of Moses* (hereafter *As. Mos.*). (Tertullian, on the other hand, had been able to cite Jude as evidence for the authority of *1 Enoch: De cultu fem.* 1.3.) These objections do not seem to have had a serious effect on the acceptability of Jude except in the Syrian church, where it was not accepted as canonical until the sixth century.

Address and Salutation (Jude 1–2)

Bibliography

Spicq, C. *Agape,* 365–67.

Translation

[1] *Jude,*[a] *a servant of Jesus Christ and brother of James, to those who are called, who are loved*[b] *in*[c] *God the Father and kept for Jesus Christ.*[d]
[2] *May mercy, peace, and love be given you in abundance.*

Notes

[a] Ἰούδας, elsewhere in English versions of the NT rendered "Judas," has traditionally been rendered "Jude" in this one instance. This commentary follows the convention of calling the writer "Jude."

[b] For ἠγαπημένοις, some MSS have ἡγιασμένοις, "sanctified" (K L P *al*). This is probably an assimilation to 1 Cor 1:2, prompted by the difficulty of the phrase ἐν θεῷ πατρὶ ἠγαπημένοις.

[c] Westcott and Hort, followed by Mayor (clxxxii–clxxxiii), suggested that the ἐν originally stood before Ἰησοῦ, not before θεῷ; the versions give some support to including ἐν before Ἰησοῦ, but not to omitting it before θεῷ. The difficulty of the present text is better tackled by exegesis.

[d] Ἰησοῦ Χριστῷ: dative of advantage. The meaning "by Jesus Christ" is unlikely, since God should be the agent implied in both ἠγαπημένοις and τετηρημένοις, "kept," and the dative of agent is rare in NT. To take Ἰησοῦ Χριστῷ as governed by the ἐν which precedes θεῷ (Wand) is highly unnatural.

Form/Structure/Setting

The opening was the most stereotyped part of the ancient letter, and Jude here follows the form of the Jewish letter of his day, in which the opening normally contained (a) a parties' formula, naming the sender and the recipient(s), and (b) a salutation.

(a) *The parties' formula* (v 1) follows the form "X to Y" (found in the Aramaic and Greek letters from Naḥal Ḥever, as well as in all the NT letters which have letter-openings). An extended Christian theological characterization of the recipients is common in early Christian letters (cf. Rom 1:7; 1 Cor 1:2; 1 Thess 1:1; 2 Thess 1:1; 1 Pet 1:2; 2 Pet 1:2; *1 Clem.* inscr.; and all the letters of Ignatius), and the binitarian form can also be paralleled (1 Thess 1:1; 2 Thess 1:1; *1 Clem.* inscr.; all the letters of Ignatius mention God the Father and Jesus Christ in describing the recipients).

Most early Christian letters specify in the parties' formula a destination, a specific church or group of churches, to which they are sent. Jude's failure to do this has led to the view, traditional from an early period, that his letter is a "catholic letter," addressed to all Christians. This view is expressed in the addition of the phrase τοῖς ἔθνεσι ("to the Gentiles") in v 1 in a few minuscule manuscripts and the Syriac version. Among modern scholars it is still held by Plummer (376), Windisch, Reicke, Krodel (92), and Wisse ("Jude"). Most modern commentators, however, have recognized that Jude addresses a specific situation in which false teachers of a specific kind were active, and so he must have intended his letter for a specific church or group of churches. It is possible that the destination was omitted when the letter was copied for wider circulation, perhaps in the second century when its relevance to the problem of Gnosticism throughout the church was seen. Alternatively, Jude did not include the destination in his parties' formula, either because his messenger would in any case know where to deliver it, probably with additional verbal messages, or perhaps because it was intended for a large group of churches which Jude intended the messenger to visit in turn, allowing each church to make its own copy.

(b) *The salutation* (v 2) is somewhat closer than many other early Christian examples to Jewish forms. This kind of salutation originates from blessing formulae (K. Berger, "Apostelbrief und apostolische Rede," *ZNW* 65 [1974] 191–201): the writer desires God to bless the recipients. All such salutations wish peace to the recipients, some add mercy (ἔλεος, corresponding to חסד). The one extant example in a Jewish letter is *2 Apoc. Bar.* 78:2: "Mercy and peace be with you" (for the text see P. Bogaert, *Apocalypse de Baruch* [SC 144–45; Paris: Editions du Cerf, 1969] 1, 68, 70; cf. 2, 142), but non-epistolary blessings provide other parallels (Num 6:25–26; Tob 7:12 א; cf. *1 Enoch* 5:6; and for "mercy" in blessings, cf. also 2 Sam 2:6; 15:20; Ps 33:22). In early Christian letters ἔλεος occurs in 1 Tim 1:2; 2 Tim 1:2; 2 John 3; Pol. *Phil.* inscr.; *Mart. Pol.,* inscr. (cf. also Gal 6:16, in a letter-ending): like Jude's, these represent a continuation of Jewish practice. The third element in Jude's salutation, however, is a Christian addition to the formula: ἀγάπη ("love") is found in no Jewish example, and in only one other early Christian example, the salutation in *Mart. Pol.* (though cf. also 2 Cor 13:14; Eph 6:23; "*3 Cor.*" 3:40, in letter-endings). Finally, the use of "increase" (πληθύνειν, Aramaic שגא) again derives from blessings formulae (K. Berger, "Apostelbrief und apostolische Rede," *ZNW* 65 [1974] 195–96 and n.29; and to his references add Herm. *Sim.* 9:24:3), and is found in both Jewish and early Christian letter salutations (G. R. Driver, *Aramaic Documents of the Fifth Century* B.C. [Oxford: Clarendon Press, 1957] nos. I, II, III, XIII; A. Cowley, *Aramaic Papyri of the Fifth Century* B.C. [Oxford: Clarendon Press, 1923] nos. 38–42; Dan 3:31 [Aram.]; Dan 4:1 θ; 4:37c LXX; 6:26 [Aram.], θ; *b.Sanh.* 11ᵇ; *y.Sanh.* 18ᵈ; 1 Pet 1:2; 2 Pet 1:2; *1 Clem.* inscr.; Pol. *Phil.* inscr.; *Mart. Pol.* inscr.; *Ep. Apost.* 1). It is used as a "divine passive" to wish that God may give blessings abundantly.

Thus, apart from the addition of ἀγάπη, Jude's salutation follows the form of Jewish letters. It should be noted that Jude does *not* adopt two other Christian adaptations of the salutation which are extremely common in early Christian letters. One of these, the use of χάρις ("grace"), is nearly universal: it occurs in all the NT letters which have this kind of salutation (all Pauline letters; 1 Pet 1:2; 2 Pet 1:2; 2 John 3; Rev 1:4) and in *1 Clem.* Among early Christian letters which have this kind of salutation, χάρις is lacking only in Jude; Pol. *Phil.;* and *Mart. Pol.*

The other common feature of early Christian letter salutations which Jude does not adopt is the indication of the source of blessings by a binitarian formula such as "from God our Father and our Lord Jesus Christ" (all Pauline letters except Col 1:2, which has "from God our Father," and 1 Thess 1:1; also 2 John 3; Rev 1:4–5; *1 Clem.* inscr.; Pol. *Phil.* inscr.; *Mart. Pol.* inscr.; Ps-Clementine *Epistle of Peter to James*).

Also unusual is the threefold form of Jude's salutation, though three NT letters have the formula "grace, mercy, and peace" (1 Tim 1:2, 2 Tim 1:2; 2 John 3), and Jude's triad "mercy, peace, and love" reappears in the *Mart. Pol.* (cf. also "*3 Cor.*" 3:40: "peace, grace, and love"—a letter-ending). We cannot therefore be sure that Jude himself invented his form of salutation by adding ἀγάπη, but he certainly chose it according to his marked stylistic preference for triple expressions.

The unusual form of Jude's salutation is a minor indication that he belongs to Jewish-Christian circles somewhat apart from those represented by the bulk of the early Christian literature we possess. The closest parallel is the salutation in the *Mart. Pol.* ("May mercy, peace, and love, from God the Father and our Lord Jesus Christ, be given abundantly"), which also, it may be noted, has a doxology (20:2) similar to Jude's (vv 24–25). Whether the *Mart. Pol.* reflects the influence of Jude, or the influence of the tradition to which Jude himself was indebted, it is impossible to tell.

Comment

1. Ἰούδας. The name was common among Jews of the first century. The following identifications of this Judas (traditionally known in English as Jude) have been made:

(1) The overwhelming majority of scholars have understood this Judas to be Judas the brother of Jesus, who is mentioned in Matt 13:55; Mark 6:3; and Hegesippus (*ap.* Eusebius, *Hist. Eccl.* 3.19.1–20.6), though they are divided on whether Jude himself wrote the letter or a later writer wrote under his name. This view seems to give the best explanation of the two phrases by which Jude is described in v 1: "a servant of Jesus Christ and brother of James." The brothers of the Lord were not known as "apostles" in the early Church, and so Jude's authority to address his readers is expressed by the term "servant" rather than "apostle" (see below). The second phrase, which distinguishes this Judas from others of the same name, does so by mentioning his relationship to the only man in the primitive church who could be called simply "James" with no risk of ambiguity (see below). The only difficulty in this view is to understand why Jude is not here *called* "brother of the Lord" or "brother of Jesus Christ." It is easier to explain this if the letter is authentic than if it is pseudepigraphal. Palestinian Jewish-Christian circles in the early church used the title "brother of the Lord" not simply to identify the brothers, but as ascribing to them an authoritative status, and therefore the brothers themselves, not wishing to claim an authority based on mere blood-relationship to Jesus, avoided the term (see below).

(2) Some older commentators (e.g. Calvin, Matthew Henry) identified the author as the apostle "Judas of James" (Luke 6:16; Acts 1:13: Ἰούδας Ἰακώβου). But (a) "Judas of James" naturally means "Judas son of James" rather than

"Judas brother of James" (the latter translation, found in AV, derives from the assumption that this apostle is the same person as Judas the Lord's brother); (b) Jude does not call himself "apostle."

(3) H. Koester ("ΓΝΩΜΑΙ ΔΙΑΦΟΡΟΙ," *HTR* 58 [1965] 297) suggested that Jude is the apostle Thomas, who in Syrian Christian tradition was known as Judas Thomas or Judas "the twin" (Eusebius, *Hist. Eccl.* 1.13.11; *Acts Thom.; Gos. Thom.; Thom. Cont.;* John 14:22 sy[c]). Since Thomas is almost certainly not a personal name but a surname meaning "the twin," the apostle must have had another name and it is possible that tradition has correctly preserved it as Judas. But this does not mean, as Koester thinks, that Judas "the twin" was the twin brother of Jesus and therefore identical with Judas the Lord's brother. It is true that later tradition interpreted the surname "the twin" as meaning *Jesus'* twin (*Acts Thom.* 31; 39; *Thom. Cont.* 138:4–8), but the idea was usually not that he was a blood-brother of Jesus but that he bore a close physical resemblance to Jesus (A. F. J. Klijn, "John xiv 22 and the Name Judas Thomas," in *Studies in John: presented to Professor Dr J. N. Sevenster* [NovTSup 24; Leiden: E. J. Brill, 1970] 88–96) or that he was a kind of spiritual twin (cf. J. J. Gunther, "The Meaning and Origin of the Name 'Judas Thomas,' " *Mus* 93 [1980] 113–148). Only at a late stage was Judas Thomas, Jesus' "twin," confused with Judas the blood-brother of Jesus.

This suggestion therefore cannot explain "brother of James," and encounters the same difficulty as (2) in explaining why Jude does not call himself "apostle."

Sidebottom (69, 79) adopted the same suggestion in arguing that Jude is a pseudonymous work of the early second century directed against gnostic heresy. Against the objection that Judas the Lord's brother was too obscure a figure to be used as a pseudonym, Sidebottom points out that Judas Thomas was an important figure in gnostic literature (*Gos. Thom.; Thom. Cont.*). This argument, however, rests, like Koester's, on the mistaken assumption that Judas Thomas was identified with Judas the Lord's brother. Second-century Gnostics would not have recognized Judas Thomas under the description "Judas . . . brother of James."

(4) Several scholars (Selwyn, *Christian Prophets,* 148; du Plessis, "Authorship," developing an earlier argument by W. J. Fournier; Ellis, "Jude"; and cf. Plumptre, 85–86) have identified the author with Judas Barsabbas (Acts 15:22, 27, 32). But this Judas might be expected to distinguish himself from others of the same name by using his surname Barsabbas, rather than "brother of James," even if this can be taken to refer to spiritual fraternity (du Plessis, "Authorship," 197; for Ellis's interpretation of "brother" here, see below).

(5) B. H. Streeter (*The Primitive Church* [London: Macmillan, 1929] 178–80) thought Jude was written by the third bishop of Jerusalem, whom the *Apostolic Constitutions* 7:46 called "Judas of James," and that "brother" is a later addition to the text of Jude 1. This enabled him to date the letter in the early second century without regarding it as pseudonymous. Much earlier, Grotius had thought the author was Judas, the last Jewish bishop of Jerusalem according to Eusebius (*Hist. Eccl.* 4.5.3) (see Chase, *DB*(*H*) 2, 804 n.), who was perhaps the same man. These suggestions would be at all plausible only if the evidence for so late a date for Jude were compelling, but even then

it would be hard to understand how the work of such an author could have come to be widely regarded as authoritative throughout the church by the end of the second century.

(6) Moffatt (244–46) thought the author was probably an otherwise unknown Judas, brother of an equally unknown James. This fails to take account of the fact that to identify oneself by reference to one's brother, rather than one's father, was extremely unusual and requires explanation. (The only theory which does explain it is that which identifies James as *the* James whom everyone knew.)

The traditional identification (1) remains the best. On whether the letter is an authentic writing of the Lord's brother, or a pseudepigraphal letter written under his name, see Introduction.

Ἰησοῦ Χριστοῦ δοῦλος, "a servant of Jesus Christ." The phrase occurs in letter-openings at Rom 1:1; Phil 1:1 (plural, of Paul and Timothy); Jas 1:1 ("servant of God and the Lord Jesus Christ"); 2 Pet 1:1. Elsewhere, Paul uses it of himself (Gal 1:10), of Epaphras (Col 4:12), of Timothy (2 Tim 2:24), and of Christians in general (1 Cor 7:22; Eph 6:6). In the background lies the Jewish term "servant of God," used especially as an honorific title for leaders such as Abraham (Ps 105:42), Moses (Neh 9:14: Rev 15:3; Josephus, *Ant.* 5:39), David (Ps 89:3), Daniel (Dan 6:20). The Jewish title was sometimes used of Christians (1 Pet 2:16; Rev 7:3; *1 Clem.* 60:2) or the apostles (Tit 1:1), but the more characteristic Christian phrase became "servant of Jesus Christ," suggesting the idea that Christians have been bought by Christ from captivity or slavery and now belong to him as his slaves (1 Cor 7:23). All Christians were therefore "servants of Jesus Christ," but the phrase could be used of those called to special service, Christian workers, not as an indication of privileged rank, but, as in the case of the term διάκονος ("servant"), indicating that the Christian worker exemplifies the servant role which all God's people are called to play. Probably in this context as Jude's self-designation, it contains a claim to authority, but an authority based on his call to serve the Lord rather than on his family relationship with the Lord. Though the term "servant of Jesus Christ" could be used of apostles, it was not in itself equivalent to "apostle" (cf. Rom 1:1; 2 Pet 1:1), and so we should probably infer that, while Jude exercised some kind of leadership role in the church, he was not given the title "apostle." James 1:1 (whether or not the letter is authentic) indicates that "apostle" was not thought an appropriate title for his brother either. On the other hand, Jude 17 (see *Comment* on that v) does not necessarily exclude Jude from the category of the apostles.

Whether Paul included the Lord's brothers among the apostles is not quite clear (1 Cor 9:5; 15:7; Gal 1:19). Paul's understanding of the "apostle" as one who had received a missionary call from the risen Lord in person might exclude James, who was not a missionary; other brothers, probably including Jude, did exercise a missionary role (1 Cor 9:5), but whether they had seen the risen Christ we do not know (possibly Acts 1:14 permits a guess that they had). Perhaps what these Pauline texts really indicate is that although James and the other brothers of Jesus might be regarded as *qualifying* for the title "apostles," by Paul's criteria, they were not usually *called* "apostles," simply because their usual title was "the Lord's brothers." Their blood-relationship to Jesus put them in a special category, in the eyes of the first Christians, and they preferred a title for them which indicated this special category, rather than including them in the general category of apostles. Hence Paul seems to class them *with* the apostles, but early Christian literature never explicitly calls them "apostles." Jewish-Christian tradition, represented by Hegesippus (*ap.* Eusebius, *Hist. Eccl.* 2.23.4) and the Pseudo-Clementines, distinguished James from the apostles. (Of course, we do not know for certain that Paul's understanding of apostleship was accepted in the cirles in which Jude moved, and another possibility is that the restriction of the title "apostle" to the Twelve is not a late feature in Acts, but a characteristic of Palestinian Christianity from the first. In that case, Jude did not see himself as an apostle because he was not one of the Twelve.)

If the brothers of the Lord were not known as "apostles," it is natural that they should not call themselves "apostles." But from Jude 1 and (if it is authentic) Jas 1:1, it seems that they also avoided calling *themselves* by the title which others used of them: "brother of the Lord." This is not surprising. It is perfectly credible that they should have been more conscious than their followers of the fact that mere blood-relationship to Jesus could give them no authority (cf. Mark 3:33–35). It is not so much because of modesty, as many commentators have suggested, that they refrain from mentioning their relationship to Jesus. The point is rather that the self-designation in the letter-opening must establish their authority to address their readers, as Paul's habitual mention of his apostleship in his letter-openings does. For this purpose they adopt the designation "servant of Jesus Christ" (as Paul and Timothy, who was not an apostle, did in Phil 1:1).

It seems reasonable, therefore, to see Jude 1 and James 1:1 as reflecting the characteristic way in which the brothers described themselves. This is much more plausible than attributing the description to later writers, using the pseudonyms of James and Jude at a time when, not only were they regularly called "the Lord's brothers," but also Jewish Christians increasingly looked to the family of Jesus as authoritative precisely by virtue of their kinship to the Lord. It is incredible that Jude should be a pseudepigraphal product of this "dynastic Christianity" (as Rowston, *NTS* 21 [1974–75] 554–63, and *Setting,* argues), and yet not state Jude's kinship to Jesus explicitly. There is no evidence for Kelly's suggestion that growing reverence for the Lord made the claim to blood-relationship seem presumptuous.

ἀδελφὸς δὲ Ἰακώβου, "and brother of James." After the death of James the son of Zebedee, only one early Christian leader was commonly called simply "James," without the need for further identification (Acts 12:17; 15:13; 21:18; 1 Cor 15:7; Gal 2:9, 12); and only one pair of brothers called James and Judas are known from the NT (Mark 6:3). Jude therefore uses this phrase to identify himself by reference to his more famous brother. Of course, he must have been known to the churches he addresses, but Judas was too common a name, even among Christian leaders, to identify him alone (cf. Luke 6:16; John 14:22; Acts 15:22). Unlike Ἰησοῦ Χριστοῦ δοῦλος, "servant of Jesus Christ," this phrase must be simply for identification, not to establish Jude's authority. If mere kinship to Jesus should convey no authority, still less should mere kinship to James. But if Jude could not use his usual title "brother of the Lord" to establish his authority, why could he not use it simply to identify himself? The answer may be that it was generally understood as conferring authoritative status and could not be used without this implication. Moreover, "servant and brother of Jesus Christ" may have seemed an incongruous combination.

Ellis argues that ἀδελφός means not "blood-brother" but "co-worker" ("Jude," 227), and this enables him to identify Jude as Judas Barsabbas, one of the "brothers" of the Jerusalem church (Acts 15:22). But it is unlikely that ἀδελφοί in Acts ever means more than "Christians" (against E. E. Ellis, "Paul and his Co-Workers," *Prophecy and Hermeneutic in Early Christianity* [WUNT 18; Tübingen: J. C. B. Mohr, 1978] 15–17). Pauline usage is another matter; sometimes, at least, ἀδελφοί seems to approximate to a technical term for Paul's fellow-workers in the Christian mission (Ellis, 14–15). But this is not a very secure basis for supposing that ἀδελφὸς Ἰακώβου could be easily understood to mean "one of James' co-workers."

ἐν θεῷ πατρὶ ἠγαπημένοις, "who are loved in God the Father." It is possible that all three terms with which Jude describes his readers derive from the Servant Songs of Isaiah, where Israel is described as called, loved and kept by God (called: Isa 41:9; 42:6; 48:12, 15; 49:1; 54:6; loved: 42:1; 43:4; cf. 44:2 LXX; kept: 42:6; 49:8). Following early Christian usage, Jude applies them to the church as the eschatological people of God. According to the OT, God's love for Israel (cf. Deut 7:7–8; Jer 31:3: Hos 11:1; 14:4; *2 Apoc. Bar.* 78:3) is shown especially in the salvation-event of the Exodus and in the eschatological salvation-event of the new Exodus, which the NT sees fulfilled in Christ. In the LXX, (ὁ) ἠγαπημένος becomes almost a title for Israel (Deut 32:15; 33:5, 26; 2 Chr 20:7; Ps 28:6; Isa 5:1; 44:2; Bar 3:37) and in the prayer in 3 Macc 6:11 the Jews are οἱ ἠγαπημένοι σου, "your loved ones." In Pauline usage, ἠγαπημένοι applied to Christians is closely associated with other terms transferred from the old Israel to the new ("chosen": 1 Thess 1:4, ἐκλογή; 2 Thess 2:13, εἵλατο; Col 3:12, ἐκλεκτοί; "holy": Col 3:12, ἅγιοι), just as Jude associates it with τετηρημένοι ("kept") and κλητοί ("called") (cf. also Ign. *Trall.* inscr.). This transference of titles from the old Israel to the church as the eschatological Israel was universal in primitive Christianity, and there is no need to see Jude's use of ἠγαπημένοι as influenced by Paul.

The perfect participle (ἠγαπημένοι) implies that God's love, once bestowed on his people, remains (cf. Jer 31:3; Rom 8:39).

The unexpected phrase ἐν θεῷ πατρί, "in God the Father," has been much discussed. Since it is clear that Jude is speaking not of his own love for his readers, but of God's love, it is natural to expect a reference to God as agent (cf. 1 Thess 1:4: ἠγαπημένοι ὑπὸ θεοῦ; 2 Thess 2:13: ἠγαπημένοι ὑπὸ κυρίου). But it is unlikely that the instrumental use of ἐν can be extended, even by a Semitism, to give the meaning "loved by God" (1 Cor 6:2, ἐν ὑμῖν, is not a real parallel because it is a technical for forensic usage), and such uses as "in the sight of" (cf. 1 Cor 14:11, ἐν ἐμοί), and "in the department of" (Moulton, *Grammar,* 103) give no sense that Jude can have preferred to that of ὑπὸ θεοῦ. Most commentators therefore try to give meaning to the local sense, "in God the Father": "by God" must be implicit in ἠγαπημένοι, and ἐν θεῷ πατρί must convey some further idea.

The Pauline usage of ἐν χριστῷ, "in Christ," and ἐν κυρίῳ, "in the Lord," is hardly relevant; in the Pauline corpus only 1 Thess 1:1 and 2 Thess 1:1

use ἐν θεῷ πατρί (adding καὶ κυρίῳ Ἰησοῦ Χριστῷ) in a (probably) local sense. Johannine usage, however, speaks more often of Christians' being "in God," as one side of the reciprocal relationship between Christians and God (John 17:21; 1 John 2:24; 3:24; 4:13, 15, 16). This usage seems particularly relevant since it is closely related to love: the indwelling is that of an intimate love relationship (see especially 1 John 4:16). It should be noted that Jude 21 ("keep yourselves in the love of God") also approximates to a Johannine idea (John 15:9–10; 1 John 4:16). Jude may therefore mean that those whom God loves are taken into the intimate fellowship of God's love, embraced and enfolded by his love. To be in God's love is to be "in God."

Ἰησοῦ Χριστῷ τετηρημένοις, "kept for Jesus Christ." This phrase has an eschatological sense: Christians are kept safe by God for the Parousia of Jesus Christ when they will enter into their final salvation in his kingdom. (Perhaps the metaphor is: Christians are the property of Jesus Christ, kept safe for him until he comes to claim it; cf. 1 Pet 1:4, where the inheritance of Christians is kept safe [τετηρημένην] for them in heaven until, at the Parousia, they can claim it.) For this eschatological sense, cf. 1 Thess 5:23 ("may your spirit and soul and body be kept [τηρηθείη] sound and blameless at the coming of our Lord Jesus Christ"); 1 Pet 1:5 ("guarded [φρουρουμένους] by God's power through faith for a salvation ready to be revealed in the last time"); and Jude 24 (where φυλάσσειν has the same sense as τηρεῖν, "to keep," here, cf. John 17:12). The idea that God must keep Christians safe (also in John 17:11, 15; Rev 3:20) clearly belongs to no one tradition of early Christianity but was widespread (Chaine, 277, thinks it is from the common primitive catechesis). It has a special appropriateness at the beginning of Jude's letter, with its concern that its readers be kept safe from the influence of the false teachers. The eschatological orientation also belongs to the letter as a whole (cf. v 21).

Again the perfect participle (τετηρημένοις) expresses the secure state of being in God's safekeeping.

τοῖς . . . κλητοῖς, "to those who are called." This is another title transferred to Christians from OT Israel, especially from Deutero-Isaiah (41:9; 42:6; 48:12, 15; 49:1; 54:6; cf. also Hos 11:1; the Qumran community applied the title to themselves as the faithful of Israel: CD 2:9; 4:4). Israel's "calling" is closely linked with God's "choice" or "election" of Israel (Isa 41:8, 9; 42:1; 43:10; 44:1, 2; 49:7; cf. CD 4:4): God's choice takes effect in his call to Israel to be his servant people. The idea expresses the divine initiative to which man must respond in faith, and in the NT καλεῖν ("to call") becomes a technical term for the process of Christian salvation. It refers to God's call to men and women, through the gospel, to enter his kingdom, to belong to the new people of God. Alongside the OT background, there may be the influence of Jesus' parables in which the call to enter the kingdom is represented by the invitation (καλεῖν) to a marriage feast (Matt 22:3–9, 14; Luke 14:8, 16–24; Rev 19:9). With the technical use of καλεῖν goes also the use of κλητός as a substantive (as here) as a technical term for Christians. Both are characteristic of Pauline usage, but by no means confined to Paul. Christians are κλητοί not only in Rom 1:6–7; 8:28; 1 Cor 1:2, 24 (as noun: Rom 1:6; 1 Cor 1:24), but also in Matt 22:14; Rev 17:14; *1 Clem.* inscr.; *Barn.* 4:13–14; *Sib. Or.* 8:92 (as noun: Rev 17:14; *1 Clem.* inscr.; *Sib. Or.* 8:92;

cf. Heb 9:15, *οἱ κεκλημένοι*). In the parties' formula of a letter, *κλητοῖς* is found in Rom 1:7; 1 Cor 1:2; *1 Clem.* inscr., as well as in Jude 1.

2. *ἔλεος ὑμῖν καὶ εἰρήνη καὶ ἀγάπη πληθυνθείη*, "May mercy, peace, and love be given you in abundance." The Jewish greeting, "Mercy and peace" (cf. *2 Apoc. Bar.* 78:2), is a comprehensive expression of God's blessing, which Jude asks God to lavish on his readers. "Mercy" (OT חסד, "steadfast love") is the divine attitude of kindness toward the covenant people, "peace" (OT שלום) is the well-being which results. No doubt Jude's readers would read the Jewish greeting with Christian overtones: God's mercy shown in Christ, and Christian salvation in Christ. The Christian interpretation is reinforced by the addition of *ἀγάπη*, "love," found in no Jewish salutation (though it may be worth noticing that *2 Apoc. Bar.* 78:3, following the salutation, continues: "I bear in mind, my brothers, the love of him who created us, who loved us from of old . . ."). The central Christian perception of the love of God in Christ was expressed in the frequent use of this word in primitive Christianity, and this distinctive Christian sense of God's love accounts for the addition of *ἀγάπη* here, even though the Jewish greeting already contained the idea of God's love in the word *ἔλεος* ("mercy"). The love of God is a favorite theme of Jude (vv 1, 2, 21).

Explanation

Jude identifies himself as the brother of James (i.e. James "the Just" of Jerusalem, the Lord's brother). His authority to address his readers does not rest on his kinship to Jesus, which he omits to mention, but on his commission to serve Jesus Christ. Although (as one of "the Lord's brothers") he was not known in the early church by the title "apostle," he should probably be understood to have exercised a leadership role alongside the apostles, which is expressed in the term "servant of Jesus Christ."

He addresses his readers in terms drawn from the descriptions of Israel in Isa 40–55, applied now to Christians as members of the eschatological people of God. They are those whom God has called into his kingdom, who are embraced by God's love, and whom God is keeping safe through the dangers of their life in this world until Jesus Christ at his Parousia claims them for his own. In the light of the rest of the letter, it appears that the terms of this description have been carefully chosen. Threatened by the false teachers, these Christians are in danger of apostatizing from their calling and incurring the judgment which awaits the false teachers at the Parousia. Jude knows that the divine action in calling, loving, and keeping safe must be met by a faithful human response, and when he takes up the themes of v 1 in v 21 it is to put the other side of the matter: his readers must *keep themselves* in the love of God and faithfully *await* the salvation which will be theirs at the Parousia. The divine action does not annul this human responsibility. But in his final doxology Jude will return to the note on which he began: his confidence that the God who is their Savior through Jesus Christ can keep them safe until they come to their eschatological destiny (v 24).

The salutation is a Jewish form, invoking divine blessing in abundance, but adapted by the addition of "love" to make reference to the blessings of God's love in Christ.

Occasion and Theme (Jude 3–4)

Bibliography

Maier, F. "Zur Erklärung des Judasbriefes (Jud 5)." *BZ* 2 (1904) 377–97. **Whitaker, G. H.** "Faith's Function in St Jude's Epistle." *ExpTim* 29 (1917–18) 425.

Translation

[3] *My dear friends, although I am very eager to write to you about our common salvation, I find* [a] *it necessary to write appealing to you to carry on the fight for the faith which was once and for all delivered to the saints.* [4] *For certain persons have infiltrated* [b] *among you, who were long ago designated for this condemnation, as ungodly men, who pervert the grace of our God into immorality and deny our only Master and Lord Jesus Christ.*

Notes

[a] ἔσχον: epistolary aorist, more naturally rendered as a present tense in English. (Greek uses a tense appropriate from the standpoint of the readers at the time of reading, English a tense appropriate at the time of writing.)

[b] The meaning is the same whether παρεισεδύησαν (B) or παρεισέδυσαν (all other MSS) is read.

Form/Structure/Setting

These verses correspond to the "body-opening" of the Greek letter, i.e. the introduction to the body of the letter: this is "the point at which the principal occasion for the letter is usually indicated" (White, *Body,* 18).

As in spoken conversation, a starting point common to both parties must be established (White, *Body,* 19), and this may be the formal function of Jude's reference to his intended letter about "our common salvation." He then proceeds to indicate the purpose of his actual letter, and to do so employs the form of the "petition," the form in which both official and private requests were presented in the literature of the period. T. Y. Mullins ("Petition as a Literary Form," *NovT* 5 [1962] 46–54) does not include Jude 3–4 in his list of NT petitions, presumably because παρακαλεῖν ("to appeal") is not in the first person, but Jude 3–4 should be seen as a minor adaptation of the petition form with παρακαλεῖν, which, of the four verbs generally used for petitions, was "the most personal and intense," the favorite verb in personal letters (Mullins, "Petition," 48–49). Mullins analyzes the petition into three basic elements: (a) background, (b) petition verb, (c) desired action, with optional elaborations including (d) the address. Jude 3–4 has these four elements: (a) v 4, following the petition and introduced by γάρ, as in 1 Cor 1:11 (cf. White, *Body,* 74); (b) παρακαλῶν, "appealing"; (c) ἐπαγωνίζεσθαι, κ.τ.λ., "to carry on the fight" (v 3); (d) Ἀγαπητοί, ὑμῖν, "My dear friends, you" (v 3).

A close formal parallel, at a comparable point in a NT letter, is 1 Cor 1:11–12 (cf. also Philem 8–10).

It is important to notice how vv 3–4 relate to the rest of the letter. The section vv 5–19 consists of a midrash intended to establish from Scripture (and other prophecies) the statement of v 4, namely that the sin and judgment of the false teachers has been prophesied. In other words, vv 5–19 really belong to the background of Jude's petition, to his explanation of the situation which requires his appeal in v 3. The petition itself is not further explained until v 20. This means that vv 20–23 are in no sense an appendix to Jude's homily ("closing exhortations," as commentaries sometimes call them): they are actually the section which spells out the content of Jude's petition, which v 3 announces as the purpose of the letter. Jude's appeal to his readers to contend for the faith is contained in vv 20–23.

Thus v 3, the appeal, is the statement of theme for the exhortatory section vv 20–23, while v 4, the background, forms a statement of theme for the midrash section, vv 5–19. These relationships are reinforced by the catchword connections: in v 3 *ἁγίοις πίστει* with *ἁγιωτάτῃ . . πίστει* (v 20); in v 4 *κρίμα . . . ἀσεβεῖς* with *κρίσιν* (vv 6, 15), *ἀσεβείς, ἀσεβείας, ἠσέβησαν* (v 15), *ἀσεβειῶν* (v 18).

Ἀγαπητοί (also in vv 17, 20) is a common address in Christian letters (Rom 12:19; 2 Cor 7:1; 12:19; Heb 6:9; 1 Pet 2:11; 4:12; 2 Pet 3:1, 8, 14, 17; 1 John 2:7; 3:2, 21; 4:1, 7, 11; *1 Clem* 1:1; 7:1; 12:8; 21:1; 24:1–2; 35:1; 36:1; 50:1; 53:1; cf. *1 Enoch* 91:3).

The marked alliteration of the "p" sound in vv 3–4a is a rhetorical feature.

If, as is argued in the *Comment*, *δεσπότην* ("Master," v 4) refers to Christ, the end of v 4 presents a binitarian formula with the two members in parallelism:

(1) *τὴν τοῦ θεοῦ ἡμῶν χάριτα μετατιθέντες εἰς ἀσέλγειαν*
(2) *καὶ τὸν μόνον δεσπότην καὶ κύριον ἡμῶν Ἰησοῦν χριστὸν ἀρνούμενοι.*
(1) "Who pervert the grace of our God into immorality"
(2) "and deny our only Master and Lord Jesus Christ."

Comment

3. *πᾶσαν σπουδὴν ποιούμενος*, "although I am very eager." The expression *σπουδὴν ποιεῖν* is good classical Greek, and *πᾶσαν σπουδὴν ποιεῖν*, where *πᾶσαν* means "the utmost," is frequently found (Chaine, 293; Moulton and Milligan, *Vocabulary*, 586). The phrase means either "to be very eager to" or "to make every effort to," and so could indicate either that Jude was intending to write (RSV) or that he was already engaged in writing (NEB). The former seems the more usual meaning and makes good sense here.

πᾶσαν σπουδὴν ποιούμενος γράφειν ὑμῖν . . . ἀνάγκην ἔσχον γράψαι, "although I am very eager to write to you . . . I find it necessary to write." Does Jude here refer to two letters or only one? Our translation (rendering the participial phrase "although . . .") embodies the exegesis, adopted by a majority of scholars, according to which Jude had been intending to write one letter, a general treatment of the Christian faith, but interrupted this plan to write another letter which the urgent necessity of the moment required. Some scholars, however (Knopf, Windisch, Reicke; Rowston, *Setting,* 114–18), adopt a different exegesis (with the participial phrase meaning "when . . ." or "because . . .") according to which Jude refers to only one letter, which he was intending to write and then actually wrote. The following are the main considerations in the issue:

(a) The contrast between the present infinitive γράφειν ("to write") and the aorist infinitive γράψαι (cf. 3 John 13; *Barn.* 4:9; 21:9) is probably not decisive. If it is to be pressed, the distinction will be between the general intention of writing (or perhaps the process of writing already begun) and the concrete action actually carried out. But this distinction could apply either to one letter, intended and then actually written (Reicke), or two letters, one intended, the other written.

(b) Does περὶ τῆς κοινῆς ἡμῶν σωτηρίας ("about our common salvation") describe the letter Jude actually wrote? According to Windisch, it is synonymous with "the faith which was once and for all delivered to the saints." In that case, Jude does not mean that he intended to write about the *content* of "our common salvation," but an appeal to his readers to stand up for it against heresy. This is just possible, but it is easier to take "about our common salvation" to refer to an exposition of the content of the Christian gospel, and Jude's actual letter is clearly not that.

(c) The view that Jude refers to only one letter "makes the sentence unnecessarily laboured and repetitive" (Kelly), in contrast to Jude's normally terse style.

(d) Rowston (*Setting,* 117) objects to the view that Jude is an emergency letter, dashed off in immediate response to the news of the crisis, on the grounds that it is a polished literary product. This is true, but the view that Jude refers to two letters need not mean that he could not have taken reasonable time and trouble to compose the letter he actually wrote. The contrast is simply between the letter he had been planning, probably at considerable length, on a general theme, and the short letter to which he turned his attention instead, when the news from the church(es) required a letter specifically about the danger from the false teachers.

If, then, Jude refers to a letter he intended to write, but, so far as we know, never in fact wrote, there is some force in Zahn's contention (*Introduction,* 269) that this is an indication of the authenticity of our letter. Such a reference makes little sense in a pseudepigraphal letter; it is very unlikely that there was a well-known work in Jude's name (now lost) to which the author might be supposed to be referring, but even if there was, one would not then expect such a vague reference to Jude's intention of writing it.

Robinson, arguing for the authenticity of Jude, thinks that Jude later fulfilled his intention of writing "about our common salvation," and that the result was 2 Peter, written by Jude as Peter's agent (*Redating,* 193–4). The proposed subject matter ("our common salvation") is somewhat more appropriate to 2 Peter than to Jude, but the difficulties in the way of attributing both letters to the same author are insuperable (see Introduction to 2 Peter). A.-M. Dubarle ("Rédacteur et destinataires de l'Epître aux Hébreux," *RB* 48 [1939] 506–29) suggested that the intended letter is Hebrews, of which Jude was the redactor, while the "word of exhortation" mentioned in Heb 13:22 is the letter of Jude; but, apart from anything else, the problems of the churches addressed in Hebrews and Jude seem wholly different.

περὶ τῆς κοινῆς ἡμῶν σωτηρίας, "about our common salvation." The phrase ἡ κοινὴ σωτηρία was used in secular Greek to mean "the safety of the state" (references in BAG, *s.v.* κοινός): Jude's use might be a Christian adaptation of the secular phrase, but could be merely coincidental. The term σωτηρία, "salvation," had a religious sense in the mystery religions, but also in Judaism (LXX Isa 45:17; 46:13; 52:7, 10; Wis 5:2; *Ps. Sol.* 16:5) before being quite widely adopted in primitive Christianity to refer to the eschatological deliverance, accomplished and to be fulfilled by "God our Savior" (v 25) through Jesus Christ. Chase (*DB*(*H*) 2, p. 805; and in Mayor, 19) thought Jude wrote "our *common* salvation" as a Jewish Christian writing to Gentile Christians; this is possible, but it is likely that Jude's readers were predominantly Jewish Christians, and the phrase would be quite natural in any case. "It brings out the corporate nature of salvation as understood by Judaism, with its consciousness of being the people of God, and even more vividly by Christianity, with its conviction of fellowship in Christ" (Kelly). But there is no ground for Kelly's further assertion, that "salvation" here lacks the eschatological aspect it has in Paul and in 1 Pet 1:5; on the contrary, in view of v 21, we might expect that Jude's intended treatise would have stressed the salvation which is coming for the faithful at the Parousia.

ἐπαγωνίζεσθαι τῇ . . . πίστει, "to carry on the fight for the faith." ἐπαγωνίζεσθαι seems often to be used, in place of the simple ἀγωνίζεσθαι, in the sense of "to continue the struggle" or "to follow up" previous contests (examples in Mayor, *LPGL;* cf. Whitaker, *ExpTim* 29 [1917–18] 425); the dative of advantage is not common with ἐπαγωνίζεσθαι (but some examples in Mayor, xi, 22; *LPGL*), but must be the sense here (cf. Phil 1:27: συναθλοῦντες τῇ πίστει τοῦ εὐαγγελίου, "striving together for the faith of the gospel").

The verb is an example of the common metaphorical use of terms from the athletic contests of the Greek games. Such metaphors had been popularized especially by their use in Stoicism for life as a moral contest, but their connotations were not necessarily those of Stoic moral philosophy. They were widely used in Hellenistic Judaism (V. C. Pfitzner, *Paul and the Agon Motif* [NovTSup 16; Leiden: E. J. Brill, 1967] chap 3) and are found even in Palestinian Jewish writings (4 Ezra 7:92, 127–28; *2 Apoc. Bar.* 15:7–8). In the primitive church they occur especially in the Pauline corpus (Rom 15:30; 1 Cor 9:24–27; Phil 1:27–30; 4:3; Col 1:29–2:1; 4:12–13; 1 Tim 6:12; 2 Tim 4:7), but also elsewhere (Heb 10:32; *1 Clem.* 2:4; 5; 7:1; 35:4; *2 Clem.* 7; 20:2; *Barn.* 4:11). We need not therefore see Jude's usage as influenced by Paul. The metaphor frequently became a very pale metaphor, often suggesting little more than striving or exertion, without much hint of its original reference to the games (Pfitzner, *Paul,* 72). To what extent it retains a live metaphorical sense in this verse is difficult to tell.

Pfitzner has shown that Paul does not use the athletic metaphors in the Stoic way to refer to life as a moral contest. He uses them primarily to characterize his apostolic mission as a struggle for the gospel. They refer to Paul's exertions in the cause of the gospel, including his struggle against opposition to it. Although the contest is primarily that of Paul and his co-workers, the missionaries (Phil 4:3; 1 Tim 6:12), all Christians share in it (Rom 15:30; Phil 1:27–30). Perhaps the best Pauline parallel to Jude 3 is Phil 1:27–30. Like Paul, Jude uses the metaphor for the contest on behalf of the gospel ("the faith," see below). It should be noted that, neither for Paul nor for Jude, is this contest simply a *defense* of the gospel; it is offensive, promoting the gospel's advance and victory. Nor is the contest fought only verbally. For Paul it involves a way of life which is faithful to the gospel (Phil 1:27; 1 Tim 6:11; cf. Heb 10:32–34), and Jude's idea of contending for the faith includes the exhortations of vv 20–21. His phrase should not therefore suggest primarily the negative task of opposing the false teachers. He appeals to his readers to continue the positive exertions of Christian life in the service of the gospel. But to do this they must resist the influence of the false teachers, since the latter have betrayed the cause of the gospel and given up the struggle by denying the moral implications of the gospel.

The structure of the letter is most important for establishing what Jude intended his readers to do to continue the fight for the faith (see *Form/Structure/Setting* section). What his appeal means he spells out in vv 20–23, which contain entirely positive exhortations. The common mistake of supposing that, for Jude, contending for the faith means denouncing opponents, arises from a misunderstanding of the significance of vv 5–19. Those verses are intended to awaken Jude's readers to the dangerous reality of their situation which makes Jude's appeal necessary, but it is only when he has done this that Jude goes on (in vv 20–23) to explain how they must continue the fight for the faith.

τῇ ἅπαξ παραδοθείσῃ τοῖς ἁγίοις πίστει, "the faith which was once and for all delivered to the saints." Since this phrase has often been taken as a mark of "early Catholicism" in Jude (e.g. Windisch, Schelkle), it must be examined carefully. It is said to reflect the idea of a fixed body of orthodox doctrine, the "deposit" of tradition, unalterable and normative, authoritatively transmitted from the past. Clearly it is not difficult to read this idea into Jude's words, if a late date for the letter is already presupposed, but it is much less clear that Jude's words demand this interpretation. The contrast set up between Jude and the Christianity of the first generation generally results from (1) underestimating the role of tradition in Christianity from the first, and (2) exaggerating the extent to which Jude's language implies a fixed body of formal doctrine.

The word *πίστις* ("faith") here refers to the content of what is believed (*fides quae creditur*, not *fides qua creditur*). This usage can already be found in Paul, most clearly in Gal 1:23 (*εὐαγγελίζεται τὴν πίστιν*, "preaches the faith"), where *πίστις* is equivalent to "the gospel," "the Christian message." Greek had a well-established "objective" use of *πίστις* to mean "a belief, a conviction" (e.g. Josephus, *C. Apion.* 2:163), but this is probably not the main source of the early Christian usage. In Gal 1:23 *τὴν πίστιν* does not mean "the *Christian* faith," as distinguished from other faiths, so much as "the *faith,*" the message which demands faith. It was because the Christian gospel was characteristically a message demanding faith (Rom 10:8: "the word of faith") that it could come to be called "the faith." Thus "to obey the faith" (Acts 6:7; and perhaps Rom 1:5; 16:26) is equivalent to "to obey the gospel" (Rom 10:16; 2 Thess

1:8; 1 Pet 4:17); it means to respond to the gospel in faith. (Other instances in Paul where πίστις may mean "the gospel" or "the Christian religion" are 1 Cor 16:13; Gal 3:23, 25; 6:10; Phil 1:25; Col 1:23; cf. Eph 4:5; and see Bultmann in *TDNT* 6, 213.) The objective use of πίστις ("faith") as *fides quae creditur* becomes especially common in the Pastorals (1 Tim 3:9; 4:1, 6; 2 Tim 4:7; other instances are less certain) and is occasional in the apostolic Fathers (Ign. *Eph.* 16:2; Pol. *Phil.* 3:2 ?), but since it goes back to Paul there is no ground for treating Jude's use of it as evidence of a late date. Moreover, there is no reason to suppose that Jude means by πίστις anything other than "the gospel." It need not refer to confessional formulae (Grundmann), though such formulae were already known in Paul's time, nor does it imply the idea of a defined body of orthodox doctrines, which commentators frequently attribute to Jude. Jude's readers are to contend, not for some particular formulation of Christian belief, but for the central Christian message of salvation through Jesus Christ. (In fact this is probably still the meaning in the later instances of πίστις as "the faith" in Ign. *Eph.* 16:2; Pol. *Phil.* 3:2.)

The faith is that which has been "delivered to the saints." As most commentators recognize (against Spitta), "the saints" are not the apostles, who received the gospel from Jesus Christ, but the Christians of the church(es) to which Jude writes, who received the gospel from the apostles who founded the church(es). (The use of οἱ ἅγιοι, "the saints," for Christians, though apparently not common to all strands of early Christian tradition, was not peculiarly Pauline: cf. Acts 9:13, 32, 41; Heb 6:10; 13:24; Rev 5:8; 8:3; 11:18; 13:7, 10; 14:12; Herm. *Vis.* 1:1:9; 1:3:2; *Asc. Isa.* 4:13, 14, 16; *Did.* 16:7; Ign. *Smyrn.* 1:2.) Almost certainly it is the apostles who are the agents implied in παραδοθείσῃ ("which was delivered"). The technical use of παραδιδόναι ("to hand on, deliver" a tradition, equivalent to Hebrew מסר ל) with its correlative παραλαμβάνειν ("to receive" a tradition, equivalent to קבל מן) was taken over by early Christianity from its use with reference to Jewish tradition: "in the Pauline epistles we find the whole Jewish *paradosis* terminology" (O. Cullmann, "The Tradition," in *The Early Church* [London: SCM Press, 1956] 63). Jude's idea of the tradition of the gospel conforms exactly to the Pauline usage (on which see Cullmann, "Tradition," 59–99; P. Fannon, "The Influence of Tradition in St Paul," *SE* 4/1 [= TU 102; Berlin: Akademie-Verlag, 1968] 292–307; G. E. Ladd, "Revelation and Tradition in Paul," in W. W. Gasque and R. P. Martin (eds.) *Apostolic History and the Gospel* [F. F. Bruce Festschrift; Exeter: Paternoster, 1970] 223–30; and most recently, J. I. H. McDonald, *Kerygma and Didache* [SNTSMS 37; Cambridge: Cambridge University Press, 1980] chap. 4). Paul uses παραδιδόναι ("to deliver") and παραλαμβάνειν ("to receive") with reference to his initial instruction of the churches he founded: he delivered the traditions to the churches and they received them from him (1 Cor 11:2, 23; 15:3; Gal 1:19; Phil 4:9; Col 2:6; 1 Thess 2:13; 2 Thess 2:15; 3:6; cf. Rom 6:17). The central content of these traditions was the gospel itself (1 Cor 15:1; Gal 1:9), but they also included traditions about the life of Jesus (1 Cor 11:23) and instructions on Christian conduct and church practice (1 Cor 11:2; Phil 4:9; 2 Thess 3:6). Probably these various elements should not be distinguished too sharply. Particularly noteworthy are Paul's injunctions that his readers should "hold fast" or "maintain" (again technical terminology, cf. Mark 7:8) these traditions (1 Cor 11:2; 15:2; 2 Thess 2:15), and his appeal to them as a standard by which teaching and practice may be judged (2 Cor 11:3–4; Gal 1:8–9; Col 2:6–8; 2 Thess 3:6; implicitly in 1 Cor 11:2, 17; 2 Thess 2:15).

Jude's appeal to his readers to contend for the gospel they originally received does not go beyond these Pauline ideas. The word ἅπαξ ("once and for all") emphasizes that because the gospel is the message of the "once and for all" salvific action of God in Christ (Rom 6:10; Heb 9:12; 9:26–28; 10:10; 1 Pet 3:18) it cannot change, and so it is the gospel as they first received it when they became Christians to which Jude's readers must remain faithful. This emphasis, too, is thoroughly in line with Paul, who similarly, when confronted with false teaching, appealed to the gospel as originally received by the churches from their founding apostles (Rom 16:17; 2 Cor 11:4; Gal 1:9). Both Paul and Jude are reflecting a common principle of the early Christian mission.

Jude's concern is especially with the moral implications of the gospel (not with doctrinal orthodoxy; hence the idea that "the faith" means a set of doctrinal formulae is quite inappropriate). No doubt he has in mind particularly the instruction in Christian conduct which accompanied the gospel in the initial teaching given by the apostles, but he refers to the gospel itself, ἡ πίστις, because it is the gospel itself for which his readers will be fighting when they remain faithful to its moral demand and resist the antinomianism of the false teachers. Antinomianism is a perversion of the gospel itself, and so just as Paul in Galatians opposes the imposition of circumcision as contrary to the gospel his converts first received from him, so Jude opposes antinomianism as contrary to the gospel his readers first received from the apostles.

Two differences between Jude and Paul are sometimes invoked at this point, in support of a later date for Jude. In the first place, it is pointed out that in Paul's understanding of tradition it is not seen as the rigid preservation of fixed formulae, as excluding the necessary role of the Spirit in inspiring and interpreting the tradition, or as ruling out the kind of theological development to which Paul himself subjects the tradition. All this is true, but the corresponding claim that these implications *are* present in Jude's understanding of tradition has no basis in the evidence. They cannot be deduced from his strong opposition to what he sees as a gross distortion of the gospel, any more than they can be deduced from Paul's equally strong opposition to what *he* sees as gross distortions of the gospel.

Secondly, with rather more justification, it is said that Jude does not seek to refute his opponents by theological argument, as Paul does. This observation, however, may simply tell us that Jude is not Paul, rather than that Jude is later than Paul. Theological argument of the Pauline kind is not Jude's style, but it was quite probably not the style of many of Paul's fellow apostles either. In fact Jude offers his own style of theological argument in the midrash of vv 5–19.

A parallel to v 3 has been noticed in *T. Mos.* 4:8: "the two tribes shall remain in the faith first laid down for them" (in the Latin version: *permanebunt in praeposita fide sua*). Jude was acquainted with the *T. Mos.* (see vv 9, 16) and perhaps the phrase had stuck in his mind, but his words are fully explicable on the basis of early Christian usage.

4. παρεισεδύησαν γάρ τινες ἄνθρωποι, "For certain persons have infiltrated among you." The verb παρεισδύ(ν)ειν, "to infiltrate" (only here in NT; other examples in Mayor, xi, 24) need not invariably, but tends to carry the connotation of secrecy or stealth (cf. the noun παρείσδυσις used of the activity of the devil in *Barn* 2:10; 4:9; Paul's use of παρεισάκτος and παρεισέρχεσθαι in Gal 2:10; παρεισάγειν in 2 Pet 2:1, of heretical teachings; παρεισπορεύεσθαι used with λεληθότως in 2 Macc 8:1). The use of τινες ("certain persons") to designate a definite group of people, well-known to the readers, is common (Rom 3:8; 1 Cor 4:18; 15:34; 2 Cor 3:1; 10:12; Gal 1:7; 1 Tim 1:3, 19; 2 Pet 3:9; Ign. *Eph.* 7:1; 9:1): it is often used of opponents, with a hint of disparagement.

Jude's language suggests that the troublemakers were itinerant prophets or teachers, perhaps with a group of followers. Such wandering teachers were a feature of early Christianity, as of the contemporary religious world in general, and frequently occur in early Christian literature as the cause of trouble in the churches (Matt 7:15; 2 Cor 10–11; 1 John 4:1; 2 John 10; *Did.* 11–12; Ign. *Eph.* 9:1). Jude is not reflecting a theological claim that heretical teaching must come from outside the church (Wisse, "Jude," 136), because he means only that the false teachers have come from outside the particular church(es) to which he writes, and vv 5–6 imply that he regards them as apostate believers; he is reflecting the reality of the situation.

οἱ πάλαι προγεγραμμένοι εἰς τοῦτο τὸ κρίμα, "who were long ago designated for this condemnation." This phrase bristles with difficulties. The adverb πάλαι usually means "long ago," but can sometimes mean simply "in the past" and refer to the recent past (classical examples in Chaine, 296); with the perfect προγεγραμμένοι it could mean "for a long time." At any rate πάλαι seems to indicate that προ in προγεγραμμένοι should have a temporal sense ("written beforehand," as in Acts 1:16; Rom 15:4; Eph 3:3, rather than "placarded publicly," as in Gal 3:1, or "enlisted," as in 1 Macc 10:36), but some have pointed to the technical use of προγράφειν with reference to "the proscribed," i.e. those whose names were entered on a register of outlaws, according to Roman practice (Polybius, *Hist.* 32.5.2; 6.1; Lucian, *Tim.* 51). For the interpretation of the words οἱ πάλαι προγεγραμμένοι there are three main possibilities:

(1) The false teachers and their condemnation have been recorded in the heavenly books (Clement of Alexandria, Windisch, Kelly). (This idea can incorporate the meaning "proscribed" for προγεγραμμένοι.) Many of the Jewish texts usually cited in this connection are not relevant, since the idea they employ is that the sins of the wicked are recorded at the time when they are committed, so that they can be brought in evidence at the last judgment (Rev 20:12; *2 Apoc. Bar.* 24:1; *1 Enoch* 89:61–71; 98:7; 104:7). Rather different and less common is the predestinarian idea that the condemnation of the wicked is already set down in the heavenly books, before they sin (*1 Enoch* 108:7—an appendix to *1 Enoch* which Jude is unlikely to have known). This idea really belongs to the deterministic notion of the heavenly tablets of destiny, on which the whole of history is set down in advance (*1 Enoch* 81:1–2; 93:1, 3; 103:2; 106:19; *T. Asher* 7:5). Jude could have taken up this idea of the heavenly tablets of destiny from *1 Enoch,* but how did he know what was written on them? Had he been granted a special revelation of their con-

tents, like Enoch (*1 Enoch* 81:1–2)? The only plausible reply to this is that Jude applied to the false teachers the prophecies of judgment on the wicked which he found in *1 Enoch,* where they allegedly derived from *Enoch*'s reading of the heavenly tablets. But in that case it is much simpler to suppose that *προγεγραμμένοι* refers directly to the prophecies of Enoch, rather than to the heavenly books (see interpretation (3) below).

(2) The false teachers and their condemnation have been prophesied in an apostolic prophecy, either 2 Pet 2:1–3:4 (Zahn, *Introduction,* 249–52), or other prophecies such as the one Jude quotes in vv 17–18 (cf. Acts 20:29–30; 1 Tim 4:1–3; 2 Tim 3:13). Zahn's case depends on his interpretation of *τοῦτο τὸ κρίμα* ("this condemnation") as referring back to *παρεισεδύησαν* ("infiltrated"), so that the prophecy is about the infiltration of the false teachers in the particular church(es) to which Jude writes. This is unlikely (see below), but without it we need a written apostolic prophecy of the condemnation of the false teachers, which neither Jude's quotation (v 18) nor any other extant apostolic prophecies, except 2 Peter, seem to supply. This view therefore really depends on the priority of 2 Peter.

(3) The false teachers and their condemnation have been prophesied in pre-Christian prophecy, either in the form of the OT types of vv 5–7, 11 (Maier, *BZ* 2 [1904] 384–91; Grundmann) or in the book of Enoch (Mayor, Chaine, Cantinat). This interpretation gives full weight to *πάλαι,* "long ago," and can make better sense of *τοῦτο τὸ κρίμα* ("this condemnation") than (1) or (2) can (see below).

It also provides a more satisfactory link with the following verses. This structural consideration, however, requires a modification of this interpretation, for vv 5–19 are really a unity, in which Jude cites a series of types and prophecies to substantiate the claim made in v 4, that the false teachers and their doom have been prophesied. Thus the whole section vv 5–19 serves as explanation of *οἱ πάλαι προγεγραμμένοι εἰς τοῦτο τὸ κρίμα,* and it is unnecessary to select only part of vv 5–19 as containing the prophecy Jude has in mind in v 4. Not even the apostolic prophecy of v 18 need be excluded from Jude's thought in v 4, for if it is only one of a series of prophecies referred to in v 4 it need not contain a reference to the false teachers' condemnation or bear the full weight of *πάλαι.* Nor need the types and prophecies of vv 5–19 exhaust the prophecies Jude has in mind in v 4: *οἱ πάλαι προγεγραμμένοι* is a general statement, which Jude backs up by expounding some examples, not necessarily an exhaustive list.

εἰς τοῦτο τὸ κρίμα, "for this condemnation." The main difficulty in this phrase is to explain *τοῦτο* ("this"); the following suggestions have been made:

(1) *τοῦτο* refers backward, either to v 3b, which implies the condemnation of the false teachers in the defense of orthodoxy (Mayor), or to *παρεισεδύησαν* ("infiltrated," v 4a), understood as a judgment on the churches in which the false teachers have appeared (Zahn, *Introduction,* 249). Both these explanations are very unnatural.

(2) *τοῦτο* refers forward to the immediately succeeding words in the rest of v 4, understood as the verdict pronounced by prophecy on the false teachers (Spitta). However, although *κρίμα* ("condemnation") does refer to the verdict rather than to the punishment, it seems very weak in this context to take it

as a mere statement of their sin; it should be the judicial sentence pronounced on their sin and leading to punishment.

(3) τοῦτο refers forward to part or all of vv 5–19 (Clement of Alexandria, Cantinat, Grundmann). The difficulty here is that the point of reference is too remote, but the difficulty is at least eased by the following considerations: (a) The rest of v 4 (ἀσεβεῖς . . . ἀρνούμενοι) is not simply additional description of τινες ἄνθρωποι ("certain persons"), but should be taken closely with οἱ πάλαι προγεγραμμένοι εἰς τοῦτο τὸ κρίμα ("who were long ago designated for this condemnation"), not in the sense of constituting the condemnation, as in (2) above, but in the sense of specifying the sins for which prophecy has said they will be condemned. In other words, it is *as* ungodly men, who pervert God's grace into immorality and deny the Lord, that prophecy has designated them for condemnation. In the following verses (5–19) Jude substantiates from prophecy *both* their sins *and* the condemnation which their sins will incur. This makes the separation of τοῦτο from its point of reference by v 4b less difficult, since v 4b belongs with τοῦτο τὸ κρίμα to a statement which as a whole looks forward to vv 5–19. (b) The use of τοῦτο will seem more natural once it is seen that v 4 is the announcement of the theme which Jude expounds in vv 5–19. (c) This intimate connection with vv 5–19 is strengthened by the observation that in v 4 Jude is already using his exegetical method of linking text and exegesis by means of catchwords, so that εἰς τοῦτο τὸ κρίμα, "for this condemnation," (v 4) links up with εἰς κρίσιν (v 6) and κρίσιν, "judgment" (v 15). The latter link is especially clear since ἀσεβεῖς ("ungodly"), immediately following κρίμα in v 4, is emphatically linked with the double ἀσεβεῖς in Enoch's prophecy in v 15.

Thus τοῦτο τὸ κρίμα refers to the condemnation at the Parousia, which is prophesied typologically in vv 5–7, 11, and directly in vv 14–15. That Jude uses κρίμα, referring to the sentence of condemnation more than to the punishment, fits his purpose of countering the antinomianism of the false teachers. He does not wish to prove simply that they are heading for destruction, but that their immoral behavior will incur divine condemnation.

ἀσεβεῖς ("ungodly") "may be almost said to give the keynote to the Epistle (cf. vv 15, 18) as it does to the Book of Enoch" (Mayor). Certainly this is the word which sums up Jude's indictment of the false teachers. His brief letter contains six occurrences of the words in the word-group ἀσεβ- (ἀσεβής, ἀσέβεια, ἀσεβεῖν), which is more than any other writing of the NT and the apostolic Fathers (except *Barn.,* which also has six). However, no less than four of these occurrences are in the quotation from *1 Enoch* (vv 14–15) and Jude has probably there followed the vocabulary of the Greek translation. Nevertheless he will have selected the quotation partly because of its strong emphasis on the "ungodliness" of those who are to be judged. He then picked up the term in his wording of the apostolic prophecy (v 18). Here in v 4 ἀσεβεῖς is a catchword, linking this statement forward to the two prophecies (vv 14–15, 17–18) which clinch Jude's argument for it.

Jude's (and the Greek *Enoch*'s) use of the ἀσεβ- words must be understood against the background of their use, not in secular Greek, but in Jewish Greek, especially the LXX. The words are common in the LXX (translating especially רשע), and especially in the Wisdom literature, which contrasts the way of life of the ἀσεβεῖς with that of the righteous. They are also quite common in the *T. 12 Patr.*, with their strong ethical concern (and less common in the Greek of *1 Enoch:* only 1:9; 5:6–7; 8:2; 10:20; 13:2). In this Jewish usage the basic sense of irreverence is given a strong ethical direction. Because, for the Jew, God's commandments regulate the whole of man's conduct, the irreverent attitude to God is manifested in unrighteous conduct. All evil deeds are ἀσέβειαι, "godlessnesses," and ἀσεβής, "godless" is equivalent to ἁμαρτωλός, ἄδικος, or ἄνομος. It is not surprising that, as in Jude, the ἀσεβ-words occur frequently in the context of the judgment that overtakes such wickedness (*1 Enoch* 10:20; *T. Zeb.* 10:3; Rom 1:18; 1 Pet 4:18; 2 Pet 2:6; 3:7; *1 Clem.* 14:15; 57:7–8; *2 Clem.* 10:1; 18:1; *Barn.* 10:5; 11:7; 15:5; *Mart. Pol.* 11:2).

The word is appropriate to Jude's purpose because it sums up the antinomianism of the false teachers: unrighteous behavior stemming from an irreverent rejection of the moral authority of God's commandments. It describes, not theoretical atheism, but practical godlessness.

τὴν τοῦ θεοῦ ἡμῶν χάριτα μετατιθέντες εἰς ἀσέλγειαν, "who pervert the grace of our God into immorality." The grace of God is that free favor of God which the Christian experiences through Jesus Christ, forgiving him and liberating him from sin and the condemnation of the Law. (The word χάρις in this sense, though typical of Pauline theology, is not a uniquely Pauline term: cf. John 1:14, 16; Heb 4:16; 10:29; 12:15; 1 Pet 1:10; *1 Clem.* 16:17.) Jude complains that the false teachers pervert this grace into ἀσέλγεια, "immorality," which in the Greek of this period designates sensual indulgence, especially sexual immorality (cf. 1 Pet 4:3; Rom 13:13; 2 Cor 12:21). In other words, they interpret the Christian's liberation by God's grace as liberation from all moral restraint (cf. 2 Pet 2:19). They justify immoral behavior by an antinomian doctrine.

The danger of such a libertine misinterpretation of Christian freedom was recognized in primitive Christianity, by Paul (Rom 3:8; 6:1, 15; Gal 5:13) and others (1 Pet 2:16), and apparently realized at Corinth in Paul's time (1 Cor 5:1–6; 6:12–20; 10:23) and in the churches of Asia when Revelation was written (Rev 2:14, 20). The libertinism in Jude's churches has a good deal in common with that at Corinth (see also v 19), and there is some ground for thinking that in both cases it was Paul's own teaching on Christian freedom from the Law which was exaggerated and distorted. Whether we should postulate a "gnostic" influence is much less certain: there is no definite evidence of specifically gnostic traits in Jude's opponents.

A certain emphasis on sins of the flesh (ἀσέλγεια, "immorality," cf. vv 8, 10; 1 Cor 6:12–20; Rev 2:14, 20) may reflect, on the one hand, a standard Jewish tendency to view the sexual indulgence which was typical of pagan society with particular abhorrence, and, on the other hand, the temptations of life in pagan society (if Jude's churches were located in pagan society) and the libertines' determination to demonstrate their freedom by flouting the more obvious kinds of conventional morality. It is much less likely that we should attribute to them the dualistic belief that the spiritual man transcends the concerns of the material body; this would be more definitely an incipient Gnosticism.

The suggestion that the charges of immorality are merely conventional polemic against heretics (Wisse, "Jude," 137) is unacceptable, since all of Jude's charges against the false teachers are of teaching and practicing antinomianism. He has not first labeled them heretics for some other, purely doctrinal, error, and then concluded that, like all heretics, they must lead immoral lives. Their rejection of the moral demands of the gospel is his only concern.

τὸν μόνον δεσπότην καὶ κύριον ἡμῶν Ἰησοῦν χριστόν, "our only Master and Lord Jesus Christ." Does the whole phrase refer to Jesus Christ, or does *τὸν μόνον δεσπότην* ("the only Master") refer to God the Father? The absence of the article before *κύριον* ("Lord") cannot decide the issue because the article is often omitted before *κύριος*. The term *δεσπότης* ("Master") was widely used of God in Judaism (LXX, Philo, Josephus), and the phrase *ὁ μόνος δεσπότης* is found (Josephus, *BJ* 7:323, 410; *Ant.* 18:23: in all three cases God as the one *δεσπότης* is contrasted, not with other gods, but with Roman rule). Early Christianity took over this usage, especially in prayer and liturgical formulae, and used *δεσπότης* almost always of God the Father (Luke 2:29; Acts 4:14; Rev 6:10; *1 Clem.* 7:5; 8:2; 9:4; 11:1; 20:8, 11; 24:1, 5; 33:1, 2; 36:2, 4; 40:1; 48:1; 52:1; 56:16; 59:4; 61:1–2; *Did.* 10:3; *Barn.* 1:7; 4:3; Herm. *Vis.* 2:2:4–5; *Sim.* 1:9; *Diogn.* 8:7; Justin, *1 Apol.* 61:3). This evidence might seem decisive, and it is not surprising that several manuscripts and the Syriac version clarify the text by inserting *θεόν* ("God") after *δεσπότην*. There are, however, three pieces of evidence which point in the other direction:

(1) 2 Pet 2:1, which is the only NT text (apart from Jude 4) to use *δεσπότης* of Christ, evidently understood Jude 4 in that sense. This is not decisive, but it does show that the weight of early Christian usage of *δεσπότης* did not prevent one early reader of Jude 4 from taking *δεσπότης* to refer to Christ.

(2) According to Julius Africanus, who lived at Emmaus in the late second century, the family of Jesus were known as *οἱ δεσπόσυνοι* (*ap.* Eusebius, *Hist. Eccl.* 1.7.14). This distinctive usage must imply that Jesus was known as *ὁ δεσπότης*, "the Master," in the Palestinian Jewish circles in which his family was known. It therefore brings us close—perhaps closer than the other early Christian usage listed above—to the terminology current in Jude's own milieu.

(3) The term *δεσπότης* is appropriate to the image of Jesus as the Master of his household slaves. This is how it is used in 2 Pet 2:1 ("the Master who bought them"), and it is how the equivalent term *οἰκοδεσπότης*, "the master of the house," is used, figuratively, of Jesus in Matt 10:25 and, in parables, in Mark 13:27; Luke 13:25 (where P[75] has *δεσπότης*). Of course, *κύριος* was used in the same way, but as a Christological title it rapidly acquired much broader and more exalted connotations. Perhaps, then, it was in order specifically to invoke the image of Christ as the Master of his Christian slaves that *δεσπότης* was used in (2) above, and this will explain why Jude should *add* *δεσπότης* to *κύριος*. For Jude, *κύριος* is the title of Jesus' divine authority as the one who exercises the divine function of judgment (v 14, and perhaps vv 5–6, 9); in v 4 he adds *δεσπότης* to convey the thought that, as Christians, the false teachers belong to Jesus as his slaves whom he has bought. They are both disowning him as Master and flouting his authority as universal Judge.

A minor issue is the parallel in *1 Enoch* 48:10: "They denied the Lord of

Spirits and his Messiah" (tr. Knibb). Jude has sometimes been thought to have modeled his words on this, but it occurs in the Parables of Enoch (*1 Enoch* 37–71), a section of *1 Enoch* which has not been found among the Qumran fragments and which is now commonly dated in the late first century A.D. It seems unlikely that Jude knew the Parables; there is very little other indication in the letter that he did (but v 14, cf. *1 Enoch* 60:8). This parallel can therefore scarcely be invoked in favor of referring *δεσπότην* to God.

Jude's use of *μόνον*, "only," with *δεσπότην* seems at first sight to favor the reference to God (cf. v 25: *μόνῳ θεῷ*, "only God") but a reference to Christ as the only Master is intelligible if Jude is here concerned with the immoral behavior of the false teachers (see below, on *ἀρνούμενοι*). To indulge in such behavior is to serve other masters (cf. Matt 7:24; Rom 6:12–23; Gal 4:3, 8–9; 2 Pet 2:19). Thus, by their conduct, the false teachers disown Christ, the only Master of Christians, and subject themselves to other masters.

ἀρνούμενοι, "deny." Does this refer to doctrinal denial or ethical denial? Those who think the reference is to doctrinal error usually suppose that some kind of Gnostic belief is in view: denying the one God (if *δεσπότην* refers to God) by postulating a demiurge as creator of the material world, and denying the Lord Jesus by a docetic Christology (cf. 1 John 4:2–3; 2 John 7). But the rest of the letter provides no evidence of such beliefs, and if the false teachers did believe in a gnostic demiurge it is remarkable that Jude accuses them only of blaspheming angels (v 8). It is more consistent with the evidence of the letter as a whole to take the denial of Christ as a further reference to their libertinism (so Luther, Plummer, Chaine, Cantinat, Grundmann, and so on), thus creating a parallelism of meaning between the two participial phrases at the end of v 4. The ungodly behavior of the false teachers (*ἀσεβεῖς*) is (1) in relation to God the Father, a perversion of his grace, and (2) in relation to Christ, a denial of his lordship.

The idea of denial of God by conduct is attested in Judaism and early Christianity (*1 Enoch* 38:2; 41:2; 45:2; 46:7; 48:10; 67:8, 10—but all these examples are from the Parables; Titus 1:16: "They profess to know God, but they deny him by their deeds"). The Rabbis taught that to reject one's obligation to obey God's commandments is to deny God (references in E. P. Sanders, *Paul and Palestinian Judaism,* [London: SCM Press, 1977] 136): a concept relevant to Jude's libertines. References to denial of Christ by deeds are rarer, but *2 Clem.* 17:7 says of the wicked who are punished at the Last Judgment that they "denied Jesus by their words or by their deeds" (and cf. 3:1–4), while the thought, though not the terminology, is found in Matt 7:21–23. Jude means that by refusing to obey Christ's moral demands the false teachers are in effect, though not in words, disowning him as Master and rejecting his authority as Sovereign and Judge. "They regard themselves, not Him, as their Lord" (Luther).

Explanation

In this section Jude explains the background and purpose of his letter. It is not the extended discussion of Christian salvation which he has been planning to write, but a more *ad hoc* work, called forth by the disturbing news he has received from the church(es) he addresses.

A group of itinerant prophets has arrived in the church(es). Jude describes them as people of irreligious conduct, who pervert the grace of God into an excuse for immorality. Evidently, like the Corinthians whose slogan was "All things are lawful for me" (1 Cor 6:12; 10:23), they take Christian freedom to mean that the really spiritual man is free from the restraints of conventional morality. Especially they seem intent on flouting accepted standards of sexual ethics, in line with the greater permissiveness of pagan society. Although they claim to be followers of Jesus Christ, Jude says that by rejecting his moral demands they are in fact disowning him as their Master and repudiating his authority as Lord.

This description of the false teachers, however, is more than empirical observation. For just such people, Jude claims, were long ago described in prophecy, which also predicted their condemnation by God. This is the claim which Jude will go on to substantiate by means of his midrash on a series of types and prophecies in vv 5–19.

Jude's purpose in seeking to demonstrate that the false teachers and their condemnation have been prophesied is not to comfort his readers with the assurance that all is happening according to God's plan—though this may be an incidental effect. Still less is he indulging in mere denunciation. The point is to prove that the libertine teaching and practice of these people puts them into a class of people who, according to Scripture, incur God's wrath and condemnation, and that therefore they constitute a severe danger, which Jude's readers must resist, to the churches. Jude is alerting them to one of the great dangers of the last times in which they are living. The method of argument he will adopt is therefore appropriately the method of apocalyptic interpretation of OT types and prophecies (vv 5–19).

This danger (v 4, substantiated in vv 5–19) is really the presupposition for Jude's main purpose in writing his letter, stated in the appeal of v 3. He writes to urge his readers to continue the fight on behalf of the Christian gospel. In the false teachers' attack on the moral implications of the gospel, Jude sees the gospel itself ("the faith") at stake, and here he is at one with all the NT writers. God's purpose in the gospel is to save sinners, not to promote sin.

Like other NT writers, Jude identifies the true gospel as the one which the apostles who founded the churches preached to the first converts. This appeal to the past, and to a form of tradition, is not to be seen as an "early Catholic" fossilization of the faith into fixed formulae of orthodox belief. Rather it was present in early Christianity from the start, bound up with the notion of the apostolate, and necessarily inherent in a message about God's saving action in historical events. It excludes neither the living inspiration of the Spirit nor legitimate theological development, but requires that they be tested against the standard of the original gospel.

Jude's appeal to contend for the faith is not further developed until vv 20–23, in which he will explain what it involves.

Three Old Testament Types (Jude 5–10)

Bibliography (including Bibliography for the Excursus on Jude 9)

Barrett, C. K. "Things Sacrificed to Idols." *NTS* 11 (1964–65) 138–53. **Berger, K.** "Der Streit des guten und des bösen Engels um die Seele: Beobachtungen zu 4QAmr[b] und Judas 9." *JSJ* 4 (1973) 1–18. **Berger, K.** "Hartherzigkeit und Gottes Gesetz, die Vorgeschichte des anti-jüdischen Vorwurfs in Mc 10[5]." *ZNW* 61 (1970) 1–47. **Black, M.** "Critical and exegetical notes on three New Testament texts Hebrews xi. 11, Jude 5, James i. 27." *Apophoreta: Festschrift für Ernst Haenchen.* BZNW 30. Berlin: Alfred Töpelmann, 1964. 39–45. **Charles, R. H.** *The Assumption of Moses.* London: A. & C. Black, 1897. **Cramer, J. A.** ed. *Catenae Graecorum Patrum in Novum Testamentum.* vol.8. Oxford: Oxford University Press, 1844. 160–63. **Daniel, C.** "La mention des Esséniens dans le texte grec de l'épître de S. Jude." *Mus* 81 (1968) 503–21. **Delcor, M.** "Le mythe de la chute des anges et de l'origine des géants comme explication du mal dans le monde dans l'apocalyptique juive. Histoire des traditions." *RHR* 190 (1976) 3–53. (= Delcor, M. *Etudes bibliques et orientales de religions comparées.* Leiden: E. J. Brill, 1979. 263–313.) **Denis, A. M.** *Fragmenta Pseudepigraphorum Graeca.* In *Pseudepigrapha Veteris Testamenti Graeca* 3, ed. A. M. Denis and M. de Jonge. Leiden: E. J. Brill, 1970. 63–67. **Denis, A. M.** *Introduction aux Pseudépigraphes grecs d'Ancien Testament.* SVTP 1. Leiden: E. J. Brill, 1970. 128–41. **Dubarle, A. M.** "Le péché des anges dans l'épître de Jude." *Memorial J. Chaine.* Lyons: Facultés Catholiques, 1950. 145–48. **Glasson, T. F.** *Greek Influence in Jewish Eschatology.* London: S. P. C. K., 1961. 62–67. **Haacker, K.** and **Schäfer, P.** "Nachbiblische Traditionen vom Tod des Mose." *Josephus-Studien: Untersuchungen zu Josephus, dem antiken Judentum und dem Neuen Testament: Otto Michel zum 70. Geburtstag gewidmet,* ed. O. Betz, K. Haacker, M. Hengel. Göttingen: Vandenhoeck & Ruprecht, 1974. 147–74. **Hanson, A. T.** *Jesus Christ in the Old Testament.* London: S. P. C. K., 1965. 136–38. **James, M. R.** *The Lost Apocrypha of the Old Testament.* London: S. P. C. K./New York: Macmillan, 1920. 42–51. **Kee, H. C.** "The Terminology of Mark's Exorcism Stories." *NTS* 14 (1968) 232–46. **Kellett, E. E.** "Note on Jude 5." *ExpTim* 15 (1903–4) 381. **Laperrousaz, E. M.** *Le Testament de Moïse,* 29–62. **Loewenstamm, S. E.** "The Death of Moses." *Studies on the Testament of Abraham,* ed. G. W. E. Nickelsburg, Jr. SBLSCS 6. Missoula, MT: Scholars Press, 1976. 185–217. **Maier, F.** "Zur Erklärung des Judasbriefes (Jud 5)." *BZ* 2 (1904) 377–97. **Mees, M.** "Papyrus Bodmer VII (P[72]) und die Zitate aus dem Judasbrief bei Clemens von Alexandrien." *CDios* 181 (1968) 551–59. **Milik, J. T.** "4Q Visions de 'Amram et une citation d'Origène." *RB* 79 (1972) 77–97. **Reicke, B.** *Diakonie,* 355–59. **Schlosser, J.** "Les jours de Noé et de Lot: A propos de Luc, XVII, 26–30." *RB* 80 (1973) 13–36. **Sickenberger, J.** "Engels- oder Teufelslästerer im Judasbriefe (8–10) und im 2. Petrusbriefe (2, 10–12)?" *Festschrift zur Jahrhundertfeier der Universität zu Breslau,* ed. T. Siebs = *MSGVK* 13–14 (1911–12) 621–39. **Wikgren, A.** "Some Problems in Jude 5." *Studies in the History and Text of the New Testament in honor of Kenneth Willis Clark,* ed. B. L. Daniels and J. M. Suggs. SD 29. Salt Lake City: University of Utah Press, 1967. 147–52.

Translation

[5] *Now I should like to remind you, though you have been informed of all things once and for all,*[a]

that the Lord[b]

who saved a people out of the land of Egypt, on the second occasion destroyed those who did not believe. [6] *The angels, too, who did not keep their own position of authority, but abandoned their proper home, he has kept in eternal chains in the nether darkness*[c] *until the judgment of the great day.* [7] *Similarly Sodom and Gomorrah and the neighboring towns, which practiced immorality in the same way as the angels and hankered after*[d] *strange flesh, are exhibited as an example by undergoing the punishment of eternal fire.*

[8] *Yet in the same way also these people, on the strength of their dreams, defile the flesh, reject the authority of the Lord, and slander the glorious ones.*

[9] *But when Michael the archangel, in debate with the devil, disputed about the body of Moses, he did not presume to condemn him for slander,*[e] *but said, "May the Lord rebuke you!"*

[10] *But these people slander whatever they do not understand, while by the things they do understand, instinctively, like unreasoning animals, they are destroyed.*

Notes

[a] *ἅπαξ* is placed by some MSS (ℵ 1739 *al*) after *κύριος*, "Lord," but this reading (though defended by Mayor and Black, "Notes") should probably be seen as an attempt to supply a "first time" corresponding to the difficult *τὸ δεύτερον*, "the second occasion." The opposition to *τὸ δεύτερον* is possible (examples in Mayor, 29), but *ἅπαξ* strictly means "once only" rather than "first in a series," and v 3 supports the connection with *εἰδότας*, "having been informed."

[b] Most MSS read *κύριος* (or *ὁ κύριος*), but some important MSS and versions (A B vg cop[sa, bo] eth Origen) have Ἰησοῦς, a few have *ὁ θεός*, and P[72] has *θεὸς χριστός*. Probably *κύριος* should be preferred since it could have given rise to the other readings as attempts to resolve the ambiguity in *κύριος* (cf. the similar readings at 1 Cor 10:9). It is not likely that Jude would have used Ἰησοῦς of the preexistent Christ (despite Hanson, *Jesus Christ,* 165–67; F. F. Bruce, *This is That* [Exeter: Paternoster, 1968] 35–36): other NT examples (2 Cor 8:9; Phil 2:5–6; and perhaps Heb 2:9) have the Incarnation directly in view. Nor could Jude have used Ἰησοῦς for the OT Joshua (as Jerome, *In Jovin.* 1.21, thought; also Kellett, "Note"; Wikgren, "Problems," 148–49) since Joshua did not destroy the unbelievers (v 5b) or keep the angels in chains (v 6). In the second century, however, the coincidence of names between Joshua son of Nun and Jesus Christ was frequently exploited in the interests of typology (*Barn.* 12:8; Justin, *Dial.* 24.2; 75.1–2; Clement Alex., *Paed.* 1.60.3), and Joshua as a type of Jesus could be said to have led the people out of Egypt (Justin, *Dial.* 120.3). This typology could not have been intended by Jude (since it could not apply to v 6, which has the same subject), but could have attracted a scribe (who could miss its pitfalls) and account for his changing *κύριος* to Ἰησοῦς, rather than to Χριστός (which would, as Spitta objects, be expected otherwise, and is the corresponding variant in 1 Cor 10:9).

[c] Lucifer and one MS of the Old Latin add *ἁγίων ἀγγέλων* before *ὑπὸ ζόφον*; Clement Alex. adds *ἀγρίων* (read *ἁγίων*?) *ἀγγέλων* after *ὑπο ζόφον*. It is possible that this addition belongs to the original text, and refers to Raphael and Michael, who, in *1 Enoch* 10:4–5, 11–12, are responsible for chaining the fallen angels (cf. Milik, *Enoch,* 177), but Mees (*CDios* 181 [1968] 555–6) considers it an explanatory gloss.

[d] lit. "went after" (*ἀπελθοῦσαι ὀπίσω*), cf. the LXX idiom *πορεύεσθαι ὀπίσω θεῶν ἑτέρων* "to go after other gods" (Judg 2:12; 3 Kgdms 11:10).

[e] *κρίσιν ἐπενεγκεῖν βλασφημίας*. Many translations and commentators take *βλασφημίας* to be a "genitive of quality," equivalent to a Semitic adjectival genitive (Moule, *Idiom Book,* 175; Chaine, 276): "a reviling judgment" (RSV), "a slanderous accusation" (NIV). This appears to fit the context in Jude, and is also in line with 2 Pet 2:11 (*βλάσφημον κρίσιν*, "a slanderous judgment"). But the meaning of Jude's phrase must be determined in the first place by his source, according to which Satan had "slandered" (*ἐβλασφήσει κατά*) Moses by accusing him of murder, and Michael, not tolerating this slander (*βλασφημία*), appealed to God's judgment against him (see texts D,

M and N in the Excursus). From this context it seems the point is not that Michael refrained from slandering the devil, nor even that he refrained from bringing a *charge* of slander against the devil (NEB Margin: "to charge him with blasphemy"), since Michael's words virtually amount to such a charge. The point is that he refrained from taking it upon himself to pronounce judgment on Satan for his slandering of Moses. Only God could judge Satan's accusation to be false, i.e., slanderous. Thus a κρίσιν βλασφημίας would be a condemnation of the devil for his slander.

Form/Structure/Setting

At the beginning of this section Jude moves from the opening to the main body of his letter by means of a version of the stylistic device which White, in his study of the form of the Greek letter, calls "the fuller disclosure formula." The standard form of this is "I wish you to know that . . ." (examples from the papyri in White, *Body,* 3; some NT examples are Rom 1:13; 11:25; 2 Cor 1:8; 8:1; Gal 1:11). Jude's version, "I wish to *remind* you that . . ." is superficially an example of conventional polite style (cf. Rom 15:14–15; 2 Pet 1:12; *1 Clem.* 53:1) but also makes a serious point (see *Comment*). The "fuller disclosure formula" signifies a major transition (White, *Body,* 38), which Jude does not again indicate until he uses a similar form at v 17. This supports the exegesis that what Jude wishes to "remind" his readers covers not just vv 5–7 but the whole section vv 5–16, which comprises his OT prophetic material.

This section contains, in vv 5–7, the first of Jude's four citations of types and prophecies of the ungodly people of the last days and their doom, followed by his interpretation, in vv 8–10, which establishes the fulfillment in the false teachers now troubling the churches to which Jude writes. In this case the citation consists of a summary of scriptural material relating to three OT types (the first of two sets of three types, cf. v 11), and Jude's stylistic preference for triple expressions is evident not only in the selection of three types, but also in the three characteristics of the false teachers which he lists in the interpretation in v 8 (reinforced, whether intentionally or not, by the rhyme: μαίνουσιν . . . ἀθετοῦσιν . . . βλασφημοῦσιν: "they defile . . . reject . . . slander").

Verse 9 is a free quotation (from the *T. Mos.,* see below) which is linked back to v 8 and forward to v 10 by the catchword βλασφημοῦσιν/βλασφημίας, "they slander"/"slander." But this does not mean that vv 9–10 are an independent section comprising text (v 9) and interpretation (v 10). Rather, v 9 is a secondary quotation introduced in the course of the interpretation of the types of vv 5–7. This is shown by the fact that v 9 does not supply a type or prophecy of the false teachers, but an example with which they are contrasted. Moreover, v 10 does not simply interpret v 9 but continues the interpretation begun in v 8. Thus v 9 (as the catchword βλασφημίας indicates) relates to the last clause of v 8, which v 10 therefore takes up again in its first clause. But v 10 then continues by reverting to the subject of the first clause in v 8, and finally (with ἐν τούτοις φθείφονται) ends the exposition of the three types by making explicit what v 8 had not yet mentioned: that the antitypes, like the types, have incurred judgment.

The structure of the section is therefore: citation (vv 5–7), followed by interpretation (vv 8, 10), with a secondary quotation (v 9) introduced to help the interpretation. (This introduction of a secondary quotation in the course of the exegesis can be found occasionally in Qumran pesharim: 4QFlor 1:4, 12–13, 15–17; 4QpIsa^c, see M. P. Horgan, *Pesharim: Qumran Interpretations of Biblical Books* [CBQMS 8; Washington, D.C.: Catholic Biblical Association of America, 1979] 95.)

The pattern of citation and interpretation is marked by the change of tense (past tenses in vv 5–7, except *πρόκεινται*, "are exhibited," and v 9; present tenses in vv 8, 10) and the use of *οὗτοι*, "these people," to introduce the interpretation (vv 8, 10). The latter requires some discussion.

Jude's Use of οὗτοι

Each of Jude's sections of interpretation, following the reference to types or the citation of a prophecy, begins with the word *οὗτοι* ("these people") which he appears to use as a formula, though in somewhat varying forms: *ὁμοίως μέντοι καὶ οὗτοι* and *οὗτοι δέ* (followed by verbs, vv 8, 10), *οὗτοι εἰσιν* (followed by predicates, v 16), and twice *οὗτοι εἰσιν οἱ* (followed by participles, vv 12, 19).

The last three instances in particular have often been compared to the standard formula ("This is . . . ," "These are . . .") used in the interpretation of apocalyptic dreams and visions (Dan 5:25–26; Zech 1:10, 19–20; 4:10, 14; Rev 7:14; 11:4; 14:4; *1 Enoch* 46:3, and so on). Recently Ellis ("Jude," 225) has compared Jude's use of *οὗτοι* to the use of the similar formula sometimes used in the pesher exegesis of Qumran to introduce the interpretation of a text (4QpIsa^b 2:6: "These are the scoffers who are in Jerusalem"; 2:10: "This is the congregation of scoffers who are in Jerusalem"; 4QFlor 1:2: "This is the house which . . ."; 1:3, 11, 17–18; 2:1; 4QpIsa^a 3:9; cf. CD 4:14). Although this formula is rare in the Qumran texts, as compared with the more usual formulae including the word "pesher," it is perhaps significant that it occurs especially in the "thematic pesher" 4QFlor, which resembles Jude's midrash more than the "continuous pesharim." An example of a similar usage in the NT is Gal 4:24 ("These women are . . .").

In both of these formulae, the apocalyptic formula and the pesher formula, the demonstrative pronoun refers to that which is to be interpreted, a figure in the vision or an object mentioned in the text. Thus 4QpIsa^b 2:6–7 means: "These (people to whom the text refers) are the scoffers who are in Jerusalem (in our time)." In the two instances where Jude uses *οὗτοι εἰσιν οἱ* (vv 12, 19), "these are the ones who . . ." (exactly equivalent to the Qumran: (אלה הם . . . אשר . . .), he conforms to this usage. In v 12 *οὗτοι* refers to the people mentioned in v 11; in v 19 *οὗτοι* are the scoffers of whom the apostles prophesied (v 18).

But Jude's use of the formula is flexible, and in the other cases *οὗτοι* does not refer to that which is to be interpreted, but to those people to whom the interpretation applies, the contemporary fulfillment of the text (so vv 8, 10, 16): it means "these people we are talking about, the people who have infiltrated your churches." Here the formula is used to introduce a statement about the false teachers which demonstrates that they are the fulfillment of the type or the prophecy, but it does not state the identification directly in the way that the more usual use of the formula does. Perhaps this variation results from Jude's desire, not simply to *assert* that these types and prophecies refer to the false teachers, but to show that the false teachers' behavior corresponds to them.

A partial parallel to this use of *οὗτοι*, especially in v 8, can be found in 1 Tim 3:8: "As Jannes and Jambres . . . , so also these people . . ." (*οὕτως καὶ οὗτοι*).

For Jude's use of *τούτοις* (v 14) in the introduction to a quotation, see on v 14.

The Background and Sources of vv 5–7

For his list of three examples of divine judgment on sinners in vv 5–7, Jude has drawn on a traditional schema in which such examples were listed. Other passages which provide evidence of this tradition are Sir 16:7–10; CD 2:17–3:12; 3 Macc 2:4–7; *T. Napht.* 3:4–5; *m. Sanh.* 10:3; 2 Pet 2:4–8 (partially dependent on Jude). Most of these passages are studied by Berger, *ZNW* 61 (1970) 27–36; and Schlosser, *RB* 80 (1973) 26–34, who demonstrate the connections between them; but Berger's interpretation of Sir 16:6–10 is corrected by D. Lührmann, "Noah und Lot (Lk 17[26-29]) — ein Nachtrag," *ZNW* 63 (1972) 131. The variations in the examples listed in these passages are clearly variations in a traditional list:

Sirach	*CD*	*3 Macc*	*m. Sanh.*
	Watchers		
giants	giants	giants	
	generation of the Flood		generation of the Flood
	sons of Noah		generation of the dispersion
Sodom		Sodom	Sodom
	sons of Jacob		
Canaanites	Israel in Egypt	Pharaoh and Egyptians	spies
generation of the wilderness	Israel at Kadesh		generation of the wilderness
			company of Korah

Jubilees	*T. Naphtali*	*Jude*	*2 Peter*
giants	Sodom	generation of the wilderness	Watchers
Sodom	Watchers	Watchers	generation of the Flood
		Sodom	Sodom

Jude's three examples in fact form the core of the traditional list. (The Watchers and their sons the giants are closely related examples. Israel at Kadesh [the wilderness generation] is omitted for good reason in 3 Macc 2, where the historical context has led to the substitution of Israel's enemies the Egyptians, and in *T. Napht.* 3 and *Jub.* 20:5, which are represented as spoken before Exodus.) It should be noted that the lists usually follow chronological order: only the *T. Napht.* and Jude diverge from this order.

The main context of the traditional schema was Jewish paraenesis in which the hearers were warned not to follow these examples (cf. especially the contexts in Sir 16:6–14; CD 2:14–17; *T. Napht.* 3:1–4; *Jub.* 20:2–7; but in 3 Macc 2 the tradition is used in the context of a prayer for similar divine judgment), and usually the examples follow, as illustrations, a general maxim about God's punishment of sin (Sir 16:6; CD 2:16; 3 Macc 2:3–4a; cf. *T. Napht.* 3:3). Apart from 3 Macc 2, the emphasis is on sin as apostasy (Sir 16:7, 10: revolt, hardness of heart; CD 2:17–3:12: stubbornness of heart, rebelling against and not keeping God's commandments, choosing their own will; *T. Napht.* 3:2–5: departure from the God-given order of their nature), and Jude also reflects this emphasis on apostasy.

Probably this Jewish schema had been taken up in the paraenesis of the primitive church and used in the initial instruction of converts: hence Jude can refer to it as already well-known to his readers (v 5a). But the use Jude makes of it is not paralleled in the Jewish texts. In Jude the examples are not given as warnings to his readers, but as prophetic types of which the false teachers (οὗτοι, v 8) are the antitypes. So instead of a general maxim and paraenetic application of the examples, Jude adds in vv 8–10 an interpretation of the three types, applying them to the false teachers. In doing so, he treats his version of the tradition practically as a scriptural citation, no doubt because it represents a traditional summary of scriptural material. Was Jude's use of the tradition as typological prophecy of the false teachers his own innovation, or had it already been adapted in this way in the Christian tradition with which his readers were familiar? In favor of the latter, it could be urged that such use of OT types is found elsewhere in NT writings (1 Tim 3:8–9; Rev 2: 14, 20; cf. CD 5:18–19).

There are some detailed contacts with the tradition which should be noted. The idea of Sodom as an example (δεῖγμα, v 7) is found in 3 Macc 2:5 (παράδειγμα). The stylistic link between Jude's second and third examples (ὡς . . . ὅμοιον, v 7), and between the three examples and the false teachers (ὁμοίως μέντοι καί, v 8), is used in *T. Napht.* 3:5 to link the two examples of Sodom and the Watchers (ὁμοίως δὲ καί; cf. also 4:1); it must have been a feature of the tradition as Jude knew it. Moreover, the parallelism between the *kinds* of sin of which Sodom and the Watchers were guilty, which this stylistic link conveys in *T. Napht.*, reappears in Jude.

For the detailed description of his second example, the Watchers, Jude has drawn on the account in *1 Enoch* (see the passages quoted in the Comment), which he knew well. The fact that Jude's *vocabulary,* however, does not reflect that of the Greek version of *1 Enoch,* while at one point ("the judgment of the great day," see *Comment*) he seems to depend on a phrase as it stands in the Aramaic, but not in the Greek as we have it, may indicate that he knew *1 Enoch* in its original Aramaic form rather than in its Greek translation. (Much stronger evidence for this conclusion will be found in v 14.)

The Background and Source of v 9

See the detailed discussion in the Excursus, where it is argued that Jude has drawn his information from the lost ending of the *T. Mos.* and the story he found there is reconstructed. It belonged to a tradition of stories in which Satan, as the accusing angel, and the chief of the angels, acting as the patron of God's people, engaged in legal disputes over the people of God. This tradition goes back to Zech 3, from which Jude's source drew the words ("May the Lord rebuke you!") with which Michael appeals to God against the devil's slanderous accusation.

The story in the *T. Mos.* about the burial of Moses was one of a number of legends which grew up around the death and burial of Moses, stimulated by the account in Deut 34:1–6, in which Moses, though debarred by God from entering the Promised Land, was granted the unique privilege of burial by God himself, in a grave unknown to man. In line with the general tendency of intertestamental literature, the *T. Mos.* ascribed the burial to Michael, acting as God's agent. At Moses' death on Mount Nebo, the archangel was sent by God to remove the body to another place where he was to bury it, but before he could do so he encountered the devil, intent on a last attempt to gain power over Moses. The *T. Mos.* may have attributed to him the desire to bring Moses' body to the Israelites for them to make it an object of worship. He certainly wished to deprive Moses of the honor of burial by the archangel.

The devil therefore engaged in a dispute with Michael for possession of the body. This was a legal dispute, in which Satan played his traditional role of accuser, albeit a malicious accuser. He endeavored to prove Moses unworthy of honorable burial by charging him with murder, on the grounds that he had killed the Egyptian (Exod 2:12).

The *T. Mos.*, however, described this accusation as slander (*βλασφημία*), and related how Michael, not tolerating the devil's slander, said to him, "May the Lord rebuke you, devil!" This was an appeal to God to assert his authority over Satan and dismiss Satan's case against Moses. The devil was thereby silenced and took flight. Michael was now able to take the body away for burial.

The story functioned primarily to demonstrate that, in spite of the apparent blemishes on his record, God vindicated Moses as his servant, worthy of the unique honor of burial by his archangel, against Satan's attempt to claim him as a sinner.

In Jude's reference to the story the words *τῷ διαβόλῳ διακρινόμενος διελέγετο περὶ τοῦ Μωϋσέως σώματος* ("in debate with the devil, disputed about the body of Moses") are probably quoted from the *T. Mos.* (cf., in similar stories, 4Q ʿAmram[b] 1:10–11: "disputed about me . . . were carrying on a great contest about me"; Origen, *Hom.15* on Luke: "disputing"; and text B in the Excursus), as are the words "May the Lord rebuke you!" (texts A, E, M, N in the Excursus).

Comment

5. *Ὑπομνῆσαι δὲ ὑμᾶς βούλομαι, εἰδότας ἅπαξ πάντα*, "Now I should like to remind you, though you have been informed of all things once and for all" is more than a tactful formula, complimenting his readers on their knowledge (such as we find in *1 Clem.* 53:1). Like similar NT passages (Rom 15:14–15; 1 Thess 4:9; 1 John 2:21, 27) it has theological significance. *ἅπαξ* ("once and for all") recalls v 3. The apostolic faith, in which Jude's readers were thoroughly instructed at the time of their conversion, is definitive and complete; it does not need supplementing. Therefore Jude need not give fresh information, as perhaps the false teachers did, but need only remind his readers.

"Reminding" and "remembering" (v 17) are essential to biblical religion as grounded in God's acts in history (cf. B. S. Childs, *Memory and Tradition in Israel* [SBT 37; London: SCM Press, 1962]). As Jewish writers urged their readers to "remember" the tradition of God's redemptive acts (especially in Deuteronomy) and commandments (e.g. Num 15:39–40; Mal 4:4; *Jub.* 6:22; *2 Apoc. Bar.* 84:2, 7–9), so early Christian writers recalled their readers to the tradition of the apostolic gospel (Rom 15:15; 1 Cor 11:2; 2 Thess 2:5; 2 Tim 2:8, 14; 2 Pet 1:12; 3:1–2; Rev 3:3). Though this becomes especially prominent in contexts where the faithful preservation of the tradition against heretical deviations needs emphasis, there is no need to regard it as a late feature in Jude (against, e.g., Schelkle). Nor need such an emphasis imply stale repetition; it is by recalling the gospel that its meaning is more deeply understood and its relevance freshly experienced.

πάντα ("all things") could mean simply "all that I wish to tell you" (so Spitta, Mayor clxxxiv, Grundmann), but with *ἅπαξ*, "once and for all," more naturally means "all the essentials of the faith in which the apostles instructed you at the time of your conversion" (cf. v 17). In this original instruction the specific subjects of Jude's reminder here (vv 5–16) were included. This need not mean that all the detailed content of these verses was already familiar to Jude's readers, but since his references to OT and apocryphal materials are not always self-explanatory, he may be drawing to a considerable extent on traditional material. In vv 5–7 his examples, which follow a traditional Jewish list (see *Form/Structure/Setting* section), may have been used in Christian, as in Jewish, paraenesis as illustrations of the general maxim that sin, especially apostasy, incurs divine judgment, and in that case it is Jude himself who *interprets* the tradition as typological prophecy of the false teachers and their coming judgment. Similarly in vv 11 and 14–15 it may be that Jude himself is responsible for the application of traditional material to the false teachers. On the other hand, for the comparison of the false teachers of the last days with OT prototypes, 2 Tim 3:8–9 and Rev 2:14, 20 provide parallels which suggest that Jude's OT types may already have been interpreted in this way in the traditions he used. At any rate it is certain that his readers' original Christian instruction did include the warning that false teachers of immoral life were prophesied for the last days, along with their inevitable divine judgment (Jude 17).

κύριος ("the Lord"). In the *Notes* we have argued for this reading rather than Ἰησοῦς, but the question remains whether *κύριος* itself refers to God or to the preexistent Christ (as Bigg; Hanson, *Jesus Christ,* 137; Ellis, "Jude," 232 n.40, argue). The former is the interpretation presupposed in 2 Pet 2:4, but this cannot decide the issue. The latter, it should be noticed, involves attributing not only the events of the Exodus, but also the imprisonment of the angels (v 6) to Christ.

A decision must involve two considerations: (1) Are references to the activity of the preexistent Christ in OT history rare in the NT (John 12:41; 1 Cor 10:4, 9 are the most commonly admitted) or very common (as Hanson argues)? Few have found Hanson's case fully convincing. (2) Does Jude use *κύριος* consistently of Jesus? The evidence may not be sufficient to decide this. Jude uses *κύριος* four times with "Jesus Christ" (vv 4, 17, 21, 25), once in a quotation from an apocryphal writer (v 9) who certainly meant "God" but could have been interpreted by Jude to refer to Jesus, and once as an interpretative gloss in a quotation (v 14), where Jude certainly intended a reference to Jesus. Moreover, v 5 follows immediately the reference to "our Lord Jesus Christ" in v 4. It is also true that NT writers rarely use *κύριος* of God, outside OT quotations, and sometimes (though by no means always) interpret the *κύριος* of OT texts (representing the Tetragrammaton) as Jesus (John 12:41; Rom 10:13; Heb 1:10; cf. 1 Cor 10:9).

It is difficult to weigh these factors, but it may be that, in view of Jude's general usage, he has used *κύριος* here of Jesus, not so much because he is concerned to explain the preexistent activity of Christ, but rather because in his typological application of these OT events to the present it is the Lord Jesus who has saved his people the church and will be the Judge of apostates.

τοὺς μὴ πιστεύσαντας ἀπώλεσεν, "destroyed those who did not believe," refers to the account of Num 14, where, discouraged by the report of the majority of the spies returning from Canaan, the people of Israel "murmured," showing lack of faith in God's promises to give them the land and so refusing to go into Canaan. As a result, God decreed that all the Israelites guilty of disbelief, i.e. all aged twenty and over, with the exception of Joshua and Caleb, should die in the wilderness. (Num 26:64–65 records the fulfillment.) Jude's specific reference to disbelief (an act of disbelief indicated by the aorist participle) identifies the occasion he has in mind, for disbelief is mentioned in Num 14:11 and in other references to the same incident (Deut 1:32; 9:23; Ps 106:24; *Bib. Ant.* 15:6; Heb 3:19; 4:2); it was, of course, disbelief which issued in disobedience (Deut 9:23; Ps 106:25; Heb 3:19; 4:6, 11). Since virtually the whole generation was guilty of disbelief and died in the wilderness, Jude will intend no contrast between the λαός ("people") whom the Lord saved and the unbelievers whom he destroyed. His point, reinforced also by the participial construction, is that precisely those people whom the Lord saved afterward incurrred judgment (so Maier, *BZ* 2 [1904] 393–94).

This apostasy and judgment of Israel in the wilderness was a well-known example of sin and judgment, used both in the traditional schema which Jude follows in these verses (note especially CD 3:7–9, where it receives special emphasis; Sir 16:10) and elsewhere (Ps 95:8–11; Heb 3:7–4:11). The rabbis debated whether the wilderness generation would have a share in the world to come (*m. Sanh.* 10:3). Paul in 1 Cor 10:7–11 refers not to this but to other examples of sin and judgment in the wilderness, but his comment that these things "were written down for our instruction, upon whom the end of the ages has come" (10:11 RSV), together with the extended use of the example in Heb 3–4, show how Christian tradition used the experiences of the people of God in the period of the Exodus as instructive for the eschatological people of God in the period of the new Exodus. Jude depends on this typological tradition for his own application to the false teachers.

Probably it was this especially close parallel between Israel and the church which led Jude to make this the first of his three types, out of chronological order. It recalls the judgment of the very people whom God had saved by the great salvation-event of the Exodus, and so was of special relevance to apostate Christians. Jude's use of it implies that he did consider the false teachers to be apostate Christians.

τὸ δεύτερον ("on a second occasion") is hard to explain with precision. To suggest that a second destruction of Israel in A.D. 70 is in mind (Zahn, *Introduction,* 253–55, 261–62) makes Jude's point improbably involved. Some (Spitta; Berger, *ZNW* 61 [1970] 36) suggest a second occasion of disbelief, corresponding to a first occasion at the Red Sea (Exod 14:10–12; Ps 107:7), but (1) there were many other intervening instances of unbelief (Num 14:22; Ps 78:40–41), and (2) in that case we should expect τὸ δεύτερον to follow τούς. It is more likely that Jude intends to distinguish a first occasion on which God acted to save his people (at the Exodus) and a second occasion on which he acted to judge their disbelief (Chaine, Schelkle, Kelly, Cantinat, Grundmann). In that case the point of τὸ δεύτερον is to emphasize that this is an act of judgment on apostasy; the people whom the Lord had saved were not thereby immune from subsequent judgment. Applied to the antitypes, Jude means that the first occasion on which the Lord acted in relation to Christians, to save them, will be followed by a second occasion, the Parousia, when he will judge apostate Christians.

6. ἀγγέλους are the angels (known as the Watchers) who, according to

Jewish tradition, descended from heaven to marry human wives and corrupt the human race in the period before the Flood. This was how the account of the "sons of God" in Gen 6:1–4 was universally understood (so far as our evidence goes) until the mid-second century A.D. (*1 Enoch* 6–19; 21; 86–88; 106:13–15, 17; *Jub.* 4:15, 22; 5:1; CD 2:17–19; 1QapGen 2:1; *Tg. Ps.-J.* Gen. 6:1–4; *T. Reub.* 5:6–7; *T. Napht.* 3:5; *2 Apoc. Bar.* 56:10–14), though the tradition took several varying forms. From the time of R. Simeon b. Yohai in the mid-second century A.D., the traditional exegesis was replaced in Judaism by an insistence that the "sons of God" were not angels but men. In Christianity, however, the traditional exegesis had a longer life, questioned only in the third century and disappearing in the fifth century.

Originally the fall of the Watchers was a myth of the origin of evil (so *1 Enoch* 6–19), but by the first century A.D. its importance was already waning as the origin of evil was focused rather on the fall of Adam (e.g. Rom 5; 4 Ezra). This is no doubt why there are only a few allusions to it in the NT (1 Pet 3:19–20; 2 Pet 2:4; perhaps 1 Cor 11:10; 1 Tim 2:9). But it was still widely known and accepted, especially in those Jewish Christian circles where the Enoch literature remained popular. Perhaps it was largely owing to the influence of those circles and the continuing popularity of the Enoch literature in second-century Christianity that the fall of the Watchers retained its place in the Christian tradition longer than in Judaism, where the Enoch literature fell out of favor in rabbinic circles.

Jude's reference is directly dependent on *1 Enoch* 6–19, which is the earliest extant account of the fall of the Watchers (from the early second century B.C. at the latest: Milik, *Enoch,* 22–25, 28, 31), and he shows himself closely familiar with those chapters. They tell how, in the days of Jared (Gen 5:18), two hundred angels under the leadership of Šemiḥazah and ʿAśa'el, filled with lust for the beautiful daughters of men, descended on Mount Hermon and took human wives. Their children, the giants, ravaged the earth, and the fallen angels taught men forbidden knowledge and all kinds of sin. They were therefore responsible for the total corruption of the world on account of which God sent the Flood. The Watchers were punished by being bound under the earth until the Day of Judgment, when they will be cast into Gehenna. Their children, the giants, were condemned to destroy each other in battle (10:9), but their spirits became the evil spirits responsible for all evil in the world between the Flood and the Day of Judgment (15:8–16:1). It is clear that for the author of these chapters the judgment of the Watchers and men at the time of the Flood prefigured the final elimination of all evil at the Last Judgment. The parallel will also have been in Jude's mind when he used the Watchers as a type of the false teachers of the last days.

It is unnecessary to suppose that Jude is dependent on the Greek myth of the Titans, recounted in Hesiod's *Theogony.* The resemblances between the Greek and Jewish myths is probably largely due to their common derivation from ancient Near Eastern myth. The Greek myth may have had some minor influence on the Jewish tradition (cf. Glasson, *Influence,* 63–67; Delcor, *RHR* 190 [1976] 30, 39–40, 44) and certainly some Jewish writers identified the Titans with the fallen angels or with their sons the giants (see *Comment* on 2 Pet 2:4). But Jude's use of δεσμοί ("chains") and ζόφος ("darkness"), which are also used of the Titans chained in the darkness of Tartarus (Hesiod, *Theog.* 718, 729) is insufficient to show that he made this identification or knew Hesiod.

Older exegetes understood Jude 6 to refer to the fall of Satan and his angels before the fall of Adam; but Jude's dependence on *1 Enoch* is clear from the close parallels in this verse (see below) and also from the allusion in v 7 (see below) to the fact that the angels' sin was sexual intercourse with mortal women. Dubarle ("Péché") accepts the allusions to *1 Enoch* in v 6, but suggests that Jude is making primary reference, in terms of the myth of the fallen angels, to the spies (*ἀγγέλους* = messengers) in Num 13, who forsook their eminent position (*ἀρχήν*) among the people and abandoned the land (*οἰκητήριον*) which God had promised them. But it is hard to see how Jude's readers could have detected this supposedly primary layer of meaning, and again the allusion in v 7 to the angels' intercourse with women rules it out.

ἀρχήν here means a position of heavenly power or sphere of dominion, which the angels exercised over the world in the service of God (cf. *Jub.* 2:2; 5:6; *1 Enoch* 82:10–20; 1QM 10:12; 1QH 1:11; Justin, *2 Apol.* 5.2). (Cf. *ἀρχαί* as a rank of angels in *T. Levi* 3:8; *2 Enoch* 20:1; and as cosmic powers in Rom 8:38; Eph 1:21; 3:10; 6:12; Col 1:16; 2:15.) Papias (*ap.* Andr. Caes., *in Apoc.* 34:12) says that to some of the angels God "gave dominion (*ἄρχειν*) over the affairs of the earth, and ordered them to rule (*ἄρχειν*) well . . . . But their order (*τάξιν*) ended in nothing."

ἀπολιπόντας τὸ ἴδιον οἰκητήριον, "abandoned their proper home": cf. *1 Enoch* 12:4; 15:3: "you left (Greek: *ἀπελίπετε*) the high, holy and eternal heaven"; 15:7: "the spirits of heaven, in heaven is their dwelling" (Greek: *ἡ κατοίκησις αὐτῶν*).

The two participial phrases, in synonymous parallelism, stress the apostasy of the angels, which Jude intends to compare with that of the false teachers. The fact that sexual immorality was also involved in the angels' sin will become apparent in v 7.

εἰς κρίσιν μεγάλης ἡμέρας, "until the judgment of the great day": cf. *1 Enoch* 10:12 (= 4QEn^b 1:4:11, Milik, *Enoch,* 175): Michael is to bind the fallen angels "for seventy generations in the valleys of the earth, until the great day of their judgment." The adjective "great," lost in the Greek and Ethiopic versions of *1 Enoch,* is now found in the 4Q Aramaic fragment (Aramaic: עד יומא רבא). The precise phrase "great day of judgment" is unusual, cf. *1 Enoch* 22:11; 84:4; *Tg. Neof.* Deut. 32:34; more usual is "great day of the Lord" (Joel 2:11, 31 [= Acts 2:20]; Zeph 1:14; Mal 4:5; *2 Enoch* 18:6), cf. Rev 6:17 ("great day of their wrath"); 16:18 ("great day of God Almighty"); *1 Enoch* 54:6 ("that great day").

δεσμοῖς ἀϊδίοις ὑπὸ ζόφον τετήρηκεν, "he has kept in eternal chains in the nether darkness": cf. *1 Enoch* 10:4–6: "Bind ʿAśʾel hand and foot, and cast him into the darkness (Greek: *σκότος*): and make an opening in the desert, which is in Dadduʾel (see Milik, *Enoch,* 30), and cast him therein. And place upon him rough and jagged rocks, and cover him with darkness (*σκότος*), and let him abide there forever, and cover his face that he may not see light. And on the day of the great judgment he shall be cast into the fire."

Jude's language reflects both this judgment on ʿAśaʾel and the judgment on Šemiḥazah and the rest of the fallen Watchers in 10:12 (quoted above). His phrase ὑπὸ ζόφον (not in the Greek Enoch) is commonly used in Greek poetry for the underworld (Homer, *Il.* 21:56; *Od.* 11:57, 155; 20:356; Hesiod, *Theog.* 729; Aeschylus, *Pers.* 839; *Sib. Or.* 4:43).

The chains, to which Jude refers, are very prominent in the tradition of the fall of the Watchers (cf. *1 Enoch* 13:1; 14:5; 54:3–5; 56:1–4; 88:1; 4QEnGiants[a] 8:14 [Milik, *Enoch,* 315]; *Jub.* 5:6; *2 Apoc. Bar.* 56:13; Origen, *C. Cels.* 5.52; Oxford MS. 2340 § 19, quoted Milik, *Enoch,* 332).

The angels' imprisonment is only temporary, until the Day of Judgment when they will be transferred to the fire of Gehenna, but the chains are called "eternal" (ἀΐδιος, synonymous with αἰωνιος v 7, no doubt chosen for stylistic variation, cf. 4 Macc 10:15). Jude's terminology seems here to depend on *1 Enoch* 10:5, where ʿAśaʾel is bound "forever" (Greek C: εἰς τοὺς αἰῶνας; S: εἰς τὸν αἰῶνα) until the judgment. Here "forever" must mean "for the duration of the world until the Day of Judgment" (= the seventy generations of 10:12). The same usage appears in 14:5 (= 4QEn[c] 1:6:15, Milik, *Enoch,* 193, 195): "to bind you (the fallen angels) for all the days of eternity" (Aramaic: [עד כול יומי על[מא); *Jub.* 5:10 (evidently dependent on *1 Enoch* 10): "they were bound in the depths of the earth forever, until the day of the great condemnation." (Cf. also Josephus, *BJ* 6.434, where δεσμοῖς αἰωνίοις, "eternal chains," refers to life imprisonment.)

With τετήρηκεν, "kept," cf. *2 Enoch* 7:2: the Watchers, imprisoned in the second heaven, are "reserved for and awaiting the eternal judgment"; 18:4: they are "kept in great darkness" in the second heaven, until (18:6) they are "punished at the great day of the Lord." The coincidences of language with Jude are striking, but may reflect only common dependence on *1 Enoch* (with "kept" as a chance coincidence), or even the influence of Jude 6 on *2 Enoch.* Cf. also *T. Reub* 5:5 (of women such as those who seduced the Watchers): εἰς κόλασιν τοῦ αἰῶνος τετήρηται, "has been kept for eternal punishment."

One reason for Jude's use of τηρεῖν, "to keep," here is to make a grim play on words with μὴ τηρήσαντας ("did not keep") in the first part of the verse. Since the angels have not *kept* their position, the Lord now *keeps* them chained. This is an example of the common practice of describing a sin and its judgment in corresponding terms, so that the punishment fits the crime (*lex talionis;* cf., e.g., 1 Cor 3:17; Rev 16:6). τηρεῖν seems to be one of Jude's catchwords (cf. vv 1, 13, 21). The angels contrast with faithful Christians who should *keep* their position in God's love (v 21) and whom God *keeps* safe, not for judgment but for salvation at the Last Day (v 1). Such plays on the word are not unlikely, since τηρεῖν, a common word in early Christian (especially Johannine) vocabulary, is similarly played on elsewhere (John 17:6, 11–12; Rev 3:10).

7. Σόδομ καὶ Γόμορρα, "Sodom and Gomorrah," had long been regarded as the paradigm case of divine judgment (Deut 29:23; Isa 1:9; 13:19; Jer 23:14; 49:18; 50:40; Lam 4:6; Hos 11:8; Amos 4:11; Zeph 2:9; Sir 16:8; 3 Macc 2:5; *Jub.* 16:6, 9; 20:5; 22:22; 36:10; *T. Asher* 7:1; Philo, *Quaest. in Gen.* 4:51; Josephus, *BJ* 5.566; Matt 10:15; 11:24; Mark 6:11; Luke 10:12; 17:29).

αἱ περὶ αὐτὰς πόλεις, "and the neighboring towns." The five Cities of the

Plain were Sodom and Gomorrah, Admah, Zeboiim and Zoar, but Zoar was spared the judgment (Gen 19:20–22).

τὸν ὅμοιον τρόπον τούτοις ἐκπορνεύσασαι καὶ ἀπελθοῦσαι ὀπίσω σαρκὸς ἑτέρας, "which practiced immorality in the same way as the angels and hankered after strange flesh." The second clause explains the first. As the angels fell because of their lust for women, so the Sodomites desired sexual relations with angels. The reference is to the incident in Gen 19:4–11. *σαρκὸς ἑτέρας*, "strange flesh," cannot, as many commentators and most translations assume, refer to homosexual practice, in which the flesh is not "different" (*ἑτέρας*); it must mean the flesh of angels. The sin of the Sodomites (not, strictly, of the other towns) reached its zenith in this most extravagant of sexual aberrations, which would have transgressed the order of creation as shockingly as the fallen angels did. The two cases are similarly brought together in *T. Napht.* 3:4–5.

In Jewish tradition the sin of Sodom was rarely specified as homosexual practice (though Philo, *Abr.* 135–36 is a notable account of Sodomite homosexuality, and cf. *Mos.* 2.58). The incident with the angels is usually treated as a violation of hospitality, and the Sodomites are condemned especially for their hatred of strangers (Wis 19:14–15; Josephus, *Ant.* 1:194; *Pirqe R. El.* 25), their pride and selfish affluence (Ezek 16:49–50; 3 Macc 2:5; Josephus, *Ant.* 1.194; Philo, *Abr.* 134; *Tg. Ps.-J.* Gen 13:13; 18:20), or their sexual immorality in general (*Jub.* 16:5–6; 20:5; *T. Levi* 14:6; *T. Benj.* 9:1). So it is not very likely that Jude means to accuse the false teachers of homosexual practice (Kelly), and we can hardly speculate that they desired sexual relations with angels—even in their "dreams" (v 8).

Jude's intention in stressing here the peculiar sexual offenses of both the Watchers and the Sodomites is probably to highlight the shocking character of the false teachers' violation of God-given order. This is the emphasis in *T. Napht.* 3, which belongs to the same tradition as Jude uses here ("Sun, moon and stars do not change their order; so should you also not change the law of God by the disorderliness of your deeds . . . that you become not as Sodom, which changed the order of her nature [*ἐνήλλαξε τάξιν φύσεως αὐτῆς*]. In the same way also the Watchers changed the order of their nature . . ."; and cf. the same idea of sin as violation of the created order in *1 Enoch* 2–5). In rejecting the commandments of God, the false teachers were rebelling against the divinely established order of things as flagrantly as the Watchers and the Sodomites had done. Moreover, in doing so they were motivated, like the Watchers and the Sodomites, by sexual lust, and, like the Sodomites, insulted angels (v 8).

πρόκεινται δεῖγμα, "are exhibited as an example" (cf. Josephus, *BJ* 6:103: *ὑπόδειγμα πρόκειται*, "an example is exhibited"). According to 3 Macc 2:5, God made the Sodomites "an example (*παράδειγμα*) to those who should come afterward." *δεῖγμα* means "sample," and so here "example" in the sense of an actual instance of sinners punished (E. K. Lee, "Words denoting 'Pattern' in the New Testament," *NTS* 8 [1961–62] 167), which serves as proof of divine punishment for later generations, who can still view it (*πρόκεινται*, present tense). The idea is that the site of the cities, in antiquity located on the south of the Dead Sea, a scene of sulfurous devastation, provided ever-present evidence of the reality of divine judgment. This is partly why the example was so often cited, and why the particular features of the judgment of Sodom and Gomorrah (fire and brimstone, the smoking, uninhabitable waste) (Gen 19:24–25, 28) became stock imagery of future judgment (Deut 29:23; Isa 34:9–10; Jer 49:17–18; Ezek 38:22; *Sib. Or.* 3:504–7; Rev 14:10–11; 19:3; 20:10). So, according to Wis 10:7, the wickedness of the Cities of the Plain "is still attested by a smoking waste" (NEB); Josephus says that "vestiges of the divine fire" can still be seen there (*BJ* 4.483); and according to Philo, "even to this day the visible tokens of the indescribable disaster are pointed out in Syria—ruins, cinders, brimstone, smoke and murky flames which continue to rise from the ground as from a fire still smoldering beneath" (*Mos.* 2.56; cf. *Abr.* 141). (It is interesting to note that according to another tradition the hot springs and sulfurous nature of the Dead Sea region resulted from the fact that the prison of the fallen angels was located beneath it: *1 Enoch* 67:4–13; Origen, *c. Cels.* 5.52.)

πυρὸς αἰωνίου, "eternal fire" (the same phrase is used in 4 Macc 12:12; 1QS 2:8; *T. Zeb.* 10:3; *3 Apoc. Bar.* 4:16; Matt 18:8; 25:41) could be taken with *δεῖγμα* or with *δίκην*, but perhaps better with the latter. Jude means that the still burning site of the cities is a warning picture of the eternal fires of hell.

8. *ὁμοίως μέντοι καὶ οὗτοι*, "Yet in the same way also these people." The sins of the false teachers to be described in this verse correspond to those of their types as described in the preceding three verses. But the three sins specified in v 8 cannot be correlated each with one of the three types: both the Watchers and the Sodomites defiled the flesh, all three types flouted the authority of the Lord, only the Sodomites abused angels. All three sins, it should be noted, are attributable to the Sodomites, and it may be that in terms of the sins specified in v 8, Jude's list of three types was constructed to reach a climax with the third. In one sense, as we argued above, Israel in the wilderness was the most forceful analogy for Christians and was therefore placed first, but in terms of specific sins it may be the Sodomites who most resemble the false teachers. Thus while *ὁμοίως μέντοι*, "yet in the same way," relates generally to all three types, its immediate relation to the third is appropriate. *μέντοι* ("yet") will mean: in spite of these well-known examples of divine punishment, and particularly in spite of the fact that Sodom's punishment is evident for all to see, these people commit the same sins.

ἐνυπνιαζόμενοι, "on the strength of their dreams." This participle (lit. "dreaming") relates to all three main verbs, and so cannot, with *σάρκα μιαίνουσιν* ("defile the flesh"), refer to erotic dreams. Nor does it refer simply to imagination, which is not a usual sense of *ἐνυπνιαζέσθαι*, "to dream," or to the slumbers of those sunk in the torpor of sin (Calvin, Plummer) or "hypnotized" (Reicke). The reference, as most modern commentators agree, is to dreams as the medium of prophetic revelation, and Jude will have chosen the term since, although it can refer to authentic revelation (Dan 2:1; Joel 2:28 = Acts 2:17; and cf. *1 Enoch* 85:1), it is used rather often in the OT of the dreams of false prophets (*ἐνυπνιαζέσθαι*, in LXX Deut 13:2, 4, 6; Isa 56:10; Jer 23:25; 36:8; and cf. *ἐνύπνια ψευδῆ*, "false dreams," Jer 23:32; Zech 10:2). He may also have remembered *1 Enoch* 99:8: the sinners of the last days "will sink into impiety because of the folly of their hearts, and their eyes will be blinded through the fear of their hearts, and through the visions of their dreams" (tr. Knibb). (Daniel, *Mus* 81 [1968] 503–21, thinks ἐνυπνιαζόμενοι translates חוזים, "seers," which he takes to be the Essenes' name for themselves, but one would expect οἱ ὁρῶντες, "the seers," as usually in LXX.)

This information about the false teachers is not derived from the types in vv 5–7, and must indicate that they claimed visionary experiences in which they received revelation (cf. 2 Cor 12:1–3; Col 2:18). This is the first real hint that Jude's opponents were guilty not simply of antinomian *practice,* but also of antinomian *teaching,* for which they claimed the authority of prophetic revelations. Since, however, it is in the next section (vv 11–13) that Jude will focus on their character as teachers and corrupters of other people, we should probably take the reference to their visions here as indicating primarily the authority they claim for their own antinomian practice, rather than the authority they claim in teaching others to sin, though no doubt their visions did also serve the latter function.

Visionary revelations were common to apocalyptic Judaism, primitive Christianity, and contemporary paganism, and so we cannot say that this characteristic identifies the false teachers as Gnostics.

The relation of the particle ἐνυπνιαζόμενοι to the three main verbs should probably be taken to mean, not that they committed these offenses while experiencing visions, but that it was the revelations received in their visions which authorized their practices.

σάρκα μὲν μιαίνουσιν, "they defile the flesh." *1 Enoch* repeatedly refers to the sin of the fallen Watchers as "defiling themselves" with women (Greek μιαίνεσθαι, "to defile themselves": *1 Enoch* 7:1; 9:8; 10:11; 12:4; 15:3, 4; cf. 69:5; 4QEnGiants[c], Milik, *Enoch,* 308; Oxford MS. 2340, quoted Milik, *Enoch,* 331), while according to *Jub.* 16:5 the Sodomites "defile themselves and commit fornication in their flesh." Jude is therefore identifying the sin of the false teachers as corresponding to that of the second and third types, and must intend a reference to sexual immorality (for the precise phrase σάρκα μιαίνειν, "to defile the flesh," cf. *Sib. Or.* 2:279; Herm. *Mand.* 4:1:9; *Sim.* 5:7:2; and cf. μιαίνειν τὸ σῶμα, *T. Asher* 4:4 *v.l.*; cf. also *Apoc. Pet.* A 32; E 10; *Acts Paul & Thecla* 10). See *Comment* on v 4 (ἀσέλγειαν).

κυριότητα δὲ ἀθετοῦσιν, "reject the authority of the Lord." The word κυριότης here (which is the abstract noun from κύριος, "Lord," meaning "lordship") has been interpreted in three ways: (1) human authorities, ecclesiastical or civil (Calvin, Luther): but this seems out of place in a verse which is applying the types of vv 5–7 to the false teachers, and Jude shows no other sign of concern for this issue; (2) the class of angels known as κυριότητες (Col 1:16; Eph 1:21; *Greek Legend of Ascension of Isaiah* 2:22; cf. *2 Enoch* 20:1; and angels called κύριοι in *Apocalypse of Zephaniah,* quoted Clement Alex., *Strom.* 5.11.77) (so Werdermann, *Irrlehrer,* 31; Moffatt): but in that case the singular κυριότητα is difficult (the variant reading κυριότητας in א and Origen is an attempt to eliminate the difficulty), and this clause would mean the same as the next; (3) the lordship of God (as in *Did.* 4:1) or of Christ (as in Herm. *Sim.* 5:6:1) (so most modern commentators). In view of Jude's exegetical method of using catchword connections, we should link κυριότητα with κύριος (v 5), and "reject the authority of the Lord" then becomes equivalent to "deny our only Master and Lord Jesus Christ" (v 4). As in v 4, the rejection will probably be practical: the false teachers were not teaching Christological heresy, but by their libertine behavior they effectively rejected the judicial authority of the Lord who (according to vv 5–7) judges sin.

δόξας δὲ βλασφημοῦσιν, "slander the glorious ones." The term δόξαι (lit. "glories") for angels is attested in the Dead Sea Scrolls (נכבדים: 1QH 10:8; and perhaps 11QPs[a]Zion 22:13) and in apocalyptic and Gnostic literature (*2 Enoch* 22:7, 10; *Asc. Isa.* 9:32; Codex Brucianus, in C. Schmidt and V. MacDermot, *The Books of Jeu and the Untitled Text in the Bruce Codex* [NHS 13; Leiden: E. J. Brill, 1978] 248–49, 266–69; *Allogenes* 50:19; 52:14; 55:17–18, 34; 57:25; probably also Exod 15:11 LXX). Probably they are so called because they participate in or embody the glory of God (cf. *T. Jud.* 25:2; *T. Levi* 18:5; Heb 9:5; Philo, *Spec. Leg.* 1.8.45). It is true that נכבדים can also refer to illustrious men, noblemen (Isa 3:5; 23:8; Nah 3:10; Ps 149:8; 1QpHab 4:2; 4QpNah 2:9; 3:9; 4:4; 1QM 14:11), but in these cases the Septuagint does not use δόξαι, and one would expect a more idiomatic Greek rendering if this were Jude's meaning. It is in any case an unlikely meaning, especially in view of the parallel statement in v 10a. Clement of Alexandria already interpreted Jude's δόξαι as angels.

The false teachers "slander" (or "revile, insult") the angels. This is unlikely to be merely an implication of their antinomian behavior (like rejecting the authority of the Lord), but must mean that for some reason they spoke disparagingly of angels. It is important, for assessing the character of the false teaching, to notice that while Jude apparently cannot accuse the libertines of teaching which is *explicitly* blasphemous toward God or Christ, he does accuse them of slandering angels. This feature appears to be unique among the false teachings combated in the NT (except 2 Pet 2:10), a fact which confirms the view that Jude confronts a specific and actual case of false teaching, not a generalized caricature of heresy.

Some commentators have thought that the δόξαι must be, or at least include, evil angels, partly on the grounds that v 9 provides an example of respect for the devil. But this is a misinterpretation of v 9 (see below). The term δόξαι is not elsewhere used of evil angels, and seems intrinsically unsuitable for such a use (Sickenberger, "Engels," 626–29). It also seems most improbable that Jude should have objected so strongly (both here and in v 10a) to insults directed at evil angels. There are no parallels to the idea that evil angels should be treated with respect (at Qumran there were liturgies for the cursing of Satan and his followers: 4Q 280–82, 286–87). While the angels in question may have been regarded as evil by the false teachers, Jude must have seen them as angels of God who deserve to be honored. This conclusion is reinforced by the close connection between this clause and the preceding. It is unthinkable that Jude should, in the same breath, have accused his opponents of rejecting the authority of the Lord and slandering the forces of Satan. Moreover, if the connection with vv 5–7 is to be preserved, it is relevant that the angels insulted by the Sodomites were messengers of God.

This already eliminates two principal interpretations of the false teachers' behavior, which regard them as either underestimating the power or denying the existence of the supernatural forces of evil. These are: (1) in their confident immorality the false teachers are contemptuous of the demonic powers. As free spiritual men they are victorious over the forces of Satan, and so if they are accused of falling into their power they mock them as powerless and inferior to themselves (Werdermann, *Irrlehrer,* 33). (2) C. K. Barrett (*NTS* 11 [1964–65] 139–40) suggests that the problem of food sacrificed to idols is in view (cf. 1 Cor 8; Rev 2:14, 20). Like the Corinthians (1 Cor 8:4) the false teachers deny the idols any real existence, but in doing so fail to recognize the demonic powers (1 Cor 10:20) who are at work in pagan religion. But, apart from the objections above, neither of these interpretations adequately explains the word *βλαφημοῦσιν*, "they slander."

Another interpretation (3) explains the false teaching in the light of second-century Gnosticism, in which the creation of the world was attributed to the angels or archons. In this case the angels are the powers of this material world, enemies of the transcendent God and of the Gnostic, who reviles them to demonstrate his victory over them (cf. Sidebottom; Bultmann, *Theology of the New Testament,* tr. K. Grobel [London: SCM Press, 1952] 1, 170). This view has the merit of explaining the angels as good angels in Jude's view but evil angels in his opponents' view. But it depends on a developed gnostic dualism of which there is no clear evidence in the NT, and which, if Jude's opponents held it, we should expect him to oppose much more directly and forcefully. If they were really teaching that the material world was created not by God but by inferior powers hostile to God, is it likely that Jude should merely hint at this doctrine and combat it so ineffectively? The citation in v 9 is a ludicrously weak response to such teaching.

It is possible (4) that the false teachers' contempt for the angels was simply an expression of their superiority, as spiritual men who in their visions entered the heavenly realms, exalted above the angels (cf. 1 Cor 6:3). Such visionary experience seems, however, to have normally promoted excessive reverence for angels (Col 2:18; cf. Rev 19:10; 22:8) rather than the opposite.

Much more plausible is (5) the view that it was the angels as givers and guardians of the law of Moses whom the false teachers slandered (Chaine)—and, we may add, the angels as guardians of the created order. This view has the advantage of cohering with what we know for certain about the false teachers—their antinomianism—and of making the three accusations in v 8 a closely connected series. All three are their rejection of the moral order over which the angels preside.

According to Jewish belief, the law of Moses was mediated by angels (*Jub.* 1:27–29; Josephus, *Ant.* 15.136; Acts 7:38, 53; Heb 2:2) and angels watched over its observance (Herm. *Sim.* 8:3:3). They were also, more generally, the guardians of the created order (the office from which the Watchers apostatised, v 6), and (according to the most probable interpretation of 1 Cor 11:10) it is to this function of the angels that Paul refers when he recommends proper conduct in the Christian assembly "because of the angels." We can well imagine that the false teachers, reproached for conduct which offended the angels as the administrators of the moral order, justified themselves by proclaiming their liberation from bondage to these angels and speaking slightingly of them. They understood Christian freedom to mean freedom from moral authority and therefore from the authority of the angels. No doubt they aligned the angels with the forces of evil from whose power the Christian was delivered, and accused them of imposing the Law out of envy and malice toward men. In other words, their "slandering" of the angels was a way of detaching the Law from God and interpreting it simply as an evil.

It is tempting to suppose that at this point they were taking up Pauline teaching about the Law. For Paul, too, was able to use the traditional role of the angels to the disadvantage of the Law (Gal 3:19), and in associating the angels of the Law closely with *τὰ στοιχεῖα τοῦ κόσμου*, "the elemental (powers) of the world" (Gal 4:3, 9; cf. Col 2:8–23; Rom 8:33–39) imply a strongly negative attitude toward them. The Law and its guardians belonged to the old era of slavery from which Christ has delivered the Christian (see especially B. Reicke, "The Law and This World According to Paul" *JBL* 70 [1951] 259–76). It is quite possible that in this respect the false teachers were closer to Pauline teaching than Jude was, though Jude's precise attitude to the Law cannot be inferred from his brief letter. On the other hand, for Paul the Law is "holy and just and good" (Rom 7:12), its moral content is the permanent divine standard of righteousness, and he firmly resisted such antinomian conclusions as the false teachers drew. If they were inspired by Paul, they represent an exaggerated and seriously distorted Paulinism. Against such antinomianism, Jude and Paul are agreed that the Christian is liberated for, not from, righteousness.

The attitude of Jude's opponents to the Law and its angels can be found in later Gnosticism (cf. Irenaeus, *Adv. Haer.* 1.23.4, on Simonianism; 1.24.5, on Basilides; *Treat. Seth* 64:1–10; *Testim. Truth* 29:11–30:17; and on gnostic libertinism, see G. W. MacRae, "Why the Church Rejected Gnosticism," in *Jewish and Christian Self-Definition,* vol. 1, ed. E. P. Sanders [London: SCM Press, 1980] 128–30), often as an interpretation of Paul (Pagels, *Paul,* 66–67). But in Gnosticism it became part of a much more thorough-going dualism in which the creation of the material world was also attributed to the archons. Without this cosmological dualism—which Jude's opponents lack—we cannot really speak of Gnosticism. Perhaps the antinomianism combated in Jude was one of the streams which flowed into later Gnosticism, but in itself it is not specifically gnostic.

Finally on v 8, it is worth noticing that Jude's use of *μὲν . . . δὲ . . . δέ* has the effect of dividing the list of three sins between, on the one hand, *σάρκα μὲν μιαίνουσιν* ("defile the flesh"), and, on the other hand, *κυριότητα δὲ ἀθετοῦσιν, δόξας δὲ βλασφημοῦσιν* ("reject the authority of the Lord and slander the glorious ones"). The first item of the list is the immoral behavior of the false teachers, the latter two items are their rejection of authority (of the Lord himself and of his ministers) on which the behavior is based. The division corresponds to that, in v 4, between *τὴν τοῦ θεοῦ ἡμῶν χάριτα μετατιθέντες εἰς ἀσέλγειαν* ("pervert the grace of our God into immorality"), and *τὸν μόνον δεσπότην καὶ κύριον ἡμῶν Ἰησοῦν Χριστὸν ἀρνούμενοι* ("deny our only Master and Lord Jesus Christ"). This supports our view of the significance of *δόξας δὲ βλασφημοῦσιν* ("slander the glorious ones"). In v 10 the same twofold characterization of the false teachers' error is found, this time (because v 10 takes up the end of v 8 and v 9) in the reverse order.

9. Μιχαὴλ ὁ ἀρχάγγελος, "Michael the archangel." In Dan 12:1 and rabbinic

usage (*b. Ḥag.* 12b; *Menaḥ.* 110a) Michael is "the great prince" (השר הגדול; Dan. 12:1 *θ*: ὁ ἄρχων ὁ μέγας), and in Dan 10:13 "one of the chief princes" (אחד השרים הראשנים; *θ*: εἷς τῶν ἀρχόντων τῶν πρώτων). The Greek ἀρχάγγελος (in NT only here and 1 Thess 4:16) came into use as equivalent to these expressions, usually applied either to the four (cf. *1 Enoch* 40) or to the seven chief angels (*1 Enoch* 20:7), otherwise called "the angels of the Presence." In either case Michael is included in the group, and often takes the leading role (cf. *Asc. Isa.* 3:16: "Michael the chief of the holy angels"), especially as the patron of Israel (Dan 12:1; 1QM 17; probably *T. Mos.* 10:2) and therefore the opponent of Satan (cf. Rev 12:7). He played these roles in the story about the burial of Moses to which Jude alludes. In that story, as the *T. Mos.* told it, Moses was the advocate for God's servant Moses in a legal dispute with Satan his accuser.

τῷ διαβόλῳ διακρινόμενος διελέγετο περὶ τοῦ Μωϋσέως *σώματος*, "in debate with the devil, disputed about the body of Moses." The words refer to a legal dispute (*διακρινόμενος* as in Joel 4:2 LXX). The devil in his ancient role as accuser tried to establish Moses' guilt, in order to prove him unworthy of honorable burial and to claim the body for himself. (See details of the story in *Form/Structure/Setting* section and the Excursus.)

οὐκ ἐτόλμησεν κρίσιν ἐπενεγκεῖν βλασφημίας, "he did not presume to condemn him for slander." The translation given is justified (see the *Note*) from the context of the story to which Jude alludes. In that story it was the devil who brought a slanderous accusation (*βλασφημία*) against Moses. There is no question of Michael slandering the devil. The point is rather that Michael, who was the advocate and not the judge, did not take it on himself to reject the devil's accusation as malicious slander; instead he appealed to the Lord's judgment.

Most commentators, however, prefer the translation: "he did not presume to pronounce a reviling judgment upon him" (RSV), on the grounds that it "fits the context better" (Kelly). Jude has complained (v 8) that the false teachers speak abusively of Moses, and so (it is said) he now contrasts their behavior with that of the archangel Michael himself who treated even the devil with respect, not using abusive language against him. If this interpretation has the merit of being relatively simple, it also seems an odd way for Jude to have made his point. The idea that the devil should not be insulted is an unparalleled idea in Jewish and early Christian literature, a questionable principle in itself, and not a necessary deduction from Jude's text. It is worth asking whether closer attention to the story to which Jude refers can make better sense of his reference to it.

In the first place, we should notice that the connection between *βλασφημοῦσιν* (vv 8, 10) and *βλασφημία* (v 9) is primarily a *catchword* connection. It creates a verbal, rather than necessarily a strict conceptual, link between the quotation and its application to the false teachers. It is therefore not necessary to insist that *κρίσιν βλασφημίας* means "a slanderous judgment" on the grounds that the false teachers' abuse of the angels must be paralleled by Michael's not abusing the devil.

So far as we can tell, the principal characteristic of the false teachers was their claim to be free from moral authority. We have argued that they "slandered" the angels (v 8) as the givers and guardians of the Law. They held that it was only out of envy and ill-will toward men that the angels had imposed the law of Moses. If it was pointed out to them that their behavior laid them open to the accusation of sin by the standards of the Law, they rejected the accusation as founded only on the malice of the angels who gave the Law. They were free men, not subject to the Law, and in rejecting its accusations needed to appeal only to their own authority as spiritual men. The authority by which spiritual men will judge angels (1 Cor 6:3) is sufficient to reject any accusation made against them by the angels whose mouthpiece is the Law.

To expose the presumption in this attitude, Jude reminds his readers of the story, which they presumably knew, of the dispute between Michael and the devil over the body of Moses, in which the devil charged Moses with murder, i.e. with sin according to the standards of the Law itself. This was a story in which an accusation in the name of the Law was made by an angelic accuser (the devil) who was undoubtedly motivated by malice. Moreover, it was brought against Moses himself. According to the current Jewish estimate of Moses, if anyone was entitled to reject such an accusation as slanderous, it was Moses. Yet, as Jude points out, Moses' advocate Michael, the archangel himself, did not take it on himself to condemn the devil for malicious slander. In countering the devil's accusation, he could not dismiss it as unjustified, on his own authority. He could only appeal to the Lord's judgment.

The point of contrast between the false teachers and Michael is not that Michael treated the devil with respect, and the moral is not that we should be polite even to the devil. The point of contrast is that Michael could not reject the devil's accusation on his own authority. Even though the devil was motivated by malice and Michael recognized that his accusation was slanderous, he could not himself dismiss the devil's case, because he was not the judge. All he could do was ask the Lord, who alone is judge, to condemn Satan for his slander. The moral is therefore that no one is a law to himself, an autonomous moral authority. Even if it were true—as the false teachers alleged—that when the Law accused them of sin it was only the malice of the angels which prompted those accusations, they would still not be justified in rejecting them on their own authority. Even if they were as righteous as Moses and had the authority of an archangel, they would not be above accusations of sin under the Law. They remain subject to the moral authority of the Lord.

This interpretation has several advantages. It makes Jude's choice of this text for use against his opponents more intelligible. When its reconstructed context in the *T. Mos.* is brought into the picture it can be seen to fit the case of the false teachers much better than if considered in isolation. This interpretation also allows Jude to be making a much more serious point than the questionable idea that even the devil should not be insulted. It is not a question of respect for the devil as such. Jude's argument hinges on the devil's role of *accuser,* bringing accusations under the Law. Not Michael's respect for the devil himself, but his response to the devil's accusation, is exemplary. Finally, this interpretation exempts Jude from the charge that his own polemic against the false teachers is more insulting than Michael's response to the devil. It is not a question of insulting language. Jude's treatment of the false teachers is in fact quite consistent with his own principle; he does not condemn them on his own authority, as though he were judge over them, but appeals to the coming judgment of the Lord (vv. 14–15).

Ἐπιτιμήσαι σοι κύριος, "May the Lord rebuke you!" The words were already quoted from Zech 3:2 (LXX: *Ἐπιτιμήσαι κύριος ἐν σοί, διάβολε*, "the Lord rebuke you, O devil") in the *T. Mos.* (see Excursus). As Kee has shown, *ἐπιτιμᾶν*, as a translation of גער, frequently has a stronger sense than "reprimand." These words "carry the connotation of divine conflict with the hostile powers, the outcome of which is the utterance of the powerful word by which the demonic forces are brought under control" (Kee, *NTS* 14 [1968] 238): hence they are used for God's eschatological subjugation of his enemies (e.g. *2 Apoc. Bar.* 21:23; *Asc. Isa.* 4:18) and in the accounts of Jesus' exorcisms (Mark 1:25 etc.). Something of this sense is appropriate in Zech 3:2 and the *T. Mos.*, though there is no eschatological reference and we must remember the context of legal dispute in both cases. Satan's power over men (over Joshua and his people in Zech 3:2, over the body of Moses in the *T. Mos.*) rests on his ability to sustain accusations against them. Thus when the angel (reading מלאך יהוה in Zech 3:2) asks God to "rebuke" Satan, he asks him to dismiss Satan's accusation and thereby assert his authority over Satan (cf. Kee, *NTS* 14 [1968] 239).

For Jude, the point of the words is their appeal to *God* to assert *his* authority over Satan. Our interpretation of Jude's intention here (see above) receives some support from *b. Qidd.* 81[a-b] (Str-B 1, 140), which evidently illustrates later rabbinic use of the words, "May the Lord rebuke you." This story tells how Pelimo used to say every day, "An arrow in Satan's eyes!", i.e. a defiant curse. One day, however, Satan got the better of him, and then asked him why he always cursed him in these terms. Pelimo asked Satan what words he ought to use in order to repel him. Satan replied, "You should say, 'The Merciful rebuke Satan!' " The contrast is apparently between Pelimo's habitual curse, which was a defiant expression of his own ability to overcome Satan, and the words quoted from Zech 3:2, which are an appeal to God to overcome Satan. Probably further evidence of this kind of understanding of the words from Zech 3:2 in Judaism is provided by *Adam and Eve* 39:1, in which Seth silences the Serpent's accusations against Eve with the words, "God the Lord revile thee" (tr. in *APOT*).

In Zech 3:2 and the *T. Mos. κύριος*, of course, referred to God, but it is probable that Jude interpreted the term as a reference to Jesus (see *Comment* on v 5). Jesus had the authority to rebuke Satan, both during his ministry (Mark 8:33) and at the Last Day (*Asc. Isa.* 4:18).

10. *οὗτοι δὲ ὅσα μὲν οὐκ οἴδασιν βλασφημοῦσιν*, "But these people slander whatever they do not understand." Having illustrated the proper response to accusations under the Law, Jude resumes the direct attack on the false teachers. Their attitude to the angelic guardians of the Law shows that they have no real understanding of the actual role of the angels as the ministers of the divine Lawgiver and Judge. The clause is probably direct polemic against the false teachers' claims to understanding, for no doubt it was precisely the heavenly world of the angels into which, like the apocalyptic and

gnostic visionaries, they had ascended in their visions and into which they claimed special insight. At the same time, the Sodomites' treatment of the angels may still be in Jude's mind, for *T. Asher* 7:1 speaks of "Sodom which knew not (ἠγνόησε) the angels of the Lord, and perished for ever."

ὅσα δὲ φυσικῶς ὡς τὰ ἄλογα ζῷα ἐπίστανται, "while by the things they do understand, instinctively, like unreasoning animals." This clause corresponds to *σάρκα μὲν μιαίνουσιν* ("defile the flesh") in v 8, with *φυσικῶς*, "instinctively," corresponding to *σάρκα*, "flesh," and no doubt refers to the sexual indulgence of the false teachers. This is what they do understand—on the level of merely instinctual knowledge. Though they claim to be guided by special spiritual insight gained in heavenly revelations, they are in fact following the sexual instincts which they share with the animals.

ἄλογα ζῷα is a standard phrase (Wis 11:15; 4 Macc 14:14, 18; Josephus, *C. Apion.* 2.213; *Ant.* 10.262) for the animals as contrasted with human rationality. (Cf. Xenophon, *Cyropaed.* 2.3.9, quoted by Mayor and Windisch, for a similar comparison between what men and beasts know [*ἐπιστάνται*] by instinct [*φύσει*].) For the comparison of sin with the behavior of animals, cf. 4 Ezra 8:29–30.

ἐν τούτοις φθείρονται ("they are destroyed"): not that by their sexual indulgence they contract fatal diseases, but that they incur judgment, as Israel in the wilderness and the Cities of the Plain were destroyed (cf. 1 Cor 3:17). (The idea which 2 Pet 2:12 introduces, that destruction is the natural fate of unreasoning animals, was probably not in Jude's mind.)

Explanation

To help his readers resist the influence of the false teachers, Jude reminds them that their initial instruction by the apostles at their conversion and baptism included teaching about God's judgment on disbelief and disobedience, and specific warnings of false teachers who would incur this judgment.

To illustrate this, he takes up first a well-known traditional list of OT examples of divine judgment: the extermination of the faithless wilderness generation of Israel after the Exodus, the punishment of the angels who abandoned their heavenly position for the sake of illicit relations with mortal women, and the destruction of the Cities of the Plain. For Jude, these are not just warning examples from the past, but also types. In common with Jewish apocalyptic and early Christian writers generally, he sees the great acts of God in the salvation-history of the past as prefiguring the eschatological events. The examples he gives are therefore typological prophecies of the eschatological judgment at the Parousia which threatens apostate Christians in these last days.

The first of the three types, whose significance Jude highlights by placing it first out of chronological order, makes especially clear that the Lord's own people, who have experienced his salvation, are not therefore less but more in danger of judgment if they repudiate his lordship. The other two types are probably cited also for the outrageous extremes of immorality they illustrate, including the Sodomites' insult to the angels.

In v 8 Jude applies the three types to the false teachers, instancing sins which correspond to the types and which therefore put them under threat of divine judgment corresponding to that of the types. Like the Watchers and the Sodomites, the false teachers indulge in sexual immorality. Like all three types, they reject the Lord's authority by repudiating his commandments, and like the Sodomites they insult the angels. The last accusation probably means that they justify their transgression of the Law by denigrating the angels as its authors and guardians. Thus all three sins are aspects of their antinomianism. In addition, all three rest, for their pretended religious authority, on visionary revelations, which Jude probably intends, by the use of the word "dreaming," to condemn as false prophecy.

In vv 9–10a Jude takes up, for further treatment, the charge of slandering angels. The presumptuousness involved in the false teachers' attitude to the angels of the Law is highlighted by comparison with the behavior of the archangel Michael in the story about the burial of Moses, which Jude and his readers knew from the *T. Mos.* The devil, in his traditional role of malicious accuser, had accused Moses of murder. Michael, disputing with the devil as advocate for Moses, knew the accusation to be slander, but did not presume to condemn the devil for his slander. Instead he referred the matter to the divine Judge who alone has the authority to rule out an accusation brought under the Law. Michael's behavior contrasts with that of the false teachers when they reject the accusations which the angels, as spokesmen for the Law, bring against them. They do so because they claim to be above all such accusations, subject to no moral authority. In fact, even if they had the status of Moses or Michael, they would remain subject to the divine Lawgiver and Judge. Given the context of the allusion, which Jude's readers knew, v 9 effectively exposes the spiritual conceit of the false teachers, whose attitude to the angels reveals a resistance to moral authority which will not even be subject to God.

In slandering the angels (v 10) they show how little they actually understand the heavenly world which they purport to explore in their visions. If they really understood the angelic world, they would recognize the angels as the ministers and messengers of God, but like the Sodomites they fail to do this. On the other hand, their behavior demonstrates that what they understand only too well is how to follow their sexual drives. In doing so, these people who claim to be spiritual men, superior to the angels, prove themselves to be living only on the subhuman level of the beasts.

The section concludes, most effectively, with the final respect in which the three types correspond to their antitypes, the false teachers. This is the real point of the whole comparison. Since the false teachers resemble the types in their sins, they will also resemble the types in their destruction.

Excursus: The Background and Source of Jude 9

Although the source of Jude's story of the dispute over the body of Moses is not extant, a wealth of material is available from which it should be possible to reconstruct the story which Jude knew. Much of this material has been assembled before (Charles, *Assumption,* 106–10; James, *Apocrypha,* 42–51; Denis, *Fragmenta,* 63–67), but it has not been subjected to the kind of critical investigation which is necessary if it is to provide reliable access to the content of Jude's source.

The discovery of 4Q^cAmram has recently stimulated some fresh discussion of the background to Jude 9 (Milik, *RB* 79 [1972] 77–97; Berger, *JSJ* 4 [1973] 1–18), and it has become clear that the reconstruction of Jude's source must take account of the general background which is provided by other comparable stories. Awareness of the tradition in which Jude's story belongs will aid investigation of the evidence for the story itself. We shall therefore begin by discussing this general background before turning to the extant sources which may preserve the actual story Jude knew.

I. General Background

Evidently the words of Michael, quoted in Jude's source, derive from Zech 3:2. The vision in Zech 3:1–5 is a courtroom scene in which the accusing angel, "the adversary" (השטן), and the angel of the Lord confront each other in a legal dispute in which the defendant is the high priest Joshua. Evidently Joshua's guilt, as representative of Israel, has placed him in the power of Satan his accuser. When the angel of the Lord (Jude's source must have read מלאך יהוה "the angel of the Lord" for MT יהוה "Lord" in Zech 3:2), as the Lord's representative, silences Satan with the words, "May the Lord rebuke you, Satan," he dismisses Satan's case against Joshua. As Kee observes (*NTS* 14 [1968] 237), the translation "rebuke" is rather weak: גער here denotes more than a reprimand. It refers to God's commanding word which asserts his authority over Satan, delivering Joshua and his people from Satan's power (cf. Pss 9:5; 68:30; Isa 17:13; Mal 3:11; and Kee's discussion of גער: *NTS* 14 [1968] 235–38).

The idea of a contest between Satan and the angel of the Lord was later applied to other episodes in the history of Israel. *Jub.* 17:15–18:16 tells the story of the sacrifice of Isaac within the framework of a heavenly trial of Abraham (cf. Job 1–2), in which the prince of the Mastema (= Satan) again appears as accuser, arguing that Abraham's faithfulness should be tested. When Abraham proves faithful, it is the angel of the presence who, on God's behalf, intervenes to save Isaac (cf. Gen 22:11–12), while "the prince of the Mastema was put to shame" (*Jub.* 18:12). (With this account compare the tradition preserved in *Yal. Rub.* 43:3, quoted by Chaine, 311: "When Isaac was bound, there was a debate between Michael and Satan. Michael brought a ram to free Isaac, but Satan wanted to keep him off so that Isaac should be sacrificed.")

The book of Jubilees makes further use of the theme of the contest between Satan and the angel, especially in chap 48, to illuminate the career of Moses and the Exodus. According to 48:2–3, it was the prince of the Mastema (not the Lord, as in Gen 4:24) who tried to kill Moses, and it was the angel of the presence who delivered Moses from his power (48:5). Though Satan's motivation here plainly derives from his enmity toward God and God's people (48:4), it may be that the author still intends him to be seen in the role of accuser: it was Moses' failure to circumcise his son (Gen 4:25) which put him into Satan's power.

Then the prince of the Mastema opposed Moses in his confrontation with Pharaoh, and aided the Egyptian magicians against him (48:9), while the angels of the presence assisted Moses by destroying them (48:11). This particular confrontation is recalled also by the Damascus Rule (CD 5:17–18): "Moses and Aaron arose by the hand of the Prince of lights and Satan in his cunning raised up Jannes and his brother" (tr. Vermes). However, according to Jubilees, the victory over the magicians did not yet result in the "shaming" of Satan (48:12) because he took further action: the Egyptians' pursuit of Israel (48:12, 16–17). The angels then delivered Israel from him at the Red Sea (48:13). Again it should be noticed that in this account Satan's power against Israel seems to rest on his power to "accuse them" (48:15, 18): as the leader of the forces of evil against the good angels he has not entirely lost his legal function of accusation (cf. also Rev 12:10).

These stories provide the principal background for the story to which Jude 9 alludes. It fits readily into the same pattern. At Moses' death, Satan makes a last attempt to assert his power over him. As we shall see, he does so by accusing Moses of murdering the Egyptian. By this accusation he intends to claim Moses' body and deprive him of the honor of burial by the archangel. Michael, however, silences Satan by his appeal to God to assert his authority over Satan ("May the Lord rebuke you!"), and thereby not only rescues Moses' body from Satan's power, but also vindicates Moses as the servant of God against Satan's attempt to claim him as a sinner.

Another text which clearly belongs in broadly the same tradition is 4QVisions of ᶜAmram (or Testament of ᶜAmram), in which Moses' father ᶜAmram relates a dream in which he saw two angels engaged in a legal dispute over him. The two angels (of whose names only Melkirešaᶜ survives in the text) are the two chief angels, the Prince of light and the Prince of darkness, who between them "have power over all the sons of Adam" (1:12). The dispute is plainly over whether ᶜAmram is a "son of light" belonging to the Prince of light or a "son of darkness" belonging to the Prince of darkness, but the text as it survives gives us no reason to suppose that it is a question of ᶜAmram's fate after death. (The vision took place during ᶜAmram's stay in Hebron, after which he returned to Egypt, and so some time before his death.) At one point the text is strikingly close to Jude 9: "behold, two of them of them disputed about me and said . . . and they were carrying on a great contest about me" (1:10–11). The similarity can scarcely be accidental, but probably we should not, as Milik does (*RB* 79 [1972] 95), conclude that Jude's source was inspired by 4QᶜAmram. The similarity may be sufficiently explained by the broader tradition of contests between the devil and the chief of the angels. The idea of the verbal dispute derives from the original courtroom context of accusation and defense.

Berger (*JSJ* 4 [1973] 1–18) has sought to link both 4QᶜAmram and Jude 9 to a tradition in which two angels, or two groups of angels, contend for possession of the departed soul at death. For this tradition he marshalls a wealth of evidence from later Christian apocalyptic texts, and clearly he has identified a very influential form which the tradition of contests between the devil and the angel took in relation to the fate of the soul at death. None of his texts, however, is as early as Jude 9 (though *T. Asher* 6:4–6 may be early evidence of his tradition; the earliest indisputable evidence is Origen's quotation from an apocryphal text about the death of Abraham: *Hom. 35 on Luke*). Berger recognizes that Jude 9, which is not about the fate of the soul at death, represents an adaptation of the tradition for a specific purpose. It is better, however, to see Jude 9 as a specific instance of the *general* tradition of contests between the devil and the angel, 4QᶜAmram as another specific instance of this general tradition, and Berger's tradition of texts about the fate of the soul at death as a particular form which that tradition took, perhaps at a later date than the time of writing of Jude's source and certainly without any direct relation to Jude's source. Again the recurrence of the idea of dispute (among Berger's texts, note especially: Origen, *Hom.* 35: *super Abrahae salute et interitu disceptantes,* "debating about the salvation and death of Abraham"; Syriac *Apoc. Paul* 11: "a dispute between those good angels and those bad angels") derives from the common dependence on the general tradition, rather than from a dependence by Jude 9 on the specific tradition identified by Berger.

II. The Lost Ending of the Testament of Moses

There is widespread agreement that Jude's source in v 9 was the lost ending of the work preserved for us only in Latin translation, in the incomplete and rather poor text of a sixth-century manuscript in Milan, a work sometimes known as the *As. Mos.,* but more appropriately known as the *T. Mos.* This work, of Palestinian origin, has commonly been dated at the beginning of the first century A.D., though some have argued for its origin in the Maccabean period, with some revision in the early first century A.D. It seems likely that Jude in v 16 made use of that part of the work which is now extant (see *Comment* on v 16), and may therefore have used its lost ending in v 9. Moreover, although some have argued that Jude's story of the dispute over Moses' body seems to belong to a different kind of literature from what we have of the *T. Mos.,* it could be argued, from our text of the *Testament,* that it must have ended with a story of Moses' death and burial, since (1) testaments usually end with an account of the subject's death and burial (*T. 12 Patr., T. Abr., T. Job*), and (2) *T. Mos.* 11:6–8 raises the question of Moses' burial and seems to require an account of his burial in an unknown grave.

Although the ending of the *T. Mos.* is no longer extant, a number of Christian sources seem to have preserved the substance of the story it contained. These require detailed discussion in turn:

A. *Palaea Historica*

Of the death of Moses. And Moses said to Jesus the son of Nave, "Let us go up into the mountain." And when they had gone up, Moses saw the land of promise, and he said to Jesus, "Go down to the people and tell them that Moses is dead." And Jesus went down to the people, but Moses came to the end of his life. And Samuel (Σαμουήλ) tried to bring his body (σκύνωμα) down to the people, so that they might make him (it) a god (θεοποιηθῶσιν αὐτόν, *v.l.* αὐτό). But Michael the chief captain (ἀρχιστράτηγος) by the command of God came to take him (it) and remove (συνστεῖλαι) him (it), and Samuel resisted (ἀνθίστατο) him, and they fought (διεμάχοντο). So the chief captain was angry and rebuked him, saying, "May the Lord rebuke you, devil!" (ἐπιτιμᾷ σε κύριος, διάβολε). And so the adversary (ἀντικείμενος) was defeated and took flight, but the archangel Michael removed the body (σκύνωμα) of Moses to the place where he was commanded by Christ our God, and no one saw the burial-place (or, burial: ταφήν) of Moses.

(Greek text in A. Vassiliev, *Anecdota Graeco-Byzantina* [Moscow: Imperial University Press, 1893] 257–58. The *Palaea* is a Byzantine collection of biblical legends. For its value in preserving old Jewish traditions, see D. Flusser, "Palaea Historica: An Unknown Source of Biblical Legends," *ScrHie* 22 [1971] 48–79.)

This text is almost certainly independent of Jude 9: there is a striking lack of coincidence in vocabulary (only διαβόλος and ἀρχάγγελος), except in the words of rebuke, but even here the words are not quoted from Jude (who has ἐπιτιμήσαι σοι κύριος). If the author drew these words from Jude 9, he also missed Jude's point, which is that Michael himself did *not* rebuke the devil, but appealed to the Lord to rebuke him.

The following features of the text should be noted:

(1) The death of Moses raises no problem for this tradition. There is no trace of that resistance to the idea that Moses should have to submit to the fate of sinful men, which is found in so many Jewish traditions about the death of Moses (see especially Loewenstamm, "Death of Moses"). There is no trace of the idea of the bodily assumption of Moses which was current in some circles as early as the first century A.D. (reflected, though countered, in the accounts of Moses' death in Josephus, *Ant.* 4.326, and *Bib. Ant.* 19:16; see Haacker and Schäfer, "Traditionen," 155–56; Loewenstamm, "Death," 197–98; and rabbinic passages in Str-B 1, 754–55). Nor is there any trace of the idea of Moses' own reluctance to die, and of the unwillingness of the angels and the inability of the angel of death to receive his soul, which were elaborated in the rabbinic traditions (*Sipre Deut.* 305; *Deut. Rab.* 11:10; *Midr. Peṭirat Moše*). There is not even any question of the ascension of Moses' soul to heaven. In this account the death of Moses is straightforwardly related, and the interest focuses on the question of the burial of his corpse. This is precisely what we should expect in a conclusion to the extant text of the *T. Mos.*, in which Moses looks forward to his death in a matter-of-fact way, accepting it without argument (1:15; 10:12, 14) and without implying that there would be anything remarkable about it. (The word *receptione* (10:12), which may mean "assumption," has generally been regarded as a loss; see section (III) below.) The unique dignity of Moses leads Joshua to expect, not a unique manner of death for Moses, but a unique form of burial (11:5–8). Burial by the archangel Michael in an unknown grave fulfills this expectation.

(2) The account begins with Joshua accompanying Moses up the mountain, before Moses sends him down again. This feature, which does not derive from the biblical text, is rare in the traditions of Moses' death (but cf. Josephus, *Ant.* 4.326). It would, however, have followed on well from the text of the *Testament of Moses* as we know it. There it is Joshua whom Moses addresses throughout the book, who is commissioned to succeed Moses (10:15), who responds with consternation to the news that Moses must die (11) and has to be reassured by Moses (12).

(3) The name Σαμουήλ, i.e., Sammaʾel, for the devil is known from the *Asc. Isa.* (where in 1:8 he is identified with Malkira, i.e. the Melkirešaʿ of 4QʿAmram, and in 11:41 with Satan) and from rabbinic sources ("the chief of all the satans," *Deut. Rab.* 11:10). In rabbinic traditions of Moses' death he appears as the angel of death, commanded by God to take Moses' soul but unable to do so. A remnant of his dispute with Michael survives in these traditions, but transposed from the context of Moses' burial to that of his death (*Midrash Peṭirat Moše* 11; *Deut. Rab.* 11:10).

(4) The removal of Moses' body (*συνστέλλειν* must here mean "remove," despite the rarity of this meaning)—to be buried elsewhere—corresponds to the tradition found in *Tg. Ps.-J.* Deut 34:6 and *Sipre Deut.* 355, in which God or his angels carry the body four miles from the place of his death to bury it (see Haacker and Schäfer, "Traditionen," 165–66). This feature is intended to explain Deut 34:6.

(5) Unlike the rabbinic traditions of Moses' burial, however, this account ascribes the burial not to God himself but to Michael, carrying out God's command. It is typical of the Jewish literature of the intertestamental period to introduce angels as God's agents, in actions which the OT attributes directly to God. In relation to Moses' burial (by God, according to Deut 34:6 MT) the LXX ("they buried") may already intend to introduce angelic agents. The later rabbinic traditions, however, lay great stress on the fact that God himself ("none other than God," according to *m. Soṭa* 1:9) buried Moses, in order to enhance the unique dignity of Moses (Haacker and Schäfer, "Traditionen," 165). Our text probably preserves a tradition which antedates that tendency.

(6) Our text is alone in suggesting that Satan tried to take Moses' body to the people for them to worship it, but the idea that Moses' grave was unknown so that

idolatrous use should not be made of it is a widespread feature of the traditions of Moses' burial (*Midrash Leqaḥ Tob,* cited by Loewenstamm, "Death," 204; Origen, *Selecta in Num., PG* 12. 578B; Theodoret of Cyrus, *Quaest. in Deut.* 32, *PG* 80. 447C; Armenian *History of Moses* [M. E. Stone, "Three Armenian Accounts of the Death of Moses," in G. W. E. Nickelsburg (ed.), *Studies on the Testament of Moses* (SBLSCS 4; Missoula, MT: Scholars Press, 1973) 118–21]; Josephus, *Ant.* 4.326 hints at the danger of deification, though not in relation to the burial of the body). Moreover, it is possible that *T. Mos.* 11:7 already hints at the danger of deification of Moses' body. However, when we consider text C below, we shall find some grounds for wondering whether this feature of A is secondary: it is hard to be sure whether it belonged originally to the story as found in the lost ending of the *T. Mos.*

(7) Alone among the texts to be considered in this section, this account represents the contest between the devil and Michael (here in his military capacity as ἀρχιστράτηγος) as a physical conflict rather than as a verbal dispute in which Satan brings accusations. This makes Michael's words, "May the Lord rebuke you," taken from the context of verbal dispute (Zech 3:2), less appropriate. In this respect this account is very probably less original than the other texts to be discussed in this section. (It probably reflects the increasing militarization of the figure of Michael in the later Christian tradition, demonstrated by J. P. Rohland, *Der Erzengel Michael, Arzt und Feldherr* [BZRGG 19; Leiden: E. J. Brill, 1977].) The motif of the devil's resistance, which occurs also in texts E, M, and N below, derives probably from Dan 10:13.

Thus, with the exception of point (7), and perhaps also of point (6), this account seems to preserve material which can plausibly be attributed to the lost ending of the *T. Mos.*

B. *The Slavonic Life of Moses 16*

But at the end of the same year in the twelfth month, on the seventh day (that is, in March), Moses the servant of God died and was buried on the fourth of the month September on a certain mountain by the Chief Captain (*Archistrategos*) Michael. For the devil contended with the angel, and would not permit his body to be buried, saying, "Moses is a murderer. He slew a man in Egypt and hid him in the sand." Then Michael prayed to God and there was thunder and lightning and suddenly the devil disappeared; but Michael buried him with his (own) hands. (Translation in James, *Apocrypha,* 47–48, from the German translation in N. Bonwetsch, "Die Mosessage in der slavischen kirchlichen Litteratur," NGWG.PH (1908) 607, but the opening words corrected according to the suggestion of E. Turdeanu, "La *Chronique de Moïse* en russe," *RESl* 46 [1967] 55. Turdeanu shows that the Slavonic *Life of Moses* is a [fifteenth-century] version of the medieval Hebrew *Chronicle of Moses,* similar to that in the *Chronicles of Jeraḥmeel;* the episode of the dispute over Moses' body is not found in *Jeraḥmeel,* and Turdeanu regards it as an interpolation in the original *Chronicle,* but an interpolation made in the Hebrew *Chronicle* before its translation.)

This text, again not dependent on Jude 9 and also, it seems, independent of the account in the *Palaea,* is of interest mainly because it preserves the devil's accusation against Moses. Whereas in text A the idea of a legal dispute has been largely transformed into a physical combat, in B the legal context is preserved through the retention of the devil's charge. The devil retains his ancient role of accuser. This must be an original feature of the tradition, not only on the general grounds that Satan retains his accusing role in the general background to Jude 9 (section I above), but more specifically because the words of the archangel, "May the Lord rebuke you!" which Jude's source quoted from Zech 3:2, must originally have been a reply to Satan's accusation, as they are in Zech 3:1–2. It is an impressive indication of the complementary value of the divergent accounts A and B, that A preserves the archangel's words without the accusation, whereas B preserves the accusation without the archangel's reply. The accusation from B and the archangel's reply from A together form a coherent summary of the dispute. We may therefore be confident that the devil's charge of murder against Moses formed part of the lost ending of the *T. Mos.* which Jude read.

On the other hand, the other new feature in B—the thunder and lightning—looks like a late embellishment.

C. *Pseudo-Oecumenius, In Jud. 9*

It is said that Michael the archangel served the burial of Moses. For the devil would not accept this, but brought an accusation because of the murder of the Egyptian, on the grounds that Moses was guilty of it, and because of this would not allow him to receive honorable burial. (Greek text in Denis, *Fragmenta,* 67. The translation "on the grounds that Moses was guilty of it" follows the emendation of *αὐτοῦ* to *αἰτίου* proposed by A. Hilgenfeld, "Die Psalmen Salomo's und die Himmelfahrt des Moses, B," *ZWT* 22 [1868] 299; the text as it stands is meaningless.)

D. *From Cramer's Catena*

When Moses died on the mountain, Michael was sent to remove (*μεταθήσων*) the body. When the devil slandered Moses (*κατὰ τοῦ Μωϋσέως βλασφημοῦντες*) and proclaimed him a murderer because he smote the Egyptian, the angel, not tolerating the slander against him, said to the devil, "May God rebuke you!" (*ἐπιτιμήσαι σοι ὁ θεός*). (Greek text in Cramer, *Catenae,* 163, lines 18–22; and in Denis, *Fragmenta,* 67; Charles, *Assumption,* 109–10.)

Several scholia and anonymous comments in the *Catenae* are very similar to C and D (see Denis, *Fragmenta,* 67, and texts M and N below). The points of contact with A and B should be noticed: D agrees with A that Michael's mission was to remove the body (for burial elsewhere); both agree with B on the accusation. It is also of interest, for the exegesis of Jude 9, that D refers to the devil's accusation as *βλασφημία* against Moses.

A point of conflict between C and A is the question of the devil's motivation. In A he wishes to present the body to the people for use as an idol, whereas in C he simply wishes to prevent Moses from receiving the unique dignity of burial by an archangel, arguing that, as a murderer, Moses is unworthy of this. The two motives are not necessarily incompatible, but if a choice must be made between them, the version in C should be preferred as more original, since it belongs to the devil's proper role as accuser in a legal dispute. The motive in A, although, as we have seen, it draws on an old tradition, may be a later introduction into the story, required by the fact that A has lost sight of the devil's *accusing* role. On the other hand, it is possible that the original story contained both motives of the devil, each fulfilling a different function in the narrative: the motive in C serves the story's intention by showing that Moses deserved the unique honor of burial by the archangel, while the motive in A serves to explain why Michael removed the body and buried it in a *secret* grave (as a precaution against idolatrous reverence for the body). Both these general themes are to be found in the Jewish traditions about the death of Moses, and it is quite possible that the conclusion of the *T. Mos.* incorporated both.

E. *Severus of Antioch*

Here [in Deut 34] by means of a bodily image God set forth a mystery which occurs concerning the soul. For when the soul separates from the body, after its departure hence both good angelic powers and a very evil band of demons come to meet it, so that according to the quality of the deeds, evil and good, which it has done, either one group or the other may carry it off to the appropriate place, to be guarded until the last day, when we shall all be presented for judgment, and led away either to eternal life or to the unending flame of fire. God, wishing to show this also to the children of Israel by means of a certain bodily image, ordained that at the burial of Moses, at the time of the dressing of the body and its customary depositing in the earth, there should appear before their eyes the evil demon as it were resisting and opposing, and that Michael, a good angel, should encounter and repel him, and should not rebuke him on his own authority, but retire from passing judgment against him in favor of the Lord of all, and say, "May the Lord rebuke you!", in order that by means of these things those who are being instructed might learn that there is a conflict over our souls after their departure hence and that it is necessary to prepare oneself by means of good deeds in order to secure the angels as allies, when the demons are gibbering jealously and bitterly against us. And when this divine image had appeared before their eyes, it seems that then some cloud or shining of light came upon that place, obscuring it and walling it off from the onlookers, so that they might not know his grave. Therefore also the holy Scripture says in Deuteronomy, "And Moses the servant of the Lord died there in the land of Moab by the word of the Lord. And they buried him in the land of Moab near the house of Phogor. And no one saw his death (*τελευτήν*) (or, his grave [*ταφήν*]) until this day." [Deut 34:5–6] . . . These things, it is said, are found in an apocryphal book which contains the more detailed account (*λεπτοτέραν ἀφήγησιν*) of the genesis or creation. (Greek text in Cramer, *Catenae,* 161, line 20–162, line 17; and partly in M. R. James, *The Testament of Abraham* [TextsS 2/2; Cambridge: Cambridge University Press, 1892] 17, whose text includes the last sentence, not in Cramer. With this text, cf. also Cramer, *Catenae,* 161, lines 9–18, attributed to Severus in James, *Apocrypha,* 46; and the further quotations from Severus in Cramer, *Catenae,* 162, lines 17–30; 162, line 31–163, line 10.)

This passage contains a number of new features:

(1) The explicit statement that Michael, in saying, "May the Lord rebuke you!", was refraining from giving a judgment on his own authority, looks as though it depends on Jude's interpretation of his source in Jude 9, rather than on the source itself. It was Jude's use of the source, rather than the source's own interest, which required this point to be made explicit.

(2) In explaining that the contest between Michael and the devil was shown to the people to teach them what happens to the soul at death, Severus makes contact with the tradition represented by the texts which Berger has assembled (see section I above). It is, however, a somewhat unsatisfactory use of the story of the contest, which was over Moses' body, not his soul, and must be regarded as a secondary, homiletical adaptation of the story.

(3) The idea of the dazzling cloud which prevented the onlookers from seeing where Moses was buried is found in other accounts (Josephus, *Ant.* 4.326; *Memar Marqah* 5:3 [tr. J. Macdonald, vol. 2 (BZAW 84; Berlin: Töpelmann, 1963) 202]; quotation from "an apocryphal and mystical codex" in a *catena,* quoted Charles, *Assumption,* xlviii). It was evidently a fairly widespread tradition, but in these other accounts the cloud hides Moses from view already *before* he dies. In Severus' source it has been transposed to follow the dispute between Michael and the devil, since the latter has become a public spectacle. The transposition is evident in the quotation from Deut 34:5–6, which is quoted in a form designed to show that no one saw Moses *die* (*τελευτήν*), but then is glossed according to the usual form of the text, to convey the sense

that no one saw his burial or grave (ταφήν). This is a further indication that the exhibition of the dispute over the body to the people is a secondary feature of the tradition. Whether the luminous cloud originally played any part in the narrative of Moses' death in the *T. Mos.* it is impossible to tell.

(4) As James points out (*Apocrypha,* 46) Severus apparently ascribes his account to the book of *Jubilees* (also known as *Leptogenesis*). This must be a mistake, but Severus seems to have had his information at second-hand, at best. An apocryphon containing an account of Moses' death could easily have been regarded as a sequel to *Jub.* and attached to it: this may be the cause of the error. But what was this apocryphon? Plainly not the *T. Mos.,* but probably a later work which took from the *T. Mos.* the story of the contest between Michael and the devil, but adapted it to illustrate the general principle of the contest for the soul at death. If the explanation that Michael refrained from passing judgment on the devil on his own authority is to be attributed to Severus' source, rather than to Severus himself, then the apocryphon was perhaps a Christian work acquainted with Jude 9. In any case, Severus provides us with no reliable information about the source which Jude himself used.

F. *From Cramer's Catena*

> Michael, since he lacked the authority, did not bring upon him (the devil) the punishment appropriate to blasphemy (τῆς βλασφημίας), but left him to the judgment of his Master. For when he brought Moses onto the mountain where the Lord was transfigured, then the devil said to Michael, "God lied in bringing Moses into the land which he swore he should not enter." (Greek text in Cramer, *Catenae,* 161, lines 4–8.)

This text is clearly a Christian attempt to explain Jude 9 without any knowledge of its Jewish background. Assuming that the devil's βλασφημία, mentioned in Jude 9, was blasphemy *against God,* the writer tried to explain what such blasphemy, in connection with a dispute over the body of Moses, might have been. Not realizing that Jude 9 refers to the time of Moses' burial, he placed the dispute at the time of the transfiguration of Jesus, when Moses' appearance on the mountain apparently contradicted God's declaration that Moses should not enter the promised land.

Although James (*Apocrypha,* 47–48), relying on text N below, supposed these words of the devil to come from the conclusion of the *T. Mos.,* they cannot do so, because (a) they are incomprehensible apart from the Christian story of the transfiguration of Jesus, and (b) they do not constitute an accusation *against Moses,* but an accusation *against God,* which is out of keeping with the devil's role in the story of the dispute at the burial of Moses.

This concludes the review of texts which could provide reliable evidence of the story of the dispute over Moses' body as Jude knew it, i.e. in the form in which it was told in the lost ending of the *T. Mos.* (Other texts which have been thought to provide such evidence, but in fact probably reflect another version of the story, will be discussed in section III below.) Discounting texts E and F (which have been shown not to be reliable evidence of the story Jude knew), and secondary features of other texts (the physical combat in A, the thunder and lightning in B), we may reconstruct the outline of the story as follows:

> Joshua accompanied Moses up Mount Nebo, where God showed Moses the land of promise. Moses then sent Joshua back to the people to inform them of Moses' death, and Moses died. God sent the archangel Michael to remove the

body of Moses to another place and bury it there, but Samma'el, the devil, opposed him, disputing Moses' right to honorable burial. The text may also have said that he wished to take the body to the people for them to make it an object of worship. Michael and the devil therefore engaged in a dispute over the body. The devil brought against Moses a charge of murder, because he smote the Egyptian and hid his body in the sand. But this accusation was no better than slander (*βλασφημία*) against Moses, and Michael, not tolerating the slander, said to the devil, "May the Lord rebuke you, devil!" At that the devil took flight, and Michael removed the body to the place commanded by God, where he buried it with his own hands. Thus no one saw the burial of Moses.

Evidently the intention of the story was primarily to dramatize the issue of Moses' supreme worthiness in God's sight. In spite of the apparent blemishes on his record, to be found in the biblical account and brought in evidence against him by Satan, Moses was vindicated as worthy of the unique honor of burial by God's archangel. (That the account of Moses' killing the Egyptian in Exod 2:12 was something of a problem to Jewish exegetes can be seen from Josephus, *Ant.* 2.254, where the explanation of Moses' flight from Egypt omits to mention this incident, and from Philo, *Mos.* 1.44, which justifies Moses' action.) If the motif of Satan's desire to make the body an idol is original, the story had the secondary function of explaining why Moses was buried in a secret grave (Deut 34:6).

III. The Assumption of Moses

Before the conclusion reached in section II can be allowed to stand, it is necessary to consider the evidence of several of the Fathers who refer to a work called the *As. Mos.* as supplying the source of Jude 9 and ascribe to that work details of a dispute between Michael and the devil which seems to diverge from the story given in the texts in section II. It will be convenient to list all the relevant texts before discussing them.

G. *Clement of Alexandria, Fragm. in Ep. Jud.*
(On Jude 9:) This corroborates the Assumption of Moses (*Assumptionem Moysi*). (Latin text in Charles, *Assumption,* 107.)

H. *Didymus the Blind, in ep. Jud. enarr.*
They take exception to the present epistle and object to the Assumption of Moses (*Moyseos Assumptioni*), on account of that place where the archangel's word to the devil concerning the body of Moses is indicated. (Latin text in Charles, *Assumption,* 108.)

I. *Origen, De Princ. 3:2:1*
In Genesis the serpent is described as having deceived Eve, and with regard to this, in the Ascension of Moses (*in Adscensione Mosis*) (a book which the apostle Jude mentions in his epistle), Michael the archangel, disputing with the devil about the body of Moses, says that the serpent, inspired by the devil, was the cause of the transgression of Adam and Eve. (Latin text in Charles, *Assumption,* 108.)

J. *Gelasius Cyzicenus, Hist. Eccl. 2.17.17*
. . . as it is written in the book of the Assumption of Moses (ἐν βίβλῳ ἀναλήψεως Μωσέως), Moses having summoned Jesus the son of Nave and disputing with him, said, "And God foresaw me before the foundation of the world to be the mediator of his covenant." (Greek and Latin texts in Denis, *Fragmenta,* 63.)

K. *Gelasius Cyzicenus, Hist. Eccl. 2.21.7*
And in the book of the Assumption of Moses, Michael the archangel, disputing (διαλεγόμενος) with the devil, says, "For from his holy Spirit we were all created." And again he says, "From the face of God his Spirit went forth, and the world was made." (Greek text in Denis, *Fragmenta,* 64.)

L. *From Cramer's Catena*
For the devil resisted (ἀντεῖχε), wishing to deceive, (saying) "The body is mine, for I am the Master of matter," and was answered by the angel, "May the Lord rebuke you," that is, the Lord of the spirits of all flesh. (Greek text in Cramer, *Catenae,* 160 line 29–161 line 1.)

M. *A scholion on Jude 9*
When Moses died on the mountain, the archangel Michael was sent to remove (μεταθήσαν) the body. But the devil resisted (ἀντεῖχε), wishing to deceive, saying, "The body is mine, for I am the Master of matter," or slandering (βλασφημοῦντος κατά) the holy man, because he smote the Egyptian, and proclaiming him a murderer. The angel, not tolerating the slander against the holy man, said to the devil, "May God rebuke you!" (Greek text in Denis, *Fragmenta,* 67; Charles, *Assumption,* 110.)

N. *A scholion on Jude 9*
For the devil resisted (ἀντεῖχεν) wishing to deceive, saying, "The body is mine, for I am the Master of matter," and was answered by, "May the Lord rebuke you," that is, the Lord who is Master of all the spirits. Others say that God, wishing to show that after our departure hence demons oppose our souls on their upward course, permitted this to be seen at the burial of Moses. For the devil also slandered (ἐβλασφήσει κατά) Moses, calling him a murderer because he smote the Egyptian. Michael the archangel, not tolerating his slander, said to him, "May the Lord God rebuke you, devil!" He also said this, that God had lied in bringing Moses into the land which he swore he should not enter. (Greek text in James, *The Testament of Abraham,* [TextsS 2/2; Cambridge: Cambridge University Press, 1892] 18, from MS. Bodl. Arch. E.5.9; translation adapted from James, *Apocrypha,* 46.)

Texts L, M and N have been included in this list because it is clear that they supply the words of the devil ("The body is mine, for I am the Master of matter") to which Michael replies in text K, and so must provide information from the same source as text K explicitly quotes. Texts M and N, however, are clearly conflated accounts. Text M combines the tradition represented by D with the tradition represented by L, while text N has brought together material from a whole series of divergent traditions, represented by texts D, E, F and L. These conflated versions are not evidence that all these elements derive from a single source, but represent the scholiasts' attempts to gather together the various versions of the story which they found in their sources. The material derived from the traditions already discussed in section II can therefore be discounted as evidence of the content of the *As. Mos.*

Texts I, K, L, M, and N provide an outline of Michael's dispute with the devil which is quite distinct from that of the texts in section II. Here the devil claims that the body of Moses belongs to him because he is the Master of matter. Michael evidently rejects this claim by arguing that the material world, including human bodies, was created by the Holy Spirit of God, and therefore belongs to God. The devil is not the rightful Lord of the material world, but a rebel who, from the time of Adam and Eve, has tempted God's creatures to sin against God. Therefore when Michael, with the words, "May the Lord rebuke you!", appeals to the judgment of God, he appeals to the one Creator of the world to whom Satan, like all other spiritual beings, is subject.

There have been attempts to combine this dispute with the dispute found in the texts in section II (James, *Apocrypha,* 48–49; Charles, *Assumption,* 105–7; Loewenstamm, "Death," 209–10), but these attempts are mistaken. The two versions of the dispute exist in two distinct sets of texts, and are brought together only by the late *scholia* (M and N) which themselves indicate that they are found in distinct sources. Moreover, the role of the devil and the character of the dispute are quite different in the two versions. In the texts in section II, the devil remains the malicious accuser of Jewish tradition, trying to prove Moses' guilt. In the alternative version, the devil has become a kind of gnostic demiurge, claiming to be lord of the material world, and Michael's refutation of his claim is the anti-gnostic assertion that the one God, to whom the devil himself is subject, created the material world. The whole concern of the narrative has now become the debate with gnostic dualism. Each version provides a coherent account in its own terms, but the attempt to combine them into one narrative can only produce incoherence.

If the story of the dispute over Moses' body existed in these two versions, were we correct to identify the version in section II with the lost ending of the *T. Mos.* and the source of Jude 9? At first sight, the texts in this section seem to indicate that it was the *As. Mos.,* with its anti-gnostic version of the dispute, which Jude read and which included the text represented by the Latin manuscript we have called the *T. Mos.,* for (a) texts G, H, and I explicitly link Jude 9 with the *As. Mos.;* and (b) text J quotes from the *As. Mos.* (evidently the same work as is quoted in text K) words which are found in the Latin *T. Mos.* (1:14). A reply to (a) is not difficult. If the Alexandrian Fathers knew only that version of the dispute over Moses' body which was found in the *As. Mos.,* they would naturally have linked that version with Jude 9, especially as both versions seem to have contained the words, "May the Lord rebuke you!", which Jude quotes.

However, the quotations in texts J and K constitute a more serious difficulty. They require us to suppose *either* that the text represented by the extant Latin manuscript was concluded by the anti-gnostic version of the dispute over Moses' body, and known as the *As. Mos.; or* that the *As. Mos.* was a *revised version* of the earlier *T. Mos* in which some material, including *T. Mos.* 1:14, remained unchanged. (Laperrousaz, *Testament,* 60–61, simply rejects the testimony of texts J and K as unreliable, since Gelasius' account of the Council of Nicaea, in which they occur, is widely regarded as historically untrustworthy. But this is not an adequate ground for suspecting Gelasius' attributions of the quotations to the *As. Mos.*) Of these two alternatives, the second is preferable. It is hard to believe that a Palestinian work of the early first century A.D. would have included the kind of refutation of dualism which the texts quote from the *As. Mos.* It is much more plausible to attribute the *As. Mos.'* version of the dispute over Moses' body to the concerns of Christian anti-gnostic argument in the second century A.D.

Of course, if Jude were written against teachers of precisely this kind of gnostic dualism, as some have argued, then it might perhaps be thought appropriate that Jude 9 should refer to this anti-gnostic version of the dispute over Moses' body. In fact, however, there is no evidence in the letter that Jude's opponents did espouse a developed Gnosticism or believe in a demiurge who was lord of the material world. If they did, it is incredible that Jude should refer to the story in the *As. Mos.,* but *not* exploit it as an argument against their dualism. For the purposes of his polemic, Jude seems interested only in the fact that Michael appealed to the judgment of God against the devil.

The anti-gnostic version of the dispute over Moses' body in the *As. Mos.* may, however, have been connected with Jude 9 in another way. If Jude was not written against developed Gnosticism, it must have been *used* against developed Gnosticism in the second and third centuries. (Clement of Alexandria thought Jude wrote prophetically against the Carpocratians; Didymus the Blind took his opponents to be the disciples of Simon Magus.) Perhaps it was the fact that Jude, understood as an anti-gnostic tract, made polemical use of the dispute over the body of Moses, that inspired a second-century Christian to rewrite that dispute in the form of a refutation of gnostic dualism.

We have not yet discussed the title Ἀνάληψις Μωσέως, "Assumption of Moses." It might be considered a further sign that the traditions in section II do not derive from this work, that they contain no hint of an assumption either of Moses' body or of his soul. Moreover, the extant section of the *T. Mos.* contains no expectation of an assumption, except perhaps in the word *receptione* (10:12), which if it does mean "assumption" (see below) is so out of keeping with the rest of the work (cf. 1:15; 10:14; 11:4–8) that most scholars have considered it a gloss. On the other hand, the texts (given above) which explicitly quote the *As. Mos.* are equally silent about an assumption. There are, however, accounts of an assumption of Moses, given without naming their sources by Clement of Alexandria and Origen, who knew the *As. Mos.* It is a fair conclusion that these derive from the *As. Mos.* (The accounts are in Clement. *Strom.* 6.15.2–3; Origen, *In lib. Jesu Nave Hom.* 2:1; cf. also Evodius of Uzala, *Epist. ad Aug.* 158:6; and a further reference to Moses' ἀνάληψις ("assumption") in Clement, *Strom.* 1.23.1: texts printed in Denis, *Fragmenta,* 64–66.) The assumption described is one in which Moses was seen in one form ascending to heaven with angels, while in another form he was buried in the earth. (On this story, cf. J. D. Purvis, "Samaritan Traditions on the Death of Moses," in G. W. E. Nickelsburg (ed.) *Studies on the Testament of Moses* [SBLSCS 4; Cambridge, Mass.: Scholars Press, 1973] 113–14; Philo, *Mos.* 2.291; Denis, *Introduction,* 132. The combination of the burial of the body and the assumption of the soul is paralleled in other Hellenistic Jewish testaments: *T. Job, T. Abr.*) It is therefore a kind of assumption which is compatible with the story of the dispute over the body of Moses which the *As. Mos.* contained. Thus we may conclude that the fragments of an account of Moses' assumption preserved by the Alexandrian Fathers derive from the second-century work which they knew as the *As. Mos.*

The word *receptione* in *T. Mos.* 10:12 (*morte receptionem,* usually corrected to *morte receptione mea,* "my death (and) reception") remains to be considered. It has generally been taken to be a translation of ἀνάληψις ("assumption"), and in that case constitutes the only hint of an assumption of Moses to be found in the extant Latin text of the *Testament.* Laperrousaz (*Testament,* 41–46) argues that it need describe nothing more than a normal death (cf. *T. Mos.* 11:5: "What place will receive (*recipiet*) you?", i.e., "be your grave"), but it remains a plausible translation of ἀνάληψις (see Laperrousaz, *Testament,* 42 n. 3, 43) and should probably be taken in that sense. If so, it may be a gloss added by a scribe who knew the tradition of Moses' assumption. Alternatively, it is possible that the revision which transformed the *Testament* into the *As. Mos.* was almost entirely confined to the concluding part of the work, leaving the part covered by the Latin fragment untouched except for this gloss (cf. Charles, *Assumption,* xlix, 44, 89), but this is perhaps less likely.

Finally, our hypothesis of a *T. Mos.* which was subsequently rewritten and entitled the *As. Mos.,* would explain the presence of two works, a *T. Mos.* (Διαθήκη Μωϋσέως) and an *As. Mos.* (Ἀνάληψις Μωϋσέως), in the ancient lists of apocryphal books. Charles's argument, that the *As. Mos.* to which the lists refer was a work dealing only with the death and assumption of Moses, founders on the length assigned to the *As. Mos.* in the *Stichometry* of Nicephorus (1400 *stichoi,* compared with the *Testament*'s 1100 *stichoi*): it seems much too long for such a work. If the *Assumption* was a revised version of the *Testament,* the *Stichometry*'s statement of its length can be more easily believed.

Three More Old Testament Types (Jude 11–13)

Bibliography

Boobyer, G. H. "The Verbs in Jude 11." *NTS* 5 (1958–59) 45–47. **Jones, H. S.** "ΣΠΙΛΑΣ.—ΑΠΑΡΧΗ ΠΝΕΥΜΑΤΟΣ." *JTS* 23 (1922) 282–83. **Knox, A. D.** "ΣΠΙΛΑΔΕΣ." *JTS* 14 (1913) 547–49. **Knox, A. D.** "Σπιλάς." *JTS* 16 (1915) 78. **Oleson, J. P.** "An Echo of Hesiod's *Theogony* vv. 190–2 in Jude 13." *NTS* 25 (1978–79) 492–503. **Reicke, B.** *Diakonie,* 352–67. **Spicq, C.** *Agape,* 368–72. **Spicq, C.** *Notes de Lexicographie Néo-Testamentaire.* vol. 2. OBO 22/2. Fribourg: Editions Universitaires/Göttingen: Vandenhoeck & Ruprecht, 1978. 809–11. **Vermes, G.** "The story of Balaam—The scriptural origin of Haggadah." *Scripture and Tradition in Judaism: Haggadic studies.* SPB 4. Leiden: E. J. Brill, 1961. 127–77. **Vermes, G.** "The Targumic Versions of Genesis 4:3–16." *Post-Biblical Jewish Studies.* SJLA 8. Leiden: E. J. Brill, 1975. 92–126.

Translation

11 *Woe to them!*
For they walked [a] *in the way* [b] *of Cain,*
they plunged [a] *into Balaam's error for profit,*
and through the controversy of Korah they perished.
12 *These are the people* [c] *who feast with you at your fellowship meals,* [d] *without reverence,*
like dangerous reefs. They are shepherds who only look after themselves. They are
clouds blown along by the wind without giving rain; autumnal trees bearing no fruit,
dead twice over, uprooted;
13 *wild waves of the sea casting up the foam of their*
abominations; wandering stars for whom the nether gloom of darkness has been reserved
for ever.

Notes

[a] For the translation of these verbs, see *Comment* section.

[b] For the dative ὁδῷ in this expression, cf. Acts 14:16; Herm. *Mand.* 6:1:2; BDF § 198, 5.

[c] *οἱ* is omitted by ℵK *al,* probably because they connected it with *σπιλάδες*, "reefs," which is feminine; in fact it relates to *συνευωχούμενοι*, "feasting together," with *σπιλάδες* in apposition.

[d] For *ἀγάπαις ὑμῶν*, "your agapes," A reads *ἀπάταις αὐτῶν*, "their deceptions": a correction because the presence of the false teachers at the agapes seemed too scandalous (cf. 2 Pet 2:13).

Form/Structure/Setting

Jude 11 is a woe oracle, a form of speech which, although it may have Wisdom origins, was used with great frequency by the OT prophets and occurs in the OT almost exclusively in the prophetic books (a useful review of recent study of the OT woes is D. E. Garland, *The Intention of Matthew 23* [NovTSup 52; Leiden: E. J. Brill, 1979] 72–80). It was a flexible form, adaptable to different purposes, but within and after the OT (although it could still be used primarily as a lament: "alas!": cf. Matt 24:19; *Gos. Pet.* 7) it developed an increasingly imprecatory character, becoming a prophetic pronouncement of judgment on sinners. This, for example, is the function of the large number of woes (thirty-two, more than in any other ancient Jewish work) in *1 Enoch* 92–105 (on which see G. W. E. Nickelsburg, "The apocalyptic message of *1 Enoch* 92–105," *CBQ* 39 [1977] 309–28; R. A. Coughenour, "The Woe-Oracles in Ethiopic Enoch," *JSJ* 9 [1978] 192–97). Even there, however, a note of sadness and lament for the fate of sinners is not excluded (*1 Enoch* 95:1).

The form of woe oracles varies. Those in *1 Enoch* (also Jdt 16:17; Sir 41:8–9) follow the pattern: (1) "Woe!" (frequently with a second person address, "to you"); (2) specification of the sins of the wicked; (3) pronouncement of judgment. But there are woes which lack (3) (Luke 11:42–44), and, very rarely, woes which lack (2) (*Barn.* 6:2). Frequently a *ὅτι* clause, as in Jude, is used, specifying the cause of the exclamation, but this can be either the sin (Luke 11:42–44, 46–47, 52) or the coming judgment (Luke 6:25; *1 Enoch* 99:16). Jude, in the three clauses which follow his *ὅτι*, specifies *both* the sins *and* the judgment to which they lead, by reference to the OT types. His "Woe *to them!*" is very unusual (cf. Hos 7:13 LXX), since the more usual forms are impersonal ("Woe to those who . . .") or direct address ("Woe to you!"), but it is determined by his context and purpose.

The use of a woe implies prophetic consciousness on the part of the speaker or writer, as one authorized to announce divine judgment (Nickelsburg, "Apocalyptic message," 317), and the prophetic character of v 11 is confirmed by the three aorist verbs, representing the Semitic use of a "prophetic perfect." This means either that Jude himself here delivers a prophetic oracle, or that he quotes an already existing oracle, presumably of an early Christian prophet (as Ellis, "Jude," 224, suggests). It is scarcely possible to decide between these alternatives. It might be argued that just as he cites his first set of types (vv 5–7) according to a traditional list, so he cites the second set according to a well-known oracle. One rabbinic text (*t. Soṭa* 4:9, quoted Vermes, "Balaam," 134) lists Cain, Korah, and Balaam as a group of notorious sinners, but this is insufficient evidence to show that they were a well-known set of three in established Jewish tradition. At least in the cases of Balaam and Korah, however, Jude was not the only early Christian to use these types with reference to false teachers in the church (Balaam: Rev 2:14; Korah: an application to false teachers is implied in 2 Tim 2:19, quoting Num 16:5; *1 Clem.* 51:3–4; and cf. the Jewish evidence on Korah given in the *Comment* section), and this may well point to a piece of Christian prophetic teaching well-known in the early church (and known to Jude's readers according to v 5). On the other hand, it is possible that Jude, though taking up an established typology, has himself cast his reference to it in the form of a woe oracle.

In either case, v 11 stands here as equivalent to an OT text, which Jude then applies to the false teachers in vv 12–13 (beginning *οὗτοί εἰσιν*, as in vv 16 and 19). This is the only case in which Jude's "text" appears to refer directly to the false teachers, but it does so only in saying that they conform to the types. It is vv 12–13 which actually describe the errors of the false teachers in order to show that they do conform to the types. The pattern is therefore the same as in the exposition of the first three types in vv 8–10, and just as that exposition introduced an additional text (v 9) to help the exposition, so vv 12–13 contain allusions to other texts (Ezek 34:2; Prov

25:14; Isa 57:20; *1 Enoch* 80:6). The link between the original "text" and the exposition is helped by the catchword connection πλάνη, "error" (v 11)/ πλανῆται, "wandering" (v 13). Finally, just as the exposition in vv 8–10 concluded by inferring the judgment of the false teachers, so does the exposition in vv 12–13.

The remarkable accumulation of metaphors (six in all) is unusual in Jewish literature, but cf. the series of similes in Wis 5:9–12, 14; Ep Jer 70–71; and 1QH 3:6–7; the series of metaphors for the writer's enemies in 1QH 5:6–8; and the accumulated imagery in 4 Macc 7:1–5; Jas 3:2–8.

The last four of Jude's metaphors comprise a set of four images from nature, probably inspired by reflection on *1 Enoch* 2:1–5:4; 80:2–8, and selected to represent the four regions of the universe (see *Comment* section). Like much of Jude's letter, these verses are carefully composed, and the accumulated imagery, culminating in the image of judgment, is rhetorically effective.

Comment

11. What distinguishes this second set of types (v 11), with their exposition (vv 12–13), from the first set (vv 5–7), with their exposition (vv 8–10)? Most commentators assume that Jude varies his illustrations, but largely repeats his charges. Having compared the false teachers with three notorious groups of sinners, he now compares them with three notorious individual sinners from the OT. Closer examination, however, suggests that Jude's purpose is more precise. Whereas in vv 5–10 he portrayed the false teachers simply as sinners, in vv 11–13 he portrays them as false *teachers* who lead other people into sin. This interpretation will give a unity of theme to the section vv 11–13, and will enable vv 12–13 to be seen as an application of the three types of v 11 to the false teachers, rather than as simply a series of loosely connected denunciations.

It is therefore largely this section which will justify regarding Jude's opponents as false *teachers.* They were not simply members of the church guilty of immoral conduct (Chase, *DB*(*H*) 2, 804; Plummer, 390), but people who *taught* antinomianism, no doubt on the authority of their visions (v 8), and thereby enticed other Christians into sin (cf. the teaching of "Balaam" and the prophetess "Jezebel" in Rev 2:14, 20).

τῇ ὁδῷ τοῦ Κάϊν ἐπορεύθησαν, "they walked in the way of Cain." In postbiblical Jewish tradition, Cain became not simply the first murderer, but the archetypal sinner and the instructor of others in sin. Some writers saw him as the prototype of hatred and envy toward one's brothers (*T. Benj.* 7:5; 1 John 3:11; *1 Clem.* 4:7). Josephus (*Ant.* 1.52–66) portrayed him as guilty of greed, violence and lust, and as the great corrupter of mankind ("he incited to luxury and pillage all whom he met, and became their instructor in wicked practices": 1.61, Loeb tr.). For Philo Cain was the archetypal egoist (*Det.* 32, 78), and the leader of others in the ways of sin (*Post.* 38–39). Several of these characteristics, but perhaps especially Cain's role of enticing others to sin, make him appropriate as a type of Jude's opponents.

In addition, however, it is possible that Jude also has in mind a tradition found in the Targums, which represented Cain as the first heretic. All the

Targums, except Onqelos, include at Gen 4:8 a haggadic expansion of the biblical text in which Cain's murder of Abel is represented as the outcome of an argument about the righteousness of God (see Vermes, "Targumic Versions"; P. Grelot, "Les Targums du Pentateuque: Etude comparative d'après *Genèse,* IV, 3–16," *Sem* 9 [1959] 59–88). The argument takes place in two stages (though the *Frg. Tg.* combines them into one exchange between the brothers). In the first stage Cain complains that God's acceptance of Abel's offering and rejection of Cain's offering is unjust; it shows that God does not govern the world justly. Abel replies that the world is governed justly, and it was because of the righteousness of Abel's deeds that his offering was accepted. Only this first stage is given in the Geniza fragment of the Palestinian Targum, but Pseudo-Jonathan and Neofiti take the argument into a second stage, in which Cain denies that there will be justice in a future life. He says: "There is no Judgment, there is no Judge, there is no other world, there is no gift of good reward for the just and no punishment for the wicked" (*Tgs. Ps.-J., Neof.,* cf. *Frg.;* tr. in Vermes, "Targumic Versions," 97–99). To this Abel replies: "There is Judgment, there is a Judge, there is another world. There is the gift of good reward for the just and punishment for the wicked" (*Tgs. Ps.-J., Neof.,* cf. *Frg.;* tr. in Vermes, "Targumic Versions," 97, 99; *Tg. Neof.* adds: "in the world to come"). Particularly in this second stage of the argument, Cain is represented not only as a wicked man, but also as the first heretic: he indulges in wickedness on the strength of religious skepticism about the divine righteousness and the reality of future judgment.

With regard to the dating of this tradition great caution is required. Probably the second stage of the argument is a later development than the first stage, but it may still be as early as the first century A.D. (Vermes, "Targumic Versions," 116; but the argument of S. Isenberg, "An Anti-Sadducee Polemic in the Palestinian Targum Tradition," *HTR* 63 [1970] 433–44, that it reflects polemic against the Sadducees' denial of a future life is not decisive evidence of date). If this tradition was familiar to Jude and his readers, the mention of Cain would suggest a man who makes denial of future judgment a pretext for wickedness, and Jude's heretics would thus be followers of Cain not only in their immorality, but also in their religious teaching that there will be no future judgment in which God will punish their immorality. Though we are never explicitly told that this was part of their teaching, it seems a reasonable inference that it was: their freedom from the Law entailed immunity from any future judgment.

The sense of "walked in the way of Cain" is probably that they have followed in Cain's footsteps by imitating his sin. (For the expression, cf. LXX 3 Kgdms 15:26: ἐπορεύθη ἐν ὁδῷ τοῦ πατρὸς αὐτοῦ; 15:34; 16:2, 19, 26; 4 Kgdms 8:18, 27; 16:3; 2 Chron 11:17; 21:6; Ezek 23:31; in all these cases it means to follow someone's moral example. πορεύεσθαι, "to walk," frequently, in Jewish Greek, refers to conduct or manner of life.) Boobyer (*NTS* 5 [1958–59] 45–47), however, argues that all three verbs in this sentence are used synonymously to refer to the destruction which the false teachers have incurred on account of their sin. πορεύεσθαι would then be used as a euphemistic expression for going to one's death (cf. LXX 3 Kgdms 2:2: πορεύομαι ἐν ὁδῷ πάσης τῆς γῆς; 2 Chron 21:20; Luke 22:22), equivalent to ἀπώλοντο, "they perished." Boobyer translates: "they go to death in the path of Cain." But: (1) this is not the most natural meaning of the phrase (Kelly, 269), and (2) although Cain was sometimes used as an example of judgment (*T. Benj.* 7:5; cf. Wis 10:3; *Jub.* 4:31), the emphasis was often on the mitigation of his punishment (Gen 4:13–15; Josephus, *Ant.* 1.58; *Tgs.* Gen. 4:13, 24), which made him less suitable as an example of judgment. It seems best to reject Boobyer's suggestion, though it is possible that Jude's choice of expression contains a hint that to follow in Cain's path will lead to Cain's fate.

τῇ πλάνῃ τοῦ Βαλαὰμ μισθοῦ ἐξεχύθησαν, "they plunged into Balaam's error for profit." Again, Jude's reference to Balaam is dependent on the development of traditions about Balaam in postbiblical Judaism (on which see Vermes, "Balaam"; Ginzberg, *Legends* 3, 354–82), in which Balaam was almost always portrayed in a bad light, as "Balaam the villain," one of the great enemies of the people of God. The disciples of Balaam are contrasted with the disciples of Abraham (*Pirqe ʾAbot* 5:22: the disciples of Balaam have "an evil eye, a greedy soul, and a haughty spirit," and "go down to Gehenna").

Although according to the biblical account Balaam refused to be persuaded to curse Israel for the sake of monetary reward (Num 22:18; 24:13; but cf. Deut 23:4; Neh 13:2), Jewish traditional exegesis represented him as accepting Balak's invitation out of greed for the large rewards promised him (*Tgs.* Num 22:7; Philo, *Mos.* 1.266–68; *Mig.* 114; *ʾAbot R. Nat.* 1.29; *Num Rab.* 20:10). Although Balaam of course failed to curse Israel, he made up for the failure, according to haggadic tradition, by advising Balak to entice Israel into sin (cf. Num 31:16). Balak's advice, in Pseudo-Philo's version, was: "Select the most beautiful women among you and in Midian, and set them before them naked, adorned with gold and jewels. And it shall come to pass that when they see them, they will sin against the Lord their God and they will fall into your hands, for otherwise you cannot overcome them" (*Bib. Ant.* 18:13; cf. *Tg. Ps.-J.* Num 24:14, 25; 31:8; Philo, *Mos.* 1 295–300; Josephus, *Ant.* 4. 126–30; *y. Sanh.* 10.28d; and cf. Rev 2:14). In this way Balaam was regarded as responsible for the apostasy of Israel recorded in Num 25:1–3, and the resulting divine judgment which caused the death of 24,000 Israelites (Num 25:9; cf. Num 31:16, which gave rise to this interpretation). The fact that Balaam was with the Midianite kings when the Israelites killed him (Num 31:8; Josh 13:21–22) was explained in the exegetical tradition by the supposition that Balaam had returned to collect his reward for his successful advice: "What business had Balaam there? R. Jonathan said: He went to receive his reward for the 24,000 Israelites whose destruction he had encompassed" (*b. Sanh.* 106a, Soncino tr.; cf. *Num. Rab.* 20:20; 22:5; *Sipra Numbers* 137).

Thus, by highlighting and developing certain aspects of the biblical account (especially Num 31:16), Jewish tradition remembered Balaam primarily as a man of greed, who for the sake of reward led Israel into debauchery and idolatry. The parallel with Jude's opponents will be that, like Balaam, they were enticing the people of God into sexual immorality (idolatry, though mentioned in Rev 2:14, does not appear in Jude), and doing so because they received financial rewards for their teaching. It may also be relevant that Balaam was in some sense a prophet, who received revelation in dreams and visions; sometimes Jewish exegetes saw him as a true prophet who had become a mere soothsayer or interpreter of dreams (*b. Sanh.* 106a; cf. *Tgs.* Num 22:5; *Bib. Ant.* 18:2; *Num. Rab.* 20:7)

The precise meaning of τῇ πλάνῃ τοῦ Βαλαὰμ μισθοῦ ἐξεχύθησαν, "they plunged into Balaam's error for profit," is not easy to determine. Boobyer again argues that the verb should be synonymous with ἀπώλοντο, and translates, "they are themselves cast away in the error of Balaam" (cf. RV Margin: "they cast themselves away through the error of Balaam"), but his parallels to this use of the verb are not really convincing. On the other hand, this verb (passive of ἐκχεῖν or ἐκχύνειν, "to pour out") can be used in the sense of "to abandon oneself to" or "to plunge into" (examples in Mayor, and BAG *s.v.*), occasionally with the dative instead of the more usual εἰς. In that case πλάνῃ (equivalent to εἰς πλάνην) will be that into which the false teachers plunged.

Although the verb is appropriate to sexual immorality (cf. *T. Reub.* 1:6) and although Jewish tradition sometimes accused Balaam of this (bestiality with his ass: *Tg. Ps.-J.* Num 22:30), this sense is ruled out here by μισθοῦ ("for profit"). The false teachers cannot be said to give themselves up to sexual indulgence for the sake of financial gain. Probably Jude refers to the idea, found in the Jewish exegesis, that Balaam, enticed by the prospect of reward, hurried with great eagerness to go and curse Israel (*Num. Rab.* 20:12; *b. Sanh.* 105b, interpreting Num 22:21); and, by telescoping the story, this would mean that he hurried to give the advice that led Israel into immorality. Similarly, the false teachers, greedy for money, have rushed to follow his example.

At the same time, Jude may well intend a hint that to plunge into this error of Balaam's is to plunge to destruction. For Balaam's eagerness, which Jewish exegesis found in Num 22:21, was connected with the words of God in the preceding verse. This verse was understood to mean that because Balaam so much wished to go, God let him have his desire, but in doing so sent him to his destruction ("Villain! I have no wish that the wicked should perish, but seeing that you are eager to go and to perish out of the world, rise up, go!": *Num. Rab.* 20:12, Soncino tr.; cf. *Bib. Ant.* 18:8). The same interpretation was given to Num 22:35 (Philo, *Mos.* 1.274; *Num. Rab.* 20:15; cf. Ginzberg, *Legends,* 3, 367).

Balaam's "error" (πλάνη means literally "wandering" from the right path) must refer primarily to his advice to Balak which led Israel into sin. It was for this advice that he was rewarded. πλάνη should therefore be taken in an active sense (as in Matt 27:64; 2 Thess 2:11): his leading others astray. But the passive sense need not be excluded: in leading others astray, he himself went astray (cf. πλανῆται, "wandering stars," v 13: the false teachers are themselves stars which have wandered from their courses; and 2 Tim 3:13). Again, there may also be a hint of judgment, cf. *Num. Rab.* 20:9: "Balaam appeared on the scene and led mankind astray into lewdness. And as he led others astray so he was himself led astray. By the counsel that he gave he was himself tripped up. And the Holy One, blessed be he, led him astray; for so it is in fact written, 'He causeth the nations to err, and destroyeth them' (Job 12:23)" (Soncino tr.).

For their antinomian teaching the false teachers take payment (μισθοῦ, cf. Philo, *Mig.* 114: ἐπὶ μισθῷ, referring to the fact that the Moabites "hired"

Balaam; LXX Deut 23:5; Neh 13:2: ἐμισθώσαντο). In the primitive church the traveling missionary's or prophet's right to be supported by the churches (1 Cor 9:4; *Did.* 13:1) was all too easily abused (Rom 16:18; 1 Tim 6:5; Titus 1:11; *Did.* 11:5–6, 12). Hence the concern, which is frequent in the NT, to protect the church's leaders from any suggestion that they might be making profit out of their work (cf. Acts 20:33–34; 1 Thess 2:9; 2 Thess 3:8; 1 Tim 3:3, 8; Titus 1:7; 1 Pet 5:2; *Did.* 15:1; Pol. *Phil.* 5:2).

τῇ ἀντιλογίᾳ τοῦ Κόρε ἀπώλοντο, "through the controversy of Korah they perished." Korah, who with Dathan and Abiram led a rebellion against the authority of Moses and Aaron (Num 16:1–35; 26:9–10; cf. Ps 106:16–18; Sir 45:18–19), was a notorious figure in Jewish tradition. He became the classic example of the antinomian heretic. This was partly because, in addition to the material already in the biblical text of Num 16, Jewish exegetical tradition, represented by Pseudo-Philo (*Bib. Ant.* 16:1) and *Tg. Pseudo-Jonathan* (to Num 16:1–2), interpreted Korah's revolt in connection with the immediately preceding account of the law of the fringes (Num 15:37–41). Korah and his fellow-conspirators complained that this was an intolerable law (*Bib. Ant.* 16:1). In contravention of it they "made garments with completely blue fringes, which the Lord had not commanded" (*Tg. Ps.-J.* Num 16:2; cf. *Num. Rab.* 18:3). Korah accused Moses of adding his own inventions to the Torah (*Num. Rab.* 18:3, 12). Later rabbinic tradition attributed to Korah the heresy of the *Minim* that God gave only the Decalogue, and represented Korah as claiming, "The Torah is not from heaven" (Vermes, "Decalogue," 173; cf. Ginzberg, *Legends,* 6, 100–101).

It should also be noticed that the Targums (*Neof.* Num 16:1; 26:9; *Ps.-J.* Num. 26:9) say that Korah, Dathan and Abiram "made a schism" (literally "divided," פלג; perhaps cf. 4QpNah 4:1). This characterization of them as schismatic is also reflected in *1 Clem.* 51:1–4, which compares those "who set themselves up as leaders of rebellion and dissension" (στάσεως καὶ διχοστασίας) with Korah and his fellows, who rebelled (στασιαζόντων) against Moses (cf. also *1 Clem.* 4:12). The implication of Num 16:2, that Korah, with Dathan, Abiram, and On, was responsible for inciting others to rebel, is strengthened by *Num. Rab.* 18:2, which interprets "took men" to mean that Korah "drew their hearts with persuasive words" (cf. Josephus, *Ant.* 4.15–21). Korah was therefore a natural type for heretical teachers, and 2 Tim 2:19 (along with *1 Clem.* 51:1–4) suggests that Jude was not the only early Christian writer to apply this type to false teachers within the church. The allusive character of the reference in 2 Tim 2:19 (quoting Num 16:5) suggests a well-established tradition.

Jude's use of Korah as a type of the false teachers has often been thought to indicate that he accuses them of rebelling against ecclesiastical authorities (Zahn, *Introduction,* 244–45; Werdermann, *Irrlehrer,* 58; Bigg, Windisch, Barnett, Kelly, Reicke), but this is not necessarily the case. Korah's rebellion was against God as much as against Moses and Aaron (Num 16:11; 26:9), and Jude may have seen Moses in this context as representing the Law. It is likely that the real significance of Korah for Jude is as one who denied the divine authority of the Law.

For Korah's rebellion, Jude does not use στάσις ("sedition"; as in *1 Clem.* 51:1, 3; Josephus, *Ant.* 4.12–13) or ἐπισύστασις, "uprising" (as in LXX Num

26:9), but ἀντιλογία, "controversy" (used of Korah's rebellion in *Prot. Jas.* 9:2; LXX uses it to translate Meribah in Num 20:13; 27:14; Deut 32:51; 33:8; Ps 80:8; 105:32). Although ἀντιλογία can, by extension, refer to opposition in act (Moulton and Milligan, *Vocabulary, s.v.*), its root and common meaning is *verbal* opposition, quarrel, dispute. It is appropriate to Korah as a heretical leader who advanced antinomian opinions in controversy with Moses (cf. *Pirqe ʾAbot* 5:22: "the controversy [מחלקת] of Korah").

We have argued that in the cases of Cain and Balaam, Jude has referred primarily to their sins, though perhaps also hinted at their judgment. In the case of Korah, however, he refers explicitly to Korah's judgment. This (as Boobyer rightly points out) is not likely to be because he sees Korah as the most heinous sinner of the three. It is more probably because the exceptional character of Korah's fate made it a much more striking example of divine judgment than those of Cain and Balaam. This will also explain why Jude has placed Korah last, out of chronological order (cf. *t. Soṭa* 4:19, which lists them in chronological order: Cain, Korah, Balaam). The sequence of three clauses reaches a climax in the final word ἀπώλοντο ("have perished").

Although Korah was sometimes thought to have been consumed by the fire (Num 16:35; Josephus, *Ant.* 4.56), he was usually held to have shared the fate of Dathan and Abiram, when the earth swallowed them up and they went down alive to Sheol (Num 26:10; *Bib. Ant.* 16:6; *Prot. Jas.* 9:2; cf. *Num. Rab.* 18:19). This unique (Num 16:30) fate was frequently cited as a warning example of divine judgment (Num 26:10; Ps 106:17; Sir 45:19; Josephus, *BJ* 5.566; *Bib. Ant.* 57:2; *1 Clem.* 4:12: 51:4; *Prot. Jas.* 9:2). According to Pseudo-Philo, Korah and his company remain alive in Sheol until the Last Day, when they will be destroyed without sharing in the resurrection (*Bib. Ant.* 16:3; cf. *ʾAbot R. Nat.* 36:2; *Num. Rab.* 18:13).

The aorist ἀπώλοντο is equivalent to a "prophetic perfect," i.e. it views the future judgment of the false teachers with the certainty of an event which has already occurred. This perspective necessarily also puts the sins of the false teachers into the completed past; hence the aorist tense of the two preceding verbs.

12. *ἐν ταῖς ἀγάπαις ὑμῶν*, "in your fellowship meals." This is the earliest occurrence of the term "agape" in the sense of the Christian fellowship meal, a usage which afterward becomes fairly frequent (2 Pet 2:13 *v.l.;* Ign. *Smyrn.* 8:2; *Ep. Apost.* 15; *Acts Paul & Thecla* 25; Clement Alex., *Paed.* 2.1.4; *Strom.* 3.2.10; Tertullian, *Apol.* 39; *De jejun.* 17–18). It is equivalent to the much less frequent term "the Lord's supper" (*κυριακὸν δεῖπνον*: 1 Cor 11:20; Hippolytus, *Apost. Trad.* 26.5; Clement Alex., *Paed.* 2.2, quoting 1 Cor 11:20).

In the background to the practice lie the common meals of Judaism (e.g. the meals of the *ḥaburoṯ* and those of the Qumran sect and the Therapeutae) and the communal living of the earliest Christian community (Acts 2:44–46), but more especially the meals, including the Last Supper, which the disciples of Jesus celebrated with him both before and after his resurrection. The agape or Lord's Supper was a real meal (1 Cor 11:20–34; Acts 2:46), held in the evening (Acts 20:7, 11), and was not, in the NT period, distinct from the Eucharist (see M. J. Townsend, "Exit the Agape?" *ExpTim* 90 [1978–79] 356–61; I. H. Marshall, *Last Supper and Lord's Supper* [Exeter: Paternoster,

1980] 110–11) for which NT writers have no term which distinguishes it from the agape. Probably Ignatius still uses the term ἀγάπη to include the Eucharist (*Smyrn.* 8:2), and the close association of agape and Eucharist continued well into the second century (*Ep. Apost.* 15), though by the time of Justin the two had become separate, at least in some places. The agapes to which Jude refers certainly included, as their focal point, the sharing of the loaf and the cup which was later distinguished as the Eucharist. Their name must derive from the dominant early Christian sense of the love of God reaching men through Jesus Christ and creating a fellowship of love among Christians. This fellowship was expressed and enacted in the fellowship meal.

The mention of the agapes here is probably not, as has often been thought, because they were subject to particular abuse by the dissolute false teachers (cf. Clement of Alexandria on the agapes of the Carpocratians: *Strom.* 3.2), but because they were the focal point of the common life of the Christian community, and so the presence of the false teachers, behaving in their usual irreverent manner (ἀφόβως), was there especially dangerous.

σπιλάδες, "dangerous reefs." The meaning of σπιλάδες here has been much discussed.

(1) The majority of the commentators (Spitta, Knopf, Bigg, Windisch, Sidebottom, Grundmann, Cantinat; Spicq, *Agape,* 368–69; and already the Vulgate: *maculae*) and most English translations take σπιλάς to be here equivalent to σπίλος, meaning "blot, blemish, spot." This is supported mainly by 2 Pet 2:13 (σπίλοι), and Jude's own use of the verb σπιλοῦν ("to defile") in v 23. But this meaning of σπιλάς, which presumably arose by confusion with σπίλος, is extremely rare (apparently only one known instance: the Orphic book *Lithaca* 614, from the fourth century A.D.). In view of Jude's good command of Greek vocabulary it is not likely that he simply confused the two words.

(2) A few take σπιλάς as an adjective, "dirty" or "polluted," equivalent to ἐσπιλωμένος (v 23), and so here: "polluted persons" (so apparently Didymus: *maculati;* Hesychius: μεμιασμένοι; Zahn, *Introduction,* 245, 258 n.5; cf. BDF § 45). Jude means that the false teachers participate in the fellowship meals "polluted by their unchastity" (Zahn, *Introduction,* 258). This gives a slightly different sense from (1), and accords with Jude's description of the false teachers in v 8. But the usage is hard to parallel.

(3) Knox (*JTS* 14 [1913] 547–49; *JTS* 16 [1915] 78; cf. Jones, *JTS* 23 [1922] 282–83) has argued that σπιλάς can mean "foul wind" (adjectival σπιλάς with ἄνεμος understood). But even if his evidence for this use is accepted, it gives no good sense in Jude 12, where it occurs too early to be connected with the later wind metaphor.

(4) The usual meaning of σπιλάς is "rock," especially at sea or on the shore, and hence a reef which can cause shipwreck (examples in Mayor, Spicq, *Lexicographie,* 809–10, and BAG). This interpretation (adopted by Ps.-Oecumenius, Plummer, Mayor, Reicke, Green, Kelly) is not only the natural meaning of the word; it also makes excellent sense. In context the word should indicate the danger which the false teachers present to Jude's readers by their close association with them in the fellowship meals. The false teachers, he says, are like dangerous reefs; close contact with them will result in shipwreck. (For the metaphor, cf. 1 Tim 1:19; *Barn.* 3:6; and cf. the more common

metaphors of the snare and the rock of stumbling: of persons, Isa 8:14–15; Matt 13:41; 16:23. It is in keeping with Jude's style that he substitutes a less common and livelier metaphor.) σπιλάδες are sometimes said to be hidden, submerged rocks (cf. Etymologicum Magnum, quoted Mayor; Kelly, Reicke) but this need not be the case (see especially *Anth. Pal.* 11.390, quoted Bigg; Josephus, *BJ* 3.420; Plummer, 428). They can be visible rocks, jutting out from the seashore, and such rocks are also a danger to shipping. Jude certainly does not think the false teachers are in any way "hidden"; they are identifiable by their teaching and scandalous conduct. His point is that close proximity to such people is dangerous, and should be avoided, as a sailor keeps his ship clear of the rocks.

It is not impossible, in view of Jude's use of catchword connections (cf. πλάνη, "error" (v 11) and πλανῆται, "wandering" (v 13) in this section; and the remarks on τηρεῖν in the *Comment* on v 6) and his use of σπιλοῦν, "to defile," in v 23, that Jude intends the pun σπιλάδες/σπίλοι, "dangerous reefs/blots."

οἱ . . . συνευωχούμενοι ἀφόβως, "the people who feast with you . . . without reverence." The article οἱ relates not to σπιλάδες, which is feminine, but to συνευωχούμενοι, (cf. the same construction in v 19); σπιλάδες is in apposition (Chaine, Kelly).

συνευωχούμενοι could mean simply "feasting together," by themselves (Spitta, Bigg, RSV), and this could be supported by the following phrase ἑαυτοὺς ποιμαίνοντες ("feeding themselves"), if this refers directly to their behavior at table, and by v 19 (ἀποδιορίζοντες, "making divisions"): they formed their own group at table (cf. 1 Cor 11:18–21). But whether or not they did this, it is not likely to be the point Jude is making. After ἐν ταῖς ἀγάπαις ὑμῶν ("in your fellowship meals") the natural meaning of συνευωχούμενοι is "feasting with you" (thus C and 2 Pet 2:13, which add ὑμῖν, are correct interpretations). In line with the theme of this section—the false teachers as those who entice others to sin—Jude's point relates to the danger of such close association with them.

There is not necessarily anything reprehensible about "feasting" at the agape, but coupled with ἀφόβως, "without reverence," there may be the implication that, in accordance with their sensuality (v 10), the false teachers treat it as a *mere* banquet, an occasion for gratifying their appetites, rather than for fellowship with the Lord and their fellow-Christians (cf. 1 Cor 11:20–22, 33–34). Some take ἀφόβως with the following phrase (Zahn, *Introduction,* 258; Mayor, Bigg), but when understood as "irreverently" (as in LXX Prov 15:16) it goes well with συνευωχούμενοι and supplies the note of condemnation which would otherwise be lacking in this phrase. The irreverent attitude (also at Corinth: 1 Cor 11:27–29) probably relates to the spiritual arrogance of the false teachers, who behave as though they were their own masters, not subject to the Lord. There is no reason to think they made the agape an occasion for blatant debauchery. The danger Jude sees is from the influence of their general attitude and behavior. We should also remember that the agape was probably also a time when prophecy and teaching took place (cf. Acts 20:7, 11), so that the false teachers' presence exposed the church to their teaching. It may be that in this way this opening phrase of v 12 connects fairly directly to the rest of vv 12–13, which concern the teaching activity of the false teachers.

The danger of close association with the false teachers may have been connected in Jude's mind especially with Korah (v 11), since the account of Korah's revolt lays great stress on the danger to the rest of Israel from proximity to Korah and his company (Num 16:24, 26–27, 34; *Bib. Ant.* 16:7).

ἑαυτοὺς ποιμαίνοντες, "shepherds who only look after themselves." This phrase has often been taken closely with the preceding: they selfishly concentrate on having a good meal themselves, like the Corinthians who could not wait for their brothers before starting their own meal (1 Cor 11:21) (so Plummer, Moffatt, Kelly). But *ποιμαίνοντες*, "shepherding," is the activity of shepherds, and the metaphor of shepherding for Christian leadership was so common in early Christianity (John 21:16; Acts 20:28; 1 Cor 9:7; Eph 4:11; 1 Pet 5:2; Ign. *Phld.* 2:1; Ign. *Rom.* 9:1; cf. CD 13:9–10) that it must be implied here. Bigg thinks the phrase refers to the rebelliousness of the false teachers; instead of submitting to the pastors of the church, they wish to be their own shepherds. But the more natural meaning is that they claim to be leaders in the church, but instead of tending the flock they only look after themselves. This meaning becomes certain when it is seen that Jude is alluding to Ezek 34:2, which indicts the shepherds (i.e. rulers) of Israel for feeding themselves at the expense of the sheep. The sheep provide them with meat and wool, but they do not tend the sheep (34:3). Similarly the false teachers are making a good living out of the church. (Cf. also *Asc. Isa.* 3:24: "many elders will be lawless and violent shepherds to their sheep and will become ravagers [of the sheep], since they have no holy shepherds": tr. in *NTApoc* 2, 648.) The phrase connects with the example of Balaam (v 11), the prophet who hired out his services for financial gain.

Jude's allusion is evidently to the Hebrew of Ezek 34:2 (LXX has *μὴ βόσκουσιν ποιμένες ἑαυτούς*; "do shepherds feed themselves?" cf. Symmachus: *οἱ ποιμαίνοντες ἑαυτούς*, "shepherds who only look after themselves").

νεφέλαι ἄνυδροι ὑπὸ ἀνέμων παραφερόμεναι, "They are clouds blown along by the wind without giving rain." This is the first of four metaphors from nature, all of which relate to the false teachers' claim to be prophets and teachers. This metaphor probably derives from Prov 25:14: "Like clouds and wind without rain is a man who boasts of a gift he does not give" (RSV). (Again Jude must be dependent on the Hebrew text, for the LXX completely obscures this sense.) On summer days on the coasts of Palestine and Syria, clouds are sometimes seen approaching land, promising rain, but then pass, blown on by the wind, without producing any rain. Similarly, the false teachers are all empty promise. They make great claims for the value of their teaching, but it provides nothing beneficial at all.

δένδρα φθινοπωρινὰ ἄκαρπα, "autumnal trees bearing no fruit." The precise significance of *φθινοπωρινός* is disputed: (1) some hold that it refers to a time when the trees are bare, after the season when the fruit is harvested (Bigg, Chaine, Kelly); (2) others take it to refer to the end of the season of harvest, when any tree's fruit, if it has any, should be ripe (this view is argued in Mayor's long note, 55–59). It seems that evidence can be cited for either usage, no doubt because the reckoning of seasons varied. But (1) seems an unsatisfactory sense in context; a tree cannot be blamed for bearing no fruit when the season for fruit has passed. The second suggestion provides a good parallel with the previous phrase; just as the clouds promise rain but give none, so the trees promise fruit but yield none. Like the fig tree in the parable (Luke 13:6), these trees are bare when fruit is expected.

The image of a tree and its fruits is common in the biblical literature, with various meanings (Ps 1:3; Jer 17:6, 8; Wis 4:3–5; Sir 6:3; Matt 3:10 par. Luke 3:9; Jas 3:12; Herm. *Sim.* 4); of particular relevance is Matt 7:16–20 (cf. Matt 12:33 par. Luke 6:43–44), where false prophets are known by their evil fruits. It may be, however, that Jude's image was primarily inspired by a passage in *1 Enoch* which describes how "in the days of the sinners" (80:2) the regularity of nature will be interrupted: "all things on earth will change, and will not appear at their proper time" (80:2; on the relevance of this passage as a whole to vv 12–13, see below). One instance of this is that "the fruits of the trees will be withheld at their proper time" (80:3, tr. Knibb). In this picture of lawless nature Jude saw a metaphor of the lawless men troubling his churches.

δὶς ἀποθανόντα ἐκριζωθέντα, "dead twice over, uprooted." The metaphor of the trees is an advance on that of the clouds, in that it describes the judgment of the false teachers, picturing it, as in v 11, as though already accomplished. This extension of the tree metaphor is traditional (trees cut down: Matt 3:10 par. Luke 3:9; Matt 7:19; Luke 13:9; uprooted: Ps 52:5; Prov 2:22; Wis 4:4; Matt 15:13). It is hard to give "twice dead" a botanical meaning; Mayor suggests that they "may be called doubly dead, when they are not only sapless, but are torn up by the root, which would have caused the death even of a living tree." But the term has clearly been chosen for its application to the false teachers. Some think it is as apostates that they are doubly dead; they have returned to their preconversion condition of spiritual death (Mayor, Bigg, Green, Grundmann). More probably Jude refers to the term "the second death," by which the fate of the wicked after the Last Judgment was known (Rev 2:11; 20:6, 14; 21:8; for "the second death" in the Targums, see I. Abrahams, *Studies in Pharisaism and the Gospels,* 2nd Series [Cambridge: Cambridge University Press, 1924] 41–49; McNamara, *Targum,* 117–25).

13. *κύματα ἄγρια θαλάσσης ἐπαφρίζοντα τὰς ἑαυτῶν αἰσχύνας*, "wild waves of the sea casting up the foam of their abominations." This third of the metaphors from nature is probably based on Isa 57:20: "the wicked are like the tossing sea; for it cannot rest, and its waters toss up mire and dirt" (RSV). (The last clause is missing in LXX; so again it is clear that Jude depends on the Hebrew.) It is noteworthy that this verse of Isaiah is twice echoed in the Qumran hymns, to describe the assaults of the wicked on the writer (1QH 2:12–13: "they have roared like turbulent seas, and their towering waves have spat out mud and slime"; 1QH 8:15: "they cast up their slime upon me": tr. Vermes; for the wicked as wild waves, cf. also 1QH 2:27–28; 6:23). (Note also that *T. Jud.* 21:9 predicts false prophets like storms at sea.)

In his paraphrase of Isa 57:20, Jude shows his command of good literary Greek (for the use of *ἄγριος* for a turbulent sea, and the rare word *ἐπαφρίζειν*, "to cause to splash up like foam"; cf. Euripides, *Hercules furens* 851: *θάλασσαν* ἀγρίαν; Moschus, *Idyll.* 5:5: ἁ δὲ θάλασσα κυρτὸν ἐπαφρίζῃ; Wis 14:1: ἄγρια κύματα; *Sib. Or.* 3:778: ἄγρια κύματα Πόντου, "wild waves of Pontus"), but there is no reason to think he depends on any particular Greek source. Oleson (*NTS* 25 [1978–79] 492–503) argues that Jude alludes to the myth of Aphrodite's birth in Hesiod, *Theog.* 147–206, with a secondary allusion to Euripides, *Hercules furens* 850–52, but there is no *verbal* contact with the former except that Hesiod uses ἀφρός, "foam," while the connection Oleson makes with the passage in Euripides is tenuous in the extreme.

Jude's language has broken through his metaphor: the abominations belong to the false teachers, not to the waves, but Jude compares them with the filth which the waves cast up on the shore. It is not certain whether the "abominations" (lit., "shames") are shameful *deeds* (so most commentators; and cf. the refs. for this usage in BAG) or shameful *words* (Reicke). In either case, the metaphor makes a rather different point from those of the clouds and the trees. They produced nothing; the waves produce something, but the product is horribly unlike the teaching and conduct of the true Christian prophet. Instead of edifying other Christians, it soils them like the dirt thrown up by a stormy sea.

ἀστέρες πλανῆται, "wandering stars." It is widely agreed that Jude has borrowed this image from *1 Enoch.* Jewish apocalyptic thought of the heavenly bodies as controlled by angels (see, e.g., *1 Enoch* 82), and inherited Oriental myths in which the apparently irregular movements of the planets were attributed to the disobedience of heavenly beings, and probably also such phenomena as comets and meteors were interpreted as heavenly beings falling from heaven (cf. Isa 14:12–15; Rev 8:10; 9:1). Thus in *1 Enoch* 18:13–16; 21:3–6, the Watchers (whose fall from heaven and judgment Jude mentioned in v 6) are represented as seven stars "which transgressed the command of the Lord from the beginning of their rising because they did not come out at their proper times" (18:15, tr. Knibb; cf. 21:6). This imagery is taken up in the later Book of Dreams (*1 Enoch* 83–90), which in its allegory of world history represents the fall of the Watchers as the fall of stars from heaven (86:1–3); then, in a passage corresponding to *1 Enoch* 10 (which Jude quoted in v 6) the archangels cast the stars down into the darkness of the abyss and bind them there (88:1, 3) until their judgment at the End, when they will be cast into the abyss of fire (90:24). If Jude is alluding to these passages, as many think (Plummer, Mayor, Windisch, Chaine, Kelly; Milik, *Enoch,* 239), then he is once again, as in v 6, comparing the false teachers with the fallen angels. His phrase ἀστέρες πλανῆται ("wandering stars") was normally used of the planets (references in *TDNT* 6, 229 n.7), and was still so used, even though in Jude's day astronomers were aware that in fact their movements are regular (Cicero, *De natura deorum* 2.51, quoted Mayor). This corresponds to Enoch's reference to "*seven* stars" (*1 Enoch* 18:13; 21:3), though the fall of the stars (86:1–3) would perhaps better suit comets or meteors.

A minor criticism of this view would be that in *1 Enoch* darkness is the *temporary* fate of the fallen angels (*1 Enoch* 88:1; cf. 10:4–5), as it is in Jude 6, until at the Last Judgment they are thrown into the fire (*1 Enoch* 90:24; cf. 10:6, 13; 21:7–10). In Jude 13 darkness is the eternal destiny of the stars. But this may indicate only that Jude is using his source material flexibly.

There is, however, another passage in *1 Enoch* which may have a better claim to have been immediately in Jude's mind: the passage already mentioned, in *1 Enoch* 80, which describes the lawlessness of nature in the last days: "And many heads of the stars in command will go astray, and these will change their courses and their activities, and will not appear at the times which have been prescribed for them" (80:6, tr. Knibb). The following verse describes how they thereby lead people astray. These "wandering stars" Jude takes as an image of the false teachers who stray from the path of obedience to God in order deliberately to entice others into sin. The use of *πλανῆται*, "wandering," establishes a catchword connection with Balaam (v 11), the prophet who went astray in leading others astray (*πλάνη*).

The words *πλανᾶν* ("to lead astray") and *πλάνη* ("error") were regularly used to describe the activity of the false prophets of the last days (Matt 24: 4–5, 11, 24; 1 Tim 4:1; 2 Tim 3:13; 1 John 4:6; Rev 2:20; 13:14; cf. *TDNT* 6, 241, 246–49). Clement of Alexandria, applying Jude's image of the wandering stars to the Carpocratians, correctly perceived its force: "For these are the 'wandering stars' (*ἀστέρες πλανῆται*) referred to in the prophecy, who wander (*πλανώμενοι*) from the narrow road of the commandments into a boundless abyss of the carnal and bodily sins" (*Letter to Theodorus* 1.6–7, tr. in M. Smith, *Clement of Alexandria and a Secret Gospel of Mark* [Cambridge, Mass.: Harvard University Press, 1973] 446). Theophilus of Antioch (*Ad Autol.* 2.15.17–19), whether or not inspired by Jude, saw the fixed stars as images of righteous men who observe God's laws and the planets as representing men who have strayed from God and abandoned his laws.

οἷς ὁ ζόφος τοῦ σκότους εἰς αἰῶνα τετήρηται, "for whom the nether gloom of darkness has been reserved for ever." In *1 Enoch* the place of final damnation is usually represented by fire, but Jewish thought also knew the idea of consignment to eternal darkness (Tob 14:10; *1 Enoch* 46:6; 63:6; *Pss. Sol.* 14:9; 15:10; cf. Matt. 8:12; 22:13; 25:30), and the two images were sometimes combined (*1 Enoch* 103:8; 108:14; *Sib. Or.* 4:43; 1QS 2:8; 4:13; *2 Enoch* 10:2). Jude will have chosen the image of darkness here because it is a more appropriate fate for stars. Unlike the true Christian teachers who are to shine like the stars in heaven (Dan 12:3), the misleading light of the false teachers will be extinguished in darkness for ever.

With regard to the whole group of four images from nature, two final observations can be made. Firstly, as Reicke points out, it may be significant that Jude has chosen an image from each of the four regions of the physical world: clouds in the air, trees on the earth, waves in the sea, stars in the heavens. But this observation is really only significant when connected with the second (first made by Spitta), that this sequence of metaphors is related to *1 Enoch* 2:1–5:4 and 80:2–8. The first of these passages follows immediately the verse of *1 Enoch* (1:9) which Jude quotes in vv 14–15, and at 5:4 it returns to the theme of 1:9. It forms a kind of comment on 1:9, addressed directly to the wicked whose judgment is foretold in 1:9, and it is therefore likely that Jude had reflected on it.

The theme of the section is that the works of God in nature conform to the laws which God has ordained for them, by contrast to the wicked who transgress God's law. The illustrations of this include the four natural phenomena which Jude takes up: "Consider the summer and the winter, how the whole earth is full of water, and clouds and dew and rain rest upon it" (2:3, tr. Knibb); "Contemplate how the trees are covered with green leaves, and bear fruit" (5:1, tr. Knibb); "Behold how the seas and rivers likewise accomplish and do not alter their tasks from his commandments" (5:4, tr. from Greek); "Contemplate all the events in heaven, how the lights in heaven do not change their courses, how each rises and sets in order, each at its proper time, and they do not transgress their law" (2:1, tr. Knibb). But in contrast to these pictures of law-abiding nature, Jude has chosen corresponding examples of nature transgressing these laws, not fulfilling its appointed functions. His examples from nature are therefore not (as in *1 Enoch*) contrasts but parallels to the lawless behavior of the wicked.

Jude will probably also have known a later passage of *1 Enoch* (in the "astronomical" section) which predicts the last days ("the days of the sinners," 80:2), when nature will no longer present a law-abiding contrast to the ways of wicked men, but will itself go astray into lawlessness. Here parallels to three of Jude's four images may be found: "the rain will be withheld, and heaven will retain it" (80:2); "the fruits of the trees will be withheld at their proper time" (80:3); "many heads of the stars in command will go astray" (80:6).

It seems likely that these two passages in *1 Enoch* have inspired Jude's series of metaphors. He represents the lawlessness of nature, prophesied for the last days, by selecting an example from each of the four regions of the world, and sees in them figures of the lawless teachers who are also prophesied for the last days. He has then filled out this general conception by working in allusions to Prov 25:4 and Isa 57:20.

Explanation

In this section Jude focuses on the false teachers as teachers and corrupters of others, and shows that in this capacity, too, they conform to OT types of sin and its judgment. Again he uses prophetic types probably already familiar to his readers from the catechetical tradition, and he refers to them in the form of a prophetic woe oracle against the false teachers, an authoritative pronouncement of judgment, which he either quotes from earlier Christian prophecy or utters on his own prophetic authority.

The oracle compares the false teachers first to Cain, the great prototype of sinners, who corrupted the race of Adam, and also (if this tradition can be dated to Jude's time) the first heretic, who justified his antinomian behavior by denying divine righteousness and judgment. Secondly, they are compared to Balaam, the prophet who, in his greed for financial gain, hurried eagerly to give the advice which led Israel into the disastrous apostasy at Beth-peor. Thirdly, they are compared to Korah, the archetypal schismatic, who contested the authority of Moses and disputed the divine origin of certain laws, gathering followers around him. The mention of judgment is reserved for this third type, since it is the spectacular fate of Korah which illustrates most effectively the doom which awaits Jude's opponents.

The detailed application of the oracle to the false teachers (vv 12–13) opens with a reference to the church's agapes or fellowship meals, which were at this period not distinguished from the Eucharist and were the center of the church's life of worship and fellowship. In these fellowship meals the false teachers participated fully, and with their customary lack of reverence, so that the danger which their influence constituted for the church as a whole is focused on their presence at the fellowship meals. It is encapsulated in the first of six metaphors with which Jude describes them in this section; they are dangerous reefs, and if Jude's readers come too close to them they risk shipwreck.

With a reference to Ezek 34:2, the second metaphor describes the way they exploit the roles of leadership which they claim in the community, probably by requiring the church to support them at a high standard of living. They are shepherds, who instead of tending the sheep, look after themselves at the sheep's expense.

The four metaphors which follow are drawn from nature, one from each region of the universe (air, earth, water, heavens) and each an example of nature failing to follow the laws ordained for her. In this lawlessness of nature, such as apocalyptic writers expected to characterize the last days, Jude sees pictures of the lawlessness of the false teachers of the last days.

The first two of these images—the clouds which fail to give rain and the trees which fail to provide fruit—make the same point: despite the claims they make for the value of their teaching, the false teachers are of no benefit to the church at all. Therefore, just as a barren tree is uprooted, they will incur the second death.

Not only do these teachers have no beneficial effect. Like the turbulent sea which throws up filth on the shore, they have an actually harmful effect, corrupting those who come under their influence.

Finally, they are compared to stars which go astray from their God-ordained courses, as the planets did in the old astrological myths, misleading those who look to them for guidance. The traditional judgment of such disobedient stars is to be extinguished in the eternal blackness of the underworld.

Much of the impact of this passage derives from its imaginative force. Many of Jude's readers no doubt found the false teachers impressive and persuasive, and part of Jude's task must be to shift their whole imaginative perception of the false teachers and show the false teachers in a wholly different light. With this aim he provides a series of imaginatively powerful images which will influence the range of mental associations with which his readers perceive the false teachers.

The Prophecy of Enoch (Jude 14–16)

Bibliography

Bauckham, R. J. "A Note on a Problem in the Greek Version of I Enoch i. 9." *JTS* 32 (1981) 136–38. **Black, M. ed.** *Apocalypsis Henochi Graece.* In *Pseudepigrapha Veteris Testamenti Graeca* 3, ed. A. M. Denis and M. de Jonge. Leiden: E. J. Brill, 1970. **Black, M.** "The Christological Use of the Old Testament in the New Testament." *NTS* 18 (1971–72) 1–14. **Black, M.** "The Maranatha Invocation and Jude 14, 15 (I Enoch 1:9)." *Christ and Spirit in the New Testament: in honour of Charles Francis Digby Moule,* ed. B. Lindars and S. S. Smalley. Cambridge: Cambridge University Press, 1973. **Charles, R. H.** *The Book of Enoch or I Enoch.* 2nd ed. Oxford: Clarendon Press, 1912. **Knibb, M. A.** *The Ethiopic Book of Enoch.* Vol. 2. **Laperrousaz, E. M.** *Le Testament de Moïse,* 51–58. **Milik, J. T.** *The Books of Enoch.* **Osburn, C. D.** "The Christological Use of I Enoch i. 9 in Jude 14, 15." *NTS* 23 (1976–77) 334–41. **vander Kam, J.** "The Theophany of Enoch I 3b-7, 9." *VT* 23 (1973) 129–50.

Translation

14 *It was also about these* [a] *that Enoch, the seventh in descent from Adam, prophesied, saying,*

Behold, the Lord came [b] *with his tens of thousands of holy ones,* [c] 15 *to execute judgment on all, and to convict all the ungodly of all the ungodly deeds which they had committed in their ungodliness,* [d] *and of all the hard things* [e] *which ungodly sinners had spoken against him.*

16 *These people are discontented murmurers, who follow their own desires. Their mouths utter arrogant words and they show partiality for the sake of gain.*

Notes

[a] This use of the dative τούτοις is odd, but must bear this meaning.

[b] The aorist ἦλθεν represents a 'prophetic perfect.'

[c] On the variant readings see Osburn, *NTS* 23 (1976–77) 337–38. The addition of ἀγγέλων in some manuscripts, including P[72], is probably an explanatory gloss, since ἅγιοι alone, in ordinary Christian usage, came to mean Christians, rather than angels.

[d] This phrase is intended to represent in the English the repetition of the stem ἀσεβ-, which in the Greek is contained in the verb ἠσέβησαν.

[e] The addition of λόγων (א etc.), as in *1 Enoch* 1:9 (C), is probably an explanatory gloss.

Form/Structure/Setting

This is the only section of his midrash in which Jude provides a formal quotation from a written source as his text, and he indicates this by using a standard formula of introduction (cf. 4QpIsa[b] 2:7; 4QFlor 1:16; Acts 2:16; 4:11) in which τούτοις, "these," identifies the false teachers as those to whom the prophecy applies. In accordance with early Christian practice he makes certain modifications of the text (see below) which reflect his exegesis of it (cf. Osburn, *NTS* 23 [1976–77] 340–41).

In the interpretation (v 16) the use of the phrase *κατὰ τὰς ἐπιθυμίας αὐτῶν πορευόμενοι*, "following their own desires," creates a catchword connection with the next quotation (v 18).

The Test of the Quotation from 1 Enoch

In these verses Jude quotes *1 Enoch* 1:9. For the text of this verse we have a fragment of the original Aramaic, from Qumran (4QEn[c] 1:1:15–17: Milik, *Enoch,* 184 and Plate IX), the Greek version in Codex Panopolitanus (C) (given in the table from Black's edition), the Ethiopic version (given in the table in Knibb's translation), and a Latin version in Pseudo-Cyprian, *Ad Novatianum* 16 (text in Charles, *Enoch,* 275), which has been widely regarded as derived directly from 1 Enoch rather than from Jude. Comparison of Jude with these witnesses to the text of *1 Enoch* 1:9 raises two questions: (a) Has Jude followed the Greek version (C) or made his own translation from the Aramaic? (b) Has Jude adapted the text to meet his own requirements?

The following points where Jude diverges from C need to be considered:

(1) *ἰδού*: here Jude agrees with Ethiopic and Ps.-Cyprian against (C), and almost certainly follows the Aramaic text (so vander Kam, *VT* 23 [1973] 147–48; Black, "Maranatha," 195; Osburn, *NTS* 23 [1976–77] 335–36; against Milik, *Enoch,* 186). (Both *ἰδού* and C's *ὅτι* may derive from an original ארי [as Knibb, *Enoch,* 59, suggests], or perhaps from an original ארי הא, the phrase with which the Targum renders כי הנה in Mic. 1:3 [a theophany text on which 1 Enoch 1:4–6 depends] where the LXX has *διότι ἰδού*; cf. vander Kam, *VT* 23 (1973) 147–48.)

(2) *ἦλθεν*: Jude's aorist (agreeing with Ps.-Cyprian) represents a Semitic "prophetic perfect," and will be the more literal translation of the Aramaic, whereas C and Ethiopic are more idiomatic renderings (vander Kam, *VT* 23 [1973] 148; Osburn, *NTS* 23 [1976–77] 337; for the Aramaic prophetic perfect, see Black, *NTS* 18 [1971–72] 10 n.; "Maranatha," 196).

(3) *κύριος*. In *1 Enoch* the subject of the sentence is God, named in 1:4. Jude's *κύριος*, which has no support from the other versions, has no doubt been supplied by him, probably as a Christological interpretation, in order to apply the verse to the Parousia of Jesus Christ (Black, "Maranatha," 195; Osburn, *NTS* 23 [1976–77] 337), but perhaps also by analogy with other theophany texts (Isa 40:10; 66:15; Zech 14:5; cf. *1 Enoch* 91:7) which were also applied to the Parousia in primitive Christianity.

(4) *ἐν ἁγίαις μυριάσιν αὐτοῦ*: here Jude agrees with the Ethiopic and the Aramaic fragment against C. (For an attempt to explain C's longer reading, as a Christian interpretation of the text, see Bauckham, "A Note.") Even if the expansion of the text in C is the result of a secondary gloss or scribal error in the Greek version, the fact that Jude uses the Semitism *ἐν* instead of C's *σύν* shows that he is not here following the Greek (cf. Zahn, *Introduction,* 287).

(5) *καὶ ἐλέγξαι πάντας τοὺς ἀσεβεῖς*. Comparison of the versions shows that Jude has here abbreviated the text. According to the Ethiopic, Ps.-Cyprian and C, there are three purposes of God's coming: (a) to judge, (b) to destroy, (c) to convict. By combining (b) and (c) into one phrase Jude omits the idea of destruction, which one might have expected him to retain (cf. vv. 5, 10), but he also omits the original object of (c): "all flesh." This omission has the effect of applying the text exclusively to the *ἀσεβεῖς*, whom Jude wishes to identify as the false teachers (cf. Osburn, *NTS* 23 [1976–77] 338). The omission of "destroy," (which comes

4QEn^c 1:1:15–17	*Ethiopic*	*Greek (C)*	*Jude*	*Ps.-Cyprian*
	And behold! he	ὅτι	ἰδοὺ	Ecce
	comes with ten	ἔρχεται σὺν	ἦλθεν κύριος ἐν	venit cum multis
[רבו]את	thousand holy ones,	ταῖς μυριάσιν αὐτοῦ	ἁγίαις μυριάσιν	milibus nuntiorum
קדישו[הי]		καὶ τοῖς ἁγίοις αὐτοῦ,	αὐτοῦ,	suorum
	to execute judgment	ποιῆσαι κρίσιν	ποιῆσαι κρίσιν	facere iudicium
	upon them	κατὰ πάντων,	κατὰ πάντων,	de omnibus
	and to destroy	καὶ ἀπολέσει	καὶ ἐλέγξαι	et perdere
		πάντας τοὺς	πάντας τοὺς	omnes
	the impious	ἀσεβεῖς	ἀσεβεῖς	impios
	and to contend	καὶ ἐλένξει		et arguere
[ב]שרא	with all flesh	πᾶσαν σάρκα		omnem carnem
על	concerning every-	περὶ πάντων	περὶ πάντων τῶν	de omnibus
עובד[ין]	thing which the	ἔργων τῆς	ἔργων	factis
	sinners and the	ἀσεβείας αὐτῶν	ἀσεβείας αὐτῶν	impiorum
	impious have done	ὧν ἠσέβησαν	ὧγ ἠσέβησαν	quae fecerunt impie
[רב]רבן	and wrought	καὶ	καὶ περὶ πάντων	et de omnibus
וקשין		σκληρῶν ὧν	τῶν σκληρῶν ὧν	verbis impiis quae
		ἐλάλησαν λόγων,	ἐλάλησαν	de Deo locuti sunt
		καὶ περὶ πάντων		
		ὧν κατελάλησαν		
	against him.	κατ᾽ αὐτοῦ	κατ᾽ αὐτοῦ	
		ἁμαρτωλοὶ ἀσεβεῖς.	ἁμαρτωλοὶ ἀσεβεῖς.	peccatores.

rather oddly before "convict" in *1 Enoch*) emphasizes their judicial conviction, which must precede their destruction.

(6) περὶ πάντων τῶν σκληῶν ὧν ἐλάλησαν κατ' αὐτοῦ. The longer text in C may be explained by dittography (Charles, *Enoch,* 8; Knibb, *Enoch,* 60), unless Jude has again abbreviated the text, as the Ethiopic has certainly done here. Against all the versions, the Aramaic fragment has "*great and* hard," as in 5:4 (Greek: μεγάλους καὶ σκληροὺς λόγους; Ethiopic: "proud and hard words"). Jude has the sense of this in v 16 (ὑπέρογκα).

Jude's divergences from C do not seem to be explicable by the supposition that he was quoting the Greek version from memory (Chaine, Kelly). At points (3) and (5) he has deliberately adapted the text to suit the interpretation he wishes to put on it, but at points (1), (2), (4) and perhaps (6) he seems to be closer to the Aramaic original than to C. On the other hand, elsewhere his translation coincides closely with C. This coincidence might just possibly be accidental, assuming in both cases a literal rendering of the Aramaic (cf. Milik's reconstruction of the Aramaic), but this is unlikely.

The simplest explanation is that Jude *knew* the Greek version, but made his own translation from the Aramaic. Other possibilities are that the text in C is a corruption of the Greek version which Jude quotes, or that the translator of the Greek version was a Christian who knew Jude's letter (Zahn, *Introduction,* 287).

Comment

14. Ἐπροφήτευσεν, "prophesied." While this word indicates that Jude regarded the prophecies in *1 Enoch* as inspired by God, it need not imply that he regarded the book as canonical Scripture. At Qumran, for example, the Enoch literature and other apocryphal works were evidently valued without being included in the canon of Scripture.

ἕβδομος ἀπὸ Ἀδαμ, "the seventh in descent from Adam": a traditional description of Enoch (*1 Enoch* 60:8; 93:3 = 4QEn[g] 1:3:23–24; *Jub.* 7:39; *Lev.Rab.* 29:11), arrived at by reckoning the generations inclusively (Gen. 5:3–19). As the number of perfection, it indicates Enoch's very special character in the genealogy of the patriarchs, as the man who walked with God and was taken up to heaven (Gen 5:24)—the root of all the legends and literature about Enoch in intertestamental Judaism. The description here is probably intended to stress, not so much Enoch's antiquity, as his special status which gives authority to his prophecy.

ἦλθεν κύριος, "the Lord came." κύριος ("the Lord") is probably Jude's interpretative gloss on the text (see *Form/Structure/Setting* section above), by which he applies a prophecy of the eschatological coming of God (*1 Enoch* 1:4) to the Parousia of the Lord Jesus. In doing so he follows what seems to have been a widespread practice in primitive Christianity, of applying OT theophany texts to the Parousia (e.g. Isa 40:10 [Rev. 22:12]; Isa 63:1–6 [Rev 19:13, 15]; Isa 66:15 [2 Thess 1:7]; Zech 14:5 [1 Thess 3:13; *Did.* 16:7]). The opening section of 1 Enoch is in fact based on a series of such OT texts, especially those which depict the coming of the Divine Warrior (see vander Kam, *VT* 23 [1973] 129–50).

That early Christians expected the eschatological theophany to take the form of the Parousia of the Lord Jesus has considerable importance for the study of the earliest Christological developments, for it was one route by which divine language came to be used of Christ. Like most early Christology, this was a functional identification of Jesus with God; as God's representative he will carry out the divine function of eschatological judgment (and salvation, see on v 21). Even though Jewish messianic expectation could also transfer such functions to the Messiah (4 Ezra 12:31–33; 13:37–38; *2 Apoc. Bar.* 40:1; 72:2), it is noteworthy that much early Christian thinking about the Parousia did not derive from applying OT messianic texts to Jesus but from the direct use of OT texts about the coming of God. Jude is clear evidence that this took place in Palestinian Jewish Christianity.

Black (*NTS* 18 [1971–72] 10–11; "Maranatha") suggests that *1 Enoch* 1:9, in the form given in Jude 14, is the source of the *Maranatha* formula, but this presupposes (1) that *1 Enoch* 1:9 was widely used in early Christianity, and (2) that *κύριος* is not Jude's own but a traditional Christian adaptation of the text. If (1) were acceptable, (2) would be plausible enough, but Jude's use of 1 Enoch is rather exceptional among NT writers (by contrast with second-century Christian writers, who surprisingly allude to *1 Enoch* more frequently), and we cannot be very confident that *1 Enoch* 1:9 was used of the Parousia much outside the circles to which Jude belongs. It is of course possible that Jude is one of our very few witnesses from precisely those Aramaic-speaking Christian circles in which *Maranatha* originated. But it would be safer to connect the formula more generally with the early Christian use of OT texts which refer to the coming of the Lord (Deut 33:2; Ps 68:17; Isa 40:10; 66:15; Mic 1:3; Zech 14:5). It is with one of these other texts (Isa 40:10) that the formula seems to be linked when it is used in Revelation (22:12, 20).

ἐν ἁγίαις μυριάσιν αὐτοῦ, "with his tens of thousands of holy ones." The author of *1 Enoch* 1:9 derived the phrase from Deut. 33:2 (understanding the text as "tens of thousands of holy ones with him," as in *Tg. Onq.;* cf. Ps. 68:17, and vander Kam, *VT* 23 [1973] 148–50), in accordance with the mention of Sinai in *1 Enoch* 1:4. The "holy ones" are angels, the heavenly army of the Divine Warrior, as in Zech 14:5, which was probably the main source of the early Christian expectation that the Lord at his Parousia would be accompanied by a retinue of angels (Matt 16:27; 25:31; Mark 8:38; Luke 9:26; 2 Thess 1:7; perhaps 1 Thess 3:13; see Bauckham, "A Note").

15. *ποιῆσαι κρίσιν κατὰ πάντων*, "to execute judgment on all." The phrase refers to adverse judgment, condemnation (cf. v 4, *κρίμα*), and, especially in Jude's adaptation of the text, not to all men but to all the ungodly (*ἀσεβεῖς*).

ἀσεβεῖς, "the ungodly": see *Comment* on v 4. The quotation is remarkable for its repetition of the stem *ἀσεβ-* (*ἀσεβεῖς* twice, *ἀσεβείας*, *ἠσέβησαν*), and this must be one reason why Jude chose it. It is probable that for him this was really the key text which demonstrates that the false teachers and their judgment are prophesied, and that v 4 (*οἱ πάλαι προγεγραμμένοι εἰς τοῦτο τὸ κρίμα, ἀσεβεῖς*) points forward, not exclusively, but especially, to this quotation.

περὶ πάντων τῶν σκληρῶν ὧν ἐλάλησαν κατ' αὐτοῦ, "of all the hard things which . . . had spoken against him." The ungodly are to be condemned both for their deeds and (in this phrase) for their words. It is on the latter aspect that Jude will concentrate in his interpretation (v 16), probably because he has already dealt with the former aspect quite fully (vv 5–10) and is now more concerned with the false teachers as teachers. To speak "hard things" (cf. *1 Enoch* 5:4; 27:2; 101:3; also LXX Gen 42:7, 30; 1 Kgdms 20:10; 3 Kgdms 12:13) is associated in *1 Enoch* 5:4 with being "hard-hearted," and probably in *1 Enoch* means to express stubborn resistance to God's will.

16. *γογγυσταί*, "murmurers." The connotations of the phrase "hard things" (*σκληρῶν*) in the quotation from *1 Enoch* take Jude's mind back to the Israelites in the wilderness (cf. Ps 95:8; and for Israel in the wilderness as the classic case of "hardness of heart," see Berger, *ZNW* 61 [1970] 1–47), whom he has already cited as types in vv 5 and 11. For the verbal expressions of Israel's stubbornness, her complaints against God and resistance to his will, are again and again in the Pentateuch and later literature described as "murmuring" (לון, רגן; LXX: *γογγύζειν, διαγογγύζειν, γογγυσμός*; and see K. H. Rengstorf in *TDNT* 1, 728–37). (Jude's *γογγυσταί* is a *hapax* in LXX and NT, but is found in Symmachus, Prov 26:22: Isa 29:24; and Theodotion, Prov 26:20.) Israel's disbelief at Kadesh, to which Jude referred in v 5, was expressed in "murmuring" (Num 14:2, 27, 29, 36; Deut 1:27; Ps 106:25; CD 3:8), as was Korah's revolt (Num 16:11; for other instances of Israel's murmuring in the wilderness, see Exod 15:24; 16:2, 7–9, 12; 1 Cor 10:10; 4 Ezra 1:15–16). Though, of course, the word could be used in other contexts (Sir 10:25; *Ps. Sol.* 16:11; 1QH 5:23; 1QS 11:1; Matt 20:11; Luke 5:30; John 6:41, 43, 61; 7:32; *Did.* 3:6; *3 Apoc. Bar.* 8:5; 13:4), its associations with Israel in the wilderness were so strong that Jude must intend them here.

The reference is not to the false teachers' complaints against the church authorities (Werdermann, *Irrlehrer,* 58–59; Zahn, *Introduction,* 247), because Jude is interpreting the "hard things" of Enoch's prophecy, which the ungodly spoke *against the Lord* (*κατ' αὐτοῦ*). Jude means that the false teachers, like Israel in the wilderness, dispute the authority of God (or Christ). Instead of accepting his will for them, they resist it and complain about it (cf. Num 14:2–3). Jude is again thinking of their antinomianism. No doubt the false teachers said that no good came of keeping the commandments of the Law and regarded them as a burdensome restriction of human freedom.

μεμψίμοιροι, "discontented." This word (which should probably be taken as an adjective with *γογγυσταί*, "murmurers") adds little to the meaning of *γογγυσταί*, but strengthens the rhetorical impact. Another NT (and LXX) *hapax,* it refers to people who are discontented with their lot. Philo (*Mos.* 1.181) uses *μεμψιμοιρεῖν* of Israel's murmuring in the wilderness, and Jude may have taken the word from *T.Mos.* 7:7 (*quaeru* [. . .], restored by Charles, *Assumption,* as *quaerulosi,* which in the Vulgate at Jude 16 translates *μεμψίμοιροι*; but against this view, see Laperrousaz, *Testament,* 51–52).

The false teachers are not content with the moral restrictions God has imposed on them, and wish to throw off such restraints.

κατὰ τὰς ἐπιθυμίας αὐτῶν πορευόμενοι, "following their own desires." The corollary of their rejection of God's will is that they follow their own will. Although *ἐπιθυμία* frequently has the bad sense of sinful desire, Jude's point here is not so much that they indulge particular sinful desires, whether sexual lust or greed, but that they follow their *own* desires rather than *God's.* An illuminating comparison is with the catalogue of historical examples of sin and judgment in CD 2:14–3:12 (which is related to Jude's list in vv. 5–7), where the repeated phrases describing sin are: "walked in the stubbornness of their heart," "did not keep the commandment(s)," and "chose their own will" (cf. also CD 8:7–8; Jer 18:12). The last is the equivalent of Jude's phrase (cf. also Isa 65:2; *T. Jud.* 13:2; 2 Tim. 4:3; Aristides, *Apol.* 7).

το στόμα αὐτῶν λαλεῖ ὑπέρογκα, "Their mouths utter arrogant words." The Qumran Aramaic fragment of *1 Enoch* 1:9 (4QEn[c] 1:1:17) says that the wicked spoke "great and hard things" (רב[רב]ן וקשין): if Jude read this text, he omitted "great" in his quotation, but now takes it up in his interpretation. In any case, the phrase is repeated in *1 Enoch* 5:4 (4QEn[a] 1:2:13), which resumes the theme of 1:9: "you have spoken great and hard words (Greek: *μεγάλους καὶ σκληροὺς λόγους*) with your unclean mouth against his majesty." This passage is again echoed in *1 Enoch* 101:3: "you speak with your mouth great and hard things (*μεγάλα καὶ σκληρά*) against his majesty" (cf. also 27:2). Jude may also have recalled the same expression in *T. Mos.* 7:9 (*os eorum loquetur ingentia,* an exact equivalent of Jude's phrase) and Dan 7:8, 20 (LXX and *θ*: *στόμα λαλοῦν μεγάλα,* "a mouth uttering great things,") (cf. also Ps 12:3 [LXX 11:4]; Rev 13:5; *2 Apoc. Bar.* 67:7).

In place of the usual literal Greek rendering *μεγάλα* ("great"), Jude uses *ὑπέρογκα* (lit. "huge"; elsewhere in NT only at 2 Pet 2:18), which is better Greek idiom, since the word can be used of speech and of arrogance (see the quotations from Plutarch in Mayor; Theodotion, at Dan 11:36, has *λαλήσει ὑπέρογκα,* "he will speak arrogant words"). But the Semitic idiom must determine Jude's meaning, which is not that the false teachers are, in the usual sense, boastful (as in RSV, JB, NIV, etc.). Their big words are uttered against God (*1 Enoch* 5:4; 101:3), like those of Nebuchadnezzar (*2 Apoc. Bar.* 67:7), Antiochus Epiphanes (Dan 7:8, 20; 11:36) and the Antichrist (Rev 13:5). They express their arrogant, presumptuous attitude toward God, their insolent contempt for his commandments, their rejection of his moral authority which amounts to a proud claim to be their own moral authority.

θαυμάζοντες πρόσωπα ὠφελείας χάριν, "showing partiality for the sake of gain." Neither the connection of this phrase with what precedes nor its precise meaning is easy to understand. The expression *θαυμάζειν πρόσωπον* or *πρόσωπα* is a common translation of the Hebrew idiom נשא פנים (used in LXX: e.g. Deut 10:17; 28:50; 2 Chron 19:7; Job 13:10; 22:8; Prov 18:5; the alternative translation in LXX is *λαμβάνειν πρόσωπον*). It does not always carry a bad sense (cf. Gen 19:21; Deut 28:50), but when in the OT it does it usually means to show partiality in the administration of justice, and is often linked with perverting justice by taking bribes (Deut 10:17; 16:19; 2 Chron 19:7; Prov 28:21; Sir 35:12–13).

In Jude 16 the term has commonly been translated "flatter" (RSV, JB, NIV), but there is little precedent for this meaning (cf. Job 32:21–22). It could mean "show partiality" in a very general sense, as in Jas 2:1–9, where the fault is that of showing honor to the rich while neglecting the poor. Then, as most commentators argue, Jude means that the false teachers curry favor with the rich and influential members of the church. This gives a good sense except that it seems very loosely linked to what precedes.

It may be that the meaning is rather more precise. There are a number of passages in which the sin of "respecting persons" is linked to the activity of religious *teaching.* These are closely related to the usual judicial context of the term, since just as the judge may pervert the Law to favor the rich and powerful or for the sake of a bribe, so may the teacher of the Law adapt his teaching to what his hearers may wish to hear. He may, in his teaching, overlook the sins of those on whose favor he depends. So Mal 2:9 denounces the priests who show partiality in their teaching of the Law (LXX: *ἐλαμβάνετε πρόσωπα ἐν νόμῳ*; and cf. Mic 3:11), and the ideal of the Jewish teacher according to Luke 20:21 (cf. Matt 22:16; Mark 12:14) is one who shows no partiality (*οὐ λαμβάνεις πρόσωπον*) but truly teaches the way of God. We might also compare the instructions in the early Christian catechesis, that when it is necessary to reprove a Christian brother for a fault, it should be done without partiality (*Did.* 4:3; *Barn.* 19:4; *Ep. Apost.* 46, cf. 38, 42).

Many commentators think that Jude has *T. Mos.* 5:5 especially in mind, and if so this should settle the meaning. Although the text is somewhat corrupt (see Charles, *Assumption,* 72–75), it appears to speak of teachers of the Law (*magistri, doctores eorum*—not judges, who are mentioned later in v 6) who "respect persons" (*mirantes personas*) and pervert justice by accepting bribes. (A similar passage from a later passage of Christian apocalyptic about the false *teachers* in the Church in the last days is *Ep. Apost.* 37; and cf. also *Asc. Isa.* 3:25.)

Jude's opponents set themselves up as teachers in the church, but instead of faithfully presenting God's moral demands without fear or favor, they set them aside, because, Jude alleges, they hope in this way to make themselves acceptable to those members of the community on whose generosity they depend for their living. This interpretation has the advantage of providing an intelligible connection with the rest of the verse. The whole verse concerns their rejection of the will of God in their teaching. This reflects, says Jude, not only their presumptuous arrogance in relation to God ("Their mouths utter arrogant words"), but also their sycophancy toward men. The same teaching in which they utter their "big words" against God is intended to please their patrons because it offers them freedom from moral restraint.

Explanation

The quotation from Enoch is probably to be seen as Jude's key text in his midrash. Interpreted by the addition of the word "Lord," it speaks of the coming of the Lord Jesus to judge the wicked. Its emphatic repetition of the word "ungodly" hammers home the message of Jude's whole midrash: that those who indulge in "ungodly" conduct, as the false teachers do, are those on whom judgment will fall.

In applying the prophecy to the false teachers, Jude takes up especially its mention of the "hard things" which the ungodly have spoken against the Lord, and highlights the *words* of the false teachers as those of men who will not submit to the divine will. Like Israel in the wilderness they "murmur" against it, complaining of the restraints which the Law imposes on people. In the clash between God's will and their own, they reject the former to follow the latter. They do this with shameless arrogance, setting themselves up as a moral authority competent to set aside the commandments of God. They also do so with an eye to the favor of those members of the church on whom they depend for their prosperous living, hoping that a doctrine of moral laxity will appeal to these others as much as it appeals to themselves.

The passage adds little to our knowledge of the false teachers, but that is not its purpose. It turns entirely on the fact that they are antinomians, and it is only this fact with which Jude is really concerned. His efforts are directed to persuading his readers that such antinomian teachers belong with the sinners of all ages condemned in Scripture, and especially with the sinners of the last days whose judgment at the Parousia is prophesied. The value of the prophecy of Enoch was that it made this point very effectively.

The Prophecy of the Apostles (Jude 17–19)

Translation

[17] *But you, my dear friends, should remember the predictions of the apostles of our Lord Jesus Christ,* [18] *how they said to you,*

In the final age there will be scoffers, who will follow their own desires for ungodliness. [a]

[19] *These people are the ones who create divisions, who follow mere natural instincts, and do not possess the Spirit.*

Notes

[a] *τῶν ἀσεβειῶν* could be a genitive of quality, perhaps a Semitism ("ungodly desires"), or an objective genitive ("desires for ungodly deeds"): the plural makes the latter rather more likely. The words are an example of Jude's catchword technique, and so should not be rejected as a gloss (as Spitta proposes).

Form/Structure/Setting

The opening phrase, with the vocative *ἀγαπητοί*, "my dear friends," indicates a major transition (see White, *Body,* 15–16, 38), in which Jude repeats the thought of the opening phrase in v 5. This formal transition indicates the transition from OT types and prophecies (vv 5–16) to an apostolic prophecy (vv 17–19). Jude is still recalling his readers to the teaching they received at the time of their conversion, but he now moves from the OT material in which they were instructed to the prophecies which the apostolic founders of their church(es) gave them on their own authority.

Jude's quotation, which has no close parallel except in 2 Pet 3:3, may not be a precise quotation from a written or oral source, but a statement in his own words of the general sense of some of the prophetic material which was often included in early Christian teaching. That the words are his own is suggested by the fact that *κατὰ τὰς ἑαυτῶν ἐπιθυμίας πορευόμενοι τῶν ἀσεβειῶν* ("who will follow their own desires for ungodliness") echo, in catchword fashion, v 16 and the repeated *ἀσεβ-* words in the quotation from Enoch (v 15). On the other hand, it is also possible that Jude quotes a fixed form of words, which he has selected *because* of its use of the catchword *ἀσεβειῶν* and in v 16 deliberately anticipated its wording.

Comment

17. *ὑμεῖς δέ*, "But you," indicates a contrast with the false teachers (v 16), but not, as many commentators think, a contrast between this section and the preceding verses (5–16). It is not that Jude now turns from denouncing the false teachers to exhorting the faithful. In this section he is still explaining to his readers that the false teachers are the people of whom they were warned

in prophecy. But throughout the midrash section his intention has been that his readers, heeding these warnings, should no longer be tempted to follow the false teachers.

μνήσθητε τῶν ῥημάτων τῶν προειρημένων ὑπὸ τῶν ἀποστόλων τοῦ κυρίου ἡμῶν Ἰησοῦ Χριστοῦ, ὅτι ἔλεγον ὑμῖν, "you should remember the predictions of the apostles of our Lord Jesus Christ, how they said to you." The interpretation of this passage is crucial for the date and character of the whole letter, since it has often been understood as requiring a postapostolic date of writing. It is said to represent the age of the apostles as belonging to the past.

Against this view there are two decisive considerations: (1) The formal connection with v 5 (see *Form/Structure/Setting* section) indicates that Jude is still recalling his readers to their *original* Christian instruction, received at the time of the founding of their church(es). Once this is realized, the whole passage can be read naturally in a way which does not at all require a postapostolic date. It is not the apostles themselves who belong to the past, but simply their instruction of Jude's readers at the time of their church-founding visit to the area. (2) This interpretation is supported by the explicit information that it was Jude's readers themselves (*ὑμῖν*, "to you") whom the apostles taught. This sets the only limit that can be gathered from this passage on the length of time which had passed since the apostles' prophecies were given. It implies that most of the original converts were still living when Jude wrote. The word *προειρημένων* ("spoken beforehand") does not require that a long period of time had passed; its function is only to indicate that the predictions preceded their fulfillment.

Against this argument that Jude here refers only to his readers' initial Christian instruction, it might be objected that the imperfect *ἔλεγον* ("they said") implies that the teaching was "often repeated" (Mayor). But (1) it is doubtful whether in the case of this verb the distinction between the imperfect and the aorist can be pressed (see BDF § 329; and cf., e.g., Matt 9:34; Mark 3:21–22); (2) even if it could be pressed, the repetition need be only in the course of one visit by the apostles. Paul's Thessalonian letters provide instructive parallels, for he uses three imperfects (*προελέγομεν*, 1 Thess 3:4; *ἔλεγον*, 2 Thess 2:5; *παρηγγέλλομεν*, 2 Thess 3:10) with reference to his teaching during his one initial visit to Thessalonica. Moreover, Paul's *προελέγομεν* ("we said beforehand": 1 Thess 3:4) parallels Jude's *προειρημένων* ("spoken beforehand") as a reference to an apostolic prediction, given only a short time before, but already fulfilled at the time of writing. The parallel is closer still if Paul's prediction is interpreted as the apocalyptic expectation of the time of eschatological tribulation. A further parallel with Jude's words is found in 2 Thess 2:5 ("Do you not remember that when I was still with you I told you [*ἔλεγον ὑμῖν*] these things"): here Paul (if 2 Thessalonians is authentic) recalls his readers to the apocalyptic teaching about the coming of Antichrist which he gave them during the missionary visit when he founded their church. Unlike Paul, Jude refers in the third person to the apostles, because he himself was not one of the founding missionaries of the church(es) to which he writes. But his words do not necessarily require any longer interval of time than that between Paul's visit to Thessalonica and his writing of the Thessalonian letters.

τῶν ῥημάτων, lit. "the words." The plural seems most naturally taken as "sayings," in which case the quotation that follows is only a sample or summary of the apostles' prophecies.

τῶν ἀποστόλων τοῦ κυρίου ἡμῶν Ἰησοῦ Χριστοῦ, "the apostles of our Lord Jesus Christ," are not all the apostles, "the apostolic college" seen through the reverent eyes of a later generation (Kelly), but, naturally in the context, those apostles who founded the church(es) to which Jude writes. The full expression is not paralleled elsewhere in the NT (in the Pauline writings, the usual expression is "apostle of Christ Jesus"; but cf. Eph 3:5: "his holy apostles"), but it stresses the authority of the apostles as derived from the Lord, in a way which is quite natural from a contemporary of the apostles.

Almost all commentators think that Jude here excludes himself from the number of the apostles, but he need only be excluding himself from the number of those apostles who founded the church(es) to which he writes. In fact, as "the Lord's brother," he was probably not known as an apostle (see on v 1), but that conclusion cannot be derived from this verse.

18. *ἐπ' ἐσχάτου τοῦ χρόνου*, "in the final age." The OT expression באחרית הימים ("in the latter days") is rendered in the Septuagint and early Christian literature in a wide variety of ways, of which the most common are *ἐπ' ἐσχάτου τῶν ἡμερῶν* and *ἐν (ταῖς) ἐσχάταις ἡμέραις*. Sometimes *καιρός* ("time") is used instead of *ἡμέρα* ("day") (1 Tim 4:1; 1 Pet 1:5; *Did.* 16:2; Ign. *Eph.* 11:1), but *χρόνος* ("time") is used only here and in 1 Pet 1:20 (*ἐπ' ἐσχάτου τῶν χρονῶν*, "in the last times"). Again we have evidence of the relatively independent character of Jude's translations of Semitic material. The rather awkward expression ("improved" by those MSS which omit *τοῦ*) results from the use of *ἐσχάτου* as a substantive, equivalent to the Hebrew אחרית ("latter part"or "final part"), as in the more usual rendering *ἐπ' ἐσχάτου τῶν ἡμερῶν* (LXX Num 24:14; Jer 23:20; 25:19; Dan 10:14; Heb 1:2).

As used in the OT, the phrase usually refers simply to the future (G. W. Buchanan, "Eschatology and the 'End of Days,' " *JNES* 20 [1961] 188–93), but later, in apocalyptic literature and elsewhere, it became a standard expression for the time when the OT prophecies would be fulfilled, and hence the "eschatological" future (CD 4:4; 6:11; 1QSa 1:1; 1QpHab 2:5; 9:6; *2 Apoc. Bar.* 6:8; 41:5; 78:5). Early Christian writers, with their sense of living already in the time of fulfillment, can use it with reference to the coming of Christ in the past (Heb 1:2; 1 Pet 1:20; *2 Clem.* 14:2; *Asc. Isa.* 9:13; cf. Heb 9:26) and to their own present (*Barn.* 4:9; Ign. *Eph.* 11:1; cf. 1 John 2:18), as well as to the still outstanding future (Jas 5:3; 1 Pet 1:5; *Did.* 16:2, 3; *Asc. Isa.* 3:30). The same writer can use it with reference to both past and future (1 Pet 1:5, 20). Hence when Jude represents the apostles as predicting events for the last days, he is not denying that they saw themselves as living already in the last days. The phrase is a flexible one, which was no doubt used in apostolic predictions of the apocalyptic future in the earliest Christian teaching. For its use in contexts similar to that of Jude 18, cf. 1QpHab 2:5–6; 1 Tim 4:1; 2 Tim 3:1; *Did.* 16:3; *Asc. Isa.* 3:30.

ἐμπαῖκται, "scoffers." In the Widsom Literature of the OT the "scoffer" (לץ) is the man who despises and ignores religion and morality (Ps 1:1; Prov 1:22; 9:7–8; 13:1 etc.; and cf. 4 Ezra 7:79, 81), and it is in this general sense that Jude uses the Greek equivalent ἐμπαίκτης. This word and its cognates are typical of Jewish Greek (ἔμπαιγμα, ἐμπαιγμός, ἐμπαιγμονή, ἐμπαίκτης are found only in LXX and NT, ἐμπαίκτης only in Isa 3:4; 2 Pet 3:3; Jude 18), but usually in the context of the persecution of the righteous by the wicked who mock them (see *TDNT* 5, 633). They are never used in the Septuagint to translate לץ. Again Jude's Greek is relatively independent of Septuagint usage. (In the Qumran texts, "the scoffer" [איש הלצון] and "the scoffers" are the sect's terms, probably derived from Isa 28:14, for their enemies the Wicked Priest and his allies: CD 1:14; 4QpIsa[b] 2:6, 10.)

κατὰ τὰς ἑαυτῶν ἐπιθυμίας πορευόμενοι τῶν ἀσεβειῶν, "who will follow their own desires for ungodliness." The addition of *τῶν ἀσεβειῶν* (lit. "for ungodly deeds") to the phrase which Jude has already used in v 16 gives it a different nuance: not simply their *own* desires, but their desires to indulge in *wickedness.* (Cf. Herm. *Vis.* 3:7:3: *πορεύονται πάλιν ὀπίσω τῶν ἐπιθυμιῶν αὐτῶν τῶν πονηρῶν*, "they go once more after their evil desires"; *T. Iss.* 6:12; *T. Jud.* 13:12.)

Jude has not cited a prophecy explicitly about false prophets or false teachers, although such prophecies were common in early Christian eschatological teaching (Matt 7:15; 24:11, 24; Mark 13:22; Acts 20:29–30; 1 Tim 4:1–3; 2 Tim 4:3–4; 1 John 2:8; 4:1–3; *Did.* 16:3; *Apoc. Pet.* A 1; *Sib. Or.* 2:165–6). Probably because he wished to end his series of texts with one which again stressed the antinomian character of his opponents, he has cited a prophecy on a closely related and equally traditional theme: the apostasy of believers from true religion and morality in the last days (2 Tim 3:1–5; *Asc. Isa.* 3:21, 25–28; cf. Matt 24:12; *Did.* 16:3–4). With his conviction that such prophecies were now being fulfilled, cf. 1 John 2:18; 2 Tim 3:1–9.

19. *ἀποδιορίζοντες*, "who create divisions." This very rare word (a stronger form of *διορίζειν* or *ἀφορίζειν*) was used by Aristotle (*Pol.* 4.4) in the sense of "to define," "to make a distinction" in order to classify (see also the later occurrences in Maximus Confessor and Severus, quoted by Mayor), and some commentators have thought Jude uses it in the same sense: the false teachers make distinctions within the community. This is especially suitable for the interpretation of the false teachers as Gnostics; they classify themselves as pneumatics and the ordinary Christians as psychics (so Mayor, Windisch, Chaine, Kelly, Grundmann, NEB). But *ἀποδιορίζειν* can also (like *διορίζειν* and *ἀφορίζειν*) mean "to separate," as in *Corp. Herm.* 3:2a, where it is used of the separation of the upper from the lower elements in the creation of the cosmos, and this seems to be a more obvious sense in Jude. The false teachers are causing divisions in the church (so Spitta, Bigg, Reicke). Since they still participate in the common fellowship-meals (v 12), Jude cannot mean that they have gone into complete schism, but that they gather their own faction within the church, like Korah (see on v 11). The tendency of their teaching is divisive because it creates an élitist group who regard themselves as those who truly possess the Spirit (see below).

The fact that Jude introduces this theme in his interpretation of the apostles' prophecy (v 18) may indicate that this too was a theme of the eschatological prophecies of the early Christian missionaries. Cf. the *agraphon,* "There will be divisions and factions" (*ἔσονται σχίσματα καὶ αἱρέσεις*, Justin, *Dial.* 35.3; J. Jeremias, *Unknown Sayings of Jesus,* tr. R. H. Fuller [London: S. P. C. K.,

1957] 59–61), and 1 Cor 11:19: "there must be factions (αἱρέσεις) among you." Thus one mark which identifies the false teachers as the prophesied "scoffers" is the fact that, as prophesied, they create factions.

M. R. James (xlv) makes the interesting suggestion that Jude took the word ἀποδιορίζοντες from *T. Mos.* 7:7, where, immediately before *querulosi* (= μεμψίμοιροι, "discontented," as in Jude 16), the Latin text has *exterminatores,* "destroyers." James conjectures that this is a literal rendering of ἀποδιορίζοντες (since διορίζειν can carry the same sense as Latin *exterminare*), but it is difficult to see what ἀποδιορίζοντες could have meant in the context (admittedly fragmentary) of *T. Mos.* 7:7.

ψυχικοί, πνεῦμα μὴ ἔχοντες, "who follow mere natural instincts, and do not possess the Spirit." ψυχικός (pertaining to ψυχή, "soul" or "life") is used in 1 Cor 2:14; 15:44, in a contrast with πνευματικός (pertaining to πνεῦμα, "the Spirit"): it refers to merely physical life, the life of this world, without the eschatological gift of the Holy Spirit. In Jas 3:15 (the only other NT occurrence) ψυχικός has a similar but even more sharply negative sense: the God-given wisdom "from above" is contrasted with the wisdom that is "earthly, unspiritual, devilish" (ἐπίγειος, ψυχική, δαιμονιώδης).

Although Paul's use of πνευματικός and ψυχικός in 1 Cor 2:14–15 is widely, though not universally, regarded as echoing the terminology of his opponents at Corinth, no fully convincing source for this terminology has yet been demonstrated. The second-century gnostic use of πνευματικός and ψυχικός (B. A. Pearson, *The Pneumatikos-Psychikos Terminology in 1 Corinthians* [SBLDS 12; Missoula, MT: Scholars Press, 1973] chap. 6) derives from their exegesis of Paul (Pagels, *Paul,* 59, 163–64).

Hellenistic-Jewish Wisdom theology is a more promising source (Pearson, *Pneumatikos-Psychikos*), but not only is the terminology πνευματικός and ψυχικός itself unattested; there is not even a regular anthropological distinction between πνεῦμα ("spirit") as the higher element and ψυχή ("soul") as the lower element in man (R. A. Horsley, "Pneumatikos vs. Psychikos," *HTR* 69 [1976] 270–73, criticizing Pearson). Although some Hellenistic anthropology did distinguish the ψυχή ("soul") as a lower element from νοῦς ("mind") as the higher element, the devaluation of ψυχή ("soul") by comparison with πνεῦμα ("Spirit") must result from the early Christian belief in the Spirit not as a constituent of human nature, but as the gift of God to the believer.

Since the background to Paul's use of πνευματικός and ψυχικός is so uncertain, we cannot draw firm conclusions as to Jude's relationship to it: whether that Jude borrowed the term ψυχικός from Paul, or that Jude's opponents borrowed it from Paul, or that Jude's opponents shared it with Paul's opponents. It is safer to interpret Jude's words in their own context.

Clearly πνεῦμα μὴ ἔχοντες ("not possessing the Spirit") explains ψυχικοί: the false teachers do not possess the Spirit of God, but live purely at the level of natural, earthly life. As most commentators recognize, it is likely that Jude here contradicts his opponents' claim to possess the Spirit. Probably they connected this claim with their visionary experience and the revelations they received in their visions (v 8). The Spirit of prophetic inspiration inspired them, and as men of the Spirit they claimed to be free from moral restraint and superior to moral judgments. Jude's denial of this claim rests on their immoral behavior, which shows that they cannot be led by the Spirit of God, but merely "follow their own desires for ungodliness" (v 18). Such people are merely *ψυχικοί*, devoid of the Spirit. Whether *ψυχικοί* was the false teachers' own term for other Christians, who did not share their charismatic experience and moral freedom, is less certain. It is possible that Jude turns the tables on them in this way, but equally possible that *ψυχικοί* is simply his own judgment on them.

If there is a connection with *ἀποδιορίζοντες* ("who create divisions"), it will be that the false teachers are gathering a faction which claims to possess the Spirit by contrast with more conventional Christians. Those who see the false teachers as Gnostics find in Jude's words a reflection of gnostic anthropology; the false teachers and their followers see themselves as pneumatics (*πνευματικοί*) with a higher knowledge and destiny, while the ordinary Christians are psychics (*ψυχικοί*) (Windisch, Moffatt, Barnett, Sidebottom, Kelly, Grundmann). This fully gnostic interpretation differs from the view already suggested in that it posits not merely an élite (which others may join), but a fixed division of mankind into naturally distinct classes. But this theory cannot be shown to have been taught before the second century, and even then did not characterize all gnostic groups. There is no need to read it into Jude's words, which require not a developed heretical system of this kind, but an antinomian distortion of common early Christian notions of the Spirit.

Explanation

For his final "text" Jude turns to apostolic prophecy, reminding his readers of the apocalyptic predictions which were part of the teaching they received from the apostles who founded their church(es). The words he quotes are probably his own summary of the kind of prophecies the early Christian missionaries gave. They predict that in the final period of history there will be enemies of true religion and morality in the church. Jude sees this expectation fulfilled in the false teachers, who are now further characterized as people who cause divisions in the church. They gather an élitist faction of people who share the same kind of prophetic inspiration as they themselves claim. But this claim Jude dismisses. Their immoral behavior is for him sufficient evidence that in reality they do not possess the Spirit of God, but live purely on the level of natural, unredeemed life.

The Appeal (*Jude 20–23*)

Bibliography

Bieder, W. "Judas 22 f.: Οὓς δὲ ἐᾶτε ἐν φόβῳ." *TZ* 6 (1950) 75–77. **Birdsall, J. N.** "The Text of Jude in P[72]." *JTS* 14 (1963) 394–99. **Marshall, I. H.** *Kept by the Power of God.* London: Epworth Press, 1969. 161–63. **Mees, M.** "Papyrus Bodmer VII (P[72]) und die Zitate aus dem Judasbrief bei Clemens von Alexandrien." *CDios* 181 (1968) 551–59. **Osburn, C. D.** "The Text of Jude 22–23." *ZNW* 63 (1972) 139–44. **Spicq, C.** *Agape,* 372–74.

Translation

[20] *But you, my dear friends, build yourselves up* [a] *on the foundation of your most holy faith,* [b] *pray* [a] *in the Holy Spirit,* [21] *keep yourselves in the love of God, wait* [a] *for the mercy of our Lord Jesus Christ to grant you eternal life.*

[22] *Snatch some from the fire,*

[23] *but on those who dispute* [c] *have mercy with fear,* [d] *hating even the clothing that has been soiled by the flesh.*

Notes

[a] On the participles in these verses, probably used as imperatives, see *Form/Structure/Setting* section below.

[b] Probably the ἐπί in ἐποικοδομοῦντες, "build up," here retains the sense of "(build) *on*" (as in 1 Cor 3:12; Eph 2:20), and the dative τῇ πίστει, "the faith," therefore indicates the foundation on which the building is erected. This seems preferable to an instrumental dative (suggested by Reicke): "by means of your most holy faith."

[c] For this translation of διακρινομένους, see *Comment.*

[d] The translation of vv 22–23a follows the text of P[72]: see the note on the text below.

The Text of Jude 22–23a

It is probably impossible to reach an assured conclusion as to the original text of vv 22–23a, which is "undoubtedly one of the most corrupt passages in New Testament literature" (Osburn, *ZNW* 63 [1972] 139). The manuscripts and versions present a baffling variety of readings, which can, however, be divided into two main groups: a shorter text consisting of two clauses and a longer text consisting of three clauses. Scholars have been divided, not only in preferring either the shorter or the longer text, but also in selecting particular forms of each. The following are the principal readings, together with translations which illustrate the diversity of scholarly judgments.

(A) *The Two-Clause Text*

1. P[72]: οὓς μὲν ἐκ πυρὸς ἁρπάσατε
 διακρινομένους δὲ ἐλεεῖτε ἐν φόβῳ.

This is the text translated above. Also by Moffatt:

Snatch some from the fire,
and have mercy on the waverers, trembling as you touch them.

It is supported by Clement of Alexandria, *Strom.* 6.8.65:

> *οὓς μὲν ἐκ πυρὸς ἁρπάζετε*
> *διακρινομένους δὲ ἐλεεῖτε.*

and by the Latin version in the Liber Commicus, the Philoxenian Syriac and Sahidic versions, and the Latin version in Jerome, *Ez.* 18, omitting, like Clement, *ἐν φόβῳ* (these texts are given by Osburn, *ZNW* 63 [1972] 139–40).

2. C: *οὓς μὲν ἐλέγχετε διακρινομένους*
   οὓς δὲ σώζετε ἐκ πυρὸς ἁρπάζοντες ἐν φόβῳ.

3. K, L, P, S: *οὓς μὲν ἐλεεῖτε διακρινόμενοι*
   οὓς δὲ ἐν φόβῳ σώζετε ἐκ πυρὸς ἁρπάζοντες.

Translated by AV:

> And of some have compassion, making a difference:
> and others save with fear, pulling them out of the fire.

(Also translated by J. B. Phillips, Reicke.)

4. B: *οὓς μὲν ἐλεᾶτε διακρινομένους σώζετε ἐκ πυρὸς ἁρπάζοντες*
   οὓς δὲ ἐλεᾶτε ἐν φόβῳ.

Translated by NEB:

> There are some doubting souls who need your pity; snatch them from the flames and save them.
> There are others for whom your pity must be mixed with fear.

(Also translated by TEV (1966), JB Margin, Kelly.)

(B) *The three-clause text*

1. ℵ: *οὓς μὲν ἐλεᾶτε διακρινομένους*
   οὓς δὲ σώζετε ἐκ πυρὸς ἁρπάζοντες
   οὓς δὲ ἐλεᾶτε ἐν φὸβῳ.

Translated by RV:

> And on some have mercy who are in doubt (Margin: while they dispute with you);
> and save some, snatching them out of the fire;
> and on some have mercy with fear.

(Also translated by TEV/GNB (1976), NIV.)

2. A: *οὓς μὲν ἐλέγχετε διακρινομένους*
   οὓς δὲ σώζετε ἐκ πυρὸς ἁρπάζοντες
   οὓς δὲ ἐλεᾶτε ἐν φόβῳ.

Translated by RSV:

> And convince some, who doubt;
> save some, by snatching them out of the fire;
> on some have mercy with fear.

(Also translated by JB, NEB Margin.)

In addition to these readings, some scholars have proposed emendations not supported by any manuscript: in an attempt to achieve a satisfactory climax in the three-clause text, Windisch suggested that *ἐλεᾶτε*, "have mercy," in A be amended to ἐκβάλατε, "throw out, expel," while Wohlenberg proposed ἐλάσατε and Bieder (*TZ* 6 [1950] 75–77) ἐᾶτε. But such emendations only make it even more difficult to explain the textual confusion.

A good case for the originality of the shortest reading, in P[72], can be made, on the grounds of its attestation, its suitability to the context in Jude, and because it is possible to explain the various longer readings as expansions and adaptations of it. Birdsall (*JTS* 14 [1963] 394–99) and especially Osburn (*ZNW* 63 [1972] 139–44) have given plausible accounts of how the other readings may have originated. (The reading of P[72] was also supported, before P[72] itself became known, by Moffatt [244] and Bigg [340–42, but with σώζετε . . . ἁρπάζοντες].)

The first clause in P[72], without the interpretative σώζετε, "save," is in line with the conciseness of Jude's style and his other terse allusions to Scripture. It would be later scribes who would feel the need to explain the metaphor. In this reading διακρινομένους can be taken in the sense of "disputing" (see *Comment*), which is how Jude uses the word in v 9. Although he could easily have used it in two different senses, he seems to have had v 9 in mind when he wrote vv 22–23 (the words, "May the Lord rebuke you," quoted by the *T. Mos.* from Zech 3:2, apparently brought to his mind the passage Zech 3:1–5, to which he alludes in vv 22–23), and so there is a possibility that διακρινομένους is an echo of his earlier use of the word. The distinction of two classes of people is appropriate in the situation to which Jude writes (see *Comment*). Some (e.g. James, xxxviii) argue that the three-clause reading is supported by Jude's stylistic preference for sets of three, but this cannot be pressed against other considerations. Jude would not have manufactured artificially a threefold distinction if the situation itself only suggested a twofold one (cf. vv 20–21, where he gives four, not three, injunctions). Finally, the stylistic device in the P[72] reading, where the participle διακρινομένους takes the place of a second οὓς, is good Greek style (Birdsall, *JTS* 14 [1963] 397), but not otherwise attested in the New Testament. Mees (*CDios* 181 [1968] 558) therefore suggests that Jude would not have used it, but this is probably to underestimate Jude's competence in Greek.

In the development of the other readings, the following factors may have played a part: (1) σώζετε is an interpretative gloss to explain the metaphor ἐκ πυρὸς ἁρπάσατε, "snatch from the fire" (Osburn, *ZNW* 63 [1972] 141). (2) διακρινομένους can be understood in several senses: "doubting" (as often in the NT), "being judged" (hence Jude 22 Vulgate: *iudicatos*), "making a distinction" (hence the AV translation of διακρινόμενοι in the Received Text), or "disputing." Different interpretations of the word led to rearrangements and adaptations of the text (Birdsall, *JTS* 14 [1963] 398; Osburn, *ZNW* 63 [1972] 141). (3) ἐλέγχετε, in the sense either of "convince" or "reprove," was introduced as an appropriate treatment of doubters or disputers, and perhaps under the influence of the traditional catechesis reflected in *Did.* 2:7 (see below). (4) Attempts to bring the text into line with the disciplinary practices in the churches the scribes knew may have played a part, especially in the formation of the three-clause readings.

Finally, special mention must be made of the relationship to *Did.* 2:7:

οὐ μισήσεις πάντα ἄνθρωπον
ἀλλὰ οὓς μὲν ἐλέγξεις
περὶ δὲ ὧν προσεύξῃ
οὓς δὲ ἀγαπήσεις ὑπὲρ τὴν ψυχήν σου.

Thou shalt hate no man;
but some thou shalt reprove,
and for some thou shalt pray,
and some thou shalt love more than thine own life (Loeb trans.).

Comparison with *Barn.* 19:3–5 and the Latin *Doctrina apostolorum* (J. P. Audet, *La Didachè* [Paris: Gabalda, 1958] 142) shows that the second and third clauses were not in the "Two Ways" document on which the Didache here depends, but were probably added from Christian catechetical tradition, partly in dependence on Lev 19:17–18 LXX. Only if the text of C or A (including ἐλέγχετε) is read in Jude is there any verbal relationship to Jude, and so it is unlikely that there is any direct dependence of Jude on the *Did.* or *vice versa.* It is, however, possible that the *Did.* preserves a piece of traditional Christian teaching which distinguished two classes of sinners (some to be reproved and reclaimed; others, more hardened, for whom it was only possible to pray), and that Jude rephrased this tradition in his own words (the two-clause text). The final clause in *Did.* 2:7 (which comes from the "Two Ways" document, cf. *Barn.* 19:5) can hardly refer to a third class of sinner; presumably it refers to faithful Christians. It therefore offers no support to the three-clause readings in Jude.

Later scribes evidently tried to bring these two texts into closer correspondence. The reading ἐλέγχετε in Jude in C and A may be influenced either by the *Did.* itself or by the catechetical tradition behind the *Did.* Influence in the other direction is evident in *Apostolic Constitutions* 6:4, which reproduces *Did.* 2:7, but adds another clause, οὓς δὲ ἐλεήσεις, "and on some thou shalt have mercy," after οὓς μὲν ἐλέγξεις. Perhaps both this and the three-clause readings in Jude are attempts to adapt the texts to a three-stage system of ecclesiastical discipline (private reproof, public warning, excommunication; cf. Matt 18:15–17: four stages).

Form/Structure/Setting

These verses contain Jude's appeal to his readers to fight for the faith, as announced in v 3, and are therefore not an appendix to the letter, but its climax (see on vv 3–4, *Form/Structure/Setting* section). The opening phrase, as in v 17, again indicates a major transition, and a link with v 3 is established by the catchword connection between τῇ ἁγιωτάτῃ ὑμῶν πίστει, "your most holy faith," in v 20 and τοῖς ἁγίοις πίστει, "faith . . . to the saints," at the end of v 3. There are also links beteen v 21 and v 1, both in content and by catchwords (v 21: ἐν ἀγάπῃ θεοῦ τηρήσατε, "keep yourselves in the love of God"; v 1: ἐν θεῷ πατρὶ ἠγαπημένοις . . . τετηρημένοις "loved by God the Father . . . kept"). In vv 22–23, where Jude turns to his readers' behavior toward the false teachers and their followers, the links are with vv 7–9: πυρός (v 22) with πυρός (v 7); διακρινομένους (v 23) with διακρινόμενος (v 9); ἀπο τῆς σαρκὸς ἐσπιλωμένον (v 23) with σάρκα . . . μιαίνουσιν (v 8, cf. also σπιλάδες, v 12); and the allusions to Zech 3:2–4 (see *Comment*) with Michael's words (Zech 3:2) in v 9.

In vv 20–21 Jude selects four injunctions from traditional catechetical material. The parallels to these four injunctions elsewhere in the NT (and not only in the Pauline corpus) (see *Comment*) are evidence, not of Jude's dependence on other NT authors, but of his indebtedness to the common paraenetic tradition of primitive Christianity. It is possible that the grammatical form of his exhortations also reflects their traditional nature. He uses three participles (ἐποικοδομοῦντες, "building yourselves up"; προσευχόμενοι, "praying"; προσδεχόμενοι, "waiting") and one imperative (τηρήσατε, "keep"). There is no difficulty in explaining the construction as normal Greek usage, the participles dependent on the imperative. But in view of the fact that elsewhere in the paraenetic sections of NT letters (Rom 12:9–19; Eph 4:2–3; Col 3:16–17;

Heb 13:5; 1 Pet 2:18; 3:1, 7–9; 4:7–10) a special use of participles with an imperatival sense is found, sometimes interspersed with true imperatives, it may well be that Jude also follows this usage. The explanation of the usage is probably to be found in the theory put forward by D. Daube ("Participle and Imperative in I Peter," in E. G. Selwyn, *The First Epistle of St Peter* (London: Macmillan, 1946) 467–88) that they reflect a usage found in rabbinic Hebrew, where the participle can be used in rules and codes of conduct, though not in direct commands. In that case, the NT examples will derive from early codes of Christian conduct, originally formulated in Hebrew (or, less probably, Aramaic). (On such codes, see also W. D. Davies, *Paul and Rabbinic Judaism* [London: S. P. C. K., 1948] 122–45.) (Jude's direct address to his readers will represent his adaptation of the traditional form, such as Daube postulates in Col 3:16; 1 Pet 3:7.)

There are two patterns to be observed in the set of four injunctions. The first, third and fourth represent the familiar triad faith, love, hope, which is probably a traditional, pre-Pauline, Christian formula (A. M. Hunter, *Paul and his Predecessors,* 2nd ed. [London: SCM Press, 1961] 33–35), here expanded into a tetrad by the addition of prayer. The second, third and fourth injunctions correspond to a trinitarian formula: Holy Spirit, God, Christ. Either or both of these patterns may have guided Jude's selection of injunctions from traditional material; or perhaps he has expanded a traditional set of three injunctions which was constructed according to one of these patterns.

In vv 22–23 the allusions to Zech 3:2–4 (see *Comment*) probably indicate that Jude himself composed these instructions, but he may have been rephrasing a catechetical tradition which is also found in *Did.* 2:7 (see the note on the text of Jude 22–23a above) and which distinguished the differing treatment to be given to two different classes of sinners.

Comment

20. ἐποικοδομοῦντες ἑαυτοὺς, "build yourselves up." The concept of the Christian community as the eschatological temple goes back to the earliest Palestinian Christianity (cf. the "pillar" apostles: Gal 2:9) and is therefore found in many strands of early Christian tradition (1 Cor 3:9–15; 2 Cor 6:16; Eph 2:19–22; 1 Pet 2:5; *Barn.* 4:11; 6:15; 16; Herm. *Vis.* 3; *Sim.* 9; Ign. *Eph.* 9:1). Probably from this concept derived the image of "building" the Christian community, which was used in various ways, especially in the Pauline writings (Rom 14:19; 15:2, 20; 1 Cor 3:9–15; 8:1; 10:23; 14:3–5, 12, 17, 26; 2 Cor 10:8; 12:19; 13:10; Gal 2:18; Eph 2:18; 2:20–22; 4:12, 16; Col 2:7; 1 Thess 5:11) but also elsewhere (Matt 16:18; Acts 9:31; 15:16; 20:32; 1 Pet 2:5; *Barn.* 16:8–10; Ign. *Eph.* 9:1; Pol. *Phil.* 3:12; 12:2; *Odes Sol.* 22:12). There is no need to derive all these non-Pauline occurrences of the metaphor from Pauline usage. Paul himself will have been dependent on common Christian usage, and it is probable that exhortations to "build up" the community or to "edify" one's Christian brother, both in Paul and elsewhere (Rom 14:19; 15:2; 1 Cor 14:12, 26; 1 Thess 5:11; 1 Pet 2:5; Jude 20), go back to traditional catechetical material.

Jude does not mean that each of his readers should build himself up—

which would be contrary to the ordinary Christian use of the metaphor—but that all should contribute to the spiritual growth of the whole community. As with the metaphor of "fighting" in v 3, it is difficult to tell how far "build" retains its live metaphorical sense, how far it has become a pale metaphor, like the English "edify." The mention of a foundation, which follows, suggests that the picture of erecting a building has not entirely faded.

The use of the metaphor forms a contrast with the activity of the false teachers in the preceding verse: whereas they disrupt the church and tear it apart (ἀποδιορίζοντες), Jude's readers are to construct it.

τῇ ἁγιωτάτῃ ὑμῶν πίστει, "on the foundation of your most holy faith." *πίστις* ("faith") is here the gospel, as in v 3, and it is holy because it comes from God (for the expression "holy faith," cf. *Act. Verc.* 8). It is the faith which Jude's readers received when the gospel was first preached to them (v 3), and therefore "*your* faith," distinguished from the message of the false teachers. No doubt Jude's main thought is that when the church lives on the basis of the gospel, its life will be holy, by contrast with the immorality which results from the antinomian principles of his opponents.

Jude's view of the gospel as the foundation of the church is a different (though not contradictory) perspective from Paul's view of Jesus Christ himself as the foundation (1 Cor 3:11; cf. Eph 2:20).

ἐν πνεύματι ἁγίῳ προσευχόμενοι, ("pray in the Holy Spirit"). The phrase *ἐν (τῷ) πνεύματι* ("in the Spirit") in early Christian literature frequently means "in the control of the Spirit" or "under the inspiration of the Spirit" (Matt 22:43; Mark 12:36; Luke 2:27; 4:1; Acts 19:21; Rom 8:9; 1 Cor 12:3; Rev 1:10; 4:2; *Barn.* 9:7; *Asc. Isa.* 3:19; Polycrates, *ap.* Eusebius, *Hist. Eccl.* 5. 24. 2, 5; cf. *Did.* 11: 7–12), and with reference to prayer indicates charismatic prayer in which the words are given by the Spirit (see J. D. G. Dunn, *Jesus and the Spirit* [London: SCM Press, 1975] 239–40). Praying in the Spirit includes, but is not restricted to, prayer in tongues (1 Cor 14:15–16; Dunn, *Jesus and the Spirit,* 245–46: "A reference to charismatic prayer, including glossolalic prayer, may therefore be presumed for Jude 20").

Prayer in the Spirit is attested not only in the Pauline writings (Eph 6:18; cf. Rom 8:15–16, 26–27; Gal 4:6), but also in the Fourth Gospel (John 4:23–24). There is therefore no need to see specifically Pauline influence on Jude here, but the close verbal parallel with Eph 6:18 (*προσευχόμενοι ἐν παντὶ καιρῷ ἐν πνεύματι,* "pray at all times in the Spirit"), including perhaps in both cases the imperatival use of the participle (see *Form/Structure/Setting* section), suggests that both reflect traditional paraenetic material.

Again there is a contrast with the false teachers, who lay claim to prophetic utterance in the Spirit, but show by their behavior that they "do not possess the Spirit" (v 19).

21. *ἑαυτοὺς ἐν ἀγάπῃ θεοῦ τηρήσατε,* "keep yourselves in the love of God." Most commentators take *θεοῦ* ("of God") as a subjective genitive (God's love for you), but a few (Chaine, Cantinat) think it must be objective (your love for God), because the imperative requires an action on the part of Christians. However, in the parallel in John 15:9, "remain in my love" (*μείνατε ἐν τῇ ἀγάπῃ τῇ ἐμῇ*), the love is certainly Christ's for his disciples. They remain in it by obeying his commandments (15:10). Similarly Jude probably means

that God's love for Christians (v 1) requires an appropriate response. Without obedience to God's will, fellowship with God can be forfeited, and this is the danger with which the antinomian doctrine of the false teachers threatens the church.

The similarity to Johannine passages (John 15:9–10; 1 John 4:16) implies common dependence on paraenetic tradition. For the catchword connections of *τηρήσατε* ("keep"), see *Comment* on v 6.

προσδεχόμενοι τὸ ἔλεος τοῦ κυρίου ἡμῶν Ἰησοῦ Χριστοῦ, "wait for the mercy of our Lord Jesus Christ." "Mercy" (*ἔλεος*) was a traditional term with reference to the eschatological hope of God's people (2 Macc 2:7 *v.l.; Pss. Sol.* 7:10; 8:27–28; 10:4, 7; 14:9; 17:45; *1 Enoch* 1:8; 5:6; 27:4; *2 Apoc. Bar.* 78:7; 82:2; 4 Ezra 14:34; Matt 5:7; 2 Tim 1:18; *1 Clem.* 28:1; Herm. *Vis.* 3:9:8; *Sim.* 4:2). Usually, of course, the reference is to *God*'s mercy, and Jude's phrase "the mercy of our Lord Jesus Christ" (cf. 2 Tim 1:18: *ἔλεος παρὰ κυρίου*, "mercy from the Lord"; *2 Clem.* 16:2: *τοῦ ἐλέους Ἰησοῦ*, "the mercy of Jesus") belongs with his Christological interpretation of *1 Enoch* 1:9 in v 14: it is to the Lord Jesus that God has committed the final judgment. If Jude's readers remain faithful by following the previous three exhortations, they can expect not, like the false teachers, condemnation at the Parousia, but salvation. But of course, not even the faithful Christian escapes condemnation except by the Lord's mercy.

Throughout early Christian literature "waiting" describes the eschatological expectation (*προσδέχεσθαι*: Mark 15:43; Luke 2:25, 38; 12:36; 23:51; Acts 24:15; Titus 2:13; *2 Clem.* 11:2; *προσδοκᾶσθαι*: Matt 11:3; Luke 7:19–20; 2 Pet 3:12–14; *1 Clem.* 23:5; Ign. *Pol.* 3:2; *ἐκδέχεσθαι*: Heb 11:10; *Barn.* 10:11; *2 Clem.* 12:1; *ἀπεκδέχεσθαι*: Rom 8:23; 1 Cor 1:7; Gal 5:5; Phil 3:20; Heb 9:28; *ἀναμένειν*: 1 Thess 1:10; *2 Clem.* 11:5), though not often in exhortations (2 Pet 3:12; *2 Clem.* 12:1; cf. Hab 2:3; *2 Apoc. Bar.* 83:4). (Sir 2:7: *ἀναμείνατε τὸ ἔλεος αὐτοῦ*, "wait for his mercy," is not eschatological.) The popularity of the term may derive in part from Hab 2:3 ("wait for it"; LXX: *ὑπομεῖνον αὐτόν*, "wait for him"), which had long been a classic text for the eschatological expectation (see A. Strobel, *Untersuchungen zum eschatologischen Verzögerungsproblem auf Grund der spätjüdisch-urchristlichen Geschichte von Habakuk 2, 2 ff.* [NovTSup 2; Leiden: E. J. Brill, 1961] Part 1), and from other prophetic texts which were interpreted eschatologically (Isa 30:18; 49:23; 51:5; 60:9; 64:4, especially LXX (64:3): *ὑπομένουσιν ἔλεον*, "(they) wait for mercy"; Dan 12:12; Mic 7:7; Zeph 3:8). It does not, of course, indicate a merely passive attitude, but an orientation of the whole life toward the eschatological hope.

εἰς ζωὴν αἰώνιον, "to (grant you) eternal life." Eternal life, i.e. the resurrection life of the age to come, is the gift which Christ in his mercy will bestow on the faithful Christians at the Parousia.

22. *οὓς μὲν ἐκ πυρὸς ἁρπάσατε*, "snatch some from the fire." This is the first of two allusions in these verses to the vision in Zech 3:1–5, a passage to which Jude's attention must have been drawn as a result of his use of the *T. Mos.* in v 9, where the words, "May the Lord rebuke you," derive ultimately from Zech 3:2. In the same verse the high priest Joshua is described as "a brand plucked from the fire" (RSV); the same phrase occurs in Amos 4:11, in connection with a reference to the judgment on Sodom and Gomor-

rah, but since Jude 23 probably alludes to Zech 3:3–4 (see below), it is probable that Zechariah rather than Amos was the source of Jude's image in v 22. As usual, Jude shows no dependence on the LXX translation (Amos 4:11 and Zech 3:2: δαλὸς ἐξεσπασμένος ἐκ πυρός).

The fire is that of final judgment in hell, as in v 7. Jude does not mean that the people to whom he refers are already in the fire (Windisch), but that they are on the brink of it and can be snatched back before they fall into it. They are sinners who are in imminent danger of judgment at the Parousia (cf. vv 14–15). Here the extent to which Jude's eschatological outlook is governed by the imminent expectation of the primitive church is especially clear.

Those who are to be snatched from the fire are evidently church members who, under the influence of the false teachers, are indulging in sinful behavior, but will repent when their error is pointed out to them. It is not necessary for Jude to explain how his readers are to snatch them from the fire, because it was understood everywhere in the early church that an erring brother must be rebuked and warned in a spirit of brotherly love (Matt 18: 15–17; Luke 17:3; Gal 6:1; 2 Thess 3:15; 1 Tim 5:20; Titus 3:10; Jas 5:19–20; *Did.* 2:7; 15:3).

23. διακρινομένους could here mean "those who are under judgment" (Birdsall, *JTS* 14 [1963] 398), and would refer to those who, remaining unrepentant when reproved by the church, have been excommunicated (cf. 1 Cor 5: 3–5). Although this would make good sense in the context, there are two considerations which may carry some weight against it: (1) It is possible that the false teachers were too dominant in the church(es) for a formal procedure of excommunication to be practicable (Bieder, *TZ* 6 [1950] 75). (2) Jude used the same verb in v 9 in the sense of "dispute," and while that need not determine his use here, it should be noticed that v 9 contains the allusion to Zech 3:2 which probably suggested Jude's allusions to Zech 3:2–4 in vv 22–23. It is therefore quite likely that his earlier use of διακρίνεσθαι was in his mind when he selected it for use here.

The meaning, "those who dispute," makes good sense in the context. Jude refers to those who will not accept the rebuke of their fellow-Christians, but argue against it, trying to justify their behavior by means of the antinomian doctrines which the false teachers were propagating. The people in question will be either the false teachers themselves or disciples of theirs. Probably the two groups which Jude distinguishes in these verses are differentiated not by the degree to which they have been influenced by the false teachers, so much as by their response to the reproof. It is not out of the question that some of the false teachers themselves could be among the first group, the repentant.

Another possible meaning of διακρινομένους is "those who doubt" or "hesitate," but although this meaning is suitable in variants of the text which use the word to describe the first group (see the note on the text above), it is inappropriate in the text we are following, where it describes a group of people who must be treated more cautiously than the first group.

ἐλεεῖτε ἐν φόβῳ, "have mercy with fear." The implication is that those who persist in sin and continue to argue in support of their antinomian behavior constitute a serious danger to Jude's readers. The following phrase will explain that the danger is from contamination by their sin. The "fear" may be fear of this contamination, fear of being influenced by these people (so most commentators), but more probably it is fear of God (Kelly, Green). The motive for avoiding the dangerous influence is fear of God's judgment on sin, since Jude's readers know that antinomian behavior will incur God's judgment. In that case *ἐν φόβῳ* ("with fear") here contrasts with *ἀφόβως* ("without reverence"), which characterized the attitude of the false teachers in v 12.

The danger from these people does not, however, mean that Jude's readers should not continue to love them and to desire their salvation. They are to "have mercy" on them, imitating the divine mercy (Luke 6:36) which they themselves have received (v 1) and expect (v 23). Jude does not say how this mercy is to be expressed in action, but certainly some kind of action, not merely a benevolent attitude, is intended. Perhaps the most likely form of action is prayer (cf. *Did.* 2:7), a resource available even when the danger is such that all contact with a person has to be avoided (Ign. *Smyrn.* 4:1). Whether in this case Jude intends his readers to avoid all dealings with the sinners, so that prayer is the only possible means of having mercy on them, depends on the interpretation of the next phrase.

μισοῦντες καὶ τὸν ἀπὸ τῆς σαρκὸς ἐσπιλωμένον χιτῶνα, "hating even the clothing that has been soiled by the flesh." Probably there is an allusion to Zech 3:3–4, where Joshua is "clothed with filthy garments" (RSV). Again Jude shows no dependence on the LXX (*ἱμάτια ῥυπαρά*), and Chase (*DB*[*H*] 2, 800–1) plausibly suggests that he in fact alludes to the associations of the Hebrew word which is translated "filthy" in Zech 3:3–4 (צוֹאִים).

This word is connected with the words צֵאָה and צֹאָה, which are most often used in the OT to refer to human excrement (Deut 23:14; 2 Kgs 18:27; Prov 30:12; Isa 36:12; Ezek 4:12; in Isa 28:8 צֹאָה refers to drunkards' vomit, and in Isa 4:4 is figurative for wickedness). Jude therefore interprets the "filthy garments" to mean clothes which have been soiled by the body. The *χιτών* ("tunic") was the garment worn next to the skin.

The picture is therefore a vivid and intentionally unpleasant one, which Jude uses to suggest that whatever comes into contact with these people is contaminated by their sins. For a somewhat similar use of the image of soiled clothes, cf. Rev 3:4. Jude's reference to "the flesh" does not imply that he regards the physical body as intrinsically sinful, but rather that he is thinking primarily of the sins of the flesh in which the false teachers indulged (cf. vv 8, 10).

The phrase suggests that Jude's readers, while exercising mercy toward these people, must maintain their abhorrence of their sin and everything associated with it, lest they themselves be infected by it. Most commentators take it to mean that Jude intends his readers to have no contact with them at all, and if his words do not quite require that interpretation (Plummer), it is rendered probable by the practice of the early church attested elsewhere. Avoiding personal contact with other professed Christians was commonly demanded in two cases: those who had been excommunicated for persistence in sin (Matt 18:17; 1 Cor 5:11; Titus 3:10) and false teachers (2 John 10–11; Ign. *Eph.* 7:1; *Smyrn.* 4:1; 7:2). In the former case this was as much for the offender's good as for the church's (1 Cor 5:5), but in the latter case was largely prudential, because the influence of such people was dangerous. This seems to be the kind of situation Jude envisages.

Nevertheless, there is no question of abandoning such people to their fate. That Jude continues to hope for their salvation is suggested not only by ἐλεεῖτε ("have mercy"), but also by the source of his picture of the soiled garments in Zech 3:3–4. Joshua's "filthy garments" were removed and replaced by clean ones, as a symbol of God's forgiveness (3:4–5). Similarly, if Jude's opponents will abandon their sin and all that is associated with it, forgiveness is available for them.

Explanation

In this section Jude comes to the main purpose of his letter, which is to give his readers positive instructions about how, in the situation in which they find themselves, they are to "carry on the fight for the faith" (v 3).

Four injunctions, probably drawn from traditional catechesis, summarize the duties of the Christian life in the Christian community. First, the gospel which they received from the apostles is to be the foundation for the church's life, and on this foundation they must erect the Christian community as the eschatological temple. The church's life built on this foundation will embody the moral implications of the gospel which the antinomians are subverting. Secondly, they must engage in prayer under the inspiration of the Spirit, thereby realizing the true charismatic nature of the church, by contrast with the false claims to inspiration made by the false teachers. Thirdly, they must maintain their place in God's love by obeying his will. Finally, they must live with their hope set on the Lord's coming, when those who remain faithful to him will receive, in his mercy, final salvation. Thus the four injunctions set out a path of obedient discipleship leading to eschatological salvation, by contrast with the path of ungodliness leading to eschatological judgment, which Jude has set out as the way the antinomianism of his opponents is leading them and all who come under their influence. To "fight for the faith" against antinomianism is therefore to resist its influence and not be deflected from the positive tasks of Christian obedience.

Jude continues with instructions on how his readers are to behave toward the false teachers and those who have been influenced by their teaching. The accepted Christian practice toward erring brothers and sisters, pointing out their sin and warning them in a spirit of Christian love, will rescue from the impending judgment those who respond with repentance. But those who refuse to repent and continue, as the false teachers have done, to argue their freedom from accusations of sin, are a serious danger to Jude's readers, who must exercise Christian mercy toward them only in conjunction with the greatest care to avoid being influenced by them. They must fear the judgment of God which they too will incur if they are infected by the sins of these sinners. Just as earlier Jude had compared the false teachers to rocks, close contact with which causes shipwreck (v 12), so now he uses the metaphor of clothes soiled by the body's excretions to suggest the contaminating effect of their sin on everything around them. Probably his advice is therefore that his readers must avoid any dealings with those of the false teachers and their followers who persist in their errors. But he does not give up hope of their salvation: his readers are to continue to exercise Christian love toward them, even if prayer is now the only practical means of doing so. In these instructions Jude combines abhorrence for the sins which the false teachers are promoting and a strong belief in God's judgment on sin with a genuinely Christian concern for the reclamation of even the most obstinate.

Closing Doxology (Jude 24–25)

Bibliography

Crafer, T. W. "The connexion between St Jude and the Magnificat." *The Interpreter* 4 (1908) 187–91. **Deichgräber, R.** *Gotteshymnus und Christushymnus in der frühen Christenheit.* SUNT 5. Göttingen: Vandenhoeck & Ruprecht, 1967. 25–40, 99–101.

Translation

[24] *Now to the one who is able to keep you from stumbling, and to present you without blemish in the presence of his glory, with rejoicing,* [25] *to the only God our Savior, through Jesus Christ our Lord, belong* [a] *glory, majesty, power and authority, before all time, now and for evermore. Amen.*

Notes

[a] The verb is understood, and most translations supply "be," making the doxology a prayer. For the indicative meaning presupposed in this translation, see *Form/Structure/Setting* section below.

Form/Structure/Setting

The letter concludes with a doxology which no doubt follows a traditional liturgical form, though some of its detailed wording may be due to Jude himself.

The basic form of early Christian doxologies is given by Deichgräber (*Gotteshymnus,* 25) as:

ᾧ/τῷ/αὐτῷ/σοὶ ἡ δόξα εἰς τοὺς αἰῶνας. ἀμήν.
("To whom/him/you the glory for ever. Amen.")

It divides into four parts: (1) the person praised, usually in the dative; (2) the word of praise, usually δόξα ("glory"); (3) the indication of time; (4) "Amen" is usually added (in all NT examples except some manuscripts of 2 Pet 3:18), representing the response with which the hearers would make the prayer their own (Deichgräber, *Gotteshymnus,* 25–27). The copula is usually omitted in doxologies, and the question whether an indicative or an optative should be supplied has been discussed (see Deichgräber, *Gotteshymnus,* 30–32). Where a verb is given, it is usually indicative (ἐστιν: Pr Man 15; 1 Pet 4:11; *Did.* 8:2; 9:4; 10:5; *1 Clem.* 58:2), but sometimes optative (Clement of Alexandria, *Quis div. salv.* 42.20) or imperative (*1 Clem.* 32:4). Evidently the users of doxologies could understand them either as statements or as prayers, but the former is really more appropriate to their content, and is sometimes required by the content of a particular doxology (Deichgräber, *Gotteshymnus,* 32). In Jude 24–25 the reference to the past necessitates an indicative meaning.

The basic form of the doxology is capable of expansion in various ways, and Jude's doxology is one of the more elaborate examples. (1) is very often, as in the basic form, a pronoun only, but can be expanded (e.g. Phil 4:20; 1 Tim 1:17; Rev 5:13; *2 Clem.* 20:5). Jude's doxology belongs to a form, of which three other examples are known (Rom 16:25; Eph 3:20; *Mart. Pol.* 20:2), which begins: *τῷ δυναμένῳ* ("to him who is able . . ."). This must reflect a standard liturgical form, though what follows is different in each example (*Mart. Pol.* 20:2 resembles Jude 24 in thought, but not in wording). The expansion has the effect of making this part of the doxology effectively, though not in form, a prayer. Jude's *μόνῳ θεῷ* ("to the only God") is also paralleled in other doxologies in Rom 16:25; 1 Tim 1:17; *2 Clem.* 20:5; cf. 1 Tim 6:15–16; *1 Clem.* 43:6. (2) Though many doxologies have only **δόξα**, many follow the example of 1 Chr 29:11 in listing several attributes (see *Comment* for parallels to those in Jude). Lists of two, three, four, five, and seven are found (Deichgräber, *Gotteshymnus,* 28). The phrase **διὰ Ἰησοῦ Χριστοῦ** ("through Jesus Christ") is often found in doxologies (Rom 16:27; *Did.* 9:4; *1 Clem.* 58:2; 61:3; 64; 65:2; *Mart. Pol.* 14:3; 20:2; cf. 2 Cor 1:20; 1 Pet 4:11), and usually constitutes their only specifically Christian feature. It was added to give a Christian character to the inherited Jewish forms (Deichgräber, *Gotteshymnus,* 39–40). Since in almost all instances (but see *2 Clem.* 20:5) it is the ascription of glory that is "through Jesus Christ," this is probably the sense to be given to the phrase in Jude (see *Comment*). (3) The simple *εἰς τοὺς αἰῶνας* ("for ever") is frequently expanded into fuller formulae for eternity (Deichgräber, *Gotteshymnus,* 27–28; E. von Dobschütz, "Zwei- und dreigliedrige Formeln," *JBL* 50 [1931] 138). Twofold forms referring to past and future (*Tg. Neof.* Exod 15:18; *1 Clem.* 65:2; *Mart. Pol.* 21) or to present and future (2 Pet 3:18; *1 Clem.* 64; *Mart. Pol.* 14:3; *Acts Pet.* 39) are found, but Jude's threefold reference to past, present and future is unparalleled in Jewish and early Christian doxologies.

Several of these features of Jude's doxology Deichgräber regards as marks of a late date, but his reasons are not compelling. (a) A tendency for liturgical formulae to become fuller in later forms (*Gotteshymnus,* 28–29) cannot be invoked as a firm principle for relative dating, since simple forms certainly survived alongside more elaborate ones. (b) Longer lists of attributes are not necessarily later than shorter ones, since 1 Chr 29:11, the basic OT model for doxologies, has a list of five attributes. (c) The anarthrous form of the attributes (also in 1 Tim 1:17; 6:16; *1 Clem.* 64; 65:2; *Mart. Pol.* 14:3; 20:2; 21) cannot be a sure sign of late date, since Deichgräber himself (*Gotteshymnus,* 28 n. 3) has to see Luke 2:14, which he regards as having a Palestinian Hebrew origin, as an exception. (d) The phrase *διὰ Ἰησοῦ Χριστοῦ* ("through Jesus Christ"), Deichgräber claims, occurs only in late examples (*Gotteshymnus,* 40). But, although the authenticity of Rom 16:27 is disputed, 2 Cor 1:20 is probably evidence of the use of this phrase in doxologies in Paul's day (and cf. Rom 1:8; 5:11; 7:25; Col 3:17). (e) The fuller formulae for eternity are not necessarily later, since they have Jewish precedents (Pss 41:14; 106:48; *Tg. Neof.* Exod 15:18). Jude's threefold division of time, though not found in other doxologies, is itself traditional (*2 Apoc. Bar.* 21:9; 23:3; Heb 13:8; Rev 1:4; 4:8), and his use of it can be attributed to his preference for threefold forms of expression.

Deichgräber rightly holds that the doxology must be clearly distinguished from the benediction ("Blessed be/is God . . ."). Doxologies are rare in the literature of ancient Judaism, but common in early Christianity, whereas benedictions, which are relatively rare in early Christian literature (Deichgräber, *Gotteshymnus,* 40–43), were common in Judaism. The reason for this difference is unknown, but there is no doubt that the early Christian doxology did derive from Judaism. Deichgräber holds that in the literature of Palestinian Judaism the fixed form of the doxology as it appears in early Christian literature is not found, but only some steps toward it (1 Chr 29:11; Pss. 22: 28; 62:11–12a; Dan 2:20). These lack the indication of time, and do not, like the Christian doxologies, occur consistently at the *end* of a prayer or sermon. The fixed form of the doxology, as found in the NT, occurs first in the literature of Hellenistic Judaism (4 Macc 18:24; Pr Man 15; and 1 Esd 4:40, a doxology to "truth"; cf. 1 Esd 4:59; 5:58). Deichgräber therefore argues that the NT doxologies derive from the worship of the Hellenistic Jewish synagogues of the Diaspora. (Exceptions to this are the untypical forms found in Luke 2:14; 19:38; Rev 7:10; 19:1, where the doxology is not a closing formula, but an independent "Heilsruf" or "Siegesruf.")

The evidence for Jewish doxologies, however, does not really support this sharp distinction between Palestinian and Hellenistic Judaism. The eternity-formula is found in a Palestinian text, *Pss. Sol.* 17:3, which Deichgräber admits comes close to the Christian doxologies in form (*Gotteshymnus,* 37), in the Targums to Exod 15:18, which are more significant for the origins of the doxology than Deichgräber allows (*Gotteshymnus,* 37 n. 5; McNamara, *Targum,* 204–9, relates them to the doxologies in Revelation), and in Jewish benedictions (1 Chr 29:10; Pss 41:14; 72:19; 89:52; 106:48; Dan 2:20) which will easily have influenced the form of the doxology. It is by no means certain that the Pr Man is of Hellenistic rather than Palestinian Jewish origin (as Deichgräber asserts: *Gotteshymnus,* 38 n. 1). Moreover, while Deichgräber admits that the doxologies in the Apocalypse are evidence of Palestinian Jewish Christian usage (*Gotteshymnus,* 38–39), he mentions only 7:10 and 19:1, which are untypical in form, and omits to mention 1:5–6 and 5:13, which have the regular early Christian form. Thus we certainly cannot exclude a Palestinian Jewish origin for the doxology, and, in view of the other indications of the Palestinian background of Jude's letter, we can regard his doxology as his own adaptation of a form in liturgical use in Palestinian Jewish Christianity.

Doxologies were used to conclude prayers (Pr Man 15; Eph 3:20–21) and sermons (*2 Clem.* 20:5; cf. 1 Esd 4:40). Probably as an extension of the latter use, in early Christianity they also conclude letters (Rom 16:25–27; 2 Pet 3:18; *1 Clem.* 65:2; *Mart. Pol.* 21; *Diogn.* 12:9) or the main part of a letter before the concluding greetings (Phil 4:20; 2 Tim 4:18; Heb 13:21; 1 Pet 5:11; *1 Clem. 64; Mart. Pol.* 20:2). The peculiarity of Jude's letter-ending is the lack of any personal greetings or specifically epistolary conclusion. He ends as he might have ended a spoken homily, with a liturgical doxology.

Comment

24. φυλάξαι ὑμᾶς ἀπταίστους, "to keep you from stumbling," is probably an echo of a common metaphor in the Psalms, where the psalmist describes the disasters from which God preserves him in terms of his feet stumbling or slipping (Pss 38:16; 56:13; 66:9; 73:2; 91:12; 94; 116:8; 121:3). Perhaps in the background lurk the wicked who try to trip up the righteous or lay traps for them to fall into (Pss 140:4–5; 141:9; 142:3). God's ability to "keep" them from stumbling is prominent in Pss 121:3–8; 140:4; 141:9. New Testament references to God's guarding or keeping Christians are 2 Thess 3:3 (φυλάσσειν, "to keep"; perhaps there is here a liturgical background, as in Jude); John 17:11, 15; Rev 3:10 (τηρεῖν); 1 Pet 1:5 (φρουρεῖν); and see *Comment* on v 1. ἄπταιστος is a NT *hapax legomenon* (but cf. the metaphorical use of πταίειν in Rom 11:11; Jas 2:10; 3:2; 2 Pet 1:10), but is used in a rather similar metaphorical way in 3 Macc 6:39 (ἀπταίστους αὐτοὺς ἐρρύσατο, "saved them from disaster"). The general sense is that God will protect Jude's readers from the dangers of falling into the sinful ways of the false teachers and thereby failing to attain to final salvation.

στῆσαι κατενώπιον τῆς δόξης αὐτοῦ ἀμώμους, "to present you without blemish in the presence of his glory." Comparison with the following passages indicates that there is probably a common background in liturgical tradition: 1 Thess 3:13: "so that he may establish your hearts unblamable (ἀμέμπτους) in holiness before (ἔμπροσθεν) our God and Father"; Col 1:22: "in order to present (παραστῆσαι) you holy and blameless (ἀμώμους) and irreproachable before (κατενώπιον) him"; Eph 1:4: "that we should be holy and blameless (ἀμώμους) before (κατενώπιον) him"; Eph 5:27: "that he might present (παραστήσῃ) the church to himself in splendor, without spot or wrinkle or any such thing, that she might be holy and without blemish (ἄμωμος)" (RSV); Pol. *Phil.* 5:2: "likewise must the deacons be blameless (ἄμεμπτοι) before (κατενώπιον) his righteousness" (Loeb trans.); (cf. also 1 Cor 1:8; 1 Thess 5:23). Of these, Jude 24; 1 Thess 3:13; Eph 5:27; and Col 1:22 are eschatological in reference, and all of them use the sacrificial metaphor; Christians are to be presented before God as sacrificial victims without blemish. (For ἄμωμος of sacrificial animals, see, e.g., Exod 29:38; Lev 1:3; 3:1; Heb 9:14; 1 Pet 1:19. For sacrifices presented "before the Lord," cf. Lev 1:3; 3:1, 12.) The word κατενώπιον ("in the presence of," "before") is found in early Christian literature only in the above four passages: Jude 24; Col 1:22; Eph 1:4; Pol. *Phil.* 5:2 (and elsewhere only in LXX).

τῆς δόξης αὐτοῦ, "his glory" is a reverential periphrasis for "God himself" (cf. Tob 12:12, 15; *1 Enoch* 27:2; 63:5; 102:3; 104:1; *T. Abr.* 4 [Rec. B]): God's glory is the radiance of his very being. For this eschatological hope of coming into God's presence, cf. 4 Ezra 7:98; Matt 5:8; Rev 7:15; 22:3–4.

ἐν ἀγαλλιάσει, "with rejoicing." The word ἀγαλλίασις is found only in Jewish and Christian Greek; the phrase ἐν ἀγαλλιάσει occurs in *1 Enoch* 5:9; Luke 1:44; Acts 2:46; *Mart. Pol.* 18:3. "Rejoicing" is a traditional eschatological motif: the jubilation of God's people in the attainment of his purpose (Isa 12:6; 25:9; 60:5; 61:10; Tob 13:13; Bar 4:37; 5:5; 4 Ezra 7:98; *T. Levi* 18:14; *1 Enoch* 5:9; 103:4; *Apoc. Abr.* 29; 1 Pet 4:13; Rev 19:7). Here, in the context of the cultic picture, the eschatological joy is represented as a cultic festival (Schelkle).

25. *μόνῳ θεῷ*, "to the only God." That the God of Israel was the only true God was the distinctive Jewish religious confession, and *μόνος* ("only") was therefore frequently applied to God in Jewish confessional (2 Macc 7:37; 4 Macc 5:24) and liturgical (LXX 4 Kgdms 19:15, 19; Neh 9:6; Pss 82:19; 85:10; Dan 3:45; 1 Esd 8:25; 2 Macc 1:24–25; cf. 4QDibHam 5:8–9; *Apoc. Abr.* 17) contexts (see G. Delling, "ΜΟΝΟΣ ΘΕΟΣ," *Studien zum Neuen Testament und hellenistischen Judentum: Gesammelte Aufsätze 1950–1968* [Göttingen: Vandenhoeck & Ruprecht, 1970] 396–99). Primitive Christianity continued this usage (John 5:44; 17:3; Rev 15:4; cf. E. Stauffer, *New Testament Theology,* tr. J. Marsh [London: SCM Press, 1955] 242–44; Delling, *Studien,* 399–400), and it is not surprising to find *μόνος θεός* ("the only God") in several doxologies, probably following Jewish models (Rom 16:27; 1 Tim 1:17; *2 Clem.* 20:5; cf. 1 Esd 8:25; 1 Tim 6:15–16; *1 Clem.* 43:6). (Jude's *μόνῳ θεῷ σωτῆρι ἡμῶν*, "to the only God our Savior," comprises two distinct phrases and should not be connected with the formula *μόνος σωτήρ*, "only savior": for this formula in Greek religion and in Philo, see Delling, *Studien,* 392, 397.) It is quite unnecessary to see in this phrase opposition to gnostic speculations about the Demiurge (Moffatt, Wand, Kelly).

σωτῆρι ἡμῶν, "our Savior." Again this is a traditional Jewish term for God, translating אלהי ישענו, "the God of our salvation" (*σωτὴρ ἡμῶν* occurs in LXX Pss 64:6; 78:9; 94:1; *Pss. Sol.* 8:33; 17:3; cf. *TDNT* 7, pp. 1012–15). Whereas Christ is quite frequently called *σωτήρ* ("Savior") in early Christian literature, God is rarely so called (only Luke 1:47; 1 Tim 1:1; 2:3; 4:10; Titus 1:3; 2:10; 3:4; *1 Clem.* 59:3). Here at least the term must be a survival of Jewish usage. There is no basis at all for regarding it as peculiarly Hellenistic (Deichgräber, *Gotteshymnus,* 100).

διὰ Ἰησοῦ Χριστοῦ τοῦ κυρίου ἡμῶν, "through Jesus Christ our Lord." It is disputed whether this phrase should be taken with *σωτῆρι ἡμῶν* ("our Savior") (Spitta, Chaine, Grundmann, Green) or with the attributes which follow (Mayor, Bigg, Cantinat, Kelly), i.e., whether Christ mediates salvation to us or mediates the glory and authority of God to him. In favor of the latter, is the use of the phrase in doxologies elsewhere (Rom 16:27; *Did.* 9:4; *1 Clem.* 58:2; 61:3; 64; 65:2; *Mart. Pol.* 14:3; cf. 2 Cor 1:20; 1 Pet 4:11), but this may not be an entirely conclusive argument, since there is also one, admittedly late, doxology (*2 Clem.* 20:5) where "through whom" (i.e., Christ; *δι' οὗ*) belongs in the expansion of the first part of the doxology and refers to God's saving work through Christ, while in the doxology in *Mart. Pol.* 20:2, which closely resembles Jude 24–25, the phrase "through his only child Jesus Christ" (*διὰ τοῦ μονογενοῦς παιδὸς αὐτοῦ Ἰησοῦ Χριστοῦ*) has the same ambiguity as the phrase in Jude. Also in favor of taking the phrase with what follows, is the grammatical awkwardness of attaching it to the noun *σωτῆρι* ("Savior"). On the other hand, it is argued that Christ cannot be regarded as the mediator of glory to God "before all time" (Chaine, Green), but *1 Clem.* 65:2 provides a doxology in which this has to be the case. It can be explained either by the preexistence of Christ (Cantinat; see *Comment* on v 5) or by the lack of precision in this kind of liturgical language (Kelly). Perhaps it is not necessary to choose between the two alternative ways of interpreting the phrase: the phrase may be deliberately ambiguous, combining the two thoughts (an abbreviated form of *διὰ Ἰησοῦ Χριστοῦ, δι᾽ οὗ*, "through Jesus Christ, through whom," which is used in the doxology in *1 Clem.* 58:2; cf. 65:2). If we must choose, the dominant usage in doxologies makes the second alternative the more probable.

δόξα, "glory," is the attribute found in almost all doxologies (1 Tim 6:16; 1 Pet 5:11 are exceptions): it is the essential glory of God's being. Even if the doxology is to be understood as a prayer (which is unlikely) rather than a statement, there can be no question of the worshiper giving God glory which he does not in any case possess.

μεγαλωσύνη, "majesty," occurs in 1 Chr 29:11 (LXX), the basic OT source for the lists of attributes in doxologies, and in doxologies in *1 Clem.* 20:12; 61:3; 64; 65:2; *Mart. Pol.* 20:2; 21 (and cf. LXX Deut 32:3; Sir 39:15). It describes God's "awful transcendence" (Kelly), is used only of God in early Christian literature, and is so characteristic a divine quality as to be sometimes, like "glory," practically a periphrasis for God himself: *1 Enoch* 5:4; *T. Levi* 3:9; Heb 1:3; 8:1; *1 Clem.* 27:4; 36:2; 58:1.

κράτος, "power," is common in doxologies: 1 Tim 6:16; 1 Pet 4:11; 5:11; Rev 1:6; 5:13; *1 Clem.* 64; 65:2; *Mart. Pol.* 20:2 (and cf. *Pss. Sol.* 17:3). It is frequently used of God's power (LXX Job 12:16; Ps 61:13; Isa 40:26; Jdt 9:14; 2 Macc 3:34; 11:4; 3 Macc 1:27; Eph 1:19; etc.).

ἐξουσία, "authority," is otherwise found in a doxology only in the doxology to "truth" in 1 Esd 4:40, but is used of God's power in LXX Dan 4:17; Sir 10:4; Josephus, *Ant.* 5.109; often in Philo; Luke 12:5; Acts 1:7; Rom 9:21; Rev 16:9; Herm. *Mand.* 4:1:11. Its meaning is close to that of *κράτος*, but tends, in biblical usage, to denote the sovereign authority of God as Ruler (cf. *TDNT* 2, 562–74).

Explanation

The first part of Jude's magnificent doxology is in effect a prayer, though a confident prayer, that God will preserve the recipients of the letter from the spiritual disaster with which the false teaching threatens them and bring them to the eschatological destiny he intends for them. Having in the previous section stressed his readers' responsibilities, Jude now assures them of the divine support and protection without which all their efforts will be fruitless.

Drawing on traditional liturgical material, he pictures the last day as the eschatological festival of worship, in which the achievement of God's purposes for his people will take the form of his presentation of them as perfect sacrifices in his heavenly sanctuary, offered up to the glory of God amid the jubilation of the worshipers. All Jude's concerns in the letter, to combat the false teaching for the sake of the health of the church and the Christian obedience of its members, are finally aimed at this goal: that they should in the end be found fit to be a sacrificial offering to God.

This picture appropriately leads to the doxology proper, in which the church acknowledges the greatness of God as he is for all eternity. When the letter was read aloud, the hearers would join in the concluding "Amen."

Bibliography

A. Commentaries

These are referred to throughout the commentary by authors' names only.

Barnett, A. E. "The Epistle of Jude." *The Interpreter's Bible.* vol. 12. New York/Nashville: Abingdon Press, 1957. **Bigg, C.** *A Critical and Exegetical Commentary on the Epistles of St. Peter and St. Jude.* ICC. Edinburgh: T. & T. Clark, 1901. **Boobyer, G. H.** "Jude." *Peake's Commentary on the Bible,* ed. M. Black and H. H. Rowley. London: Thomas Nelson, 1962. **Calvin, J.** *Commentaries on the Catholic Epistles.* Tr. J. Owen. Edinburgh: Calvin Translation Society, 1855. **Cantinat, J.** *Les Epîtres de Saint Jacques et de Saint Jude.* SB. Paris: Gabalda, 1973. **Chaine, J.** *Les épîtres catholiques: La seconde épître de saint Pierre, les épîtres de saint Jean, l'épître de saint Jude.* EBib. 2nd ed. Paris: Gabalda, 1939. **Clement of Alexandria.** *Adumbrationes in epistola Judae catholica.* GCS 3, ed. O. Stählin, 206–9. Leipzig: J. C. Hinrichs, 1909. **Cranfield, C. E. B.** *I & II Peter and Jude.* TBC. London: SCM Press, 1960. **Green, M.** *The Second Epistle General of Peter and the General Epistle of Jude.* TNTC. Leicester: Inter-Varsity Press, 1968. **Grundmann, W.** *Der Brief des Judas und der zweite Brief des Petrus.* THKNT 15. Berlin: Evangelische Verlagsanstalt, 1974. **Hauck, F.** *Die katholischen Briefe.* NTD 10. 3rd ed. Göttingen: Vandenhoeck & Ruprecht, 1937. **James, M. R.** *The Second Epistle General of Peter and the General Epistle of Jude.* CGTSC. Cambridge: Cambridge University Press, 1912. **Kelly, J. N. D.** *A Commentary on the Epistles of Peter and Jude.* BNTC. London: A. & C. Black, 1969. **Knopf, R.** *Die Briefe Petri und Judä.* MeyerK 12. 7th ed. Göttingen: Vandenhoeck & Ruprecht, 1912. **Krodel, G.** "The Letter of Jude." *Hebrews, James, 1 and 2 Peter, Jude, Revelation,* by R. H. Fuller, G. S. Sloyan, G. Krodel, F. W. Danker, E. S. Fiorenza. PC. Philadelphia: Fortress Press, 1977. **Kühl, E.** *Die Briefe Petri und Judae.* Meyer K 12. 6th ed. Göttingen: Vandenhoeck & Ruprecht, 1897. **Lawlor, G. L.** *Translation and Exposition of the Epistle of Jude.* Nutley, N.J.: Presbyterian and Reformed Publishing Co., 1976. **Leaney, A. R. C.** *The Letters of Peter and Jude.* CBC. Cambridge: Cambridge University Press, 1967. **Luther, M.** "Sermons on the Epistle of St. Jude." Tr. M. H. Bertram. *The Catholic Epistles,* ed. J. Pelikan and W. A. Hansen. Luther's Works 30. St Louis, Missouri: Concordia Publishing House, 1967. **Mayor, J. B.** *The Epistle of St. Jude and the Second Epistle of St. Peter.* London: Macmillan, 1907. **Michl, J.** *Die katholischen Briefe.* RNT 8. 2nd ed. Regensburg: Verlag Friedrich Pustet, 1968. **Moffatt, J.** *The General Epistles: James, Peter, and Judas.* MNTC. London: Hodder & Stoughton, 1928. **Pseudo-Oecumenius.** *Epistula Judae apostoli catholica. PG* 119. 703–722. **Plummer, A.** *The General Epistles of St James and St Jude.* ExpB. London: Hodder & Stoughton, 1891. **Plumptre, E. H.** *The General Epistles of St Peter and St Jude.* CBSC. Cambridge: Cambridge University Press, 1892. **Reicke, B.** *The Epistles of James, Peter, and Jude.* AB. New York: Doubleday, 1964. **Schelkle, K. H.** *Die Petrusbriefe, der Judasbrief.* HTKNT 13/2. Freiburg/ Basel/ Vienna: Herder, 1961. **Schlatter, A.** *Die Briefe des Petrus, Judas, Jakobus, der Brief an die Hebräer.* Stuttgart: Calwer Verlag, 1964. **Schneider, J.** *Die Briefe des Jakobus, Petrus, Judas und Johannes: Die katholischen Briefe.* NTD 10. 9th ed. Göttingen: Vandenhoeck & Ruprecht, 1961. **Schrage, W.** *Die "katholischen" Briefe: Die Briefe des Jakobus, Petrus, Johannes und Judas,* by H. Balz and W. Schrage. NTD 10. 11th ed. Göttingen: Vandenhoeck & Ruprecht, 1973. **Sidebottom, E. M.** *James, Jude and 2 Peter.* NCB. London: Thomas Nelson, 1967. **Soden, H. von.** *Hebräerbrief, Briefe des Petrus, Jakobus, Judas.* HKNT 3/2. Freiburg i. B.: J. C. B. Mohr, 1899. **Spitta, F.** *Die zweite Brief des Petrus* *und der Brief des Judas.* Halle a. S.: Verlag der Buchhandlung des Waisenhauses, 1885. **Wand, J. W. C.** *The General Epistles of St. Peter and St. Jude.* WC. London: Methuen, 1934. **Windisch, H.** *Die Katholischen Briefe.* HNT 15. 3rd ed., ed. H. Preisker. Tübingen: J. C. B. Mohr, 1951.

B. Other Works

Berger, K. "Hartherzigkeit und Gottes Gesetz, die Vorgeschichte des anti-jüdischen Vorwurfs in Mc 10^5." *ZNW* 61 (1970) 1–47. **Bauer, W., Arndt, W. F.,** and **Gingrich, F. W.** *A Greek-English Lexicon of the New Testament and Other Early Christian Literature.* 2nd ed., ed. F. W. Gingrich and F. W. Danker. Chicago/London: University of Chicago Press, 1979. **Blass, F., Debrunner, A., Funk, R. W.** *A Greek Grammar of the New Testament and Other Early Christian Literature.* Chicago/London: University of Chicago Press, 1961. **Charles, R. H.** ed. *The Apocrypha and Pseudepigrapha of the Old Testament.* 2 vols. Oxford: Clarendon Press, 1913. **Charles, R. H.** *The Assumption of Moses.* London: A. & C. Black, 1897. **Chase, F. H.** "Jude, Epistle of." *DB(H)* 2, 799–806. **du Plessis, P. J.** "The authorship of the Epistle of Jude." *Biblical Essays:* Proceedings of "Die Ou-Testamentiese Werkgemeenskap in Suid-Afrika," and Proceedings of the Second Meeting of "Die Nuwe-Testamentiese Werkgemeenskap van Suid-Afrika." Potchefstroom, S. Africa: Potchefstroom Herald (Edms.) Beperk, 1966. 191–99. **Ellis, E. E.** "Prophecy and Hermeneutic in Jude." *Prophecy and Hermeneutic in Early Christianity: New Testament Essays.* WUNT 18. Tübingen: J. C. B. Mohr, 1978. 221–36. **Eybers, I. H.** "Aspects of the Background of the letter of Jude." *Neot* 9 (1975) 113–23. **Ginzberg, L.** *The Legends of the Jews.* Tr. P. Radin. Vols. 3 and 6. Philadelphia: Jewish Publication Society of America, 1911, 1928. **Hastings, J.** ed. *A Dictionary of the Bible.* 5 vols. Edinburgh: T. & T. Clark, 1898–1904. **Hennecke, E., Schneemelcher, W.,** and **Wilson, R. McL.** *New Testament Apocrypha.* 2 vols. London: Lutterworth Press, 1963, 1965. **Kittel, G.** *Theological Dictionary of the New Testament.* Tr. G. W. Bromiley. 10 vols. Grand Rapids, Michigan: Eerdmans, 1964–76. **Knibb, M. A.** *The Ethiopic Book of Enoch: A new edition in the light of the Aramaic Dead Sea fragments.* Vol. 2. Oxford: Clarendon Press, 1978. **Lampe, G. W. H.** ed. *A Patristic Greek Lexicon.* Oxford: Clarendon Press, 1961–68. **Laperrousaz, E. M.** *Le Testament de Moïse (généralement appelé "Assomption de Moïse"): Traduction avec introduction et notes.* = *Sem* 19 (1970) 1–140. **Leconte, R.** "Epître de Jude." *DBSup* 4, 1288–91. **McNamara, M.** *The New Testament and the Palestinian Targum to the Pentateuch.* AnBib 27. Rome: Pontifical Biblical Institute, 1966. (Midrash) **Freedman, H.** and **Simon, M.** ed. *Midrash Rabbah.* 10 vols. London: Soncino Press, 1939. **Migne, J. P.** ed. *Patrologiae Cursus Completus.* Series Graeca. 162 vols. Paris: J. P. Migne, 1857–66. **Milik, J. T.** *The Books of Enoch: Aramaic Fragments of Qumrân Cave 4.* Oxford: Clarendon Press, 1976. **Moule, C. F. D.** *An Idiom Book of New Testament Greek.* 2nd ed. Cambridge: Cambridge University Press, 1959. **Moulton, J. H.** *A Grammar of New Testament Greek. Vol. I. Prolegomena.* 3rd ed. Edinburgh: T. & T. Clark, 1908. **Moulton, J. H.** and **Milligan, G.** *The Vocabulary of the Greek Testament illustrated from the papyri and other non-literary sources.* London: Hodder & Stoughton, 1929. **Pagels, E. H.** *The Gnostic Paul: Gnostic Exegesis of the Pauline Letters.* Philadelphia: Fortress Press, 1975. **Pirot, L., Cazelles, H.,** and **Feuillet, A.** ed. *Supplément au Dictionnaire de la Bible.* Paris: Letouzey & Ané, 1928–. **Reicke, B.** *Diakonie, Festfreude und Zelos in Verbindung mit der altchristlichen Agapenfeier.* UUÅ 1951:5. Uppsala: A. B. Lundequistska/ Wiesbaden: O. Harrassowitz, 1951. **Robinson, J. A. T.** *Redating the New Testament.* London: SCM Press, 1976. **Rowston, D. J.** "The Most Neglected Book in the New Testament." *NTS* 21 (1974–75) 554–63. **Rowston, D. J.** *The Setting of the Letter of Jude.* Unpublished doctoral dissertation, Southern Baptist Theological Seminary, Louisville, KY. 1971. **Schelkle, K. H.** "Spätapostolische Briefe als frühkatholisches Zeugnis." *Neutestament-*

liche Aufsätze für J. Schmid, ed. J. Blinzler, O. Kuss, F. Mussner. Regensburg: Verlag Friedrich Pustet, 1963. 225–32. **Selwyn, E. C.** *The Christian Prophets and the Prophetic Apocalypse.* London: Macmillan, 1900. **Spicq, C.** *Agape in the New Testament.* Vol. 2. Tr. M. A. McNamara and M. H. Richter. St Louis/ London: Herder, 1965. **Strack, H. L.** and **Billerbeck, P.** *Kommentar zum Neuen Testament aus Talmud und Midrasch.* 4 vols. Münich: Beck, 1922–28. (Talmud) **Epstein, I.** ed. *The Babylonian Talmud.* 35 vols. London: Soncino Press, 1935–52. **Vermes, G.** *The Dead Sea Scrolls in English.* 3rd ed. Harmondsworth, Middx.: Penguin Books, 1968. **Vermes, G.** "The Decalogue and the Minim." *Post-Biblical Jewish Studies.* SJLA 8. Leiden: E. J. Brill, 1975. 169–77. **Werdermann, H.** *Die Irrlehrer des Judas- und 2. Petrusbriefes.* BFCT 17/6. Gütersloh: C. Bertelsmann, 1913. **White, J. L.** *The Form and Function of the Body of the Greek Letter.* 2nd ed. Missoula, MT: Scholars Press, 1972. **Wisse, F.** "The Epistle of Jude in the History of Heresiology." *Essays on the Nag Hammadi Texts in Honour of Alexander Böhlig,* ed. M. Krause. NHS 3. Leiden: E. J. Brill, 1972. 133–43. **Zahn, T.** *Introduction to the New Testament.* vol. 2. Tr. M. W. Jacobus and others. Edinburgh: T. & T. Clark, 1909.

The Second Letter of Peter

Introduction

Like the Introduction to Jude, this Introduction presupposes the exegetical discussion in the commentary.'

Form and Structure

Second Peter belongs to two literary genres, the letter and the testament. It not only calls itself a letter (3:1), but it is a real letter, whose letter-opening (1:1–2) conforms to the style of the Jewish and early Christian letter. An introductory statement of theme (1:3–11) and an explanation of the occasion for the letter (1:12–15) follow. As in many NT letters, there is a paraenetic section toward the end (3:11–18a), though, like Jude, 2 Peter closes with a doxology alone (3:18b), without any specifically epistolary conclusion or personal greetings. However, it was the letter-opening which was the really essential formal constituent of the ancient letter.

Second Peter is also a genuine letter in that it was written and sent to specific addressees: a church or group of churches which had been (among) the recipients of 1 Peter (3:1) and to which one or more letters of Paul had been addressed (3:15). Thus despite the generality of the address (1:1), it is not a "catholic letter" to all Christians, but a work written for a specific, localized audience. This is also clear from the apologetic content of 2 Peter, which is directed against specific objections to Christian teaching and a group of false teachers with specific characteristics.

However, it is equally clear that 2 Peter belongs to the genre of ancient Jewish literature known to modern scholars as the "farewell speech" or "testament." In the intertestamental period there was a considerable vogue for accounts of the last words of OT heroes, whether as independent works (e.g. *T. Mos., T.12 Patr., T. Job, 1 Enoch* 91–104) or as parts of historical or pseudo-historical works (e.g. Tob 14:3–11; 4 Ezra 14:28–36; *2 Apoc. Bar.* 57–86; *Jub.* 21–22; 35; 36:1–18; *Bib. Ant.* 19:1–5; 24:1–5; 28:3–4, 5–10; 33; *Adam and Eve* 25–29; Josephus, *Ant.* 4.309–19). Such testaments had two main types of content: (1) Ethical admonitions: before his death a patriarch gives to his children or a national leader to his people a definitive summary of his ethical and religious instruction which they are to follow in the future, often with eschatological sanctions attached. (2) Revelations of the future: in accordance with the ancient belief that the last hours of a great man were a time when he was endowed with prophetic knowledge of the future, the hero predicts the future of his descendants or the destiny of his people, often in the form of apocalyptic revelations of the last days, often as a basis for eschatological paraenesis. On these characteristics of Jewish testaments, see especially Stauffer, *Theology*, 344–47; Kolenkow, *JSJ* 6 (1975) 57–71; J. Munck, "Discours d'adieu dans le Nouveau Testament et dans la littérature biblique," in *Aux Sources de la Tradition Chrétienne* (M. Goguel Festschrift; Neuchâtel: Delachaux & Niestlé, 1950) 155–70.

The genre of the farewell discourse was rather naturally applied in the early church to the apostles (Acts 20:17–34; 2 Timothy; *Acts Pet.* 36–39; *Acts John* 106–7; *Acts Thom.* 159–60), and 2 Peter has been widely recognized to be intended as a "testament of Peter" (Munck, "Discours," 162; Spicq, 194; Reicke, 146; Grundmann, 55–56; Knoch, "Vermächtnis," 149–54; Neyrey, *Polemic,* 99–105).

The following passages identify 2 Peter as belonging to this genre: (1) The passage 1:3–11 is in form a miniature homily, which follows a pattern used in the farewell speeches of Ezra (in 4 Ezra 14:28–36) and John (in *Acts John* 106–7) (see *Form/Structure/Setting* section on 1:3–11). In the light of the references back to this passage in 1:12, 15, it is clearly intended as a definitive summary of Peter's ethical and religious teaching, set down for the instruction of readers after his death. (2) 1:12–15 is full of language typical of farewell speeches (see *Comment* on those vv) and explicitly describes the occasion for the writing of 2 Peter as Peter's knowledge of his approaching death and his wish that his teaching be remembered after his death. These two features are standard and almost universal features of the genre. (3) In two passages (2:1–3a; 3:1–4; cf. 3:17a) Peter predicts the rise of false teachers in the churches in the last days following his death (3:4: the death of the "fathers," of whom Peter was one). These four passages, but especially 1:12–15, would leave no contemporary reader in doubt that 2 Peter belonged to the genre of "testament." Perhaps we should also add, as further testamentary features, the Transfiguration as a revelation of the future to Peter (see *Form/Structure/Setting* section on 1:16–18), the apocalyptic prophecy of 3:7, 10, and the eschatological paraenesis of 3:11–15a (see *Form/Structure/Setting* section on 3:11–16).

The rest of 2 Peter is structured around the sections which clearly belong to the testament genre in the following manner. 1:3–11 provides, as the core of Peter's testament, a summary of Peter's definitive teaching of which it is the purpose of his testament to "remind" the readers (1:12–15) and which emphasizes ethics and eschatology and the link between the two. The two sections of prophecy (2:1–3a; 3:1–4) are Peter's predictions of false teachers who will undermine Christian ethics and deny the eschatological expectation. The rest of the letter defends Peter's teaching on ethics and eschatology against the objections raised by these false teachers. There are four passages which reply to a series of objections to the eschatological expectation (1:16–19; 1:20–21; 2:3b–10a; 3:5–10): in one case the false teachers' objection is specifically stated in quotation in Peter's prophecy (3:4; cf. 3:9), in the other three cases it is implicitly contained in the author's denial of it (1:16a, 20b; 2:3b). In addition to these pieces of apologetic argument, there is a long denunciation of the false teachers' libertine behavior (2:10b–22) and, by way of contrast, a passage of eschatological paraenesis which exhorts the readers to holy living on the basis of the eschatological expectation (3:11–16). Thus the two traditional characteristics of the testament—the definitive summary of Peter's ethical and religious message (1:3–11) and the revelations of the future (2:1–3a; 3:1–4)—provide a framework around which is built an apologetic defense of Peter's teaching against the false teachers.

Two further aspects of the use of the testament genre in 2 Peter remain to be considered: its combination with the letter genre, and its pseudepigraphal character. One Jewish example of a testament in the form of a letter is *2 Apoc. Bar.* 78–86. Baruch, having already made his farewell to the people in Judea, responds to their request that he also write to the people in exile, and chaps 78–86 are his farewell letter to the nine and a half tribes, largely consisting of eschatological paraenesis. This letter within the framework of a fictional history is not entirely comparable with 2 Peter, but it highlights the motive for putting a testament into letter form: the testator's desire to communicate over a distance. In most testaments the farewell speech is a homily delivered orally to immediate hearers. The speaker himself is not supposed to have written it down and in fact most testaments are not in the really strict sense pseudepigrapha, represented as having been written by the hero who is making his farewell. They are supposed accounts of oral speeches, reported in writing by an anonymous writer within a (frequently minimal) narrative framework. They are fictional, rather than strictly pseudepigraphal. But *2 Apoc. Bar.* 78–86 reproduces a testament supposedly written by Baruch himself, and the reason for this exception is Baruch's desire to give his last instructions to people who lived far away. (It happens to be set within a narrative framework which in this case is itself pseudepigraphal, told in the first person by Baruch.)

The desire to communicate at a distance is of course the reason for almost all genuine letters, and the desire to communicate religious instruction at a distance was the reason for the apostolic letters of early Christianity. The composition of Peter's testament in the form of a letter was really an obvious combination of genres if the testament were addressed not to the church of Rome, where Peter's life ended, but churches elsewhere. But the combination of genres in this case created a genre with a unique communicative capacity: a testamentary letter could communicate at a distance *in space* (like all letters) and also at a distance *in time,* for in a written testament it is possible explicitly to address not only those who read it immediately but also those who will read it after the testator's death (as 1:12–15 makes very clear). This unique capacity of the testamentary letter would make it uniquely serviceable to a pseudepigrapher. If someone wished to write an apostolic pseudepigraphon to communicate the teaching of the apostles to Christians living after their death, he faced a serious problem of literary genre. In what genre could an apostle be represented as addressing a situation which would exist only after his death? In one sense the letter was the obvious genre to use, since it was the principal genre in which the apostles had written, but letters are naturally addressed to contemporaries. A pseudo-apostolic letter could be addressed to fictional readers in the apostle's lifetime, but then the immediacy of direct address to the real readers is lost. To this dilemma the testamentary letter is the ideal solution. It is almost the only plausible way in which an apostle could be represented as directly addressing readers after his death, in a specific situation which the testament convention of deathbed prophecy allows him to foresee. If 2 Peter is pseudepigraphal, its author has invented the ideal form for his purpose. But we should not neglect the possibility that if Peter himself had really wished to address Christians living after his death, it would also have been the ideal form for his purpose. The question arises whether the debate over the pseudepigraphal character of 2 Peter can be settled on grounds of literary genre alone.

In Jewish usage the testament was a *fictional* literary genre (not usually pseudepigraphal in the strict sense: see above). The farewell discourses in the intertestamental literature were sometimes expansions and elaborations of last words recorded in the OT (e.g. *T. Mos.*), but in most cases they were entirely free invention. It is highly probable that they were normally accepted as such. It is very implausible to suppose that most Jewish readers were so naïve as to read such speeches as accurate historical reports, or that their authors were so naïve as to expect them to be so read. The writers of haggadic midrash were nowhere so free in their expansions of the OT text as in attributing speeches to OT figures. No doubt such speeches were expected to have verisimilitude—to be the *kind* of thing that might well have been said—but anyone who could compare them with the OT text itself must have known that they were an exercise in historical imagination. Farewell speeches were simply a specially popular form of this practice.

Second Peter bears so many marks of the testament genre (especially the conventional testamentary language in 1:12–15) that readers familiar with the genre must have expected it to be fictional, like other examples they knew. If they knew that it came from the Petrine circle in Rome (see section on *Authorship and Pseudonymity*), then they might trust its author to have made a good job of reporting the essence of Peter's teaching, but they would not expect Peter to have written it. At any rate the presumption would be that he had not.

This presumption might perhaps have to be overruled if there were good evidence for genuine Petrine authorship, since it always remains a possibility that someone wishing to write his own testament could have adopted the fictional genre in order to do so. (The Jewish apocalypse was a pseudepigraphal genre, but John, the author of the NT Apocalypse, wrote an apocalypse in his own name.) However, in the case of 2 Peter, the presumption that Petrine authorship is fictional is decisively reinforced for us (and would have been for the original readers too) by two considerations. One is the evidence for date (see section on *Date*), but the other is an additional literary characteristic of the work, which demonstrates that the Petrine authorship was intended to be an entirely *transparent* fiction.

Major sections of the apologetic parts of 2 Peter (2:3b–22; 3:5–10, 16b) are not really written within the testamentary genre, even though they are closely attached to passages which are (2:1–3a; 3:1–4, 15b–16a, 17). They speak of the false teachers and their followers in the present tense, as the author's contemporaries, not in the future tense, as in Peter's prophecies which predict their rise after Peter's death. In other words, the convention of prediction, necessary in a testament, is not maintained, but alternates with passages in which it is abandoned. The explanation that this is carelessness on the author's part is scarcely credible; 2 Peter is not carelessly composed. Nor is it easy to believe that the present tenses are intended to depict the future with vividness, *as though* present. The obvious explanation is that the author feels free to break the conventions of the genre he is using for the sake of a particular literary effect. Deliberate juxtaposition of Peter's prophecies of the false teachers with present-tense accounts of them conveys to 2 Peter's readers the message: these apostolic prophecies are now being fulfilled. It also enables the writer to engage in apologetic argument with the false teachers (as in 3:5). But such deliberate breaches of the fiction of Petrine authorship are possible only if the fiction was a transparent one.

For further consideration of the author's purpose in writing in the form of a testament, see section on *Authorship and Pseudonymity* below.

OUTLINE OF THE STRUCTURE OF 2 PETER

1:1–2	Address and Salutation
1:3–11	Theme: A Summary of Peter's Message
1:12–15	Occasion: Peter's Testament
1:16–18	Reply to Objection 1: (a) Apostolic Eyewitness
1:19	Reply to Objection 1: (b) The Value of OT Prophecy
1:20–21	Reply to Objection 2: The Inspiration of OT Prophecy
2:1–3a	Peter's Prediction of False Teachers
2:3b–10a	Reply to Objection 3: The Certainty of Judgment
2:10b–22	Denunciation of the False Teachers
3:1–4	Peter's Prediction of Scoffers (including Objection 4: v 4)
3:5–7	Reply to Objection 4: (a) The Sovereignty of God's Word
3:8–10	Reply to Objection 4: (b) The Forbearance of the Lord
3:11–16	Exhortation
3:17–18	Conclusion

Language

Second Peter has an even higher proportion of NT *hapax legomena* than Jude, in fact the highest proportion of any NT book (for the proportions, see Chaine, 15). There are fifty-seven words not found elsewhere in the NT. Of these thirty-two are not found in the LXX either (ἀκατάπαστος, 2:14; ἀμαθής, 3:16; ἀμώμητος, 3:14; ἀστήρικτος, 2:14; 3:16; αὐχμηρός, 1:19; βλέμμα, 2:8; βραδύτής, 3:9; διαυγάζειν, 1:19; δυσνόητος, 3:16; ἐγκατοικεῖν, 2:8; ἑκάστοτε, 1:15; ἔκπαλαι, 2:3; 3:5; ἐμπαιγμονή, 3:3; ἐξέραμα, 2:22; ἐπάγγελμα, 1:4; 3:13; ἐπίλυσις, 1:20; ἰσότιμος, 1:1; καυσοῦσθαι, 3:10, 12; κυλισμός, 2:22; μυωπάζειν, 1:9; ὀλίγως, 2:18; παραφρονία, 2:16; παρεισάγειν, 2:1; παρεισφέρειν, 1:5; πλαστός, 2:3; ῥοιζηδόν, 3:10; στηριγμός, 3:17; ταρταροῦν, 2:4; τεφροῦν, 2:6; τολμητής, 2:10; φωσφόρος, 1:19; ψευδοδιδάσκαλος, 2:1; also σειρός if this reading is preferred in 2:4), while twenty-five occur in the LXX (where LXX references are given they are the only LXX occurrences: ἄθεσμος, 2:17; 3:17; 3 Macc 5:16; 6:26; ἅλωσις, 2:12; Jer 27:46; ἀποφεύγειν, 1:4; 2:18, 20; Sir 22:22; ἀργεῖν, 2:3; LXX 6 times; βόρβορος, 2:22; Jer 45:6; ἔλεγξις, 2:16; Job 21:4; 23:2; ἐντρυφᾶν, 2:13; ἐξακολουθεῖν, 1:16; 2:2, 15; LXX 6 times; ἐπόπτης, 1:16; κατακλύζειν, 3:6; λήθη, 1:9; μεγαλοπρεπής, 1:17; μέγιστος, 1:4; μίασμα, 2:20; μιασμός, 2:10; Wis 14:26; 1 Macc 4:43; μνήμη, 1:15; μῶμος, 2:13; ὀμίχλη, 2:17; παρανομία, 2:16; σειρά, 2:4, unless the reading σειρός is preferred; στρεβλοῦν, 3:16; ταχινός, 1:14; 2:1; LXX 6 times; τήκεσθαι, 3:12; τοιόσδε, 1:17; 2 Macc 11:27; 15:12; ὗς, 2:22).

Of the thirty-two biblical *hapax legomena,* fifteen are found in other Hellenistic Jewish writers of the period (*Sib. Or., Ep. Arist.,* Philo, Josephus) (ἀμαθής, ἀμώμητος, βλέμμα, βραδύτης, διαυγάζειν, ἐγκατοικεῖν, ἔκπαλαι, ἐπάγγελμα, ἐπίλυσις, ἰσότιμος, παρεισάγειν, πλαστός, τεφροῦν, τολμητής, φωσφόρος), and two more in other Jewish versions of the OT (κυλισμός: Prov 2:18 θ; ὀλίγως: Isa 10:7 Aquila). This may begin to suggest that 2 Peter belongs to the sphere of Hellenistic Jewish Greek (like James, 1 Peter, Hebrews and the Pastorals, according to A. Wifstrand, "Stylistic Problems in the Epistles of James and Peter," *ST* 1 [1948] 170–82). Since the relevant context in early Christian literature in which 2 Peter should be placed is not the NT alone, but also the Apostolic Fathers, it should also be noted that seventeen of 2 Peter's NT *hapax legomena* occur in the Apostolic Fathers, though only four of these are biblical *hapax legomena* (βλέμμα, Herm. *Sim.* 6:2:5; δυσνόητος, Herm. *Sim.* 9:14:4; ἐγκατοικεῖν, *Barn.* 1:4; ἐπίλυσις, 6 times in Herm. *Sim.* 5–9). One more of the biblical *hapax legomena* occurs in the Greek text of the *Apoc. Pet.* (αὐχμηρός, *Apoc. Pet.* A 21).

Despite the large number of rare words in Jude, it is relevant to notice that 2 Peter has, in taking over material from Jude, taken over few rare words. Of thirty-eight words in 2 Peter which occur only once or twice elsewhere in the NT, only four occur in Jude and these are the only four words which are found exclusively in Jude and 2 Peter in the NT (ἀσεβεῖν, ἐμπαίκτης, συνευωχεῖσθαι, ὑπέρογκος, and of these ἀσεβεῖν is probably not borrowed from Jude). This suggests that, despite its dependence on other sources as well as Jude, few of 2 Peter's rare words are likely to derive from sources. They belong to the author's own vocabulary.

Of course, some of the *hapax legomena* are relatively common words (e.g. ἀμαθής, ἀργεῖν, βραδύτης, λήθη, μέγιστος, μίασμα, μνήμη, ὁμίχλη, παρανομία, ὗς), but some are very rare, including most of the thirteen not yet noted as occurring anywhere outside 2 Peter. There are three words not known elsewhere in extant Greek literature: ἀκατάπαστος, which is the best reading in 2:14 but must probably be explained as an error for ἀκατάπαυστος, which most MSS have but which is itself rare; ἐμπαιγμονή, 3:3, perhaps the author's own formation from ἐμπαίζειν (cf. ἐμπαίκτης, 3:3; Jude 18; Isa 3:4; ἐμπαιγμός, Heb 11:36; Ezek 22:4; 2 Macc 7:7; Sir 27:28; Wis 12:25; *Pss. Sol.* 2:11; ἔμπαιγμα, Ps 37:8; Isa 66:4); παραφρονία, 2:16, which is probably used instead of παραφροσύνη or παραφρόνησις (Zech 12:4, very rare) for the sake of the assonance with παρανομία. As Mayor suggests (lxii), several of 2 Peter's rare forms may be used in preference to commoner forms for the sake of euphony and rhythm, to which our author is sensitive. This may help to account for the rare κυλισμός and ἐξέραμα (2:22), as well as perhaps for ταρταροῦν (2:4) instead of the only slightly more common καταταρταροῦν. Other rare words are ἀστήρικτος (2:14; 3:16; but this belongs to the στηρίζειν word-group, a favorite of our author's, as does the biblical hapax στηριγμός, 3:17); καυσοῦσθαι (3:10, 12; elsewhere used only of fever by medical writers); μυωπάζειν (1:9 is the first known occurrence); ῥοιζηδόν (3:10); ψευδοδιδάσκαλος (2:1 is the first known occurrence; then Justin, *Dial.* 82:1, probably dependent on 2 Pet 2:1; cf. ψευδοδιδασκαλία, Pol. *Phil.* 7:2; but it is an obvious formation by analogy with other ψευδο- compounds in early Christian use, such as ψευδοπροφήτης).

The list of *hapax legomena* includes enough extremely rare words to show that the author is widely read, and fond of rather literary and poetic, even obscure words. They do not on the whole seem to be used arbitrarily where common words would suffice as well, but contribute to the author's literary and rhetorical effects. Thus ταρταροῦν, with its mythological background, is highly appropriate in 2:4; καυσοῦσθαι, and the onomatopoeic ῥοιζηδόν contribute to the poetic quality of the apocalyptic imagery in 3:10; the use of ἐμπαιγμονῇ with ἐμπαῖκται in 3:3 creates, not a genuine Hebraism, but an effective Septuagintalism; στηριγμός and ἀστήρικτος form with στηρίζειν a word-group which the author uses almost technically; μυωπάζειν is used (1:9) to form, with τυφλός, one of the author's characteristic pairs of near-synonyms, which he uses for rhetorical effect; 1:19, with the three relatively rare terms αὐχμηρός, φωσφόρος, διαυγάζειν, is deliberately poetic and effectively so; δυσνόητος and στρεβλοῦν (3:16) seem exactly the right words. There are, however, some instances where nothing but preference for a less common or more literary word seems to be operating: ἀμώμητος (3:14) instead of ἄμωμος; σπουδὴν παρεισφέρειν (1:5) instead of the common εἰσφέρειν. But what writer with literary pretensions is not occasionally guilty of this? It cannot really be said that the author *mis*uses words (the list of "solecisms," given by Chase, *DB*(*H*) 3, pp. 807–8, presupposes too much confidence in our knowledge of usage; cf. Mayor, lx–lxi).

The incidence of rare words is part of a general impression 2 Peter gives of aiming at ambitious literary effect (cf. Chase, *DB*(*H*) 3, p. 808). Moulton speaks of "an artificial dialect of high-sounding words learnt from rhetoricians and books"; "the general style is far removed from the language of daily life" (*Grammar* 2, pp. 28, 6). The author is certainly fond of rather grandiose language (cf. 1:3–4, 16–17), and has a highly characteristic stylistic habit of using pairs of synonyms or near-synonyms, sometimes as hendiadys, often apparently as a rhetorical device to increase the effect (1:3, 4, 8, 9, 10, 16, 17; 2:10, 11, 13; 3:7, 11, 14, 16). He also has a habit of repeating words. This is quite different in function from Jude's catchword technique. Sometimes the repeated words are the author's semitechnical religious terminology (ἀστήρικτος, εὐσέβεια, τηρεῖν, φθορά, προσδοκᾶν, ἐπίγνωσις, ἀπωλεία) and occasionally there is a deliberate echo or word-play (μισθὸς ἀδικίας, 2:13, 15; σπουδήν, 1:5 and σπουδάσατε, 1:10), but often there seems to be no literary intention in the repetition. It is simply that a rather unusual word has taken the author's fancy and he likes to use it more often than one would normally expect (ἀποφεύγειν, 1:4; 2:18, 20; ἐξακολουθεῖν, 1:16; 2:2, 15; δελεάζειν, 2:14, 18; ἔκπαλαι, 2:3; 3:5; δωρεῖσθαι, 1:3–4; ἐπιχορηγεῖν, 1:5, 11; ἐπάγειν, 2:1, 5; σπουδάζειν, 1:10, 15; 3:14; ταχινός, 1:14; 2:1; less remarkable examples in Bigg, 225–26; Chase, *DB*(*H*) 3, p. 808). This scarcely implies that his vocabulary is "poor and inadequate" (Chase). But it suggests a stylist rather easily captivated by the striking word and in danger of overworking it. The habit is found to a small extent in most writers; in 2 Peter it seems indulged to excess.

Second Peter's Greek style is not to the taste of many modern readers: "at times pretentiously elaborate" (Kelly, 228); "a striving after the pompous phrase" (Turner, in Moulton, *Grammar* 4, p. 142); "a somewhat artificial piece of rhetoric" (Chase, *DB*(*H*) 3, p. 809). Abbott went so far as to dub it "Baboo Greek," comparing it with a ludicrous example of Indian English (*Exp* 2/3 [1882] 204–19; and cf. his *Contrast*), but this was certainly a misconception of the writer's literary competence. As Reicke points out (146–47), 2 Peter must be related to the "Asiatic" style of Greek rhetoric which was coming into fashion in 2 Peter's time, and which, with its love of high-sounding expressions, florid and verbose language, and elaborate literary effects, was an artificial style which Reicke aptly compares with European baroque. If 2 Peter's language can seem bombastic and pompous to us, it must be judged by the taste of its age and circle, and we should not too quickly decide that the writer overreached himself in his literary ambition. In any case, there are undoubtedly successful passages, such as 1:19 and 2:12–16 (for the literary devices used there see the *Form/Structure/Setting* section on 2:10b–16), and if the long and complicated sentences are sometimes tortuously obscure (1:3–4; 3:5–6), 2:4–10 is in its own way effective.

According to Moulton the language "is employed with the uneasy touch of one who has acquired the language in later life" (*Grammar* 2, p. 28). It is difficult to judge how far this impression results from the author's adoption of an artificial literary style, but the poverty of connecting particles (Chase, *DB*(*H*) 3, p. 808), the meager use of prepositions, the tendency to ambiguity and obscurity (Turner, in Moulton, *Grammar* 4, p. 141), and what Mayor calls "an illiterate use of the anarthrous noun" (xxxiv), may point in this direction. On the other hand, it is not clear whether there are any genuine Semitisms, i.e. usages which betray a native Semitic speaker, or only Septuagintalisms which belong to the writer's deliberate style (cf. genitive of quality in place of adjective: *ἐπιθυμίᾳ μιασμοῦ*, 2:10; *ὑπέρογκα ματαιότητος*, 2:18; the use of *πᾶσα . . . οὐ*, 1:20, for *οὐδεμία*; *ὀπίσω σαρκὸς πορεύεσθαι*, 2:10; *ἐπ' ἐσχάτων τῶν ἡμερῶν*, 3:3; *κατάρας τέκνα*, 2:14; omissions of the article with a definite noun before a genitive could reflect the Hebrew construct state (Chaine, 18) but the author's use of the article is too erratic for this to be certain; *ἐν ἐμπαιγμονῇ ἐμπαῖκται*, 3:3, is a clear case of an expression which is only an imitation Septuagintalism, see *Comment; ἐν τῇ φθορᾷ . . . φθαρήσονται*, 2:12, is usually cited, but is not really even a Septuagintalism, see *Comment;* among Semitic literary devices, note also the synonymous parallelism in 2:3b; the *Tobspruch* in 2:21; the chiastic structure in 1:16–2:3; 3:4–10). A native Semitic speaker cannot be ruled out, but another possibility which should be considered, and to which the frequent improper use of the anarthrous noun might point, is a native Latin speaker (suggested, but not followed up, by Salmon, *Introduction,* 637n.; Reicke, 147). This would suit the probable Roman origin of 2 Peter (see *Authorship and Pseudonymity*).

Literary Relationships

This section includes a variety of different kinds of literary relationships. In many cases there are implications for the date and character of 2 Peter, and these will be pointed out.

1. *Old Testament*

Second Peter is not as saturated in OT allusions as Jude is, but neither are they quite as sparse as is sometimes claimed. The following are certain or very probable allusions: 1:17–18 (Ps 2:6–7); 1:19 (Num 24:17); 2:2 (Isa 52:5); 2:5 (Gen 6:17); 2:6 (Gen 19:29); 2:15–16 (Num 22:21–35); 2:22 (Prov 26:11); 3:5 (Gen 1:1); 3:8 (Ps 90 [LXX 89]:4); 3:9 (Hab 2:3); 3:10, 12 (Isa 34:4); 3:12 (Isa 60:22); 3:12–14 (Hab 2:3); 3:13 (Isa 65:17). Admittedly many of these allusions seem to be drawn by the author from sources he used: this is most probably the case in 1:17–18; 2:22; and the whole passage 3:8–13. Allusions which are possible, but not certain, are: 1:11 (Dan 7:27); 1:17 (Ps 8:5 [LXX 6]; Dan 7:14); 1:19 (Cant 2:17).

Unlike Jude, 2 Peter's allusions are habitually to the LXX. The following correspond to the language of the LXX: 1:11 (Dan 7:27 *θ*, LXX); 1:17 (Ps 8:6); 1:19 (Num 24:17); 2:2 (Isa 52:5); 2:5 (Gen 6:17); 2:6 (Gen 19:29); 3:12 (Isa 34:4); 3:13 (Isa 65:17). In the following cases the allusion is certainly not to the LXX version: 1:19 (Cant 2:17); 2:22 (Prov 26:11); 3:9, 12–14 (Hab 2:3); 3:12 (Isa 60:22), but in all except the first of these cases the author has probably taken the allusion from an intermediate source.

As evidence for the author's familiarity with the LXX, we should add the use of typically LXX phrases (e.g. *πορεύεσθαι ὀπίσω*, 2:10; *ἐπ' ἐσχάτων τῶν ἡμέρων*, 3:3; *ποῦ ἐστιν*; 3:4).

We may add that the author shows familiarity with extrabiblical Jewish haggadic traditions (2:4–5, 7–8, 15–16).

2. *Jewish Pseudepigrapha*

In the Introduction to Jude, we noted his allusions to Jewish apocryphal works as a prominent feature of his letter. These allusions are almost entirely absent from 2 Peter. Working on the assumption that 2 Peter is dependent on Jude (see section 4), we find that Jude's verbal echoes of *1 Enoch* in Jude 6 have disappeared in the rewriting in 2 Pet 2:4, though the allusion to the story of the Watchers (itself much more widespread than *1 Enoch*) remains (and if we read σειροῖς rather than σειραῖς, we have to assume that the author had independent access to traditions which are found in *1 Enoch*). Hardly anything of Jude's debt to *1 Enoch* in Jude 12–13 remains in 2 Pet 2:17, while Jude's explicit quotation from *1 Enoch* in Jude 14–15 is wholly absent from 2 Peter. We cannot be quite sure how deliberate these omissions are. In 2 Pet 2:4, 17 the author has probably not recognized Jude's allusions to *1 Enoch* and they have been accidentally lost in his rewriting. It is possible that he simply found no use for Jude 14–15 (see *Form/Structure/Setting* section on 3:1–4). But in 2 Pet 2:11, Jude 9 has apparently been misunderstood and its point generalized so as to eliminate the reference to the story of Michael and the devil in the *T. Mos.* In this case, at least, we can be sure that the author of 2 Peter has deliberately avoided taking over Jude's reference to apocryphal material. (The claim that 2 Pet 2:3 is dependent on *T. Mos.* 7:6, and 2 Pet 2:13 on *T. Mos.* 7:4, 8, is discussed and rightly rejected by E.-M. Laperrousaz, *Le Testament de Moïse* = *Sem* 19 [1970] 63–66.)

These phenomena have commonly been explained as evidence that the author of 2 Peter *disapproved* of Jude's use of apocryphal works, and this is said to reflect 2 Peter's second-century date: "II Peter is already reluctant to use this literature, whereas Jude has a naïve attitude toward it" (Kümmel, *Introduction,* 431; so also Schelkle, 177, 220–21; Kelly, 227; Grundmann, 104; Käsemann, "Apologia," 173). Second Peter is thought to reflect a later and stricter view of the canon of Scripture, which makes allusion to non-authoritative works such as *1 Enoch* and the *T. Mos.* unsuitable. However, this explanation ignores the facts about early Christian use of apocryphal works. Although the *T. Mos.* seems never to have been well-known in Christian circles, in the case of *1 Enoch* the evidence shows that, whereas there are very few allusions to it in first-century Christian literature, in the second century it became one of the most popular books in the Christian church. Second-century writers freely allude to it (*Barn.* 4:3; 16:5–6; Papias, *ap.* Andr. Caes., *In Apoc.* 34.12: Athenagoras, *Apol.* 24–26; Justin, *2 Apol.* 5; *Dial.* 79.1; Tatian, *Oratio,* 8–9, 20; *Ap. John* 29:16–30:2; Irenaeus, *Adv. Haer.* 1.10.1; 1.15.6; 4.16.2; 4.36.4; *Proof* 18; Clem. Alex., *Eclog. Proph.* 2.1; 53.4; *Strom.* 5.1.10.2; 1.17.81.4; Tertullian, *De Idol.* 3, 9, 15; *De Cult. Fem.* 1.2; 2.10; *De Orat.* 22.5; *Adv. Marc.* 5:18; *De Virgin. Vel.* 7–8; cf. H. J. Lawlor, "Early Citations from the Book of Enoch," *JP* 25 (1897) 164–225; A.-M. Denis, *Introductions aux Pseudépigraphes grecs d'Ancien Testament* [SVTP 1; Leiden: E. J. Brill, 1970] 20–24). No doubts about the authority of *1 Enoch* are recorded before Tertullian (*De Cult. Fem.* 1.3) and Origen (*C. Cels.* 5:54; *Comm. in Joh.* 6.25), and such doubts seem only to have become common in the fourth century. If the author of 2 Peter disapproved of *1 Enoch* he is most unlikely to have lived in the second century.

What the evidence seems to indicate is that until the early second century

1 Enoch was not widely known in Christian circles. It circulated only in those Palestinian Christian circles which Jude represents, where it was read in Aramaic, and may not yet have been translated into Greek. It may be that the production of the Greek version accounts for its growing popularity in the second century.

The probability is that the author of 2 Peter omitted Jude's quotation from *1 Enoch* and his allusion to the *T. Mos.*, not because he disapproved of these works, but because he was unfamiliar with them or at least assumed his readers would be unfamiliar with them. Without knowledge of these works, the material in Jude 9 and 14–15 would only have been puzzling (whereas the main outline of the story of the Watchers, to which 2 Pet 2:4 alludes, was well-known to Jews and Christians who had never read *1 Enoch*). In relation to *1 Enoch,* this conclusion points to an earlier rather than a later date for 2 Peter, before the second-century Christian vogue for *1 Enoch.*

The conclusion that the author of 2 Peter did not disapprove of Jewish apocryphal works on principle is confirmed by the probability that he himself employed one as his source in 3:4–13. In the commentary on those vv we have argued that 2 Peter is there dependent on a Jewish apocalypse, from which quotations are probably to be found in *1 Clem.* 23:3–4; *2 Clem.* 11:2–4; 16:3; and perhaps also *1 Clem.* 23:5; 27:4. This apocalypse was evidently popular in the Roman church of that period, and may well have been the *Book of Eldad and Modad* which Hermas quotes (*Vis.* 2:3:4). It would be useful if this work could be dated. We know that it was concerned with the problem of eschatological delay. Since this problem became acute in Jewish apocalyptic especially after the fall of Jerusalem in A.D. 70, and since the argument of 2 Pet 3:9 is paralleled especially in Jewish discussion in the post-70 period (see Bauckham, *TynB* 31 [1980] 3–36), it is possible that *Eldad and Modad* was one of the Jewish apocalypses produced in the aftermath of the catastrophe of A.D. 70.

3. *Other Jewish Writings*

Abbott (*Exp* 2/3 [1882] 49–63; *Contrast,* 39–41) argued that 2 Peter was dependent on Josephus. Farrar (*Exp* 2/3 [1882] 401–23; *Exp* 3/8 [1888] 58–69) thought Abbott had proved a literary relationship, but suggested that Josephus might be dependent on 2 Peter. However, Abbott's case was convincingly refuted by Salmon (*Introduction,* 638–53; cf. also Mayor, cxxvii–cxxix; James, xxv; Fillion, *DB*(*V*) 5, cols. 409–10). Some of the resemblances (in Josephus' account of Moses' last words) belong to the literary conventions of the "testament" genre (see commentary on 1:12–15), others to the literary Greek of the period and the ideas of Hellenistic Judaism.

Abbott (*Exp* 2/3 [1882] 54–56) also argued for 2 Peter's dependence on Philo (and cf. Mayor, cxxix–cxxx), but again a common background in the literature of Hellenistic Judaism is sufficient to explain the resemblances (see especially *Comment* on 1:20–21). However, these resemblances do highlight 2 Peter's closeness to Hellenistic Jewish literature, as some general resemblances to the *Sib. Or.* also indicate (see *Comment* on 2:5; 3:6–7, 10). That the author had read some of Philo's works is not at all improbable, even though it cannot be proved.

4. *Jude*

That some kind of close relationship exists between 2 Peter and Jude is obvious to all readers.The resemblances are largely between Jude 4–13, 16–18 and 2 Pet 2:1–18; 3:1–3. (These passages are given in parallel at the appropriate points in the *Form/Structure/Setting* sections of the commentary on 2 Peter.) Although various more tenuous points of contact in the earlier and later parts of the letters have often been pointed out (cf. e.g. the list in Fornberg, *Early Church,* 34), none of them is very likely to be more than accidental, except perhaps Jude 5 and 2 Pet 1:12. Precise verbal correspondence between the two works is relatively sparse (much more so than in the "Q" pericopes of Matthew and Luke, e.g.), but it is sufficient and sufficiently striking to require an explanation at the level of *literary* relationship (only Reicke, 190, seems to think an oral common source could account for them).

Four explanations have been offered (and logically these are almost the only four possible): (1) Jude is dependent on 2 Peter (so Luther and many older commentators; Spitta, 381–470, has the fullest argument; Zahn, *Introduction,* 250–51, 265–67, 285; Bigg, 216–24; Falconer, *Exp* 6/6 [1902] 218–24). (2) 2 Peter is dependent on Jude (so most modern commentators; full arguments for this position may be found in Mayor, i–xxv; Chaine, 18–24; Sidebottom, 65–69; Grundmann, 75–83). (3) Both are dependent on a common source. Robson (*Studies*) held that 2 Peter is a composite work put together from various sources, including genuine Petrine fragments and a "prophetic discourse," of which Jude also made use. Reicke (148, 189–90) thought of a common "sermonic pattern," perhaps oral, behind the two works, and Green (50–55) of an anti-heretical tract (cf. also Spicq, 197 n.1). (4) Common authorship is the hypothesis of Robinson (*Redating,* 192–95; his position was anticipated by Leaney in R. Davidson and A. R. C. Leaney, *Biblical Criticism* [PGMT 3; Harmondsworth, Middx.: Penguin Books, 1970] 319), who suggests that Jude wrote both works. Guthrie, *Introduction,* 919–27, is a good summary of the arguments for (1), (2) and (3).

Common authorship is implausible because of the considerable differences of style (see section on *Language* in both Introductions) and background (the Palestinian Jewish character of Jude, the Hellenistic character of 2 Peter), and also because it is difficult to believe that a writer would have used his own work in the way in which the author of 2 Peter uses Jude (see, e.g., the *Comment* on 2 Pet 2:11, 13, 17).

A common source is a somewhat more attractive possibility. Since Jude's midrash (vv 5–19) is explicitly based on traditional material with which his readers were already familiar (v 5), it would have some plausibility if the parallels were limited to Jude's midrash section. But the undeniable relationship between Jude 4 and 2 Pet 2:1–3 makes this view less likely. There is some force in the usual objection to this view, that the common source would have had to have covered so much of the content of Jude and Jude's own contribution would have been so small, that it is hard to see why he bothered. However, this argument loses a good deal of its force in the light of the view argued in the commentary on Jude, that the *most* important part of Jude, which fulfills the author's main purpose in writing, is the appeal (vv

20–23). These vv are precisely those (together with the opening vv 1–3 and the closing doxology) which Jude would have added to the hypothetical source. This is an intelligible procedure and the possibility of a common source cannot be entirely ruled out.

However, since it is a more complicated hypothesis than that of direct dependence, we must have good reason for preferring it to the latter. Its advocates seem to offer no such reason. It is a fallacy to suppose that it explains more clearly the *differences* between Jude and 2 Peter in the similar passages. Second Peter's style is so consistent that its author must in any case have rewritten his source fairly freely; it is as easy to suppose that he rewrote Jude as that he rewrote the hypothetical common source. The common source and Jude would not have been sufficiently different for the theory of a common source to have any advantage over that of 2 Peter's dependence on Jude. It could perhaps have advantages over the theory of Jude's dependence on 2 Peter, since it might be easier to imagine Jude borrowing from the common source than borrowing from 2 Peter. But it is likely to prove attractive only if there are strong reasons for dating 2 Peter before Jude.

The most important literary reason for preferring 2 Peter's dependence on Jude to the opposite hypothesis is that this commentary shows Jude 4–18 to be a piece of writing whose detailed structure and wording has been composed with exquisite care, whereas the corresponding parts of 2 Peter, while by no means carelessly composed, are by comparison more loosely structured. Jude's careful midrashic structure is entirely absent from 2 Peter, along with most of his many allusions to the OT and to *1 Enoch,* and the technique of catchword connections. By comparison, 2 Pet 2:3b–10a has a deliberate, though simple, literary structure, but 2:10b–18 is fairly formless. There are only a few biblical allusions (2:2, 5–6) different from those in Jude. It is reasonably easy to see how, e.g., Jude 6–8 could have been rewritten in a new literary form, with a slightly different purpose, in 2 Pet 2:3b–10a, and how an author who failed to perceive or was not interested in the midrashic structure and allusions of Jude 8c–16 could have revised the material in writing a straightforward passage of denunciation in 2 Pet 2:10b–18. It is much more difficult to imagine Jude constructing his elaborate midrash with 2 Pet 2 before him. It is easy to see how the author of 2 Peter could have seen Jude 8c–16 as useful material for composing a denunciation of the false teachers' sins, but it is difficult to see why it should have occurred to Jude to find in 2 Pet 2:10b–18 a quarry for material to use in constructing a midrash designed to show that the false teachers and their doom have been predicted in Scripture. There are cases where a more complex literary work is based on a simpler one, and *a priori* that might even seem a more likely procedure, but consideration of this particular case seems to indicate that it must be one in which the more complex work is prior. But one must judge for oneself in reading the commentary.

Only recently have the insights of redaction criticism been brought to the study of the relationship between Jude and 2 Peter (Fornberg, *Early Church,* chap 3; Neyrey, *Polemic,* chap 3; cf. also Danker, 89–90; Cavallin, *NovT* 21 [1979] 263–70). The attempts to study the details of the parallel passages in order to determine priority have always, at least in a rudimentary way, involved considerations of redaction, but usually without sufficient awareness of the possibility that an author may be adapting earlier material for a new purpose. The common assumptions that both letters were written to combat similar or even identical heretics and reflect a similar background have particularly hindered an accurate understanding of the differences between the two letters in the parallel passages. Both Neyrey and Fornberg are led by redaction-critical investigation to recognize that the two letters derive from different situations, oppose different adversaries, and therefore make appropriate changes to the material they have in common. Both Neyrey and Fornberg assume the priority of Jude as a working hypothesis, and their redaction criticism therefore consists in explaining 2 Peter's redactional treatment of Jude. The same procedure is followed in this commentary.

Fornberg thinks that by this method he has "refuted" the theory of the priority of 2 Peter (*Early Church,* 58), but this is probably too strong a conclusion. He has shown that 2 Peter's redaction of Jude is intelligible, but not that Jude's redaction of 2 Peter is unintelligible or less intelligible. Redaction criticism could *demonstrate* the priority of Jude only by considering at each point the *relative* plausibility of a redaction of Jude by 2 Peter and of a redaction of 2 Peter by Jude, and then calculating the overall relative plausibility of the two possibilities. But this would be a very complex task, because there is a great deal of room for differing interpretations of redactional changes. Neyrey, Fornberg and I disagree over the interpretation of many of 2 Peter's redactional alterations of Jude. One may produce—as I hope this commentary does produce—a convincing interpretation of 2 Peter's use of Jude, but one cannot be quite sure that an equally convincing interpretation of Jude's use of 2 Peter is impossible. No one since Spitta and Bigg has attempted it, but the analogy with Synoptic criticism perhaps suggests that their view may be ripe for revival.

Despite these qualifications, on present evidence the case for 2 Peter's dependence on Jude is a good one, and to realize its strength the reader should study the relevant sections of the commentary on 2 Peter. Moreover, the case for dating 2 Peter later than Jude does not depend on their literary relationship, but is strong on other grounds alone (see section on *Date* in both Introductions).

Finally, it should be carefully observed that the literary relationship between 2 Peter and Jude does not justify the common habit of classing these two works together as similar works, deriving from the same background and context, displaying the same theological outlook. The reuse of some of the material in one work by the writer of another no more proves that in this case than it does in the case of, e.g., Kings and Chronicles, or Mark and Luke. One clear result of the exegesis in this commentary is to show that Jude and 2 Peter are very different works, from very different historical contexts.

5. *1 Peter*

The difference in vocabulary and style between 1 and 2 Peter has been observed at least since Jerome (*Ep.* 120.11), whose solution to the problem this raises—that Peter used two different "interpreters"—has also been the usual resort of those who maintain Peter's authorship, in some sense, of both letters.

Mayor's attempt—to demonstrate statistically the difference in vocabulary by computing the ratio of words the two letters have in common to those they do not (Mayor, lxx–lxxiv)—must be judged to be unsuccessful. Holzmeister (*Bib* 30 [1949] 339–55) showed that, of the words used in 2 Peter, 38.6 percent are common to 1 and 2 Peter, 61.4 percent peculiar to 2 Peter, while of the words used in 1 Peter, 28.4 percent are common to 1 and 2 Peter, 71.6 percent peculiar to 1 Peter. These percentages do not compare badly with those for 1 and 2 Corinthians: of the words used in 1 Corinthians, 40.4 percent are common to 1 and 2 Corinthians, 59.6 percent are peculiar to 1 Corinthians; of the words used in 2 Corinthians, 49.3 percent are common to 1 and 2 Corinthians, 50.7 percent are peculiar to 2 Corinthians. To explain the somewhat lower percentage of words common to 1 and 2 Peter, Holzmeister appealed to the fact that both letters depend on sources, different in each case (Romans, Ephesians, Hebrews and James have influenced 1 Peter, according to Holzmeister, while 2 Peter used Jude). It may also be relevant (though not noted by Holzmeister) that the two Corinthian letters are considerably longer, and that 1 and 2 Peter both have a large number of NT *hapax legomena* (sixty in 1 Peter, fifty-seven in 2 Peter), which indicates that the author(s) commanded a large vocabulary.

However, these statistics fail to reveal the real differences between the two letters. The words common to the two letters are mostly very common words. Of the 154 words used in both 1 and 2 Peter, only twenty-six occur less than twenty times in the NT, and only ten occur less than ten times. In 2 Peter, there are thirty-eight words which occur only once or twice elsewhere in the NT; of these only two (ἀπόθεσις, ἀρετή,) occur in 1 Peter (whereas ten occur in Acts, eight in the Pastorals, seven in the rest of the Pauline corpus). Only one word (ἀπόθεσις) is used exclusively in 1 and 2 Peter among the NT writings. As these figures partly indicate, there are hardly any words which could be regarded as *characteristic* of the two Petrine letters. One might suggest ἀναστροφή, (six times in 1 Peter, twice in 2 Peter, five times elsewhere in NT), ἄσπιλος (once in 1 Peter, once in 2 Peter, twice elsewhere in NT), ἀρετή (once in 1 Peter, three times in 2 Peter, once elsewhere in NT; but in very different senses in 1 and 2 Peter), φιλαδελφία (once in 1 Peter, twice in 2 Peter, three times elsewhere in NT), but these do not make a very impressive case. (Other alleged resemblances in vocabulary, given in Zahn, *Introduction,* 289 n.9; Bigg, 225; Green, *Reconsidered,* 12–13, are even more flimsy.) None of the really characteristic terminology of either epistle reappears in the other. For example, 2 Peter's characteristic idea of the ἐπίγνωσις (knowledge received in conversion) of Christ (1:2, 3, 8; 2:20); the use of εὐσέβεια and εὐσεβής (1:3, 6; 2:9; 3:11); σπουδάζειν and σπουδή (1:5, 10, 15; 3:14); the ὁδός terminology (2:2, 15, 21); the idea of Christian "stability" (στηρίζειν, στηριγμός, ἀστήρικτος: 1:12; 2:14; 3:14, 17; στηρίζειν is used in 1 Pet 5:10, but with a different nuance); the title σωτήρ for Christ, and its combination with κύριος (1:1, 11; 2:20; 3:2, 18); the title κύριος ἡμῶν for Christ (1:8, 11, 14, 16; 3:18); and the use of θεῖος (1:3, 4) are all absent from 1 Peter. None of these examples derives from 2 Peter's sources or probable sources, and all are relatively independent of the special subject matter of 2 Peter. One would expect some of them to reappear in other writings by the same author. Of instances where the two letters use different terminology for the same idea (Mayor, lxxiv–lxxvi), the most striking is that whereas the second coming of Christ is his *παρουσία* in 2 Peter (1:16; 3:4; cf. 3:12), in 1 Peter it is his *ἀποκάλυψις* (1:7, 13; 4:13; cf. *φανεροῦν* in 5:4).

Of course, both letters are relatively short, are evidently directed to different issues and situations, and deal on the whole with different subjects. Even allowing for these considerations, however, the facts that common terminology is negligible and that common ideas are almost entirely confined to ideas found throughout early Christianity, weigh heavily against common authorship. By contrast, the Pauline letters (even those judged by many scholars to be inauthentic) share characteristic terminology and characteristic recurring themes. It should also be remembered that if both Petrine letters are authentic, they cannot be placed very far apart in time. It can safely be said that if 1 and 2 Peter had been anonymous documents, no one would have thought of attributing them to a single author.

Differences of terminology and ideas are more striking than differences of grammatical usage and style of writing. A. Q. Morton's computer analysis (cited by Green, 17 n.8) showed 1 and 2 Peter to be linguistically indistinguishable. Mayor, after his detailed comparison of the grammar and style of the two letters (lxxxix–civ), concluded that "there is not that chasm between them which some would try to make out" (civ). In their use of the article, e.g., they are similar (lxxxix–xc). The same habit of repeating words is said to be common to both letters (Bigg, 226–27; Mayor, civ), but in fact the phenomenon is much less remarkable in 1 Peter than in 2 Peter. 2 Peter's very striking stylistic habit of using pairs of synonyms or near-synonyms (1:3, 4, 8, 9, 10, 16, 17; 2:10, 11, 13; 3:7, 11, 14, 16), while it can be paralleled in 1 Peter (1:19, 23; 2:18, 25; 3:4; 4:7) as in most writers, is a much less prominent trait in 1 Peter than in 2 Peter, whereas triplets, not used in 2 Peter, occur in 1 Peter (1:4, 7; 3:22; cf. 5:10). Most commentators concur in the view that 1 Peter's style is simpler and more successful, while 2 Peter shows a greater liking for grandiose expressions, ambitious literary effects and bookish words.

Jerome was the first of many who have tried to maintain the common authorship of 1 and 2 Peter by attributing the differences to Peter's use of secretarial assistance, either two different secretaries for the two letters (Dillenseger, *MFOB* 2 [1907] 193; Falconer, *Exp* 6/6 [1902] 117–27; Green, 16–17; tentatively, Guthrie, *Introduction,* 840) or a secretary for one and not for the other (Spitta and Bowman, 159–60, attribute 1 Peter largely to Silvanus, 2 Peter to Peter himself; Robinson, *Redating,* 166–69, 192–95, inclines to attribute 1 Peter to Peter himself, 2 Peter to Jude; Selwyn, *Christian Prophets,* 157–63, attributes 2 Peter to Luke). However, since the most important differences are not those of grammar and style, but those of thought, themes, and theological terminology, an adequate secretary hypothesis must (as Robinson recognizes) postulate not an amanuensis, but an *agent,* i.e. a writer who had a completely free hand not only with the expression but also with the content of the letter. In other words, one or both of the letters was really composed (in the full sense of the word) by someone other than Peter, but Peter approved it and allowed it to be sent out under his name. If we imagine a circle of Christian leaders in Rome, who regarded Peter as their most senior and authoritative member, this hypothesis is not at all implausible. It does mean, however, that only an external link between 1 and 2 Peter is preserved. If Peter is the "author" of one or both letters only in the sense that he approved a letter written by someone else, then the relationship between the two letters becomes hardly at all relevant to the "authenticity" of 2 Peter, which must be considered on its own merits.

It should be borne in mind that the possible derivation of both letters from a Petrine "circle" of Christian leaders in Rome is plausible *only* if the "circle" is *not* considered a "school." Those scholars who postulate Pauline or Johannine "schools" do so to explain the theological and literary resemblances between several writings which they think cannot be ascribed to one author. But in the case of 1 and 2 Peter, there are no such resemblances to be explained. Their authors cannot both be *disciples* of Peter who share a common debt to Peter's teaching. If both letters derive from a Petrine "circle," the circle cannot be a "school" with a common theology, but simply a circle of colleagues who worked together in the leadership of the Roman church. Some of them, at least, must have been independent minds, whose religious thought owed little, if anything, to Peter (Silvanus and Mark, if 1 Pet 5:12–13, indicates that they belonged to such a Petrine "circle" [as Elliott, "Peter," thinks] would, of course, hardly have been Peter's disciples).

The lack of resemblance between the two letters is such that, not only is common authorship very improbable and derivation from a common "school" of Christian teaching equally improbable, but also the author of 2 Peter cannot, in his writing of 2 Peter, have been influenced by his reading of 1 Peter. In spite of Boobyer's attempt to demonstrate such influence ("Indebtedness"; followed by Kelly, 353; Fornberg, *Early Church,* 12–13), there is really no plausible instance of it (see the commentary on 1:1–2 [*Form/Structure/Setting*]; 1:3–11 [*Form/Structure/Setting*]; 1:3; 2:5; 3:9). The only real point of contact is between 1 Pet 3:20 and 2 Pet 2:5; 3:9, but since these vv of 2 Peter cannot derive solely from 1 Pet 3:20 but must also be independently influenced by Jewish traditions, it is simpler to explain the resemblance by common use of fairly well-known themes without regarding 1 Pet 3:20 as a source for 2 Peter. The address and salutation of 2 Peter (1:1–2) is decisive evidence against the view that the author of 2 Peter deliberately modeled his work on 1 Peter to give it a Petrine appearance, for the resemblance in the salutation (a standard formula) is outweighed by the divergence in Peter's self-designation.

Yet it is probable that 3:1 shows that the author of 2 Peter knew of 1 Peter (for his reasons for referring to it in 3:1, see *Comment*). His relationship to 1 Peter, knowing it yet uninfluenced by it, is parallel to his relationship to the Pauline letters (see section 6), but it is worth noticing that it is unlike the practice of most second-century writers of apostolic pseudepigrapha. In cases where writings attributed to their pseudonyms were extant, these writers usually echo such writings in their own pseudonymous productions. The pseudo-Pauline *Laodiceans* is nothing but a patchwork of Pauline phrases;

"3 Corinthians" is full of Pauline terminology and ideas; though less pervasive, there are clear echoes of Paul in the *Prayer of the Apostle Paul* (CG 1, 1), in the *Apoc. Paul,* in the speeches of Paul in the *Acts of Paul,* and even in the apocryphal correspondence between Paul and Seneca. The *Acts John* attributes appropriate Johannine terminology to its hero. In the case of the Petrine pseudepigrapha (see section 8), the *Apoc. Pet.* and the speeches of Peter in the *Acts of Peter* certainly echo 2 Peter, and the *Acts Pet.* probably echoes 1 Peter too. The *Ep. Pet. Phil.* (CG 8, 2) probably echoes 2 Peter and the Petrine speeches in Acts. The Gnostic *Apoc Pet.* (CG 7, 3) contains no clear echoes of other Petrine writings (but cf. 79:31 with 2 Pet 2:17), but consists mostly of Christ's words to Peter. The *Gos. Pet.* and the *Ker. Pet.* do not, in the texts we have, allude to 1 or 2 Peter, but we have only fragments and we do not know whether their authors knew other Petrine writings.

It would be hazardous to base too much on this contrast between 2 Peter's nonuse of 1 Peter and the practice of second-century pseudepigraphers, but it may at least point us in a plausible direction. The author's relationship to Peter may be neither that of a disciple who has absorbed and reflects his master's teaching, nor that of a second-century pseudepigrapher who has carefully studied his pseudonym's writings to make his fiction plausible, but that of an erstwhile colleague of Peter's, who writes Peter's testament after his death, writing in his own way but able to be confident that he is being faithful to Peter's essential message. He would not have to study 1 Peter to be confident of this, and if 1 Peter itself was written not by Peter but by another colleague in the Petrine circle, whether before or after Peter's death, he would know this and feel even less need to base his own work on it.

6. *Pauline Letters*

The author of 2 Peter knew a collection of Pauline letters, though we cannot tell how large a collection, and regarded them as "scriptures," i.e. inspired, authoritative writings, suitable for reading in Christian worship alongside the OT (3:15–16). Yet there is little sign of Pauline influence in 2 Peter. Barnett noted that our author's use of the Pauline letters "is characterized by extreme reserve" (*Paul,* 222), and the possible allusions he lists are mostly very tenuous (*Paul,* 223–28). Lindemann concludes that 2 Peter is entirely uninfluenced by Pauline theology and contains no allusion to the Pauline letters (*Paulus,* 263). In fact, only two allusions to Romans (2:19: Rom 8:21; cf. 6:16; 7:5; and 2 Pet 3:15: Rom 12:3; 15:15) and one to 1 Thessalonians (3:10: 1 Thess 5:2) seem even possible, and they are far from certain.

This knowledge of, but nonuse of, Paul is surprising. We cannot really suppose that our author himself found Paul too "hard to understand" (3:16). As Lindemann points out (*Paulus,* 262), he can hardly be thought to be putting himself in the same position as his opponents, who cannot understand Paul because they are "uninstructed and unstable" (3:16). Nor is it likely that he considered Paul too close to heresy and refers to Paul only because his opponents made much of him; 3:15–16 assumes Paul's orthodoxy as something to be taken for granted, and treats Paul as a wholly trustworthy, indeed inspired, authority. There is no trace of embarrassment or reserve in the reference to Paul. Lindemann's suggestion that the author simply did not see Paul's letters as relevant to his situation is not, as he admits, very satisfactory (*Paulus,* 262–63), at least as a complete explanation. We might not then find deliberate allusions to Paul, but we might still expect his work to show that he had absorbed some Pauline influence. Besides, the author himself asserts that Paul dealt explicitly with some of his own subject matter (3:15–16). An additional possibility is that the author's theological thinking and terminology were formed before he had much contact with Pauline theology, and that a collection of Paul's letters was only just coming into use at the time when he wrote. It is quite possible that Pauline letters were already an established authority in the churches of Asia Minor, to which he wrote (hence 3:15–16), but, apart from Romans, had only recently become known in the church of Rome, from which he wrote (see section on *Authorship and Pseudonymity*).

Such a situation would suit a date in the late first century, which is also a plausible date at which Paul's writings might be called γραφαί ("scriptures"; see *Comment* on 3:16). In general, the later we date 2 Peter, the more surprising the lack of Pauline influence becomes. This argument cannot be pressed very far, because there are second-century writers (such as Justin) who show little or no trace of Pauline influence, but on the whole 2 Peter's relation to the Pauline letters, often cited in favor of a second-century date, may point more in the direction of an earlier, though not too early, date.

7. *Gospel Traditions*

Second Peter contains four certain allusions to gospel traditions: 1:14 (a tradition which also appears in John 21:18); 1:16–18 (a tradition independent of the Synoptic accounts of the Transfiguration, but closer to Matthew than to Mark or Luke); 2:20 (Matt 12:45 par. Luke 11:26); 3:10 (probably a phrase from paraenetic tradition, based on the parable in Matt 24:43 par. Luke 12:39, cf. 1 Thess 5:2). Other possible echoes of or allusions to gospel traditions are: 1:16 (Mark 9:1 par. Matt 16:28, but if so, an independent form of this saying); 2:9 (the Lord's Prayer in the Matthean or a similar version: Matt 6:13); 2:21 (Mark 9:42; 14:21 par. *1 Clem.* 46:8); 3:4 (Mark 9:1 par.; Mark 13:30 par.). It is clear that in some cases the author is dependent on gospel materials, oral or written, independent of the Gospels we know. It is impossible to tell whether he is dependent on any of our Gospels, though of these Matthew is the most likely. Access to extracanonical gospel traditions points to an earlier rather than a later date, but was still possible well into the second century. It should also be noted (as shown in the *Form/Structure/Setting* section on 1:16–18) that the character of 2 Peter's Transfiguration tradition is primitive and quite unlike the strongly Hellenized second-century accounts.

8. *Other Petrine Pseudepigrapha*

If 2 Peter is pseudepigraphical, it is one of a large group of pseudo-Petrine writings. Those which date from the late first century and the second century are: 1 Peter (if it is pseudepigraphal); the *Apoc. Pet.*, the *Gos. Pet.*, the *Ker. Pet.* (Preaching of Peter), and the *Acts Pet.*, and perhaps (these may date from the third century) the gnostic *Apoc. Pet.* (CG 7, 3), the *Ep. Pet. Phil.* (CG 8, 2), the *Act Pet.* (BG, 8502, 4). (Of these, the *Acts Pet.*, the *Ep. Pet. Phil.*, the

Act Pet. and perhaps the *Ker. Pet.* are not pseudepigraphal in the strict sense, i.e. they do not purport to be written by Peter.) In view of Peter's stature as an apostolic figure, the proliferation of Petrine pseudepigrapha is natural enough. Their diversity of character shows that a wide variety of Christian groups, gnostic as well as "orthodox," believed they could claim Petrine authority for their views.

Some of the later Petrine pseudepigrapha are demonstrably dependent on, and some can plausibly be thought to be influenced by, the earlier Petrine writings. This is what one might expect, but the relationships seem to be relationships of literary influence, and provide no convincing evidence of a Petrine "school" or "tradition." This conclusion is confirmed by Smith (*Petrine Controversies*), who has recently studied the relationships between these Petrine writings to trace controversies around the figure of Peter in the early church. Evidence of dependence on 2 Peter can certainly be found in the *Acts Pet.* (*Act. Verc.* 12; cf. 2 Pet 2:16; 1:1; 2:2; *Act. Verc.* 20: cf. 2 Pet 1:16–18; and perhaps *Act. Verc.* 2: cf. 2 Pet 1:9; *Act. Verc.* 6: cf. 2 Pet 2:9, 15; *Act. Verc.* 7: cf. 2 Pet 1:16, 18; 2:15), and perhaps also in *Ep. Pet. Phil.* (132:13–14: cf. 2 Pet 3:15; 132:17–18: cf. 2 Pet 1:11) and the gnostic *Apoc. Pet.* (79:31: cf. 2 Pet 2:17). Smith has suggested that 2 Peter and the gnostic *Apoc. Pet.* might reflect the same controversy, but they are alike only in being strongly polemical and attributed to Peter; their theological themes are quite different.

Only the *Apoc. Pet.* shows extensive similarities with 2 Peter. In a forthcoming article we have shown that these result from literary dependence on 2 Peter. Clearly the writer of the *Apoc. Pet.* had studied 2 Peter carefully. As well as specific cases of verbal dependence, he has adopted 2 Peter's "way" terminology (2 Pet 2:2, 15, 21: *Apoc. Pet.* E 7; A 22, 28, 34; B), which is also found in the *Acts Pet.* (*Act. Verc.* 6, 7, 12), and the idea of the eschatological conflagration (though his ideas about this do not all derive from 2 Peter). These last points might perhaps suggest, in addition to literary dependence, some kind of theological "tradition," possibly that the writer of the *Apoc. Pet.* was a disciple of the author of 2 Peter, but are not really sufficient evidence for this by themselves.

The other Petrine pseudepigrapha therefore offer little help in determining the character and origin of 2 Peter, except to indicate that it was already accorded authority as a source of Petrine tradition when the *Apoc. Pet.* (probably c. 110–40) and the *Acts Pet.* (c. 180) were written.

9. *1 Clement, 2 Clement, Hermas*

When compared with the other NT documents, 2 Peter is a highly distinctive work. Some of its ideas and much of its religious terminology are hard to parallel from other NT writers. Its material links with Jude, and largely formal links with 1 Peter and Paul, do not indicate any real affinities of thought and language. Second Peter seems to represent a Christian milieu and a style of Christian discourse not otherwise represented in the NT.

However, there is a group of early Christian writings with which 2 Peter shows much closer affinities than with any NT books: *1 Clem., 2 Clem.* and the *Shepherd* of Hermas. The careful reader of this commentary will find that many parallels, in ideas and vocabulary, are pointed out throughout the commentary, and the impression will grow that these three works are 2 Peter's closest relatives in the early church. (In addition to the parallels noted throughout the commentary, it is worth noting here that of 2 Peter's fifty-seven NT *hapax legomena,* sixteen are found in *1 Clem., 2 Clem.* and Hermas, and fifteen of these not elsewhere in the Apostolic Fathers, while of the thirty-eight words in 2 Peter which occur only once or twice elsewhere in the NT, seventeen occur in *1 Clem., 2 Clem.* and Hermas, ten of these not elsewhere in the Apostolic Fathers. But the considerable length of *1 Clem.* and Hermas should be remembered when assessing these figures.)

The relationships of 2 Peter with these three works are *not* of the kind which literary dependence could explain, nor is common authorship conceivable. The four writers, despite the links between them, remain highly individual writers, each with his distinctive traits of thought and language. The kind of similarities which this commentary demonstrates are those which derive from the use of shared Christian traditions and from belonging to a shared Christian language milieu. It cannot be accidental that *1 Clem.* and Hermas are indubitably Roman works; that *2 Clem.,* whose place of origin is disputed (Rome and Corinth are the most likely possibilities), is widely admitted to be closely connected with *1 Clem.* in some way; and that 2 Peter can very plausibly be located in Rome (see section on *Authorship and Pseudonymity*). The similarities between the four works most probably indicate their common indebtedness to a tradition of Roman Christianity. (This hypothesis ought to be tested by investigation of parallels between the three works *1 Clem., 2 Clem.* and Hermas, to supplement this commentary's investigation of the parallels between 2 Peter and those three works.)

Such common indebtedness to a tradition of Roman Christianity need not necessarily imply close proximity in date, but since there is no evidence of literary dependence, we may expect the chronological span within which the four works were written to be relatively short—perhaps no more than twenty years. Unfortunately, although there is still wide agreement that *1 Clem.* should be dated c. A.D. 96, there is no scholarly agreement on the dates of *2 Clem.* and Hermas. In spite of recent arguments for an earlier date for *1 Clem.* (Robinson, *Redating,* 328–34, with references to other literature) there seems no sufficient reason to challenge the view that *1 Clem.* belongs to the 90s. In the case of Hermas, a trend of scholarly opinion toward a date c. 80–100 can perhaps be discerned (Edmundson, *Church of Rome,* 208–21; J. Daniélou, *The Theology of Jewish Christianity,* tr. J. A. Baker [London: Darton, Longmann & Todd, 1964] 39; Robinson, *Redating,* 320–22, with references to other literature; cf. R. J. Bauckham, "The Great Tribulation in the *Shepherd* of Hermas," *JTS* 25 [1974] 28–29). *Second Clement* is still commonly dated well into the second century, but the latest full study by Donfried puts it at the end of the first century, partly because he sees it as written soon after *1 Clem.,* but also for more general reasons (*Second Clement,* 1, 79–81, 124, 191). A further reason for grouping all three works within a relatively short period toward the end of the first century is the evidence in all three that they were written at a time when either the generation of the apostles or the generation of the first converts in their place of origin had almost or just passed away (*1 Clem.* 23:3; 44:1–3; *2 Clem.* 11:2; Hermas, *Vis.* 3:5:1;

Sim. 9:15:4). A similar criterion can be used to date 2 Peter in the same period (section on *Date*).

Character of the Letter

In a famous essay which contains a full-scale theological attack on 2 Peter, Käsemann calls it "from beginning to end a document expressing an early Catholic viewpoint," and "the clearest possible testimony to the onset of early Catholicism" ("Apologia," 169, 195). Although for Käsemann "early Catholicism" is not so much a historical category as a theological accusation, his verdict on 2 Peter's "early Catholic" character is endorsed by many scholars, not all of whom follow his excessive denigration of the letter: "the clearest example in the Canon of 'early Catholicism' " (R. H. Fuller, *A Critical Introduction to the New Testament* [2nd ed.; London: Duckworth, 1971] 166), "a prime example of early Catholicism" (J. D. G. Dunn, *Unity and Diversity in the New Testament* [London: SCM Press, 1977] 351), "the classic document of so-called early Catholicism" (Schrage, 118; cf. also Schelkle, "Spätapostolische Briefe"; but Fornberg, *Early Church,* 3–6, regards early Catholicism as "an artificial category which cannot do justice to a document such as 2 Peter"). As in the case of Jude, the usefulness of this categorization of 2 Peter must be investigated.

We may begin by applying the three alleged features of early Catholicism which we used in the discussion of Jude: (1) The fading of the Parousia hope. It is a serious misunderstanding of 2 Peter to suppose that its author abandons the imminent eschatological expectation of primitive Christianity. On the contrary, he assumes it as naturally as other writers do: both his opponents and his readers will experience the Parousia (1:19; 2:12; 3:14), and the eschatological judgment is coming swiftly on his opponents (2:1). Of course, in his day the delay of the Parousia has become a problem, which for his opponents justifies thorough-going eschatological skepticism (3:4, 9) and therefore he must give some explanation of the delay. But the effect of the arguments he uses is not to postpone the Parousia to the distant future; they are traditional Jewish apocalyptic arguments which belong in the context of Jewish apocalyptic's characteristic tension between the sense of eschatological imminence and a wrestling with the problem of delay (besides the commentary on chap 3, see Bauckham, *TynB* 31 [1980] 3–36). If the Parousia hope has become to some extent problematic in our author's time, he does not at all allow it to fade, but vigorously reasserts it.

Käsemann has other criticisms of 2 Peter's eschatology; that it "lacks any Christological orientation" ("Apologia," 178), that (with reference to 1:4) it is a "relapse into Hellenistic dualism" ("Apologia," 180), and that it is anthropocentric, concerned only with moral retribution ("Apologia," 179–80). It is not clear why these failings are regarded as "early Catholic," and one suspects that "early Catholic" and "non-Pauline" are being equated. This may make "early Catholic" a useful term for Käsemann's theological-critical purposes, but it makes it a useless term for historical investigation. However, to deal briefly with the charges, they are not entirely fair to 2 Peter. The first charge neglects (or misunderstands: see "Apologia," 186–

87) the appeal to the Transfiguration (1:16–18), which the author sees as a basis for the Parousia hope because it was God's installation of Jesus as the one who will exercise God's universal rule. 1:4 (see *Comment* for detailed discussion of Käsemann's charge) is not the whole of 2 Peter's eschatology, and the paradox of its Hellenistic language juxtaposed with the apocalyptic perspective of chap 3 must be faced (see below), not eliminated. Second Peter's eschatology *is* concerned with retribution and has a primarily ethical interest, but this is a concern with God's righteousness and is by no means purely man-centered. Its emphasis is continuous with that of Jewish apocalyptic eschatology, which justifies the use of a Jewish apocalyptic source in chap 3. In summary, 2 Peter's eschatology is apocalyptic for the most part, but is expressed in strongly Hellenistic terminology in 1:4. It is not clear that the label "early Catholic" helps us at all to understand this combination.

(2) Increasing institutionalization is the second mark of early Catholicism. Second Peter makes no reference at all to ecclesiastical office-holders, unless his reference to his opponents as ψευδοδιδάσκαλοι ("false teachers," 2:1) counts. On the most probable interpretation of 1:20–21, those vv have nothing to do with the exegesis of Scripture, and therefore do not insist on an authoritative interpretation of Scripture by officeholders who alone possess the Spirit (against Käsemann, "Apologia," 189–91). 3:16 does allude to the misinterpretation of Scripture by the opponents, but noticeably fails to meet the problem by restricting interpretation to authorized persons. On the contrary, 3:15 seems to be an appeal to the readers' own ability to see that the writer's view accords with their reading of Paul. The fact that 2 Peter does not refer to officeholders in the churches does not of course imply that there were none, but it does show that in the author's conception of the struggle against the false teachers, the role of the officeholders does not occupy the center of the stage. (This is recognized by Knoch, "Vermächtnis," 158–59, who thinks that the preservation of apostolic tradition against heretics had not yet become explicitly the task of the officeholders, as it has in the Pastorals.)

(3) The crystallization of the faith into set forms. Second Peter's characteristic terms for Christianity are (a) the "way" phrases: "the way of truth" (2:1), "the straight way" (2:15), and "the way of righteousness" (2:21), which (used deliberately against the opponents' libertinism) characterize Christianity not as a body of belief but as an ethical way of life; (b) "the holy commandment" (2:21) and "the commandment of the Lord and Savior" (3:2), which have a similar significance; (c) "the knowledge (ἐπίγνωσις) of Jesus Christ" (1:2, 8), which is not "orthodox doctrinal tradition" (Käsemann, "Apologia," 193), but the essential knowledge, theoretical and personal, gained in Christian conversion; (d) "the truth that you have" (1:12), which, like Jude's "the faith" (Jude 3), is simply the gospel. It is absurd to see in this last phrase the implication that "revelation is now a piece of property which is at the community's disposal" (Käsemann, "Apologia," 174). There is no evidence here for insistence on formalized creedal orthodoxy. Certainly, 2 Peter is written in defense of traditional Christian eschatology and ethics; the author believes that the expectation of the Parousia and its ethical implications were essential to the apostolic message and he defends them. But he uses no creedal formulae, and his opponents are skeptics and libertines (see section on *The Oppo-*

nents), not Gnostics who appealed to personal inspiration (Käsemann, "Apologia," 175) and against whom orthodoxy has to be formulated and tied to institutional authority.

Second Peter's response to heresy is not the "early Catholic" response of insistence on institutional authority and creedal orthodoxy. Nor does the author respond to the delay of the Parousia in the way that "early Catholicism" is supposed to have responded, by highlighting Christology or ecclesiology in compensation for the inevitable loss of the imminent expectation. On the contrary, he reasserts the primitive eschatological perspective. It is plain that the label "early Catholic" is no help in understanding 2 Peter.

Only in one respect is Käsemann's critique really relevant to determining the character of 2 Peter. He emphasizes the importance of the conception of the apostles and the normative character of apostolic tradition for the author, and connects this with his use of pseudepigraphy ("Apologia," 177). If we accept that 2 Peter is a pseudepigraphal "testament of Peter," it becomes clear that the author is conscious of living in a period when the generation of the apostles has passed, and the "scoffers" whom the apostles had predicted would arise after their death, in the critical "last days," are already on the scene (3:4). These "scoffers" consider the apostles' teaching, on eschatology and ethics, discredited. But for the author it is the norm of Christian belief. It is not, of course, to be woodenly or unintelligently repeated. In 1:3–11 he puts Peter's message very much into his own terms, for his own situation, and to maintain the credibility of the Parousia hope of the apostles he uses whatever arguments, new or old, make sense to him. Yet it is Peter's message—and for him this is simply the *apostolic* message—which he interprets and defends. To deliver the *apostolic* message in a *postapostolic* situation: this is the key to the author's conception of his task.

This task combines with the particular resources he brings to it to determine the peculiar character of the letter. On the one hand, his own background (or at least that of the Christian traditions he has made his own) appears to be in Hellenistic Judaism (see *Language* and sections 1, 3 of *Literary Relationships*), and he is familiar with the literature in which Hellenistic Jews had endeavored to express biblical faith in terms appropriate to their cultural environment. At least partly from this background in Hellenistic Judaism, as well as from his own interaction with the pagan cultural context of his church, derives his free use of Hellenistic religious and ethical terminology (especially 1:3–8). From Hellenistic Judaism comes also his understanding of scriptural inspiration (1:20–21). Second Peter's Christianity has acquired at least a glossy veneer of adaptation to a Hellenistic cultural context, but it is important to realize that this was in the first place an adaptation to a Hellenistic *Jewish* religious culture which had already adapted to its pagan context. As the commentary on 1:3–8 points out, our author uses his Hellenistic terminology with some care and skill, so that a Christian content controls it.

On the other hand, however, his letter reflects his use of Jewish apocalyptic and Jewish Christian apocalyptic sources: his tradition of the Transfiguration (1:16–18), Jude (2:1–18; 3:1–3), and the Jewish apocalypse which underlies 3:4–13. Even if, because of his cultural distance from Jude's apocalyptic midrash, he has not really understood it in detail, yet its broad intention comes through in the insistence on imminent eschatological judgment and the use of the typological material in 2:4–9. The Jewish apocalyptic ideas seem faithfully reproduced in 3:5–13. The apocalyptic interpretation of the Transfiguration is integral to his argument.

This surprising combination of Hellenism and apocalyptic is precisely the way in which the author tries to interpret and defend the apostolic message in a postapostolic generation. What appears to come most naturally to him, when he is not following a source, is a Hellenistically influenced way of *interpreting* the apostolic message which makes contact with the ideals and aspirations of the church's pagan environment (1:3–8). But he faces opponents whose Hellenism involves a critical attitude to the apostolic message and leads, in his view, to its abandonment. They advocate mere pagan skepticism about eschatology and mere compromise with pagan permissive morality. In response he must *defend* the eschatological content and the eschatologically motivated ethical content of the apostolic teaching. To aid him in this, he resorts with a sure instinct to sources close to the apocalyptic outlook of the primitive church. He sees that this must be reasserted if a Hellenized Christianity is not to become a merely paganized Christianity. Commentators have often tended to play down either the Hellenism or the apocalyptic in 2 Peter. In reality the juxtaposition of the two gives 2 Peter its special character. A similar mixture to a greater or lesser extent characterizes *1 Clem.*, *2 Clem.*, and Hermas, which belong to the same milieu as 2 Peter (section 9 of *Literary Relationships*). This group of Roman Christian leaders faced the church's perennial task of retaining the gospel's essential content while giving it meaningful expression in new cultural contexts. Second Peter's contribution to that task deserves more appreciation than it has received from modern scholars.

The Opponents

Like Jude, 2 Peter is a polemical document. Its purpose is to counter the influence of a group of teachers in the churches to which it is addressed, and to this end it employs not only denunciation but also apologetic argument in defense of the eschatological teaching of the apostles against their objections. From the objections which the author counters we can discern the main thrust of the opponents' teaching, at least as he understood it.

From 2:1–3a, 14, 18 it is clear that the opponents were teachers with disciples. The central theme of their teaching was eschatological skepticism. The Parousia of Jesus Christ had been expected during the lifetime of the apostles, but the first Christian generation had now passed away, and in the view of the false teachers this proved the primitive Christian eschatological expectation to have been wholly mistaken (3:4, 9a). There would be no eschatological judgment (2:3b), no divine intervention to eliminate evil and establish a world of righteousness. No doubt this teaching fed on disillusionment felt by some Christians when the last prominent members of the generation of the apostles, in whose final years eschatological expectation had run high, passed away and the prophecy of the Parousia remained unfulfilled. But it seems also, in the mind of the false teachers, to have belonged to a common-sense rationalistic view of the world, according to which the world continues on its course without dramatic divine interventions (3:4). Judgments are prophesied but never happen (2:3b).

To support this skepticism they held that the apostles, who undeniably preached the Parousia as central to the Christian message, had invented the idea themselves (1:16a), perhaps as an instrument of moral control. As for the passages of OT prophecy traditionally interpreted with reference to the Parousia, these were not divinely inspired but simply the prophets' own mistaken attempts to interpret their dreams and visions (1:20–21a). The eschatological expectation was not based on divine promise, but on human invention.

The opponents' eschatological skepticism was advanced not simply in the interests of intellectual honesty, but in the interests of moral freedom. They claimed to be emancipating people from the fear of divine judgment (2:19a). Petty moral restraints could be safely ignored. They were not impressed when stricter Christians warned them of judgment to come, nor when they warned them of the danger of falling into the power of the forces of evil and sharing their fate, eschatological destruction. On the contrary, they laughed at the supposed power of the devil and his angels (2:10b). "Freedom" was their catchword, and evidently they felt free to indulge in sexual immorality, drunkenness and sensual excesses generally (2:2, 10a, 13–14, 18). No doubt the easy compromise with pagan moral standards which their teaching allowed was one source of their popularity (2:18).

Since they apparently still regarded themselves as Christians, they may have sought some support for their views in authoritative Christian writings, and, since Paul was a major authority in their churches (3:15), they may have appealed to Pauline teaching about Christian freedom and justification by faith (cf. 2:19; 3:16). But 3:15–16 may mean that they misinterpreted Paul and other authoritative writings in an unfavorable sense, i.e. they interpreted passages about the imminence of the Parousia as unfulfilled and therefore false prophecy. At any rate, it would go beyond the evidence to speak of a real Pauline influence on them, let alone to regard them as radical Paulinists. In spite of the reference to Paul in 3:15–16, the evidence for a Pauline background to the false teaching in 2 Peter is less convincing than in the case of Jude's opponents.

This sketch of the opponents has attempted to stay close to the evidence which 2 Peter offers and to do justice to the centrality of the eschatological question in the debate. It should also be observed, from the author's redaction of Jude, that he omits material in Jude relating to Jude's opponents' claims to possess the Spirit and to be the recipients of prophetic revelations (Jude 8: cf. 2 Pet 2:10; Jude 19), and also Jude's reference to their antinomian perversion of grace (Jude 4: cf. 2 Pet 2:1–3). As far as we can tell, the opponents in 2 Peter claimed to be teachers but not prophets (2 Pet 2:1) and set no store by charismatic experiences (cf. also *Comment* on 2:16). Their ethical libertinism had more to do with their eschatological skepticism than with an antinomian understanding of grace. The angels they mocked were the powers of evil, not angelic guardians of the Law (2 Pet 2:10–11: cf. Jude 8–9). Thus redaction-critical study reveals the false teachers in 2 Peter to be very different from the opponents in Jude. The only certain point of substantial resemblance between the two is their ethical libertinism, which is what accounts for 2 Peter's use of Jude.

The most plausible background to the attitudes of the false teachers in 2 Peter is their pagan environment (so Fornberg, *Early Church,* 65, 104–5, 119–20, 126, 132; note especially 120: "the adversaries consisted of theologically unaware Christians who compromised with ideas current in the world around them"). Neyrey (*Polemic,* chap 4; *JBL* 99 [1980] 407–31) has shown the extent to which the eschatological debate in 2 Peter resembles pagan Hellenistic controversy over the views of the Epicureans on providence and eschatology, and these parallels have been pointed out at relevant points in the commentary. It is also important to remember the extent to which eschatology of the Jewish apocalyptic kind was alien to Hellenistic thinking, even including much Hellenistic Jewish thinking. The opponents' charges in 1:16a and 1:20–21a also seem to belong to Hellenistic debate (involving Hellenistic Judaism) about prophecy and oracles (see *Comment* on those vv). The opponents' ethical practice, in which sexual immorality seems prominent, is plausibly seen as accommodation to the permissiveness of pagan society, a perennial temptation in the early church, especially when Christian morality impeded participation in the social life of the cities. The false teachers may therefore be seen as aiming to disencumber Christianity of its eschatology and its ethical rigorism, which seemed to them an embarrassment in their cultural environment, especially after the evident failure of the Parousia expectation. From a general familiarity with Hellenistic religious debate they were able to deploy current skeptical arguments about eschatology and divine revelation. Perhaps they saw themselves as rather daring young radicals trying to clear a lot of traditional nonsense out of the church. Whether they also had any positive religious teaching our evidence does not allow us to say. The analogy with radicals in other generations suggests that a largely negative message could have sounded impressive enough (cf. 2:18a).

The opponents in 2 Peter are not Gnostics. Although the identification of them as Gnostics has been the common opinion since Werdermann (*Irrlehrer*), it has recently been rejected by Fornberg (*Early Church, passim*) and Neyrey (*CBQ* 42 [1980] 506), both of whom have studied the opponents in 2 Peter carefully, without confusing its opponents with Jude's. The present commentary confirms their conclusion. As in the case of Jude, there is no evidence that the false teachers in 2 Peter held the cosmological dualism which is the essential mark of true Gnosticism. There is no evidence that their ethical libertinism was based on such dualism, or that their eschatological skepticism resulted from a gnostic concentration on realized, at the expense of future, eschatology. If they resembled some second-century Gnostics in denying the divine inspiration of OT prophecy (1:20–21a), they did so by attributing it to a merely human origin, not to the demiurge, as second-century Gnostics did. There is no hint in 2 Peter of controversy about bodily resurrection, which was usually a main focus of anti-gnostic discussion of eschatology, because of the link between this issue and gnostic dualism (cf., e.g., 1 Cor 15; 2 Tim 2:18; *1 Clem.* 24; *2 Clem.* 9; Pol. *Phil.* 7:1; "*3 Cor.*"—though not all these need be anti-gnostic). Conversely, there is no evidence that the delay of the Parousia, so important in 2 Peter, featured in second-century Gnostic argument against traditional eschatology.

Support for identifying the opponents as Gnostics has been sought in the reference to "myths" (1:16), but this is the opponents' charge against the apostles, not the author's charge against the opponents. When he does turn the charge against the opponents (2:3a), it is notable that the word "myths" does not recur: evidently the opponents had false (skeptical) arguments, but nothing so positive as "myths." The use of the "knowledge" theme in 2 Peter has also been regarded as aimed against heretical *gnosis,* but careful study shows that in fact "knowledge" in 2 Peter (ἐπίγνωσις and γνῶσις) is free of polemical overtones and cannot have been a catchword of the opponents (see especially *Comment* on 1:2; 2:12).

Only insofar as eschatological disillusionment may have contributed to the rise of the Gnostic movement can the opponents in 2 Peter be seen even as forerunners of Gnosticism.

Date

No book in the NT has been assigned such a wide range of dates as 2 Peter. Even within the last twenty years, commentaries and reference books have placed 2 Peter in almost every decade from 60 to 160 A.D. (only the decade 70–80 seems to be unrepresented). This suggests that the usual arguments about its date are unusually inconclusive. Fortunately, our investigation suggests a wider range of chronological indications, and a relatively new perspective on the problem of date.

The evidence for date from the study of literary relationships can be summarized thus:

(1) Documents known to 2 Peter

c. 50–60	Pauline letters
(c. 55–59	Romans)
c. 50–60	Jude
? c. 60–65 or 65–75	1 Peter
? c. 70–80	Jewish apocalypse used in 2 Pet 3.

(2) Documents roughly contemporary with 2 Peter

c. 80–100	Hermas, *The Shepherd*
c. 80–100	*2 Clement*
c. 96	*1 Clement*

(3) Documents dependent on 2 Peter

c. 110–140	*Apocalypse of Peter*
c. 180	*Acts of Peter*

In addition (from the investigations in *Literary Relationships*) we should note that the author's relation to and attitude to a collection of Pauline letters could point to, and is certainly consistent with, a late first-century date (section 6; and *Comment* on 3:16), while the use of Gospel traditions is inconclusive with regard to date, but again is consistent with a late first-century date (section 7). The nonuse of *1 Enoch* also seems to point to a first-century rather than a second-century date (section 2).

This evidence, though it is inevitably dependent on other dates which are very much in dispute (e.g. those of 1 Peter and Jude), seems to point to a date for 2 Peter in the period 75–100, though on this evidence an early second-century date cannot be entirely excluded. Other features of 2 Peter support a late first-century date. The christology of the letter (*Comment* on 1:1; 3:18) is consistent with such a date. The language of 1:4, sometimes held to require a late date, merely shows the influence of Hellenistic Judaism (see *Comment*), possible at any stage of the development of Christianity outside Palestine. The "early Catholic" response to heresy, which stresses the role of institutional officeholders and might point to a relatively late date, is absent from 2 Peter (see *Character of the Letter*). The imminent eschatological expectation remains important (see *Character of the Letter*). The opponents are not second-century Gnostics (see *The Opponents*).

This converging evidence is impressive, but 2 Peter contains one further strong clue to its date, whose probable significance has not often been seen: 3:4. Significantly, even defenders of Petrine authorship do not treat this verse as a real prediction, but as an objection which was being raised at the time of the writing of 2 Peter (Spitta, Green; Dillenseger, *MFOB* 2 [1907] 207–9). The fathers who are dead are not the fathers of the scoffers, but the first Christian generation, the generation of the apostles. Of course, it is not possible to date the death of a generation, but what is required is an estimate of the date at which the scoffers could plausibly have claimed that the first Christian generation had died, so that the promise of the Parousia within their lifetime was invalidated. The generation of the apostles would consist of people born no later than c. A.D. 10. Assuming that in the first century it was rare to live beyond seventy years, we may suppose that c. A.D. 80 was the time at which contemporaries with their hopes set on the Parousia in the lifetime of the apostolic generation would begin to feel acutely that this generation had virtually died out. The scoffers' objection in 3:4 becomes plausible in the decade 80–90.

In the *Comment* on 3:4 we have argued that this objection belongs in the context of the *immediate* crisis provoked by the passing of the first generation (so also Fornberg, *Early Church,* 65). It appealed to the disillusionment felt immediately after a period of high eschatological expectation (cf. especially *Asc. Isa.* 4:13), and represents a crisis which was surmounted and forgotten before long. The death of the first generation was no longer an issue in the second century.

Thus 3:4 alone enables us to date 2 Peter with considerable probability c. A.D. 80–90. The fact that a wide range of other evidence also points toward a date in the late first century gives this conclusion very high probability (other scholars who date 2 Peter c. 80 or c. 90 are Chaine, Spicq, Reicke). Contrary to established scholarly tradition, 2 Peter is probably not the latest book in the NT.

Authorship and Pseudonymity

The language alone (see *Language*) makes it improbable that Peter could have written 2 Peter, while the author's preference for Hellenistic terminology (see *Character of the Letter;* cf. section 3, of *Literary Relationships*) can only implausibly be attributed to Peter. It is likely enough that the author of 2 Peter was Jewish, but a strongly Hellenized Jew. No doubt it is true that the distinction between Palestinian and Hellenistic Judaism has often been exaggerated and misused, but we should not now react against it to the extent of missing the obvious difference between the Palestinian Jewish character of Jude and the Hellenized character of 2 Peter. The relationship of 1 and 2 Peter is ambiguous in its relevance to the question of Petrine authorship, but certainly Peter cannot be the real author of both letters (section 5 of *Literary Relationships*).

This evidence, however, would be consistent with a secretary hypothesis in which the secretary is not Peter's amanuensis but his agent. The evidence which really rules out composition *during Peter's lifetime* is that of literary genre (*Form and Structure*) and that of date (*Date*). Either of these might be fatal for any degree of Petrine authorship. Together they must be regarded as entirely conclusive against Petrine authorship. (Peter's death can be dated with a high probability in A.D. 64 or 65. See Robinson, *Redating,* 149, for an argument that 65 is more likely.)

Second Peter is fictionally represented as written shortly before Peter's death (1:14) and therefore in Rome (for the early tradition of Peter's death in Rome, see *Apoc. Pet.* R; Ign. *Rom.* 4:3; and probably *Asc. Isa.* 4:3; *1 Clem.* 5:4). This would not need to imply that it was really written in Rome if 2 Peter were not a real letter, but since it is written to specific churches (3:15) it is a likely deduction that it was sent to them from the church of Rome. This is confirmed by 3:1, which indicates that the churches addressed are those which 1 Peter addressed from Rome (1 Pet 5:13). A Roman origin is also rendered extremely probable by 2 Peter's close links with *1 Clem.* and Hermas, if not also *2 Clem.* (section 9 of *Literary Relationships*). We know that the leaders of the Roman church in that period maintained a strong pastoral interest in churches elsewhere. Not only is 1 Peter addressed to a large group of churches, both of Pauline foundation and others, in Asia Minor (1 Pet 1:1), but also *1 Clem.* was sent, on behalf of the Roman church, to the church at Corinth, to sort out its difficulties, while Hermas' visions were to be sent "to the cities abroad" (*Vis.* 2:4:3). In fact, Clement is said to have been entrusted with the task of sending out the Roman church's foreign correspondence (Herm. *Vis.* 2:4:3), which implies that letters to other churches were written quite regularly. Ignatius not long afterward congratulated the Roman church on having "taught others" (*Rom.* 3:1).

Thus 2 Peter can plausibly be set within this context of the Roman church's pastoral concern for churches elsewhere during the late first century. Like *1 Clem.,* it is not really the letter of an individual so much as of a church, written by an unknown Christian leader on behalf of the church of Rome. There is no need to postulate any personal link between its author and the churches to which he writes. These churches, either all or some of the churches in the area to which 1 Peter was addressed (1 Pet 1:1), certainly included Pauline churches (2 Pet 3:15), and 2 Peter therefore refers to Paul's letter(s) to them (3:15) as naturally as *1 Clem.* refers to 1 Corinthians when writing to the church of Corinth (*1 Clem.* 47:1).

Given a desire to write an apostolic "testament," the choice of Peter was the natural pseudonym in a letter from the church at Rome. Peter and Paul were the two apostles associated with Rome (*1 Clem.* 5; Ign. *Rom.* 4:3), and although we do not know how long either spent in Rome, the strength of later tradition can probably be trusted to the extent of indicating that, of the two, it was Peter who exercised more of a real leadership role in the church in Rome, for however brief a period. Thus, in order to explain our author's choice of pseudonym, it may not be necessary to look further than Peter's status as the most prestigious of the leaders of the Roman church. Whether a desire to use the Transfiguration tradition (1:16–18) contributed to the choice of pseudonym, or whether the prior choice of pseudonym suggested it, we cannot tell.

Apart from the Transfiguration tradition and other Gospel traditions, there is little material in 2 Peter which could plausibly be regarded as specifically Petrine tradition deriving from the historical Peter. Insofar as the summary of Peter's message in 1:3–11 is a summary of common primitive Christian teaching, it is attributable to Peter as much as to any apostle, but insofar as there is anything distinctive about it, notably the Hellenistic terminology, it must be regarded as our author's interpretation of the apostolic message in terms of (post-Petrine) Roman theology. The prophecy of the false teachers (2:1–3a) could owe something to memories of Peter's preaching, but could as well derive from generally apostolic, but not specifically Petrine, material. Our author's purpose is to defend the ethical and eschatological teaching of the apostles, whom he regards as united in preaching the same message (see 1:12, 16; 3:15, with *Comment*). To write Peter's testament he really only needed to be sure he was representing correctly the message Peter shared with all the apostles. He did not need to include peculiarly Petrine material, though in one case (1:16–18) he found it useful to do so. He may actually have made more use of the work of another apostle, Jude, than of specifically Petrine traditions.

However, there are some possible hints that the author may have had some personal connection with Peter. The use of the name *Simeon* Peter may indicate an author who remembered what Peter was called by colleagues who had known him in Palestine (*Comment* on 1:1). His disregard for 1 Peter, which is mentioned because the readers knew it (3:1) but on which, by contrast with later pseudepigraphal practice, the author conspicuously fails to model 2 Peter, may indicate a confidence, derived from personal knowledge, of his ability to speak on behalf of the dead Peter without recourse to other Petrine writings (section 5 of *Literary Relationships*). In view of the lack of specifically Petrine material, he can hardly have been a disciple of Peter who had learned his theology from Peter (and this is even less possible if 1 Peter, from which 2 Peter differs so completely, be thought to embody Peter's teaching to any degree). But he may have been a colleague of Peter's in the leadership of the Roman church in the 60s. This may be saying little more than that, when he wrote 2 Peter in the 80s, he was one of the more senior members of the circle of Roman church leaders. (If one had to guess a name or person as a candidate for the authorship of 2 Peter, a possibility might be Linus [2 Tim 4:21], whom the early Roman bishop lists, deriving from Hegesippus

[Irenaeus, *Adv. Haer.* 3.3.3; Eusebius, *Hist. Eccl.* 3.13, 21; 5.6.1], list as bishop of Rome after Peter, or Anencletus [Cletus] whom the same lists consider Linus' successor and Clement's predecessor.)

The idea of a "Petrine circle" of Christian leaders in Rome was mentioned in section 5 of *Literary Relationships.* Elliott ("Peter") has recently argued that 1 Peter derives, after Peter's death, from a Petrine group of those who had been close associates of Peter in Rome. This group would include Silvanus and Mark (1 Pet 5:12–13) and therefore Palestinian traditions would be influential in its ideas and teaching. Elliott envisages it as a fairly close-knit group, which shared Peter's theology and interests, and which therefore had a definite theological identity. One may doubt whether a group which included such mature and widely experienced men as Silvanus and Mark could have been quite as theologically homogeneous as Elliott seems to suggest. But if such a group does account for 1 Peter, it could hardly have included the author of 2 Peter, who in no sense belongs to the same theological "school" as the author of 1 Peter (section 5 of *Literary Relationships*), though he could have belonged to the same "circle," in the loose sense of a group of working associates, including a good deal of theological diversity. If Elliott's Petrine group really existed and produced 1 Peter before or soon after Peter's death, we must envisage its character changing as it evolved into the late first century group of Roman Christian leaders which included Clement and Hermas and the author of 2 Peter. Perhaps in the 60s the author of 2 Peter was on the fringe of the Petrine group: he was used to calling Peter by his Palestinian name and perhaps first came to know Jude's letter from these Palestinian colleagues, but he did not learn his theology from them. The sense in which 1 and 2 Peter both derive from a "Petrine circle" can only be that both were sent out by the leaders of the Roman church who regarded Peter as their most authoritative member, present or past.

What was implied in the author of 2 Peter's adoption of pseudonymity and of the "testament" genre? Possibly an intention of writing not as an individual but as representing the Roman church and therefore under the name of its greatest leader. More certainly, the intention of defending the apostolic message in a postapostolic age (see *Character of the Letter*). In the relatively new and largely unexpected situation of the Christian church after the death of the apostles, he assures his readers that they are not disadvantaged as Christian believers who do not have personal access to the apostolic eyewitnesses (1:1), he provides them with a "reminder" of the apostolic message (1:12–15; 3:1–2), and he interprets and defends the apostolic message in the light of his contemporary situation and in the face of contemporary challenges to the message (cf. especially Zmijewski, *BZ* 23 [1979] 161–71, on the meaning of pseudepigraphy in 2 Peter). By contrast with the false teachers, who were claiming to correct the apostles' message, our author sets no store by his own authority or any message of his own. His authority lies in the faithfulness with which he transmits, and interprets for a new situation, the normative teaching of the apostles. "Peter's testament" is the ideal literary vehicle for these intentions.

The pseudepigraphal device is therefore not a fraudulent means of claiming apostolic authority, but embodies a claim to be a faithful mediator of the apostolic message. Recognizing the canonicity of 2 Peter means recognizing the validity of that claim, and it is not clear that this is so alien to the early church's criteria of canonicity as is sometimes alleged. The case of the unfortunate author of the *Acts Paul* (Tertullian, *De Bapt.* 17; Green, *Reconsidered,* 33–34) is often referred to in this connection, together with Serapion's investigation and rejection of the *Gos. Pet.* (Eusebius, *Hist. Eccl.* 6.12.1–6; Green, *Reconsidered,* 35–36), but, apart from the fact that the *Acts Paul* is not pseudepigraphal, but fictional, both cases involved unorthodox teaching, i.e. the attribution of nonapostolic teaching to the apostles (cf. Fornberg, *Early Church,* 18–19). Somewhat more relevant to the case of 2 Peter is Origen's comment on Hebrews (*ap.* Eusebius, *Hist. Eccl.* 6.25.13–14), which he regarded as effectively Paul's because "the thoughts are the apostle's," though the composition must be attributed to a disciple (cf. also Tertullian, *Adv. Marc.* 4.5.4).

Of course, the authority of 2 Peter was disputed in the early church, in connection with its authorship (cf. Eusebius, *Hist. Eccl.* 3.3.4; 6.25.8; Jerome, *Ep.* 120.11), and it was no doubt as a product of Peter's own mind that it was generally accepted as canonical in the end. But we must reckon with a Gentile church which no longer understood the conventions of a Jewish literary genre, and which had had to sort out the genuinely apostolic from an abundance of late and often heretical pseudepigrapha. What the church actually recognized in 2 Peter was its apostolic content. That the NT canon should include a work which explicitly documents the preservation of the apostolic message through the transition from the apostolic age to the postapostolic age may be seen, from a modern perspective at least, to be appropriate. There is no reason why 2 Peter should not hold an honorable place in the canon of Scripture.

Attestation

The weakness of the second-century attestation of 2 Peter has been a major factor in the prevailing scholarly view that it must be a second-century, even a late second-century work.

Two questions need to be distinguished: evidence for the existence of 2 Peter and evidence for its canonicity. There is better evidence than is sometimes admitted for the fact that 2 Peter existed in the second century. A long list of possible allusions can be gathered from Hermas, *1 Clem., 2 Clem., Barn.,* Aristides, Theophilus, the *Letter of the churches of Lyons and Vienne,* Irenaeus, Melito, the *Ap. John* and others (details in Bigg, 204–10; Chase, *DB*(*H*) 3, 799–802; Chaine, 1–3; Dillenseger, *MFOB* 2 [1907] 179–84; A. K. Helmbold, *The Nag Hammadi Gnostic Texts and the Bible* [Grand Rapids: Baker Book House, 1967] 91), but many of these are improbable, some are possible, none can be regarded as the kind of clear evidence that is required. However, the *Apo. Pet.* (c. 110–40) is very good evidence that at least one early second-century writer knew and used 2 Peter, and is sufficient to rule out a late date for 2 Peter. However we may account for the neglect of 2 Peter in the second century, the reason cannot be that it was not written until the second half of the century. The *Acts Pet.* (c. 180) is a later, but certain, witness of 2 Peter's existence (section 8 of *Literary Relationships*). Justin, *Dial.* 82.1 is a reasonably probable allusion to 2 Pet 2:1 (see *Form/Structure/Setting* section on 2:1–3a). Although *Gos. Truth* 18:20 is not a very convincing allusion, 33:15–16 refers to the first half of the proverb in 2 Pet 2:22. The facts that it is used with reference to apostasy and that the *Gos. Truth* never alludes to the OT make an allusion to Prov 26:11 much less likely than an allusion to 2 Pet 2:22, though we cannot entirely exclude the possibility that the proverb was already in Christian use with reference to apostasy when 2 Peter quoted it. The same slight ambiguity attaches to Hippolytus' use of the second half of the proverb with reference to heresy (*Ref.* 9.7.3: the most convincing of several possible allusions to 2 Peter in Hippolytus). Whether Eusebius' statement that Clement of Alexandria commented on all the Catholic Epistles (Eusebius, *Hist. Eccl.* 6.14.1) means that he commented on 2 Peter, has been doubted, in view of the elusiveness of possible allusions to 2 Peter in Clement's extant works (list in Bigg, 202), but the newly discovered *Letter to Theodorus* includes a likely allusion to 2 Pet 2:19 (see *Comment*) in company with Clement's characteristic use of Jude against the Carpocratians, and so the probability that Clement knew 2 Peter is increased.

Evidently 2 Peter was known throughout the second century, at least in some circles, but not widely used. We can only guess at the reason for this. Quite probably the churches which originally received it, knowing it not to be Peter's own work, would not have granted it the same status in their own use as they did, e.g., to the Pauline letters, and would not have circulated it to other churches with the same eagerness with which the works of apostles were circulated. It is quite possible that during the second century 2 Peter was not especially widely known, and that those who knew it tended to put it in the same category as works like *Barn.*, *1 Clem.* and Hermas, which were valued but not as authoritative as the works of the apostles themselves. To a work in that category we should expect only occasional allusions. A less likely possibility is that 2 Peter suffered by association with other pseudo-Petrine works, some of which were of doubtful orthodoxy, and may even have been known, as some have suggested, as part of a *corpus* of Petrine writings. (But the Muratorian canon includes the *Apoc. Pet.*, but not 1 or 2 Peter!)

Whatever the reasons for its lack of wide use in the second century, this seems to have contributed to its very slow progress toward general acceptance into the canon (details in Chaine, 5–12). It is not included in the Muratorian canon, though nor is 1 Peter. Origen, the first to refer to 2 Peter by name, records doubts about its genuineness (*ap.* Eusebius, *Hist. Eccl.* 6.25.11), though it is not clear how far he shared them himself. Eusebius, who placed 2 Peter in the *Antilegomena,* seems to have been impressed by the lack of ancient testimony to it (*Hist. Eccl.* 3.3.1, 4; 3.25.3–4). Jerome had to deal with doubts arising from the linguistic differences between 1 and 2 Peter (*Ep.* 120.11), but his own firm acceptance of 2 Peter among the Catholic Epistles probably helped considerably to overcome hesitations about it. As in the case of Jude, the Syriac speaking churches were the last to accept it.

Address and Salutation (*1:1–2*)

Bibliography

Fitzmyer, J. A. "The Name Simon." *Essays on the Semitic Background of the New Testament.* London: Geoffrey Chapman, 1971. (=*HTR* 54 (1961) 91–97.)
Picirelli, R. E. "The meaning of 'Epignosis.' " *EvQ* 47 (1975) 85–93.

Translation

[1] *From Simeon* [a] *Peter, servant and apostle of Jesus Christ.*
To those who have received a faith which through the justice of our God [b] *and Savior Jesus Christ is of equal privilege with ours.*
[2] *May grace and peace be given you abundantly, in the knowledge of God and of Jesus our Lord.* [c]

Notes

[a] Many MSS have Σίμων, "Simon," ℵ A K P *al* have Συμεών, "Simeon." Probably the latter is original and has been corrected to the more usual Σίμων.

[b] The reading κυρίου for θεοῦ in ℵ is clearly an assimilation to the more usual phrase (cf. 1:11; 2:20; 3:2, 18).

[c] τοῦ θεοῦ καὶ Ἰησοῦ is omitted by P ψ *al* and this shorter reading is preferred by Spitta, Bigg, Chaine, and Zahn (*Introduction,* 220). But it can be explained as a correction to harmonize with (a) the references to a single divine person in vv 1 and 3a, (b) the writer's normal use of ἐπίγνωσις with Christ alone as the object (1:3, 8; 2:20). The same considerations account for the reading in P [72] which also makes the text refer to only one divine person, by omitting καί. Some MSS add Χριστοῦ after Ἰησοῦ: probably an adaptation to the more common expression.

Form/Structure/Setting

The opening of 2 Peter conforms to the letter style described in the commentary on Jude 1–2.

(a) *The parties' formula* (v 1) includes the common theological characterization of the recipients. The phrase τοῖς ἰσότιμον ἡμῖν λαχοῦσιν πίστιν ("those who have received a faith of equal privilege with ours") has, besides its specific meaning (see *Comment* section), a formal function, in that an expression establishing a connection between the writer and his readers often occurs early in a letter (2 *Apoc. Bar.* 78:4; Rom 1:6; 1 Cor 1:2; Titus 1:4; 1 John 1:3; Jude 3; Rev 1:9; cf. *Acts John* 106, a sermon).

Like Jude, 2 Peter does not include a destination in its parties' formula. If 2 Pet 3:1 refers to 1 Peter, the recipients must be the churches named in 1 Pet 1:1, unless 1 Peter was already so widely known that the author of 2 Peter can think of it as addressed to all Christians. Second Peter 3:15–16 (see *Comment* on those vv), however, provides clear evidence that 2 Peter does address a specific church or group of churches, which must therefore be either all the churches in the area described in 1 Pet 1:1 or a smaller group of churches or single church within that area. This view—that 2 Peter was not written as a "catholic letter" to all Christians—is supported by the situation of danger from a specific kind of false teaching. For possible reasons for the omission of the destination from the parties' formula, see the commentary on Jude.

(b) *The salutation* (v 2) uses the commonest combination of blessings to be found in early Christian letter salutations: *χάρις καὶ εἰρήνη* ("grace and peace": all Pauline letters except 1 and 2 Timothy; also 1 Pet 1:2; Rev 1:4; *1 Clem.* inscr.). The use of *πληθύνειν* ("to increase") is also common in Jewish and early Christian letter salutations (references in commentary on Jude 1–2). The whole phrase is therefore entirely natural, and the close resemblance to Jude 2 and 1 Pet 1:2 will only appear striking to those whose knowledge of salutations is limited to canonical examples. No case for 2 Peter's dependence on 1 Peter can be based on this phrase (against Boobyer, "Indebtedness," 39; Fornberg, *Early Church,* 12–13); on the contrary, if the writer of 2 Peter were deliberately following the earlier letter he would surely have modelled his parties' formula as well as his salutation on 1 Peter, instead of diverging so greatly from the apostle's self-designation in 1 Pet 1:1 ("Peter, apostle of Jesus Christ"). The fact that *χάρις καὶ εἰρήνη πληθυνθείη* ("May grace and peace be given you abundantly") occurs in 1 Peter, 2 Peter *and 1 Clem.* may perhaps point to an established convention in the church of Rome.

Most early Christian letters indicate the source of the blessings by a binitarian formula such as "from God our Father and the Lord Jesus Christ" (references in commentary on Jude 1–2). Instead of using a binitarian formula in that way, the author of 2 Peter has adapted it to his particular interest in the *ἐπίγνωσις* ("knowledge") of God and Jesus (see *Comment* section).

Comment

1. *Συμεὼν Πέτρος*, "Simeon Peter." The form *Συμεών* ("Simeon") is the Greek transliteration of the Hebrew name שמעון. Jews of this period who bore this name normally used the Greek name *Σίμων* ("Simon") as its Greek equivalent. Thus, for example, Simon Maccabeus is normally *Σίμων*, but is once called *Συμεών* (by his father: 1 Macc 2:65). In the NT nine people, apart from Peter, are called *Σίμων*, and two people, apart from Peter, the patriarch Simeon (Rev 7:7) and an ancestor of Jesus (Luke 3:30), are called *Συμεών* (Luke 2:25, 34; Acts 13:1). It seems to have been the commonest Jewish name in the period 100 B.C.–A.D. 200, no doubt partly because it was a patriarchal (and so patriotic) name which was readily assimilated to a common Greek name. The apostle Peter is normally called *Σίμων* in the NT (and always in later Christian literature); evidently this was the name by which Greek-speaking Christians knew him, along with the nickname *Πέτρος* ("Peter"; the Aramaic form "Cephas," *Κηφᾶς*, is found only in Galatians and 1 Corinthians). He is called *Συμεών* only here and in Acts 15:14, by James in the Palestinian setting of the council of Jerusalem. The combination of the Hebrew form *Συμεών* with the Greek form of his nickname, *Πέτρος*, is surprising.

The use of *Συμεών* here has been regarded either as a mark of authenticity (Bigg, Green; cf. Mayor, James) or as a deliberate archaizing touch by a pseudepigraphal writer who tried in this way to make his work look authentic (Barnett, Kelly, Schrage; Fornberg, *Early Church,* 10). It is unlikely that Peter himself wrote the letter (see Introduction on *Authorship*), but against the second alternative it must be said that (a) no other pseudepigraphal Petrine writer uses *Συμεών*; (b) if the writer aimed at authenticity and if he and his readers knew 1 Peter (see 3:1), one would have expected him to copy the wording of 1 Pet 1:1; (c) in any case, it is unlikely that he expected his readers to think that Peter himself had written the letter (see Introduction, *Authorship*). J. A. T. Robinson, who thinks Jude wrote 2 Peter, sees *Συμεών* as a mark of Jude's authorship, since it is used by Jude's brother James in Acts 15:14 (*Redating,* 194). The theory that Jude wrote 2 Peter is untenable, but Robinson may be pointing in the right general direction. The form *Συμεών* may reflect the fact that the writer was an associate of Peter's who belonged to Peter's circle in Rome. Because that circle included Jewish Christian leaders (such as Mark and Silvanus) who had known Peter in Palestine the name *Συμεών* which was current in Palestinian Christian circles continued to be used in the Roman Petrine circle.

δοῦλος καὶ ἀπόστολος Ἰησοῦ Χριστοῦ, "servant and apostle of Jesus Christ." Again it is clear that the writer is following neither 1 Pet 1:1 ("apostle of Jesus Christ") nor Jude 1 ("servant of Jesus Christ"); the suggestion that he combines the two is ludicrous. He needed no model to produce this natural pair of designations, "the one drawing attention to his ministerial role and the other underlining his authoritative commission" (Kelly; cf. Rom 1:1; Titus 1:1). For the term "servant," see commentary on Jude 1.

τοῖς ἰσότιμον ἡμῖν λαχοῦσιν πίστιν, "to those who have received a faith which is of equal privilege with ours." The faith of the recipients is here compared with "ours." This has been understood either as a comparison between Jewish Christians, of whom Peter is one, and the Gentile Christian readers (cf. Peter's words in Acts 11:17; 15:9, 11) (so Plumptre, Mayor, Boobyer, Leaney; Hanse in *TDNT* 4, 2), or as a comparison between the apostles, of whom Peter is one, and the readers, who are not apostles (so Spitta, Lumby, James, Moffatt, Reicke, Spicq; Zahn, *Introduction,* 206–7; Stählin in *TDNT* 3, 349). The latter is more probable because there is no other trace of the Jewish-Gentile issue in this letter, and because in that case the first person plural is being used in the same sense as later in the chapter (vv 16–18). There is a further dimension to the comparison: in 1:12–15 Peter is represented as writing for readers in the period after his death. The comparison is therefore between the apostles and those who live in a postapostolic generation (so Schelkle, Sidebottom, Kelly, Schrage). The faith of these later believers is not inferior to that of the apostles (cf. John 20:29 for a similar thought from the same period; *Ep. Apost.* 6; and perhaps cf. 1 Pet 1:8). This interpretation has the advantage of establishing at the outset the major concern of the letter: to communicate the apostles' teaching to a postapostolic generation.

ἰσότιμον can mean either "of equal value" (so NIV: "a faith as precious as ours"; AV, RV) or "of equal privilege" (so RSV: "a faith of equal standing with ours"; NEB). In the latter sense the word was used for equal status or rank in civil life (*TDNT* 3, 349). This sense is preferable here because it allows a good meaning for *ἐν δικαιοσύνῃ* ("through the justice . . ."; see below).

But in that case *πίστιν* can hardly have the objective sense of *fides quae creditur* (see Jude 3 and commentary) (Schelkle, Kelly, Schrage, Grundmann). It is the Christian believer's subjective faith—based, it is true, on the objective gospel—which puts him in the same privileged position as the apostles (cf. John 20:29). This faith, as the verb λαγχάνειν ("to receive by lot or by divine will") indicates, is the free gift of God (see Hanse in *TDNT* 4, 2).

ἐν δικαιοσύνῃ, "through the justice." Some take "righteousness" here to refer to the redemptive work of Christ to which Christians owe their faith (Spicq, Stöger), but elsewhere in 2 Peter "righteousness" is an ethical quality (1:13; 2:5, 7, 8, 21; 3:13) and most commentators therefore rightly connect it with *ἰσότιμον*, taking it to refer to the fairness and lack of favoritism which gives equal privilege to all Christians.

τοῦ θεοῦ ἡμῶν καὶ σωτῆρος Ἰησοῦ Χριστοῦ, "of our God and Savior Jesus Christ." Does this phrase refer to two persons ("our God and the Savior Jesus Christ") or one ("our God and Savior Jesus Christ")? The absence of the article before *σωτῆρος* ("Savior") favors the latter, but is not decisive (cf. the similar problems in Titus 2:13; Jude 4). Some scholars therefore think the phrase intends to distinguish God and Jesus (Plumptre, Mayor, Windisch; Käsemann, "Apologia," 183 n.2), but a large majority think that *θεοῦ* ("God") is here used of Jesus. The following arguments favor this view: (1) Elsewhere in the letter the writer uses the similarly constructed phrase *τοῦ κυρίου ἡμῶν καὶ σωτῆρος Ἰησοῦ Χριστοῦ* ("our Lord and Savior Jesus Christ": 1:11; 3:18; cf. 2:20; 3:2), where there is no doubt that the whole phrase refers to Jesus Christ. When, however, this writer wishes to distinguish the two persons, in 1:2, the construction is different: *τοῦ θεοῦ καὶ Ἰησοῦ τοῦ κυρίου ἡμῶν* ("of God and Jesus our Lord"). (2) The doxology addressed to Christ in 3:18 is consistent with a Christology in which *θεός* ("God") can be used of Christ. (3) Perhaps also the usage should be seen as part of the writer's use of Hellenistic religious language (Fornberg, *Early Church,* 143).

The arguments against this view are not convincing: (1) The two persons *are* distinguished in 1:2. But the use of a binitarian formula in the salutation of a Christian letter was traditional, whereas in v 1 the writer is probably composing more freely. (2) Käsemann ("Apologia," 183 n.2) argues that since the stereotyped Christological formula (used in 1:11; 2:20; 3:2, 18) is "our *Lord* and Savior Jesus Christ," the use of *θεοῦ* ("God") here must be intended to distinguish the persons. But there is no reason why variations on the stereotyped formula should not be used. (3) *θεός* ("God") is rarely used of Jesus in the NT. There are a small number of certain instances (John 1:1; 20:28; Heb 1:8–9; cf. John 1:18 *v.l.*) and a number of texts where *θεός* may, with varying degrees of probability, be used of Jesus (Titus 2:13; 1 John 5:20; Rom 9:5; 2 Thess 1:12) (on these texts see V. Taylor, "Does the New Testament Call Jesus 'God'?" in *New Testament Essays* [London: Epworth, 1970] 83–89; R. E. Brown, "Does the New Testament Call Jesus God?" in *Jesus God and Man* [London: Geoffrey Chapman, 1968] 1–38; A. W. Wainwright, *The Trinity in the New Testament* [London: S.P.C.K., 1962] 53–74). Although not all of these instances are certain, the cumulative effect of their evidence must indicate that in the later decades of the first century *θεός* ("God") was occasionally being used of Jesus. Early extracanonical Christian literature shows that by the beginning of the second century the title was not uncommon (*1 Clem.* 2:1?; Ign. *Eph.* inscr.; 1:1; 7:2; 18:2; 19:3; *Trall.* 7:1; *Rom.* 3:3; *Smyrn.* 10:1; *Pol.* 8:3; Pol. *Phil.* 12:2; *Ep. Apost.* 3 (Ethiopic); *Apoc. Pet.* E 16; cf. *2 Clem.* 1:1). (For Jesus Christ as "our God," as in 2 Pet 1:1, see Ign. *Eph.* inscr.; 18:2; *Rom.* 3:3; *Pol.* 8:3.) Thus there is no improbability in 2 Peter's use of θεός ("God") for Jesus, nor does the usage require a second-century date for the letter.

It is hardly possible to tell whether the author intends precisely to attribute full divinity to Jesus or whether the term is used in a looser sense in conformity with pagan usage. It will certainly, however, reflect the Christian religious attitude to Jesus, expressed in the doxology (3:18), which was a response to the divine functions attributed to Jesus throughout early Christianity.

The other title here given to Jesus, σωτήρ ("Savior"), is found only sixteen times as a Christological title in the NT (Luke 2:11; John 4:42; Acts 5:31; 13:23; Eph 5:23; Phil 3:20; 4:14; four times in the Pastorals: 2 Tim 1:10; Titus 1:4; 2:13; 3:6; five times in 2 Peter: 1:1, 11; 2:20; 3:2, 18). In later writings it becomes rather more frequent (*2 Clem.* 20:5; Ign. *Eph.* 1:1; *Magn.* inscr.; *Phld.* 9:2; *Smyrn.* 7:1; Pol. *Phil.* inscr.; *Mart.Pol.* 19:2; *Gos. Pet.* 4:13; Pap. Oxy. 840, lines 12, 21, 30; *Diogn.* 9:6; *Ep. Apost.* 3, 5, 6, 8, 12; Quadratus, *Apol., ap.* Eusebius, *Hist. Eccl.* 4.3.2) and from the mid-second century onward very common. The term was used of God in Judaism and occasionally in early Christianity (see *Comment* on Jude 25), and probably its application to Jesus derived originally from this Jewish usage; early Christians saw Jesus as the one who exercised the divine function of salvation. Its increasing popularity in Christian usage, however, will have been due to its great familiarity as a pagan religious term: applied to the Hellenistic savior-gods and divine rulers, especially in the cult of the Caesars (*TDNT* 7, 1004–12). Our author's predilection for the title may be another sign of his willingness to use the religious vocabulary of his Hellenistic environment to communicate the gospel meaningfully to Gentile converts.

2. *ἐν ἐπιγνώσει τοῦ θεοῦ καὶ Ἰησοῦ τοῦ κυρίου ἡμῶν*, "in the knowledge of God and of Jesus our Lord." The question of a difference of meaning between γνῶσις and ἐπίγνωσις has been much discussed (see Picirelli, *EvQ* 47 [1975] 85–93, who reviews the debate; also Mayor, 171–74). It seems clear that there is no hard-and-fast distinction, and like the corresponding verbs γινώσκειν and ἐπιγινώσκειν they can be used interchangeably. But sometimes, at least, the prefix ἐπι- has an "inceptive force" (Picirelli, *EvQ* 47 [1975] 91), i.e. it denotes *coming* to know. This accounts for what appears to be a technical usage of ἐπίγνωσις (and to a lesser extent of ἐπιγινώσκειν) in early Christianity as referring to the knowledge gained in conversion (Bultmann in *TDNT* 1, 707). This usage of ἐπίγνωσις is found in Heb 10:26; 1 Tim 2:4; 2 Tim 2:25; 3:7; Titus 1:1 (in all these cases, "knowledge of the truth"); *1 Clem.* 59:2 ("knowledge of the glory of his name"); *Mart. Pol.* 14:1 (knowledge of God); *Diogn.* 10:1 ("knowledge of the Father") (and cf. ἐπιγινώσκειν in Herm. *Sim.* 9:16:7; *Ker. Pet.*, fragm.2; and γινώσκειν in Gal 4:9; *2 Clem.* 3:1). Such terminology has its background in Hellenistic Jewish apologetic

in which Judaism as knowledge of God was contrasted with pagan ignorance of the true God (Dupont, *Gnosis,* 47–49).

It seems clear that 2 Peter's use of ἐπίγνωσις (a favorite term: 1:2, 3, 8; 2:20) conforms to this usage: it is "the decisive knowledge of God which is implied in conversion to the Christian religion" (Bultmann in *TDNT* 1, 707). In contrast to γνῶσις, which is used in 2 Peter for knowledge which can be acquired and developed in the course of the Christian life (1:5, 6; 3:18), ἐπίγνωσις always refers to that fundamental saving knowledge on which the whole of Christian life is based. Similarly ἐπιγινώσκειν (2:21 *bis*) refers to the conversion experience of coming to knowledge (whereas γινώσκειν has an ordinary sense in 1:20; 3:3).

In this verse the Jewish terminology, "knowledge of God," has been expanded to refer to the more specific knowledge involved in Christian conversion by the addition "and of Jesus our Lord" (for the double object, cf. John 17:3). Elsewhere 2 Peter refers more briefly to knowledge *of Christ* (1:2, 3, 8; 2:20; cf. 3:18). The general idea of "knowing" Christ is not very common in early Christianity (John 10:14; 14:7; 17:3; 2 Cor 5:16; Eph 4:13; Phil 3:8, 10; 1 John 2:3–4), and 2 Peter's description of the fundamental Christian knowledge as of Christ is a special feature of the letter's terminology. The closest parallels are Herm. *Sim.* 9:16:7 (ἐπέγνωσαν τὸ ὄνομα τοῦ υἱοῦ τοῦ θεοῦ, "came to know the name of the Son of God"), and *Ep. Apost.* 6, which is worth quoting in full because it offers a general parallel to several features of 2 Pet 1:1–15: "And these things our Lord and Savior revealed and showed to us [the apostles], and likewise we to you, that you, reflecting upon eternal life, may be associates in the grace of the Lord and in our service and in our glory. Be firm, without wavering, in the knowledge and investigation of our Lord Jesus Christ, and he will prove gracious and will save always and in all never ending eternity" (*NT Apoc.* 1, 194).

The knowledge in question is no doubt both a theoretical acknowledgment and a personal knowledge of God and Jesus Christ, and 2 Peter's alternative description of Christian conversion as coming to know the way of righteousness (2:21) reminds us that it is also a knowledge with strong practical and ethical implications, as will also become clear in 1:3–8. The reason for our author's emphasis on the fundamental Christian conversion-knowledge and its ethical implications is the danger of apostasy through ethical libertinism (2:20–21) which his readers faced.

In this verse the usual binitarian form of Christian letter salutations has been modified by the introduction of ἐπίγνωσις (found nowhere else in early Christian letter salutations). It is only *as Christians,* who have come to and not renounced the knowledge of God and Jesus, that the readers will experience the blessing of God's grace and peace (so Dupont, *Gnosis,* 32).

Some commentators (Plumptre, Schelkle, Reicke, Green, Kelly) think that ἐπίγνωσις in 2 Peter has a polemical reference to the false teachers' claim to γνῶσις. However, its use seems to be sufficiently explained, as above, without reference to specifically "gnostic" adversaries. Second Peter never refers directly to any such claim, and, unlike the Pastorals where γνῶσις is used only in a bad sense (1 Tim 6:20), 2 Peter freely uses both γνῶσις (1:5, 6; 3:18) and ἐπίγνωσις in good, but different, senses.

Explanation

A former colleague of the apostle Peter, probably a member of a circle of Peter's associates and disciples in Rome, writes in Peter's name to the churches which had received 1 Peter. His concern to maintain the apostles' teaching in the period after the death of most of the apostles already becomes apparent in his description of the recipients. As Christian believers of the second generation they are no less privileged than the apostles themselves who had seen the Lord, because they still have access to the apostles' teaching, which remains valid as the basis of their Christian faith and life.

The distinctive feature of the salutation is the reference to the "knowledge of God and of Jesus our Lord," which refers to the fundamental Christian knowledge gained in conversion and which again introduces at once a major purpose of the letter: to warn against apostasy in which this knowledge is effectively renounced by moral libertinism. The writer invokes God's blessing on those who have come to know God and Christ in their conversion to the Christian faith.

Theme: A Summary of Peter's Message (1:3–11)

Bibliography

Boobyer, G. H. "Indebtedness," 40–44. **Danker, F. W.** "2 Peter 1: A Solemn Decree." *CBQ* 40 (1978) 64–82. **Deissmann, G. A.** *Bible Studies,* 95–97, 360–68. **Dupont, J.** *Gnosis,* 32–33, 380–98. **Easton, B. S.** "New Testament Ethical Lists." *JBL* 51 (1932) 1–12. **Fischel, H. A.** "The Uses of Sorites (*Climax, Gradatio*) in the Tannaitic Period." *HUCA* 44 (1973) 119–51. **Gross, J.** *La divinisation du chrétien d'après les pères grecs.* Paris: Gabalda, 1938. 109–11. **Normann, F.** *Teilhabe–ein Schlüsselwort der Vätertheologie.* MBTh 42. Münster: Aschendorff, 1978. 60–65. **Spicq, C.** *Agape in the New Testament.* Tr. M. A. McNamara and M. W. Richter. Vol. 2. London/St Louis: Herder, 1965. 374–77. **Vögtle, A.** *Die Tugend- und Lasterkataloge im Neuen Testament.* NTAbh 16. 4/5. Münster: Aschendorff, 1936. 48, 90–91, 188–91. **Wibbing, S.** *Die Tugend- und Lasterkataloge im Neuen Testament und ihre Traditionsgeschichte unter besonderer Berücksichtigung der Qumran-Texte.* BZNW 25. Berlin: Alfred Töpelmann, 1959. 80–81, 84–85, 104.

Translation

3 *His divine power has bestowed on us everything necessary for a godly life, through*
the knowledge of him who called us by his own glory and might,[a] 4 *by means of*
which he has bestowed on us [b] *the very great and precious* [c] *promises, so that through them you may escape the corruption that is in the world because of sinful desire and become sharers of divine nature.*

5 *For this very reason make every effort, by your faith to produce virtue, by virtue*
knowledge, 6 *by knowledge self-control, by self-control steadfastness, by steadfastness*
godliness, 7 *by godliness brotherly affection, and by brotherly affection love.* 8 *For if*
you possess these qualities in increasing measure, they keep you from being idle or
unfruitful in the knowledge of our Lord Jesus Christ. 9 *Anyone who does not have*
them is short-sighted, blind, and has forgotten that he was cleansed from his past
sins. 10 *Therefore, my brothers, make all the more effort* [d] *to confirm your call and*
election.

If you do these things, you will never come to grief. 11 *For in this way entry into*
the eternal kingdom of our Lord and Savior Jesus Christ will be richly provided for you.

Notes

[a] ἰδίᾳ δόξῃ καὶ ἀρετῇ (ℵ A C P *al*) is clearly preferable to διὰ δόξης καὶ ἀρετῆς (P[72] B K L *al*).

[b] Most MSS have ἡμῖν, but A has ὑμῖν. Confusion between the two pronouns is easy, and it is impossible to be certain which is original: ἡμῖν could be influenced by the preceding ἡμᾶς or ὑμῖν by the following γένησθε.

[c] The order of the adjectives varies in the MSS. Mayor and Chaine prefer τίμια καὶ μέγιστα (P[72] ℵ B K L *al*) on the grounds that normal Greek style would place the superlative second (cf. also Metzger, *Textual Commentary,* 699–700), but this supplies a motive for scribal correction, and so the harder reading μέγιστα καὶ τίμια (A C P ψ *al*) may be original.

[d] The words διὰ τῶν καλῶν ἔργων (ℵ A Vg *al*) are an explanatory gloss.

Form/Structure/Setting

The particle ὡς ("seeing that"), with which this section begins, has been left untranslated in the English translation given above. It is difficult to decide whether it indicates a connection with the preceding verse, so that vv 3–4 are an elaboration of the salutation, or whether it introduces a new paragraph. In the latter case it is necessary to take vv 3–4 as a protasis, to which the corresponding apodosis is found in vv 5–7 (so Knopf, Reicke). However, the phrase καὶ αὐτὸ τοῦτο δέ ("for this very reason," v 5) is so awkward an introduction for an apodosis, that we should then have to suppose an anacolouthon, with the writer starting a fresh sentence in v 5. This grammatical awkwardness has led the majority of commentators to prefer a connection with v 2 (so Spitta, Bigg, Windisch, Schelkle, Spicq, Kelly; Zahn, *Introduction,* 220; Fornberg, *Early Church,* 86). Such an explanation of the salutation is rare, but examples are cited from the pseudo-Platonic letters (Spitta, 29) and from the letters of Ignatius (*Eph.* 1:1; *Rom.* 1:1; *Phld.* inscr.; *Smyrn.* 1:1; see Spitta, 27–29). These examples show, not so much that the salutation is expanded before the body of the letter begins, as that the opening of the body of the letter is linked syntactically to the salutation. The reader is led from the salutation into the letter itself without a break. In the case of 2 Peter, although ὡς ("seeing that") seems intended in this way to create a loose connection between v 2 and v 3, it is also clear from v 5a that vv 3–4 are closely connected with what follows. The connection with v 2 is largely stylistic, whereas the connection with vv 5–7 is fundamental to the flow of argument. We are therefore justified in indicating in the English translation the main break between vv 2 and 3, and in treating vv 3–11 as the first main section of the letter.

These verses appear to follow a scheme which K. Baltzer (*The Covenant Formulary,* tr. D. E. Green [Oxford: Basil Blackwell, 1971]) and Donfried (*Second Clement,* 41–48) have shown to be a standard homiletic pattern in Jewish and early Christian literature. (Whether Baltzer is correct in deriving this pattern from the OT covenant formulary is unimportant here.) The pattern consists of three sections:

(a) a historical (or theological) section, recalling the acts of God in salvation-history: vv 3–4. (b) ethical exhortations, based on (a) and with (c) in view: vv 5–10. (c) an eschatological section, in which salvation is promised or judgment threatened: v 11.

Two of the best examples of this pattern are to be found in 4 Ezra 14:28–36 ([a]: vv 29–33; [b]: v 34; [c]: v 35) and *Acts John* 106–107 (see Baltzer, *Covenant Formulary,* 173–75). Both of these are farewell speeches, Ezra's before his translation and John's before his death. Clearly they are intended to encapsulate the essence of each teacher's message as he intended it to be remembered after his death. The author of 2 Peter evidently wishes to present in these verses a similar "farewell sermon" of Peter, a summary of Peter's definitive teaching as he wished it to be remembered after his death (cf. 1:12–15). (Donfried, *Second Clement,* 46, attempts to apply the homiletic pattern to the whole of 2 Peter, but to do so he has to regard 1:20–3:2 as interpolated. It is better to see 1:3–11 alone as a miniature homily.) The rest of the letter will then be devoted to the defense of this teaching against the objections raised by the false teachers.

Boobyer ("Indebtedness," 40–41) argues that these verses are "a review and amplification" of 1 Pet 1:3–9, but the relationship between the two passages is extremely vague, and only if there were more definite evidence elsewhere for 1 Peter's influence on 2 Peter would it be plausible here. The author intends to summarize Peter's teaching, but does not seem to have referred to 1 Peter in order to do so. If he was an associate of Peter's he would not have had to depend on 1 Peter for his knowledge of Peter's teaching.

Danker (*CBQ* 40 [1978] 64–82) tries to show that 2 Pet 1, especially vv 1–11, is modeled on the form and style of Hellenistic imperial and civic decrees, in which communities recorded the generosity of their benefactors. But few of the parallels he adduces to particular phrases in 2 Pet 1 are very close or remarkable, and he has to postulate a very considerable modification of the decretal form. The theory is not convincing. The most that might be said is that the highly rhetorical style of vv 3–11 echoes some of the kind of language used in official decrees (cf. also Deissmann, *Bible Studies,* 360–68). It does not follow that the passage is intended to resemble a decree.

The Catalogue of Virtues (vv 5–7)

The NT letters contain numerous lists of virtues (on which see Easton, *JBL* 51 (1932) 1–12; Vögtle, *Tugend- und Lasterkataloge;* Wibbing, *Tugend- und Lasterkataloge*), but 2 Pet 1:5–7 differs from the others in two important respects:

(1) In terminology. Wibbing (*Tugend- und Lasterkataloge*) has shown that, whereas the other NT ethical lists (except Phil 4:8) are quite similar in content to the list in 1QS 4, the ethical terms in 2 Pet 1:5–7 correspond much more closely to the ethical terminology of Stoicism and the Hellenistic popular philosophy. Three terms especially in 2 Peter's list are markedly Hellenistic in character and occur only once each in other NT lists: *ἀρετή* ("virtue"; Phil 4:8), *ἐγκράτεια* ("self-control"; Gal 5:23), and *εὐσέβεια* ("godliness"; 1 Tim 6:11). These do, however, appear frequently in non-Christian lists of virtues (Vögtle, *Tugend- und Lasterkataloge,* 91, 124; Wibbing, *Tugend- und Lasterkataloge,* 104; Dupont, *Gnosis,* 383; A. Deissmann, *Light from the Ancient East,* tr. L. R. M. Strachan, 2nd ed. [London: Hodder & Stoughton, 1927], 317–18). Πίστις occurs in non-Christian lists with the meaning "loyalty" (Vögtle, *Tugend- und Lasterkataloge,* 91), but in 2 Peter means "faith" as in other Christian lists. *γνῶσις* ("knowledge") is the only one of 2 Peter's terms which corresponds to a term in the list in 1QS 4, and it occurs in Pauline lists (2 Cor 6:6; 8:7), but also frequently in non-Christian Hellenistic lists, which may therefore be the basis for its use here (so Dupont, *Gnosis,* 392–93).

The Hellenistic ethical terms which occur in 2 Pet 1:5–7 but are rare elsewhere in the NT are more frequent in the extracanonical early Christian literature (see *Comment* section for references). Whereas 2 Peter's list is the odd man out among NT ethical catalogues, it is no longer so unusual when compared with the lists in *1 Clem.* 1:2; 62:2; 64:1; *2 Clem.* 4:3; Herm. *Vis.* 3:8:7; *Mand.* 6:1:1; 8:9; 12:3:1; *Sim.* 9:15:2; *Barn.* 2:2–3; *Act. Verc.* 2; *Acts John* 29. As it happens, the list which most overlaps with that in 2 Peter is the one in the *Acts Pet.* (*Act. Verc.* 2: the Greek original of this Latin text can be reconstructed from the *Vita Abercii* 13: T. Nissen ed., *S. Abercii Vita* [Leipzig: Teubner, 1912] 12). In this list of fourteen virtues, five of the eight virtues in 2 Peter (*πίστις, ἀγάπη, γνῶσις, φιλαδελφία,* ἐγκράτεια) are found, probably coincidentally, since although the author of the *Acts Pet.* knew 2 Peter, he based his list on Gal 5:22–23.

Thus, in its ethical terminology, 2 Peter's catalogue of virtues owes more to Hellenistic moral philosophy than do the catalogues in the Pauline literature, and in this respect it is closer to *1 Clem.* and Hermas, with their strongly Hellenized ethical terminology, than it is to other NT writings. This is not to say that in important respects (see (3) below) it is not a deliberately Christian list.

(2) In form. Unlike the other NT ethical lists (except Rom 5:3–5, see below), 2 Pet 1:5–7 uses the literary device known as sorites (also called *climax* or *gradatio*). The sorites is "a set of statements which proceed, step by step, through the force of logic or reliance upon a succession of indisputable facts, to a climactic conclusion, each statement picking up the last key word (or key phrase) of the preceding one" (Fischel, *HUCA* 44 [1973] 119). It takes the form A . . . B, B . . . C, C . . . D, and so on. It was widely used and recognized in the early Christian period. Examples from early Christian literature (apart from the ethical lists discussed below) are Rom 10:14–15; 8:29–30; and the apocryphal saying of Jesus in *Gos. Thom.* 2 and *Gos. Heb.* (*ap.* Clem. Alex. *Strom.* 5.14.96).

One of the distinct types of sorites which Fischel isolates is the "ethical and ethico-metaphysical" sorites (*HUCA* 44 [1973] 132–143). Stoic and other Hellenistic ethical writers used chains of virtues in sorites form to provide a memorable summary of their view of the good life (Seneca, *Ep. Moral.* 85.2, quoted by Fischel, *HUCA* 44 [1973] 134; cf. Maximus of Tyre 16.3b, quoted in BAG *s.* ὑπομονή), and sometimes also chains of vices to illustrate the evil life (Cicero, *Pro Roscio Amerino* 27.75; Epicharmus, fragm. 148, quoted in BDF § 493 (3)). An example from Hellenistic Judaism is Wis 6:17–20:

> The beginning of wisdom is the most sincere desire for instruction,
> and concern for instruction is love of her,
> and love of her is the keeping of her laws,
> and giving heed to her laws is assurance of immortality,
> and immortality brings one near to God;
> so the desire for wisdom leads to a kingdom (RSV).

This is not so much a chain of virtues, as a sketch of how the desire for wisdom leads to eternal life. A rabbinic example (*m. Soṭa* 9:15, ascribed to R. Phineas b. Jair, c. A.D. 90) is a real chain of virtues, comparable with 2 Pet 1:5–7, but corresponds to Wis 6:17–20 in having an eschatological climax:

> Zeal leads to cleanliness,
> and cleanliness leads to purity,
> and purity leads to self-restraint,
> and self-restraint leads to sanctity,
> and sanctity leads to humility,
> and humility leads to the fear of sin,
> and the fear of sin leads to piety,
> and piety leads to the Holy Spirit,
> and the Holy Spirit leads to the resurrection of the dead.

(translation adapted from D. R. Cartlidge and D. L. Dungan, *Documents for the Study of the Gospels* [London: Collins, 1980] 180; parallel passages in rabbinic literature are listed in Fischel, *HUCA* 44 [1973] 132 n. 38). In this category belongs also Rom 5:3–5, which (especially in view of v 2) has an implied eschatological climax.

A brief example of a sorites with the contrasting theme, how evil desires lead to death, is Jas 1:15.

The best early Christian examples of ethical sorites comparable with 2 Pet 1:5–7 are in Hermas. In *Mand.* 5:2:4 there is a chain of vices: "from foolishness is engendered (γίνεται) bitterness, and from bitterness wrath, and from wrath anger, and from anger spite; then spite being composed of all these evil elements becometh (γίνεται) a great sin and incurable" (tr. Lightfoot). The chain of virtues in *Vis.* 3:8:7 is part of an allegory in which the virtues appear as women: "they follow each other, in the order in which they were born. From Faith is born Continence (ἐγκράτεια), from Continence Simplicity, from Simplicity Guilelessness, from Guilelessness Reverence, from Reverence Knowledge (ἐπιστήμη), from Knowledge Love." The passage continues with an eschatological conclusion: "Whosoever therefore shall serve these women, and shall have strength to master their works, shall have his dwelling in the tower with the saints of God" (3:8:8, tr. Lightfoot).

In view of these examples, it is clear that 2 Peter follows an established Jewish and Christian rhetorical convention, adapted from Hellenistic moral philosophy, in which a sorites encapsulates the writer's ideal of the good life and the eschatological goal to which this way of life will lead. Like Hermas, the author of 2 Peter makes the Christian virtue of love the climax of the sorites itself, but seems aware of the traditional eschatological climax, since, again like Hermas, he adds this after the sorites (1:11).

One further feature of the form and terminology of 2 Pet 1:5–7 should be noticed:

(3) There is some evidence that a catalogue of virtues beginning with πίστις ("faith") and ending with ἀγάπη ("love") was an established Christian form (Dupont, *Gnosis,* 393–98). As well as 2 Pet 1:5–7 and Herm. *Vis.* 3:8:7 (quoted above), the form is found in 2 Cor 8:7. (Herm. *Sim.* 9:15:2 is really only an apparent example, but the order in which the virtues are listed may be influenced by this form.) See also the sorites in Clem. Alex. *Strom.* 7.10.55, where the eschatological climax is added: "For it is said, 'to him who has shall be given': to faith knowledge (γνῶσις), to knowledge love, to love the [heavenly] inheritance." With such lists should be connected the thought of Ign. *Eph.* 14:1: "perfect in your faith and love toward Jesus Christ, for these are the beginning and end of life—faith is the beginning and love is the end" (tr. Lightfoot). The chain of virtues beginning with faith and ending with love is a specifically Christian form which gives the way of life encapsulated a specifically Christian character, founded on faith and culminating in love. The rest of the chain between these two fixed points was variable, and evidently each writer using the form would make his own choice of ethical terms.

The close resemblance between 2 Pet 1:5–7 and Herm. *Vis.* 3:8:7 should be particularly noted: in both cases (a) the sorites form is used; (b) the list begins with πίστις ("faith") and ends with ἀγάπη ("love"); (c) each virtue produces the next; (d) an eschatological climax is added after the sorites. It is likely that they are two variations on a form in use in the catechesis of the Roman church. Hermas has seven virtues, the obvious choice of number. Second Peter has eight. Perhaps the author thinks of faith as the foundation, to which seven virtues are added. It is less likely that he has in mind the mystical significance of the number eight (Mayor, 192; see *Comment* on 2:5), which would not be appropriate here.

Comment

3. ἡμῖν, "on us." All the pronouns in v 3 are problematic. Are "we" the apostles (as in v 1) or Christians generally, including the readers (as in v 2:

"our Lord")? Some (Spitta, Bigg, Chaine; Zahn, *Introduction,* 220) think that the connection with vv 1–2 and the change to "you" in v 4 require us to think of the apostles. But (1) if the connection with v 2 is to be pressed, v 3 must speak of the knowledge which the *readers* have received. (2) If v 3a means that "everything necessary for a godly life" has been granted *to the apostles,* it is hard to see why this statement should be made. It could only be relevant if the apostles passed these things on to the readers, but it is not stated that they did. (3) The shift from "we apostles" (v 1) to "we Christians" (v 3) is easily and naturally made, and frequently occurs in the Pauline letters. Here the transition is even more natural because of the use of "our Lord" in v 2. (4) The transition from the first to the second person in v 4 is understandable as a transition to the exhortation in v 5 (see below, on v 4). A similar movement between "you" and "we" is found in 3:11–14.

τῆς θείας δυνάμεως αὐτοῦ, "his divine power." If the longer reading in v 2b is accepted, it is impossible to be sure whether *αὐτοῦ* ("his") refers to God or to Jesus, but the latter, as the nearest antecedent, is more probable (so Grundmann; Fornberg, *Early Church,* 144).

The phrase *θεία δύναμις* ("divine power") was a standard term in Greek literature (see references in BAG and Mayor; the decree of Stratonicea, in Deissmann, *Bible Studies,* 360–61), taken up in Hellenistic Jewish writers (*Ep. Arist.* 157; *Sib. Or.* 5:249; Philo, *Det.* 83; *Abr.* 26; *Spec. leg.* 2.2; *Conf.* 115; Josephus, *Ant.* 19.69) and later Christian writers (Justin *1 Apol.* 32; Clem. Alex. *Strom.* 1.98.4; 7.37.4). This is its only occurrence in Christian literature before Justin, and is an example of 2 Peter's use of Hellenistic religious vocabulary. Of course, as Dillenseger (*MFOB* 2 [1907] 190) points out, the equivalent phrase *ἡ δύναμις τοῦ θεοῦ* ("the power of God") is frequent in the NT, and the idea that the power of God is active through Jesus is also frequent (Matt 24:30; Mark 5:30; Luke 4:14; 5:17; 6:19; Rom 1:4; 1 Cor 5:4; 2 Cor 12:9; Heb 1:3; cf. 1 Cor 1:24). There is nothing unusual about the *idea* expressed in this verse. But it is still significant that 2 Peter expresses it in this Hellenistic religious phraseology.

The adjective *θεῖος* ("divine"; also in 1:4) is found elsewhere in the NT only in Paul's Areopagus speech (Acts 17:29: *τὸ θεῖον,* "the divine"; also Acts 17:27 D). It occurs only nine times in the LXX (Exod 31:3; 35:31; Job 27:3; 33:4; Prov 2:17; Sir 6:35; 2 Macc 3:29; 4:17; 9:11), but is very frequent in the more Hellenized Jewish writers: 4 Maccabees (25 times), Philo (see C. R. Holladay, *Theios Aner in Hellenistic Judaism* [SBLDS 40; Missoula, MT: Scholars Press, 1977] 177–83) and Josephus (Holladay, *Theios Aner,* 57–66). It entered Christian usage very slowly (*1 Clem.* 40:1; *2 Clem.* 20:4; Herm. *Vis.* 3:8:7; 4:1:6; *Mand.* 11:2, 5, 7, 8, 9, 12, 21; Ign. *Magn.* 8:2; Papias, fragm. 4), probably because its very broad usage gave it a polytheistic or pantheistic flavor. It is interesting to note that most of the few early Christian occurrences are found in the three (probably closely contemporary) Roman documents 2 Peter, *1 Clem.,* and Hermas, and the closely related *2 Clem.*

θεῖος ("divine") was a very flexible word, but here it must indicate, not that Christ possesses a divine or godlike power of his own, as though he were a second god, but that he shares in God's own power (Fornberg, *Early Church,* 144). It is the same power which will be manifested at the Parousia of Christ (1:16).

τὰ πάντα . . . τὰ πρὸς ζωὴν καὶ εὐσέβειαν, "everything necessary for a godly life." For the expression *τὰ πρὸς*, "what is necessary for . . . ," cf. Judg 17:10 LXX (B: *τὰ πρὸς ζωήν σου*); Josephus, *Ant.* 1:6 (*παιδευθέντες . . . τὰ πρὸς εὐσέβειαν*); Luke 19:42; Acts 28:10. The author of 2 Peter is fond of pairs of words like *ζωὴν καὶ εὐσέβειαν* (literally "life and godliness") and they are usually closely related in meaning. Although many commentators take *ζωήν* ("life") to mean "eternal life," we should probably understand the whole expression as a hendiadys: "a life of godliness," "a godly life" (so Reicke; cf. Fornberg, *Early Church,* 90).

εὐσέβεια ("godliness"), also found in 1:6, 7; 3:11 (cf. *εὐσεβής*, 2:9), is another characteristically Hellenistic term. It is found only nine times in the LXX, but is frequent in 4 Maccabees (47 times), Philo and Josephus. In early Christian literature, outside 2 Peter, it is found only in Acts (3:12), the Pastorals (1 Tim 2:2; 3:16; 4:7–8; 6:3, 5–6, 11; Titus 1:1; 3:5), *1 Clem.* (11:1; 15:1; 32:4) and *2 Clem.* (19:1) (cf. also *εὐσεβής*: Acts 10:2, 7; *1 Clem.* 2:3; 50:3; *2 Clem.* 19:4; 20:4). It denotes piety toward the gods, but also, especially in Jewish and Christian usage, the respect for God's will and the moral way of life which are inseparable from the proper religious attitude to God.

δεδωρημένης, "has bestowed." The verb *δωρεῖσθαι* (used eight times in LXX; in early Christian literature only here and in 1:4; Mark 15:45; *Diogn.* 11:5) especially denotes royal (Esth 8:1; 1 Esdr 1:7; 8:55), official (Mark 15:45) or divine (Gen 30:20; *Diogn.* 11:5) bounty.

διὰ τῆς ἐπιγνώσεως τοῦ καλέσαντος ἡμᾶς, "through the knowledge of him who called us." As in v 2, *ἐπίγνωσις* ("knowledge") is the fundamental Christian knowledge gained in conversion (Dupont, *Gnosis,* 31–32). This was Christ's first gift, by means of which he also gave everything necessary for a God-fearing life.

Since 2 Peter usually speaks of the knowledge *of Christ* (1:8; 2:20; cf. 1:2), most commentators understand "him who called" as Christ rather than God. In the rhetorical style of this passage there is no difficulty in referring *αὐτοῦ* ("his") and *τοῦ καλέσαντος* ("him who called") to the same person. In the NT it is usually God, rather than Christ, who is the subject of the Christian's calling. The only real exceptions are passages which refer to Jesus' calling of disciples during his ministry (Mark 1:20 etc.; but cf. 2:17 par.). Those who think *ἡμᾶς* ("us") are not Christians in general, but the apostles, argue that 2 Peter here refers to the call of Peter and the other apostles by Jesus during his ministry (Spitta, Bigg, James, Chaine, Barnett, Kelly; Zahn, *Introduction,* 220). But the idea that Christ called Christians is characteristic of *2 Clem.* (1:8; 2:4, 7; 5:1; 9:5: this usage seems dependent on the saying of Jesus in Mark 2:17 par., quoted in 2:4), and is also found in Hermas (*Sim.* 9:14:5), writings which are close to 2 Peter. *2 Clem.* 5:1 has 2 Peter's precise phrase: *τοῦ καλέσαντος ἡμᾶς* ("him who called us"). Further confirmation that 2 Peter refers to the calling of Christians in general, not apostles in particular, is found in 1:10, which surely takes up the idea of calling from v 3.

ἰδίᾳ δόξῃ καὶ ἀρετῇ, "by his own glory and might." The dative can hardly give the sense "called to" (which would require *εἰς* and the accusative, as in 1 Pet 5:10), but should be taken as instrumental. The pair *δόξῃ καὶ ἀρετῇ* should be understood, like other pairs of words in 2 Peter, as closely related in meaning. It is therefore unlikely that *ἀρετῇ* here means "moral virtue"

(Bigg, Green; Zahn, *Introduction,* 220). In fact, *δόξα καὶ ἀρετή* was already a stock combination in Hellenistic writers, especially Plutarch (examples in Wettstein). In this context, *ἀρετή* is virtually synonymous with *δόξα*, and denotes the manifestation of divine power (Deissmann, *Bible Studies,* 97; *TDNT* 1, 461). The phrase is a rhetorical variation on *θεία δύναμις* ("divine power") and presumably refers to the incarnate life, ministry and resurrection of Christ as a manifestation of divine power by means of which he called men and women to be Christians.

There is no need to see here the influence of 1 Pet 2:9 (where the plural *τὰς ἀρετάς* refers to the "miraculous deeds" of God, or perhaps to his "praises," as in Isa 42:12 LXX) or 1 Pet 5:10 (where *God* has called Christians *to* his glory).

4. *δι' ὧν τὰ μέγιστα καὶ τίμια ἡμῖν ἐπαγγέλματα δεδώρηται,* "by means of which he has bestowed on us the very great and precious promises." By his saving activity Christ gave not only what is requisite for godly life in the present, but also promises for the future. *ἐπάγγελμα* ("promise"; in early Christian literature only here and in 3:13) is synonymous with *ἐπαγγελία* (3:4, 9), the usual NT word for "promise." It could mean "the thing promised" (as in Philo, *Mut.* 128), i.e. Christ has granted us the gifts which had previously been promised (in OT times?), and some of those who wish to interpret the rest of the verse as referring to Christian conversion and baptism interpret *ἐπαγγέλματα* in this way (Reicke, Spicq). But it is more natural, and in line with the letter's general emphasis on the promises for the future (3:4, 9, 13; cf. 1:11, 6, 19), to think of promises which Christ gave.

The adjectives no doubt apply to the promises because of the great things that they promise. For similar language, cf. *2 Clem.* 5:5: "the promise of Christ is great and marvelous (*μεγάλη καὶ θαυμαστή*), even the rest of the kingdom that shall be and of life eternal" (cf. 2 Pet. 1:11); and (of *God's* promises) *1 Clem.* 26:1: "the greatness (*μεγαλεῖον*) of his promise"; 34:7: "that we may be made partakers of his great and glorious promises" (*εἰς τὸ μετόχους ἡμᾶς γενέσθαι τῶν μεγάλων καὶ ἐνδόξων ἐπαγγελιῶν αὐτοῦ*). The idea of *Christ's* promises, very rare in early Christian literature, which usually speaks of *God's* promises, is another link between 2 Peter and *2 Clem.* (cf. also *Apoc. Pet.* R, but this is probably dependent on 2 Peter).

διὰ τούτων, "through them," most naturally means "through inheriting the promises," "by receiving the fulfillment of the promises," so that what follows describes the content of the promises. To explain that the promises for the future kindle faith by which the Christian participates in the divine nature in the present (Mayor, Chaine) is to strain the words excessively.

γένησθε θείας κοινωνοί φύσεως, "you may become sharers of divine nature." The change from the first person to the second person plural occurs either in the previous clause (if we read *ὑμῖν* there: see the *Note*) or in this. In either case it is probably because the writer is already thinking of his intention to exhort his readers to moral effort (v 5) so that they may be sure of inheriting the promises. If the change comes only in this clause, it is also possible that Peter, represented as addressing those who will read his letter after his death (1:15), is considered to have already, at death, attained to a share in divine nature.

In these and the following words our author uses ideas and language which had a long history in Greek philosophical and religious thought. In the context of a basic dualism which contrasted the divine world and the material world, permanence and immortality were regarded as characteristic of the divine world, while transience and mortality characterized this material world. But a strong tradition of Greek thought held that the superior, spiritual part of man really belongs to the divine world and can recover its true, godlike nature and participate in the immortality of the gods. In the mystery religions it was through the ritual, through union with the god, and, in some cases, through a life of ascetic purification of the soul, that the initiate attained a new, immortal life and expected to live with the gods after death. In the Platonic tradition the soul regained its divine state through the philosophical contemplation of the realities of the divine world, through detachment from the body and through intellectual and moral purification. In the Hermetic literature gnosis was the means of divinization. In general the soul's attainment of godlike immortality, and its liberation from the material world in which it is involved through its confinement in the body, were necessarily closely connected.

The author of 2 Peter was doubtless aware of the currency of these ideas in the Hellenistic religious world, but he was probably more immediately dependent on the literature of Hellenistic Judaism, which had already adapted the terminology of Greek religion and philosophy in order to express its own religious tradition in terms appropriate to its Hellenistic environment. In 4 Maccabees and the Wisdom of Solomon, human destiny is presented as the soul's attainment of immortality and incorruptibility after death, in the likeness of God's immortality. See, for example, 4 Macc 18:3: the martyrs "were deemed worthy of a divine share" (θείας μερίδος κατηξιώθησαν); Wis 2:23: "God created man for incorruption (ἀφθαρσίᾳ) and made him in the image of his own eternity (τῆς ἰδίας ἀϊδιότητος) (*v.l.* his own nature, ἰδιότητος)." Pseudo-Phocylides (103–4) boldly combines the Jewish doctrine of physical resurrection with the Greek language of divinization: "For in fact we hope that the remains of the departed will soon come to light again out of the earth. And afterwards they become gods (θεοὶ τελέθονται)" (tr. P. W. van der Horst, *The Sentences of Pseudo-Phocylides* [SVTP 4; Leiden: E. J. Brill, 1978] 185; and see discussion in van der Horst, 185–88; H. C. C. Cavallin, *Life After Death* Part 1 [Lund: C. W. K. Gleerup, 1974] 151–55). Above all, Philo makes copious use of the Platonic language. In the experience of mystical ecstasy and definitively after death the soul of the virtuous man is "divinized" (see especially *Quaest. Exod.* 2.29), by which Philo means, not that it becomes God in the monotheistic sense of the one God, but that, escaping the material world, it becomes incorporeal and immortal, one of the divine powers of the heavenly world (see Gross, *La divinisation,* 86–94; C. R. Holladay, *Theios Aner in Hellenistic Judaism* [SBLDS 40; Missoula, MT: Scholars Press, 1977] 155–70). None of these Jewish examples envisages any kind of pantheistic absorption into God. They do not intend to blur the distinction between God and his creatures, but they do hold that the human soul, created in God's image, is capable of resembling God in his immortality and incorruption. This is "divinization" only in the loose sense of joining the world of "divine" beings who are incorporeal and immortal but not uncreated. To become, in this sense, "divine" is, of course, for these Jewish writers the gift of God's grace, not attainable on human initiative alone.

It is not difficult to find parallels, pagan and Jewish, to the phrase *θείας κοινωνοί φύσεως* ("sharers of divine nature"). Manetho, quoted by Josephus, speaks of a sage who, because of his wisdom and knowledge of the future, was thought to share in divine nature (*θείας δοκοῦντι μετεσχηκέναι φύσεως*: *c. Apion.* 1.232). Plutarch speaks of the most virtuous of the daimons sharing fully in divinity (*θειότητος μετέσχον*: *De defectu orac.* 10: *Mor.* 415C). Philo says that the stars and planets share in divine, blessed and happy nature (*θείας καὶ μακαρίας καὶ ευδαίμονος φύσεως μετεσχηκότων*: *Decal.* 104). (For the phrase *θεία φύσις*, see also Josephus, *Ant.* 8:107; Philo, *Abr.* 144; *Conf.* 154; Heracleon, *ap.* Origen, *Comm. ad Joh.* 13.25.) Such expressions most commonly use *μετέχειν* ("to share in"), but *κοινωνεῖν* is used synonymously in parallel expressions: *φύσεως κοινωνοῦντες ἀνθρωπίνης* (inscription from Commagene, first century B.C., quoted by Deissmann, *Bible studies,* 386 n. 2); *λογικῆς κεκοινωνηκασι φύσεως* (Philo, *Som.* 1.176).

Second Peter's use of this language raises two questions: (1) *In what sense* do Christians become "divine"? In view of the background sketched above, it is not very likely that participation in God's own essence is intended. Not participation in *God,* but in the nature of heavenly, immortal beings, is meant. Such beings, in the concepts of Hellenistic Judaism, are *like* God, in that, by his grace, they reflect his glorious, immortal being, but they are "divine" only in the loose sense, inherited from Hellenistic religion, of being god*like* and belonging to the eternal world of "the gods." To share in divine nature is to become immortal and incorruptible.

In that case this famous text in fact provides less support for a developed doctrine of "deification"—as human participation in the very life and being of God—than does the Pauline concept of the Christian's participation in the Holy Spirit. The latter is closely connected with immortality, in that for Paul the resurrection life will be glorious, immortal and incorruptible because the divine Spirit is the principle of life in the risen Christ and in risen Christians (Rom 8:11; 1 Cor 15:42–53). This thought *could* be behind 2 Pet 1:4, but it is not required by the Hellenistic language there used. Ignatius is closer to Paul than to 2 Peter when he says that Christians "partake of God" (*θεοῦ μετέχητε*: *Eph.* 4:2; cf. also Heb 3:14).

(2) *When* do Christians become partakers of divine nature? A number of scholars, connecting the phrase with concepts such as regeneration, adoption, and the gift of the Spirit, and sometimes with sacramental theology, think that participation in divine nature begins with Christian conversion and baptism (Chaine, Spicq, Reicke, Green; Dillenseger, *MFOB* 2 [1907] 192–93). Others regard it as an eschatological prospect, to be attained at death or at the consummation (Moffatt, Schelkle, Kelly; Gross, *La divinisation,* 109–10; Normann, *Teilhabe,* 65; Fornberg, *Early Church,* 85–89).

In Greek thought divinization was often thought possible to some degree within this life. In book 13 of the *Cor. Herm.*, man becomes divine through an experience of regeneration (and cf. the Hermetic *Pr. Thanks.* [CG 6,7] 64:17–19: "We rejoice because while we were in the body, thou hast made us divine through thy knowledge"). Philo thought that divinization was anticipated in the experience of mystical ecstasy. But always it was at death that the soul definitively attained a godlike, immortal nature. This was necessarily so because of the connection between divinization and escape from the material world of corruption and mortality to which the body belongs.

Exegesis of the earlier part of v 4 has already led us to expect reference to a future prospect, not a present experience. This will be confirmed by our exegesis of the final part of the verse, which follows the usual Hellenistic view in connecting divinization with escape from the perishable world.

The Hellenistic language suggests divinization at death, not at a general resurrection at the end of history, of which Hellenistic thought, including most Hellenistic Jewish thought, knew nothing. At this point the writer simply adopts the Hellenistic language without suggesting any modification of its meaning. It is probable that even the false teachers, who rejected future judgment and future cosmic eschatology, would have been happy enough with the description of human destiny given in this verse. At this point the writer is content, in opposition to them, to insist on the moral qualifications for attaining this destiny (1:5–9), but that he did not accept the individualistic Hellenistic eschatology without qualification is shown by the fact that he sets alongside it the more traditional Christian eschatological language of Christ's kingdom (1:11) and by his vigorous defense of future cosmic eschatology in chap 3. He may well have thought that Christians attained a provisional experience of immortality at death, but the hope of human immortality really belongs in the broader context of the hope for a new world in which righteousness dwells (3:13). Pseudo-Phocylides, 97–115, shows that it was possible to combine the Hellenistic language of immortality with the traditional Jewish language of bodily resurrection, awkward though the combination may seem to us.

ἀποφυγόντες τῆς ἐν τῷ κόσμῳ ἐν ἐπιθυμίᾳ φθορᾶς, "having escaped the corruption that is in the world because of sinful desire." The aorist participle indicates that the escape from corruption precedes the participation in divine nature.

Some commentators interpret *φθορᾶς* as moral corruption (Lumby, Chaine, Reicke; Neyrey, *Polemic,* 51), which is a possible meaning of the word (cf Wis 14:12). But the context demands the idea of physical corruption: decay, transitoriness, mortality (Sidebottom, Kelly, Schrage; Fornberg, *Early Church,* 88–89; Harder in *TDNT* 9, 104; Köster in *TDNT* 9, 275). Throughout Hellenistic religious literature is found the contrast between the incorruptibility (*ἀφθαρσία*) of divine nature and the corruptibility (*φθορά*) of everything in this material world, including man's body (see *TDNT* 9, 103–04, 254–55; Plutarch, *Mor.* 358E; Wis 2:23; 9:15; Josephus, *BJ* 2.154; 3.372; *Ant.* 10.278; Philo, *Spec. leg.* 4.48; *Mos.* 2.194; *Conf.* 154). The same contrast is found in Paul (1 Cor 9:25), who sees the whole of this world in bondage to *φθορά* ("corruption," Rom 8:21) and Christians too awaiting the eschatological gift of *ἀφθαρσία* ("incorruptibility," 1 Cor 15:42, 52–54; Gal 6:8). (Cf. also 1 Pet 1:4, 18, 23; *2 Clem.* 6:6; *Diogn.* 6:8.) In 2 Pet 1:4 *φθορᾶς* can hardly be anything else than the mortality which the Christian believer will escape when, at death or at the Parousia, he attains to an immortal form of life. It is in line with Pauline thought that this escape is an eschatological expectation, not a present experience, for in this life the Christian still participates in decay and mortality.

However, the Hellenistic dualism is here significantly modified by the phrase ἐν ἐπιθυμίᾳ ("because of sinful desire"). Decay and mortality are not due simply to the materiality of this world, as in Greek thought, but to sin (cf. Wis 1:16; 2:24; Rom 5:12; Herm. *Mand.* 12:1). Two fairly close parallel passages are Eph 4:22; "the old man which is decaying because of deceitful lusts" (τὸν παλαιὸν ἄνθρωπον τὸν φθειρόμενον κατὰ τὰς ἐπιθυμίας τῆς ἀπάτης); and 1 John 2:17: "the world and its sinful desire pass away" (ὁ κόσμος παράγεται καί ἡ ἐπιθυμία αὐτοῦ). It is true that ἐπιθυμία is by no means out of place in a Hellenistic account of the material world: it is the bodily desires for corruptible things which drag man down and entangle him in transitory material existence (cf. Käsemann, "Apologia," 180). But in such an account materiality itself is still the basic evil. The author of 2 Peter rejects this account and finds in ἐπιθυμία ("sinful desire") itself the root cause of evil, through which φθορά ("corruptibility") has entered the world. φθορά has then to be understood as divine judgment on sin, as it is in 2:12.

Although φεύγειν ("to flee") is often used in a moral sense, of avoiding sin, and although Platonist writers sometimes speak of the soul's duty to escape from its corporeal entanglements even during this life (Plato, *Theaet.* 176, quoted by Kelly; Philo, *Mig.* 9: "Depart out of the earthly matter that encompasses you: escape [ἐκφυγών], man, from the foul prison-house, your body . . . and from the jailers, its pleasures and lusts [ἐπιθυμίας]"), we should probably take ἀποφυγόντες ("having escaped") to refer, not to renunciation of sin at baptism (Plumptre, Spicq, Kelly) or throughout Christian life, but to the escape from mortality that comes only at death or at the Parousia.

It is true that 2:20 speaks of an escape from the pollutions of the world (ἀποφυγόντες τὰ μιάσματα τοῦ κόσμου) through conversion and baptism, but the difference in the wording of the two passages is significant. In becoming a Christian a person renounces sin and escapes the world's immoral influence, but he does not yet escape the mortality which is the result of sin.

Second Peter has come in for a good deal of criticism for its use of Hellenistic religious language, and this verse in particular has been a target of attack. Käsemann writes: "It would be hard to find in the whole New Testament a sentence which, in its expression, its individual motifs and its whole trend, more clearly marks the relapse into Hellenistic dualism" ("Apologia" 180). Later in the same essay, again mainly with reference to 1:4, he condemns the "anthropocentric character" of 2 Peter's eschatology, which is orientated not to the sovereignty of God but to the human desire to escape corruption and attain apotheosis ("Apologia" 184; cf. also Schrage). Käsemann's criticism of the letter depends on the exegesis of many passages, but with reference to 1:4 the following points may be made in response:

(1) The Greek aspiration for immortality was not simply denied but taken up and critically fulfilled by the gospel of the resurrection.

(2) The task of translating the gospel into terms appropriate to a new cultural milieu was (and has always continued to be) essential to the church's missionary role. "The interpretation of experiencing salvation in Jesus is not bound up with the language of Canaan, as salvation is meant for all, including Greeks. They may relate their experience of salvation-in-Jesus *in their idiom*" (E. Schillebeeckx, *Christ: The Christian Experience in the Modern World,* tr. J. Bow-

den [London: SCM Press, 1980] 304, on this passage). Our author, like other NT writers, was able to use the bridges into Hellenistic thought which Hellenistic Jewish apologetic had already built.

(3) Of course, the use of Hellenistic terminology involved risks. The author of 2 Peter seeks to minimize these risks by juxtaposing the Hellenistic eschatology of 1:4 with the traditional Christian eschatological language of 1:11. Moreover, the danger of an anthropocentric eschatology, which would certainly be real if 1:4 stood alone, disappears when the eschatology of the rest of the letter is understood: its dominant theme is the authentic primitive Christian hope for the triumph of God's righteousness.

(4) Full account should be taken of the fact that 1:4 is probably uncontroversial—the false teachers would not have objected to it—whereas every other statement on eschatology in the letter is polemical. It is in the polemical passages that we should expect to find the author's critical assertion of specifically Christian eschatology against Hellenizing tendencies.

(5) Even in 1:4 the Hellenistic dualism is in fact modified by the attribution of corruptibility to sin.

5. *καὶ αὐτὸ τοῦτο δέ*, "for this very reason," probably refers to the whole of vv 3–4 as the salvation-historical basis for the exhortation. Moral effort is required because Christ has given us (a) everything necessary for godly life (v 3), and (b) the promises of immortality (v 4). We cannot expect to escape the mortality which is due to sin (v 4) unless we ourselves avoid sin and make moral progress, the spiritual resources for which are available to every Christian through the knowledge of Christ he received when he became a Christian (v 3).

σπουδὴν πᾶσαν παρεισενέγκαντες, "make every effort." The verb is a NT *hapax* (and very rare elsewhere), but the meaning of the phrase is no different from that of *εἰσφέρειν πᾶσαν σπουδήν*, a favorite expression in the Koine (references in BAG *s.v.* *σπουδή*; Chaine; Spicq, *Lexicographie,* 668 n. 2, 819 n. 1). The expression is too ordinary an idiom for *σπουδή* here to carry the special moral connotation that *σπουδαῖος* had acquired in Hellenistic usage (as Harder in *TDNT* 7, 567, thinks), but it is an appropriate introduction to a list of virtues and may have been part of the traditional form which the writer uses.

ἐπιχορηγήσατε ἐν τῇ πίστει ὑμῶν τὴν ἀρετήν, "by your faith to produce virtue." This verb (also in v 11) means "to furnish, to provide at one's own expense," but is difficult to translate here. The meaning of the clause must be: "by means of your faith supply virtue," i.e. each virtue is the means of producing the next. But it is difficult to capture this nuance in an English translation which can also reproduce the form of the sorites without awkwardness. The usual English rendering, "add to your faith virtue" (AV) is not what the Greek says.

It is also not easy to see how each virtue is supposed to develop out of the preceding one. To some extent the concept is conventional (see *Form/Structure/Setting* section). In Rom 5:3–5, an example of a sorites using the same principle, there is a much more intelligible train of thought. In the rabbinic example in *m. Soṭa* 9:15, the way in which each virtue leads to the next is rather more obscure. In Herm. *Vis.* 3:8:7, an allegory in which each of the virtues is the daughter of another, it is as difficult as it is in 2 Pet

1:5–7 to see how each "gives birth" to the next. We must conclude that we are dealing with a conventional form, based on the notion that the virtues are interconnected so that in the virtuous life one develops out of another. In examples like those in Hermas and 2 Peter this concept is expressed conventionally, rather than with psychological realism, in that the order in which the virtues are listed is largely random. Although some scholars (e.g. Vögtle, *Tugend- und Lasterkataloge,* 48) have attempted to explain the order in 2 Peter, their attempts are scarcely convincing. Only two virtues have a clearly intelligible place in the list: πίστις ("faith") in first place, and ἀγάπη ("love") in last place. These were the two fixed items in the traditional form which 2 Peter follows, whereas the rest of the list was variable (see *Form/Structure/Setting* section). Of the author's selection of virtues, other than πίστις and ἀγάπη we can only say that he has chosen virtues familiar from the Stoic and popular philosophical ethics of the Hellenistic world, some of them very general in meaning, to give a general impression of the kind of virtuous life which the Christian faith should foster.

πίστις ("faith") occurs in Christian ethical lists (meaning either "faith" or "faithfulness") in Gal 5:22; 1 Tim 4:12; 6:11; 2 Tim 2:22; Titus 2:2; Rev 2:19; Herm. *Mand.* 12:3:1; *Act. Verc.* 2; and occupies first place in the lists in 1 Cor 8:7; 2 Tim 3:10; *1 Clem.* 1:2; 62:2; 64:1; Herm. *Vis.* 3:8:7; *Mand.* 6:1:1; 8:9; *Sim.* 9:15:2; *Barn.* 2:2; *Acts John* 29; *Acts Paul and Thecla* 17. As the beginning point of such Christian lists, it is not the πίστις ("loyalty") which appears in some pagan Hellenistic lists of virtues (see Vögtle, *Tugend- und Lasterkataloge,* 91, 189), but the specifically Christian "faith" in the gospel which is the basis of all Christian life. By representing faith as the root of all the virtues, the writer of 2 Peter is illustrating what he said in v 3: that Christ "has bestowed on us everything necessary for a godly life, through the knowledge of" himself. That knowledge of Christ is received by faith. It should also be noticed that, although the list of virtues includes terms highly characteristic of Hellenistic ethics, the whole list is given a specifically Christian character by the position of faith at the head of the list.

ἀρετή ("virtue") appears in Christian lists of virtues only in Phil 4:8 (a strongly Hellenistic catalogue) and Herm. *Mand.* 12:3:1, but is found in pagan catalogues of virtues (Vögtle, *Tugend- und Lasterkataloge,* 91). It was a standard term of Greek moral philosophy, in the general sense of "virtue," and as such was taken up in Hellenistic Jewish usage (especially in 4 Maccabees and Philo). Doubtless because of its typically Greek connotations—virtue as the achievement of human excellence, rather than as obedience to God—it is rarely used in the LXX or in the NT (only here and Phil 4:8 in the moral sense), and only slightly more common in the Apostolic Fathers (*2 Clem.* 10:1; Herm. *Mand.* 1:2; 6:2:3; 12:3:1; *Sim.* 6:1:4; 6:2:3; 8:10:3). In *2 Clem.* and Hermas—writings close to 2 Peter—the word is given a Christian sense, especially by means of its frequent association with δικαιοσύνη ("righteousness") in Hermas (cf. also Wis 8:7; and, on ἀρετή in *2 Clem.,* Donfried, *Second Clement,* 148–49), and we may assume the same for 2 Peter. Some commentators think that the word must have a more specific sense than "virtue," but the only such meaning available is "valor" (2 Macc 10:28), which is not suitable here. It is better to allow the word its common, very general meaning of "moral excellence." Catalogues such as this often contain very general terms alongside more specific ones.

6. γνῶσει, "knowledge," may seem out of place in a list of ethical qualities, but it was common in Hellenistic catalogues of the virtues (Dupont, *Gnosis,* 384–92), meaning either philosophical knowledge or "knowledge of God" (*Corp. Herm.* 13.7–9). In Christian lists, it occurs in 2 Cor 6:6; 8:7; *1 Clem.* 1:2; *Barn.* 2:3; *Act. Verc.* 2; *Acts John* 29. It is interesting to notice that in the non-Christian lists it was usually first or last in the list. In most Christian lists it has been displaced from these positions by "faith" and "love." γνῶσις ("knowledge") is not here that fundamental knowledge of God in Christ which makes a person a Christian; for 2 Peter that is ἐπίγνωσις. γνῶσις here is the wisdom and discernment which the Christian needs for a virtuous life and which is progressively acquired. It is practical rather than purely speculative wisdom (cf. Phil 1:9).

ἐγκράτειαν, "self-control," appears in Christian ethical lists in Gal 5:23; *1 Clem.* 62:2; 64:1; *2 Clem.* 4:3; Herm. *Vis.* 3:8:7; *Mand.* 6:1:1; *Sim.* 9:15:2; *Barn.* 2:2; *Act. Verc.* 2. Again, it is a characteristically Hellenistic virtue, corresponding to the Stoic ideal of the free man who is his own master and to the kind of Hellenistic dualism which sought to minimize the soul's entanglements with material things and therefore valued self-restraint and ascetic control of the bodily passions (see *TDNT* 2, 340–41; Spicq, *Lexicographie,* 61–63). As such, ἐγκράτεια was highly esteemed by Philo, and occurs in other Hellenistic Jewish writers, implying restraint from the excessive indulgence of physical desires (Sir 18:30; Wis 8:21; 4 Macc 5:34; *Ep. Arist.* 278; Josephus, *BJ* 2:120). It was often, but not exclusively, associated with sexual restraint. Quite rare in the NT (Gal 5:23; Acts 24:25; cf. ἐγκρατεύεσθαι, "to control oneself": 1 Cor 7:9; 9:25; ἐγκρσαής, "self-controlled": Titus 1:8), it becomes especially popular in the group of writings to which 2 Peter seems closely related (*1 Clem.* 35:2; 38:2; 62:2; 64:1; *2 Clem.* 15:1; Herm. *Vis.* 2:3:2; 3:8:4, 7; *Mand.* 6:1:1; 8:1; *Sim.* 9:15:2; cf. ἐγκρατεύεσθαι: *1 Clem.* 30:3; Herm. *Mand.* 1:2; 8:1–9, 11–12; *Sim.* 5:1–5; ἐγκρατής: *2 Clem.* 4:3; Herm. *Vis.* 1:2:4; cf. also *Barn.* 2:2; Pol. *Phil.* 4:2; 5:2). It was a Hellenistic ideal which Christian writers recognized as a necessary component of Christian ethics. The Christian, too, needed to be self-disciplined and not indulge his physical desires to excess. It is perhaps worth noticing that in Gal 5:23 it occurs in the context of warning against the misuse of Christian freedom in libertinism (Gal 5:13), which is also the problem in 2 Peter (2:19) and *2 Clem.* (Donfried, *Second Clement,* 116).

ὑπομονήν, "steadfastness," occurs in Christian catalogues of virtues in Rom 5:3–4; 1 Tim 6:11; 2 Tim 3:10; Titus 2:2; Rev 2:19; *1 Clem.* 62:2; 64:1; Herm. *Mand.* 8:9; *Barn.* 2:2. The word refers to courageous and steadfast endurance in the face of suffering or evil, and as such was a recognized virtue in Hellenistic culture. But it was also an important ethical quality in Jewish and early Christian teaching, not simply as a borrowing from Hellenism but as an integral part of biblical religion. In Jewish and early Christian usage the endurance is associated not with personal bravery or Stoic detachment, but with the believer's trust in God and hope for the fulfillment of God's promises.

εὐσεβείαν, "godliness": see the *Comment* on v 3. It occurs in pagan ethical lists (Vögtle, *Tugend- und Lasterkataloge,* 91), and elsewhere in Christian lists only in 1 Tim 6:11; *1 Clem.* 1:2. This rarity in Christian lists, like that of ἀρετή, may be due not only to its Hellenistic quality, but also to its very general meaning.

7. φιλαδελφίαν, "brotherly affection," occurs in Christian ethical lists elsewhere only in 1 Pet 3:8 (φιλαδελφοί); *Act. Verc.* 2; *Acts John* 29 (cf. also ἀδελφότης: "brotherhood," Herm. *Mand.* 8:10). In non-Christian usage this word denoted family affection between physical brothers and sisters, but the early Church used it for fellow-believers, brothers and sisters in the faith (Rom 12:10; 1 Thess 4:9; Heb 13:1; 1 Pet 1:22). It is therefore a specifically Christian feature of the list in 2 Peter.

ἀγάπην, "love," occurs in Christian catalogues of virtues in 2 Cor 6:6; Gal 5:22; Eph 4:2; 1 Tim 4:12; 6:11; 2 Tim 2:22; 3:10; Titus 2:2; Rev 2:19; *1 Clem.* 62:2; Herm. *Sim.* 9:15:2; *Act. Verc.* 2. It occurs (as here) at the end of a list which began with πίστις ("faith") in 1 Cor 8:7; Herm. *Vis.* 3:8:7 (and cf. 1 Cor 13:13; Col 3:14; Ign. *Eph.* 14:1). The significance of its place at the end of the list is elucidated by the catalogue of vices in Herm. *Mand.* 5:2:4. Here (as with the virtues in 2 Peter) each vice produces the next, but of the final vice it is said: "malice (μῆνις) being composed of so many evil elements (ἐκ τοσούτων κακῶν συνισταμένη) becomes a great sin and incurable." The final member of the series comprises all the others. Similarly, in 2 Peter, love, as the crowning virtue, encompasses all the others. The thought is similar to that of Col 3:14, which probably means that love coordinates and unites all the other virtues (cf. Dupont, *Gnosis,* 395–96).

Easton (*JBL* 51 [1932] 12) points out a danger in the early Christian method of teaching by means of ethical catalogues: "Jesus' ethical achievement was his centering the moral life around the supreme virtue of love, from which all other virtues derive their meaning. Hence in teaching by means of lists of virtues there was a constant peril of sacrificing this principle of unity and so splitting up the moral vision into fragments. In a list everything has equal weight, so that 'love' and (for instance) 'self-control' are coordinated. So the neophyte, bewildered as term after term was reeled off by his teacher, could very well satisfy his conscience by selecting and concentrating on virtues which especially appealed to him." This danger is avoided in 2 Peter's sorites, because the last, climactic term of a sorites is not of equal weight with the others. This most Hellenistic of the NT ethical lists in fact preserves very faithfully the place of love in Jesus' ethical teaching, as the virtue which encompasses, coordinates and perfects the others. The other principal danger in the ethical lists which Easton notes—that terms of Stoic origin should continue to convey merely a Stoic meaning—is also avoided in this list, where the virtues borrowed from Stoicism are not only rooted in Christian faith but also encompassed by Christian love. The borrowings testify to the fact that Christian ethics cannot be totally discontinuous with the moral ideals of non-Christian society, but the new context in which they are set ensures that they are subordinated to and to be interpreted by reference to the central Christian ethical principle of love.

Boobyer ("Indebtedness," 40–41) and Klinger (*SVTQ* 17 [1973] 162–67) argue that in stressing that the virtues must be added to faith, these verses are aimed against the exaggerated Paulinism of the false teachers (cf. 3:16), who made Paul's doctrine of justification by faith an excuse for ethical libertinism. The false teachers may have used Paul in this way (but see *Comment* on 2:19 and 3:16); more certainly, they based their libertinism on a denial of future judgment. Second Peter therefore stresses here the need for virtuous living if the Christian's eschatological goal is to be attained. The passage is not, however, explicitly polemical; it is intended as a positive account of the Christian way of life which will be defended against objections later in the letter.

When Klinger further argues that 2 Peter counters the lawlessness of the false teachers by reintroducing the Law under the new form of Stoic morality, we must be more cautious. The teaching of 2 Peter here is essentially very similar to Paul's own way of counterbalancing the danger of a libertinistic misinterpretation of his teaching (Gal 5:13–26), though it must be admitted that the Christological and pneumatological grounding of Paul's argument are missing in 2 Peter. But, as in Paul, neither the Law nor Stoic ethics are introduced except as issuing from Christian faith and summed up in Christian love.

8. *οὐκ ἀργοὺς οὐδὲ ἀκάρπους καθίστησιν*, "they keep you from being idle or unfruitful." This phrase (literally, "they make you neither idle nor unfruitful") employs the figure of speech litotes: affirming an idea by denying its opposite. It cannot be literally reproduced in English.

ἀργούς ("idle") and *ἀκάρπους* ("unfruitful") are one of 2 Peter's pairs of nearly synonymous words. The same pair is found, in a quite different context, in the letter of the churches of Lyons and Vienne (Eusebius, *Hist. Eccl.* 5:1:45): possibly a reminiscence of 2 Peter, or evidence that the combination was commonly used. A similar pair is used in *1 Clem.* 34:4, with the same meaning as in 2 Pet 1:8: "to be neither idle nor indolent for every good work" (*μὴ ἀργοὺς μηδὲ παρειμένους εἶναι ἐπὶ πᾶν ἔργον ἀγαθόν*). Both words were used in early Christianity in the context of the need for Christian faith to have ethical effects in the Christian's life. *ἀργός*, which means "idle" or "inactive," describes faith without works in Jas 2:20. *ἄκαρπος* ("unfruitful") depends on the common metaphor of fruit for good works or ethical qualities (Prov 19:22 LXX; Matt 3:8, 10; 21:43; Mark 4:20; Luke 13:6–9; John 15:2–8; Gal 5:22; Eph 5:9; Col 1:10; Heb 2:11; Jas 3:18; Herm. *Sim.* 4; 9:19:2), and is used in Titus 3:14 in a way similar to here (cf. also Herm. *Sim.* 4:4). It is not very likely that 2 Peter here depends on Jude 12 (*δένδρα φθινοπωρινὰ ἄκαρπα*, "autumnal trees bearing no fruit"). See also *Odes Sol.* 11:23: "For there is abundant room in your paradise; and there is nothing in it that is idle [the Greek version has *ἀργεῖ*], but everything is filled with fruit."

εἰς τὴν τοῦ κυρίου ἡμῶν Ἰησοῦ Χριστοῦ ἐπίγνωσιν, "in the knowledge of our Lord Jesus Christ." Most commentators take this phrase to refer to the goal or product of the virtues: virtuous conduct leads to fuller knowledge of Christ (Plumptre, Mayor, Wand, Chaine, Windisch, Schelkle, Reicke, Spicq, Green, Schrage, Grundmann; also Spicq, *Agape,* 376–77). But a few commentators take the knowledge of Christ to be the root from which moral progress proceeds (Spitta, Bigg, Kelly; also Dupont, *Gnosis,* 32–33). The latter is possible if *εἰς* has the vague sense "with reference to," "in respect to," which is possible in the Koine, and is required by 2 Peter's use of ἐπίγνωσις for the knowledge gained in Christian conversion (see *Comment* on v 2) as well as by the general sense of this passage. Through the knowledge of Christ he has given Christians everything necessary for godly life (v 3); if they exercise the virtues, this knowledge will be fruitful.

9. τυφλός ἐστιν μυωπάζων, "is shortsighted, blind." The verb μυωπάζειν, which means "to be short-sighted," is very rare, and is here a NT *hapax*. Its use in combination with τυφλός ("blind") is odd, since it ought to refer to a less severe condition than blindness. Some commentators (Spitta, Spicq, Green, Kelly) refer to the word's etymological meaning, "to close the eyes," and think that it adds to τυφλός the idea of *willful* blindness, deliberate closing of the eyes (cf. Isa 6:10 LXX: "they have closed their eyes"). The difficulty with this view is that the etymological sense describes the fact that the short-sighted person screws up his eyes in his attempt to see better, not in order to avoid seeing (Mayor). We should probably conclude that the writer uses the two words as virtually synonymous, as so often he does with pairs of words, supposing that the addition of μυωπάζων ("short-sighted") would increase the rhetorical effect. Fornberg's suggestion (*Early Church,* 53) that μυωπάζων is intended to suggest μύστης, the lower grade of initiate in the Eleusinian mysteries, is far-fetched.

The metaphor of blindness, for inability or refusal to see the truth, is common in early Christian literature (Matt 15:14; 23:16, 24; Luke 6:39; John 9:40–41; 12:40; Rom 2:19; 2 Cor 4:14; *Gos. Thom.* 28; cf. *T. Sim.* 2:7; *T. Dan* 2:4; *T. Jud.* 18:3, 6; 19:4). Particularly relevant are those texts which apply the metaphor to the moral declension of Christians: 1 John 2:11; Rev 3:17; and *1 Clem.* 3:4: "each man has forsaken the fear of the Lord and has become dim-sighted (ἀμβλυωπῆσαι) in his faith and does not walk according to the laws of his commandments." Especially in view of the latter part of v 9, there may be a reference to conversion and baptism as illumination, giving sight to the blind (Heb 6:4; 10:32; *2 Clem.* 1:6). The "knowledge of Jesus Christ," received at conversion, came as illumination to those who were blind in their pagan ignorance (2 Cor 4:4), but Christians who do not carry through the moral implications of this knowledge have effectively become blind to it again.

λήθην λαβὼν τοῦ καθαρισμοῦ τῶν πάλαι αὐτοῦ ἁμαρτιῶν, "and has forgotten that he was cleansed from his past sins." The metaphor of "cleansing" (καθαρισμός, καθαρίζειν) from sin is of OT origin (LXX Lev 16:30; Job 7:21; Ps 50:4; Sir 23:10; 38:10) and was quite widely used in early Christianity (Titus 2:14; Heb 1:3; 9:14; 1 John 1:7, 9; *1 Clem.* 60:2; Herm. *Vis.* 2:3:1; 3:2:2; 3:8:11; 4:3:4; *Sim.* 5:6:2, 3). Here, as almost all commentators agree, the reference is to purification at baptism (Acts 22:16; 1 Cor 6:11; Eph 5:26; Titus 3:5; *Barn.* 11:11). For the phrase τῶν πάλαι αὐτοῦ ἁμαρτιῶν ("from his past sins"), cf. Rom 3:25; Eph 2:2; 1 Pet 1:14; 4:3; and, with reference to baptism, Herm. *Mand.* 4:3:1 (ἄφεσιν ἁμαρτιῶν ἡμῶν τῶν προτέρων, "remission of our former sins"); Justin, *1 Apol.* 61 (ἀφέσεώς τε ἁμαρτιῶν ὑπὲρ ὧ προημαρτόμεν, "the remission of sins formerly committed"). The forgiveness received in baptism is a decisive break with the old sinful life and should therefore be the beginning of a virtuous life. The Christian who does not pursue virtue must have forgotten his baptism, and is in danger of relapsing into his pre-Christian condition (2:22). For this implication of baptism, cf. Rom 6:1–14; 1 Cor 6:9–11; Herm. *Mand.* 4:3:2 ("he who has received remission of sins in baptism ought no longer to sin, but to dwell in purity"); *2 Clem.* 6:9 ("with what confidence shall we, if we do not keep our baptism pure and undefiled, enter the kingdom of God?").

10. *διὸ μαλλὸν, ἀδελφοί, σπουδάσατε*, "Therefore, my brothers, make all the more effort." *ἀδελφοί* ("brothers") is a common form of address in early Christian letters. *σπουδάζειν* ("to be zealous, to make an effort") is a natural word for moral effort (Eph 4:3; Heb 4:11; *2 Clem.* 10:2; 18:2; Ign. *Eph.* 10:3) and is something of a favorite word in 2 Peter (also 1:15; 3:14). Here it echoes *σπουδήν* ("effort") in v 5. The phrase *διὸ μᾶλλον ἐσπούδασα*, "therefore made all the more effort," occurs, in a different context, in *Barn.* 21:9.

βεβαίαν ὑμῶν τὴν κλῆσιν καὶ ἐκλογὴν ποιεῖσθαι, "to confirm your call and election." *βέβαιος* (along with *βεβαιοῦν* and *βεβαίωσις*) had acquired a legal sense, meaning "ratified," "guaranteed" (see Deissmann, *Bible Studies,* 104–7; *TDNT* 1, 602; Spicq, *Lexicographie,* 182–83). Its use here is not a precise legal metaphor, for it was the seller, not the buyer, who "guaranteed" a sale, but the word probably retains a vaguely legal sense. Christ has called the Christian into his kingdom (v 3), promising him immortality (v 4), but an appropriate moral response is required if his final salvation is to be guaranteed. It is interesting to compare the sorites in Wis 6:17–20 (see *Form/Structure/Setting*): "giving heed to [Wisdom's] laws is assurance [*βεβαίωσις*] of immortality" (6:18).

τὴν κλῆσιν καὶ ἐκλογήν ("call and election"), which echoes *τοῦ καλέσαντος* ("him who called") in v 3, is another example of our author's predilection for nearly synonymous pairs of words. The calling is based on the choice, but there is probably no great distinction between the two terms intended here. Cf. Rev 17:14: *κλητοί καὶ ἐκλεκτοὶ καὶ πιστοί* ("called and chosen and faithful"); *Apoc. Pet.* R: *τοῖς κλητοῖς μου καὶ ἐκλέκτοις μου* ("my [Christ's] called and chosen": but this passage is probably dependent on 2 Peter); and for the close association of the two concepts, cf. 1 Cor 1:26–27; 1 Pet 2:9.

This passage does not mean that moral progress provides the Christian with a subjective assurance of his election (the sense it was given by Luther and Calvin, and especially in seventeenth-century Calvinism), but that the ethical fruits of Christian faith are objectively necessary for the attainment of final salvation. Although we should not obscure the variety of NT teaching about salvation, this passage is not so obviously in conflict with Paul's doctrine of justification by faith as is often supposed. (1) The author of 2 Peter is concerned with the ethical fruits *of faith* (1:5) and with moral effort which is only possible *through grace* (1:3: "his divine power has bestowed on us everything necessary for a godly life"). (2) Paul can also regard the ethical fruits of faith as necessary for salvation, even in Galatians (5:21), when countering the dangers of libertinism. (3) If our author seems to *emphasize* man's role in his salvation, the context should be remembered (cf. Fornberg, *Early Church,* 27). His readers were in danger of moral apostasy, under the influence of teachers who evidently held that immorality incurred no danger of judgment.

Apparently in the face of a similar danger, the closely related work *2 Clem.* also emphasizes righteous living as necessary to final salvation (cf. 5:5–6; 11:6–7). Cf. also *Barn.* 4:13: "lest if we relax as those who are called (ὡς κλητοί) we should fall asleep over our sins and the prince of evil receive power against us and thrust us out from the kingdom of the Lord."

ταῦτα, "these things," either refers back (like *ταῦτα* in vv 8, 9) to the virtues in vv 5–7 (Mayor, Chaine, Kelly), or to the effort to confirm the call and election (v 9). But these amount to the same thing, and a vague reference to the whole drift of vv 5–9 could be intended.

πταίσητε, "come to grief," is literally "stumble." Many commentators think that because this metaphor means "sin" in Jas 2:10; 3:2 it must do so here (Chaine, Spicq, Schelkle, Schrage; Fornberg, *Early Church,* 95; Moffatt and Sidebottom restrict it to serious sin), but this makes the sentence virtually tautologous: "if you lead a virtuous life (or: if you confirm your calling by leading a virtuous life), you will never sin." The metaphor must rather be given the same sense as in Jude 24 (*ἄπταιστος*: see *Comment* p. 122): it refers to the disaster of not reaching final salvation (so Bigg, James, Kelly, Grundmann, Senior). Perhaps the metaphor is closely connected with the following verse, and pictures the Christian walking the road which will lead him into the eternal kingdom; if he does not stumble on the road he will reach his destination (Bigg, Grundmann). There may even be the further thought that the blind man (v 9) *will* stumble (cf. 1 John 2:10–11) (Mayor). But these suggestions may see too much significance in a pale metaphor.

11. *πλουσίως ἐπιχορηγηθήσεται*, "will be richly provided." The verb is the same as that used in v 5, but this author's habit of repeating words does not usually have the significance of Jude's catchword technique. It is possible, but not necessary, to see the principle of the eschatological *lex talionis* behind the repetition: if you provide the virtues, God will provide your entrance into the kingdom (cf. Bigg, Mayor). In combination with *πλουσίως* ("richly"; cf. Rom 10:12; Eph 1:7; 1 Tim 6:17; Titus 3:6; *Barn.* 1:3) the verb here indicates the lavish provision made by the divine generosity. In spite of the emphasis on human participation in the attainment of salvation, the section ends as it began (v 3) with an attribution of salvation to God's grace.

ἡ εἴσοδος, "entry": the article is used because this is the Christian's expectation. The idea of *entering* the kingdom derives from the Gospels (Matt 5:20; 7:21; 18:3; 19:23; Mark 10:23–25; Luke 18:17, 24–25; John 3:5; cf. *Gos. Thom.* 22, 99) and, outside of the sayings of Jesus, is rare in early Christian literature (Acts 14:22; *2 Clem.* 6:9; 11:7; Herm. *Sim.* 9:12:3–8; 9:16:2–4; *Apoc. Pet.* R). It normally refers to the future eschatological hope.

εἰς τὴν αἰώνιον βασιλείαν τοῦ κυρίου ἡμῶν, "into the eternal kingdom of our Lord." Reference to Christ's, rather than God's, kingdom, is not very common in early Christian literature (Matt 13:41; 16:28; Luke 1:33; 22:29–30; 23:42; John 18:36–37; 1 Cor 15:24–25; Col 1:13; 2 Tim 4:1, 18; Heb 1:8; *1 Clem.* 50:3; *2 Clem.* 12:2; *Barn.* 7:11; *Apoc. Pet.* R; *Ep. Apost.* 39 Ethiopic; cf. Eph 5:5; Rev 11:15). Here it is consistent with the Christological focus of the whole section 1:3–11. Of course, the kingdom of Christ is not here *distinguished* from God's kingdom; hence it is eternal, not the temporary reign of 1 Cor 15:24–25.

Surprisingly the phrase *αἰώνιος βασιλεία* ("eternal kingdom") hardly occurs at all in early Christian literature, whether with reference to Christ's kingdom or to God's kingdom. Before Justin, it is found only here and in *Apoc. Pet.* R (*εἰς τὴν αἰωνίαν μου βασιλείαν*, "into my [Christ's] eternal kingdom"), which is dependent on 2 Peter (also *Mart. Pol.* 20:2 *v.l.;* and Aristides, *Apol.* 16, where the phrase is found in the Greek but not in the Syriac version, and is probably not original). Later it occurs occasionally (Justin, *Dial.* 32.1, referring to Dan 7; *Dial.* 117.3; Melito, *Peri Pascha* 68; and cf. also Philo, *Som.* 2. 285). Its occurrence here may be dependent on Dan 7:27 (cf. 4:3), which one might have expected to have had more influence on early Christian phraseology, or perhaps dependent on pagan terminology (cf. *αἰώνιος ἀρχή* in the inscription from Stratonicea: Deissmann, *Bible Studies,* 363). The *idea* of Christ's eternal kingdom is found in Luke 1:33 (cf. Rev 11:15).

In view of the eschatology of chap 3, the eternal kingdom here is not simply "heaven," but looks forward to the cosmic reign of God in righteousness in the new heaven and new earth (3:13). This primitive Christian hope is not "spiritualized" here by the Hellenistic language of immortality in v 4 (cf. R. Schnackenburg, *God's Rule and Kingdom,* tr. J. Murray, 2nd ed. [London: Burns & Oates, 1968] 325); rather it provides the proper setting for it.

τοῦ κυρίου ἡμῶν καὶ σωτῆρος, "our Lord and Savior." The author of 2 Peter is fond of this combination of Christological titles (also in 3:18; cf. 2:20; 3:2). Elsewhere in early Christian literature it seems to occur only in the *Ep. Apost.* (3, 6, 8 Ethiopic; but where the Coptic is extant, in chap 8, it has only "our Savior"), though Ign. *Phld.* 9:2 has "the Savior our Lord Jesus Christ" (*τοῦ σωτῆρος κυρίου ἡμῶν* Ἰησοῦ Χριστοῦ). For "Savior," see *Comment* on v 1.

Explanation

In this passage the author provides a kind of miniature "farewell sermon" of Peter's, summarizing Peter's definitive teaching as he would wish it to be remembered after his death. Although the substance of the passage is no doubt faithful to the historical Peter's message, its form and terminology must be attributed to the author, whose distinctive way of expressing the Christian faith is very evident in these verses. Following the path already pioneered by Hellenistic Judaism, he employs Hellenistic religious ideas and language to interpret the gospel in terms appropriate to his Hellenistic environment. At the same time he gives these borrowings a definitely Christian context which determines their meaning.

The first section (vv 3–4) establishes the basis for Christian living, in what God in Christ has done for us. By the divine power evident in Christ's life, death and resurrection he has called men and women to be Christians, and when they come to knowledge of Christ in Christian conversion they also receive through that knowledge the grace of Christ which will enable them to live a life of obedience to God. The basis for Christian living also includes the promises which Christ gave, which set before the Christian the eschatological goal of escaping mortality and attaining immortality. This goal is the typical aspiration of Hellenistic religion and is expressed in strongly Hellenistic language in v 4b. However, the author modifies the Hellenistic concept by indicating that the corruptibility and mortality of life in this world are due not simply to materiality but to sin. Thus the promise of escape from mortality imposes a strong ethical condition (vv 5–10).

Although v 4b has been a classic prooftext for the Greek patristic and Eastern Orthodox doctrine of deification, in its own historical context it does not refer to a participation in the life or essence of God himself, but to the gift of "godlike" immortality.

The second section of the "farewell sermon" (vv 5–10) exhorts Christians to a life of moral progress, in the grace of Christ and in hope of their eschatological goal. The list of virtues (vv 5–7), although it includes some distinctively Christian items ("brotherly affection," "love"), is notable for the predominance of ethical terms drawn from Hellenistic moral philosophy ("virtue," "self-control," "godliness"). But the whole list is given Christian definition by its first and last items—the only terms whose position in the list is significant. Christian faith is the root from which all these virtues must grow, and Christian love is the crowning virtue to which all the others must contribute. In a list of this kind, the last item has a unique significance. It is not just the most important virtue, but also the virtue which encompasses all the others. Love is the overriding ethical principle from which the other virtues gain their meaning and validity. Thus the author of 2 Peter sees that some of the ethical ideals of pagan society should also be Christian ideals, but only if they are subordinated to and reinterpreted by the Christian ideal of love.

The knowledge of Christ received in Christian conversion should have these ethical consequences, and such fruits of faith are actually necessary if Christ's choice and call of Christians is to be made good and his promises to them fulfilled by their attaining final salvation. The Christian whose life does not exhibit these qualities is in fact living as though he or she had not been converted and baptized a Christian. Since that person does not see that the knowledge of Christ received in conversion must lead to virtuous living, he or she seems to be still in pagan ignorance and appears to have forgotten that clean break with his or her pagan past which the forgiveness of sins in baptism entails.

The third and final section (v 11) holds out the prospect of entry into Christ's kingdom for those whose faith is effective in virtuous living. Despite the emphasis on moral effort in the second section, this concluding statement makes it clear that final salvation is not man's achievement but the gift of God's lavish generosity.

Already in this passage the threat of the false teachers lurks in the background. The emphasis on the fact that Christian faith must have ethical results and that Christ's promises have ethical conditions no doubt has the false teachers' indifference to morality in view. But this passage is not explicitly apologetic or polemical. The author intends here to present a brief positive statement of the apostolic message of which he wishes to remind his readers (1:12). He will then devote the rest of his letter to defending this message against the objections raised by the false teachers.

Occasion: Peter's Testament (1:12–15)

Bibliography

Boobyer, G. H. "Indebtedness," 44–51. **Vögtle, A.** "Die Schriftwerdung der apostolischen Paradosis nach 2. Petr 1,12–15." *Neues Testament und Geschichte: Historisches Geschehen und Deutung im Neuen Testament,* ed. H. Baltensweiler and B. Reicke. (O. Cullmann Festschrift) Zürich: Theologischer Verlag/Tübingen: J. C. B. Mohr. 1972.

Translation

[12] *Therefore I am going to be* [a] *always reminding you of these things, even though you know them and are established in the truth that you have.* [13] *I consider it my duty, as long as I am in this body, to arouse you with a reminder,* [14] *since I know that I must soon be divested of my body, as our Lord Jesus Christ also informed me.* [15] *But I will also do my best to see that after my death you will be able to recall these things at all times.*

Notes

[a] The textual variations at this point have no doubt arisen because of the difficulty of the best reading μελλήσω, "I am going to" (see *Comment* section).

Form/Structure/Setting

This section states the occasion for the letter, namely Peter's intention of leaving a testament. Its position in the letter at this point is no doubt determined by its function as a transition from the positive summary of Peter's teaching in 1:3–11, to the apologetic defense of this teaching against objections in the rest of the letter. By introducing the idea that the letter, as a testament, is intended for the period after Peter's death, the author is able to begin dealing with objections which are being raised in his own time.

Two conventions of the testament genre appear in this section: (1) the hero knows that his death is approaching (v 14; for references see *Comment* section); (2) he wishes his teaching to be remembered after his death (v 12; for references see *Comment* section). Parallel ideas and phrases are especially to be found in two other examples of the genre: Baruch's testament in the form of a letter (*2 Apoc. Bar.* 78–86; see especially 78:5; 84:1, 7–9; 86:1–2) and Josephus' account of Moses' last words (*Ant.* 4.309–19; see especially 315–16, 318). These parallels doubtless derive from the conventions of the genre, not from literary dependence. It is this section in particular which would enable contemporary readers of 2 Peter to recognize its literary genre, including its pseudepigraphal character.

Comment

12. διό, "therefore," presumably means: because salvation (v 11) depends on following the teaching of vv 3–11 (=τούτων, "these things").

μελλήσω ἀεὶ ὑμᾶς ὑπομιμνήσκειν, "I am going to be always reminding you." The future μελλήσω is difficult. There are two possible translations: (a) "I shall be ready to . . ." (RV), i.e. "the writer will be ready in the future, as often as necessity arises, to recall to the minds of the readers truths with which they are familiar" (Zahn, *Introduction*, 211 n. 3); (b) "I shall . . . ," i.e. a periphrasis for a simple future (Bigg, Wand). In classical Greek, and rarely in the Koine (Acts 11:28; 24:15; 27:10), μέλλειν with the future infinitive means "will certainly"; in the Koine, μέλλειν with the present infinitive can serve simply as a periphrasis for the future. But there seems to be only one other example (Matt 24:6) of the *future* tense of μέλλειν, followed by the present infinitive, serving this purpose. The difficulty of the text leads Mayor to adopt Field's emendation μελήσω, "I will take care to . . ."; but the usual construction would be μελήσει μοι, "I will take care to . . . ," and although there are rare examples of μελήσω (Mayor, cxciii), their rarity is sufficient to cast doubt on the emendation. The translation found in some English versions, "I intend to . . ." (RSV) is not really possible for the future μελλήσω.

Translation (a) has the effect of excluding a reference to the present letter, and also requires that ἀεί ("always") be limited to the short time (v 14) before the apostle's death. Since the purpose of this paragraph seems to be to explain the present letter, it is better to adopt translation (b). The writer has adopted an unusual, but possible, periphrasis for ὑπομνήσω ("I shall remind").

If the writer intends to refer to the present letter, it is at first sight odd that he uses a future tense, and a similar problem arises with σπουδάσω ("I will do my best") in v 15. Usually in Greek letters a writer used the aorist tense to refer to his writing of the letter and the occasion which provoked it (e.g. Jude 3); this was the tense appropriate from the standpoint of the readers of the letter. He could use the present tense to refer to his intentions as he writes the letter (e.g. Jude 5). He could use the future tense to refer to what he is going to do in the following section of the letter (e.g. *Barn.* 1:8). But this use of the future tense cannot be our writer's use in vv 12 and 15. He cannot mean that in the rest of the letter he intends to remind his readers of what he has said in vv 3–11, because this is not what he does in the rest of the letter. If he refers to the present letter at all, it must be with primary reference to 1:3–11, and only secondary reference to the rest of the letter.

In fact, the use of the future tense with reference to the whole of the present letter, though unusual, is quite intelligible here. The apostle is represented as thinking not of the activity of writing the letter, but of the function which the letter will perform when he has written it. He intends the letter to be a *permanent* reminder of his teaching, not only to be read on one specific occasion, but to be available at all times (1:15). Thus even from the standpoint of his readers the letter's function of reminding continues into the future. So neither the epistolary aorist, which would imply that from the readers' standpoint the action of reminding is complete, nor the present tense, which would not convey the apostle's intention of writing for the future, would have been appropriate.

As the next three verses imply, ἀεί ("always") means both up to and after the apostle's death. By means of his letter, Peter will be able to remind the readers of his essential message not only in the brief time before his death, but also after his death. In other words, the future tense here, with ἀεί ("always"), expresses the intention appropriate, not to an ordinary letter, but to a testament (so, essentially, Vögtle, "Schriftwerdung," 298–300). Especially as a *written* form of the farewell discourse, the testament is intended as a permanent reminder of the apostle's definitive teaching.

This does not mean, however, that the real writer of 2 Peter, writing in Peter's name after Peter's death, was himself looking very far into the future. He himself was writing, not for the future, but for the present circumstances of his readers, which were future from the fictitious standpoint in Peter's lifetime. He wrote to combat the concrete threat of false teaching which threatened his readers at the time when he wrote the letter. Thus ἀεί ("always") is intended primarily to cover the time up to the real time of writing, and the writer wrote Peter's "testament" not to preserve Peter's teaching for the future in general, but to apply it specifically to specific readers at a specific time. Probably, although his theological account of the delay of the Parousia (3:8–9) could accommodate an indefinite delay, he did not expect the Parousia to be long delayed (cf. 1:19; 3:3, 12, 14), and certainly did not write for generations of future Christians.

The fact that the writer represents Peter as writing a testament by means of which he will be able to remind "you" (ὑμᾶς) of his teaching even after his death is an important indication that the writer is not, like some writers of pseudepigraphal apostolic letters (e.g. "*3 Corinthians*"), imagining fictitious *readers* of the letter as part of the whole pseudepigraphal device. He has deliberately used a form of pseudepigraphon, the testament, by which he can represent Peter as addressing readers *after his death.* This means that "you" are specific Christian communities about which the historical Peter knew and which he could be represented as having in mind as the recipients of this testament. (3:1 indicates that they are the communities to which 1 Peter was addressed.) To press "you" to mean that the actual members of the Christian communities addressed must have been alive before Peter's death, or that most of them had, is probably to take the argument too far (this is not implied when Polycarp, *Phil.* 3:2, tells the Philippians that Paul "came among you" and "wrote a letter to you").

The ideas of reminding and remembering, stressed both in these verses and in 3:1–2 (1:12: ὑπομιμνῄσκειν; 1:13: ὑπομνήσει; 1:15: μνήμην ποιεῖσθαι; 3:1: ὑπομνήσει; 3:2: μνησθῆναι) are very important for the writer's conception of his purpose in writing (Käsemann, "Apologia," 177). They are naturally appropriate and recurrent themes of farewell discourses (*Jub.* 22:16; *2 Apoc. Bar.* 84:7–8; *Bib. Ant.* 19:5; 24:3; Josephus, *Ant.* 4.318; John 14:16; Acts 20:31; 2 Tim 2:8, 14; *Act. Verc.* 36), a major concern of which is often that the speaker's teaching be remembered and observed after his death (cf. also *T.*

Mos. 10:11; *T. Sim.* 7:3; *T. Dan* 6:9). By adopting the literary genre of the testament, the writer of 2 Peter shows that he has no intention of presenting new teaching of his own, but reproduces only what the apostle Peter had taught and handed on (Zmijewski, *BZ* 23 [1979] 166, 169). He writes in Peter's name and claims Peter's authority because (and to the extent that) he transmits Peter's message. Of course, this transmission is at the same time an interpretation and application of Peter's message appropriate to his readers' situation at the time when he wrote. In 1:3–11 he has exercised the freedom of interpreting Peter's message in Hellenistic religious vocabulary which the apostle would doubtless not have used, and in the rest of the letter (as Neyrey, *Polemic,* 106, 109–10, stresses) his "reminding" will take the form of an apologetic *defense* of the apostolic message against the false teachers of his own time. In these ways he maintains the tradition of Peter's teaching in a living, not an antiquarian, form, but it is on its claim to be an authentic "reminder" of the apostolic message that 2 Peter's status as an "apostolic" writing, belonging within the NT canon, must be based.

περὶ τούτων, "of these things," refers back to vv 3–11, the summary of Peter's message committed to writing for the benefit of readers after his death.

καίπερ εἰδότας, "even though you know them:" see commentary on Jude 5, which may lie behind 2 Peter at this point. The content of Peter's message is no more than the basic Christian instruction which all Christians have received. Since Peter had probably not evangelized the communities addressed (see *Comment* on 3:2), the writer clearly regards Peter's message, which he transmits, as the common apostolic message. In vv 16–18 he will *defend* this message by appeal to specially Petrine testimony, but the message itself is that which all the apostles, including Paul (3:15), preached. There is no need to see this as an "early Catholic" trait which idealizes the apostolic age (so Knoch, "Vermächtnis," 154–5); despite the tensions between them, the apostles did see themselves as proclaiming the same gospel (Gal 2:7).

ἐστηριγμένους ἐν τῇ παρούσῃ ἀληθείᾳ, "are established in the truth that you have." *στηρίζειν* ("to establish"), *ἀστήρικτος* ("unstable": 2:14; 3:16) and *στηριγμός* ("stability": 3:17) are a favorite word-group in 2 Peter. The verb is quite common in a metaphorical sense in early Christian literature (examples which bear some comparison with the use in 2 Peter: Luke 22:32; Acts 18:3; Rom 16:25; 1 Thess 3:2; 1 Pet 5:10; *2 Clem.* 2:6). Here it means that the readers are well-grounded in the Christian faith, instructed in it, firmly committed to it, and therefore not likely to be easily misled by false teaching. Of course, the communities included those who were coming under the influence of the false teachers and who could therefore be described as "unstable" (2:14), while the whole letter shows the writer's concern that his readers should not "lose their stability." So there is probably an element of hopefulness in the description of them in this verse.

A particularly illuminating parallel to our author's concern for "stability" in the truth is found in the introduction to the *Ep. Apost.,* a writing which is also concerned, at a somewhat later date, with the preservation of the authentic apostolic gospel in the face of heresy. The letter is said to have been written "that you may be established and not waver, not be shaken and not turn away from the word of the Gospel that you have heard" (*Ep. Apost.* 1: *NT Apoc.* 1, 191–92).

τῇ παρούσῃ ἀληθείᾳ, "the truth that you have," is not the truth which the readers have *contrasted* with further truth which they do not yet have. The phrase simply makes the point that they do already have this truth and do not need to be given it for the first time. The phrase is 2 Peter's equivalent to Jude's "the faith which was once and for all delivered to the saints" (Jude 3: see *Comment*), and like that phrase means simply the Christian message, as taught to the readers at their conversion. ἀληθεία ("truth") was a widespread and frequent designation for the gospel from an early period (Gal 2:5, 14; 5:7; Eph 1:13; Col 1:5; 2 Thess 2:12–13; 2 Tim 2:15; Jas 1:18; 2 John 4 etc.): there is no need to read into it "early Catholic" overtones of a rigid dogmatic corpus of belief. Here, of course, the writer has in mind especially those aspects of the Christian message (moral and eschatological) which he has stressed in his summary in vv 3–11, and will defend against the false teachers in the rest of the letter.

13. ἐν τούτῳ τῷ σκηνώματι, "in this body." σκηνώμα (lit. "tent") was a current Greek term for the body, interchangeable with σκῆνος ("tent": Wis 9:15; 1 Cor 5:1, 4). Of the two, σκηνώμα appears to have been rather more popular in the early centuries A.D. As a metaphor it conveys the image of the body as a temporary dwelling-place for the soul, folded up and abandoned when the soul leaves it at death. It therefore tends to be used especially in contexts which distinguish the soul from its dwelling-place the body (*Paral. Jer.* 6:6–7: σκηνώμα as the dwelling-place of the heart, καρδία; Tatian, *Oratio* 15: σκηνώμα as the habitation of the spirit; *Sentences of Sextus* 320: τὸ σκήνωμα τῆς ψυχῆς σου, "the dwelling-place of your soul"), stress the immortal soul's temporary dwelling in the mortal body (*Diogn.* 6:8), or refer to death (*Apoc. Paul* 15: at death the soul leaves its σκήνωμα). Frequently it refers to corpses, the tents left behind by their departed inhabitants (non-Christian references in *TDNT* 7, 383; Eusebius, *Hist. Eccl.* 2.25.6; 3.31.1–2, of the burial of the bodies of Peter and Paul; *Palaea historica,* quoted in the Excursus on Jude 9, of Moses' corpse). It is therefore an appropriate term in the context of these verses, where Peter contemplates his death. No doubt it carries some connotations of the Hellenistic anthropological dualism of soul and body, and is another example of the writer's Hellenistic terminology. But it should not be overlooked that Paul also adopted the current Hellenistic metaphor when he contemplated his death in 2 Cor 5:1–4. The term was too common for there to be any likelihood that 2 Peter is here dependent on Paul (who uses σκῆνος, not σκηνώμα); still less is there any reference to Peter's offer to build "three tabernacles" (σκηνάς: Mark 9:5 par.) in the Transfiguration narrative (Plumptre, Green).

With the whole verse, cf. *2 Apoc. Bar.* 84:1 (from Baruch's "testamentary" letter): "Behold! I have therefore made known unto you these things *whilst I live;* for I said that ye should learn the things that are excellent; for the Mighty One hath commanded to instruct you; and I will set before you some of the commandments of his judgment *before I die*" (tr. Charles; and cf. 78:5; *Bib. Ant.* 19:5; Josephus, *Ant.* 4. 316, 318).

14. *ταχινή*, "soon." *ταχινός* means "quick, swift" (Isa 59:7; Wis 13:2; Sir 18:26; Herm. *Sim.* 9:26:6) and hence (like English "quick" in certain contexts) can sometimes mean "coming soon, imminent" (Herm. *Sim.* 8:9:4; 9:26:6). It has sometimes been argued (notably by Zahn, *Introduction,* 212–14; followed by Plumptre, Green; cf. Boobyer, "Indebtedness," 46) that here it must mean "sudden," in the sense of "unexpected," i.e. Peter anticipates a violent death which might come upon him at any moment. But (1) this is not a well-attested meaning (and Zahn's NT examples of *ταχέως* and *ταχύ* meaning "sudden" are misinterpretations); (2) it need not (in spite of Zahn) be the meaning of *ταχινός* in 2 Pet 2:1; (3) it is not the most natural meaning in this context. It is doubtful if it would have been suggested if the passage were not being read in the light of John 21:18.

ἡ ἀπόθεσις, lit. "the divesting": the metaphor is that of taking off clothes (cf. *ἀποτίθεναι*: 2 Macc 8:35; Acts 7:58), and with *σκηνώμα* ("tent") a mixed metaphor results, no doubt because both were such standard, and therefore pale, metaphors. For *ἀπόθεσις*, of death, cf. Clem. Alex. *Strom.* 1.19 (*σαρκὸς ἀπόθεσις*); Methodius, *Res.* 1.29 (*PG* 41:1140A); and for the metaphor, cf. *Asc. Isa.* 9:8; 2 Cor 5:3–4 (where the two metaphors are mixed, as here).

καθὼς καὶ ὁ κύριος ἡμῶν Ἰησοῦς Χριστὸς ἐδήλωσέν μοι, "as our Lord Jesus Christ also informed me." All the commentators treat this clause as explaining how Peter knows that his death is imminent, but as Vögtle ("Schriftwerdung," 301) points out, this interpretation overlooks the *καί* ("also"). *καθὼς καί* is quite common in the NT (e.g. Luke 11:1; Acts 15:8; Rom 1:13; 15:7), but in every case the *καί*, though slightly pleonastic, can be translated "also." It reinforces the comparative sense of *καθώς*. In other words, *καθὼς καί* introduces an additional fact which is compared with what precedes. The general sense of the passage must be: "I know that I am going to die soon—and this corresponds to Christ's prophecy." This would be a very odd way of saying: "I know that I am going to die soon *because* Christ has told me." The passage must mean that, even apart from Christ's revelation to him, Peter knows he must die soon.

It was a common hagiographical motif that the righteous hero received some kind of intimation of his approaching death before the event, and for obvious reasons this was one of the normal conventions of the testament genre. Sometimes there is no indication of how the hero knows he is going to die (*Jub.* 36:1; *T. Napht.* 1:3–4; *Adam and Eve* 45:2; 49:1; Acts 10:25; 2 Tim 4:6; *Acts John* 107), sometimes it is revealed to him by God (Deut 31:2, 14, 16; *T. Levi* 1:2; 4 Ezra 14:13–15; *2 Apoc. Bar.* 43:2; 76:2; *Bib. Ant.* 19:6; 21:1; *2 Enoch* 36:1–2; 55:1–2), sometimes a dream (*Jub.* 35:6; *T. Abr.* 7; *Mart. Pol.* 5:2) or a vision (*Acts Paul* 10 [PH 7]) is the means of revelation. Probably this conventional motif accounts for the statement that Peter knows (*εἰδώς*) he is soon to die. But why should the writer then add that this had also been revealed to him by Christ? The only plausible reason is that there was a well-known dominical prophecy of Peter's death which the readers of 2 Peter would know, and so it is natural for the writer to add a reference to this prophecy. Thus, whereas the clause *εἰδὼς ὅτι ταχινή ἐστιν ἡ ἀπόθεσις τοῦ σκηνώματος μου* ("I know that I must soon be divested of my body") is a conventional motif of the testament genre, the following clause *καθὼς καὶ ὁ* κύριος ἡμῶν Ἰησοῦς Χριστὸς ἐδήλωσέν μοι ("as our Lord Jesus Christ also informed me") is a piece of specifically Petrine tradition. We may compare the fact that in his farewell speech at Miletus Paul knows of his impending death (Acts 20:25), but then also Agabus prophesies it (Acts 21:11). The existence of a well-known prophecy of Peter's death would be sufficient reason for the writer of 2 Peter to refer to it. Vögtle's suggestion ("Schriftwerdung," 303) that the reference is intended to give additional authority to Peter's testament is unnecessary.

What was the prophecy to which 2 Peter refers? The extant literature offers the following five references to prophecies of Peter's death by Jesus:

(1) John 13:36. This looks like a Johannine reflection on Peter's words in Matt 26:35; Mark 14:31; Luke 23:33, in the light of Peter's martyrdom (R. E. Brown, *The Gospel according to John* [AB; London: Geoffrey Chapman, 1971] 615–16). We cannot be sure that the saying existed in the tradition before John's Gospel. Moreover, it contains no indication of the *time* of Peter's martyrdom, other than that it will be subsequent to Jesus' own death.

(2) John 21:18 is the saying to which commentators have most often thought 2 Peter refers (Plumpre, Bigg, Lumby, Green; Zahn, *Introduction,* 213–14; Chase, *DB*(*H*) 3, p. 809; Vögtle, "Schriftwerdung," 302). There are two main objections to this view: (a) John 21:18 does not indicate the *time* of Peter's death; (b) 2 Peter is unlikely to be dependent on the Fourth Gospel, both because 2 Peter may be earlier in date than the Fourth Gospel and because it is so far removed from the Fourth Gospel in theological character. But (a) John 21:18 does indicate that Peter's martyrdom will occur when he is old (γηράσῃς), and this may be sufficient indication of time to satisfy the requirements of 2 Pet 1:14. If our exegesis, according to which Peter knows that his death is imminent independently of Christ's prophecy, is correct, then the prophecy itself need not contain too precise an indication of time. (b) John 21:18 is too obscure and ambiguous as a reference to Peter's martyrdom for it to be a *post eventum* prophecy (cf. Brown, 1107–8, 1118), and therefore it cannot be the creation of the author of John 21. The saying must have been already a traditional saying of Jesus to which the author gives a *post eventum* interpretation in 21:19 (which probably interprets the prophecy as indicating death by crucifixion). Although some scholars have doubted whether the original saying intended a reference to Peter's death at all, it is difficult to find another meaning which would give the saying any real point or account for its preservation in the tradition. We may therefore assume that John 21:18 is a saying of Jesus which was widely known in the early Church, as a prophecy of Peter's martyrdom, even before Peter's death.

(3) *Apoc. Pet.* R (on this passage, see E. Peterson, "Das Martyrium des hl. Petrus nach der Petrus-Apocalypse," in *Miscellanea Giulio Belvederi* [CACat 23; Vatican City: Società "Amici delle Catacombe," 1954] 181–85). The risen Christ says to Peter: "Go into the city of the West and drink the cup which I have promised you, at the hands of the son of him who is in Hades." This is clearly a *post eventum* prophecy of Peter's martyrdom under Nero in Rome. Since it follows a passage which seems dependent on 2 Pet 1:3–11, and precedes a passage which is dependent on the accounts of the Transfiguration, including 2 Pet 1:16–18, it is probable that the prophecy is inspired by 2 Pet 1:14. This need not imply that the author of the *Apoc. Pet.* knew of no traditional saying of Jesus to which 2 Pet 1:14 could refer, for his phrase "the cup which I have promised you" (τὸ ποτήριον ὃ ἐπηγγειλάμην σοι) seems to presuppose an earlier prophecy. Thus it is possible that the *Apoc. Pet.* is evidence that there was a traditional saying of Jesus prophesying Peter's death, but it provides no reliable evidence of the form of that saying.

(4) The famous "Quo Vadis?" story in the *Acts Pet.* (*Act. Verc.* 35) relates how Peter, leaving Rome to escape arrest, met Jesus entering the city. In response to Peter's query, "Lord, whither goest thou here?" (*κύριε, ποῦ ὧδε;*), the Lord tells him, "I am coming to Rome to be crucified," and "I am being crucified again," and so Peter returns to Rome to be crucified (*NT Apoc.* 2, 317–18). A few scholars (Spitta; cf. Edmundson, *Church of Rome,* 151–53) have thought this story has a basis in fact, to which 2 Pet 1:14 refers. It is, however, unattested before the *Acts Pet.* (c. 180), and is almost certainly inspired by John 13:36. It should also be remembered that the author of the *Acts Pet.* knew 2 Peter.

(5) The Epistle of Clement to James (prefaced to the *Clementine Homilies*) chap. 2: Peter says: "Since, as I have been taught (*ὡς ἐδιδάχθην*) by my Lord and Teacher Jesus Christ, who sent me, the days of my death have drawn near (*αἱ τοῦ θάνατου μου ἠγγίκασιν ἡμέραι*). . . ." These words introduce a speech which is virtually a testament of Peter. In such a late document they could be dependent on 2 Pet 1:14, or on (2) or (4) above, or they could be an independent example of the application to Peter of the conventional testament motif.

In conclusion, the saying of Jesus in John 21:18 seems to be the only likely basis for 2 Pet 1:14. This conclusion is further supported by the observation that our exegesis favors reference to a saying of Jesus from the Gospel traditions rather than to a revelation by the exalted Lord shortly before Peter's death, since (a) Jesus' prophecy is *distinguished* from the testament motif of Peter's intimation of his approaching death, and (b) the prophecy must have been well-known to 2 Peter's readers.

Boobyer's suggestion ("Indebtedness," 44–51) that 2 Pet 1:14 is dependent on 1 Pet 5:1, read as evidence that the aged Peter expected martyrdom, together with Matt 16:21–27 or Mark 8:31–38, seems to be a relatively far-fetched explanation, which should hardly be preferred when a much simpler explanation is available.

15. *σπουδάσω δὲ καί*, "but I will also do my best to see," i.e. not only will I remind you during my lifetime (v 13), but I will also see to it that my teaching is available to you after my death. The verb *σπουδάζειν* is elsewhere used of diligence or eagerness to write a letter (*Barn.* 1:5; 4:9; 21:9; cf. Jude 3) and may be an instance of epistolary style. Especially striking is the fact that an equivalent expression is found in *2 Apoc. Bar.* 78:5 (Baruch's "testamentary" letter): "I have been the more careful to leave you the words of this epistle before I die" (tr. Charles). The future tense *σπουδάσω* is more difficult than the future tense in v 12, for whereas the apostle's action of reminding can go on after his death through his testament, it is more difficult to see how his diligence can do so. If *σπουδάσω* does refer to his diligence in writing 2 Peter, it is possible that the writer has used the future loosely because, as in v 12, he is thinking primarily of the work's future function "at all times." Alternatively, *σπουδάσω* may refer to the apostle's efforts to ensure that his testament is preserved after his death. The real writer may be hinting that his own efforts in writing 2 Peter are faithful to Peter's own concern that his teaching be preserved after his death.

In spite of the difficulty of the future tense *σπουδάσω* most commentators understand the verse as a reference to 2 Peter itself (Knopf, Chaine, Windisch, Schelkle, Kelly, Grundmann), but some insist that it must refer to another work which the apostle intends to provide in the future, either an otherwise unknown doctrinal writing by Peter (Zahn, *Introduction,* 200–201, 272), or future letters which Peter will write whenever the occasion presents itself (McNamara, *Scr* 12 (1960) 16–19, who takes *ἑκάστοτε*, "at all times" with σπουδάσω, and thinks 2 Pet 3 is one of these other letters), or Mark's Gospel (Plumptre, Bigg, Mayor cxlii-cxliv, Barnett, Green). This last idea depends on the tradition, found as early as Papias, that Mark was Peter's "interpreter" and wrote his Gospel on the basis of Peter's preaching. It is even possible (see below) that Irenaeus already interpreted 2 Pet 1:15 in this way. It should, however, be noted: (a) that none of the early representatives of this tradition sees Peter as having himself initiated the writing of the Gospel, and only Clement of Alexandria (*Hypotyp., ap.* Eusebius, *Hist. Eccl.* 2.15.1–2) reports that he authorized it; (b) that none of the clear allusions to Gospel traditions in 2 Peter correspond to Markan traditions (see Introduction, section of *Literary Relationships*); (c) that τούτων ("these things") in this verse must still refer to the summary of Peter's teaching in vv 3–11, and the Gospel of Mark cannot easily be seen as embodying Peter's teaching described in that way.

A reference to 2 Peter itself in this verse has the advantage of giving the section vv 12–15 a coherence which it would otherwise lack: the whole section explains Peter's intention that 2 Peter should be his testament.

μετὰ τὴν ἐμὴν ἔξοδον, "after my death." The use of the term ἔξοδος for death probably derives from the meaning "end" (i.e. the end of life: ἔξοδος τοῦ βίου) rather than from the meaning "departure" (see *TDNT* 7, 105, 107), though it was possible for some writers to give it the sense of "departure" (Wis 7:6; *Apoc. Paul* 14; Clem. Alex. *Exc. Theod.* 41: ἡ ἐκ τῆς σαρκὸς ἔξοδος, "the departure from the flesh"). Thus it need not here imply the soul's departure from the body. The term was used both absolutely, as here (Epictetus 4.4.38; Wis 3:2; *T. Napht.* 1:1 *v.l.;* Luke 9:31; Justin, *Dial.* 105.5; letter of the churches of Lyons and Vienne, *ap.* Eusebius, *Hist. Eccl.* 5.1.36, 55; 5.2.3; Irenaeus, *Adv. Haer.* 3.1.1; *Apoc. Paul* 14), and qualified in some way (τοῦ ζῆν: Josephus, *Ant.* 4.189; τοῦ βίου: Justin, *Dial.* 105.3; implied in Wis 7:6; πνεύματος: Sir 38:23). There seems no basis for the assertion that the unqualified use of the term was much rarer than the qualified (Green; cf. Bigg, 206). In neither form was it very common, but seems to have been becoming more common in the second century A.D. To derive all the Christian instances from the influence of its two NT occurrences is implausible.

There is sufficient evidence of the currency of the term to make it most unlikely that this verse alludes to its use in Luke 9:31 (Transfiguration narrative). Those who see in such an allusion evidence of Peter's authorship (Green; cf. Plumptre; Bigg, 231–32) fail to realize that it would in fact indicate acquaintance with the Lukan redaction of the Transfiguration account.

There is a somewhat more plausible case for an allusion to 2 Pet 1:15 in Irenaeus, *Adv. Haer.* 3.1.1: "after their deaths (μετὰ τὴν τούτων ἔξοδον) (i.e. of Peter and Paul) Mark, the disciple and interpreter of Peter, handed on to us in writing what Peter had preached." It is possible, though far from proven, that here Irenaeus interprets 2 Pet 1:15 as a reference to Mark's Gospel (Mayor).

Explanation

This section explains the character of 2 Peter as Peter's "testament," preserving Peter's teaching for Christians who will read it after Peter's death.

The author therefore represents Peter as writing shortly before his death and knowing that his death is approaching. Peter knows this both because he has some kind of intimation of it (a standard feature of "testaments") and because Jesus had predicted his martyrdom (probably an allusion to the saying preserved in John 21:18). In view of his imminent death, the apostle is making a written record of his teaching—the reference is primarily to the "farewell sermon" in 1:3–11—so that, although the readers are already familiar with the apostolic message which they received when they became Christians, Peter's "testament" may serve to remind them of it both up to and at all times after his death.

Owing to the author's use of the standard conventions of the ancient "testament" genre, contemporary readers would have recognized from this section that 2 Peter belongs to that genre and have understood the pseudepigraphal nature of the work. Behind the fictional device which made it possible for Peter to be represented as addressing them many years after his death, they would have understood the real author's intention of providing a "reminder" and defense of the apostle's message for his own time. By writing in Peter's name the author disclaims any desire to present a new teaching of his own. The literary device of the "testament" is a valid vehicle for his message insofar as he wishes only to preserve the apostolic message, while interpreting and defending it in terms appropriate to his readers' situation.

Reply to Objection 1: (*a*) *Apostolic Eyewitness* (*1:16–18*)

Bibliography

Baltensweiler, H. *Der Verklärung Jesu: Historisches Ereignis und synoptische Berichte.* ATANT 33. Zürich: Zwingli Verlag, 1959. 26–28. **Blinzler, J.** *Die neutestamentlichen Berichte über die Verklärung Jesu.* NTAbh 17/4. Münster: Aschendorff, 1937. 17–18, 30–31, 71–76, 87, 153. **Boobyer, G. H.** *St Mark and the Transfiguration Story.* Edinburgh: T. & T. Clark, 1942. 43–46. **Bretscher, P. G.** "Exodus 4^{22-23} and the Voice from Heaven." *JBL* 87 (1968) 301–11. **Klein, G.** *Die zwölf Apostel,* 102–3. **Neyrey, J. H.** "The Apologetic Use of the Transfiguration in 2 Peter 1:16–21." *CBQ* 42 (1980) 504–19. **Nineham, D. E.** "Eye-Witness Testimony and the Gospel Tradition III." *JTS* 11 (1960) 254–64. **Sabbe, M.** "La rédaction du récit de la Transfiguration." *La Venue du Messie: Messianisme et Eschatologie,* by E. Massaux *et al.* RechBib 6. Bruges: Desclée de Brouwer, 1962. **Schmithals, W.** "Der Markusschluss, die Verklärungsgeschichte und die Aussendung der Zwölf." *ZTK* 69 (1972) 379–411. **Stein, R. H.** "Is the Transfiguration (Mark 9:2–8) a Misplaced Resurrection-Account?" *JBL* 95 (1976) 79–95.

Translation

16 *For we did not follow cleverly concocted myths when we made known to you the coming of our Lord Jesus Christ in power, but we were eyewitnesses of his majesty.*
17 *For* [a] *he received honor and glory from God the Father, and a voice conveyed to him by the Majestic Glory proclaimed, "This is my Son, my Beloved, on whom I have set my favor."* [b]
18 *We ourselves heard this voice from heaven when we were with him on the holy mountain.*

Notes

[a] There is an anacolouthon in the Greek of vv 17–18. The participial phrases in v 17 require a main clause of which Jesus is the subject, but v 18 begins a fresh sentence.

[b] The readings of most MSS in this sentence (the words of the heavenly voice) are best seen as assimilations to the Synoptic Gospels (see Blinzler, *Berichte,* 17), and so the text of $\mathfrak{P}^{72}$ B, which show no such assimilation, is here translated.

Form/Structure/Setting

Neyrey (*Polemic,* 18–19, 22, 24) has identified v 16 as cast in the form οὐ . . . ἀλλά ("not . . . but") which the author uses three times (1:16, 21; 3:9) to state and refute the false teachers' arguments. This identification of an apologetic form must be followed with caution, because the οὐ . . . ἀλλά structure is a very common and natural one, which this author in fact uses on some occasions in a purely rhetorical way, not in order to reject an objection (2:4–5; 3:9b). This means that the plausibility of an apologetic form must be established in each case. In 1:16 it provides the most obvious reading of the passage, and so we may regard v 16a as the first objection which the false teachers bring against the expectation of the Parousia, while vv 16b–18 are the author's first response to this objection.

Neyrey finds interesting parallels to the οὐ . . . ἀλλά ("not . . . but") form in Philo and Diodorus of Sicily (*CBQ* 42 [1980] 507–9), all in passages defending the veracity of scriptures or oracles against the accusation that they are fabricated myths. Again, the form is too obvious and natural to allow us to base much on these parallels, but it seems clear that in this passage our author and his opponents carry on an argument whose basic pattern was familiar in the ancient world, especially in Hellenistic Judaism. Like many an apologist for divine revelation, the author of 2 Peter must answer the stock charge that the alleged revelation is only a human invention.

Some examples of the testament genre recount an apocalyptic revelation given to the hero, often during a trip to heaven, when revelations of the future are granted which provide the basis for the predictions made in the testament (*1 Enoch* 93; *2 Apoc. Bar.* 81:4; *T. Levi* 2–5, 8; *Adam and Eve* 25–29; *2 Enoch* 39:2; *Bib. Ant.* 28:4; cf. Kolenkow, *JSJ* 6 [1975] 57–71). It seems quite likely that the Transfiguration, which the writer of 2 Peter understands as eschatological revelation, is intended to supply this conventional feature of the testament.

Relationship to the Synoptic Gospels

The account of the Transfiguration in 2 Peter shows notable differences from the three accounts in the synoptic Gospels, and the question therefore arises of its relationship to these accounts. A number of scholars have concluded that it is independent of the synoptic Gospels, and embodies either personal reminiscences of Peter or independent oral tradition (see especially Spitta, 493–99; Zahn, *Introduction,* 217–18; Blinzler, *Berichte,* 71–72; A. J. Maclean, in *DAC* 2, 611–12). The points of divergence, and their significance, are:

(1) Nothing should be concluded from 2 Peter's omission of features of the synoptic accounts (details of the transfiguration of Jesus' appearance, the presence of Moses and Elijah, Peter's suggestion), since these are easily explained by our author's redactional purpose. He refers to the Transfiguration because he sees in it God's appointment of Jesus as eschatological king and judge, and features not strictly relevant to this point need not be mentioned. In particular, he is not interested in features of the synoptic accounts which suggest the theophany on Sinai and depict Jesus as the eschatological prophet like Moses.

Again, it is not significant that 2 Peter does not explicitly limit the experience to the three apostles Peter, James and John. The author had no special interest in pointing this out—though of course he takes it for granted that Peter himself was one of the witnesses—and we cannot tell whether or not his tradition specified a limited group of apostles.

(2) It would also be hazardous to find indications of independent tradition in the distinctive terminology of 2 Peter's account (τῆς ἐκείνου μεγαλειότητος, "his majesty"; τιμὴν καὶ δόξαν, "honor and glory"; φωνῆς ἐνεχθείσης αὐτῷ τοιᾶσδε ὑπὸ τῆς μεγαλοπρεποῦς δόξης, "a voice conveyed to him by the Majestic Glory"), since this terminology is characteristic of the author's style and may only show that he has put the tradition into his own words.

(3) A substantial difference is that whereas in all three synoptic accounts the

voice is said to come from the cloud, in 2 Peter it is "conveyed from heaven" (ἐξ οὐρανοῦ ἐνεχθεῖσαν, v 18). Too much importance cannot be attached to this difference. Since the cloud in the synoptic accounts is a form of divine presence, both expressions are ways of saying that the voice came from God. Since the writer of 2 Peter has had no occasion to mention the cloud, he may have preferred an expression which was self-explanatory to one which would require him to fill in more detail (Blinzler, *Berichte,* 75). Alternatively, the phrase may be further evidence of assimilation to the account of Jesus' baptism (cf. Matt 3:17; Mark 1:11; Luke 3:22), which some see in the phrase εἰς ὃν ἐγὼ εὐδόκησα ("on whom I have set my favor"). On the other hand, (a) the idea of a voice from heaven is an apocalyptic commonplace (Dan 4:31; *1 Enoch* 13:8; 65:4; *2 Apoc. Bar.* 13:1; 22:1; Rev 10:4; 11:12; 14:13), which in view of the apocalyptic character of the Transfiguration story (see Sabbe, "La rédaction"; H. C. Kee, "The Transfiguration in Mark: Epiphany or Apocalyptic Vision?" in J. Reumann ed., *Understanding the Sacred Text* [M. S. Enslin Festschrift; Valley Forge, PA: Judson Press, 1972] 137–52) would be entirely at home in a traditional version of the Transfiguration, but would be rather less likely to be added by the author of 2 Peter, who tends to use apocalyptic language only when he is following a source (as in chap 3). A similar point could be made about his other phrase in relation to the voice: ὑπὸ τῆς μεγαλοπρεποῦς δόξης ("by the Majestic Glory," v 17). The use of the word μεγαλοπρεπής, "majestic," is in keeping with our author's predilection for such terms (1:4: τίμια καὶ μέγιστα, "precious and very great"; 1:17: μεγαλειότητος, "majesty"), but such a periphrasis for God belongs to an apocalyptic context (cf. *1 Enoch* 14:20; *Asc. Isa.* 9:37; 11:32; *T. Levi* 3:4; cf. 18:6) rather than to 2 Peter's usual Hellenistic terminology. Moreover, (b) there are some indications elsewhere of a tradition of the Transfiguration story which spoke of the voice as coming from heaven. *Clem. Hom.* 3:53, whose version of the words of the voice may depend on a tradition related to 2 Peter's (see below), says: ἐξ οὐρανῶν (*v.l.* οὐρανοῦ) μάρτυς φωνὴ ἠκούσθη ("a witnessing voice was heard from heaven"), while John 12:28, which some scholars think reflects the Transfiguration traditions, also speaks of a voice from heaven (φωνὴ ἐκ τοῦ ουρανοῦ). (*Apoc. Pet.* E 17 has "a voice from heaven," but this is dependent on 2 Peter.) There is therefore some probability that in speaking of the voice as coming from heaven, 2 Peter reflects a tradition independent of the synoptic Gospels, but by itself this evidence is insufficient to prove the point.

(4) The most important evidence for independent tradition consists in 2 Peter's version of the words of the voice. The texts for comparison are as follows:

Transfiguration	
Matt 17:5:	οὗτός ἐστιν ὁ υἱός μου ὁ ἀγαπητός
Mark 9:7:	οὗτός ἐστιν ὁ υἱός μου ὁ ἀγαπητός
Luke 9:35:	οὗτός ἐστιν ὁ υἱός μου ὁ ἐκλελεγμένος
2 Pet 1:17:	ὁ υἱός μου ὁ ἀγαπητός μου οὗτός ἐστιν
Clem. Hom. 3:53:	οὗτός ἐστιν μου ὁ υἱός ὁ ἀγαπητός
Apoc. Pet. E 17:	This is my Son whom I love
Baptism	
Matt 3:17:	οὗτός ἐστιν ὁ υἱός μου ὁ ἀγαπητός
Mark 1:11 = Luke 3:22:	σὺ εἶ ὁ υἱός μου ὁ ἀγαπητός
Gos. Eb. (*ap.* Epiphanius, *Haer.* 30.13.7–8)	σύ μου εἶ ὁ υἱός ὁ ἀγαπητός οὗτός ἐστιν ὁ υἱός μου ὁ ἀγαπητός

Transfiguration

Matt 17:5:	ἐν ᾧ	εὐδόκησα	ἀκούετε αὐτοῦ.
Mark 9:7:			ἀκούετε αὐτοῦ.
Luke 9:35:			αὐτοῦ ἀκούετε.
2 Pet 1:17:	εἰς ὃν ἐγὼ	εὐδόκησα.	
Clem. Hom. 3:35:	εἰς ὃν	εὐδόκησα	τούτου ἀκούετε.
Apoc. Pet. E 17:	and in whom I have pleasure and my commandments . . . (?)		

Baptism

Matt 3:17:	ἐν ᾧ	εὐδόκησα.
Mark 1:11 = Luke 3:22:	ἐν σοὶ	εὐδόκησα.
Gos. Eb.	{ ἐν σοὶ	ηὐδόκησα.
	ἐφ᾽ ὃν	ηὐδόκησα.

Cf. also Ps 2:7 LXX: υἱός μου εἶ σύ.
Isa 42:1 LXX: ὁ ἐκλεκτός μου, προσεδέξατο αὐτὸν ἡ ψυχή μου.
Matt 12:18 (Isa 42:1): ὁ ἀγαπητός μου ὃν (*v.l.* εἰς ὃν) εὐδόκησεν ἡ ψυχή μου.
Deut 18:15 LXX: αὐτοῦ ἀκούσεσθε.
(The *Apoc. Pet.* has been included for completeness, but it is dependent on Matthew and 2 Peter and has no independent value.)

The following observations may be made:

(a) The omission of ἀκούετε αὐτοῦ ("hear him") in 2 Peter is easily explicable. The words derive from Deut 18:15 and portray Jesus as the eschatological prophet like Moses, but this theme is irrelevant to 2 Peter's purpose, which is to portray the Transfiguration as Jesus' appointment as eschatological king and judge. The writer has therefore probably deliberately omitted ἀκούετε αὐτοῦ ("hear him") along with other irrelevant features of the Transfiguration narrative.

(b) One of the writer's main interests is in the echo of Ps 2:7 in the heavenly voice (see *Comment* section), and it is possible that the variation in word order, which has the effect of bringing ὁ υἱός μου ("my Son") to the fore, is intended to emphasize this. It is also possible that the writer has introduced ἐγώ ("I") to stress that it was God who appointed Jesus as eschatological judge. But it is noteworthy that the writer has made no attempt to extend the reference to Ps 2:7 (cf. Luke 3:22 D; Justin, *Dial.* 88.8; 103.6), and therefore it seems likely that on the whole he has reproduced the words of the voice as he found them in tradition.

(c) Second Peter is alone in having ὁ ἀγαπητός μου ("*my* Beloved"). The effect of this repetition of the pronoun is that, whereas in the other versions ὁ ἀγαπητός ("beloved") qualifies υἱός ("Son") (see especially G. D. Kilpatrick, "The Order of some Noun and Adjective Phrases in the New Testament," *NovT* 5 [1962] 111–14), in 2 Peter ὁ ἀγαπητός μου ("my Beloved") should constitute a second title (though cf. (ii) below).

To evaluate this point of divergence from the other versions, it is necessary to consider the four different explanations of ἀγαπητός ("beloved") in the voices at the Baptism and the Transfiguration, which have been proposed:

(i) ἀγαπητός ("beloved") is said to derive from the Targum to Ps 2:7: "Beloved (חביב) as a son to his father you are to me." This derivation (supported by R. H. Gundry, *The Use of the Old Testament in St Matthew's Gospel* [NovTSup 18; Leiden: E. J. Brill, 1967] 30, 37) has the advantage of finding the whole phrase ὁ υἱός μου ὁ ἀγαπητός ("my beloved Son") in a version of Ps 2:7. But in fact the Targum is a clear attempt to play down the divine sonship of the Messiah, reducing it to a comparison. It may therefore be a Jewish reaction to Christian doctrine (so Lohse in *TDNT* 8, 362), and in any case is unlikely to be the source of a formula which stresses Jesus' divine sonship.

(ii) Bretscher (*JBL* 87 [1968] 301–11) argues that the original form of the words of the voice was based on a literal rendering of Exod 4:22: *ὁ υἱός μου ὁ πρωτότοκός μου Ἰσραήλ* (*ἐστιν*) ("my son, my firstborn, Israel (is)"), in which *πρωτότοκος* ("firstborn") was paraphrased as *ἀγαπητός* ("beloved") and *οὗτός* ("this") substituted for Ἰσραήλ ("Israel"). The result of this theory is that 2 Pet 1:17 provides the most original form of the words of the voice, both in retaining the second *μου* ("my") and in the word order *ὁ υἱός μου ὁ ἀγαπητός μου οὗτός ἐστιν* (cf. Bretscher, 306: "I can conceive of no way to account for this version of the heavenly declaration, except by reference to Exod 4:22"). There are, however, difficulties in this view. It is doubtful whether Bretscher has provided sufficiently strong reasons why בכור ("firstborn") should have been translated *ἀγαπητός* ("beloved"), and although there is evidence in the Gospels for the connection between Jesus' sonship and Israel's sonship, it does not seem very likely that the words at the Baptism and the Transfiguration originally expressed no more than this.

(iii) *ἀγαπητός* ("beloved") is equivalent to *μονογενής* ("only"). In this sense it was a well-known Greek idiom and was used in the LXX to translate יחיד (Amos 8:10; Jer 6:2; Judg 11:34; Zech 12:10). In particular, the source of *ὁ υἱός μου ὁ ἀγαπητός* ("my beloved Son") has been found in Gen 22:2, 12, 16, where the Hebrew בִּנְךָ יְחִידְךָ, "your son, your only one," is rendered in the LXX as *τὸν υἱόν σου τὸν ἀγαπητόν*, "your beloved son" (C. H. Turner, "Ο ΥΙΟΣ ΜΟΥ Ο ΑΓΑΠΗΤΟΣ," *JTS* 27 [1926] 113–29; Vermes, *Scripture and Tradition,* 233). This view would be more convincing if there were more evidence for an Isaac typology in the NT, but it is possible that *ἀγαπητός* ("beloved") is used in this sense to define Jesus' sonship as unique, but without presupposing an Isaac typology (M. D. Hooker, *Jesus and the Servant* [London: S.P.C.K., 1959] 71). If this view is correct, 2 Peter's version *ὁ υἱός μου, ὁ ἀγαπητός μου* ("my Son, my Beloved") can be seen as a more literal equivalent to a Hebrew phrase modeled on Gen 22:2, while the synoptic version is a rather more idiomatic rendering following the LXX.

(iv) *ἀγαπητός* ("beloved") is a translation of בחירי, "my chosen," in Isa 42:1 (LXX: *ὁ ἐκλεκτός μου*). This view is held both by those who think that the words of the voice at the Baptism are entirely based on Isa 42:1, with *υἱός μου* as a substitute for *παῖς μου* (Jeremias in *TDNT* 5. 701–2; O. Cullmann, *Baptism in the New Testament,* tr. J. K. S. Reid [SBT 1; London: SCM Press, 1950] 17; R. H. Fuller, *The Foundations of New Testament Christology* [London: Collins, 1969] 170), and by some of those who hold that they are a conflation of Ps 2:7 and Isa 42:1 (D. Hill, *The Gospel of Matthew* [NCB; London: Oliphants, 1972] 98). The disadvantage of this view is that it depends rather heavily on Matt 12:18 for evidence that *ὁ ἀγαπητός* is a likely translation of בחירי, whereas the version of Isa 42:1 in Matt 12:18 may well have been deliberately adapted to conform to the baptismal voice (Gundry, *The Use of the Old Testament,* 112). The text does, however, provide evidence that it was possible for an early Christian writer to see in *ὁ ἀγαπητός* an allusion to Isa 42:1. Such an allusion has the advantage of explaining the variations in the versions of the voice at this point: *ὁ ἐκλελεγμένος*, "the chosen one" (Luke 9:35, where, it should be noted, an allusion to Isa 42:1 is not suggested by the following phrase as it is in the Baptism accounts) and *ὁ ἐκλεκτός*, "the chosen one" (John 1:34 *v.l.;* see Jeremias in *TDNT* 5, 702) are more literal renderings of בחירי ("my chosen") in Isa 42:1 (cf. LXX: *ὁ ἐκλεκτός μου*), while *ὁ ἀγαπητός μου* (2 Pet 1:17) in retaining the pronoun is closer to בחירי than is the synoptic *ὁ ἀγαπητός*, and agrees with the rendering of Isa 42:1 in Matt 12:18 (*ὁ ἀγαπητός μου*). In that case the various versions of the voice are not all derived from Mark's two versions and adapted for redactional reasons only, but represent variant translations of the Semitic original, current in different churches. The underlying בחירי is more obvious in 2 Pet 1:17 than in the synoptic versions (other than Luke 9:35), in that *ὁ ἀγαπητός μου* is clearly a distinct title alongside *ὁ υἱός μου*, "my Son," and the pronoun is retained.

It will be seen that if any of views (ii)–(iv) is accepted, 2 Peter's phrase *ὁ ἀγαπητός μου* has a good claim to be closer to the Semitic basis than the synoptic versions, and must be regarded as at least as original as they are. It seems likely that, whatever the original source of *ἀγαπητός* in the voices at the Baptism and the Transfiguration, two interpretations of it were current in the early church. In one interpretation it was taken closely with *ὁ υἱός μου* as "my beloved Son," or "my only Son": this is clear at least from Luke 20:12 (cf. Mark 12:6; Herm. *Sim.* 5:2:6; perhaps cf. also Col 1:13; 1 John 4:9). In the other interpretation, it was a distinct title, "my Beloved" (Matt 12:18; 2 Pet 1:17; some take *ὁ ἀγαπητός* in Matt 3:17; 17:5 in this sense). With this should probably be connected the evidence for *ὁ ἠγαπημένος*, "the Beloved," as a Christological title in the early church (Eph 1:6; *Barn.* 3:6; 4:3, 8; Ign. *Smyrn.* inscr.; *Acts Paul & Thecla* 1; cf. *Odes Sol.* 3:8; and *ὁ ἀγαπητός* used throughout *Asc. Isa.;* cf. J. A. Robinson, *St Paul's Epistle to the Ephesians,* 2nd ed. [London: Macmillan, 1904] 229–33). If 2 Peter's phrase *ὁ ἀγαπητός μου* belongs to this second interpretation, that is itself sufficient evidence to regard it as based on a tradition independent of the synoptic accounts of the Transfiguration.

(d) Only Matt 17:5; 2 Pet 1:17; *Apoc. Pet.* E 17; and *Clem. Hom.* 3:53 have the clause "with whom I am well pleased" in the words of the voice at the Transfiguration. It has often been held that Matthew has here assimilated the voice at the Transfiguration to the voice at the Baptism. Similarly Matt 3:17 has (if this reading is accepted) *οὗτός ἐστιν* ("this is") in the voice at the Baptism, instead of Mark's and Luke's *σὺ εἶ* ("you are"), thus assimilating the voice at the Baptism to that at the Transfiguration, and Matthew's introductions to both voices (3:17; 17:5) are similar. Thus it could be argued that 2 Peter must at this point be dependent on the Matthean redaction of the Transfiguration narrative. Against this, however, it should be noticed: (i) The words "with whom I am well pleased" are widely thought to derive from Isa 42:1. If *ὁ ἀγαπητός* (*μου*) ("(my) beloved") was regarded as an allusion to Isa 42:1 (see above), an extension of the allusion to include the following phrase in Isa 42:1 could easily have occurred independently in different traditions and writers. It should also be noticed that Luke 9:35 alludes to Isa 42:1 in a different way, by using *ὁ ἐκλελεγμένος* ("the chosen one"). Thus a relationship of the voice at the Transfiguration to Isa 42:1 is not confined to the Matthean redaction (Gundry, *The Use of the Old Testament,* 37). (ii) Matt 17:5 (like Matt 3:17; Mark 1:11; Luke 3:22) uses the normal construction, *ἐν* with the dative of personal object, after *εὐδοκεῖν* ("to be well pleased"), but 2 Pet 1:17 agrees with *Clem. Hom.* 3:53 in using *εἰς* with the accusative. This very rare construction seems to be known (with a personal object) only in these two texts and in one reading in Matt 12:18, though it is used once elsewhere with an impersonal object (*T. Jos.* 17:3; see *TDNT* 2, 739). It is not therefore likely that its use in 2 Pet 1:17 is a variation due to nothing more than a slip of memory. Whether *ὃν* or *εἰς ὃν* should be read in Matt 12:18 is difficult to decide, but probably we should prefer the latter, since the simple accusative after *εὐδοκεῖν* ("to be well pleased") is more common, though not usual with a personal object, and it is unlikely that *εἰς ὃν* results from textual assimilation to 2 Pet 1:17. In that case it is possible that the whole phrase *ὁ ἀγαπητός μου εἰς ὃν εὐδόκησεν ἡ ψυχή μου* ("my Beloved with whom my soul is well pleased") in Matt 12:18 depends on a tradition of the words of the voice different from that used in Matt 3:17; 17:5, but related to the tradition in 2 Peter. The agreement between 2 Pet 1:17 and *Clem. Hom.* 3:53 is at this point striking, and combined with the fact that both have the voice ἐξ οὐρανοῦ ("from heaven"), must point to common tradition. The intention of the construction εἰς ὃν may be to give the sense of God's good pleasure lighting upon Jesus in election. Perhaps with the same intention the *Gos. Eb.* uses the construction ἐφ' ὃν which is also unusual.

We may conclude that the evidence is strongly in favor of the view that in his account of the Transfiguration the author of 2 Peter was not dependent on the synoptic Gospels but on independent tradition, which could perhaps be his own knowledge of Peter's preaching, or else the oral traditions current in the Roman church.

A more speculative possibility is that the saying Matt 16:28 (par. Mar 9:1 par. Luke 9:27) may also have been connected with the Transfiguration in the non-synoptic tradition known to 2 Peter, if it is to this saying that the phrase τὴν τοῦ κυρίου ἡμῶν Ἰησοῦ Χριστοῦ δύναμιν καὶ παρουσίαν ("the coming of our Lord Jesus Christ in power," 1:16) alludes. This possibility should be considered in connection with the possibility that the remarks of the scoffers (3:4) have in view that saying's apparent prediction of the Parousia within the first Christian generation.

A Resurrection Appearance?

The realization that 2 Pet 1:16–18 is not dependent on the synoptic Transfiguration narratives has led some scholars to consider the possibility that its setting is not, like the Transfiguration in the Synoptics, within the earthly ministry of Jesus but after the Resurrection. Some have argued that it refers to an event quite distinct from the Transfiguration recorded in the synoptic Gospels, namely an appearance of the risen Christ to Peter (K. G. Goetz, *Petrus als Gründer und Oberhaupt der Kirche* [UNT 13; Leipzig: J. C. Hinrichs, 1927] 89–90; O. Cullmann, *Peter: Disciple—Apostle—Martyr,* tr. F. V. Filson [London: SCM Press, 1953] 61; Baltensweiler, *Verklärung,* 26–28), while others regard it as evidence that the Transfiguration itself was originally a resurrection appearance story, which the synoptic Gospels have moved back into the earthly life of Jesus (R. Bultmann, *The History of the Synoptic Tradition,* tr. J. Marsh, 2nd ed. [Oxford: Basil Blackwell, 1968] 259 n. 2; Schmithals, *ZTK* 69 [1972] 395–97; cf. J. M. Robinson, "On the *Gattung* of Mark (and John)," in *Jesus and man's hope,* vol. 1 [Pittsburgh: Pittsburgh Theological Seminary, 1970] 117).

It is not really probable that 2 Pet 1:16–18 refers to a different event from the Transfiguration in the Synoptics. Once it is realized that 2 Peter's omission of features of the synoptic accounts does not necessarily indicate that they were not in the tradition behind 2 Peter (see above), then the differences between 2 Peter and the Synoptics are not sufficient to require two events. The heavenly voice, the mountain, and the visible majesty are enough to identify the event as the same as the Transfiguration in the Synoptics. The brevity and allusiveness of the account in 2 Peter presuppose a story well-known to the readers; it is easier to identify this story as the Transfiguration known to us from the Gospels, than to postulate a story otherwise unknown to us. Moreover, 2 Pet 1:16–18 cannot refer to the appearance of the risen Christ to Peter (Luke 24:34; 1 Cor 15:5), because although it does not indicate how many apostles were present, it is clear that Peter was not alone. The first person plural in these verses is not an epistolary plural, but a deliberate change from the singular of vv 12–15 (Stein, *JBL* 95 [1976] 93).

The general theory that the Transfiguration is a misplaced resurrection appearance narrative has been refuted by Boobyer (*St Mark,* 11–16) and especially by

Stein (*JBL* 95 [1976] 79–95; cf. also J. E. Alsup, *The Post-Resurrection Appearance Stories of the Gospel Tradition* [CThM 5; Stuttgart: Calwer/London: S.P.C.K., 1975] 141–44). If that theory is not credible, then the possibility that 2 Pet 1:16–18 refers to a resurrection appearance is accordingly diminished. It is true that many of the features of the synoptic Transfiguration narratives which do not suit a resurrection appearance (Stein, *JBL* 95 [1976] 90–94) are missing from the account in 2 Peter, partly because it is only a fragmentary reference whose larger context is not given. No doubt if we did not know the Transfiguration narratives of the Gospels we should assume that 2 Peter referred to a resurrection appearance. But since we do know the synoptic Transfiguration as an event located in Jesus' earthly ministry even according to the pre-Markan tradition, the burden of proof must be with those who think that the account in 2 Peter belongs after Easter. There are certainly no features of it which *require* a post-Easter setting. The τιμὴ καὶ δόξα ("honor and glory," v 17), which Bultmann (*History,* 259 n. 2, following Hofmann) holds must refer to the resurrection or exaltation of Jesus, are entirely appropriate to the Transfiguration as portrayed in the Synoptics (Blinzler, *Berichte,* 30–31; Boobyer, *St Mark,* 44–45; Stein, *JBL* 95 [1976] 88; and see *Comment* section). Appeal to the fact that being a witness of the resurrection was the basic qualification for apostleship (Robinson, "On the *Gattung,*" 117) reflects a misunderstanding of 2 Peter, which is not attempting to establish Peter's apostolic authority by reference to this event (see *Comment* section).

It has often been thought surprising that to find a basis in the history of Jesus for the expectation of the Parousia, the author of 2 Peter goes to the Transfiguration rather than to the resurrection. In fact, however, the Gospel traditions as we know them appear to connect the Parousia with the Transfiguration (Mark 9:1 par.; and cf. Boobyer's argument, *St Mark,* 48–87, to the effect that Mark saw the Transfiguration as an anticipation of the Parousia much as 2 Peter does), but fail to connect it explicitly with the resurrection (though cf. Acts 1:11). If, as we suggested above, the connection of the Transfiguration with the saying in Mark 9:1 par. was also made in the tradition the writer of 2 Peter knew, then this, together with the interpretation of Ps 2 which we shall argue lies behind 2 Pet 1:17–18 (see *Comment* section), may sufficiently explain why the writer chose to refer to the Transfiguration.

Finally, the *Apoc. Pet.* cannot be used as evidence for reference to a resurrection appearance in 2 Pet 1:16–18. The *Apoc. Pet.* does place the Transfiguration story in a post-resurrection setting, or (perhaps more accurately) it uses the Transfiguration traditions to compose an account of a revelation of paradise to the disciples by the risen Lord and an Ascension story. But since this account is based not only on 2 Peter but also on the Gospel of Matthew, it cannot be argued that the author of the *Apoc. Pet.* understood 2 Pet 1:16–18 as a resurrection appearance. On the contrary, he apparently identified it as the same event as the Transfiguration in Matthew, but then felt at liberty to reuse material from both these sources in the postresurrection setting which was normal for second-century apocryphal works, just as in chap 1 of his *Apoc.* he had transferred material from Matt 24 into a postresurrection setting.

The character of the Transfiguration in 2 Peter compared with other versions

Sabbe ("La rédaction") and H. C. Kee ("The Transfiguration in Mark: Epiphany or Apocalyptic Vision?" in J. Reumann ed., *Understanding the Sacred Text* [M. S. Enslin Festschrift; Valley Forge, PA: Judson Press, 1972] 137–52) have shown that the Transfiguration in the synoptic Gospels is not to be understood, in Hellenistic style, as an epiphany in which Jesus' divine essence is disclosed. Rather it is in form and content an apocalyptic revelation in which God installs Jesus as his eschatological vicegerent. "The transfiguration scene is not a theophany *to,* nor an epiphany *of,* Jesus, but a proleptic vision of the exaltation of Jesus as kingly Son of Man granted to the disciples as eschatological witnesses" (Kee, 149). This understanding of the Transfiguration is preserved in 2 Peter (see *Comment* section). In fact it is clearer in 2 Peter than in the synoptic accounts that the Transfiguration itself is not a disclosure of Jesus' hidden divine being, but a bestowal of glory on him by God (v 17), while it is significant that both in the Synoptics and in 2 Peter the climax of the narrative is the heavenly voice, though exegetes of 2 Peter have frequently neglected this.

Thus, although the author of 2 Peter is prone to borrowing Hellenistic religious vocabulary, when he wishes to combat the false teachers' denial of future eschatology he uses material from the apocalyptic eschatological traditions of primitive Christianity. This is as true of his Transfiguration account as it is of the material in chaps 2 and 3. The significance of 2 Peter's understanding of the Transfiguration for the date and character of the work will be better appreciated if it is compared with second-century versions of the Transfiguration.

The *Apoc. Pet.* (E 15–17) is still basically within the apocalyptic eschatological tradition, but the Transfiguration material is largely diverted to a new function: the revelation of the glory of the redeemed in paradise. Thus it appears that the text does not refer to the glorification of Jesus himself, but transfers the Transfiguration language to Moses and Elijah, as representatives of the inhabitants of paradise. Even the phrase "honor and glory," from 2 Pet 1:17, is applied, not to Jesus, but to the destiny of Christians (E 16).

Like the *Apoc. of Pet.,* the account of the Transfiguration in the *Acts Pet.* (*Act. Verc.* 20) is dependent on Matthew and 2 Peter, but it makes very different use of the material. The Transfiguration is understood as Christ's revelation of his majesty to the disciples. The emphasis is on the unbearable glory of Christ's true divine being revealed to Peter. Peter falls to the ground (cf. Matt 17:6) not in response to the heavenly voice, but overpowered by Christ's radiant appearance and by Christ's own voice. There is no reference to the cloud or to the heavenly voice or to God the Father at all.

Acts Thom. 143 refers to the Transfiguration in a rather similar way, though very briefly: "his appearance we saw transfigured with our eyes, but his heavenly form we could not see upon the mount" (*NT Apoc.* 2, 518). Presumably this means that they could not bear the sight of his divine glory.

More gnostic accounts appear in *Gos. Phil.* 26 and *Acts John* 90, both in contexts which describe the diversity of different forms which Jesus assumed on earth. "Some indeed saw him, while they thought they were seeing themselves, but when he appeared to his disciples in glory on the mount he was not small. He became great, but he made the disciples great, that they might be able to see him in his greatness" (*Gos. Phil.* 26, or 106:3–10, tr. R. McL. Wilson, *The Gospel of Philip* [London: Mowbray, 1962] 91).

The Gospel fragment from the Strasbourg Coptic papyrus, if it is rightly understood as alluding to the Transfiguration, conforms to the general trend of second-century interpretation. Christ promises to reveal his glory to the apostles, together with their power as apostles. "Our eyes penetrated all places, we beheld the glory of his godhead and all the glory of [his] dominion. He clothed [us with] the power [of our] apostle[ship]" (*NT Apoc.* 1, 230).

Comparison with these plainly Hellenistic versions of the Transfiguration demonstrates how far removed the account in 2 Peter is from them and how mistaken is the view (of, e.g., Käsemann, "Apologia," 186) that for 2 Peter the Transfiguration is an epiphany of Jesus' hidden divinity.

Comment

16. *σεσοφισμένοις μύθοις ἐξακολουθήσαντες*, "following cleverly concocted myths." Neyrey's identification of the *οὐ . . . ἀλλά* ("not . . . but") form in which the author of 2 Peter refutes objections (see *Form/Structure/Setting* section) implies that this phrase contains the opponents' charge that the apostles followed myths (so also Kelly, Green). This is a much more straightforward reading of the verse than the alternative view that the phrase contains the author's charge that his opponents followed myths (Schelkle, Grundmann, Schrage): that requires too involved a train of thought. Thus there is no question here of gnostic myths or of comparing the usage of the Pastorals, where the opponents' "myths" are rejected (1 Tim 1:4; 4:7; Titus 1:14; cf. Ign. *Magn.* 8:1). There is no need to ask what kind of myths the text refers to, for it refers to no myths except the apostolic preaching, which the false teachers slandered by calling it "myths."

What did they mean by this charge? The connotations of the term *μῦθος* in the first century A.D. were almost as various as those of the modern English "myth." The old Greek myths, the stories about the gods, could be seen as stories which were not literally true but expressed religious, moral or philosophical truth in pictorial form. They could be subjected to allegorical interpretation, as by the Stoics. The Hellenistic age was in many respects one which showed a "growing preference for *μῦθος* [myth] over *λόγος* [rational argument] as a means of expressing truth. This preference is characteristic of gnosticism: the saving gnosis is often cast in the form of a myth" (C. K. Barrett, "Myth and the New Testament: The Greek Word *μῦθος*," *ExpTim* 68 [1956–57] 345). On the other hand, there was a strong tradition of criticism and repudiation of myths, as morally unedifying, or as childish, nonsensical or fabulous. Here *μῦθος* can come, like "myth" in much modern English usage, to mean a story which is *not true,* a fable or fairy story (again in the derogatory senses). Strabo and Diodorus of Sicily oppose myth to history (Spicq, *Lexicographie,* 580); Plutarch contrasts a myth and a true account (*ἀληθεῖ λόγῳ*: *Cam.* 22.3; further examples in Spicq, *Lexicographie,* 580–81; H. D. Betz ed., *Plutarch's Ethical Writings and Early Christian Literature* [SCHNT 4; Leiden: E. J. Brill, 1978] 456); and *μῦθος* is associated with *πλάσμα* ("invention") and related terms in opposition to *ἀλήθεια* ("truth") (*TDNT* 4, 770, 784–85 and n. 139). We should also note the special contempt of the Epicurean school for myths of all kinds, including myths of providence and post-mortem punishments for the wicked (*TDNT* 4, 779 and n. 102; Neyrey, *Polemic,* 185, 194–95; and cf. Justin, *2 Apol.* 9).

Surprisingly, it is characteristic of Philo to distinguish the biblical history from myth, as truth from fiction (Spicq, *Lexicographie,* 581; *TDNT* 4, 790; Neyrey, *CBQ* 42 [1980] 507). His concern is not only to reject the pagan myths, but to repudiate the suggestion, no doubt made by Hellenized Jews as well as by pagans, that the biblical stories were mythical. Neyrey notes several occasions where Philo uses the same *οὐ . . . ἀλλά* ("not . . . but") form as we find in 2 Peter, to oppose the suggestion that a narrative or a prophecy in Scripture is a "myth" (*CBQ* 42 [1980] 507–8). The form itself is too obvious for the parallel to be remarkable, but it is interesting to find

Philo opposing the same kind of charge as the writer of 2 Peter faces, since the two writers to some extent share a similar relationship to a Hellenistic environment.

It has become clear that the charge of "myths" can be leveled not only at stories, but also at accounts of the next world (as with the Epicureans) and at prophecies (as with Philo's defense of prophecies in Genesis: *Mut.* 152; *Som.* 1.172). The very general sense in which the charge could be leveled at Christianity is evident from *2 Clem.* 13:3: "the Gentiles, when they hear from our mouth the oracles (λόγια) of God [the Scriptures], marvel at them for their beauty and greatness; then, when they discover that our works are not worthy of the words which we speak, they turn to blasphemy, saying that it is a myth and a delusion (*μῦθόν τινα καὶ πλάνην*)." There is therefore no difficulty in supposing that it was the Christian eschatological teaching about the Parousia which the false teachers rejected as "myths."

σεσοφισμένοις, "cleverly concocted," corresponds to the common description of myths as *πλαστοί* ("invented, fabricated," cf 2:3: *πλαστοῖς λόγοις*, "fabricated arguments"; see *TDNT* 7, 785 n. 139; and for many examples of Philo's association of *μῦθος* with *πλάσσειν* and *πλάσμα*, see Neyrey, *CBQ* 42 [1980] 507), but is more expressive in incorporating the idea of "cleverness" in a bad sense (for this bad sense of *σοφίζεσθαι*, cf. *Barn.* 9:4; Pap. Oxy. 840, line 1). The eschatological teaching of the apostles is held to be, not prophecy inspired by God, but the fabrication of merely human cleverness, doubtless with some unworthy motive. The Epicureans held that the Greek stories of punishment in the afterlife were invented as instruments of moral control, to keep men in fear, and the false teachers combated in 2 Peter may have said something similar about the Christian belief in future judgment.

The phrase *μύθοις ἐξακολουθήσαντες* ("following myths") is used by Josephus in contrasting Moses, who did not invent fictional stories, with other legislators, who followed fables (*Ant.* 1.22, cf. 15–16). The verb, only used in 2 Peter in the NT, recurs in 2:2, 15, where it is turned against the false teachers.

ἐγνωρίσαμεν ὑμῖν, "we made known to you." The verb is frequently used in the NT for imparting revelation. Here it is used of the apostles' preaching of the gospel, which included the expectation of the Parousia. The first person plural now refers to the apostles in general (as in v 1). In view of 3:1 ("your apostles"), it is unlikely that Peter himself was one of the missionaries who founded the churches addressed. Rather, the writer is thinking of the apostles in general, some of whom founded the churches to which he is writing, and of whom Peter was a prominent representative. This interpretation may appear awkward since in the rest of this verse and in vv 17–18 "we" becomes the apostles who witnessed the Transfiguration, i.e. Peter, James and John, none of whom is likely to have founded the churches to which 2 Peter is addressed, but really this variation is quite natural. Though to some extent all the apostles were eyewitnesses, they were not all eyewitnesses of every important event in the ministry of Jesus, and so their common message was in part based on the eyewitness testimony of only some of their number. The writer's real concern is to claim that the common apostolic teaching about the Parousia was based on eyewitness testimony, and this concern overrides the grammatical technicality that "we" is used of two mutually exclusive groups of apostles (those who preached to the gospel to the churches addressed in the letter, and those who witnessed the Transfiguration). Once again we should notice that the writer presupposes that all the apostles preached the same message.

τὴν τοῦ κυρίου ἡμῶν Ἰησοῦ Χριστοῦ δύναμιν καὶ παρουσίαν, "the coming of our Lord Jesus Christ in power." As usually with 2 Peter's pairs of words, δύναμιν καὶ παρουσίαν (lit. "power and coming") should be taken closely together, even as a hendiadys: "coming in power" (so Reicke; Fornberg, *Early Church,* 79). παρουσία, "coming," is the usual term for Christ's eschatological coming in glory, in a variety of early Christian traditions (Matt 24:3, 27, 37, 39; 1 Cor 15:23; 1 Thess 3:13; 4:15; Jas 5:7–8; 1 John 2:28), though not, it should be noted, in 1 Peter, which always uses ἀποκάλυψις ("revelation": 1 Pet 1:7, 13; 4:13). It is in this usual sense that 2 Peter uses παρουσία in 3:4, 12. It is true that Ignatius (*Phld.* 9:2) and the *Ker. Pet.* (*ap.* Clem. Alex. *Strom.* 6.15.128) use it of Christ's first coming, in incarnation and resurrection, but otherwise this usage is not attested until Justin (who uses παρουσία seventeen times of Christ's first coming, nineteen times of his future coming). These facts of usage suggest that παρουσία here refers to Christ's future coming in glory, and this is confirmed by the whole argument of the letter, which implies that it is the eschatological teaching of the apostles which needs to be defended against the charge of falsity and invention. Although a few scholars argue for a reference to the first coming (Spicq; Marín, *EE* 50 [1975] 225–26), the vast majority see a reference to the Parousia in the usual sense (Kelly, 317–18, and Fornberg, *Early Church,* 79–80, refute Spicq's arguments).

δύναμις ("power") is, like δόξα ("glory"), associated with the Parousia (Matt 24:30; Mark 9:1; 13:26; Luke 21:27; cf. *2 Clem.* 17:5: κράτος, "power"). Although in 1:3 our author has spoken of Christ's divine power at work in his incarnate life and resurrection, the close association of δύναμιν here with παρουσίαν ("coming") requires us to restrict its reference to the future Parousia (against Zahn, *Introduction,* 215). It is possible that the whole phrase is a reminiscence of Matt 16:28 par Mark 9:1 (see *Form/Structure/Setting* section above). The phrase is used by Josephus (*Ant.* 9:55; 18.284), but in the Hellenistic sense of an epiphany of divine power, not with eschatological significance. However much our author's account of the Transfiguration might resemble such Hellenistic conceptions of divine epiphany, his understanding of it is completely unhellenistic in that he sees it as a prophetic anticipation of the eschatological future.

ἐπόπται, "eyewitnesses." The word is a NT *hapax.* It means "observer, spectator" (Aeschylus, *Prom.* 298–99), and then also "overseer" (Josephus, *C. Apion.* 2.187, of priests). In the latter sense it is used of God (LXX Esth 5:1; 2 Macc 3:39; 7:35; 3 Macc 2:21; *Ep. Arist.* 16; *1 Clem.* 59:3; cf. 2 Macc 9:5). The term was also used technically for the higher grade of initiates in the Eleusinian mysteries (*TDNT* 5, 374; Fornberg, *Early Church,* 123), evidently as those who had seen the vision of the divine mysteries. Most commentators think that this technical usage is echoed in 2 Peter. In view of the writer's propensity for using Hellenistic religious vocabulary, this is quite possible, and it would be quite appropriate: the apostles at the Transfiguration witnessed the revelation of Christ's divine majesty. But it should be noted that the term did have a quite ordinary use, and that the corresponding verb ἐποπτεύειν, "to observe," is used in this ordinary sense in 1 Pet 2:12; 3:2. We cannot be sure that 2 Peter follows the mystical sense. It is in any case improbable that further overtones of a higher esoteric gnosis, accessible only to the select view, are intended (against Käsemann, "Apologia," 186; Klinger, *SVTQ* 17 [1973] 161; Green).

It is sometimes said that an emphasis on eyewitness testimony is characteristic of the later NT documents (Nineham, *JTS* 11 [1960] 254–64; Fornberg, *Early Church,* 11). What the evidence adduced really proves is that a stress on the apostolic eyewitnesses occurs when there is a need for apologetic defense of the Christian message in some way by reference to its historical basis. This accounts for the early example of this emphasis in 1 Cor 15:3–8, as well as for the anti-docetic apologetic involved in the adducing of eyewitness testimony in the Fourth Gospel (19:35) and 1 John (1:1–3; 4:14), perhaps for Luke's emphasis on the apostles as eyewitnesses in Acts, as the story of the Christian mission, and obviously for later works such as the *Gos. Pet.* (7:26–27; 14:59–60) which have a clear apologetic concern. Second Peter fits this pattern not simply as a relatively late document, but as a work concerned to defend one aspect of Christian teaching against objections. To do so the author adduces apostolic eyewitness testimony to the Transfiguration, which provides a historical basis for the expectation of the Parousia.

Many comments on this passage and its stress on the eyewitnesses are beside the point because they suppose that its purpose is to base the apostles' authority on their presence at the Transfiguration (so, e.g., Klein, *Die zwölf Apostel,* 102–3; Käsemann, "Apologia," 185–87). The defense of apostolic authority is not at all the author's intention. He wishes only to show that one aspect of the apostles' teaching, namely the expectation of the Parousia, is soundly based on what the apostles witnessed, namely the Transfiguration. This means that it is also beside the point to connect the emphasis on eyewitness testimony with the pseudepigraphal nature of the letter. The author is not trying to bolster his own authority by claiming, falsely, to be an eyewitness of the Transfiguration. He is simply adducing Peter's testimony as evidence that the event took place as he narrates it, and puts it in the first person form because of the literary convention he is following. In another sort of literary work he could have reported Peter's testimony in the third person, to the same effect.

Of course, it may seem that if the historicity of the Transfiguration is at stake, this second- or third-hand report of Peter's testimony does not have the value it would have if it were really first-hand testimony from Peter's own pen. This must be granted. But it is unlikely that the writer expected his readers to question the historicity of the Transfiguration. They would no doubt already know, in oral or written form, a tradition of the Transfiguration account and would accept it with the rest of the Gospel traditions as resting on the eyewitness testimony of the apostles. What the author of 2 Peter does is to point out to them that this tradition forms a basis for the expectation of the Parousia. His argument is that one reason why the apostles were so confident in their teaching about the Parousia is that (as the readers know and accept) they witnessed the Transfiguration. Since the readers accept this eyewitness testimony to the Transfiguration as reliable, they can also rely on the teaching which the apostles based on it: the prophecy of the Parousia. Thus the emphasis on eyewitness testimony in this passage is neither an attempt to convince otherwise skeptical readers that the Transfiguration happened, nor a spurious attempt to give authority to the work. It is an attempt to draw the readers' attention to the fact that this undisputed evidence is relevant to the matter that is disputed: the Parousia.

τῆς ἐκείνου μεγαλειότητος, "his majesty." This term, though not used exclusively of God (LXX Jer 40:9; Dan 7:27; 1 Esdr1:4; 4:40), was most commonly used of divine grandeur and majesty (Josephus, *Ant.* 1.24; 8.111; *C. Apion.* 2.168; Luke 9:43; Acts 19:27 [of Artemis]; *1 Clem.* 24:5; Ign. *Rom.* inscr. [of God and Christ]; *Diogn.* 10:5; cf. *τὸ μεγαλεῖον*, *1 Clem.* 49:3), sometimes in the first century of the divine majesty of the Emperor (Spicq, *Lexicographie,* 544). Here, as the next verse makes clear, it refers to the divine majesty which Jesus received from God.

17. *λαβὼν γάρ παρὰ θεοῦ πατρὸς τιμὴν καὶ δόξαν*, "for he received honor and glory from God the Father." Probably God is called Father here because the sentence goes on to stress Jesus' sonship in the words of the heavenly voice. *τιμὴν καὶ δόξαν* ("honor and glory") are a natural pair (Ps 8:6 LXX, quoted Heb 2:7, 9; 1 Pet 1:7; and often in doxologies). Some commentators think the reference is to the glorification of Jesus' appearance (Bigg, Windisch), some think it refers to the dignity conferred on Jesus by the heavenly voice (Grundmann; Chase, *DB*(*H*) 3, p. 808; H.-P. Müller, "Die Verklärung Jesu: Eine motivgeschichtliche Studie," *ZNW* 51 [1960] 57), and many think that *τιμή* ("honor") refers to the abstract dignity given by the voice, while *δόξα* ("glory") refers to the visible transfiguration (Mayor, Wand, Chaine, Schelkle, Green, Kelly). But 2 Peter's pairs of words are not divisible in this way; so it seems we must choose between the abstract honor and the visible glorification. The connection with the following words cannot determine the sense: both participles are dependent on a main verb which, by anacolouthon, is never expressed. In favor of a reference to the visible transfiguration is the fact that *ἐπόπται* ("eyewitnesses," v 16) requires some mention of what the apostles saw. The meaning of the double expression may be that God conferred honor on Jesus by glorifying his appearance. This sense of *δόξα* permits the inference that at the Transfiguration Jesus received from God the glory in which he will be seen by all at the Parousia. *δόξα* is always in the synoptic Gospels (except at Luke 2:9; 9:32) used of the Parousia (Matt 16:27; 19:28; 24:30; 25:31; Mark 8:38; 10:37; 13:26; Luke 9:26; 21:27; 24:26), and it is often so used elsewhere (Phil 3:21; Col 3:4; 2 Thess 1:9; Titus 2:13; 1 Pet 4:13; 5:1; *2 Clem.* 17:5). It is not used in the synoptic accounts of the Transfiguration except at Luke 9:32, but it is an entirely appropriate term for the transfiguration they describe, and there is no reason to follow Bultmann's view that *τιμὴν καὶ δόξαν* ("honor and glory") here can only refer to the resurrection or exaltation of Jesus (*The History of the Synoptic Tradition,* tr. J. Marsh, 2nd ed. [Oxford: Basil Blackwell, 1968] 259 n. 2).

It is important to notice that Jesus *receives* honor and glory *from* God. Jesus is here no Hellenistic *θεῖος ἀνήρ* ("divine man"). The Transfiguration is no epiphany of Jesus' hidden divine nature. Rather, 2 Peter's conception of the Transfiguration still belongs to the primarily functional and apocalyptic

Christology of primitive Christianity. Jesus is invested with the divine glory because he is appointed to the task of carrying out God's eschatological judgment and reign.

The phrase τιμὴν καὶ δόξαν ("honor and glory") could derive from Ps 8:6 LXX (where the two terms occur in reverse order). If so, the interpretation is different from that in Heb 2:9, where the honor and glory are given to Jesus at his resurrection, but the author of 2 Peter would no doubt agree with Heb 2:8 that the subjection of all things to Jesus (Ps 8:7) is yet to come, at the Parousia. Thus in the Transfiguration Jesus was given the status of the one to whom all things will be subdued when he comes as eschatological judge (cf. 1 Cor 15:24–28; and Ps 2:8–9, on which see below). At any rate Ps 8:6 shows how appropriate τιμή and δόξα are in a depiction of the enthronement of God's vicegerent. Alternatively, there may be a reference to Dan 7:14 (θ: ἡ τιμή, "the honor"), where the Son of Man receives universal dominion (so Sabbe, "La rédaction," 76), especially if this OT chap. was the source of τὴν αἰώνιον βασιλείαν τοῦ κυρίου ἡμῶν καὶ σωτῆρος ("the eternal kingdom of our Lord and Savior") in 1:11.

φωνῆς ἐνεχθείσης αὐτῷ τοιᾶσδε ὑπὸ τῆς μεγαλοπρεποῦς δόξης, "a voice conveyed to him by the Majestic Glory." The curious expression, "a voice conveyed to him by" God, is a way of protecting the transcendence of God by avoiding the idea that God himself speaks directly. Although this exact form of expression does not seem to be paralleled, the same concern is evident in apocalyptic references to a voice from heaven, which avoid directly identifying it as God's voice (Dan 4:31; *1 Enoch* 13:8; 65:4; *2 Apoc. Bar.* 13:1; 22:1; Rev 4:4, 8; 11:12; 16:1; cf. John 12:28; Acts 10:13–15; 11:7, 9; *Mart. Pol.* 9:1) and in the rabbinic idea of the baṯ qôl (cf. *TDNT* 9, 288–90). "The Majestic Glory" is a periphrasis for God; cf. "the great Glory" (*1 Enoch* 14:20; 102:3; *T. Levi* 3:4; *Asc. Isa.* 9:37; 11:32; cf. Sir 17:13: μεγαλεῖον δόξης; and Jude 24, with *Comment*), and "the Majesty" (μεγαλωσύνη: Heb 1:3; 8:1). μεγαλοπρεπής ("majestic," only here in NT) and its corresponding noun μεγαλοπρέπεια ("majesty") are frequently used of God and his works in the LXX (Deut 33:26; Pss 8:2; 28:4; 67:35; 70:8; 95:6; 110:3; 2 Macc 8:15) and in *1 Clem.* (9:1; 19:2; 60:1; 61:1; 64:1), which shares with 2 Peter a predilection for grandiose terms of this kind. We find τὴν μεγαλοπρέπειαν τῆς δόξης ("the glorious majesty") and τὴν δόξαν τῆς μεγαλοπρεπείας ("the majestic glory") in Ps 144:5, 12 LXX, and the same phrase as 2 Peter's used as a periphrasis for God in *1 Clem.* 9:2 (τῇ μεγαλοπρεπεῖ δόξῃ αὐτοῦ). It also occurs in later Greek liturgies and may already have been liturgical at the time of 2 Peter and *1 Clem.* (Chase, *DB*(*H*) 3, p. 799).

It is possible that this description of God as "the Majestic Glory" is connected with the cloud in the synoptic accounts of the Transfiguration. The synoptic accounts are strongly influenced by the OT accounts of the Sinai theophany (Sabbe, "La rédaction," 77–80; B. D. Chilton, "The Transfiguration: Dominical Assurance and Apostolic Vision," *NTS* 27 [1980–81] 120–21), in which "the glory of the Lord" comes down onto Mount Sinai in the Shekinah cloud (Exod 24:16). But it is unlikely that the author of 2 Peter expects his readers to see an allusion to Sinai, for he has dropped all features of the Transfiguration tradition which suggest a Moses typology, including (the most clearly deliberate omission) the words "hear him" (Deut 18:15) from the divine declaration. He is presenting Jesus as eschatological divine vicegerent, not as eschatological prophet.

It may be noted that although our author reproduces the traditional form of the words of the voice in which they are addressed not to Jesus but to the disciples ("This is . . ."), he says that the voice was conveyed by God *to Jesus* (αὐτῷ "to him"). If we are correct in supposing that he understands the voice to be the divine decree of Ps 2:7 (see below), it is relevant that the Lord's words there are addressed to the Messiah (LXX: πρὸς μέ, "to me"). This point also indicates that the writer of 2 Peter sees the Transfiguration not just as the *revelation* of Jesus' kingship to the disciples, but also as his actual appointment by God to be the eschatological king.

ὁ υἱός μου, "my Son." Although not all scholars agree that this phrase in the words of the voice at Jesus' baptism and transfiguration was originally seen as an allusion to Ps 2:7 (see *Form/Structure/Setting* section above), it is clear that it was interpreted as such from quite an early stage (Luke 3:22 D; *Gos. Eb.;* Justin, *Dial.* 88.8; 103.6; cf. Heb 1:5; 5:5; Bretscher, *JBL* 87 [1968] 302). That the writer of 2 Peter saw here an allusion to Ps 2:7, and in this the principal key to the significance of the Transfiguration, is suggested by the phrase "the holy mountain" in v 18 (see below).

Psalm 2, which was already interpreted in a messianic sense in Judaism (4QFlor 1:18–2:1; *Pss. Sol.* 17:23–24; rabbinic references in E. Lövestam, *Son and Saviour: A Study of Acts 13, 32–37* [*ConNT* 18; Lund: C. W. K. Gleerup/ Copenhagen: E. Munksgaard, 1961] 17–21) describes the enthronement of God's anointed king on Mount Zion, in the context of the rebellion of the hostile nations against divine rule. The Messiah is appointed by God and declared his son (v 7) with immediate reference to his subjugation of the nations and universal dominion (vv 8–9). This theme of the royal Messiah's conquest of the rebellious nations was prominent whenever Ps 2 was given a messianic reference in Jewish interpretation (Lövestam, 15–23). There is evidence that this was also the case in early Christian application of the psalm to Jesus; Jesus, as God's Son, had been designated the one who will exercise eschatological judgment and implement God's universal dominion at his Parousia in glory. The book of Revelation combines reference to Jesus' sonship (Ps 2:7) and to Jesus' judgment of and rule over the nations (Ps 2:9) in this way (2:26–28; 12:5; 19:15; cf. other allusions to the psalm in 11:15–18). Note especially how Rev 2:27–28 implies that as the Son of God Jesus has already received from the Father the authority to rule the nations which he was to exercise at the Parousia. L. C. Allen ("The Old Testament Background of (προ)ὁρίζειν in the New Testament," *NTS* 17 [1970–71] 105) also argues that the references in Acts 10:42; 17:31 to Jesus' appointment (ὁρίζειν) by God to be the eschatological judge are allusions to the divine "decree" (חק) of Ps 2:7.

Probably the most common early Christian application of Ps 2:7 was to the Resurrection (Acts 13:33; Rom 1:4; cf. Heb 1:5; 5:5; 7:28), but a connection with the Transfiguration could easily be made, because the Transfiguration story was already, in the pre-synoptic tradition, understood as an apocalyptic vision in which Jesus' enthronement as the royal Messiah was proleptically revealed to the disciples. In accordance with this general view of the Transfiguration, the tradition on which 2 Peter evidently depends interpreted the heavenly voice on the mountain of the Transfiguration as the divine decree of Ps 2:7, in which God appointed Jesus the one who was to judge and rule the nations. At the same time he invested Jesus with his kingly glory, a participation in the divine majesty given to the one who is to exercise the divine rule. The Transfiguration is the basis for the Parousia expectation because it is God's appointment of Jesus to a rôle which he has not yet exercised but will exercise at his coming in glory. This view of the significance of the Transfiguration in 2 Peter also accounts for the great emphasis which these verses place on the divine voice, to the exclusion of other aspects of the Transfiguration.

Although no doubt Ps 2:7 originally meant that the king's enthronement was his adoption to divine sonship, it is unlikely that the author of 2 Peter understood the heavenly voice in that way. Most probably he interpreted it to mean that *because* Jesus was already God's Son, he has appointed him to be his vicegerent.

ὁ ἀγαπητός μου, "my Beloved." Depending on the OT background to the words of the voice at this point (see *Form/Structure/Setting* section above), there are two possible interpretations. The phrase may be a literal version of the Hebrew יחידי, "my only one" (cf. Gen. 22:2, 12, 16), in which case it is closely connected with the preceding phrase and indicates the uniqueness of Jesus' divine sonship. Alternatively it may represent בחירי, "my chosen," in Isa 42:1, in which case it should be connected with the following phrase and God's election of Jesus to messianic office. The special love of God the Father for his Son involves a special calling in God's purpose. The same thought is no doubt behind the use of *ὁ ἀγαπημένος* and *ὁ ἀγαπητός* as a Christological title, "the Beloved" (Eph 1:6; *Barn.* 3:6; 4:3, 8; Ign. *Smyrn.* inscr.; *Acts Paul & Thecla* 1; *Odes Sol.* 3:8; *Asc. Isa.* 1:4, 5, 7, 13; 3:13; etc.).

εἰς ὃν ἐγὼ εὐδόκησα, "on whom I have set my favor." The phrase derives from Isa 42:1, and carries the special sense of God's *electing* good pleasure (see Schrenk in *TDNT* 2, 739–41; and *1 Enoch* 37:4; 39:9). The very rare construction *εἰς ὃν* (see *Form/Structure/Setting* section) probably carries the sense of God's favor selecting Jesus by coming to rest on him, while the aorist indicates an act of election. Presumably the election is considered as having already occurred, in God's eternity; it is now declared at the moment of Jesus' official appointment to the task for which God has elected him.

The author of 2 Peter may have added the emphatic *ἐγώ* ("I") to the form of the words which he knew in the tradition. It stresses that Jesus is the one whom *God* himself has selected to be his vicegerent. Thus the expectation of the Parousia is not a humanly contrived myth (v 16), but is firmly grounded in God's declared will as the apostles themselves heard it spoken.

Probably the author of 2 Peter sees no further significance in the allusion to Isa 42:1 as such, since the role of the Servant in that passage was not connected with the Parousia in Christian traditional exegesis. But reference to eschatological judgment could have been found in the context (Isa 41:25; 42:4).

18. *ἐξ οὐρανοῦ*, "from heaven." A voice from heaven is a standard feature

of apocalyptic visions (Dan 4:31; *1 Enoch* 13:8; 65:4; *2 Apoc. Bar.* 13:1; 22:1; Rev 10:4, 8; 11:12; 14:13) and, although the phrase is not used in the synoptic accounts of the Transfiguration, it is entirely appropriate to the primitive Christian understanding of the Transfiguration as an apocalyptic revelation and may well have belonged to the tradition 2 Peter here follows (see *Form/Structure/Setting* section).

ἐν τῷ ἁγίῳ ὄρει, "on the holy mountain." As a designation for the mountain of the Transfiguration the phrase occurs in *Apoc. Pet.* E 15 and *Act. Verc.* 20, but these passages are dependent on 2 Peter. Of course, there was no veneration of a supposed site of the Transfiguration as a holy place until much later, and so 2 Peter's expression cannot allude to a well-known locality. Some (Bigg, James, Green) think that the phrase is used simply because the theophany made the place holy. Many see it as a mark of a late date (Chaine, Schelkle, Spicq; Fornberg, *Early Church,* 146). Those who look in 2 Peter for signs of the Transfiguration's connection with the Sinai theophany find a symbolic reference to Sinai (Sabbe, "La rédaction," 75). However, although of course the OT implies the holiness of Sinai when God is present there (Exod 3:5; 19), Sinai is never called "the holy mountain" in the OT (although Philo calls it *θεῖος*, "divine," in *Leg. All.* 3.142; *Mos.* 1.115, and *ἱερωτάτος*, "most sacred," in *Mos.* 2.79; *Spec. Leg.* 3.125). The phrase "holy mountain" (usually, but not always, "my holy mountain") always in the OT designates Zion. The best explanation of the phrase here is as a deliberate echo of Ps 2:6 LXX: "I have been appointed king by him on Zion his holy mountain" (*ἐπὶ Σιων ὄρος το ἅγιον αὐτοῦ*). Of course, there is no intention of locating the Transfiguration historically on Mount Zion; the point is to identify the event with the prophecy in Ps 2 to explain its theological significance. The apostles, claims 2 Peter, were there with Jesus when God appointed him his king, and they themselves heard the divine decree.

Explanation

This section begins the author's defense of the eschatological teaching of the apostles against the attacks of the false teachers, which continues through much of the rest of the letter. The first charge to which he replies is that when the apostles preached the expectation of the future Parousia of Jesus Christ as judge and king, their message was not based on authentic divine revelation but was a mere human invention, a "myth" in the sense of a tale which is not true. The opponents may have argued that the apostles deliberately invented the notion of eschatological judgment at the Parousia as a means of moral control through fear.

To answer this charge the author first appeals to the apostles', especially Peter's, own eyewitness testimony to the transfiguration of Jesus—an event with which his readers would already be familiar through the Gospel traditions. In line with the primitive Christian apocalyptic understanding of the Transfiguration, our author sees it as God's appointment of Jesus as his eschatological vicegerent. In particular, he sees it as the fulfillment of the messianic prophecy in Ps 2, where, on the basis of the divine decree (v 7) which was echoed by the heavenly voice at the Transfiguration, the Son of God (v 7) is enthroned as God's anointed king (v 6), on God's "holy mountain" (v 6), with the task of subduing the rebellious world to divine rule (vv 8–9). On the mountain of the Transfiguration Jesus was appointed to this task which he will exercise in the future when he comes in glory as the eschatological judge and ruler. The author is therefore pointing out to his readers that the Transfiguration, to which the apostles bore witness, is a basis for the expectation of the Parousia.

Thus the author tells how, at the Transfiguration, Jesus received from God the Father a share in the divine majesty, because he was appointed to a divine task, and how the apostles saw him clothed in this visible glory in which he will be seen by all at the Parousia. They also heard, in a voice from heaven, the divine declaration that God's Son had been selected by God to be his Messiah. The emphasis of the account is that *God himself* has elected Jesus to be his vicegerent, appointed him to the office and invested him with glory for the task. If the apostles' witness to this is trustworthy, then their message about the Parousia is not a human invention, but is based on this divine action and declaration.

Reply to Objection 1: (b) The Value of Old Testament Prophecy (1:19)

Bibliography

Boehmer, J. "Tag und Morgenstern? Zu II Petr i 19." *ZNW* 22 (1923) 228–33. **Neyrey, J. H.** "The Apologetic Use of the Transfiguration in 2 Peter 1:16–21." *CBQ* 42 (1980) 504–19. **Sibinga, J. S.** "Une citation du Cantique dans la Secunda Petri." *RB* 73 (1966) 107–18. **Spicq, C.** *Lexicographie,* 953–54.

Translation

[19] *Moreover, we place very firm reliance on the prophetic word, to which you would do well to attend, as you would to a lamp shining in a murky place, until the day dawns and the morning star rises in your hearts.*

Form/Structure/Setting

This verse contains a second reply to the objection stated in v 16a.

Comment

19. *καὶ ἔχομεν βεβαιότερον τὸν προφητικὸν λόγον*, "moreover, we place very firm reliance on the prophetic word." Commentators have usually given *βεβαιότερον* its proper comparative force, "more certain, more reliable," but have then been divided as to its significance. Some think that prophecy is said to be a more solid argument for the Parousia than the Transfiguration is (Plumptre, Bigg, Green). But this would be a rather surprising argument in the context, since it appears to relativize the value of the apostolic eyewitness testimony which has been so stressed in vv 16–18. It is true that the rabbis held prophetic Scripture to be more reliable than a *baṯ qôl* (Green), but the Transfiguration was more than a voice from heaven. It was the visible investiture of Jesus with his kingly glory, the beginning of the fulfillment of scriptural prophecy. In view of this, the majority opinion of scholars takes this verse to be saying that the Transfiguration has confirmed OT prophecy. As an anticipatory fulfillment of prophecy the Transfiguration makes the still awaited future fulfillment at the Parousia yet more certain. Hence the translation: "we have the prophetic word *made more sure*" (RSV). However, this is not a very natural meaning of the Greek. The expression *ἔχειν τι βέβαιον* (Thucydides 1.32; Appian, *Bell. Civ.* 5.3) normally means "to have a firm hold on something"; the phrase does not use *βέβαιος* in the legal sense of "confirmed." In this phrase the comparative *βεβαιότερον* is used either as a true comparative (Isocrates, *Ad Dem.* 36) or, as often in the Koine, with superlative (elative) meaning ("very firm": Stobaeus, *Ecl.* 4.25.31). It is best to adopt the latter sense here (Reicke; Neyrey, *CBQ* 42 [1980] 515). No comparison need be intended.

The phrase τὸν προφητικὸν λόγον ("the prophetic word") has been held to refer to (1) OT messianic prophecy (Bigg, Mayor, Moffatt, Wand, Chaine; Käsemann, "Apologia," 187); (2) the whole OT understood as messianic prophecy (Schelkle, Spicq, Kelly, Grundmann); (3) one specific OT prophecy (Fornberg, *Early Church,* 82–83); (4) OT and NT prophecies (Plumptre, Sidebottom); (5) 2 Pet 1:20–2:19 (Robson, *Studies,* 44–48); (6) the Transfiguration itself as a prophecy of the Parousia (Neyrey, *CBQ* 42 [1980] 514–16).

All other known occurrences of the phrase refer to OT Scripture, except *2 Clem.* 11:2, which refers to an apocryphon which the writer presumably regarded as part of OT Scripture (cf. *1 Clem.* 23:3). Although Fornberg argues that it is always used of specific scriptural passsages, this judgment is not accurate. It seems in fact to be interchangeable with the term "Scripture" and, like that term, can refer to specific passages (Philo, *Leg. All.* 3.43; *Sob.* 68; *Acts Paul* 10 [PH, p. 8]; Justin, *Dial.* 56.6; 77.2; 110.3; also the plural προφητικοὶ λόγοι in Justin, *Dial.* 39.4; *1 Apol.* 54), or to several specific passages (Philo, *Plant.* 117–19), or to the OT generally, with particular passages not specified (Justin, *Dial.* 128.4). Justin, *Dial.* 129.1, makes it especially clear that the term is virtually synonymous with "Scripture." This equivalence came about because in the current Jewish understanding all inspired Scripture was prophecy.

Thus the use of the term favors view (2), though of course the author is thinking of the OT prophecies which early Christian exegesis normally applied to the Parousia. He may have one or more specific passages in mind (e.g. Ps 2:9; Dan 7:13–14; Num 24:17), but since he does not make this clear it is more likely that he is speaking generally. In view of 2 Pet 3:16, where Paul's writings are called γραφαί ("Scriptures"), it is perhaps not impossible that NT writings are included, but against this we should consider: (1) Even Justin does not use the term προφητικὸς λόγος ("prophetic word") of NT Scripture. (2) Our writer is not likely to be representing *Peter* as saying that he and his fellow-apostles based their preaching of the Parousia on apostolic writings. The best sense of the whole passage 1:16–19 is that the apostles based their eschatological message on (a) their own eyewitness testimony (vv 16–18), and (b) OT prophecies (v 19). (3) 2:1a, referring to false prophets in the OT period, presupposes that the preceding verses are about the OT Scriptures.

Against Neyrey's view (6) that the Transfiguration itself is the προφητικὸν λόγον ("prophetic word"), the normal usage of the term is decisive. Moreover, he is obliged to interpret vv 20–21 also as a defense of the Transfiguration as prophecy (*CBQ* 42 [1980] 516–19), but this is a most unnatural interpretation of a passage which explicitly discusses inspired *writings* (προφητεία γραφῆς). Finally, on his view, we should expect v 19 to begin with some more explicit connection with the preceding passage, such as "thus" or "therefore," rather than simply καί ("and").

It is commonly thought that the first person plural ἔχομεν (lit. "we have") now (in contrast to the preceding verses) includes all Christians. But this is unnecessary. The author is still arguing that when the apostles preached the Parousia, they were not following myths. On the contrary, they had reliable authorities for their message: the Transfiguration, which they witnessed, and the OT, which is inspired by God.

καλῶς ποιεῖτε,"you would do well," is often equivalent to "please" (Acts 10:33; Phil 4:14; 3 John 6), but probably has a slightly stronger force here, as elsewhere in paraenesis (Acts 15:29; Jas 2:8).

ὡς λύχνῳ φαίνοντι ἐν αὐχμηρῷ τόπῳ, "as to a lamp shining in a murky place." The comparison of the Word of God to a lamp was common (Ps 119 (118): 105; Wis 18:4; *2 Apoc. Bar.* 17:4; 59:2; 77:16; *Bib. Ant.* 9:8; 15:6; 19:5; Theophilus, *Ad Autol.* 2:13). It was sometimes extended to those who teach God's Word (John 5:35; *2 Apoc. Bar.* 77:13, 15; cf. Sir 48:1), and so in 4 Ezra 12:42 Ezra is compared to "a lamp in a dark place." Since the purpose of lamps is to shine in darkness (cf. also Job 29:3; *2 Apoc. Bar.* 59:2), this coincidence with 2 Peter is unremarkable.

αὐχμηρός, a rare word, is used by Aristotle (*De Color.* 3) as the opposite of *λαμπρός* ("bright") and synonymous with *ἀλαμπής* ("without light"). It is also used in *Apoc. Pet.* A 21, describing hell.

No doubt the world or, more probably, the human mind, is pictured as dark when it is ignorant of God's prophetic message and therefore without hope (so Grundmann). Into this darkness the prophetic Scripture casts a ray of light by awakening hope.

ἕως οὗ ἡμέρα διαυγάσῃ, "until the day dawns." Sibinga (*RB* 73 [1966] 107–18) finds evidence that Origen knew a Greek version (not LXX) of Cant 2:17 which read: *ἕως οὗ διαυγάσῃ ἡ ἡμέρα* ("until the day dawns"). In that case it is possible that 2 Peter here alludes to that OT text (which in the Hebrew should refer to the evening, not dawn). The Jewish allegorical interpretation of the Song, which found the history and future hope of God's people portrayed in it, may well go back to the first century A.D.

In any case, the day here is a symbol for the eschatological age which will dawn at the Parousia. The absence of the article is not very significant in 2 Peter (see Mayor, xxx–xxxv) and cannot itself disprove a reference to "the day of the Lord" (cf. 3:10). But such a reference is unlikely, except perhaps as a secondary allusion, since it is clear that "day" is mentioned here as the time of *light,* in contrast to the preceding darkness. It is therefore probably a symbol for the eschatological age as a whole (cf. Rom 13:12; 2 Pet 3:18: *ἡμέραν αἰῶνος,* "the day of eternity"), which is daylight in contrast to the darkness of the present time (so Boehmer, *ZNW* 22 [1923] 228–29). Prophecy's function of illuminating the darkness of ignorance will be superseded when the full light of eschatological revelation floods the hearts of God's people.

καὶ φωσφόρος ἀνατείλῃ, "and the morning star rises." Some have argued that because this clause follows the mention of daybreak, *φωσφόρος* (lit. "lightbearer") cannot refer to the morning star, which rises before dawn, but must refer to the sun (for this sense of *φωσφόρος,* cf. F. J. Dölger, *Antike und Christentum* 5 [Münster: Aschendorff, 1936] 10–11). But as a substantive *φωσφόρος* normally refers to the morning star, Venus (*TDNT* 9, 312; Spicq, *Lexicographie,* 954), which accompanied the first glimmerings of dawn and could therefore be thought of as introducing daylight into the world.

As almost all commentators agree, there is here an allusion to Num 24:17: "a star shall rise out of Jacob" (LXX: ἀνατελεῖ ἄστρον ἐξ Ιακωβ), which was already interpreted messianically in Judaism (*T. Levi* 18:3; *T. Jud.* 24:1; 1QM 11:6–7; 4QTestim. 9–13; CD 7:18–20; *y. Taᶜan.* 68d). It is interesting to notice that in *T. Levi* 18:3–4; *T. Jud.* 24:1, the two images of the star and the sunrise (with reference to Mal 4:2) are closely associated. Probably this association suggested the interpretation of the star as the *morning* star, which is found, applied to Jesus, in Rev 22:16 (ὁ ἀστὴρ ὁ λαμπρὸς ὁ πρωϊνός, "the bright morning star"; cf. 2:28). (Other suggested allusions to Num 24:17 in the NT are Luke 1:78; Matt 4:16; but they are not at all certain, cf. Isa 61:1–2; Mal 4:2.) Thus the writer of 2 Peter no doubt follows Christian exegetical tradition, though it is in line with his predilection for Hellenistic religious vocabulary that he chooses a term (φωσφόρος) which was used of Greek divinities and kings (Spicq, *Lexicographie,* 953).

Thus the rising of the morning star is a symbol for the Parousia of Christ which inaugurates the eschatological age.

ἐν ταῖς καρδίαις ὑμῶν, "in your hearts." Many have found this phrase surprising in a reference to the Parousia. Therefore some have denied that the section *ἕως οὗ ἡμέρα διαυγάσῃ καὶ φωσφόρος ἀνατείλῃ ἐν ταῖς καρδίαις ὑμῶν* ("until the day dawns and the morning star rises in your hearts") refers to the Parousia at all, and have interpreted it instead as referring to an experience of enlightenment in this life (Plumptre, Mayor, James, Spicq, Grundmann; Delling in *TDNT* 2, 953; Käsemann, "Apologia," 189). Others accept the eschatological reference, but find in this phrase evidence that the primitive Christian hope is being individualized or "spiritualized" (Schelkle, Kelly, Schrage; cf. Green).

Neither of these views is justified. The phrase ἐν ταῖς καρδίαις ὑμῶν ("in your hearts") no longer appears surprising, once it is realized that only one specific aspect of the Parousia is being discussed, namely the Parousia as the full revelation of God to Christian believers (Fornberg, *Early Church,* 85). The only point being made is that prophecy, as a partial revelation pointing forward to the full eschatological revelation, will become superfluous when the full revelation arrives. Naturally it will be "in their hearts" that Christian believers will receive and perceive this revelation. In a similar argument (1 Cor 13:8–12) Paul uses equally subjective and individual terms with reference to the age to come. Neither in Paul's case nor in 2 Peter's does this language exclude or replace the expectation of the Parousia as an objective and cosmic event (cf. 2 Pet 3:7–13).

One further point about this reference to the Parousia should be noticed. Like most NT writers, the author of 2 Peter writes as if his readers will survive until the Parousia (cf. also 3:14). Thus his recognition of the delay of the Parousia (3:8–9) does not, as has often been thought, imply an indefinite postponement and a loss of the "imminent expectation."

Explanation

To the charge that the apostles preached cleverly invented myths, the author replies, secondly, that their eschatological teaching was solidly based on OT prophecy. He takes the opportunity briefly to indicate the value of such prophecy for his Christian readers. The lamp of prophecy lights up the darkness of this present world's hopeless ignorance with a bright beam of hope. But just as a lamp is used during the night but becomes superfluous when dawn comes, so prophecy's role is to give partial illumination to those whom it enables to hope for the full eschatological revelation of God. When Christians experience that full revelation at the Parousia of Jesus Christ, it will be like the daylight which dispels all the darkness of the night, and Jesus Christ himself will be like the morning star whose rising signals the dawn.

Reply to Objection 2: The Inspiration of OT Prophecy (1:20–21)

Bibliography

Boys-Smith, E. P. " 'Interpretation' or 'Revealment'." *ExpTim* 8 (1896–97) 331–32. **Curran, J. T.** "The Teaching of 2 Peter i. 20." *TS* 4 (1943) 347–68. **Durand, A.** "Le Sens de IIª Petri, I, 20." *RSR* 2 (1911) 187–89. **Louw, J.** "Wat wordt in II Petrus 1:20 gesteld." *NedThT* 19 (1964–65) 202–12. **Molland, E.** "La thèse 'La prophétie n'est jamais venue de la volonté de l'homme' (2 Pierre I, 21) et les Pseudo-Clémentines." *Opuscula Patristica.* BTN 2. Oslo: Universitetsforlaget, 1970. (=*ST* 9 [1955] 67–85.) **Neyrey, J. H.** "The Apologetic Use of the Transfiguration in 2 Peter 1:16–21." *CBQ* 42 (1980) 504–19. **Spence, R. M.** "Private Interpretation." *ExpTim* 8 (1896–97) 285–86. **Thomson, P.** " 'Interpretation' or 'Revealment.' " *ExpTim* 8 (1896–97) 331.

Translation

[20] *Above all, you must understand that no prophecy of Scripture derives from the prophet's own interpretation,* [21] *because prophecy never came by the impulse of man, but men impelled by the Holy Spirit spoke from God.*[a]

Notes

[a] The reading ἀπὸ θεοῦ in P[72] B P *al* is probably preferable to ἅγιοι θεοῦ in ℵ A and most MSS, and ἀπὸ θεοῦ ἅγιοι in C. ἅγιοι is a conventional epithet for the prophets (cf. 3:2) and could easily have resulted from misreading.

Form/Structure/Setting

To support his appeal to OT prophecy in v 19, the author must now respond to a second objection, against the inspiration of OT prophecy. This objection is closely related to that stated in v 16a, but is set out as a distinct thesis to be rejected in v 20 and perhaps also in v 21a. Neyrey finds the apologetic οὐ . . . ἀλλά ("not . . . but") form in v 21 (*CBQ* 42 [1980] 518), as in v 16, but it is necessary to be cautious about this. It is v 20 which clearly rejects an assertion by the opponents, and v 21 is the ground for this rejection. The οὐ . . . ἀλλά form of v 21 is paralleled in some of the similar statements about inspiration quoted below in the *Comment* section (Philo, *Mos.* 1.281; Hippolytus, *Antichr.* 2; Justin, *1 Apol.* 36) and it is not possible to be sure that all of these are polemical. However, it seems quite likely that v 21a may be the denial of a statement the false teachers made.

Both verses use the standard terminology of discussions of prophetic inspiration in Hellenistic Judaism and early Christianity (ἰδίας, "own"; ὑπὸ πνεύματος ἁγίου φερόμενοι, "impelled by the Holy Spirit"; ἀπὸ θεοῦ, "from God"). It is not impossible that 2 Peter is dependent on Philo (as Abbott, *Exp* 2/3 [1882]

54–56, argued), but the common theological language of Hellenistic Judaism is sufficient to explain the resemblances.

The introductory phrase *τοῦτο πρῶτον γινώσκοντες* ("above all understanding this") recurs in 3:3. (The fact that in 3:3 the participle is ungrammatical shows how formalized the phrase is, and that in 1:20 it need not be taken closely with *προσέχοντες* in v 19.) It is not necessarily a citation formula (as Robson, *Studies,* 33–35, argues), but a way of marking out the statement it introduces for special attention (cf. similar phrases in Luke 12:39; Gal 3:7; 2 Tim 3:1; Heb 13:3).

Comment

20. *πᾶσα προφητεία γραφῆς ἰδίας ἐπιλύσεως οὐ γίνεται,* "no prophecy of Scripture derives from the prophet's own interpretation." If we leave aside some very improbable suggestions, two main interpretations of this clause are possible: (1) "no prophecy of Scripture is a matter of one's own interpretation" (most commentators and translations); (2) "no prophecy of Scripture derives from the prophet's own interpretation" (Calvin, Plumptre, Lumby, Green; NIV). The clause refers either (1) to the interpretation of prophecy in the present, or (2) to the origin of prophecy. To decide between these alternatives requires careful discussion both of the terminology and of the context and polemical intention of the statement.

Terminology

ἰδίας. In view of v 21, it is now generally agreed that *ἰδίας* here means "(someone's) own" as opposed to "the Spirit's" (see especially Curran, *TS* 4 [1943] 362), not "private" as opposed to "general" (Mayor) or "authoritative." The question is whether it means "one's own" or "the prophet's own," i.e. whether the *ἐπιλύσις* ("interpretation") is that of the contemporary exegete or that of the original author of the prophecy (other possibilities are rightly ruled out by Curran, *TS* 4 [1943] 358–59). A reference to the prophet's own interpretation (supported by Oecumenius, *PG* 119:592; Theophylact, *PG* 125:1264; Bede, *PL* 93:73) is grammatically awkward, since the prophet has not been mentioned, and therefore most modern commentators and translations prefer "one's own."

However, it is relevant to notice that *ἴδιος* is used in a series of Hellenistic Jewish and early Christian statements which deny the human *origin* of prophecy, and seems to have been virtually a technical term in such assertions:

> Philo, *Quis Her.* 259: "For a prophet utters (*ἀποφθέγγεται*) nothing that is *his own* (*ἴδιον οὐδέν*), but everything he utters belongs to another (*ἀλλότρια*), since another is prompting him (*ὑπηχοῦντος ἑτέρου*)." (Abbott, *Exp* 2/3 [1882] 54–55, thinks 2 Peter is actually dependent on this passage.)
>
> Philo, *Mos.* 1.281: "I [Balaam] say nothing that is *my own* (*οὐδὲν ἴδιον*), but only what is prompted by the divine (*ὑπηχήσῃ τὸ θεῖον*)."
>
> Philo, *Mos.* 1.286: "Nothing which he [Balaam] said was *his own* (*οὐδὲν ἴδιον*), but being possessed and inspired he expressed the things of another (*διερμηνεύοι τὰ ἑτέρου*)." (For this sense of *διερμηνεύειν* in Philo, see A. C. Thistleton, "The "Interpretation" of Tongues: a new Suggestion in the Light of Greek Usage in Philo and Josephus," *JTS* 30 [1979] 15–36.)

Philo, *Spec. Leg.* 4.49: "A prophet declares nothing at all that is *his own* (οὐδὲν ἴδιον ἀποφαίνεται τὸ παράπαν), but is a spokesman (ἑρμηνεύς) of another who suggests (ὑποβάλλοντος ἑτέρου) everything he utters."

Philo, *Quaest. Gen.* 3.10: "The prophet seems to say something, but he does not give *his own* oracle but is the interpreter [i.e. ἑρμηνεύς, "spokesman"] of another, who puts things into his mind" (Loeb tr. from the Armenian).

Hippolytus, *Antichr.* 2: "For they [the prophets] did not speak from *their own* power (ἐξ ἰδίας δυνάμεως ἐφθεγγοντο) . . . nor did they proclaim what they wished, but first they were endowed with true wisdom through the Word, and then they were correctly taught about the future through visions."

Pseudo-Justin, *Cohortatio* 8: The prophets "taught us nothing from *their own* imagination (μηδὲν ἀπὸ τῆς ἰδίας αὐτῶν φαντασίας) . . . [but] they received from God the knowledge which they also taught us. . . . For neither by nature nor by human thought (ἐννοίᾳ) is it possible for men to know such great and divine things."

Methodius, *Convivium* 8.10: The Ebionites hold that "the prophets spoke from *their own* inspiration (ἐξ ἰδίας κινήσεως)."

Cf. also Jer 23:16 LXX: The false prophets "speak from *their own* heart (ἀπὸ καρδίας αὐτῶν) and not from the mouth of the Lord."

Ezek 13:3 LXX: The false prophets "prophesy from *their own heart* (ἀπὸ καρδίας αὐτῶν)."

Josephus, *Ant.* 4.121: Balaam says, "For once he [God] has entered, nothing within us is any longer *our own* (ἡμετερον)."

Philo, *Spec. Leg.* 1.65: The prophet "will say nothing that is *his own* (οἰκεῖον οὐδέν)."

Besides these texts which use ἴδιος in discussions of the *origin* of prophecy, there is also one text which uses it with reference to the *interpretation* of prophecy: *Clem. Hom.* 2:22: Simon "interprets allegorically the things of the law by his own preconception (ἰδίᾳ προλήψει)."

This evidence cannot determine the meaning of ἰδίας in 2 Pet 1:20, except to make it quite certain that the implied opposite of ἰδίας is ἀλλότριος ("another's"), i.e. God's or the Spirit's. If, as many think, the sense of vv 20–21 is that because prophetic Scripture was not of human origin (v 21) it is not a matter of human interpretation (v 20), then the author could have adopted ἴδιος from the standard language about the origin of prophecy and applied it to the interpretation of prophecy. On the other hand, if v 20 refers to the origin of prophecy and therefore to the *prophet's* interpretation, the grammatical awkwardness of taking ἰδίας to mean "the prophet's own" is very much alleviated by the semitechnical nature of ἴδιος in this context.

ἐπιλύσεως. In the interests of referring v 20 to the origin, rather than to the exegesis, of prophecy, several scholars have tried to find a meaning other than "interpretation" for ἐπίλυσις: "revealment" (Spence, *ExpTim* 8 [1896–97] 285–86), "setting forth" (Boys-Smith, *ExpTim* 8 [1896–97] 331–32), "prompting" (E. R. Andry, *JBL* 70 [1951] xvii), "inspiration" or "ecstasy" (Louw, *NedThT* 19 [1964–65] 202–12). But these translations have no support from the known usage of ἐπίλυσις and ἐπιλύειν. In the relevant metaphorical usage of these words (well summarized by Curran, *TS* 4 [1943] 351–52) they refer to the "explanation" or "interpretation" of puzzling or mysterious statements, omens, dreams, visions, myths, parables.

This evidence of usage is often thought to support interpretation (1). In fact, although it permits that interpretation, it gives it no strong support, since there seems to be no instance of ἐπίλυσις or ἐπιλύειν used of the interpretation of Scripture (though cf. Clem. Alex. *Paed.* 2.1.14). Interpretation (2) receives stronger support from the usage of the word. In Aquila's version ἐπίλυσις and ἐπιλύειν are used of Joseph's interpretations of the baker's and the butler's dreams (Gen 40:8; 41:8, 12), which are explicitly said to be God-given interpretations (Gen 40:8). Probably the Greek version of 4 Ezra 10:43 (Latin *absolutio*) used ἐπίλυσις of the interpretation of the seer's vision, given him by the angel. Hermas (who probably belongs to the same milieu as 2 Peter) constantly uses ἐπίλυσις and ἐπιλύειν to refer to the interpretation, given him by the "shepherd," of his "parables," which are in most cases symbolic visions (*Sim.* 5:3:1–2; 5:4:2–3; 5:5:1; 5:6:8; 5:7:1; 8:11:1; 9:10:5; 9:11:9; 9:13:9; 19:16:7). Hermas' prophecies are thus the God-given interpretations (ἐπιλύσεις) of his visions. This conforms to a widely accepted view of the nature of prophecy, according to which the prophet is given a sign (e.g. Amos 7:1; Jer 1:11, 13), a dream (e.g. Zech 1:8; Dan 7:2) or a vision (e.g. Dan 8:1), and then its interpretation. In true prophecy this interpretation is not the prophet's own explanation of his vision, but an inspired, God-given interpretation. Thus it is possible that 2 Pet 1:20 counters a view which held that the prophets may have received visions, but that their prophecies, found in the OT, are only their own interpretation of the visions, mere human guesswork. This was one way of denying the divine origin of scriptural prophecy.

This explanation of v 20 receives support from a striking pagan parallel, in which a prophetess's unfavorable interpretation of an omen is rejected with the complaint, "You gave the sign your own interpretation" (σὺ σεαυτῇ ἐπέλυσας τὸ σημεῖον: Pseudo-Callisthenes, *Historia Alex. Magni* 2.1.5, quoted in BAG *s.v.* ἐπίλυσις). This parallel is especially noteworthy in view of the probability that the main motivation of the false teaching which 2 Peter opposes was rationalistic skepticism derived from the pagan Hellenistic environment.

γίνεται could, of course, mean simply "is," but the meaning "arises, comes about, derives (from)" is common. The interpretation of the verb really depends on the sense of the genitive ἐπιλύσεως. Interpretation (1) sees this as a possessive genitive or genitive of pertinence (cf. Heb 12:11), giving the meaning "belongs to, comes under the scope of, is the object of one's own interpretation" (Mayor, Spicq; Curran, *TS* 4 [1943] 353–54). Interpretation (2) takes ἐπιλύσεως as a genitive of origin. This would normally, after γίνεσθαι, require the preposition ἐκ (Rom 1:3; Gal 4:4; 1 Tim 6:4), and this is perhaps the weakest point in the case for interpretation (2), but the meaning "arises from" with the simple genitive cannot be said to be impossible. On either view, the force of the genitive is somewhat unusual.

Context and Polemical Intention

If the terminology is not entirely decisive, the relationship of v 20 to v 21, and the possible polemical thrust of the two verses, must help us to decide between the alternative interpretations of v 20. Most commentators agree that these two verses must be in some way aimed against the writer's opponents. The following explanations of the polemical intention of v 20 are offered:

(i) The usual view, following interpretation (1), is that this verse represents the author's charge against his opponents: they interpret prophecy in an arbitrary fashion, giving it their own interpretation, rather than the interpretation accepted in orthodox circles, which is assumed to be the Spirit's interpretation. This view has strong support from 3:16, according to which the opponents twist the Scriptures, but encounters the following difficulties: (a) It is difficult to combine it (as, e.g., Molland, *Opuscula,* 61–77, does) with the view that v 21a represents the opponents' position, that OT prophecy is of human origin. If they thought it was of human origin, they are unlikely to have troubled to interpret it. However, it is not necessary to read v 21a as containing the opponents' view. (b) The section 1:16–19, with which vv 20–21 appear to be closely connected, is, as we have seen, defensive rather than offensive, concerned with rebutting charges rather than with making them. It is likely that vv 20–21 continue this defense, and that attack begins only in 2:1, where the false teachers are explicitly mentioned for the first time. (c) If v 20 is the author's rejection of the opponents' interpretation of Scripture, v 21 must give his basis for this rejection. But the basis is extremely weak. The train of thought is usually explained as: Scripture cannot be subject to merely human interpretation, because it is inspired by the Spirit and so requires an interpretation inspired by the Spirit. This means that the author has left his main point—the need for Spirit-inspired interpretation—implicit rather than explicit. But even if this is allowed, the cogency of the argument requires a further crucial step: that the interpretation followed by the author *is* inspired by the Spirit, while that proposed by the false teachers is not. Surely this point could not have been left unstated if this were the argument intended.

(ii) Neyrey, also following interpretation (1), takes v 20 to be a rejection of the opponents' charge against the author: that his interpretation of prophecy is idiosyncratic (*CBQ* 42 [1980] 516–19). However, the connection with v 21 tells against this view too. The inspiration of Scripture may be a reason why it *should* not be given an idiosyncratic interpretation, but it cannot be a proof that the author's interpretation *is* not an idiosyncratic one.

(iii) Although no commentator seems to have suggested it before, it is possible, again following interpretation (1), that v 20 rejects the opponents' charge that OT prophecy is thoroughly ambiguous, so that anyone can interpret it any way he likes and no one can say which way is correct. Then v 21 would imply that, because Scripture is inspired by God, it must have the meaning God intended. This view makes quite good sense of the connection with v 21, and is probably the only way in which interpretation (1) can be sustained in context. But it requires rather a lot to be read into ἰδίας ἐπιλύσεως οὐ γίνεται.

(iv) If interpretation (2) is correct, then v 20 rejects the opponents' charge that OT prophecy is only the prophet's own human interpretation of his visions. Against interpretation (2) it has sometimes been argued that v 21 is then not a reason for the statement in v 20, but only a repetition of it (Kelly). But this is not the case. The reason why scriptural prophecy is not simply a product of human interpretation is that its authors did not speak of their own volition but under the inspiration of God. The weight of emphasis falls on v 21b as the basis for v 20. On this view it is possible (though not necessary) to see v 21a also as rejecting a charge made by the opponents: that prophecy is of human origin (see below). The two charges would be consistent with each other (contrast (i) above).

Thus (i) and (ii) are unlikely, (iii) is possible, but (iv) seems more probable. This, combined with the evidence given in the discussion of *ἰδίας* and *ἐπιλύσεως* above, tips the balance in favor of interpretation (2).

If interpretation (2) is correct, this verse says nothing about the *interpretation* of Scripture, and therefore nothing about an authoritative teaching office in the Church to which all interpretation must be subject (Käsemann, "Apologia," 189–90) or about the charism of teaching (Curran, *TS* 4 [1943] 364–67). Nor is there any implication that there were no longer Christian prophets active in the church (Grundmann): the question of Christian prophets simply does not arise here.

21. *οὐ γὰρ θελήματι ἀνθρώπου ἠνέχθη προφητεία ποτέ, ἀλλὰ ὑπὸ πνεύματος ἁγίου φερόμενοι ἐλάλησαν ἀπὸ θεοῦ ἄνθρωποι*, "because prophecy never came by the impulse of man, but men impelled by the Holy Spirit spoke from God." The repetition of the verb *φέρειν* in the Greek (*ἠνέχθη, φερόμενοι*) is difficult to render in English; in this translation the use of "impulse" (for *θελήματι*, lit. "will") and "impelled" (for *φερόμενοι*) is an attempt to provide an equivalent repetition. It should be noted that *φέρειν* (lit. "to bear") was also used in vv 17–18 of the heavenly voice. The author's concern there to stress that the words at the Transfiguration came from God, is comparable with his concern here to stress that the words of OT prophecy also came from God.

The phrase *ὑπὸ πνεύματος ἁγίου φερόμενοι* (lit. "borne by the Holy Spirit") recalls the pagan Greek use of words such as *θεοφόρος*, "bearing a god" (or *θεόφορος*, "borne by a god"), *θεοφόρητος*, and *θεοφορεῖσθαι*, to describe prophetic inspiration. The same words were used by Philo (and later by Justin); they were part of the technical vocabulary of prophetic inspiration in Hellenistic Judaism. Even closer to 2 Peter's phrase is the word *πνευματοφορος* (accented *πνευματοφόρος*, it means "bearing *pneuma* [spirit]"; accented *πνευματόφορος*, it means "borne by *pneuma* [spirit]"), used to describe prophets in LXX Hos 9:7; Zeph 3:4, though oddly in those verses it seems to be used in a derogatory sense. Theophilus of Antioch used it to describe the inspiration of the OT prophets (*Ad Autol.* 2:9, 22; 3:12).

The extent to which the whole verse is expressed in the standard terminology used in discussion of prophetic inspiration in Hellenistic Judaism and early Christianity dependent on Hellenistic Judaism can be seen by comparison with the following passages:

> Philo, *Spec. Leg.* 1.65: "A prophet inspired by God (*θεοφόρητος*) will appear and give divine oracles (*θεσπιεῖ*) and prophesy."
>
> Justin, *1 Apol.* 33: "Isaiah inspired (*θεοφορούμενος*) by the prophetic Spirit . . ."
>
> Justin, *1 Apol.* 36: "But when you hear the utterances of the prophets . . . you must not suppose that they are spoken from the inspired men themselves (*ἀπ' αὐτῶν τῶν ἐμπεπνευσμένων*) but from the divine Word who moves them (*ἀπὸ τοῦ κινοῦντος αὐτοὺς θείου λόγου*)."
>
> Justin, *1 Apol.* 37: "the things taught through the prophets from God (*ἀπὸ τοῦ θεοῦ*) . . ."

Theophilus, *Ad Autol.* 2:9: "The men of God, who were inspired by a holy Spirit (πνευματοφόροι—or πνευματόφοροι—πνεύματος ἁγίου) and became prophets, were inspired (ἐμπνευσθέντες) and given wisdom by God himself."

In Hellenistic Jewish writers (Philo, *Mos.* 1.283; *Quis Her.* 266; *Spec. Leg.* 1.65; 4.49; *Som.* 1.2; Josephus, *Ant.* 4.119) such language is often associated with a basically pagan understanding of the psychology of prophetic inspiration, as irrational ecstasy in which the prophet is a purely passive instrument of the divine Spirit, unconscious of the words the Spirit utters through him. But the language of 2 Peter does not in itself require such a depreciation of the human role in prophecy. What it says is in conformity with the OT prophets' own testimony to the nature of prophecy: that the true prophet, unlike the false (Jer 14:13; 23:16; 18:21–22, 26; Ezek 13:3), does not speak on his own initiative (cf. Amos 3:8; Jer 20:9) or proclaim a message which is the product of his own mind, but speaks "the word of the Lord" when it comes to him. The only point which the author of 2 Peter is concerned to deny is that the prophets themselves were the originating source of their message. To counter this view he affirms that the Holy Spirit was the source of their prophecy, enabling them to speak as God's own spokesmen (cf. also Acts 3:21, attributed to Peter).

Since v 20 is certainly aimed polemically against the opponents' charge that prophecy was only the prophets' own interpretation of their visions, it is quite possible that the negative clause in v 21 is also a specific denial of the false teachers' assertion that prophecy is of human origin. Molland (*Opuscula,* 64–65) provides evidence that the Ebionites, who recognized no prophets after Moses, were accused of holding this: Methodius, *Convivium* 8.10 (quoted above, on v 20); Epiphanius, *Pan.* 30.18.5: "they say that the prophets are prophets of (their own) intelligence (συνέσεως) and not of truth." Molland (*Opuscula,* 66–77) also finds evidence in the Jewish-Christian material in the Pseudo-Clementines of this radical attitude to the OT prophets, as men who did not attain to the truth. This does not prove that the opponents in 2 Peter were Ebionite or proto-Ebionite Jewish Christians, which is unlikely. Rather it shows that both the author of 2 Peter and the Ebionites carried on their discussions in the standard terms of debates about true and false inspiration, of which the quotations from Philo, Justin and Hippolytus, given above, are also evidence, and which indeed go back to the OT prophets themselves (Jer 14:13; 23:16–22; Ezek 13:1–7). Neyrey (*Polemic,* 196–99) also compares the Epicurean polemic against oracles, and it may be that pagan skepticism had more to do with the false teachers' attitude to prophecy than Jewish-Christian heresy did. In any case, it should be carefully noted that 2 Peter combats the view that OT prophecy was of purely human origin, not the typical second-century gnostic view that it was inspired by the Demiurge.

Finally, confirmation of the view that the opponents in 2 Peter rejected the divine inspiration of OT prophecy in the interests of denying the expectation of the Parousia, may be found in the section of the *Asc. Isa.* which is in the form of an apocalyptic prophecy of the last times (3:21–4:18). This passage dates from the late first century (see 4:13) and is therefore contemporary with 2 Peter. Under the guise of prophecy, the author depicts the condition of the church in his own time, when there will be "many heresies" (*αἱρέσεις πολλαί*, 3:22), and when "they will set aside the prophecies of the prophets which were before me [Isaiah] and also pay no attention to these my visions, in order to speak (forth from the) torrent of their heart" (3:31, tr. in *NTApoc.* 2, 648; cf. also "*3 Cor.*" 1:10).

Explanation

The author's appeal to the authority of OT prophecy in support of the expectation of the Parousia (v 19) must now be defended against a second objection made by the opponents. They rejected the authority of OT prophecy by denying its divine origin. They said that while it may be true that the prophets received signs and dreams and visions, their prophecies were their own human interpretations of these, not God-given interpretations. The OT prophecies were therefore just products of the human mind, like the apostolic message (v 16a).

In reply, the author denies this view, and reasserts, in the standard terms used by Hellenistic Jewish writers, the divine origin of OT prophecy. No prophecy in the OT Scriptures originated from human initiative or imagination. The Holy Spirit of God inspired not only the prophets' dreams and visions, but also their interpretations of them, so that when they spoke the prophecies recorded in Scripture they were spokesmen for God himself.

Peter's Prediction of False Teachers (2:1–3a)

Bibliography

Barrett, C. K. "Ψευδαπόστολοι (2 Cor 11, 13)." *Mélanges Bibliques en hommage au R. P. Béda Rigaux,* ed. A. Descamps et A. de Halleux. Gembloux: J. Duculot, 1970. 380–83. **Repo, E.** *Der "Weg,"* 102–7.

Translation

[1] *But there were also false prophets among the people, just as there will be false teachers among you, who will insinuate heresies that lead to destruction, who will even deny the Master who bought them, and bring swift destruction on themselves.* [2] *Many will follow their dissolute practices, and because of them the way of truth will be maligned.* [3] *In their greed they will exploit you with fabricated arguments.*

Form/Structure/Setting

The author of 2 Peter dislikes abrupt transitions, and his mention of the false prophets of OT times (2:1a) is designed to effect a smooth transition from the discussion of OT prophecy (1:20–21) to the prediction of the false teachers (2:1b–3a). But the mention of the false prophets also has another structural function, because (as Marín, *EE* 50 [1975] 226, points out) the section 1:16–2:3 has a chiastic structure:

A. apostles (1:16–18)
B. OT prophets (1:19–21)
B. OT false prophets (2:1a)
A. false teachers (2:1b–3)

This structure may be reinforced by an *inclusio* formed by σεσοφισμένοις μύθοις ἐξακολουθήσαντες ("following cleverly concocted myths," 1:16) and ἐξακολουθήσουσιν ("will follow," 2:2), πλαστοῖς λόγοις ("with fabricated arguments," 2:3). The chiastic structure makes possible a correlation and contrast between the apostles and the false teachers.

The transition to the second part of this chiastic structure also marks a transition from defense (answering the opponents' charges) to attack (making charges against the opponents, which predominates in chap. 2, although vv 3b–10a are in part defensive), which is possible now that the prediction of the false teachers at last brings them explicitly into view. For the purpose of this attack the author now begins to make use of the Letter of Jude, on which he is dependent for much of the passage 2:1–3:3. This dependence is never slavish. The author takes what he wants from Jude, whether ideas or words, and uses it in a composition which is very much his own. In this passage he borrows from Jude 4: ἀσέλγειαν ("immorality") . . . δεσποτὴν ("Master") . . . ἀρνούμενοι ("denying"). He may also be dependent on other traditional apocalyptic predictions (see *Comment* section), and in v 2b echoes Isa 52:5 LXX.

The relation of 2:1 to Justin, *Dial.* 82.1 also calls for comment in this connection.

Justin, *Dial.* 82.1: ὅνπερ δὲ τρόπον καὶ ψευδοπροφῆται ἐπὶ τῶν παρ᾽ ὑμῖν γενομένων ἁγίων προφητῶν ἦσαν, καὶ παρ᾽ ἡμῖν νῦν πολλοί εἰσι καὶ ψευδοδιδάσκαλοι· οὓς φυλάσσεσαι προεῖπεν ὁ ἡμέτερος κύριος. "Just as there were false prophets in the time of your [the Jews'] holy prophets, so there are now many false teachers among us, of whom our Lord forewarned us to beware."

Dillenseger (*MFOB* 2 [1907] 177–79) regards this passage as clearly dependent on 2 Pet 2:1. Chase (*DB*(*H*) 3, p. 801) thinks the resemblance is merely coincidental, but this is scarcely likely. The comparison of false prophets (ψευδοπροφῆται) in OT Israel and false teachers (ψευδοδιδάσκαλοι) in the church does not seem to appear in early Christian literature outside these two passages. Moreover, the word ψευδοδιδάσκαλοι is found only in these two passages in literature up to the time of Justin (ψευδοδιδασκαλία occurs once, in Pol. *Phil.* 7:2). Doubtless, as Chase points out, it was an obvious formation by analogy with many other ψευδο- ("false") compounds. But early Christian predictions of the last days normally refer to ψευδοπροφῆται ("false prophets": Matt 24:11, 14; Mark 13:22; 1 John 4:1; *Did.* 16:3; *Apoc. Pet.* A 1; Hegesippus, *ap.* Eusebius, *Hist. Eccl.* 4.22.6), and this is what Justin himself normally does, following the prophecies in Matt 7:15; 24:11, 24 (*Dial.* 35.3; 51:2; 82.2). No doubt these are the prophecies he has in mind when he refers to Christ's warnings in this passage. Moreover, the context of this passage is Justin's assertion (82.1) that the prophetic gifts of the OT prophets are now present in the Christian church. For all these reasons, we should have expected him to compare ψευδοπροφῆται of OT Israel with ψευδοπροφῆται, not ψευδοδιδάσκαλοι, in the Church. Of course, it is possible that desire for merely stylistic variation produced ψευδοδιδάσκαλοι, but if so the coincidence with 2 Pet 2:1 is more remarkable than Chase allows.

Chaine (3) points out that the resemblance could result from common use of traditional catechetical material (which is the suggestion that requires its discussion here), and in view of the probability that 2 Peter is dependent on traditional material in this passage, this is certainly a possible explanation. (Certainly this more probably explains the coincidence of αἱρέσεις, "heresies," in 2 Pet 2:1 and Justin, *Dial.* 51.2 than Dillenseger's suggestion of dependence on 2 Peter by Justin in that passage.) Against this, however, it must be said that the comparison of the false prophets of old and the Christian false teachers in 2 Pet 2:1 seems to bear every mark of having been created for its context. It is designed to link the preceding and succeeding material and create the chiastic structure (see above), while the use of ψευδοδιδάσκαλοι ("false teachers") for the Christian heretics is explained by the fact that ψευδοπροφῆται ("false prophets") would not have been appropriate for these teachers who did not claim prophetic inspiration (see *Comment* section). It is therefore more probable (though not certain) that the resemblance results from Justin's dependence on 2 Peter, a conclusion which would probably have been more widely accepted if the general opinion of the date of 2 Peter had not impeded it.

By writing in Peter's name a prediction of the false teachers who will trouble the churches after Peter's death, the writer is still using the conventions of the testament genre. A testament could include predictions of the last times (Tob 14:4–7; *T. Mos.* 5–10; *Jub.* 45:14; *T. Levi* 1:1; 4:1; 10:1–5; 14:1–18:14; *T. Jud.* 18:1; 21:6–25:5; *T. Iss.* 6:1–2; *T. Zeb.* 9:5–10:3; *T. Dan.* 5:4–13; *T. Napht.* 4:1–5; 8:1–3; *T. Gad* 8:2; *T. Asher* 7:2–7; *T. Benj.* 9:1–5), and in NT examples announcements of false teachers to appear in the churches are the main element in such predictions (Acts 20:29–30; 2 Tim 3:1–5; 4:3–4; cf. *T. Jud.* 21:9).

Comment

1. *ἐγένοντο δὲ καὶ ψευδοπροφῆται ἐν τῷ λαῷ*, "But there were also false prophets among the people." In addition to the true prophets, the authors of the OT prophecies, mentioned in 1:21, Israel also had false prophets. This mention of the false prophets is partly a stylistic device (see *Form/Structure/Setting* section), but it also marks the beginning of the author's turning from defense to attack, in which the opponents' charges against the apostles are turned against themselves. The opponents charged the apostles with basing their message of the Parousia on prophecies which were only human inventions (1:20–21a), i.e. on the words of false prophets. In reply, the author now asserts that it is in fact not the apostles but the false teachers who stand in succession to the false prophets of Israel.

The term *ψευδοπροφῆται* ("false prophets") is used of the OT false prophets in LXX, Josephus and Luke 6:26. It also occurs quite often in prophecies of the false prophets of the last times (*T. Jud.* 21:9; Matt 24:11, 24; Mark 13:22; 1 John 4:1; Rev 16:13; 19:20; 20:10; *Did.* 16:3; *Apoc. Pet.* A 1; Hegesippus, *ap.* Eusebius, *Hist. Eccl.* 4.22.6; Justin, *Dial.* 35.3; 51.2: 82.2; cf. Matt 7:15), which makes it even more notable that 2 Peter *prophesies* not *ψευδοπροφῆται* ("false prophets") but *ψευδοδιδάσκαλοι* ("false teachers"; see below).

Since, however, the author does *compare* the false teachers with the false prophets of OT times, it is relevant to note (with Neyrey, *Polemic,* 39–40) three prominent characteristics of the OT false prophets which can also be applied to the opponents in 2 Peter: (1) unlike the true prophets (1:20–21) they did not speak with divine authority (Deut 18:20; Jer 14:14; 23:21, 32; Ezek 13:2–7); (2) frequently their message was one of peace and security in contrast to the prophecies of future judgment uttered by the true prophets (Jer 4:10; 6:14; 14:13, 15; 23:17; 27:9, 16–18; Ezek 13:10; Mic 3:5, 11); (3) they were condemned to punishment by God (Jer 14:15; 23:15; 28:16–17; cf. Deut 18:20).

ὡς καὶ ἐν ὑμῖν ἔσονται ψευδοδιδάσκαλοι, "just as there will be false teachers among you." Early Christian prophecies of the last days more commonly refer to false *prophets* (see above), though the Pastorals refer to teachers of heresy (2 Tim 4:3: *διδασκάλους*; cf. 1 Tim 4:1) and Pol. *Phil.* 7:2 refers to "false teachings" (*ψευδοδιδασκαλίας*) in a context which suggests the apostasy of the last days. Of course, it is possible that 2 Peter here uses *ψευδοδιδάσκαλοι* merely as a stylistic variation after *ψευδοπροφῆται* ("false prophets"), but, unlike the opponents in Jude, the false teachers in 2 Peter do not appear to have claimed prophetic inspiration, and so it is probable that the author here deliberately avoids calling them *ψευδοπροφῆται* ("false prophets").

Barrett ("Ψευδαπόστολοι," 382–83) points out that the *ψευδο-* ("false") prefix can mean either that they falsely claimed for themselves the office of teacher, to which they had no right, or that the content of their message was false. Although, as Barrett says ("Ψευδαπόστολοι," 380), it may not be necessary to choose between the two, the author of 2 Peter is really more interested in the latter. He has not, as we have seen, justified the message of the apostles by alleging their authority to teach, but by appealing to the reliable basis on which the truth of their message rests. The chiastic structure of 1:16–2:3 (see *Form/Structure/Setting* section) makes the false teachers the counterpart of the apostles, teaching a false message of human invention rather than the apostolic message which is based on the divine words.

The future tense is used, of course, because although the author is referring to a reality of his own time, he is writing in the person of Peter, and so, as was appropriate in a testament (see *Form/Structure/Setting* section), he represents Peter as prophesying the advent of the false teachers after his death. Nor is this sheer fiction; the preaching of the apostles certainly did include apocalyptic predictions of the apostasy of the last days (cf. *Comment* on Jude 17–18). The author of 2 Peter may know a genuine tradition of Peter's teaching, which in this chapter he supplements with (equally apostolic) material from Jude, to show its fulfillment in his own day.

οἵτινες παρεισάξουσιν αἱρέσεις ἀπωλείας, "who will insinuate heresies that lead to destruction." The verb *παρεισάγειν* (only here in NT; but cf. *παρείσακτος*, "brought in," Gal 2:4) means simply "to bring in" and need not have a bad sense, but it is often used with the connotation of something underhanded or surreptitious (used of heretics also by Hegesippus, *ap.* Eusebius, *Hist. Eccl.* 4.22.5; Hippolytus, *Ref.* 5.17; 7.29): "insinuate" (Moffatt, JB) has the right nuance. If the term was suggested to the author by *παρεισεδύησαν* ("infiltrated") in Jude 4, he has substituted *παρεισάξουσιν* because he did not want to suggest that his false teachers, like Jude's, had entered the churches from outside, but that they brought in teachings from outside. Probably, therefore, we may conclude that the false teachers in 2 Peter are not, like those in Jude, itinerants who have arrived in the churches to which 2 Peter is addressed from outside, but members of those churches. They have brought their teachings in from outside, in the sense that these teachings are contrary to the apostolic message and so do not belong in the church. Perhaps the author implies—as appears to have been the case—that the false teachers were influenced by pagan skepticism about prophecy and eschatology.

αἵρεσις ("heresy") was the term used for a school of thought, whether the Greek philosophical schools or, in Hellenistic Jewish usage, the Jewish religious schools (Essenes, Sadducees, Pharisees: Josephus, *BJ* 2.118; *Ant.* 13.171, 293; *Vit.* 12; cf. Acts 5:17; 15:5; 26:5; and in Acts 24:5, 14; 28:22, of Christianity in this sense). It could also designate the particular teaching of such a school. In these uses it is a neutral, not a pejorative term. In Gal 5:20; 1 Cor 11:18 it is acquiring the pejorative sense of "faction," but the charge is divisiveness rather than heretical teaching. Possibly it could have that sense here, but in the context of reference to false *teachers* it is more natural to understand it of their teachings, though the overtone of "factions" may remain. *αἵρεσις* is already used in the sense of heretical teaching in Ignatius (*Eph.* 6.2; *Trall.* 6:1), but whereas Ignatius can use the word alone in a bad sense, in 2 Pet 2:1 the pejorative meaning is not conveyed by the word alone, but by the addition of *ἀπωλείας* ("that lead to destruction"). The evolution of the word's meaning may not yet have reached the unequivocally pejorative phase which emerges with Ignatius.

The real difficulty in this v is the use of the plural *αἱρέσεις*. In normal usage the singular αἵρεσις refers to one school of thought or its distinctive teaching as a single body of doctrine, and this is also the way in which later Christian writers use it of the Christian heresies (*Mart. Pol.* epil.Mosq. 1; Theophilus, *Ad Autol.* 2:14; Hegesippus, *ap.* Eusebius, *Hist. Eccl.* 4.22.5). It is not normally used to refer to a single doctrine, so that one false teacher could teach a whole collection of αἱρέσεις. Perhaps this difficulty was felt by the author of *Apoc. Pet.* A 1, which is probably dependent on 2 Pet 2:1, but paraphrases it: "they will teach ways and various doctrines of destruction" (ὁδοὺς καὶ δόγματα ποικίλα τῆς ἀπωλείας διδάξουσιν). It is hard to believe that the author of 2 Peter means that there are several different heretical schools of thought in the churches to which he is writing; certainly his response is not adapted to such variety. The explanation of his unusual usage may be that in this section of "prophecy" he is deliberately echoing the traditional apocalyptic warnings, and in this instance may be alluding to the agraphon, "There will be divisions and heresies" (ἔσονται σχίσματα καὶ αἱρέσεις: Justin, *Dial.* 35.3; J. Jeremias, *Unknown Sayings of Jesus,* tr. R. H. Fuller [London: S. P. C. K., 1957] 59–61; perhaps referred to also in 1 Cor 11:18; and cf. Justin, *Dial.* 51.2: γενήσεσθαι αἱρέσεις ψευδοπροφῆτας ἐπὶ τῷ ὀνόματι αὐτοῦ, "heresies and false prophets would arise in his name"; *Asc. Isa.* 3:22: ἔσονται αἱρέσεις πολλαί, "there will be many heresies").

Their teachings are "heresies of destruction" (αἱρέσεις ἀπωλείας) probably in the sense that they lead to destruction (Plumptre, Spicq, Chaine, Schelkle, Grundmann), i.e. they bring those who follow them under eschatological judgment. As the rest of chap 2 makes clear, they do this because they encourage immorality. Neyrey (*Polemic,* 40–41) may be right that ἀπωλείας is ironical; the false teachers actually taught freedom from destruction (cf. 2:19), they believed there would be no eschatological judgment, but in reality their teaching incurs precisely that judgment which they denied. ἀπωλεία ("destruction") is a favorite term in 2 Peter (twice in this v; also 2:3; 3:7, 16; cf. ἀπόλλυναι in 3:6, 9) and refers consistently to eschatological judgment (as also in Matt 7:13; John 17:12; Rom 9:22; Phil 1:28; 2 Thes 2:3; Heb 10:39; Rev 17:8, 11; *Apoc. Pet.* A 1–2).

καὶ τὸν ἀγοράσαντα αὐτοὺς δεσπότην ἀρνούμενοι, "who will even deny the Master who bought them." The very rare use of δεσπότης ("Master") for Christ is borrowed from Jude (see *Comment* on Jude 4), but 2 Peter adds a phrase which is highly appropriate to the title. Jesus is the Master of his Christian slaves because he has bought them (at the cost of his death, it is implied—the only allusion to the cross in 2 Peter). This image of redemption as the transferral of slaves to new ownership was fairly common in early Christianity (1 Cor 6:20; 7:23; Rev 5:9; 14:3–4, which use ἀγοράζειν, "to buy"; also Acts 20:28; 1 Pet 1:18; cf. Rom 6:17–18; and on the whole subject, see I. H. Marshall, "The Development of the Concept of Redemption in the New Testament," in R. Banks (ed.), *Reconciliation and Hope,* L. L. Morris Festschrift [Exeter: Paternoster; Grand Rapids: Eerdmans, 1974] 153–69); it is one form of the rather variously used idea of ransom or redemption. Thus 2 Peter does not deny that the false teachers are Christians, but sees them as apostate Christians who have disowned their Master.

What form did their denial take? In Jude 4 the thought is of practical denial by deeds, but the meaning in Jude cannot determine the sense here.

Heretical views of the person of Christ (Moffatt) or obedience to other political masters intent on revolution (Reicke) are unlikely explanations. The content of the rest of 2 Peter gives us a choice between (1) denial of Christ by denying his Parousia (Chaine), and (2) denial of Christ by teaching and practicing immorality (Bigg, Grundmann). The latter is more probable because it suits the image of Christ as *δεσπότης* ("Master"): immoral living is flouting his authority as Master of his slaves who should obey him. (It is also the sense which denial of Christ has in the closely related work *2 Clem.:* chaps. 3–4.) Moreover, this explanation gives a better link with the next phrase; it is immorality, rather than simply doctrinal error, which brings down eschatological judgment on its practicers.

ἐπάγοντες ἑαυτοῖς ταχινὴν ἀπώλειαν, "and bring swift destruction upon themselves." *ταχινήν* (see *Comment* on 1:14) does not mean "sudden," but "coming soon, imminent." Probably the author has in mind the false teachers' jibe that the Lord is slow in coming to exercise judgment (3:9), and therefore the sense will be that judgment at the Parousia is imminent. Contrary to the usual view of 2 Peter, there is no diminution of the sense of eschatological imminence, although an explanation is offered for the fact of delay (3:8–9).

Ironically, the false teachers incur judgment by teaching that there will be no future judgment and thereby leading themselves and others into immorality.

2. *καὶ πολλοὶ ἐξακολουθήσουσιν αὐτῶν ταῖς ἀσελγείαις*, "many will follow their dissolute practices." The author is fond of the verb *ἐξακολουθεῖν*, "to follow" (1:16; 2:2, 15; nowhere else in NT); here it means that the false teachers' immoral behavior is the authority which their adherents obey, perhaps in contrast to Christ the Master (*δεσπότης*, v 1) or in contrast to following "the way of truth." *ἀσελγεία* tends to mean sensual indulgence, especially sexual immorality, and the plural (cf. Herm. *Vis.* 2:2:2) designates acts of sensual excess. If the author of 2 Peter has deliberately not reproduced Jude's assertion that they "pervert the grace of God into immorality" (Jude 4), it may be because he associated the immorality of his opponents not so much with an antinomian interpretation of grace (as in Jude), but rather with their notion of freedom from future judgment. If the hypothesis is correct that the false teachers' denial of future eschatology was influenced by pagan skepticism, it may be that their immorality also should be seen as primarily a relapse into pagan ways. When stricter Christians rebuked their behavior with warnings of divine judgment, they defended themselves by mocking the notion of future judgment.

δι' οὓς ἡ ὁδὸς τῆς ἀληθείας βλασφημηθήσεται, "and because of them the way of truth will be maligned." A characteristic of 2 Peter's terminology is the use of phrases with *ὁδός* ("way"); equivalent to *ἡ ὁδὸς τῆς ἀληθείας* ("the way of truth") are *εὐθεῖαν ὁδόν* ("the straight way," 2:15) and *τὴν ὁδὸν τῆς δικαιοσύνης* "the way of righteousness," 2:21). The use of "way" as a metaphor for "way of life," ethical behavior, is very common in the OT, interestamental literature, and Philo (see *TDNT* 5, 50–64), and becomes particularly specialized in the "two ways" concept, and in the use of "the way" at Qumran to designate the sect's way of life as obedience to the Law (CD 1:13; 2:6; 1QS 8:13–14; 9:17–18; 10:20–21; this usage apparently derived from Isa 40:3).

This absolute use of "the way" for a whole moral and religious way of life reappears in the designation of Christianity as "the way" (Acts 9:2; 19:9, 23; 24:14, 22; Letter of the churches of Vienne and Lyons, *ap.* Eusebius, *Hist. Eccl.* 5.1.48; and perhaps *Act. Verc.* 7), which can be further specified as "the way of the Lord" (Acts 18:25), "the way of God" (Acts 18:26), and "this way" (Acts 19:9; on the whole subject of this early Christian usage, see Repo, *Weg*). It is clear from the context that 2 Peter uses the phrases "the way of truth," "the way of righteousness," and "the straight way" in a similar manner, to designate the Christian way of life, Christianity considered not as a body of doctrine but as a way of life, a religious message which takes effect in an ethical life style (cf. Grundmann, 90–91). The *Apoc. Pet.*, which may here be continuing a traditional usage rather than simply depending on 2 Peter, uses "the way of righteousness" (E 7 = A 22; A 28) and "the way of God" (A 34, B), as designations of the Christian way of life considered as the righteous way of life, and, as in 2 Pet 2:22, uses "the commandment of God" as virtually synonymous (E 8, A 30, E 10). (Cf. also *Acts John* 22: "thy (Christ's) way"; *Act. Verc.* 6: "the right way which is in Jesus Christ.")

The specific phrase used here, "the way of truth," is used in LXX Ps 118:30; Wis 5:6; Jas 5:19 *v. l.; 1 Clem.* 35:5, and in all these cases has the general meaning of the ethical way of life which God commands (cf. also the plural in CD 3:15; 1 QS 4:2; Tob 1:3; *1 Enoch* 104:13 Greek). As a term specifically for the Christian way of life, it occurs in early Christian literature elsewhere only in the *Acts Pet.* (*Act. Verc.* 12, "the ways of the truth of Christ": *viae veritatis Christi*), and perhaps in Aristides, *Apol.* 16 (but its occurrence in the Greek text of Aristides is suspect, since the Syriac lacks this passage). (Cf. also Herm. *Vis.* 3:7:1: τὴν ὁδὸν αὐτῶν τὴν ἀληθινήν, "their true way," but there the metaphor belongs to a larger metaphorical context; *Gos. Truth* 18:19–21: "He gave them a way and the way is the truth which he showed them.") In view of its Semitic background, the expression could be simply equivalent to "the true way," the way which God commands, but in 2 Peter's usage may well mean "the way which is based on and corresponds to the truth of the gospel" (cf. 1:12, where "the truth"=the gospel). By contrast with the false message of the opponents which results in immoral living, the true Christian way is a true message which results in an ethical way of life.

δι' οὓς . . . βλασφημηθήσεται ("because of whom . . . will be maligned") alludes to Isa 52:5 (LXX: δι' ὑμᾶς διὰ παντὸς τὸ ὄνομά μου βλασφημεῖται ἐν τοῖς ἔθνεσιν, "because of you my name is continually maligned among the Gentiles"). Quotations of and allusions to this text were used in two different ways in early Christianity: (1) against the Jews (Rom 2:24; Justin, *Dial.* 17.2); (2) in exhortations to Christians not to cause offense to pagans by immoral living (Rom 14:16 ?; 1 Tim 6:1; Titus 2:5; *1 Clem.* 47:7; *2 Clem.* 13:2; Ign. *Trall.* 8:2; Pol. *Phil.* 10:3). The allusion here depends on the second usage; the adherents of the false teachers, by their scandalously immoral behavior, are giving Christianity a bad name among their non-Christian neighbors (the closest parallel to this use of Isa 52:5 is Herm. *Sim.* 6:2:3). In such allusions to Isa 52:5 the words τὸ ὄνομα μου ("my name") are frequently replaced by some other term (cf. 1 Tim 6:1; Titus 2:5; Ign. *Trall.* 8:2; Pol. *Phil.* 10:2), as here by "the way of truth."

3. καὶ ἐν πλεονεξίᾳ πλαστοῖς λόγοις ὑμᾶς ἐμπορεύσονται, "in their greed they will exploit you with fabricated arguments." The meaning is that the false teachers make a good financial profit out of their followers, who are taken in by their teaching and contribute to their support. See *Comment* on Jude 11. πλάττειν λόγους, "to forge words," is a classical expression (examples in Bigg, Mayor; *T. Reub.* 3:5) for deceitful speech, but myths were so regularly described as πλαστοί (see *Comment* on 1:16) that we are inevitably reminded of the σεσοφισμένοις μύθοις ("cleverly concocted myths") of 1:16. This correlation is confirmed by the chiastic structure of 1:16–2:3a (see *Form/Structure/Setting* section), in which the apostles in 1:16 find their counterpart in the false teachers of 2:1b–3a. It becomes clear that the author is turning the opponents' charge against the apostles (1:16) back on themselves. It is not the apostles' message, but the false teachers', that is based on sheer invention.

Explanation

The apostles had predicted false prophets and apostasy in the last days. Drawing on traditions of such apostolic prophecies, the author puts into Peter's mouth a "prediction" about his own contemporaries, the false teachers in the churches to which he writes, to identify these people as among those whom the apostles had predicted.

The comparison with the false prophets in Israel in OT times serves to link this passage with the preceding vv (1:20–21), and is also the first of two occasions in this section when the author turns his opponents' charges against the apostles back on themselves. In denying the inspiration of OT prophecy (1:20–21a) the opponents had accused the apostles of basing their eschatological teaching on false prophecy. In the author's view, however, it is his opponents, not the apostles, who are the true successors to the false prophets of OT times.

The fact that he does not call his opponents false *prophets* may be one indication that they did not claim prophetic inspiration. But they certainly set themselves up as teachers. Ironically, because their teaching that there will be no eschatological judgment encourages immorality, it will lead them and their followers to suffer eschatological judgment. They disown their Master, who by his death bought them as his slaves; they flout his moral authority, and they are bringing on themselves imminent destruction at the Parousia, for all that they scoff at its late arrival (3:9).

The immorality their teaching permitted was, no doubt, largely a relapse into the ways of pagan society, always a strong temptation in the early Christian churches. But in a society where every opportunity of maligning Christians and Christianity was taken, Christians whose moral standards were no higher than their pagan neighbors' were a scandal. Instead of witnessing to their neighbors, they were bringing discredit on the Christian way of life.

Finally, they succumbed to another common temptation: that of making financial profit out of their disciples. But the author ends this section by again throwing back at his opponents a charge they made against the apostles: not the apostles' message, but theirs, is a mere human invention (cf. 1:16a).

Reply to Objection 3: The Certainty of Judgment (2:3b–10a)

Bibliography

Berger, K. "Hartherzigkeit und Gottes Gesetz, die Vorgeschichte des anti-jüdischen Vorwurfs in Mc 10[5]." *ZNW* 61 (1970) 1–47. **Dalton, W. J.** "The Interpretation of 1 Peter 3, 19 and 4, 6: Light from 2 Peter." *Bib* 60 (1979) 547–55. **Glasson, T. F.** *Greek Influence in Jewish Eschatology.* London: S. P. C. K., 1961. 62–64. **Lührmann, D.** "Noah und Lot (Lk 17[26-29])—ein Nachtrag." *ZNW* 63 (1972) 130–32. **Pearson, B. A.** "A Reminiscence of Classical Myth at *II Peter* 2.4." *GRBS* 10 (1969) 71–80. **Rappaport, S.** "Der gerechte Lot." *ZNW* 29 (1930) 299–304. **Schlosser, J.** "Les jours de Noé et de Lot: A propos de Luc, XVII, 26–30." *RB* 80 (1973) 13–36.

Translation

[3b] *The condemnation pronounced on them long ago is not idle; their destruction is not asleep.*

[4] *For if God did not spare the angels when they sinned, but cast them into hell and committed them to fetters* [a] *of nether darkness, there to be kept* [b] *until the judgment;*
[5] *if he did not spare the ancient world, but preserved Noah the eighth person, a preacher of righteousness, when he brought the deluge on the world of ungodly people;*
[6] *if he reduced the cities of Sodom and Gomorrah to ashes and condemned them to extinction, making them an example of what is going to happen to the ungodly,* [c]
[7] *and rescued the righteous man Lot, who was distressed by the dissolute behavior of the lawless* [8] *(for when that righteous man was living among them his righteous soul was day after day tormented by the sight and sound of their unlawful doings* [d]*),*
[9] *then the Lord is well able* [e] *to rescue the godly from trial,* [f] *but to keep the wicked to be punished* [g] *at the day of judgment,* [10] *especially those who in polluting lust* [h] *indulge the flesh and flout the authority of the Lord.*

Notes

[a] It is almost impossible to decide between the two readings σειραῖς, "cords, ropes, chains" (K L P P[72] vg syr boh *al*) and σειροῖς (=σιροῖς), "pits" (ℵ A B C 81[vid] cop[sa] *al*). σειραῖς is a more unusual word than Jude's δεσμοῖς (Jude 6) and the author of 2 Peter may have used it in accordance with his habit of substituting more elegant and unusual vocabulary for Jude's. But a scribe could have corrected σειροῖς to σειραῖς to conform to Jude 6. Pearson (*GRBS* 10 [1969] 78–80, followed by Fornberg, *Early Church,* 52–53) attempts to show that pagan Greek usage makes σιρός (which often means an underground pit for grain storage) a suitable term for the underworld, but his argument is not convincing. It is more likely that the reading σειροῖς, whether original or not, derives from the Jewish tradition of the fall of the Watchers: cf. *1 Enoch* 10:12 (Greek νάπας); 10:4; 18:11; 21:7; 22:2; 88:1, 3; *Jub.* 5:10. Since 2 Peter shows no other sign of direct knowledge of *1 Enoch,* it is perhaps more likely that a later scribe familiar with *1 Enoch* (as many second- and third-century Christians were) and perhaps finding the phrase σειραῖς ζόφου difficult, corrected σειραῖς to σειροῖς. The phrase σειραῖς ζόφου is the kind of rhetorical expression we might expect in 2 Peter. But the possibility that σειροῖς was the original reading certainly cannot be ruled out.

[b] τηρουμένους (B C K L P) should probably be preferred to κολαζουμένους τηρεῖν (ℵ A), which has probably been influenced by v 9.

[c] The reading ἀσεβέσιν, "to the ungodly" ($\mathfrak{P}^{72}$ B P syr[ph,h]) is preferable to ἀσεβεῖν, "to act ungodly" (ℵ A C K). The latter could easily have been suggested by the common construction of μελλόντων, followed by the infinitive, whereas the former makes better sense in context (Mayor, Chaine, Kelly, NIV).

[d] It is impossible to translate this sentence quite literally. It makes no good sense to take βλέμματι καὶ ἀκοῇ, "by sight and sound," with δίκαιος, "righteous."

[e] οἶδεν here means "knows how to" and so "is able to."

[f] The plural πειρασμῶν, "trials," is very poorly attested.

[g] For the translation of κολαζομένους, "to be punished," see *Comment* section.

[h] μιασμοῦ is better taken as a genitive of quality (common in 2 Peter) than as an objective genitive ("desire for pollution").

Form/Structure/Setting

Verse 3b is closely connected by οἷς ("on whom") with what precedes, but this should not deter us from recognizing a transition in the argument. The transition is signalled by the change from the future tense (vv 1–3a) to the present tense (v 3b). This could perhaps be simply in the interests of vivid personification in v 3b, but in view of the fact that the present tense continues in vv 10–22, it much more probably indicates that the author has turned from writing prophecy in Peter's name to considering the false teachers as his own opponents in the present. An exactly similar transition occurs in chap 3, where the future tense of the prophecy in v 3 changes to the present tense in v 5. It is noteworthy that in both cases the transition occurs when the author begins to answer an objection raised by his opponents; direct argument with the opponents cannot easily be conducted in the fictional form of prediction *ex eventu*. But this does not mean, as most commentators think, that the author simply *lapses* into the present tense, forgetting for the moment his pretense of writing prophecy. The author of 2 Peter is not so careless a writer as that. He can move between future and present tenses because his pseudepigraphal device is not an attempt at deceit which must be maintained, but a literary convention which his readers understand. Such a convention can be transgressed deliberately for literary effect. By juxtaposing passages of prophecy which maintain the convention with passages in the present tense which transgress it, the writer is able to indicate that the apostles' prophecies of false teachers are now being fulfilled. (The same device seems to be used in 2 Tim 3:1–9, in another testamentary letter.)

Verse 3b is probably to be understood as a denial of an assertion made by the opponents (see *Comment*). The rest of this section then provides the basis for that denial.

Verses 4, 6, 10a are partially dependent on Jude 6–8:

2 Pet 2	*Jude*
4. εἰ γὰρ ὁ θεὸς ἀγγέλων ἁμαρτησάντων οὐκ ἐφείσατο, ἀλλὰ σειραῖς ζόφου ταρταρώσας παρέδωκεν εἰς κρίσιν τηρουμένους, . . .	6. ἀγγέλους τε τοὺς μὴ τηρήσαντας τὴν ἑαυτῶν ἀρχὴν ἀλλὰ ἀπολιπόντας τὸ ἴδιον οἰκητήριον εἰς κρίσιν μεγάλης ἡμέρας δεσμοῖς ἀϊδίοις ὑπὸ ζόφον τετήρηκεν·

6. καὶ πόλεις Σοδόμων καὶ Γομόρρας τεφρώσας καταστροφῇ κατέκρινεν, ὑπόδειγμα μελλόντων ἀσεβέσιν τεθεικώς, . . .	7. ὡς Σόδομα καὶ Γόμορρα καὶ αἱ περὶ αὐτὰς πόλεις, τὸν ὅμοιον τρόπον τούτοις ἐκπορνεύσασθαι καὶ ἀπελθοῦσαι ὀπίσω σαρκὸς ἑτέρας, πρόκεινται δεῖγμα πυρὸς αἰωνίου δίκην ὑπέχουσαι.
10a. μάλιστα δὲ τοὺς ὀπίσω σαρκὸς ἐν ἐπιθυμίᾳ μιασμοῦ πορευομένους καὶ κυριότητος καταφρονοῦντας.	8. Ὁμοίως μέντα καὶ οὗτοι ἐνυπνιαζόμενοι σάρκα μὲν μιαίνουσιν, κυριότητα δὲ ἀθετοῦσιν, . . .

2 Pet 2	*Jude*
4. For if God did not spare *the angels* when they sinned, but cast them into hell and committed them to fetters of *nether darkness,* there to be *kept until the judgment;* . . .	6. *The angels,* too, who did not keep their own position of authority, but abandoned their proper home, he has *kept* in eternal chains in the *nether darkness until the judgment* of the great day.
6. if he reduced the cities of *Sodom and Gomorrah* to ashes and condemned them to extinction, making them an example of what is going to happen to the ungodly, . . .	7. Similarly *Sodom and Gomorrah* and the neighbouring towns, which practiced immorality in the same way as the angels and hankered after strange *flesh,* are exhibited as an example by undergoing the punishment of eternal fire.
10a. especially those who in polluting lust indulge the *flesh* and flout *the authority of the Lord.*	8. Yet in the same way also these people, on the strength of their dreams, defile the *flesh,* reject *the authority of the Lord,* . . .

However, as well as the clear dependence on Jude, there are strong indications that in vv 4–9 2 Peter is independently drawing on a paraenetic tradition similar to that which lies behind Jude 5–7 (see the *Form/Structure/Setting* section in the commentary on Jude 5–7). (1) οὐκ ἐφείσατο ("did not spare") (vv 4–5) is used in Sir 16:18, in a passage which represents a version of the traditional schema on which Jude is dependent. But the expression is common (LXX 1 Kgdms 15:3; Ps 77:50; Jer 13:14; 21:7; Lam 2:17; Jonah 4:11; Zech 11:6; Acts 20:29; Rom 11:21) and so the coincidence may not be significant. (2) Second Peter's examples, unlike Jude's, are in chronological order, as in other versions of the traditional schema. But again this could be coincidental. (3) The general lesson which the examples illustrate is stated in vv 9–10a. Jude, who uses the examples as typological prophecy, not illustrations of a general principle, has no such statement. But it is a standard feature of the traditional schema (Sir 16:6, 11–14; CD 2:16–17; 3 Macc 2:3–4a; and cf. (8) below). (4) Second Peter adds to Jude's examples of sinners the example of the generation of the Flood (v 5), which is also found in CD 2:20–21; *m. Sanh.* 10:3 (and Josephus, *BJ* 5.566). (5) The most notable difference from Jude is that 2 Peter adds two counterexamples of righteous persons delivered when the ungodly were judged: Noah corresponding to the generation of the Flood (and probably also to the angels), Lot corresponding to Sodom and Gomorrah. Such counterexamples occur also in CD 3:2–4 (Abraham, Isaac and Jacob); 3 Macc 2:7 (the Israelites at the Exodus). Comparison should also be made with Wis 10 (not discussed in the commentary on Jude 5–7), which is a catalogue of examples of God's (Wisdom's) deliverance of the righteous (Adam, Noah, Abraham, Lot, Jacob, Joseph, Israel at the Exodus), with counterexamples of his punishment of the wicked (Cain, the generation of the dispersion, the cities of the Plain, the Egyptians). Moreover, Philo has a passage which describes the judgments of the Flood and of Sodom and Gomorrah, and then dwells on the fact that God saved one family, Noah's, and one man, Lot, from these destructions (*Mos.* 2.53–65). (6) ἐφύλαξεν ("preserved," v 5), ἐρρύσατο ("rescued," v 7) and ῥύεσθαι ("to rescue," v 9) correspond to the verbs used in Wis 10: διαφυλάσσειν ("to preserve," vv 1, 5, 12) and ῥύεσθαι ("to rescue," vv 6, 9, 13, 15). (7) The description of Lot as δίκαιος ("righteous," v 7) also occurs in Wis 10:6. (8) *1 Clem.* 11:1 seems to belong to the same general tradition: the example of Lot's deliverance at the time of the judgment of Sodom illustrates a general maxim about God's deliverance of the righteous and punishment of the wicked (cf. 2 Pet 2:9).

Thus the author of 2 Peter has supplemented the material he drew from Jude with material drawn from his independent knowledge of a paraenetic tradition which listed examples of God's deliverance of the righteous as well as of his punishment of the wicked. Wis 10 is not 2 Peter's source, but another, distinctive, development of the same tradition.

Jude's echoes of *1 Enoch,* with which the author of 2 Peter was probably not familiar, are lost in his rewriting of Jude 6 (2 Pet 2:4), while he introduces echoes of the LXX in vv 5 (Gen 6:17) and 6 (Gen 19:29). Jewish haggadic traditions are reflected in vv 5, 7, and probably 8. There may be an echo of the Lord's Prayer (Matt 6:13) in v 9 (see *Comment*).

Comment

3. *οἷς τὸ κρίμα ἔκπαλαι οὐκ ἀργεῖ, καὶ ἡ ἀπώλεια αὐτῶν οὐ νυστάζει,* "the condemnation pronounced on them long ago is not idle; their destruction is not asleep." Neyrey (*JBL* 99 [1980] 415–16; *Polemic,* 27–30) is probably correct in seeing v 3b as a denial of the opponents' mocking claim that divine judgment is "idle" and "asleep." This is shown by comparison with 3:9a, which certainly refutes a similar claim that the Lord is late in coming to judgment. No doubt the author has phrased the opponents' jibe in his own words, and has made his denial of it into a powerful pronouncement of judgment in poetic parallelism, almost a prophetic oracle of doom (Windisch).

The two terms *κρίμα* ("condemnation") and *ἀπώλεια* ("destruction") are personified, and so *ἀργεῖ* should retain the personal sense "is idle," though the meaning is that the condemnation is not ineffective. Behind the personification of *κρίμα* and *ἀπώλεια* lies, of course, the personality of God whose judgment they represent. That God is asleep can be a skeptical taunt (2 Kgs 18:27); and the psalmist can in faith beg God, when he fails to intervene in judgment, to wake out of sleep (Ps 44:23); but the divine Guardian of Israel, it is said, will not slumber (*νυστάξει*) nor sleep (Ps 120:4 LXX); and the nations who execute God's vengeance will not slumber (*νυστάξουσιν*) nor sleep (Isa 5:27 LXX). These OT passages may have influenced the author, but if it was the opponents themselves who suggested that God's judgment was idle or asleep, it is more relevant to note that these ideas were used by pagan skeptics to mock the inactivity of the gods who seem so rarely to intervene in the world. An Epicurean opponent of providence asks: "Why did these deities suddenly awake into activity as world-builders after countless ages of slumber (*dormierint*) . . . Why did your Providence remain idle (*cessaverit*) all through that extent of time of which you speak?" (Cicero, *De natura deorum* 1.21–22, Loeb tr.; cf. also Oenomaus of Gadara, *ap.* Eusebius, *Praep. Evan.* 5.19.2; Celsus, *ap.* Origen, *C.Cels.* 6.78).

ἔκπαλαι ("long ago"; cf. πάλαι, Jude 4) must mean that the condemnation of the false teachers was pronounced long ago, though this is grammatically rather awkward. But the author of 2 Peter does not indicate when or where this condemnation was pronounced. It is just possible that he regards the OT condemnation of false prophets as a condemnation which includes the false teachers of his own time (Mayor, Wand), but this is not very likely. Jude saw the condemnation of the false teachers in the whole series of OT types and prophecies set out in Jude 5–18 (see *Comment* on Jude 4), and it may therefore be that the author of 2 Peter sees it in the OT examples of sinners judged which he gives in vv 4–6. At first sight, it looks as though these examples are not, as in Jude, prophetic types, but only illustrations of the general principle that God judges (v 9). But although this impression is given by the maxim with which, following the paraenetic tradition (see *Form/Structure/Setting* section), the author concludes, the details of his account of the judgments in vv 5–6 makes it clear that he did see those as prototypes of the eschatological judgment (see below). Alternatively, he may have simply taken over from Jude the idea of condemnation long ago without feeling the need to substantiate the point.

The condemnation pronounced on the false teachers long ago is not, as they allege, ineffective: it will soon take effect. The destruction which is due to them is not, as they say, "asleep": it will soon overtake them.

4. εἰ γὰρ ὁ θεὸς ἀγγέλων ἁμαρτησάντων οὐκ ἐφείσατο, "for if God did not spare the angels when they sinned." For the basis of this interpretation of Gen 6:1–4 in *1 Enoch,* see the commentary on Jude 6. The author of 2 Peter has followed Jude. He may not himself have known *1 Enoch* and probably in any case could not expect his readers to be familiar with it (see *Introduction,* section 2 of *Literary Relationships*), but he must have known the story of the fall of the Watchers, which was well known in contemporary Judaism, Hellenistic as well as Palestinian. In his rewriting of Jude 6 the specific verbal echoes of *1 Enoch* have mostly been lost (a fact which is most easily explained if Jude is prior to 2 Peter), but this is probably accidental rather than a deliberate attempt to avoid echoes of *1 Enoch.* No significance should be seen in the fact that 2 Peter omits to specify the sin of the angels (the sexual aspect of which even Jude only alludes to: Jude 7). Those who (later) objected to the idea that angels could have mated with women did not suggest that the angels sinned in some other way, but that "the sons of God" in Gen 6:1 were not angels at all, but men. If the author of 2 Peter and his readers knew the story of the fall of the Watchers at all, they must have known it as an interpretation of Gen 6:1–4 and have known that the angels sinned by taking human wives. But instead of specifying the sins of each of his three OT examples

of sinners in turn, the author has chosen to sum up the sins of all three in the words of v 10a, which in fact give a strong emphasis to sexual indulgence.

ἀλλὰ σειραῖς ζόφου ταρταρώσας παρέδωκεν, "but cast them into hell and committed them to fetters of nether darkness." The verbs *ταρταροῦν* and (rather more common) *καταταρταροῦν* mean "to cast into Tartarus," and were almost always used with reference to the early Greek theogonic myths, in which the ancient giants, the Cyclopes and Titans, were imprisoned in Tartarus, the lowest part of the underworld, by Uranos, Kronos and Zeus (Pearson, *GRBS* 10 [1969] 76–78). They are not used in the Greek version of *1 Enoch,* though *τάρταρος* ("Tartarus") is used of the place of divine punishment in *1 Enoch* 20:2, as elsewhere in Jewish Greek literature (LXX Job 40:20; 41:24; Prov 30:16; *Sib. Or.* 4:186; Philo, *Mos.* 2.433; *Praem.* 152). But Hellenistic Jews were aware that the Greek myth of the Titans had some similarity to the fall of the Watchers (though Philo, *Gig.* 58, rejects any comparison). Sometimes the Watchers' sons, the giants (the Nephilim), were compared with the Titans (Josephus, *Ant.* 1.73; cf. LXX Ezek 32:27; Sir 16:7) but in Jdt 16:6 (and also the Christian passage *Sib. Or.* 2:231) the Watchers themselves seem to be called *τιτᾶνες* ("Titans"). Thus in using a term reminiscent of the Greek myth of the Titans the author of 2 Peter follows Hellenistic Jewish practice.

If *σειραῖς* ("fetters") is the correct reading (see the *Note*), the author has interpreted Jude's "chains" (*δεσμοῖς*; see *Comment* on Jude 6) metaphorically of the darkness (*ζόφος* is the gloom of the underworld: see *Comment* on Jude 6) in which the angels are confined. In a highly rhetorical description of the Egyptian plague of darkness, Wis 17:16 says that the Egyptians "were bound with one chain of darkness" (*μιᾷ ἁλύσει σκότους ἐδέθησαν*; cf. also 17:2), and it is not impossible that the author of 2 Peter recalled this expression. If, however, the correct reading is *σειροῖς* ("pits"), we must suppose that the author of 2 Peter had independent knowledge of the tradition of the fall of the Watchers as it was told in *1 Enoch,* for this reading must refer to the "valleys" (*1 Enoch* 10:12: *νάπας*; cf. 10:4; *Jub.* 5:10) or the abyss (*1 Enoch* 18:11; 21:7; 88:1, 3) which served as a dungeon for the fallen angels. This is by no means impossible, since the author elsewhere augments his borrowings from Jude with details independently drawn from Jewish haggadic tradition (see vv 5, 7, 16), and may have drawn on independent knowledge of a catechetical tradition similar to that which lies behind Jude 5–7 (see *Form/Structure/Setting* section).

εἰς κρίσιν τηρουμένους, "to be kept until the judgment." The judgment (*κρίσιν*) is undoubtedly, as in Jude 6, *the* (eschatological) judgment (cf. 2:9; 3:7), and *τηρεῖν* ("to keep"), which 2 Peter has adopted from Jude but uses without Jude's ironic wordplay, always in 2 Peter has reference to eschatological judgment (2:9, 17; 3:7). Throughout this section the author emphasizes that the examples of judgment he has chosen prefigure the final judgment.

5. *καὶ ἀρχαίου κόσμου οὐκ ἐφείσατο*, "and did not spare the ancient world." The story of the Watchers was closely connected with the Flood (in *1 Enoch* the Flood comes as a consequence of the activity of the Watchers and their sons), and this connection is found in other examples of the traditional paraenetic schema which this passage follows (3 Macc 2:4; *T. Napht.* 3:5). This

close connection explains why Noah appears in this verse to serve as the example of deliverance which is the counterpart to two examples of judgment: the angels (v 4) and the "ancient world" (v 5). *κόσμος* ("world") here means primarily the inhabitants of the world (cf. *1 Clem.* 9:4: Noah preached "to the world": *κόσμῳ*), but the word also emphasizes the universal scope of the Flood and invites comparison with the coming eschatological judgment, the second such universal judgment (cf. 3:6–7). The author of 2 Peter seems to have thought of three successive worlds: the ancient world before the Flood, the present world, and the new world to come (3:13) after the eschatological judgment (Chaine). (For *ἀρχαίου*, "ancient": cf. Sir 16:7: "the ancient giants"; and for the idea, cf. *Clem. Hom.* 9:2:1: *τοῦ πάλαι κατακλυσθέντος κόσμου*, "the ancient world which was deluged.")

ὄγδοον Νωε, "Noah the eighth person," is a classical Greek idiom (cf. 2 Macc 5:27; other examples in BAG *s.v.* *ὄγδοος*) and means "Noah with seven others." The reference is to Noah, his wife, his three sons and their wives (Gen 8:18). I have retained a literal translation because the author may have seen a special significance in the number eight here. Some think the number is mentioned to stress the small number of those who were saved (Mayor, Wand, Green; cf. *Jub.* 5:19; 4 Ezra 3:11), but there seems no particular reason why that point should be emphasized here. It is stressed in 1 Pet 3:20 (*ὀλίγοι*, "few"), which also mentions the number eight, but there is no good reason for thinking 2 Peter is here dependent on that verse (against Dalton, *Bib* 60 [1979] 551–52): the only real point of contact between 1 Pet 3:20 and 2 Pet 2:5 is the number eight, and this probably indicates that for some reason Christian tradition was in the habit of specifying that there were eight persons who were saved out of the Flood. Noah is also called "eighth" (*ὄγδοος*) in *Sib. Or.* 1:280–81, a passage which may be Jewish (Kurfess in *NT Apoc* 2, 707), and the number eight is stressed in Theophilus' account of the Deluge (*Ad Autol.* 3.19).

The reason for this stress is perhaps to be found in the eschatological symbolism of the number eight, which represented an eighth day of new creation, following the seven days of the old creation's history (cf *2 Enoch* 33:1–2; *Barn.* 15:9). Early Christians associated this symbolism with Sunday, the "eighth day" (*Barn.* 15:9: Justin, *Dial.* 24.1: 41.4; 138.1). Sunday was the eighth day because it was the day of Christ's resurrection in which the new creation was begun, and this symbolism is linked by Justin to the eight people saved in the Flood (*Dial.* 138.1). It would be very appropriate in 2 Pet 2:5, and so may well have been in the author's mind.

Noah, preserved from the old world to be the beginning of the new world after the Flood, is a type of faithful Christians who will be preserved from the present world to inherit the new world after the judgment.

δικαιοσύνης κήρυκα, "a preacher of righteousness." Noah's preaching is not mentioned in Genesis, but was well-known in Jewish tradition. It is especially prominent in the first book of the Sibylline Oracles, a product of Hellenistic Judaism, in which a long sermon of Noah's is given (*Sib. Or.* 1:148–98). Normally Noah was said to have preached repentance to his wicked contemporaries (*Sib. Or.* 1:129: *κήρυξεν μετάνοιαν*, "he preached repentance"; Josephus, *Ant.* 1.74; *Gen. Rab.* 30:7: "one herald arose for me in the generation of the flood"; *Eccles. Rab.* 9:15; *Pirqe R. El.* 22; *b. Sanh.* 108; cf. also Theophilus, *Ad Autol.* 3.19; Methodius, *Conviv.* 10.3; *Apoc. Paul* 50: οὐκ ἐπαυσάμην . . . κήρυσσειν, Μετανοιεῖτε, "I did not cease to preach, Repent"; *Book of Adam and Eve* (ed. Malan) 3:2, 4; Noah's preaching of repentance may also be implied in 1 Pet 3:20: ἀπειθήσασιν, "did not obey"). The fact that this tradition appears also in *1 Clement* (7:6: ἐκήρυξεν μετάνοιαν, "he preached repentance"; cf. 9:4) does not prove that Clement knew 2 Peter; on the contrary, his use of μετάνοιαν ("repentance") shows that he had independent access to the tradition about Noah's preaching. But it is one of many signs that the two works belong to a common milieu.

Second Peter no doubt uses δικαιοσύνης ("righteousness"), meaning that Noah exhorted his contemporaries to righteous living, in order to contrast with ἀσεβῶν ("ungodly people"). (Some commentators find a parallel in *Jub.* 7:20, where Noah exhorts to righteousness, but this is irrelevant because it refers to Noah's instruction of his sons after the Flood.)

Jewish tradition also regarded the period before the Flood as a period in which God delayed judgment to give men time for repentance (*Tgs.* to Gen 6:3; *Pirqe 'Abot* 5:2; Philo, *Quaest. Gen.* 2.13; also 1 Pet 3:20) and in view of 3:9 this idea would fit well into 2 Peter's typology. But the fact that the author uses δικαιοσύνης ("righteousness") rather than μετάνοιας ("repentance," which would create a link with 3:9) seems to indicate that he did not have this aspect of the typology in mind here.

ἐφύλαξεν ("preserved"), cf. διαφυλάσσειν, "to preserve, protect," in Wis 10:1, 5, 12, a chapter which, like this section of 2 Peter, gives examples of God's protection and rescue of the righteous when the wicked are judged. The example of Noah appears in Wis 10:4.

κατακλυσμὸν κόσμῳ ἀσεβῶν ἐπάξας, "when he brought the deluge on the world of ungodly people," is an echo of Gen 6:17 LXX (ἐπάγω τὸν κατακλυσμὸν ὕδωρ ἐπὶ τὴν γῆν, "I am bringing the flood of water upon the earth"; and cf. *Sib. Or.* 1:189: κόσμος ἅπας ἀπειρεσίων ἀνθρώπων, "the whole world of countless people"). For the Flood as a punitive judgment in Jewish literature, see Schlosser, *RB* 80 [1973] 15–16. It was sometimes seen as a prototype of the eschatological judgment (this is implicit throughout *1 Enoch* 1–16; cf. 93:4: the Flood as "the first end"; 1QH 10:35–36; Matt 24:37–39), and our author certainly understood it in this way (3:6–7). For ἀσεβῶν ("ungodly"; also in 2:6; 3:7) see *Comment* on Jude 4; the word does not have in 2 Peter the catchword significance it has in Jude. As in the case of the angels, the sins of the generation of the Flood are not here specified, but in view of v 10a, it is relevant to note that Jewish tradition usually held them to be guilty of the same series of vices as it attributed to the Sodomites (Schlosser, *RB* 80 [1973] 18–25).

6. πόλεις Σοδόμων καὶ Γομόρρας τεφρώσας καταστροφῇ κατέκρινεν, "he reduced the cities of Sodom and Gomorrah to ashes and condemned them to extinction." τεφροῦν ("to reduce to ashes"), a NT *hapax,* is used of Sodom and Gomorrah by Philo (*Ebr.* 223). (The smoking ashes were thought to be still in evidence on the site of Sodom and Gomorrah: Wis 10:7; Josephus, *BJ* 4.483; Philo, *Mos.* 2.56; 4 (5) Ezra 2:9; cf. Strabo 16.2.44, where the region around the Dead Sea is called γῆ τεφρώδης, "land of ash.") καταστροφή ("ex-

tinction, destruction") is used of Sodom and Gomorrah in Gen 19:29 LXX, where Lot's deliverance from the destruction is mentioned. Neyrey (*Polemic,* 132–33) is probably correct in suggesting that the alliteration (*καταστροφῇ κατέκρινεν,* "he condemned to extinction") has the effect of reinforcing the parallelism with the preceding example of destructive judgment (*κατακλυσμὸν κόσμῳ,* "the deluge on the world," v 5).

ὑπόδειγμα μελλόντων ἀσεβέσιν τεθεικώς, "making them an example of what is going to happen to the ungodly." *ὑπόδειγμα* (on which see E. K. Lee, "Words denoting 'Pattern' in the New Testament," *NTS* 8 [1961–62] 168–69; Spicq, *Lexicographie,* 907–9) means here a *warning* example; cf. Jude 7 (*δεῖγμα*); 3 Macc 2:5 (God made the Sodomites "an example to those who should come afterward": *παράδειγμα τοῖς ἐπιγινομένοις*); *Clem. Hom.* 9.2.1 ("you have the example of the ancient world deluged," *τοῦ πάλαι κατακλυσθέντος κόσμου τὸ ὑπόδειγμα*). For the judgment of Sodom and Gomorrah as an exemplary judgment, see the *Comment* on Jude 7. It should also be noticed that, as in 2 Peter, the Flood and the destruction of Sodom and Gomorrah were sometimes linked together as the two signal examples of divine judgment (*Jub.* 20:5; *T. Napht.* 3:4–5; cf. Josephus, *BJ* 5.566; Schlosser, *RB* 80 [1973] 13–14, 23–24; Lührmann, *ZNW* 63 [1972] 130), sometimes as the two prototypes of eschatological judgment (Luke 17:26–30). In this connection it should be noted that together they exemplify the pattern of two destructions by water and by fire (Fornberg, *Early Church,* 41; Neyrey, *Polemic,* 133–34), which is used later in 2 Pet 3:5–7. Undoubtedly the author sees the judgment of Sodom and Gomorrah by fire as a pattern for the fiery judgment of the ungodly at the Parousia (3:7). This conclusion is strengthened by the words *μελλόντων ἀσεβέσιν* ("what is going to happen to the ungodly"), which have the ungodly contemporaries of the author, i.e. the false teachers and their followers, especially in view.

The author seems consistently to omit Jude's references to the eternity of punishment (vv 4, 6, 17; cf. Jude 6, 7, 13). Is this because his attention is focused on preliminary punishment in the intermediate state (cf. perhaps 2:9; but see the discussion of this v below) or because he prefers to see the fate of the wicked at the day of judgment as annihilation?

7. *δίκαιον Λωτ καταπονούμενον ὑπὸ τῆς τῶν ἀθέσμων ἐν ἀσελγείᾳ ἀναστροφῆς ἐρρύσατο,* "rescued the righteous man Lot, who was distressed by the dissolute behavior of the lawless." Genesis does not portray Lot as entirely blameless (see Gen 19:30–38), but Jewish tradition interpreted Abraham's plea on behalf of the righteous in Sodom (Gen 18:23–32) as referring to Lot (*Pirqe R. El.* 25; *Gen. Rab.* 49:13), and so could speak of him as a righteous man (Wis 10:6; 19:17: *δίκαιος*; cf. *1 Clem.* 11:1: Philo, *Mos.* 2.58). His exemplary deliverance from the fate that overtook his wicked fellow-citizens is mentioned in Wis 10:6; Philo, *Mos.* 2.58; and *1 Clem.* 11:1, which seem to belong to the same paraenetic tradition as 2 Pet 2:4–9 (see *Form/Structure/Setting* section). *ἐρρύσατο* ("rescued") is used four times in Wis 10 (vv 6, 9, 13, 15), once with reference to Lot (10:6) and once in a generalizing summary (10:9) comparable with 2 Pet 2:9a. Note the contrast between Lot as *δίκαιον* ("righteous") and the Sodomites as *ἀθέσμων* ("lawless").

8. *βλέμματι γὰρ καὶ ἀκοῇ ὁ δίκαιος ἐνκατοικῶν ἐν αὐτοῖς ἡμέραν ἐξ ἡμέρας ψυχὴν*

δικαίαν ἀνόμοις ἔργοις ἐβασάνιζεν, "for when that righteous man was living among them his righteous soul was day after day tormented by the sight and sound of their unlawful doings." The point of this extended description of Lot's righteous distress must be to heighten the contrast between the righteous whom God delivers and the wicked he punishes, and hopefully to echo the feelings of 2 Peter's readers in their own situation. It may be dependent on haggadic tradition which has not come down to us elsewhere. It must refer to Lot's inner distress (cf. Herm. *Mand.* 4:2:2, for ψυχὴν βασανίζειν), his sense of impotent outrage at the evil all around him (cf. Ezek 9:4), not to his outward suffering at the hands of the wicked (Bigg). This inner suffering was his πειρασμός (2:9), "trial" in the sense of suffering through confrontation with evil, from which God delivered him.

9. οἶδεν κύριος εὐσεβεῖς ἐκ πειρασμοῦ ῥύεσθαι, "then the Lord is well able to rescue the godly from trial." This v is the apodosis of the long conditional sentence vv 4–10a. Putting the lesson concerning the righteous first enables the writer to end emphatically with the lesson concerning the wicked, applied to his opponents.

πειρασμοῦ ("trial, test, temptation") must be interpreted in the light of the examples of Noah and Lot, to which in the first instance it refers. It cannot therefore mean temptation to sin, for Noah and Lot are not represented as being attracted by evil, but as reacting against it (Chaine). Rather πειρασμός refers to the good man's situation in a world in which the powers of good and evil confront each other and he is therefore exposed to attack from evil (K. G. Kuhn, "New Light on Temptation, Sin, and Flesh in the New Testament," in K. Stendahl (ed.), *The Scrolls and the New Testament* [London: SCM Press, 1958] 108–9). It can therefore refer generally to the afflictions which the righteous suffer in an evil world (Luke 8:13; Acts 20:19; Jas 1:2; 1 Pet 1:6). Since the reference here is in the first place to Noah and Lot the πειρασμός cannot be simply *the* ordeal of the last days (Rev 3:10; 1 Pet 4:12), but this overtone may be intended so far as the application to 2 Peter's readers is concerned. Since the Flood and the judgment of Sodom and Gomorrah are prototypes of eschatological judgment, the situations of Noah and Lot are typical of the situation of Christians in the final evil days before the Parousia.

There is quite a good parallel in Sir 33:1 (RSV: "No evil will befall the man who fears the Lord, but in trial (ἐκ πειρασμῷ) he will deliver (ἐξελεῖται) him again and again"), as well as in Wis 10:9 (RSV: "Wisdom rescued (ἐρρύσατο) from troubles (ἐκ πόνων) those who served her"). Some have detected an echo of the Lord's Prayer (Matt 6:13: μὴ εἰσενέγκῃς ἡμᾶς εἰς πειρασμόν, ἀλλὰ ῥῦσαι ἡμᾶς ἀπὸ τοῦ πονηροῦ), and this is quite possible, especially in view of the other echoes of Gospel traditions in 2 Peter. Verse 9a could be a summary of the last two petitions of the Matthean version of the Prayer. But since the wording of 2 Peter is quite natural and explicable without such an echo, we cannot be sure of it. (With even less certainty can this v be used to help reconstruct a hypothetical original version of the last petition of the Prayer, as G. Schwartz, "Matthäus vi. 9–13/ Lukas xi. 2–4," *NTS* 15 [1968–69] 241 n. 3, proposes.)

ἀδίκους δὲ εἰς ἡμέραν κρίσεως κολαζομένους τηρεῖν, "but to keep the wicked to be punished at the day of judgment." The present participle κολαζομένους (lit. "being punished") should, strictly, describe an action contemporaneous with τηρεῖν ("to keep"), and therefore some commentators, along with most English translators, understand it to refer to a preliminary punishment before the last judgment ("to keep the wicked under punishment until the last judgment": RV, RSV, NEB, NIV, GNB; Spitta, Mayor, Wand, Barnett, Boobyer, Kelly, Schrage; *TDNT* 3, 816; Fornberg, *Early Church,* 45). In favor of this, it can be argued: (a) This is the proper grammatical sense. (b) It draws the moral of v 4, where the angels are held under punishment in Tartarus awaiting their final doom. (c) Current Jewish belief did hold the wicked to be suffering in the intermediate state before the judgment (*1 Enoch* 22:10–11; 4 Ezra 7:79–87; Luke 16:23–24). On the other hand, a majority of commentators take κολαζομένους to refer to punishment at the day of judgment (Calvin, Chaine, Windisch, Schelkle, Reicke, Spicq, Michl, Green, Grundmann; AV, JB). In favor of this, it can be argued: (a) In the Greek of this period the future participle is rare, and the future passive participle extremely rare (Heb 3:5 contains the only NT example), so that a loose use of κολαζομένους with a future sense is possible. In 3:11 our author uses the present participle λυομένων (lit. "being dissolved") with future sense (other likely NT examples of the present participle with future sense are Matt 26:25; Luke 1:35; John 17:20; Acts 21:2–3; cf. Moulton, *Grammar* 3, 87). (b) In v 4 (as in *1 Enoch*) the angels are held in detention awaiting judgment, and this was also the common Jewish view of the state of the wicked dead, whose suffering in the intermediate state (*1 Enoch* 22:11) can be portrayed as that of remorse and anticipation (4 Ezra 7:79–87, cf. 93). κολαζομένους ("being punished") seems too strong a term for this detention, while both κολάζειν ("to punish") and κόλασις ("punishment") are elsewhere used of the last judgment and hell after the last judgment (κολάζειν: *2 Clem.* 17:7; *Apoc. Pet.* A 21; Herm. *Sim.* 9:18:2; κόλασις: Matt 25:46; *2 Clem.* 6:7; *Apoc. Pet.* A 21: *Mart. Pol.* 2:3; 11:2). (c) While punishment in the intermediate state might be appropriate in view of the examples in vv 4–6, it is not relevant to the case of the false teachers, whom the author also has in mind (vv 3b, 10a) and whose judgment at the imminent Parousia is the point at issue (v 3b). It seems odd that the author should emphasize preliminary rather than final punishment.

It is not easy to decide between the two alternatives, but the second seems somewhat preferable. In that case v 9, while drawing the general lesson of vv 4–8, does so with special reference to the eschatological deliverance of the righteous at the Parousia and the eschatological punishment of the wicked at the Parousia (cf. 3:7).

The *dual* conclusion—deliverance and punishment—is the most prominent respect in which 2 Peter diverges from Jude 6–8, where the examples are only of punishment. But the dual conclusion, and the examples on which it is based, no doubt come from the catechetical tradition which our author knew: cf. *1 Clem.* 11:1, which draws a similar double moral from the case of Sodom and Lot; and Philo, *Mos.* 2.57, where both aspects of the Flood and of the ruin of Sodom are brought out (cf. also Sir 16:11–14). Evidently our author wished to stress the discriminating character of divine justice. The fact that the wicked go unpunished raises the double problem of God's justice in judging the wicked *and* the suffering of the righteous while the wicked flourish. Second Peter's assertion of God's intervention in judgment aims to meet this double problem.

10. *μάλιστα δὲ τοὺς ὀπίσω σαρκὸς ἐν ἐπιθυμίᾳ μιασμοῦ πορευομένους*, "especially those who in polluting lust indulge the flesh." This phrase seems to echo two phrases in Jude: "went after strange flesh" (*ἀπελθοῦσαι ὀπίσω σαρκὸς ἑτέρας*: Jude 7, of the Sodomites), and "defile the flesh" (*σάρκα . . . μιαίνουσιν*: Jude 8, of the false teachers). For Jude's *ἀπελθοῦσαι ὀπίσω*, "went after," 2 Peter has substituted the more familiar LXX phrase *πορεύεσθαι ὀπίσω* (LXX Deut 4:3; 6:14; 28:14; 3 Kdgms 11:10; Hos 11:10; for contexts comparable to this, cf. Isa 65:2; *T. Jud.* 13:2; Herm. *Vis.* 3:7:3), which implies that they follow the flesh as a god or a master (cf. v 2). *σάρξ* ("flesh") here seems to have a less neutral sense than in Jude, and means sensuality as an evil power, or at least as a power for evil when it is allowed to dominate.

This phrase and the next are intended to summarize the sins of the three examples in vv 4–8, in such a way that they also apply to the false teachers.

κυριότητος καταφρονοῦντας, "flout the authority of the Lord," is modeled on *κυριότητα . . . ἀθετοῦσιν* ("reject the authority of the Lord," Jude 8). We cannot simply assume that *κυριότης*, "lordship," is intended in the same sense as it bears in Jude (see *Comment* on Jude 8), but in fact it is likely that it is. Human authorities cannot be intended, because this summary must be applicable to the examples listed in vv 4–8. As in Jude, the class of angels known as *κυριότητες* can hardly be meant by the singular *κυριότητος*. So the meaning must be the authority of God or Christ (so Bigg, Chaine, Spicq, Kelly, Schrage, Grundmann; Neyrey, *Polemic,* 44). Since *κύριος*, "Lord," in v 9 presumably (cf. v 4) refers to God, *κυριότητος* could be held to refer more naturally to God's than to Christ's authority; alternatively, the parallel with v 1 ("deny the Master") points to Christ's authority. The author may not have made a clear distinction.

The reference will be to practical disregard for divine authority by ethical misconduct. Those who subject themselves to the flesh cannot be subject to the Lord. Thus v 10a specifies the same two sins as vv 1–2 ("deny the Master," "dissolute practices").

Explanation

The false teachers mocked the idea of the eschatological judgment, which they claimed should have arrived by now if it were coming at all. If there is such a thing as divine judgment, they said, it must be taking time off or taking a nap. Our author's negation of this claim in v 3b amounts to a solemn pronouncement of their doom. The condemnation which was long ago pronounced on them in the prophetic Scriptures will not be without effect.

For the time being the author does not attempt to tackle the problem of the alleged delay of the eschatological judgment, but is content to demonstrate its certainty against the claim that it is ineffective. He does so by citing three of the best-known examples of divine judgment in OT times: the judgment of the angelic Watchers, the Flood, and the destruction of Sodom and Gomorrah by fire. These examples show that God is able to punish the wicked, and therefore that he will certainly also punish the false teachers and their followers who claim impunity and live accordingly. However, the OT examples are more than instances which establish the general rule (v 9b) that God punishes the wicked. They are also typological prophecies of the eschatological judgment. They foreshadow the doom of the wicked of the last days, among whom the false teachers and their followers are numbered, and so in their dual character as *prophetic* instances of judgment they make the eschatological judgment certain. If the false teachers doubt the verbal prophecies of judgment, they should consider that there have also been *acted* prophecies.

The details of the references to the three examples in vv 4–6 bring out their typological character. The angels are detained in Tartarus awaiting condemnation and punishment at the final universal assize—which is to be the day of reckoning for all the wicked (cf. v 9b). The Flood destroyed a whole world of ungodly people, thus prefiguring the only other universal judgment which the world is to suffer, the coming eschatological judgment (cf. 3:6–7). The burning of Sodom and Gomorrah was a warning example of the fate in store for the wicked in the future, especially of the cosmic conflagration which threatens the ungodly of the last days (cf. 3:7).

Into this argument about the certainty of punishment for the wicked, the author has woven a second theme: the deliverance of the righteous. If, as the false teachers allege, there is to be no eschatological judgment, then there will also be no deliverance of the righteous from their sufferings in a world where the wicked flourish. But the same examples which show the certainty of judgment on the wicked show the certainty of deliverance for the righteous. For God did not destroy the godly and ungodly indiscriminately. When he bound the angels in hell and destroyed the world in the Flood, he rescued Noah and his family, and when Sodom and Gomorrah perished, their single righteous inhabitant escaped.

Just as the OT judgments prefigured the eschatological judgment, so Noah and Lot are described in terms which make them types of the faithful Christians who will be delivered at the Parousia. Noah was a man who tried to teach his contemporaries righteousness. The detail that, with his seven relatives, he was the "eighth" person, evokes the eschatological symbolism of the number eight. As the "eighth" person he stands for the new creation which will succeed the old, the "eighth" day after the week of creation's history. Saved from the world of the ungodly in which he alone preached righteousness, he was able to enter a new world, in which, for a time, only the righteous lived. Similarly, faithful Christians, persisting in righteousness and preaching it in this present world where the ungodly flourish, will be delivered from it and enter the new world in which righteousness dwells (3:13).

The description of Lot focuses on the predicament from which he was rescued: the mental torment of the conscientious person surrounded by blatant evil and helpless to prevent it. This picture of Lot is extremely significant. It goes beyond the common apocalyptic theme of the suffering of the righteous at the hands of the wicked and their deliverance from this suffering. Lot suffers not because he is a victim of the wicked, but because he is a genuinely righteous man, a man who loves righteousness, who longs to see righteousness done in the world, and is afflicted by its absence. If 2 Peter's readers can identify with him, they too may hope for deliverance.

This assurance of deliverance is no mere consolation for 2 Peter's readers. It provides the eschatological condition for their persistence in righteousness, just as the false teachers' denial of eschatology undermines the Christian practice of righteousness. In biblical thought adherence to righteousness requires the expectation that in the end God's righteousness will prevail over all opposition to it. Only such an expectation satisfies the love of righteousness and sustains the practice of righteousness.

If the theme of deliverance is important, the certainty of judgment is the main point of this section as a refutation of the false teachers' objection to Christian eschatology, and so the section ends on that note. The OT examples show that judgment comes especially on those who allow themselves to be dominated by sensual desires, and who, in ignoring the Lord's commandments, treat his moral authority with contempt. Since these are the two categories of sin to which vv 1–2 referred, the implication is plain that the false teachers and their followers incur the same judgment.

Denunciation of the False Teachers (a) (2:10b–16)

Bibliography

Abbott, E. A. "On the Second Epistle of St. Peter. II. Had the Author read St. Jude?" *Exp* 2/3 (1882) 142–48. **Bishop, E. F. F.** *Apostles,* 218–21. **Farrar, F. W.** "Dr Abbott on the Second Epistle of St. Peter." *Exp* 2/3 (1882) 415–18. **Reicke, B.** *Diakonie, Festfreude und Zelos in Verbindung mit der altchristlichen Agapenfeier.* UUÅ 1951:5. Uppsala: A. B. Lundequistska/ Wiesbaden: O. Harrassotwitz, 1951. 352–67. **Sickenberger, J.** "Engels- oder Teufelslästerer im Judasbriefe (8–10) und 2. Petrusbriefe (2, 10–12)?" *Festschrift zur Jahrhundertfeier der Universität zu Breslau,* ed. T. Siebs = *MSGVK* 13–14 (1911–12) 621–39. **Skehan, P. W.** "A note on 2 Peter 2,13." *Bib* 41 (1960) 69–71. **Vermes, G.** "The story of Balaam—The scriptural origin of Haggadah." *Scripture and Tradition in Judaism: Haggadic Studies.* SPB 4. Leiden: E. J. Brill, 1961. 127–77.

Translation

10b *These reckless and headstrong people are not afraid to insult* [a] *the glorious*
ones, 11 *whereas angels, although they are greater in strength and power, do not use*
insults when pronouncing judgment on them from the Lord. [b] 12 *But these people are*
like unreasoning animals, which are born creatures of mere instinct, to be caught
and destroyed. They are ignorant of those whom they insult, but when they are destroyed
they themselves will also perish in the same destruction, 13 *suffering harm* [c] *in reward*
for the harm they have done. For [d] *self-indulgence in broad daylight is their idea of*
enjoyment. They are spots and blemishes, indulging in their deceitful pleasures [e] *while*
they feast with you. 14 *Their eyes are full of adulterous lust and always on the lookout* [f]
for sin. They ensnare unstable people and have hearts well trained in greed. They
are under God's curse. 15 *Leaving the straight way they have gone astray, and have*
followed the way of Balaam the son of Bosor, [g] *who loved the reward of wrongdoing.* [h]
16 *But he was rebuked for his offense: a dumb ass spoke with a human voice and*
restrained the prophet's madness.

Notes

[a] For τρέμειν, "to tremble," with the participle, see BDF §415.

[b] The reading παρὰ κυρίου (P[72] *al*) must be preferred, as the more difficult reading, to the better attested παρὰ κυρίῳ (ℵ B C K P *al*). To avoid attributing the βλάσφημον κρίσιν, "slanderous judgment," to the Lord, scribes either changed παρὰ κυρίου to παρὰ κυρίῳ or omitted the phrase altogether (A *al*). It is true that παρὰ κυρίῳ would make good sense: the angels pronounce judgment before God's judgment seat in the heavenly courtroom. But παρὰ κυρίου is explicable as 2 Peter's equivalent of Jude's Ἐπιτιμήσαι σοι κύριος, "May the Lord rebuke you" (Jude 9; see *Comment* section).

[c] ἀδικούμενοι, "suffering harm" (P[72] ℵ* B P *al*) is preferable to κομιούμενοι, "receiving" (ℵ[c] A C K *al*). Scribes will have changed ἀδικούμενοι to κομιούμενοι to obtain a simpler construction and avoid the apparent attribution of wrongdoing to God.

[d] The participles which follow seem to be loosely dependent on φθαρήσονται, "they will perish" (v 12), presumably as explaining the ἀδικίας ("the harm they have done") for which they will be destroyed.

[e] αὐτῶν shows that the reading ἀπάταις, "deceitful pleasures" ($\mathfrak{p}^{72}$ ℵ A* C K P *al*) is original, and ἀγάπαις, "love-feasts" (A^c B *al*) is an assimilation to Jude 12.

[f] On ἀκαταπάστους (A B *al*) see Mayor, cxcvii–cxcviii; the word is unknown and is doubtless a mistake for ἀκαταπαύστους, "unceasing" (most MSS).

[g] Βοσορ, "Bosor," is by far the best attested reading, but since this form of the name of Balaam's father is not found elsewhere, it has been corrected to the LXX form Βεωρ, "Beor," in a few MSS and versions.

[h] "The reward of wrongdoing" translates the same phrase (μισθὸν ἀδικίας) which is translated "reward for the harm they have done" in v 13. Unfortunately it is impossible in English to translate the phrase in the same way in both vv while also preserving the word-play in v 13 and the intentional ambiguity of the phrase in v 15 (see *Comment* section).

Form/Structure/Setting

The whole passage 2:10b–22 is a loosely structured series of denunciations of the false teachers, which for convenience we can divide after v 16, where there seems to be a slight pause in the rapid flow of accusations.

These vv draw heavily on Jude 8–12:

2 Pet 2	*Jude*
10b. τολμηταὶ αὐθάδεις, δόξας οὐ τρέμουσιν βλασφημοῦντες, 11. ὅπου ἄγγελοι ἰσχύϊ καὶ δυνάμει μείζονες ὄντες οὐ φέρουσιν κατ᾽ αὐτῶν παρὰ κυρίου βλάσφημον κρίσιν.	8. . . . δόξας δὲ βλασφημοῦσιν. 9. Ὁ δὲ Μιχαηλ ὁ ἀρχάγγελος, ὅτε τῷ διαβόλῳ διακρινόμενος διελέγετο περὶ τοῦ Μωϋσέως σώματος, οὐκ ἐτόλμησεν κρίσιν ἐπενεγκεῖν βλασφημίας, ἀλλὰ εἶπεν, Ἐπιτιμήσαι σοι κύριος.
12. οὗτοι δὲ, ὡς ἄλογα ζῷα γεγεννημένα φυσικὰ εἰς ἅλωσιν καὶ φθοράν, ἐν οἷς ἀγνοοῦσιν βλασφημοῦντες, ἐν τῇ φθορᾷ αὐτῶν καὶ φθαρήσονται, 13. ἀδικούμενοι μισθὸν ἀδικίας.	10. οὗτοι δὲ ὅσα μὲν οὐκ οἴδασιν βλασφημοῦσιν, ὅσα δὲ φυσικῶς ὡς τὰ ἄλογα ζῷα ἐπίστανται, ἐν τούτοις φθείρονται.
ἡδονὴν ἡγούμενοι τὴν ἐν ἡμέρᾳ τρυφήν, σπίλοι καὶ μῶμοι ἐντρυφῶντες ἐν ταῖς ἀπάταις αὐτῶν συνευωχούμενοι ὑμῖν	12. Οὗτοι εἰσιν οἱ ἐν ταῖς ἀγάπαις ὑμῶν σπιλάδες συνευωχούμενοι ἀφόβως. . . .
15. καταλείποντες εὐθεῖαν ὁδὸν ἐπλανήθησαν, ἐξακολουθήσαντες τῇ ὁδῷ τοῦ Βαλααμ τοῦ Βοσορ, ὃς μισθὸν ἀδικίας ἠγάπησεν	11. οὐαὶ αὐτοῖς, ὅτι τῇ ὁδῷ τοῦ Καιν ἐπορεύθησαν, καὶ τῇ πλάνῃ τοῦ Βαλααμ μισθοῦ ἐξεχύθησαν, καὶ τῇ ἀντιλογίᾳ τοῦ Κορε ἀπώλοντο.

2 Pet 2	*Jude*
10b. These reckless and headstrong people are not afraid to *insult the glorious ones,*	8. . . . and *slander the glorious ones.*
11. whereas *angel*s, although they are greater in strength and power, do not use insults when pronouncing *judgment* on them from *the Lord.*	9. But when Michael the arch*angel,* in debate with the devil, disputed about the body of Moses, he did not presume to *condemn* him for slander, but said, "May *the Lord* rebuke you!"

12. *But these people are like unreasoning animals,* which are born creatures of mere *instinct,* to be caught and destroyed. They are ignorant of those whom they *insult,* but when they are destroyed they themselves will also *perish* in the same destruction,	10. *But these people slander* whatever they do not understand, while by the things they do understand, *instinct*ively, *like unreasoning animals,* they are *destroyed.*
13. suffering harm in reward for the harm they have done. For self-indulgence in broad daylight is their idea of enjoyment. They are spots and blemishes, indulging *in* their deceitful pleasures *while they feast with* you	12. These are the people *who feast with* you *at* your fellowship meals, without reverence, like dangerous reefs . . . .
15. Leaving the straight way they have gone astray, and have followed *the way of Balaam* the son of Bosor, who loved *the reward* of wrongdoing	11. Woe to them! For they walked in *the way* of Cain, they plunged into *Balaam's* error *for profit,* and through the controversy of Korah they perished.

The author has freely adapted material from Jude to suit his own purposes. He has omitted reference to the story of Michael's dispute with the devil, probably because he and his readers were unfamiliar with the story. He has also omitted Jude's references to Cain and Korah, to concentrate on the single figure of Balaam. Probably this is because he brought in the reference to Balaam to illustrate his opponents' greed (v 14). Cain and Korah were not relevant to this point. Had he known the Jewish tradition which represented Cain as a heretic who denied the reality of eschatological judgment (see *Comment* on Jude 11), a comparison of the false teachers with Cain would have been highly appropriate, but he may not have known this tradition.

It is characteristic of our author's use of Jude that he gets an idea from Jude and then gives it a fresh twist or development of his own (vv 12, 13, 16).

In addition to Jude, the author may be dependent on Jewish haggadic tradition about Balaam (see *Comment* on v 16).

The author's "improvement" of Jude includes some ingenious literary devices: the word-play (paronomasia) *ἀδικούμενοι . . . ἀδικίας* (v 13); *σπίλοι καὶ μῶμοι* (v 13), echoing *ἄσπιλοι καὶ ἀμώμητοι* (3:14); *ἀπάταις* (v 13), an ironic pun on *ἀγάπαις*; the parechesis *παρανομίας . . . παραφρονίαν* (v 16); the paronomasia *ἄφωνον . . . φωνῇ* (v 16).

Comment

10b. *τολμηταὶ αὐθάδεις,* "these reckless and headstrong people." *τόλμα* ("daring, audacity") and *αὐθάδεια* ("arrogance, willfulness") are a natural pair which quite often occur together (*1 Clem.* 30:8, with *θράσος,* "boldness"; Spicq, *Lexicographie,* 160 n. 1). *τολμηταί* (lit. "daring people") was suggested to our author by *οὐκ ἐτόλμησεν* ("did not presume") in Jude 9: where the archangel Michael feared to tread, these fools rush in. *αὐθάδης* (cf. especially

Titus 1:7; *1 Clem.* 1:1; Herm. *Sim.* 9:22:1; *Did.* 3:6; LXX Prov 21:24) means basically "self-willed," with the implications of presumptuousness, arrogance, and obstinacy.

11b. *δόξας οὐ τρέμουσιν βλασφημοῦντες,* [11] *ὅπου ἄγγελοι ἰσχύϊ καὶ δυνάμει μείζονες ὄντες οὐ φέρουσιν κατ᾽ αὐτῶν παρὰ κυρίου βλάσφημον κρίσιν*, "are not afraid to insult the glorious ones, whereas angels, although they are greater in strength and power, do not use insults when pronouncing judgment on them from the Lord." The interpretation of this obscure passage hinges on the meaning of *δόξας* (lit. "glories") and *κατ᾽ αὐτῶν* ("against them").

The possibility that *δόξας* refers to human authorities, ecclesiastical (Bigg, Green) or civil (Luther, Calvin, Reicke), can be ruled out at once, for it can make no good sense of v 11. We must take *δόξας*, as in Jude 8, to refer to angelic powers. In that case there are two possible interpretations. Either (a) *δόξας* are evil angels and *κατ᾽ αὐτῶν* refers to these *δόξας* (so most commentators); or (b) *δόξας* are good angels, identical with the *ἄγγελοι*, and *κατ᾽ αὐτῶν* refers to the false teachers (Sickenberger, "Engels"; Wand; also Neyrey, *Polemic,* 138–42, who holds that v 11 gives the false teachers' own blasphemous statement about the angels). In the first case, the false teachers are accused of insulting devils—something which not even the angels do. In the second case, they are accused of insulting angels, and this behavior is contrasted with that of the angels toward the false teachers.

In Jude 8, *δόξας* ("glories") are good angels (see *Comment*), but this cannot determine the meaning of our author, who could have misunderstood or reinterpreted Jude. Since the false teachers opposed by Jude are not the same as those opposed in 2 Peter, there is no reason why the same accusation should be made in Jude 8–9 and 2 Pet 2:10b–11. The most natural reading of v 11 is that the *ἄγγελοι* ("angels") are to be distinguished from the *δόξαι* ("glories"), and that *κατ᾽ αὐτῶν* ("against them") refers back to *δόξας*, which must therefore designate evil angels.

This reading of v 11 is supported by its relationship to Jude 9. The true significance of Jude 9 depends on a knowledge of the apocryphal story to which it alludes (see *Comment* on Jude 9). Probably the author of 2 Peter did not know the story, and therefore he misunderstood the point of Jude 9, in the same way in which many modern commentators have misunderstood it. He thought the story of Michael and the devil must be intended as an example of an angel's respect for the devil, contrasting with the false teachers' disrespect for the *δόξας* (Jude 8). This implied that the *δόξας* were, or at least included, evil angels, of whom the devil is one. Not wishing to baffle his readers with Jude's obscure allusion to the story of Michael and the devil but wishing to retain what he took to be its significance, the author of 2 Peter substituted a general reference to the behavior of angels. For Jude's *ὁ Μιχαηλ ὁ ἀρχάγγελος* ("Michael the archangel") he wrote *ἄγγελοι* ("angels"), and for Jude's *τῷ διαβόλῳ* ("the devil") he wrote *αὐτῶν* ("them"), referring back to *δόξας* ("the glorious ones"). He also took Jude's *κρίσιν βλασφημίας*, as someone who did not know the story most naturally would, to mean "a reviling judgment," and accordingly wrote *βλάσφημον κρίσιν* ("a reviling judgment"). His *παρὰ κυρίου* ("from the Lord") replaces the words of Michael in Jude 9 (Ἐπιτιμήσαι σοι κύριος, "May the Lord rebuke you!"), which he took to indicate that Michael pronounced God's judgment on the devil, while avoiding insulting language.

The phrase *ἰσχύϊ καὶ δυνάμει μείζονες ὄντες* ("although they are greater in strength and power") compares the angels either (a) with the *δόξας* ("glorious ones"), or (b) with the false teachers. Either would make good sense: (a) Even the angels, who are more powerful than the devils, do not insult them. How foolhardy of the false teachers, who are less powerful than the devils, to do so! (b) The false teachers venture to insult the devils, whereas even the angels, who are so much more powerful than the false teachers, do not do so. It is probably slightly more natural to read the phrase in sense (a) (in which case both *μείζονες* ("greater") and *αὐτῶν* ("them") refer back to *δόξας*), but the general significance is the same in either case. What is important to notice is that this phrase implies that the false teachers are being rebuked for ignoring the *power* of the *δόξας* ("glorious ones"). The same implication is to be found in *οὐ τρέμουσιν* ("are not afraid," v 10b). The *δόξαι* ("glorious ones") are powerful beings whom the false teachers ought to be afraid of insulting. Since *οὐ τρέμουσιν* ("are not afraid") and *ἰσχύϊ καὶ δυνάμει μείζονες ὄντες* ("although they are greater in strength and power") are not borrowed from Jude, but have been added in the author's redaction of Jude, it is clear that this was the particular point he was intending to make.

The significance of the false teachers' behavior toward the powers of evil is also clarified by the two terms (*τολμηταὶ αὐθάδεις*, "reckless and headstrong people") with which the author has so emphatically introduced this sentence. The arrogant audacity of the false teachers is seen in the fact that they dare to abuse the powers of evil.

This accusation must correspond to some real characteristic of 2 Peter's opponents. If the author had not thought the material in Jude 8c–9 relevant to his polemic against his own opponents he could have simply omitted it, as he omitted other parts of Jude. Moreover, he has redacted it, not only to eliminate the obscure reference to Michael's dispute with the devil, but also to emphasize the arrogant audacity of the false teachers. He has clearly adapted Jude's material deliberately for use in his own attack on his own opponents.

It is not likely that the false teachers slandered the angelic guardians of the Law (as Jude's opponents did) or that, as Gnostics, they reviled the demiurge and his angels. In these cases the author of 2 Peter would have regarded the *δόξαι* ("glorious ones") as good angels, whereas in fact he seems to share his opponents' view of them as evil angels. The most plausible view is that in their confident immorality the false teachers were contemptuous of the demonic powers. When they were rebuked for their immoral behavior and warned of the danger of falling into the power of the devil and sharing his condemnation, they laughed at the idea, denying that the devil could have any power over them and speaking of the powers of evil in skeptical, mocking terms. They may have doubted the very existence of supernatural powers of evil. This explanation has the advantage of accounting for 2 Peter's redactional emphasis on the false teachers' foolhardy disregard for the power and might of the *δόξαι* ("glorious ones"). It is also consistent with the general attitude of skeptical rationalism which seems to characterize the opponents' stance.

As an explanation of Jude 8c, this interpretation was rejected in the commentary on Jude, because neither *δόξαι* nor *βλασφημεῖν*, "to slander," are appropriate terms for a contemptuous attitude to evil angels. This objection, however, has much less force in the case of 2 Pet 2:10b, where the terms have not been used spontaneously but have been taken over from Jude.

12. *ὡς ἄλογα ζῷα γεγεννημένα φυσικὰ εἰς ἅλωσιν καὶ φθοράν*, "like unreasoning animals, which are born creatures of mere instinct, to be caught and destroyed." The author has borrowed *ἄλογα ζῷα . . . φυσικά*, "unreasoning animals . . . creatures of mere instinct," from Jude 10, but has expanded the comparison. The false teachers are like animals not only in their irrationality, but also in being destined for destruction. The idea that certain animals were born to be slaughtered and eaten was common in the ancient world (Juvenal 1.141; Pliny, *Hist. Nat.* 8.81; *b. B. Meṣ.* 85a). *φθορά* here must mean "destruction" (not "corruption") and this determines the sense of *φθορᾷ . . . φθαρήσονται*, "destruction . . . they will perish," later in the v.

ἐν οἷς ἀγνοοῦσιν βλασφημοῦντες, lit. "insulting those of whom they are ignorant." In classical Greek *βλασφημεῖν* is followed by *εἰς* (as in Mark 3:29), *περί* or *κατά*, but in the NT usually by the accusative (as in 2 Pet 2:10). However, the Koine sometimes uses *ἐν* for *εἰς*, and so probably *ἐν οἷς* is here simply the object of the opponents' insults. It is usually taken to represent *ἐν τούτοις ἅ* ("[in] those things which," "[in] matters which"), but could (with Spitta) be taken to represent *ἐν τούτοις οὕς* ("those whom"), with reference to the *δόξαι* (v 10; the masculine *οἷς* is natural in spite of the fact that *δόξαι* is feminine). It is true that the underlying phrase in Jude has an indefinite neuter object (*ὅσα μὲν οὐκ οἴδασιν βλασφημοῦσιν*), but this is required in Jude for the sake of the parallel with the contrasting phrase which follows (*ὅσα δὲ φυσικῶς ὡς τὰ ἄλογα ζῷα ἐπίστανται*). Since the author of 2 Peter has not reproduced this parallelism, he did not need to follow Jude in giving *βλασφημοῦντες* a neuter object. From the context in 2 Peter alone, it seems more natural to give *ἐν οἷς* a personal reference, continuing the thought of v 10. If the false teachers understood how powerful the evil angels really are, they would not scoff at them.

There is no need to see *ἀγνοοῦσιν* ("are ignorant") as a polemical reference to the opponents' claim to *gnosis.* In fact, in rewriting Jude 10, our author has reduced the stress on the theme of knowledge, as he would not have done if he were countering Gnostic claims. Instead he has put the emphasis on the coming judgment of the false teachers, in line with his general apologetic concern to counter their denial of divine retribution.

ἐν τῇ φθορᾷ αὐτῶν καὶ φθαρήσονται, "but when they are destroyed they themselves will also perish in the same destruction." This clause has been understood in a variety of ways: (1) Reicke takes *ἐν τῇ φθορᾷ* with *βλασφημοῦντες*, and translates from *ἐν οἷς* onward as: "by those whom they do not recognize, but defame in their corruption, they will also be destroyed." But a connection between *φθορᾷ* and *φθαρήσονται* must be intended. Furthermore, Reicke's translation depends on his view that the *δόξαι* are the civil magistrates.

(2) "They will quite certainly destroy themselves by their own work of

destruction" (JB; similarly RV, Wand). But this active sense of φθορᾷ is not the most natural.

(3) They "shall utterly perish in their own corruption" (AV; Plumptre).

(4) In their own destruction they shall be destroyed—i.e. a Hebraism conveying emphasis (cf. 3:3: ἐν ἐμπαιγμονῇ ἐμπαῖκται, "scoffers with scoffing") (so James, Green). The author of 2 Peter would be familiar with similar phrases in the LXX (e.g. Exod 18:18: φθορᾷ καταφθαρήσῃ, "you will be destroyed with destruction"; Isa 24:3: φθορᾷ φθαρήσεται, "it will be destroyed with destruction"; Mic 2:10: διεφθάρητε φθορᾷ, "you have been destroyed with destruction"). But in this case αὐτῶν seems redundant. Moreover, (2), (3) and (4) are obliged to give καί the unnatural sense of "certainly," rather than its expected sense "also."

(5) They "will be destroyed in the same destruction with them," i.e. the animals (RSV; similarly NEB, NIV). The majority of modern commentators take αὐτῶν to refer to ζῷα ("animals"). Some of them then interpret the clause as meaning that in the coming eschatological destruction of the world animals and ungodly people will perish together, as they did in the Flood (Windisch, Schrage). But most interpret it as meaning that the false teachers will suffer a destruction similar (in its suddenness and violence, or in its finality) to the slaughter of animals by hunters (Bigg, Mayor, Chaine, Schelkle, Sidebottom, Kelly, Grundmann; Fornberg, *Early Church,* 46).

(6) They will be destroyed together with the evil angels whom they insult (Spitta, Senior). οἷς is the nearest antecedent for αὐτῶν and so, if it is correct to take οἷς as masculine, referring to the evil angels (see above), this interpretation becomes the most natural. The false teachers will share the fate of the powers of evil who will be eliminated at the day of judgment. The objection that this interpretation destroys the connection between the first φθορά, "destruction," in this v (that of the animals) and the second (Mayor) is not valid. The comparison of the false teachers' fate with that of the animals has already been made in the first part of the v and does not need to be repeated in the phrase ἐν τῇ φθορᾷ αὐτῶν. This phrase introduces a second comparison, with the fate of the evil angels.

13. ἀδικούμενοι μισθὸν ἀδικίας, "suffering harm in reward for the harm they have done." Skehan (*Bib* 41 [1960] 69–71; followed by Spicq) places a colon after ἀδικούμενοι, and takes μισθὸν ἀδικίας with ἡδονὴν ἡγούμενοι, translating: ". . . in their corruption will suffer the harm of being corrupted. They, who think that the wages of iniquity is pleasure . . ." But (1) if φθαρήσονται means, as it must, "will be destroyed," it hardly needs the addition of ἀδικούμενοι; (2) the play on words, ἀδικούμενοι and ἀδικίας, must be intentional.

If ἀδικούμενοι μισθὸν ἀδικίας constitutes a phrase, there are two possible interpretations: (1) "being defrauded of the profits of their evil-doing" (Wand, Moffatt, Reicke, Green; Fornberg, *Early Church,* 46; Moffatt's translation attempts to render the play on words: "done out of the profits of their evil-doing"). The meaning "defraud" for ἀδικεῖν is attested in the papyri (Moulton and Milligan, *Vocabulary, s.v.*), though not this use of the accusative (of respect?) μισθόν with it. The advantage of this interpretation is that it gives μισθὸν ἀδικίας the same sense as it has in v 15, i.e. the profit which the false teachers expected to get from their iniquity. However, it may be doubted whether this sense is the one which a reader would naturally give the phrase in this context. It is true that Acts 1:18 uses μισθὸς τῆς ἀδικίας, "reward of wrongdoing," of the money Judas received for his betrayal of Jesus, but this is clear from the context. In *Diogn.* 9:2, ὁ μισθὸς αὐτῆς (sc. τῆς ἀδικίας), "its (i.e., wrongdoing's) reward," and in *Barn.* 4:12 μισθὸς τῆς πονηρίας, "the reward of wickedness" refer to the punishment due to iniquity (cf. also Rev 22:12; *1 Clem.* 34:3; *Barn.* 21:3), and this seems the more obvious sense in 2 Pet 2:13. It may be that in v 15 also, while the primary reference must be to the money Balaam expected to be paid for his evil-doing, there is a secondary ironic reference to the reward he would receive at the hands of divine justice (see below). (2) "suffering the recompense for their wrong-doing" (so, essentially, Mayor, Chaine, Schelkle, Kelly, Grundmann). ἀδικεῖν ("to wrong, injure") can take two accusatives, of the person injured and the injury done, but the latter is normally restricted to τι (Phlm 18), οὐδέν (Acts 25:10; Gal 4:12; *Mart. Pol.* 9:3) and ἀδίκημα. It is, however, credible that the author should have somewhat strained normal usage in order to achieve his play on words, which embodies an example of eschatological *jus talionis:* the false teachers will suffer *wrong* (ἀδικούμενοι) in recompense for the *wrong* they have done (ἀδικίας). However, since ἀδικεῖν can mean simply "to harm" (passive in this sense: Wis 14:29; 3 Macc 3:8; Rev 2:11), there is no attribution of *wrong*doing to God. Unfortunately, in English it is impossible to translate ἀδικούμενοι with a morally neutral term and ἀδικίας with a morally pejorative term, while retaining the play on words.

ἡδονὴν ἡγούμενοι τὴν ἐν ἡμέρᾳ τρυφήν, "self-indulgence in broad daylight is their idea of enjoyment." τρυφή (elsewhere in NT only in Luke 7:25) can have a good sense ("delight": *2 Clem.* 10:4; Herm. *Sim.* 6:5:7), but is frequent in Hermas in the sense of "self-indulgence" (see especially *Sim.* 6:5:5 for a definition), and can be associated with drunkenness and other forms of sensuality (Herm. *Mand.* 6:2:5; 8:3; 12:2:1). Most commentators agree that ἐν ἡμέρᾳ is best taken to mean "in the daylight" (cf. 3 Macc 5:11; John 11:9b; Rom 13:13). Drinking or feasting in the daytime was a standard mark of degeneracy (Eccl 10:16; Isa 5:11; *T. Mos.* 7:4; Juvenal 1.103).

It is not clear whether this phrase already refers to the agapes, which are the subject of the rest of the verse (as Grundmann holds). The verbal link between τρυφήν ("self-indulgence") and ἐντρυφῶντες ("indulging") would suggest that it does. But we do not know whether the agapes were held in daylight hours at this period (as they were by the time of Hippolytus, to avoid scandal: *Apost. Trad.* 26).

σπίλοι καὶ μῶμοι, "spots and blemishes." This phrase is the author's substitute for Jude's σπιλάδες ("dangerous reefs"), which perhaps puzzled him as it has puzzled many modern commentators. Like some of them he may have thought Jude really meant σπίλοι ("spots"). His "improvement" of Jude is in its own way very apt, for it is in contrast to his own description of what the church must aim to be at the Parousia: ἄσπιλοι καὶ ἀμώμητοι ("without spot or blemish": 3:14). The latter was probably a fixed liturgical or paraenetic phrase (see references in *Comment* on 3:14) and so the readers of 2 Peter would readily see the point of describing the false teachers as "spots and blemishes" in the church. Like the blemishes on an animal not fit for sacrifice

(Lev 1:3) or on a man not fit for priestly service (Lev 21:21), these immoral people were frustrating the church's aim of holiness and could make the church unfit to be presented as a sacrifice to God.

ἐντρυφῶντες ἐν ταῖς ἀπάταις αὐτῶν συνεωχούμενοι ὑμῖν, "indulging in their deceitful pleasures while they feast with you." ἐντρυφᾶν ἔν τινι (in a good sense: LXX Isa 55:2; Herm. *Mand.* 10:3:1) means "to delight in, indulge in something." ἀπάτη ("deceit") had also come to mean "pleasure," especially sinful pleasures which entice people with an illusion of enjoyment (Spicq, *Lexicographie,* 116–18). Hermas often associates τρυφή and ἀπάτη (*Mand.* 11:12; *Sim.* 6:2:1–2, 4; 6:4:4; 6:5:1, 3–4, 6), and τρυφᾶν and ἀπατᾶν (*Sim.* 6:4:1; 6:5:3), as almost interchangeable terms (see especially *Sim.* 6:5:6). Thus, especially against the background of the Roman Christianity to which both Hermas and 2 Peter belong, the phrase ἐντρυφῶντες ἐν ταῖς ἀπάταις αὐτῶν ("indulging in their deceitful pleasures") is a very natural and readily intelligible one.

However, it must also be noticed that ἐν ταῖς ἀπάταις αὐτῶν συνευωχούμενοι ὑμῖν is evidently based on Jude's words ἐν ταῖς ἀγάπαις ὑμῶν . . . συνευωχούμενοι, "eating with you at your fellowship meals" (Jude 12). Although confusion of ἀπάταις and ἀγάπαις would have been a very easy scribal error, the change of pronouns makes it unlikely that the variant reading ἀγάπαις in 2 Peter is correct, or that the copy of Jude used by the author of 2 Peter already had the corrupt reading ἀπάταις. The author of 2 Peter must have made a deliberate alteration. It is possible that he wished to exclude any reference to the agapes (Schrage), but in that case it is odd that he has done so by substituting the similar-sounding ἀπάταις for ἀγάπαις. The suggestion that he intended a deliberate pun is more likely, and he might have expected his readers to see the pun (συνευωχούμενοι ὑμῖν, "while they feast with you," would naturally suggest the agapes) even if they were not familiar with Jude's letter. The meals which were defiled by the gluttonous and riotous behavior of the false teachers could not be called ἀγάπαι, but they might be called "deceits" (the basic meaning of ἀπάταις).

The αὐτῶν ("their") does not imply that the false teachers hosted their own meals (Windisch), because ἀπάταις primarily means "pleasures," and only as a punning overtone alludes to the meals. The author had to change Jude's ὑμῶν ("your") to αὐτῶν ("their") when he changed ἀγάπαις to ἀπάταις, and made it part of the phrase ἐντρυφῶντες ἐν ταῖς ἀπάταις αὐτῶν ("indulging in their deceitful pleasures"). But he added ὑμῖν ("with you," not in Jude) to make it clear that he was talking about the common meals of the church.

14. ὀφθαλμοὺς ἔχοντες μεστοὺς μοιχαλίδος, lit. "They have eyes full of an adulteress": a vivid expression which means that their eyes are always looking for a woman with whom to commit adultery. There was a well-known rhetorical tag according to which the shameless man does not have κόρας ("pupils" or "maidens"—a pun) in his eyes, but πόρνας ("harlots": Plutarch, *Mor.* 528E; the reverse, of a chaste man, is attributed to Timaeus (4th century B.C.) in Pseudo-Longinus, *De sub.* 4.5). It is possible that our author echoes this saying, as he does other well-known sayings (2:19, 22).

δελεάζοντες ψυχὰς ἀστηρίκτους, "they ensnare unstable people." The verb means "to entice with a bait," a metaphor from fishing and snaring (used in a similar way by Philo, *Praem.* 25). ψυχάς (lit. "souls") is here virtually "people" (cf. Acts 2:41; 1 Pet 3:20). The "unstable" are those not firmly grounded in Christian teaching, who are easily led astray; see *Comment* on 1:12.

καρδίαν γεγυμνασμένην πλεονεξίας ἔχοντες, "they have hearts well trained in greed." *γεγυμνασμένην* (lit. "trained," a metaphor from athletics) contrasts with *ἀστηρίκτους* ("unstable"). Unlike their inexperienced pupils the false teachers are experts—in greed! They make disciples in order to make a profit out of them (cf. 2:3a).

κατάρας τέκνα, lit. "children of a curse," is a "Hebraism," which the author has probably formed by analogy with similar phrases in the LXX (Isa 57:4: *τέκνα ἀπωλείας*, "children of destruction"; Hos 10:9: *τέκνα ἀδικίας*, "children of wrongdoing") and in Christian usage (Eph 2:3; 5:8; 1 Pet 1:14; *Barn.* 7:1; 9:7; 21:9; Ign. *Phld.* 2:1; and cf. Deissmann, *Bible Studies,* 161–66). It means simply that the false teachers are under God's curse (cf. Sir 41:9–10).

It is impossible to tell whether this exclamation is intended to conclude the preceding denunciations or to introduce the following. If the idea derives from Deut 11:26, 28 (Fornberg, *Early Church,* 102–3), then it connects with v 15a (cf. Deut 11:28).

15. *καταλείποντες εὐθεῖαν ὁδὸν ἐπλανήθησαν*, "leaving the straight way they have gone astray." This idea was suggested by Jude's *τῇ πλάνῃ τοῦ Βαλααμ* ("Balaam's error," Jude 11). For the use of phrases with "way" to designate Christianity in 2 Peter, see *Comment* on 2:2. The metaphorical use of "straight way" for the path of obedience to God was common (*ὁδὸς εὐθεία*: LXX 1 Kgdms 12:23; Ps 106:7; Prov 2:16; Isa 33:15; *1 Clem.* 7:3; *ὁδοὶ εὐθειαί*: LXX: Prov 2:13; Hos 14:10; Acts 13:10; *ὁδὸς ὀρθή*: Herm. *Mand.* 6:1:2; Philo, *Det.* 22; *Agr.* 101; *via recta: Act. Verc.* 6; cf. also *2 Enoch* 42:10), while "leaving" and "going astray" were obvious metaphors to use with it (LXX Deut 11:28: *πλανηθῆτε ἀπὸ τῆς ὁδοῦ ἧς ἀνετειλάμεν ὑμῖν*, "you go astray from the way which I commanded you"; Prov 2:13: *οἱ ἐγκαταλείποντες ὁδοὺς εὐθείας*, "those who forsake the straight ways"; 21:16: *πλανώμενος ἐξ ὁδοῦ δικαιοσύνης*, "going astray from the way of righteousness"; Wis 5:6: *ἐπλανήθημεν ἀπὸ ὁδοῦ ἀληθείας*, "we strayed from the way of truth"; Philo, *Det.* 22: "they have gone astray (*πεπλανημένοι*) because of their inability to see clearly the straight way (*τὴν ὀρθὴν ὁδὸν*)"; *Apoc. Pet.* A 34: *οἱ ἀφέντες τὴν ὁδὸν τοῦ θεοῦ*, "those who forsook the way of God"; cf. also *Apoc. Pet.* B; 1QS 10:20–21; CD 1:13; 2:6; Jas 5:19–20; *Did* 6:1).

ἐξακολουθήσαντες τῇ ὁδῷ τοῦ Βαλααμ τοῦ Βοσορ, "they followed the way of Balaam the son of Bosor." The idea of Balaam's "way" (*ὁδός*) is borrowed from Jude 11, which speaks of Cain's "way" (*τῇ ὁδῷ τοῦ Καιν*), but the author of 2 Peter may also have in mind the emphasis on Balaam's "way" (*ὁδός*), both literal (Num 22:23 LXX) and metaphorical (Num 22:32 LXX), in Num 22:21–35, the passage to which v 16 refers. The false teachers are Balaam's followers on the road of disobedience to God for the sake of financial profit.

Βοσορ, "Bosor," is an otherwise unattested form of the name of Balaam's father Beor (בעור, LXX *Βεωρ*). Zahn (*Introduction,* 292) suggested that it reflects Peter's Galilean pronunciation. A more plausible suggestion is that the form reflects a Jewish tradition of a play on the name and the word בשר ("flesh"). Balaam's immoral character would be indicated by calling him "son of flesh" (so already Luther; Wettstein; Vitringa, cited by Bigg). Although this explanation of the name is not known from Jewish sources, a rather similar explanation connected בעור ("Beor") with בעיר ("beasts") in order to accuse Balaam of bestiality (*b. Sanh.* 105a).

ὃς μισθὸν ἀδικίας ἠγάπησεν, "who loved the reward of wrongdoing." For Balaam's greed and reward in Jewish tradition, see *Comment* on Jude 11. To Jude's μισθοῦ ("reward") the author of 2 Peter has added ἀδικίας ("of wrongdoing"), probably to repeat the phrase already used in v 13. Literally, the μισθὸν ἀδικίας, "reward of wrongdoing," is the money Balaam expected to receive from Balak for cursing Israel and for his evil advice (cf. Acts 1:18, where μισθὸς τῆς ἀδικίας is the money Judas received for betraying Jesus). But by using this phrase (cf. *Diogn.* 9:2; *Barn.* 4:12) the author probably intends an ironical secondary reference to the recompense which Balaam would receive for his iniquity from God's justice. Jewish exegetes implied a similar irony when they explained that Balaam was killed with the Midianite kings (Num 31:8) because he had gone to them to receive his reward (*b. Sanh.* 106a; *Num. Rab.* 22:5; and especially *Sip̱re Num.* 157: the Israelites "killed Balaam son of Beor with the sword. The Israelites paid him his full salary and did not deprive him"; cf. Neyrey, *Polemic,* 92–93; Philo, *Mut.* 203).

16. ὑποζύγιον ἄφωνον ἐν ἀνθρώπου φωνῇ φθεγξάμενον ἐκώλυσεν τὴν τοῦ προφήτου παραφρονίαν, "a dumb ass spoke with a human voice and restrained the prophet's madness." In the ancient world animals were called mute because they do not speak language (Horace, *Sat.* 1.3.100; Tacitus, *Hist.* 4.17). The story of the donkey's speech is told in Num 22:21–35 (and cf. Josephus, *Ant.* 4.109: φωνὴν ἀνθρωπίνην ἀφεῖσα, "cried out with a human voice"). Commentators have often pointed out that there the rebuke is really administered by the angel rather than the ass, who merely complains of ill-treatment. The author of 2 Peter could simply have cited the story rather freely for the sake of the point he wanted to make, but it is likely that he is dependent on Jewish haggadic tradition. The Targums to Num 22:30 (*Frg. Tg., Tg. Ps.-J., Tg. Neof.*) attribute to the donkey a speech in which she rebukes Balaam for his foolishness in supposing that he can curse Israel when he is unable even to curse his donkey.

This targumic tradition also accounts for the mention of Balaam's παραφρονίαν ("madness"): the ass rebukes Balaam for his foolishness (*Tg. Ps.-J.* Num 22:30: "Woe to you, Balaam, you fool!"; *Frg. Tg.* Num 22:30: "You have no understanding and there is no wisdom in you"). The idea of Balaam's foolishness or madness is quite common in the haggadic expansions of the Balaam story (Philo, *Mut.* 203: Balaam died "stabbed by his own madness [φρενοβλαβείας]"; *Mos.* 1.293: when Balaam failed to curse Israel, Balak called him "very foolish" (ἀνοητότατε) and "mad" (φρενοβλαβής) for sacrificing the wealth he could have had as a reward for cursing Israel; cf. also the Aramaic Balaam text from Deir ʿAlla (8th–7th century B.C.), in which it seems that those who reject Balaam's prophecy accuse him of "foolishness and silliness": J. Hoftijzer and G. van der Kooij (eds.), *Aramaic Texts from Deir ʿAlla* [DMOA 11; Leiden: E. J. Brill, 1976] 181, 246–47). It was embodied in an explanation of his father's name (*Tg. Ps-J.* Num 22:5: "the son of Beor, who was insane from the magnitude of his knowledge"; cf. בער, "to be brutish, stupid"), and Philo explained the name "Balaam" as meaning "foolish people" (*μάταιος λαός*: *Cher.* 32; *Conf.* 159; *Mig.* 113; *Det.* 71; cf. *Conf.* 66).

The word *παραφρονίαν* ("madness") is not found elsewhere in extant Greek literature. The author has probably used this form (rather than *παραφροσύνη* or *παραφρόνησις*) for the sake of its assonance with *παρανομία* ("offense"). The two words are closely connected, representing two aspects of Balaam's behavior in Num 22. His transgression was his determination to curse Israel for the sake of financial profit. His madness lay in supposing that he would be able to do so. His greed swayed his judgment and made the crime seem feasible.

That Balaam was in some sense a prophet, in spite of himself, is implied in the OT account of his prophetic blessings on Israel (Num 23–24) and was widely accepted in Jewish tradition (cf. *Tgs. Neof.* and *Ps.-J.* Num 23:7; *Frg. Tg.* Num 23:1; 24:4; *Bib. Ant.* 18:12; Philo, *Mut.* 203; *b. Sanh.* 106a; *Num. Rab.* 20:7, 10). It is mentioned here, no doubt, to enhance the irony: the prophet who should know God's will foolishly failed to perceive it, while a mere donkey uttered a prophetic rebuke. Philo (who avoids mention of the ass's *speech*) perceives a similar irony in the story: "The unreasoning animal (*ἀλόγου ζῴου*) showed a superior power of sight to him who claimed to see not only the world but the world's Maker" (*Mos.* 1.272, Loeb tr.).

It is not likely that by calling Balaam *προφήτου* ("prophet") the author intends to allude to a claim to prophetic inspiration by his opponents, because in that case he would have had to make clear that he saw Balaam as a *false* prophet. As it stands, his statement most naturally reflects the belief that Balaam proved a true prophet against his will.

Why did our author include v 16 (an addition to Jude's reference to Balaam)? Probably because he saw the opportunity of taking up a theme already mentioned in v 12: the false teachers are like *ἄλογα ζῷα* ("unreasoning animals"). The same point is now made with humorous emphasis, by comparing them to Balaam, whose irrational behavior (*παραφρονίαν*) was rebuked by an unreasoning animal speaking in rational speech (cf. Philo, *Mos.* 1.272, quoted above). He was so carried away by his cupidity that even a donkey knew better than he. Similarly the false teachers. That the author intended the donkey to represent his simple Christian readers (Reicke) is much less certain.

Explanation

Having concluded the previous section (v 10a) with a reference to the vices of his opponents, the author now begins a more expansive denunciation of their sins.

He refers first to their arrogant recklessness in speaking contemptuously of the demonic powers. They are brazen in their immoral behavior and take no notice of the danger they run of falling into the grip of the powers of evil and sharing their fate. When they are warned of this danger, they pour scorn on the devil and his forces. The author highlights the foolhardiness of this attitude by pointing out that even the angels, when they pronounce God's judgment on the demons, have a healthy respect for their power and refrain from treating them with contempt. They do so in spite of the fact that they have the strength to master the demons, which the false teachers certainly do not.

Their attitude to the powers of evil is gross stupidity and will lead to their downfall. The author continues his insistence that, despite their denial of eschatological judgment, they are in fact heading for it. He compares them, in their stupidity, with the irrational animals whose natural destiny is to be hunted and slaughtered. Similarly the false teachers, who do not know what they are talking about when they scoff at the powers of evil, are on the way to sharing their fate when all evil is eliminated on the day of judgment. This will be no more than justice.

The author turns to condemn their sensuality. Accustomed to feasting and reveling in broad daylight, they evidently turn even the church's fellowship meals into occasions for self-indulgence. By means of a bitter pun the author implies that in consequence these meals are no longer fit to be called "love-feasts," but only "deceits." When he calls the false teachers "spots and blemishes" on the church's community life, he alludes to the church's aim of becoming a sacrifice fit for offering to God, "without spot or blemish" (3:14), at the Parousia. The immoral behavior of the false teachers is frustrating this aim. After a reference to their sexual lust, and the greed with which they lure immature Christians into their following to make financial profit out of them, the author pronounces them under God's curse.

Their greed prompts comparison with Balaam. Like Balaam the false teachers have wandered from the "straight way" of obedience to God's commandments in their greed for "the reward of wrongdoing." This phrase contains the ironic overtone that, also like Balaam, they will in fact receive their just reward.

Balaam's judgment was swayed by his greed so that he actually thought he could succeed in his plan of opposing God's will. Similarly the false teachers, who deny the reality of God's judgment, foolishly imagine they can sin with impunity. But in Balaam's case even his donkey knew better!

Denunciation of the False Teachers (b) (2:17–22)

Bibliography

Aubineau, M. "La thème du 'bourbier' dans la Littérature grecque profane et chrétienne." *RSR* 33 (1959) 185–214. **Bishop, E. F. F.** *Apostles,* 218–19. **Hemmerdinger-Iliadou, D.** "II Pierre, II, 18 d'après l'Ephrem grec." *RB* 64 (1957) 399–401. **Marshall, I. H.** *Kept by the Power of God: A Study of Perseverance and Falling Away.* London: Epworth Press, 1969. 165–66. **Quacquarelli, A.** "Similitudini sentenze e proverbi in S. Pietro." Associazione Biblica Italiana, *San Pietro,* 425–42. **Wendland, P.** "Ein Wort des Heraklit im Neuen Testament." SPAW.PH (1898) 788–96.

Translation

[17] *These people are wells without water, mists driven by a squall. For them* [a] *the nether gloom of darkness has been reserved.* [18] *For by their high-flown empty talk, with lusts of the flesh and dissolute practices* [b] *they ensnare people who are only just* [c] *escaping* [d] *from those who live in error.* [19] *They promise them freedom, but they themselves are slaves of corruption; for "a man becomes the slave of him who overpowers him."* [20] *For if, having once escaped the pollutions of the world through the knowledge of the* [e] *Lord and Savior Jesus Christ, they are again entangled in them and overpowered by them, "their final state has become worse than the first."*
[21] *For it would have been better for them never to have come to know the way of righteousness than, having come to know it, to turn back from* [f] *the holy commandment which was delivered to them.* [22] *What has happened to them is what the true proverb says, "A dog which returns to its vomit, and a sow which after washing returns to wallow in the mire."*

Notes

[a] οἷς refers to οὗτοι, not to πηγαί and ὁμίχλαι.

[b] σαρκός is probably best taken with ἐπιθυμίαις rather than with ἀσελγείαις (cf. Gal 5:16, 24; Eph 2:3; 1 Pet 2:11; 1 John 2:16; *Did* 1:4). ἀσελγείαις seems to be, rather awkwardly, in apposition to ἐπιθυμίαις. The reading ἀσελγείας (P *al*) is probably an attempt to avoid the awkwardness of the dative here.

[c] ὀλίγως, "just" (P[72] A B *al*) is to be preferred to ὄντως, "really" (א K L P *al*) and ὄντας: see Metzger, *Textual Commentary,* 704. Hemmerdinger-Iliadou (*RB* 64 [1957] 399–401) defends the reading τοὺς λόγους ἀποφεύγοντας τοὺς εὐθεῖς καὶ τοὺς ἐν πλάνῃ ἀναστρεφομένους, found in the Greek version of Ephraim Syrus, but this is not really a superior reading in the context (which deals with apostasy: vv 20–22) and is easily explained as an attempt to make sense of a text which had λόγους, "words," by mistake for ὀλίγως, "just."

[d] The present participle ἀποφεύγοντας is better attested than the aorist ἀποφύγοντας (K L P), which could be the result of assimilation to v 20.

[e] It is difficult to know whether or not to read ἡμῶν (after κυρίου: P[72] א A C P and most MSS). The expression occurs with ἡμῶν in 1:11; 3:18; without ἡμῶν in 3:2. It could have been omitted by mistake (in B K *al*) or added from the more familiar form of the expression.

[f] ὑποστρέψαι ἐκ (P[72] B C P *al*) is the best attested reading, but ἐπιστρέψαι (K L *al*) or εἰς τὰ ὀπίσω ἀνακάμψαι ἀπό (א A *al*), which looks like an explanatory gloss, would make little difference to the meaning.

Form/Structure/Setting

In the first part of this section the author continues to draw inspiration from Jude:

2 Pet 2	*Jude*
17. οὗτοί εἰσιν πηγαὶ ἄνυδροι καὶ ὁμίχλαι ὑπο λαίλαπος ἐλαυνόμεναι,	12. Οὗτοί εἰσιν . . . νεφέλαι ἄνυδροι ὑπὸ ἀνέμων παραφερόμεναι, δένδρα φθινοπωρινὰ ἄκαρπα δὶς ἀποθανόντα ἐκριζωθέντα, 13. κύματα ἄγρια θαλάσσης ἐπαφρίζοντα τὰς ἑαυτῶν αἰσχύνας, ἀστέρες
οἷς ὁ ζόφος τοῦ σκότους τετήρηται.	πλανῆται, οἷς ὁ ζόφος τοῦ σκότους εἰς αἰῶνα τετήρηται . . . .
18. ὑπέρογκα γὰρ ματαιότητος φθεγγόμενοι δελεάζουσιν ἐν ἐπιθυμίαις σαρκὸς ἀσελγείαις τοὺς ὀλίγως ἀποφεύγοντας τοὺς ἐν πλάνῃ ἀναστρεφομένους.	16. Οὗτοί εἰσιν γογγυσταὶ μεμψίμοιροι, κατὰ τὰς ἐπιθυμίας αὐτῶν πορευόμενοι, καὶ τὸ στόμα αὐτῶν λαλεῖ ὑπέρογκα . . . .

2 Pet 2	*Jude*
17. *These people are* wells *without water,* mists driven *by* a squall.	12. *These people are* . . . clouds blown along *by* the wind *without giving rain;* autumnal trees bearing no fruit, dead twice over, uprooted; 13. wild waves of the sea casting up the foam of their abominations;
For them the nether gloom of darkness has been reserved.	wandering stars *for whom the nether gloom of darkness has been reserved* for ever . . . .
18. For by their *high-flown,* empty talk, with *lusts* of the flesh and dissolute practices they ensnare people who are only just escaping from those who live in error.	16. These people are discontented murmurers, who follow their own *desires.* Their mouths utter *arrogant words* . . . .

The omission of the rest of the metaphors in Jude 12–13 is probably because the author of 2 Peter, having expanded the first of Jude's metaphors into two, felt the rest to be redundant. But it leaves the last clause of 2:17 without the special appropriateness it has in Jude. Another effect is to eliminate the allusions to *1 Enoch* in Jude 12–13, but this must be accidental. If the author of 2 Peter objected to allusions to *1 Enoch* on principle, he is unlikely to have been sufficiently familiar with *1 Enoch* to detect the allusions in Jude 12–13.

The omission of Jude's explicit quotation from *1 Enoch* (Jude 14–15) may, however, indicate that the author of 2 Peter and/or his readers were not familiar with the book (see Introduction, section 2 of *Literary Relationships*). On the other hand, the author of 2 Peter is not in this section concerned with *prophecies* of the false teachers and their doom, as Jude was when he quoted from *1 Enoch* 1:9; it is possible that the author of 2 Peter simply found the quotation irrelevant to his purpose.

After 2:18, he leaves aside Jude until 3:2, probably because he wanted to include a fuller and more explicit treatment of the false teachers' *apostasy* than he found in Jude. A notable feature of 2:19–22 is its reliance on proverbial material. Verse 19b quotes a current proverb (see *Comment*); v 20b quotes a saying of Jesus, but one with a proverbial ring to it; v 21 is cast in the proverbial form of the *Tobspruch* (a saying expressing the idea "better . . . than": see below), perhaps on the model of sayings of Jesus; and v 22 explicitly quotes a proverb (*παροιμίας*).

The saying of Jesus quoted in v 20b occurs in identical words in Matt 12:45 and Luke 11:26, and so it is impossible to tell whether the author is dependent on either of these Gospels or on their common source (Q) or on oral tradition.

The two sayings in v 22, which derive originally from Prov 26:11 and the proverb in *Aḥikar* 8:15/18 (see *Comment*), seem to be cited as a single proverb and were probably already combined in this form in a source on which 2 Peter depends. Since one saying is biblical and the other oriental, the source was most likely a Jewish Hellenistic work, perhaps a collection of proverbs (so Bigg; cf. Olivier, "Correction," 147–48). Bigg (228) suggests that this work could have been in iambic verse, which might account for the rare words *ἐξέραμα* ("vomit") and *κύλισμα* ("wallowing"). However, since the author of 2 Peter is himself fond of obscure terms and somewhat poetic rhythms and effects, we cannot be sure that he has not rewritten his source.

2:21 is a "better . . . than" saying. Such sayings (sometimes known as *Tobsprüche:* see G. F. Snyder, "The *Tobspruch* in the New Testament," *NTS* 23 [1976–77] 117–20) are found in OT Wisdom literature (e.g. Prov 15:16, 17; Eccl 7:1, 2, 5), but NT examples are closer in form and function to those found in rabbinic literature (e.g. *b. Ketub.* 67b: "It would be better for a man to throw himself into a fiery furnace than publicly to put his neighbor to shame"; cf. *b. Šabb.* 56b).

The form of the saying in 2 Pet 2:21 corresponds with that of other early Christian *Tobsprüche:* (1) *κρεῖττον* is found in 1 Cor 7:9; 1 Pet 3:17; *1 Clem.* 46:8 (cf. LXX Prov 16:19, 32); (2) the personal pronoun in the dative is normal (Matt 5:29, 30; 18:6, 8, 9; 26:24; Mark 9:42; 14:21; *1 Clem.* 46:8; Ign. *Rom.* 6:1); (3) the particle *ἤ* is frequently used (Matt 18:8, 9; Mark 9: 43, 45, 47; 1 Cor 7:9; 1 Pet 3:17; *1 Clem.* 46:8; 51:3; Ign. *Rom.* 6:1).

Though the precise function of NT examples varies, they are often, like rabbinic examples, admonitory, designed to emphasize the heinousness of a certain course of action. In function, the examples closest to 2 Pet 2:21 are Mark 9:42 (par. Luke 17:2; Matt 18:6) and Mark 14:21 (par. Matt 26:14). These two Jesus *logia* are quoted together and applied to those who are creating factions in the Corinthian church in *1 Clem.* 46:8, which also gives them a more complete *Tobspruch* form (*καλὸν ἦν αὐτῷ . . . ἤ . . .* , "it were good for him . . . rather than . . ."; *κρεῖττον ἦν αὐτῷ . . . ἤ . . .* "it were better for him . . . than . . .") like that used in 2 Pet 2:21. It therefore seems possible that the saying in 2 Pet 2:21 was in fact modeled on these Jesus *logia,* either in a tradition on which the author of 2 Peter draws or by the author himself.

Comment

17. *πηγαὶ ἄνυδροι καὶ ὁμίχλαι ὑπὸ λαίλαπος ἐλαυνόμεναι,* "wells without water, mists driven by a squall." The author has expanded Jude's phrase "waterless clouds blown along by the wind" (*νεφέλαι ἄνυδροι ὑπὸ ἀνέμων παραφερόμεναι,* Jude 12) into two distinct images. Perhaps he objected to "waterless clouds" because all clouds in fact carry water. Perhaps the feature of Palestinian weather to which Jude refers was less familiar to a writer resident in Italy (but cf. Virgil, *Georg.* 3.197). In any case, he has substituted two equally effective metaphors. The dried up spring or well is a "bitter symbol of disillusionment to the thirsty traveller or anxious farmer" (Kelly; cf. Jer 14:3). Instead of the damp mists which refresh the countryside in hot weather (Sir 43:22), *ὁμίχλαι* ("mists") are the haze which heralds dry weather (Aristotle, *Meteor.* 1.346B; Theophrastus, *De signis* 4) and is quickly dispersed by a gust of wind (cf Wis 2:4).

Probably the significance of both metaphors is the same as that of Jude's. They depend on the standard use of the image of water for religious teaching, which sustains spiritual life as water does natural life (Prov 13:14; Sir 24:25–26; CD 6:4; and for *πηγαὶ ἄνυδροι,* "wells without water," cf. especially Jer 2:13; Gnostic *Apoc. Pet.* [CG 7, 3] 79:31). The false teachers supply their followers with no such life-giving teaching.

οἷς ὁ ζόφος τοῦ σκότους τετήρηται, "for them the nether gloom of darkness has been reserved." This clause comes *verbatim* from Jude 13, but the omission of *ἀστέρες πλανῆται* ("wandering stars") deprives it of the metaphorical appropriateness it has in Jude. It remains intelligible, however, because darkness was a standard image of the eschatological fate of the wicked (see *Comment* on Jude 13). For the omission of Jude's phrase *εἰς αἰῶνα* ("for ever"), cf. *Comment* on 2:6.

18. *ὑπέρογκα γὰρ ματαιότητος φθεγγόμενοι,* "for by their high-flown, empty talk." Although *ὑπέρογκα,* "high-flown," is borrowed from Jude 16, it has probably lost the nuance of arrogant speech against God, which it has there. Here its significance is found in the contrast with *ματαιότητος* ("vanity, emptiness, folly"; for this word and cognates used of words, cf. LXX Ps 37:13; 143:8; 1 Tim 1:6; Titus 1:10; Ign. *Phld.* 1:1; Pol. *Phil.* 2:1). The words of the false teachers sound very impressive, but they are deceptive; in reality, they are worthless. Perhaps *ματαιότητος* was suggested to the author by the traditional description of Balaam as *μάταιος* (Philo, *Cher.* 32; *Conf.* 159; *Mig.* 113; *Det.* 71; see above, on v 16). Probably *γάρ* ("for") introduces an explanation of the previous v.

δελεάζουσιν ἐν ἐπιθυμίας σαρκὸς ἀσελγείαις, "with lusts of the flesh and dissolute practices they ensnare." See *Comment* on vv 2 and 10a, and, for *δελεάζουσιν* ("ensnare") on v 14. "Grandiose sophistry is the hook, filthy lust is the bait" (Bigg). By removing the sanction of eschatological judgment, the false teachers were encouraging their followers to return to the morally lax ways of pagan society.

τοὺς ὀλίγως ἀποφεύγοντας τοὺς ἐν πλάνῃ ἀναστρεφομένους, "people who are only just escaping from those who live in error." *ὀλίγως* could mean "to a small extent" and indicate that these new converts have not yet completely broken free of the influence of pagan society, or (more probably) "for a short while, recently," indicating that, as recent converts, they have not yet become "established" (1:12) in the faith, and so may easily slip back into pagan ways.

"Those who live in error" are pagans (for πλάνη, "error," as the condition of non-Christians, see Rom 1:27; Titus 3:3; *2 Clem.* 1:7; *Barn.* 4:1; 14:5).

19. ἐλευθερίαν αὐτοῖς ἐπαγγελλόμενοι, "they promise them freedom." This phrase continues the explanation of the message with which they entice their followers: they use the catchword "freedom," with all its deep attraction and ambiguity. *From what* did they promise freedom? The following answers have been given: (1) Freedom from moral law (Plumptre, James, Windisch, Green, Kelly; Fornberg, *Early Church,* 106–7): this is the common view of those who see 2 Peter's opponents as comparable with the Corinthian libertines (cf. 1 Cor 8:9; 10:23) or Jude's antinomians, or as extreme Paulinists who misused Paul's doctrine of justification by faith and freedom from the Law. That Christian "freedom," as taught by Paul and others, was open to this kind of antinomian abuse, is clear enough (Rom 3:8; Gal 5:13; 1 Pet 2:16; and for later Gnostic examples, cf. Irenaeus, *Adv. Haer.* 1.23.4; 1.24.4–5), while 2 Pet 3:16 could mean that the false teachers misused Paul in this way. (2) The Gnostic's freedom from the archons or the demiurge. The Gnostic saw himself as freed through knowledge from the inferior powers who created the world, and as subject to no authority whatever, the truly free man (Irenaeus, *Adv. Haer.* 1.23.4; 1.24.4–5; 1.25.2–3). However, there is no evidence in 2 Peter that the false teachers held the dualistic gnostic theory of inferior creators. (3) Freedom from φθορά, "perishability" (Harnisch, *Existenz,* 100; cf. Käsemann, "Apologia," 171): the "realised eschatology" of the opponents taught that Christians were already beyond the power of mortality. This view has the merit of finding an explanation within v 19 itself, but it cannot be regarded as certain that the author intended "slaves . . . to corruption" (δοῦλοι . . . τῆς φθορᾶς) to imply also "freedom from corruption" as the promise the false teachers made. Although it is frequently assumed that the false teachers believed in a "realised eschatology," 2 Peter itself provides no evidence of this. It indicates only that they were skeptical of future eschatology. (4) Political freedom (Reicke). But Reicke's attempt to read the controversy in 2 Peter in political terms has no real basis in the text. (5) Freedom from fear of judgment at the Parousia (Neyrey, *Polemic,* 46–49; *JBL* 99 [1980] 419–20). The false teachers deny the reality of eschatological judgment (see *Comment* on 2:3b) and so they and their followers escape from moral accountability and punishment. This view has the merit of linking the promise of freedom with the eschatological skepticism which we know to have been characteristic of the false teachers. View (1) need not be entirely rejected: freedom from moral restraint is a consequence of freedom from fear of judgment, and the false teachers may indeed have appealed to Paul's doctrine of Christian freedom (see *Comment* on 3:16). If "freedom" was one of their catchwords, they could have given it a broad spectrum of significance: freedom from judgment, freedom from moral constraint, perhaps also freedom from fear of the powers of evil (cf. v 10). But so far as we can tell, freedom from fear of eschatological judgment will have been the fundamental freedom. If φθορά

is understood as God's judgment (as in v 12, and see below), then the view (3) that the author implies that the false teachers promised freedom from φθορά is also acceptable (so Neyrey, *Polemic,* 202).

Neyrey (*JBL* 99 [1980] 418–19) compares the controversy between Epicureans and their opponents; Epicurus offered freedom from fear of divine retribution in this life and after it, and thereby, his opponents held, encouraged immorality (Lactantius, *Div. Inst.* 3.17).

αὐτοὶ δοῦλοι ὑπάρχουντες τῆς φθορᾶς, "they themselves are slaves of corruption." Many commentators think that φθορᾶς must mean "moral corruption," but, although this might be a secondary overtone, the word is best given the same basic meaning as it has in 1:4 (see *Comment*). It designates that "corruptibility" or "mortality" which is the consequence of sinful desire (1:4) and which ends in eschatological destruction (Schelkle, Kelly, Schrage). The false teachers are "slaves of corruption" because by yielding to sin they put themselves in the power of corruptibility and destruction (φθορά is here personified as a power, Destruction). From another point of view, φθορά can be seen as the divine judgment on sin (2:12). The false teachers who promise freedom from retributive judgment are themselves subject to it.

The phrase δοῦλοι . . . τῆς φθορᾶς ("slaves . . . of corruption") is reminiscent of Rom 8:21, where also φθορά is personified: "the creation itself will be set free from its bondage to decay (ἐλευθερωθήσεται ἀπὸ τῆς δουλείας τῆς φθορᾶς) and obtain the glorious freedom (ἐλευθερίαν) of the children of God" (RSV). For the general thought of this v, cf. also Rom 6:16; 7:5. It is possible that the author of 2 Peter, who is almost entirely uninfluenced by Pauline theology, here shows some influence from Paul. It is noteworthy that the parallels are from Romans, a letter with which the author must have been acquainted if 2 Peter was written from Rome.

(There is also a striking parallel in the description of the Carpocratians in Clem. Alex., *Letter to Theodorus* [M. Smith, *Clement of Alexandria and a Secret Gospel of Mark* (Cambridge, Mass.: Harvard University Press, 1973)] 1.6–7: καυχώμενοι ἐλευθέρος εἶναι, δοῦλοι γεγόνασιν ἀνδραποδώδων ἐπιθυμιῶν, "boasting that they are free, they have become slaves of servile lusts." In view of the quotations from Jude 13 in 1.3, 6, this may well be an allusion to 2 Pet 2:19.)

The point of v 19a is that the false teachers promise what they cannot give because they themselves do not have it. Neyrey (*Polemic,* 419) makes the attractive suggestion that in using the term ἐπαγγελλόμενοι ("promise") the author is turning back on his opponents the charge of unfulfilled prophecy. They complain that the "promise" (ἐπαγγελία) of the Parousia is unfulfilled (3:4, 9), but are themselves guilty of making unfulfilled promises.

The vocabulary of vv 18–20 seems to echo that of 1:3–4 (ἐπιγνώσις: 1:3; 2:20; ἐπιθυμία: 1:4; 2:18; φθορά 1:4; 2:19; ἀποφεύγειν: 1:4; 2:18, 20; κόσμος: 1:4; 2:19; ἐπαγγέλμα, ἐπαγγελλέσθαι: 1:3; 2:19). The resemblance results from the fact that this is the vocabulary in which our author expresses the essential content of Christianity. That was his subject matter in 1:3–4, his positive exposition of the Christian message, and it recurs again in 2:18–20, which deals with apostasy from Christianity. But the correspondence between the two passages suggests a contrast between the promises of Christ, through which Christians will escape from corruption (1:3–4), and the promises of the false teachers, which will only result in slavery to corruption (2:19).

ᾧ γάρ τις ἥττηται, τούτῳ δεδούλωται, "for a man becomes the slave of him who overpowers him." This saying, widely quoted in later centuries, was doubtless already a common proverb (cf. Hippolytus, *In Dan.* 3.22.4: *ᾧ γὰρ ἄν τις ὑποταγῇ τούτῳ καὶ δεδούλωται*; *Clem. Rec.* 5.12; Origen, *In Exod. Hom.* 12; "Adamantius," *De recta in Deum fide* 1, calls it *ὁ ἔξωθεν λόγος*, "the saying current among non-Christians"; cf. also Rom 6:16; John 8:34). It derives from the practice of enslaving enemies overpowered in battle. The Greek can mean "him who overpowers" or "whatever overpowers," an ambiguity which allows the metaphor from human activity to be applied to impersonal forces. The English translation "him" preserves the metaphor and the implicit personification of *φθορά* ("corruption").

20. *εἰ γὰρ ἀποφύγοντες τὰ μιάσματα τοῦ κόσμου ἐν ἐπιγνώσει τοῦ κυρίου καὶ σωτῆρος* Ἰησοῦ Χριστοῦ, "for if, having once escaped the pollutions of the world through the knowledge of the Lord and Savior Jesus Christ." This phrase refers to conversion to Christianity: for this significance of *ἐν ἐπιγνώσει* ("through the knowledge") see the *Comment* on 1:2 (and cf. Dupont, *Gnosis,* 31). With *τὰ μιάσματα τοῦ κόσμου* ("the pollutions of the world"), cf. *T. Benj.* 8:3: *μιασμοῖς τῆς γῆς* ("pollutions of the earth"). "They" are most naturally understood as the false teachers themselves, rather than their followers (so Mayor, Green, Senior, against Spitta, Bigg, Chaine, Kelly; cf. Marshall, *Kept,* 166). The false teachers are in the state of definite apostasy described in vv 20–22; their followers are doubtless in severe danger of joining them in it, and so these vv serve as a serious warning to the followers, but the author no doubt hopes that the warning will be effective in preventing them from sharing the false teachers' doom. Whether he held out any hope for the reclamation of the false teachers themselves we do not know, but vv 20–22 do not rule it out (cf. *Comment* on 3:9).

On "the Lord and Savior," see *Comment* on 1:11.

τούτοις δὲ πάλιν ἐμπλακέντες ἡττῶνται, "they are again entangled in them and overpowered by them." For the notion of being "overpowered" by sins, cf. Rom 6:12–19; Titus 3:3; *Barn.* 4:1; *2 Clem.* 10:1; Herm. *Mand.* 12:2:3; 12:5:1.

γέγονεν αὐτοῖς τὰ ἔσχατα χείρονα τῶν πρώτων, "their final state has become worse than the first." This is a practically *verbatim* quotation (only substituting *αὐτοῖς* for *τοῦ ἀνθρώπου ἐκείνου*) of the saying of Jesus: *γίνεται τὰ ἔσχατα τοῦ ἀνθρώπου ἐκείνου χείρονα τῶν πρώτων* ("the last state of that man has become worse than the first," Matt 12:45 = Luke 11:26), which concludes the story of the return of the unclean spirit (Matt 12:43–45 par. Luke 11:24–26). There seems to be an allusion to this saying in another passage about apostasy, Herm. *Sim.* 9:17:5, and the whole story seems to have inspired Herm. *Mand.* 5:2:7; 12:5:4, which also describe the backsliding of Christians into immorality. Thus it appears that the author of 2 Peter was familiar with an application of this passage of Jesus' teaching to apostasy, current in the church of Rome in the late first century A.D.

Herm. *Sim.* 9:17:5–18:2 is worth quoting in full, as a parallel to the thought of 2 Pet 2:20–21: ". . . some of them defiled themselves (*ἐμίαναν ἑαυτούς*) and were expelled from the people (*γένους*) of the righteous, and became again such as they were before, or rather even worse (*πάλιν ἐγένοντο οἷοι πρότερον ἦσαν, μᾶλλον δὲ καὶ χείρονες*). 'Sir,' I said, 'how did they become worse, after they had known God? (*πῶς . . . ἐγένοντο χείρονες, θέον ἐπεγνώκοτες*).' 'He that does not know (*γινώσκων*) God,' he said, 'and commits wickedness, has a certain punishment for his wickedness. But he who knows (*ἐπιγνούς*) God ought not any longer to commit wickedness, but to do good. So if he who ought to do good commits wickedness, does he not seem to do greater wickedness than he who does not know (*γινώσκοντα*) God? Therefore those who have not known (*ἐγνωκότες*) God and commit wickedness, are condemned to death, but those who have known (*ἐγνωκότες*) God and seen his mighty works and (still) commit wickedness, shall be doubly punished, and shall die eternally (*εἰς τὸν αἰῶνα*)."

For the seriousness of the state of the apostate, which to the postapostolic generations of the early church seemed extreme, cf. also Heb 10:26; *Acts John* 107; the "elder" quoted by Irenaeus, *Adv. Haer.* 4.27.2. To sin in ignorance, as the heathen do, is one thing; to sin deliberately when "the way of righteousness" (2:21) is known and to spurn the gift of salvation is far more culpable.

21. *ἐπεγνωκέναι τὴν ὁδὸν τῆς δικαιοσύνης*, "to have come to know the way of righteousness." For *ἐπεγνωκέναι* ("to have come to know"), see *Comment* on 1:2. For the use of phrases with "way" to describe Christianity in 2 Peter, see *Comment* on 2:2. For "the way of righteousness," see LXX Job 24:13; Prov 21:16, 21; *Jub.* 23:26; *1 Enoch* 82:4; Matt 21:32; *Barn.* 1:4; *Apoc. Pet.* E 7; A 22, 28; *Clem. Rec.* 2:21:7 (cf. also, plural: LXX Prov 8:20; 12:28; 16:31; Tob 1:3; *1 Enoch* 91:18–19; 94:1; 99:10; 1QS 4:2; "the righteous way": LXX Job 24:4, 11; 28:4; Ps 2:12; *2 Clem.* 5:7; *Barn.* 12:4), and especially *Barn.* 5:4: "a man shall justly perish who, having the knowledge of the way of righteousness, holds to the way of darkness" (and cf. Repo, *Weg*, especially 204–11). As a designation of Christianity as an ethical way of life, "the way of righteousness" is especially appropriate in this context, where the apostasy is fundamentally a moral matter (though based on denial of future judgment).

τῆς παραδοθείσης αὐτοῖς ἁγίας ἐντολῆς, "the holy commandment which was delivered to them." "The holy commandment" is here used in the same way as "the way of righteousness," as a description of Christianity considered as a body of ethical teaching (for the use of the singular "commandment," cf. Rom 7:12, of the OT law; and, with reference to Christian ethical teaching, 1 Tim 6:14; *Ep. Apost.* [Ethiopic] 26, 27, 36, 39, 46, 50; the plural "commandments of the Lord" is frequent in *2 Clem.:* 3:4; 4:5; 6:7; 8:4; 17:1, 3, 6). "Delivered" (*παραδοθείσης*, perhaps a reminiscence of Jude 3) indicates that this teaching was given them in their initial Christian instruction (see *Comment* on Jude 3).

22. *τῆς ἀληθοῦς παροιμίας*, "the true proverb." The author probably intends the citation which follows as one proverb, not two. Although the two sayings about the dog and the sow originally derive from distinct sources (see below), they are so closely parallel as given here (especially if *ἐπιστρέψασα*, "returns," is to be understood in the second) that the author probably found them

together in the form he quotes, no doubt in some Hellenistic Jewish collection of proverbs. Dogs and pigs, both dirty and despised animals, were often associated in sayings of this kind (Horace, *Ep.* 1.2.26; 2.2.75; Pap. Oxy. 840, lines 33–34; and a similar pair of proverblike sayings in Matt 7:6).

κύων ἐπιστρέψας ἐπὶ τὸ ἴδιον ἐξέραμα, "a dog which returns to its vomit." This is from Prov 26:11 (RSV: "Like a dog that returns to its vomit is a fool that repeats his folly"; cf. also *Gos. Truth* 33:15–16, which may be dependent on 2 Peter), but the translation here is quite different from LXX. The point of both the sayings is that the animal, having got rid of its filth, returns to it. The dog cannot leave its vomit alone but goes back to sniff around it. The observation of this habit confirmed the ancient oriental's dislike of dogs, which in Jewish literature were usually the pariah dogs that roamed the streets scavenging and were thought of as dirty and disgusting animals.

ὗς λουσαμένη εἰς κυλισμὸν βορβόρου, "a sow which after washing returns to wallow in the mire." There is no need to make *εἰς κυλισμὸν βορβόρου* ("to wallow in the mire") dependent on *λουσαμένη* ("after washing"), which would be a very awkward construction ("a sow that washes herself by wallowing in the mire," suggested in BAG *s.* *βόρβορος*), because verbs are often omitted in proverbial expressions, and in any case *ἐπιστρέψασα* ("which returns") can easily be supplied here from the previous phrase.

In the Hellenistic world there was a well-known saying, deriving at least in one form from Heraclitus (see G. S. Kirk (ed.), *Heraclitus, The Cosmic Fragments* [Cambridge: Cambridge University Press, 1954] 76–80), according to which pigs delight to wash in mud rather than in pure water (e.g. Sextus Empiricus, *Hypot.* 1.14.56: *σύες . . . ἥδιον βορβόρῳ λούονται . . . ἢ ὕδατι . . . καθαρῷ*; cf. Clem. Alex., *Protr.* 10.92.4; *Strom.* 1.1.2.2; 2.15.68.3; and many other references in Aubineau, *RSR* 33 [1959] 201–4; for versions which use *κυλίειν* or *κυλινδεῖσθαι,* "to wallow," and cognates, see 204 ns. 106–7). If 2 Peter's proverb were simply a version of this saying, we should have to adopt either the translation rejected above, or Bigg's interpretation, according to which the pig, having once washed in the mud, returns to do so again. In neither case would there be any reference to washing clean in water. But the parallel with the dog, which gets rid of its filth before returning to it, as well as the application of the proverb to the false teachers, seems to demand the usual interpretation, according to which the sow first washes itself clean in water but then returns to wallowing in the mud.

This interpretation, more appropriate to the context, can be sustained by referring to another proverb, an oriental proverb preserved in the ancient *Story of Aḥikar* (whether this proverb has any connection with the Hellenistic saying is uncertain: observation of the pig's love of mud is too universal to make a connection necessary). In the Syriac version (8:18) it runs: "My son, thou hast been to me like the swine that had been to the baths, and when it saw a muddy ditch, went down and washed in it, and cried to its companions: come and wash." The Arabic version (8:15) is perhaps rather closer to 2 Peter's: "thou hast been to me like the pig who went into the hot bath with people of quality, and when it came out of the hot bath, it saw a filthy hole and it went down and wallowed in it" (*APOT* 2, p. 772; and F. C. Conybeare, J. R. Harris, and A. S. Lewis, *The Story of Aḥikar,* 2nd ed. [Cambridge: Cambridge University Press, 1913] 125, 158, cf. the Armenian version on p. 54). The point is that pigs do enjoy bathing in water (cf. Pap. Oxy. 840, line 33) and may even visit the public baths, but they are so indifferent to cleanliness that they will immediately return to the mud. This proverb is undoubtedly the origin of 2 Peter's (and perhaps we should even translate λουσαμένη as "when it has been to the baths": so Conybeare, Harris and Lewis, lxviii), even if its Greek translation has employed vocabulary familiar from the well-known Hellenistic saying. (It should be noted that the Hellenistic saying was never given a *moral* significance in non-Christian writers: Aubineau, *RSR* 33 [1959] 205–6. Most recent commentators, as well as Olivier, "Correction," 146–48, recognize the proverb in *Aḥikar* as the original of 2 Peter's.)

Both sayings of course illustrate the false teachers' apostasy. Having been "cleansed from their past sins" (1:9) in conversion and baptism, they are now reverting to the immorality of their pagan past. Many commentators see an allusion to baptism in the sow's "washing," but this theme is so integral to the pre-Christian proverb that its suggestion of baptism can be no more than a happy coincidence.

This verse is the author's final extension of his comparison of the false teachers with ἄλογα ζῷα ("unreasoning animals," 2:12, cf. 16). He sees them now as unclean animals, dogs and pigs, which to the Jewish mind symbolized the immorality of Gentile life (cf. Rev 22:15).

Explanation

The two metaphors with which this section begins condemn the author's opponents as people who purport to be religious teachers. Like dry wells which disappoint the thirsty, and hazy mists which are blown away without relieving the heat of the atmosphere, these people have in reality nothing to offer those who look to them for spiritual sustenance. Consequently they are doomed to eschatological judgment. Of course, they do make disciples—especially of young Christian converts who have scarcely had time to break with pagan ways—but they do so by means of talk which only sounds impressive, and especially by denying the need for strict morality. "Freedom" is their promise—freedom from fear of divine judgment, and so from moral restraint. But this is a promise which they cannot fulfill, for ironically they themselves are not free. By yielding to sin they have subjected themselves to the power of corruption and mortality, the consequence of sin and the means of God's judgment on sin. Unlike Christ who has promised his followers escape from mortality and eschatological destruction (1:4) and can fulfill his promise, these people can provide no escape from destruction, for they themselves have been overpowered by Destruction and become its slaves. The author clinches his point by quoting a common proverb.

The rest of this section concerns the seriousness of the apostasy involved when a Christian returns to the immoral ways of his pagan past. This applies primarily to the false teachers themselves, but is clearly also a warning to their followers who are also being enticed into apostasy. Because moral apostasy involves sinning with full knowledge of God's moral demands and spurning the grace which is available through Christ for holy living, its culpability is much greater than that of the sins committed in ignorance during a person's pre-Christian life. Like the man in Jesus' story to whom the dispossessed demon returned with seven companions more evil than itself, the apostate does not simply return to his pre-Christian condition, but enters a worse state, in danger of more severe judgment.

Again the point is clinched with a proverb, which is peculiarly appropriate because it continues the animal theme of this chapter (cf. vv 12, 16) and because it concerns animals which to the Jewish mind were dirty and disgusting, like the immoral life style of pagan society. Christians who return to their former pagan ways are like a dog which vomits, but instead of leaving well enough alone goes back to sniff round its vomit, or like a sow, which has a good wash in clean water, but cannot resist the urge to wallow in the mud again.

Peter's Prediction of Scoffers (3:1–4)

Bibliography

Allmen, D. von. "L'apocalyptique juive et le retard de la parousie en II Pierre 3:1–13." *RTP* 16 (1966) 256–58. **Boobyer, G. H.** "Indebtedness," 36–39. **Harnisch, W.** *Eschatologische Existenz,* 99–104. **Ladeuse, P.** "Transposition Accidentelle dans la IIª Petri." *RB* 2 (1905) 543–52. **McNamara, M.** "The Unity of Second Peter: A Reconsideration." *Scr* 12 (1960) 13–19. **Talbert, C. H.** "II Peter and the Delay of the Parousia." *VC* 20 (1966) 137–45. **Vögtle, A.** *Zukunft,* 124–33. **Zmijewski, J.** "Apostolische Paradosis." *BZ* 23 (1979) 161–71.

Translation

1 *My dear friends, this is now my second letter to you, and in this one, as in the*
first, I am arousing your sincere understanding with a reminder, 2 *that you should*
remember the predictions of the holy prophets and the commandment of the Lord
and Savior through your apostles. 3 *Above all you must understand this, that in the*
last days scoffers will come, scoffing, following their own lusts, 4 *and saying, "Where*
is the promise of his coming? For since the fathers fell asleep, everything remains
just as it has been since the beginning of the world."

Form/Structure/Setting

Verses 1–2, which mention 1 Peter and echo 1:12–15, are doubtless intended to reestablish in the readers' minds the fact that it is Peter's testament they are reading, after a long section in which this has not been evident. In 2:10b–22 the author has been writing about the false teachers in the present tense, as his own contemporaries, but he now wishes to return to the conventions of the testament genre, in order to provide a second prophecy (cf. 2:1–3a) in which Peter foresees the false teachers who are to arise after his death. This device enables the author not only to remind his readers that the apostles predicted such false teachers as they are now encountering, but also to emphasize that these false teachers are a phenomenon of the end-time which was still future from Peter's perspective (v 3). For the first time in the letter the false teachers' objection to the expectation of the Parousia is given in explicit quotation (v 4), though doubtless phrased in the author's own words (see *Comment*), to prepare for his final and full refutation of it.

In vv 2–3 the last extensive borrowing from Jude occurs:

2 Pet 3	*Jude*
1. . . . ἀγαπητοί . . .	17. Ὑμεῖς δέ, ἀγαπητοί,
2. . . . μνησθῆναι τῶν	μνήσθητε τῶν ῥημάτων τῶν
προειρημένων ῥημάτων ὑπὸ	προειρημένων ὑπὸ
τῶν ἁγίων προφητῶν καὶ τῆς	
τῶν ἀποστόλων ὑμῶν ἐντολῆς	τῶν ἀποστόλων τοῦ κυρίου
τοῦ κυρίου καὶ σωτῆρος,	ἡμῶν Ἰησοῦ Χριστοῦ,
3. τοῦτο πρῶτον γινώσκοντες,	18. ὅτι ἔλεγον ὑμῖν,
ὅτι ἐλεύσονται ἐπ᾽ ἐσχάτων	Ἐπ᾽ ἐσχάτου
τῶν ἡμερῶν ἐν ἐμπαιγμονῇ	τοῦ χρονοῦ ἔσονται
ἐμπαῖκται κατὰ τὰς ἰδίας	ἐμπαῖκται κατὰ τάς ἑαυτῶν
ἐπιθυμίας αὐτῶν πορευόμενοι.	ἐπιθυμίας πορευόμενοι
	τῶν ἀσεβειῶν.

2 Pet 3	*Jude*
1. *My dear friends*	17. But you, *my dear friends,*
2. . . . *you should remember the*	*should remember the*
predictions of the holy prophets	*predictions of*
and the commandment *of the Lord*	*the apostles of* our *Lord*
and Savior through your *apostles.*	Jesus Christ,
3. Above all you must under-	18. how they said to you,
stand this, that *in the last* days	"*In the final* age there will be
scoffers will come, scoffing, *follow-*	*scoffers, who will follow* their
ing their	own *desires* for ungodliness."
own *lusts*	

The following modifications of Jude are especially important: (1) The author of 2 Peter introduces the predictions of the prophets (v 2), in line with his stress in 1:19–21 that the Christian expectation of the future is based not only on the apostolic witness but also on OT prophecies. (2) Whereas Jude quotes a prediction by the apostles, 2 Peter puts the prediction directly into Peter's mouth, since it is Peter's testament. (3) Whereas for Jude ἐμπαῖκται ("scoffers") is a general term for people who despise religion and morality, in 2 Peter it has in view particularly their mockery of the Parousia-hope, as the continuation in v 4 shows. The importance of the eschatological issue distinguishes the opponents in 2 Peter from those in Jude, and our author's concern with it explains why at this point he finds no further value in following Jude, but turns to another source in which the problem of eschatological delay was explicitly treated.

In the commentary on the rest of the chapter it will become clear that the writer is rather closely dependent on Jewish apocalyptic ideas, and the hypothesis of a written Jewish apocalyptic source for parts of the chap. has already been suggested by others (notably by von Allmen, *RTP* 16 [1966] 256–64, who tries to distinguish between the material borrowed from a Jewish apocalypse and the author's own contributions; cf. also the rather different analysis of Marín, *EE* 50 [1975] 228–34, who distinguishes traditional apocalyptic material from the author's didactic-exhortatory material). It is possible, however, that this source need not remain purely hypothetical, and that our author's use of it begins in v 4. *1 Clem.* 23:3–4 and *2 Clem.* 11:2–4 both preserve a fragment of an unknown apocryphal work in which the problem of eschatological delay was confronted. The beginning of the fragment bears comparison with 2 Pet 3:4:

1 Clem. 23:3	*2 Clem. 11:2*	*2 Pet 3:4*
πόρρω γενέσθω ἀφ' ἡμῶν	λέγει γὰρ καὶ	
ἡ γραφὴ αὕτη, ὅπου λέγει·	ὁ προφητικὸς λόγος·	
Ταλαίπωροί εἰσιν οἱ	Ταλαίπωροί εἰσιν οἱ	
δίψυχοι, οἱ διστάζοντες τὴν	δίψυχοι, οἱ διστάζοντες τῇ	
ψυχήν, οἱ λέγοντες· Ταῦτα	καρδίᾳ, οἱ λέγοντες· Ταῦτα	καὶ λέγοντες, Ποῦ ἐστιν ἡ
ἠκούσαμεν	πάλαι (v.l. πάντα) ἠκούσαμεν	ἐπαγγελία τῆς παρουσίας αὐτοῦ
καὶ ἐπὶ τῶν πατέρων ἡμῶν,	καὶ ἐπὶ τῶν πατέρων ἡμῶν,	ἀφ' ἧς γὰρ οἱ πατέρες
καὶ ἰδοὺ	ἡμεῖς δὲ ἡμέραν ἐξ ἡμέρας	ἐκοιμήθησαν, πάντα οὕτως
γεγηράκαμεν καὶ οὐδὲν ἡμῖν	προσδεχόμενοι οὐδὲν τούτων	διαμένει ἀπ' ἀρχῆς κτίσεως·
τούτων συνβέβηκεν.	ἑωράκαμεν.	

1 Clem. 23:3	*2 Clem. 11:2*	*2 Pet 3:4*
Let this scripture be	For the prophetic word	
far from us, where he	also	
says, Wretched are the	says, Wretched are the	
double-minded, who	double-minded who	
doubt in their soul,	doubt in their heart,	
and say, "These things	and say, "These things	and saying, "Where is
we heard in the	we heard of old in the	the promise of his coming?
days of our fathers	days of our fathers	For since the fathers
also, and behold we have	also, yet we have	fell asleep, everything
grown old, and none	waited day after day	remains just as it has
of these things has	and have seen none of	been since the beginning
happened to us.	these things.	of the world."

The resemblance, which has often been noticed, may not at first sight seem sufficient to suggest 2 Peter's dependence on the apocryphal work quoted in *1 Clement* and *2 Clement.* But the following considerations make such dependence a strong possibility: (1) The close similarities of distinctive ideas and terminology between 2 Peter and *1 Clement* and *2 Clement,* which have been observed throughout this commentary, probably indicate that all three works derive from a common milieu: the theology of the church of Rome in the late first century. From the manner in which the apocryphal work is (independently) quoted in *1 Clem.* 23:3 (ἡ γραφὴ αὕτη, "this scripture") and *2 Clem.* 11:2 (ὁ προφητικὸς λόγος, "the prophetic word": for the meaning of this phrase, see 2 Pet 1:19, with *Comment*), it is clear that it was highly esteemed in the church of Rome at that time, and must therefore have been known to the author of 2 Peter. (2) Second Pet 3:10, 12 resemble a further quotation from an unknown apocalyptic source in *2 Clem.* 16:3 (see *Form/Structure/Setting* section on 3:8–10). It is an economical hypothesis to attribute *2 Clem.* 11:2–4 and *2 Clem.* 16:3 to the same Jewish apocalypse, and to account for the resemblance between 2 Pet 3:4 and *2 Clem.* 11:2, and between 2 Pet 3:10, 12 and *2 Clem.* 16:3, by postulating common dependence on this Jewish apocalypse. (3) Second Pet 3:8–9, 12 tackles the problem of eschatological delay by means of arguments which were current in Jewish apocalyptic (see *Comment* on those vv). This suggests that 2 Pet 3 is indebted to a Jewish apocalypse concerned with the problem of delay. The work quoted in *1 Clem.* 23:3–4 and *2 Clem.* 11:2–4 was an apocalypse, probably Jewish, and very probably known to the author of 2 Peter, in which the issue of eschatological delay was explicitly posed. (4) If the quotation given above inspired 2 Pet 3:4, clearly our author has not copied his source but rewritten it in accordance with the needs of his own work (see *Comment* section for an explanation of his changes). This would be comparable with the freedom he shows in his use of Jude.

It is therefore a plausible hypothesis that, just as our author has followed Jude in 2:1–3:3, so in 3:4–13 he follows the Jewish apocalypse quoted in *1*

Clem. 23:3–4; *2 Clem.* 11:2–4. There is much to be said for Lightfoot's guess that this work was the *Book of Eldad and Modad,* of which we have only one certainly identified fragment quoted in Herm. *Vis.* 2:3:4. But where the text of this work is not attested elsewhere, it will be hazardous to try to determine precisely what our author owes to it, just as it would have been impossible to determine what parts of 2:1–3:3 derive from Jude if we did not possess Jude's letter.

Comment

1. *ταύτην ἤδη, ἀγαπητοί, δευτέραν ὑμῖν γράφω ἐπιστολήν*, "my dear friends, this is now my second letter to you." To what letter does the author here refer as Peter's first letter? The following answers have been given:

(1) An earlier part of 2 Peter. The theory that chap 3 was originally a separate letter, first proposed by Grotius, has been revived by McNamara (*Scr* 12 [1960] 13–19), who suggests that chap 1 is the first letter and chap 3 is one of the further letters promised in 1:15. He points to the abrupt transition between chap 2 and 3:1, and argues that 3:1 would more appropriately open a letter than the concluding section of a letter. One major difficulty in this view is that the author's borrowing from Jude continues up to 3:3. 1:15 is better understood as referring to the whole of 2 Peter (see *Comment*), and 3:1 can be adequately explained in its present context following chap 2 (see below).

(2) Jude. Robinson holds that Jude wrote both the letter of Jude and (as Peter's agent) 2 Peter, which is the longer letter which, according to Jude 3, Jude put aside to write "the letter of Jude." In 2 Pet 3:1 Jude refers to his own previous letter (*Redating,* 195). As suggested by Robinson, this theory presupposes the common authorship of Jude and 2 Peter: but the author of 2 Peter does not use material from Jude in the way in which a writer would use his own material. Smith (*Petrine Controversies*) also suggests that the first letter is Jude, but, unlike Robinson, regards 2 Peter as late and pseudepigraphal. He holds that either the author of 2 Peter was also the author of the (pseudepigraphal) letter of Jude, or (less probably) referred to the highly respected letter of Jude as a way of authenticating his own work. It is, however, extremely unlikely that readers of 2 Peter could have recognized a reference to Jude in this v, for 2 Peter is written in *Peter*'s name. Probably they recognized the pseudepigraphal device as a literary convention, but the convention consists in the fact that the "I" of the letter is Peter. Our author does deliberately break the literary convention in one respect (when he uses the present tense in 2:10b–22; 3:5, 16), but it is most unlikely that he is doing so in 3:1, because the purpose of this v is to introduce a *prophecy* by Peter (3:1–4). In 3:1 he is in fact deliberately reestablishing the fact that he writes in Peter's name (see below). The first letter must therefore have been a letter written in Peter's name.

(3) A lost letter. Spitta, Zahn (*Introduction,* 197–98) and Green, who all regard 2 Peter as written by Peter himself, hold that the reference is to a lost Petrine letter, and urge that there must have been many such letters. It is obviously impossible to rule out this possibility, though the notion that

Peter wrote many letters, now lost, is not perhaps as self-evident as these writers assume. But if there is a known document which meets the requirements of the reference we should not resort to the hypothesis of a lost document.

(4) First Peter. The majority of commentators accept that the reference is to the letter we know as 1 Peter. Against this, Spitta argued 2 Peter was written to Jewish Christians, 1 Peter to Gentile Christians, and that the readers of 2 Peter were known personally to Peter, while those of 1 Peter were not. But neither of these assertions about 2 Peter is justified (for the latter, see *Comment* on 1:16). More commonly it is said that 1 Peter does not answer to the description of the contents of the first letter in 3:2 (there is no need to regard 3:3 as included in the contents of the first letter). Ladeuse (*RB* 2 [1905] 544) connects *μνησθῆναι* ("that you should remember," v 2) with *γράφω* ("I am writing," v 1), so that 3:2 describes the intention of the second letter only, but it is more natural to connect *μνησθῆναι* ("that you should remember") with *διεγείρω* ("I am arousing," v 1), so that v 2 describes the contents of both letters. But if so, 3:2 is in fact sufficiently appropriate as a description of 1 Peter, which refers to the predictions of the OT prophets (1:10–12) and largely consists of reminders of the ethical implications of the Gospel. If in 3:2 the author of 2 Peter has in mind especially the expectation of judgment at the Parousia and the consequent need for holy living in the present, these too could be seen as themes of 1 Peter (1:13–17; 4:3–5, 7, 17; 5:4). It is quite unnecessary to seek any closer similarity between the two letters, because the author's real purpose in 3:1–2 is (a) to link his own letter to 1 Peter (see below), and (b) to describe the intention of his own letter. He wrote 3:2 *primarily* to describe his own purpose in writing 2 Peter, and so it need not describe the first letter as accurately as it does the second.

If the reference is to 1 Peter, why did the author make it? Not because he himself had written 1 Peter (see Introduction, section 5 of *Literary Relationships*), nor because (as Boobyer, "Indebtedness," thinks) he was influenced by 1 Peter and modeled his own letter on 1 Peter. Second Peter in fact provides no evidence that its author was influenced by or made any use of 1 Peter when writing 2 Peter (see Introduction, section 5 of *Literary Relationships*). He probably had two reasons for referring to 1 Peter: (1) Evidently the author was a member of the same Petrine circle in Rome from which 1 Peter derives, whether 1 Peter was written, like 2 Peter, after Peter's death, or, as seems to me more probable, before. Moreover, 2 Peter was probably addressed to the same churches as had received 1 Peter (this is implied by 3:1; and see below, *Comment* on 3:2 and 3:15). The reference to 1 Peter is therefore a way of identifying (not the author but) the source of the letter for its readers. But this reason is probably only a secondary one. (2) After the long passage 2:10b–22, in which the author has abandoned the conventions of the testament genre to describe the false teachers in the present tense, he now needs to reestablish the fact that he is writing in Peter's name. He must do this so that he can cast 3:3–4 in the form of a prophecy in the future tense, in which Peter foresees the "scoffers" who will arise after his death. 3:1, both by recalling 1:12–15 and by referring to 1 Peter, serves to remind the readers that they should be reading this passage as though it were written by Peter.

ἐν αἷς διεγείρω ὑμῶν ἐν ὑπομνήσει τὴν εἰλικρινῆ διάνοιαν, "and in this one, as in the first, I am arousing your sincere understanding with a reminder." These words recall 1:13. For the idea of "reminding" in 2 Peter, and the implication that the teaching is already known to the readers, see *Comment* on 1:12. *εἰλικρινής* means "pure, unmixed, uncontaminated," and hence, in a moral sense, "sincere, honest." It often describes purity or sincerity of motive or thought (cf. Plato, *Phaedo* 66A: *εἰλικρινεῖ τῇ διανοίᾳ*, "pure reason," but in a different sense from 2 Peter's; *Phaedo* 81C: *ψυχὴ εἰλικρινής*, "a pure soul"; *2 Clem.* 9:8: *ἐξ εἰλικρινοῦς καρδίας*, "from a sincere heart"; Theophilus, *Ad Autol.* 2.35: *εἰλικρινεῖ γνώμῃ*, "with a sincere mind"; *T. Benj.* 6:5: "the good mind (*διάνοια*) has a pure disposition (*εἰλικρινῆ . . . διάθεσιν*)"; for sincerity of understanding, cf. also *1 Clem.* 32:1), and here probably means that the readers' understanding is not (or the author hopes it will not be) distorted or led astray by immoral desires, as the thinking of the "scoffers" was (3:3–4).

2. *τῶν προειρημένων ῥημάτων ὑπὸ τῶν ἁγίων προφητῶν*, "the predictions of the holy prophets." For the epithet *ἁγίων* ("holy"), cf. Wis 11:1; Luke 1:70; Acts 3:21 (in a speech of Peter). In this v the writer appeals to the same two authorities, prophets and apostles, whose testimony was invoked to validate the preaching of the Parousia in 1:16–21. It is therefore certain that the OT prophets are meant, not (as Sidebottom thinks) the Christian prophets.

Vögtle (*Zukunft,* 125–26) thinks that in view of vv 3–4 the author must be thinking primarily of the prophets' preaching against scoffers who mock the delayed judgment of God (Amos 9:10; Mal 2:17; cf. Ezek 12:22; Zeph 1:12) and their predictions of divine judgment on them (Isa 5:18–20; Jer 5:12–24; Amos 9:10). The author's use of the *ποῦ ἐστιν* ("Where is?") formula in v 4 probably indicates that such passages in the prophets are in his mind, but there is no need to restrict the meaning of v 2 to predictions of the scoffers and their judgment. In v 2 he is still referring to the general purpose and content of 1 Peter and especially of 2 Peter. The teaching of which 2 Peter is intended to remind the readers is the teaching about the Parousia, and about the moral requirements of the gospel, which are related to the eschatological expectation. So, as in 1:19, the predictions of the OT prophets mentioned here are predictions of the Parousia and eschatological judgment.

τῆς τῶν ἀποστόλων ὑμῶν ἐντολῆς τοῦ κυρίου καὶ σωτῆρος, "the commandment of the Lord and Savior through your apostles." The double possessive genitive in this expression is awkward. It must mean that the commandment is primarily Christ's, but also in a secondary sense the apostles' because they were the people who preached it to the readers. Since most commentators think the apostles here are all the apostles, the apostolic "college," and that the readers are all Christians, *ὑμῶν* ("your") has caused some difficulty. Some think that, from a second-century perspective, all the apostles are seen to belong to all Christians (Moffatt, Schelkle, Kelly, Schrage; Zmijewski, *BZ* 23 [1979] 166)—others that "your" distinguishes the true apostles from the false teachers (Bigg, Sidebottom). However, the natural meaning of "your apostles" is *those* apostles who preached the gospel and founded the churches in the area to which 2 Peter is addressed, contrasted implicitly with the rest of the apostles (so Spitta, Mayor; Zahn, *Introduction,* 204–5; Fornberg, *Early Church,* 146 n. 22; cf. 1 Pet 1:12; *1 Clem.* 44:1, where "our apostles" are the apostles who founded the Roman church), and this meaning causes no difficulty once it is acknowledged that 2 Peter is addressed to specific churches (see *Comment* on 3:15). Evidently the readers' apostles included Paul (3:15).

It is therefore not true that, as has often been asserted, the writer here lapses into an expression which Peter himself could not have used. It is not even the case that the phrase "your apostles" necessarily excludes Peter himself (see Spitta; Zahn, *Introduction,* 218 n. 7; Dillenseger, *MFOB* 2 [1907] 204–5), but it is perhaps rather more natural if it does so. If the churches addressed are those addressed in 1 Pet 1:1, then Peter would be excluded.

The "commandment" is used here in the same way as in 2:21 (see *Comment* on that v): it emphasizes the ethical aspect of the Christian message because it is on this, along with the eschatological expectation, that the author wishes to insist, in opposition to the false teachers.

It is not especially surprising to find the apostolic message set side by side with OT prophecy as an authority (3:16, which puts Paul's *writings* on the same level with OT Scripture is a little more remarkable), but for similar passages which couple the prophets and the apostles, or the prophets and the Gospel, cf. *2 Clem.* 14:2; Ign. *Phld.* 5:1–2; 9:1–2; Pol. *Phil.* 6:3; "*3 Cor.*" 3:36; *Act. Verc.* 13.

3. *τοῦτο πρῶτον γινώσκοντες,* "above all you must understand this." On this expression, see *Form/Structure/Setting* section on 1:20–21. The nominative case here prevents the phrase from being too closely linked with the preceding v, and it is difficult to tell whether the author intends the prediction of the scoffers (vv 3–4) to be part of the content of the predictions of the prophets and the commandment of the apostles which the readers are to remember (v 2). Appropriate passages can be found in the prophets (see above) and prophecies of the false teachers of the last days were common in early Christian teaching (see *Comment* on Jude 18). But it appears that whereas Jude 18 quoted the teaching of the apostles, the author of 2 Peter has introduced the phrase *τοῦτο πρῶτον γινώσκοντες* precisely in order to be able to attribute the prophecy directly to Peter.

ἐπ' ἐσχάτων τῶν ἡμερῶν, "in the last days." The author has substituted the more familiar expression (LXX Gen 49:1; Jer 37:24; Ezek 38:16; Dan 2:28; Hos 3:5; Mic 4:1; Θ Dan 10:14; *T. Dan* 1:1; *2 Clem.* 14:2; *Barn.* 12:9; 16:5; Herm. *Sim.* 9:12:3) for Jude's unusual *ἐπ' ἐσχάτου τοῦ χρόνου,* "at the end of time." For its use with reference to the eschatological future, see *Comment* on Jude 18. The appearance of the "scoffers" is a phenomenon of the last days, a period still future from the fictional standpoint in Peter's lifetime, but to be identified as the present in which the writer and his readers are living. This is important for our assessment of the writer's eschatological perspective: like Jude, he sees the appearance of the false teachers as a sign that the last stage of history before the Parousia has arrived. There is also, as Fornberg (*Early Church,* 61) notes, "an ironic ring to the passage: The adversaries who denied the Parousia were themselves a proof of its imminence." It follows that their appearance ought not to disturb the faithful, but rather to confirm their faith in the prophecies (Vögtle, *Zukunft,* 129–30).

ἐν ἐμπαιγμονῇ ἐμπαῖκται, lit. "scoffers with scoffing." Second Peter has borrowed the term *ἐμπαῖκται* ("scoffers") from Jude 18; for its OT background, see *Comment* on Jude 18. It denotes people who scorn and despise God's revelation, both moral and prophetic. ἐν ἐμπαιγμονῇ ("with scoffing"), which 2 Peter adds to ἐμπαῖκται ("scoffers"), is probably a Septuagintalism, imitating the frequent occurrence in the LXX of a cognate noun with a verb (e.g. Gen 31:30; Exod 21:20; Deut 7:26; 13:16; 20:17) as a rendering of the Hebrew use of the infinitive absolute for emphasis. The fact that the author of 2 Peter uses ἐν ἐμπαιγμονῇ with a cognate *noun* (ἐμπαῖκται) shows that he is not thinking in Hebrew, but merely imitating LXX style.

κατὰ τὰς ἰδίας ἐπιθυμίας αὐτῶν πορευόμενοι, "following their own lusts." See *Comment* on Jude 16 and 18. The emphasis is on the fact that they follow their *own* desires, not the will of God (cf. Jude 16), but ἐπιθυμία ("desire") has a consistently bad sense in 2 Peter (1:4; 2:10, 18) and so it is probably taken for granted that their desires are for evil, even though 2 Peter omits Jude's τῶν ἀσεβειῶν (Jude 18), which makes this explicit. In 2 Peter this immoral behavior is to be seen as closely connected with their denial of future judgment (v 4).

It may be that the scoffers are portrayed in vv 3–4 in deliberate antithesis to v 2. Whereas the readers are to remember the predictions of the prophets and the apostolic commandment, the scoffers reject the commandment by following their own lusts (v 3), and the predictions of the prophets by mocking the Parousia hope (v 4).

4. ποῦ ἐστιν ἡ ἐπαγγελία τῆς παρουσίας αὐτοῦ; "where is the promise of his coming?" The rhetorical question beginning ποῦ ἐστιν . . . ; ("Where is . . . ?") is a standard form in the OT. "Where is your/their God?" is the taunt of the psalmist's enemies, when God does not intervene to rescue him from trouble (LXX Ps 41:4, 11), or of the Gentile nations when God does not intervene on behalf of his people (LXX Pss 78:10; 113:10; Joel 2:17; Mic 7:10). Especially relevant are Mal 2:17, where those who doubt that God is concerned to punish the wicked and reward the good ask cynically, "Where is the God of justice?" and Jer 17:15, where Jeremiah's enemies scoff at the nonfulfillment of his prophecies, with the words, "Where is the word of the Lord? Let it come true!" The form is therefore highly appropriate to express the sarcastic rejection of the prophecy of divine intervention in judgment at the Parousia of Jesus Christ, on the grounds of its nonfulfillment. Although Strobel (*Untersuchungen,* 96–97 and n. 3) thinks the alliteration points to an actual current saying, circulating perhaps in "enlightened" Jewish circles (cf. the "proverb" expressing similar skepticism in Ezek 12:22), it is much more likely that the author of 2 Peter has himself put his opponents' skeptical attitude into this particular form of words, following OT models. (Similarly, the Letter of the churches of Lyons and Vienne [*ap.* Eusebius, *Hist. Eccl.* 5.1.60] attributes to pagans, who have watched the Christian martyrs die, the jibe, "Where is their God?": ποῦ ὁ θεὸς αὐτῶν;)

In the *Form/Structure/Setting* section we have argued that 2 Peter is now partly following a Jewish apocalypse, which puts a complaint about the failure of eschatological expectation into the mouth of doubters. For other expressions of eschatological skepticism arising from the nonfulfillment of prophecy, cf. Ezek 12:22; Sir 16:22; *b. Sanh.* 97b.

Of course, the author of 2 Peter has made the specifically Christian expectation of the Parousia of Jesus Christ the target of his opponents' skepticism. The "promise" (ἐπαγγελία) may include reference to OT prophecy (cf. v 2), but is likely to refer primarily to Jesus' own promise, both because of the possible echo of 1:4 (ἐπαγγέλματα, "promises") and because the rest of the v seems to have in view especially those sayings of Jesus which apparently set a temporal limit on the expectation of the Parousia (see below).

ἀφ' ἧς γὰρ οἱ πατέρες ἐκοιμήθησαν, "for since the fathers fell asleep." "Sleep" was an accepted metaphor for death, which did not necessarily imply any particular understanding of death or life beyond death (see R. E. Bailey, "Is 'Sleep' the proper biblical term for the Intermediate State?," *ZNW* 55 [1964] 161–67; G. Rochais, *Les récits de résurrection des morts dans le Nouveau Testament* [SNTSMS 40; Cambridge: Cambridge University Press, 1981] 193–97, for references and discussion; and add *1 Clem.* 44:2; Herm. *Vis.* 3:5:1; 3:11:3; *Mand.* 4:4:1; *Sim.* 9:15:6; 9:16:5, 7). Those who wish to maintain that "the fathers" are the OT patriarchs or prophets (Bigg, Lumby, Green) have the weight of usage on their side. In early Christian literature, continuing Jewish usage (on which see *TDNT* 5, 976), οἱ πατέρες ("the fathers") means the OT "fathers," i.e. the patriarchs or, more generally, the righteous men of OT times (John 7:22; Acts 13:32; Rom 9:5; Heb 1:1; *Barn.* 5:7; 14:1; *Apoc. Pet.* E 16; *Ep. Apost.* [Coptic] 28); apart from our passage, the only possible exception is *2 Clem.* 19:4, which could refer to dead Christians but most probably refers to the OT saints (note the parallel with *Apoc. Pet.* E 16).

However, in spite of this consistent usage, there are difficulties in the way of supposing 2 Peter to refer to the OT fathers, and almost all modern commentators understand οἱ πατέρες ("the fathers") to be the first Christian generation. If they are the OT fathers, then the argument of the scoffers must be that since the death of those to whom the promise of the Parousia of Jesus Christ was first given, in OT times through the OT prophets, everything has remained the same. This would be a general argument for the nonfulfillment of prophecy over the course of many centuries. Such an argument might be plausible in a purely Jewish context (cf. *2 Apoc. Bar.* 21:24), but it is an odd argument in an early Christian context. Early Christianity constantly argued that many OT prophecies, after remaining unfulfilled for centuries, had quite recently been fulfilled in the history of Jesus. The fulfillment of eschatological prophecy had begun and would be completed in the future with the fulfillment of those OT prophecies which they held to be as yet unfulfilled. From this perspective it would not be very relevant to object that these prophecies had remained unfulfilled *since OT times.* Even if the false teachers denied that OT prophecies had been fulfilled in the life and work of Jesus, one would expect some reference to this fulfillment in 2 Peter's response.

It could be suggested that in 2 Pet 3 the author is following, with minor Christian modifications, a *Jewish* apocalypse, and that in v 4 he has taken over an objection based on the nonfulfillment of OT prophecy which really belongs in a *Jewish* context. However, as suggested above in the *Form/Structure/Setting* section, it is probable that we have the relevant fragment of the Jewish apocalypse which inspired 2 Pet 3, in the quotations in *1 Clem.* 23:3 and *2*

Clem. 11:2. In this fragment the doubters complain that they heard the eschatological promises "in the days of our fathers" (ἐπὶ τῶν πατέρων ἡμῶν) but they have not been fulfilled. Here it is clear that "our fathers" (τῶν πατέρων ἡμῶν) are the actual physical fathers, the immediate forebears, of the speakers. If 2 Pet 3:4 is a free rewriting of this source, adapted to our author's requirements, then he has made two important changes: (1) he has changed "*our* fathers" to "*the* fathers" (οἱ πατέρες); (2) he explicitly states, what is only implied in the Jewish apocalypse, that the fathers have *died.*

What is the significance of these changes? The first change means that the author of 2 Peter can hardly be referring to the actual physical fathers of the scoffers, i.e. the first generation of Christians in the churches to which he writes (as Spitta thought). οἱ πατέρες ("the fathers"), without ἡμῶν ("our"), would be very unnatural in that sense. But it is possible that he deliberately dropped ἡμῶν ("our") from his source, so that his reference should be, not to the fathers of the scoffers, but to *the* first Christian generation, the generation of the apostles. That generation of the original disciples, the founders of the churches, might appropriately be called οἱ πατέρες, the Christian "patriarchs," as it were. Although this usage is unattested elsewhere, it is a natural one, which perhaps the author of 2 Peter coined when he changed τῶν πατέρων ἡμῶν ("our fathers") in the Jewish apocalypse to οἱ πατέρες ("the fathers") in his own work.

The reason for this change becomes apparent in connection with his second change, the emphasis on the *death* of the fathers. In a Christian context a special significance attached to the death of the generation of the apostles, for there were several well-known sayings of Jesus which seemed to predict his Parousia within the lifetime of his contemporaries (Matt 16:28 par. Mark 9:1 par. Luke 9:27; Matt 24:34 par. Mark 13:30 par. Luke 21:32; John 21:22–23; cf. Matt 10:23). Thus the critical point for the nonfulfillment of the promise of the Parousia came at the time when it could be said that the generation of the apostles had died. The objection of the scoffers was not just that a long time had elapsed since the promise was given, but that the promise itself had set a time-limit within which it would be fulfilled and this time-limit had passed.

There are two possible problems about this explanation of the words of the scoffers: (1) Their objection ought to be, not that nothing has happened *since* the fathers died, but that nothing happened *before* they died (cf. Vögtle, *Zukunft,* 130). Since the attempts of Spitta and von Allmen (*RTP* 16 [1966] 258 n. 2) to give a different sense to the scoffers' words by a strained interpretation of ἀφ' ἧς, "since," cannot be allowed (see Zahn, *Introduction,* 237–38), in strict logic there is a problem here. But in terms of polemical argument, 2 Peter's wording is quite understandable. The scoffers are saying: "The Parousia was promised before the death of the fathers. Well, the fathers have died and *still* nothing happens." (2) Second Peter does not *answer* the objection that a specific time-limit has passed. The reason for this may be that the author does no more than reproduce the answers to the problem of eschatological delay which he found in his Jewish apocalyptic source, and these answers were, of course, designed to meet the general problem of eschatological delay rather than the specifically Christian problem of nonfulfillment within the lifetime of the apostles. In addition, however, it may be said that 3:9, while not mentioning the problem of the time-limit, does contain the most adequate response to it that could have been made: if God has extended the time-limit, he has done so in his grace, to give people the opportunity for repentance (cf. J. Jeremias, *New Testament Theology: Part 1,* tr. J. Bowden [London: SCM Press, 1971] 140). In effect, vv 8–9 raise the issue of eschatological delay above the level of calculating dates, and in doing so are faithful to the intentions of the sayings of Jesus which posed the problem, since the real concern of these sayings was not with a datable time-*limit* but with the imminence of God's judgment (Jeremias, *New Testament Theology,* 139).

If 2 Pet 3:4 does refer to the death of the first Christian generation, then it is clear that the author lived at a time when the first generation could be said to have passed away. He is not looking forward to such a time, since v 5 speaks of the "scoffers" in the present tense, as his own and his readers' contemporaries. But it is not, as many commentators think, a blunder on his part to have put a mention of the death of the first Christian generation into *Peter's* mouth in v 4. In v 4 he is using the pseudepigraphal device quite correctly, for he represents Peter as *prophesying* that *after his death* there will be scoffers who speak of the death of the fathers.

Many commentators think that the words "since the fathers fell asleep" indicate that the author is writing *long* after the death of the first generation. Two reasons are given for this: (1) "the use of the term οἱ πατέρες, [the fathers] in itself implies a considerable lapse of time. The founders of a movement are not called 'the fathers' till a later age looks back upon their work" (Chase, *DB*(*H*) 3, 812). This argument would be more cogent if other examples of the use of the term were given, but in fact 2 Peter seems to be unique in the literature of the first two Christian centuries in referring to the first Christian generation as "the fathers." Since the apostles had a unique role in Christian history and the second Christian generation who lived after their death was very conscious of being the second generation (Herm. *Sim.* 9:15:4; cf. *1 Clem.* 44:1–3), it would not be unnatural for a writer soon after the death of the first generation to call them "the fathers."

(2) The words "since the fathers fell asleep everything remains just as it has been . . ." are said to presuppose a considerable lapse of time since the death of the fathers (Chase, *DB*(*H*) 3, p. 812; cf. Kelly). But this is not necessarily so. We must imagine that in the years when only a few prominent Christians of the first generation were known to be still alive (cf. *Asc. Isa.* 4:13; Herm. *Vis.* 3:5:1) eschatological expectation would have reached a high pitch in many circles. The Parousia would be expected from year to year, but as year after year passed and the few survivors of the first generation passed away, skeptics would have more and more reason to call the expectation disproved. In such circumstances each year in which the promise remained unfulfilled was a long time, and the words of the scoffers in 2 Peter would be quite natural as soon as it was widely admitted that the first generation had in fact passed away.

In fact the probability is that the death of the first generation was a *temporary* problem for Christian eschatology for a short period in the late first century when the problem had first to be confronted (cf. *1 Clem.* 23:2–5; *2 Clem.*

11:1–7; Herm. *Vis.* 3:4:3; 3:5:1; 3:8:9), but once the immediate crisis was surmounted the issue was forgotten and is never mentioned in the literature of the second century. The problem of the death of the first generation was never, so far as we know, raised as an objection to traditional eschatology by second-century Gnostics. Even the more general question of the delay of the Parousia was very rarely raised in the second century (cf. L. W. Barnard, "Justin Martyr's Eschatology," *VC* 19 [1965] 86–98). The probability is therefore that 2 Peter dates from the period, late in the first century, when the death of the first generation was a fresh and challenging issue. It played its part in ensuring that it was not an enduring issue.

πάντα οὕτως διαμένει ἀπ᾽ ἀρχῆς κτίσεως, "everything remains just as it has been since the beginning of the world." The sentence, with its two parallel temporal clauses, is rather awkward, but must have the sense given it in this translation. κτίσεως ("creation") here refers to the created world, not the act of creation, and so is best translated "world," even though this rather obscures the fact that the word κτίσεως prepares for the idea of creation in v 5 (Vögtle, *Zukunft,* 133).

Many have seen in these words an assertion of the immutability and indestructibility of the universe (Bigg, Moffatt, Spicq, Sidebottom, Green; von Allmen, *RTP* 16 [1966] 257): the scoffers deny the eschatological expectation, which involves cosmic dissolution (vv 10, 12), because the stability of the cosmos makes such a prospect inconceivable. There are, however, some difficulties with this interpretation:

(1) The phrase ἀπ᾽ ἀρχῆς κτίσεως ("since the beginning of the world") is not presented as a distinct argument against the expectation of the Parousia, but as part of the argument that the Parousia prophecy has failed. The scoffers point out that since the death of the fathers everything remains the same. The phrase ἀπ᾽ ἀρχῆς κτίσεως ("since the beginning of the world") clarifies this: everything goes on as it has always done. There is no assertion that the nature of the universe is such that everything *must* go on as it has always done.

The force of this objection must be granted. But in vv 5–7 the author treats the phrase ἀπ᾽ ἀρχῆς κτίσεως ("since the beginning of the world") as though it contained an assertion which requires refutation. He argues that the world is dependent on the word of God, and that it is not in fact true that everything has always continued unchanged. Thus it appears that, although the phrase ἀπ᾽ ἀρχῆς κτίσεως ("since the beginning of the world") in v 4 is not a separate argument, the author sees in it an unjustified assumption which strengthens the scoffers' main argument about the nonfulfillment of the Parousia prophecy, and which is therefore worth refuting.

(2) Vögtle (*Zukunft,* 132–33) argues that the function of ἀπ᾽ ἀρχῆς κτίσεως ("since the beginning of the world") is not to report a view held by the scoffers, but to give the author a starting-point for his discussion of the Creation and the Flood in vv 5–7. Of course, it does provide such a starting-point, but if it does not also correspond to anything the scoffers actually thought, then the force of vv 5–7 as a *reply* to the scoffers' objection is much diminished. Even if they did not explicitly argue that there will be no Parousia because nothing ever changes, the author must have attributed to them a

general view of the world which left the Creation and the Flood out of account. He correctly saw that their denial of future eschatology was at home in such a world-view.

(3) Vögtle (*Zukunft,* 131–32) also argues that when the scoffers assert that "everything remains just as it has been since the beginning of the world," they are not denying the destruction of the physical universe, but the intervention of God in the course of history. This objection is partially correct. From 2:3b–10a (see *Comment* on that section) it has already become clear that what the opponents deny and what the author intends is the expectation of divine intervention in judgment. It will also become clear that in 3:5–13 the author's primary concern is with the Parousia as judgment, rather than as cosmic dissolution. However, it is also clear that the coming divine intervention in judgment will take the form of cosmic catastrophe. The destruction of the physical universe is involved in God's judgment of its human inhabitants. Just as his judgment of Sodom and Gomorrah (2:6) was a physical event, and just as his judgment of the whole human race at the time of the Flood was a physical catastrophe of cosmic proportions (2:5; 3:6), so his universal judgment at the Parousia is conceived as a cosmic conflagration. Thus, while it is true that the scoffers intend to reject divine intervention in history, we cannot, with Vögtle, draw a sharp distinction between human history and the physical universe.

In the light of the above discussion, we must modify the view that the scoffers advanced the "scientific" dogma of the indestructibility of the universe as an argument against the possibility of the Parousia. The phrase ἀπ' ἀρχῆς κτίσεως ("since the beginning of the world") is intended by the author to highlight an assumption the scoffers made, but not necessarily an argument they advanced, and it may be too precise to describe this assumption as the indestructibility of the universe. The scoffers assumed that God does not intervene in the world. The course of the world, i.e. of human history and of the physical world in which it is set, has always continued without the catastrophic intervention of divine judgment. Obviously this view of the past coheres with the scoffers' skepticism about future judgment, even though we cannot be sure they used it as an argument against future judgment. In challenging their view of the past the author of 2 Peter will be able to challenge their skepticism about future judgment.

It is not necessary to seek the background to the scoffers' ideas in the Aristotelian belief in the imperishability of the world, which was denied by Epicureans and Stoics. They are not influenced by cosmology as much as by a rationalistic skepticism about divine intervention in the world, to which the Epicurean denial of providence seems the closest pagan parallel (Neyrey, *JBL* 99 [1980] 420; *Polemic,* 203–5).

There is nothing in this v (or elsewhere in 2 Peter) to support the view that the scoffers' denial of future judgment was based on a Gnostic belief in a wholly realized eschatology. On that view, "their question about the delay of the Parousia, just as their appeal to the stability of the universe, is but an argument used to justify a position already held on other grounds" (Talbert, *VC* 20 [1966] 143; so also Werdermann, *Irrlehrer,* 67–68; von Allmen, *RTP* 16 [1966] 265; Harnisch, *Existenz,* 102). But this is a highly speculative view, which requires us to believe that we can know more about our author's opponents' views than he himself tells us. Clearly their denial of the Parousia was not *solely* motivated by the apparent nonfulfillment of the prophecy of the Parousia, since their skepticism about future judgment was evidently linked with ethical libertinism. But the delay of the Parousia was apparently their central argument (cf. 2:3b; 3:9) and, since our author gives it so much attention, the most effective in gaining followers for them. Our author would not have dealt so extensively with the issue of the delay of the Parousia, nor would his letter have been preserved, if that issue had not been a real source of concern for his contemporaries (cf. Fornberg, *Early Church,* 65).

Explanation

The reference to Peter's first letter (1 Peter) identifies the present letter as deriving from the Petrine circle in Rome, and also marks the author's return to the "testament" convention of writing in Peter's name, in order to prepare for a second Petrine "prediction" (cf. 2:1–3a). The purpose of 2 Peter, like that of 1 Peter, is to "remind" (cf. 1:12–15)—specifically, to recall the eschatological prophecies of the OT prophets and the ethical implications of the Christian gospel, the two points that need emphasis in opposition to the false teachers. The reminder is reinforced with an example of Peter's own apocalyptic prophecy, in which he predicts the false teachers, this time under the guise of "scoffers," i.e. skeptics who mock divine revelation, both moral and prophetic. Thus the scoffers are libertines, who follow their own evil desires instead of the commandment of Christ, and they scornfully reject the prophecy of the Parousia of Jesus Christ as unfulfilled and disproved.

The prophetic form of vv 3–4 enables the writer to portray his contemporaries, the false teachers, as a phenomenon of the last days, which the apostles predicted. The readers need not be disturbed by them. On the contrary, the false teachers, who reject eschatological prophecy, should in fact be a confirmation of the readers' faith in eschatological prophecy, since they themselves are a fulfillment of prophecy!

The quotation from the scoffers in v 4 is the author's own formulation of the objection his opponents were making to the expectation of the Parousia. The Parousia had been expected during the lifetime of the first Christian generation, but that generation had now passed away and still nothing had happened. The objection reflects what for a period in the late first century was evidently an acute problem for Christian eschatology until it was successfully surmounted and forgotten. The false teachers were no doubt able to exploit a genuine source of perplexity for 2 Peter's readers, as the serious attempt the author makes to meet the problem shows. But the last phrase of v 4 reveals a further dimension to the skepticism of the false teachers. The failure of the Parousia hope only confirms their assumption that divine interventions in history do not happen. The world continues unchanged just as it always has done. This rationalistic assumption about the past probably contributed as much to their eschatological skepticism as the fact of the delay of the Parousia did, and so the author will challenge that assumption first before tackling directly the issue of delay.

Reply to Objection 4: (a) The Sovereignty of God's Word (3:5–7)

Bibliography

Allmen, D. von. "L'apocalyptique juive et le retard de la parousie en II Pierre 3:1–13." *RTP* 16 (1966) 260–61. **Chaine, J.** "Cosmogonie aquatique et conflagration finale d'après la *secunda Petri.*" *RB* 46 (1937) 207–16. **Harnisch, W.** *Eschatologische Existenz,* 104–5. **Testa, P. E.** "La distruzione del mondo per il fuoco nella seconda epistola di san Pietro." *RivB* 10 (1962) 252–81 (not available). **Vögtle, A.** *Zukunft,* 133–36.

Translation

[5] *For in maintaining this, they overlook the fact that long ago there were heavens and an earth, created* [a] *out of water and by means of water by the word of God.* [6] *By these* [b] *the world of that time was deluged with water and destroyed.* [7] *But by the same word the heavens and the earth which now exist have been held in store for fire, and are being kept until the day of judgment and destruction of ungodly people.*

Notes

[a] Since the whole argument of these vv requires a statement that the heavens, as well as the earth, were created by the word of God, it is best to take *συνεστῶσα*, "created," with *οὐρανοί* as well as with *γῆ* and to explain its feminine singular form by attraction to the nearest subject, *γῆ*.

[b] One minuscule (69) has *δι' ὃν* instead of *δι' ὧν* and this reading is accepted by Mayor (cxcix) and Wand. It gives excellent sense, by contrast with the difficult *δι' ὧν*, but must therefore be regarded as a correction.

Form/Structure/Setting

The section 3:4–10 is chiastically structured: vv 5–7 take up the last words of v 4 and then vv 8–10 respond to the main statement of v 4. The mention of creation (κτίσεως) at the end of v 4 provides a starting-point for the author's response in v 5, while v 6 is a contradiction of the assumption in v 4b that everything has remained the same from the beginning of the world. Out of this response to v 4b the author creates an argument for the certainty of eschatological judgment (v 7). The present tense in v 5a shows that the author has again abandoned the "testament" convention of prophecy, in favor of direct present-tense argument with his contemporaries.

In view of the Jewish apocalyptic parallels to the correlation of the Flood and the eschatological conflagration (see *Comment* section), von Allmen (*RTP* 16 [1966] 260–61) suggests that these vv, apart from the introductory v 5a, are dependent on a Jewish apocalyptic source. It is likely that the author is following the source we have already postulated for the section 3:4–13, and this suggestion is confirmed by a parallel in *1 Clem.* 27:4: ἐν λόγῳ τῆς μεγαλωσύνης αὐτοῦ συνεστήσατο τὰ πάντα, καὶ ἐν λόγῳ δύναται αὐτὰ καταστρέψαι, "By a word of his majesty he created all things, and by a word he can destroy them." The use of *συνιστάναι* (transitive here; contrast the intransitive use in 2 Pet 3:5) for God's creation of the world is not uncommon (Philo, *Leg. All.* 3.10; Josephus, *Ant.* 12.22; *Corp. Herm.* 1.31; cf. *1 Enoch* 101:6) and of course the idea of creation by the word of God is very common, but the parallel between creation by word and destruction by word is rare and strikingly similar to 2 Pet 3:5, 7 (cf. also *Apoc. Pet.* E 4, probably dependent on 2 Pet 3:5, 7). This could be just one of the many similarities between *1 Clem.* and 2 Peter, but the v in *1 Clem.* occurs in a passage defending future eschatology (23–27) which began with the quotation from an apocryphal work (23:3–4) which resembles 2 Pet 3:4. It is therefore quite likely that *1 Clem.* 27:4 echoes the same Jewish apocalypse on which 2 Pet 3:5–7 is dependent.

Comment

5. *λανθάνει γὰρ αὐτοὺς τοῦτο θέλοντας*, "for in maintaining this they overlook the fact." There are two possible translations: "For they deliberately ignore this fact" (cf. AV, RV, RSV, JB, GNB, NIV; Plumptre, Bigg, Mayor, Moffatt, Spicq), or "For in maintaining this, they overlook the fact" (cf. NEB; Spitta, Windisch, Schelkle, Reicke, Kelly, Schrage). It is impossible to be sure which is correct, but the position of *τοῦτο* ("this") makes it rather more likely that it should be taken as the object of *θέλοντας*, "maintaining," as in the latter translation (see especially Kelly's discussion). The point of *γάρ* ("for") will be that the scoffers are only able to maintain the views expressed in v 4 because they overlook the facts of the Creation and the Flood.

ὅτι οὐρανοὶ ἦσαν ἔκπαλαι καὶ γῆ ἐξ ὕδατος καὶ δι' ὕδατος συνεστῶσα τῷ τοῦ θεοῦ λόγῳ, "that long ago there were heavens and an earth, created out of water and by means of water by the word of God." This clause contains no implication that the heavens were created before the earth (against Spitta), but simply echoes the reference to "the heavens and the earth" in Gen 1:1. According to the creation account in Gen 1, and in accordance with general Near Eastern myth, the world—sky and earth—emerged out of a primeval ocean (Gen 1:2, 6–7, 9; cf. Ps 33:7; 136:6; Prov 8:27–29; Sir 39:17; Herm. *Vis.* 1:3:4). The world exists because the waters of chaos, which are now above the firmament, beneath the earth and surrounding the earth, are held back and can no longer engulf the world. The phrase *ἐξ ὕδατος* ("out of water") expresses this mythological concept of the world's emergence out of the watery chaos, rather than the more "scientific" notion, taught by Thales of Miletus, that water is the basic element out of which everything else is made (cf. *Clem. Hom.* 11:24:1). The second phrase *δι' ὕδατος* ("by means of water") is more difficult to explain. Since the reference is to the creation of the world, it cannot refer to the sustenance of life on earth by rain (Bigg, Green). Some give *διά* a local sense, "between, in the midst of the waters" (RV, JB; Mayor, James, Chaine, Wand, Spicq), which accords well with the creation account (Gen 1:6–7, 9), but would be an unusual use of the preposition (Gen 1:6 LXX expresses this thought by *ἀνὰ μέσον ὕδατος καὶ ὕδατος*), especially as *δι' ὧν* in the next v means "by means of which." So it is best to translate "by means of water" (Knopf, Windisch, Kelly; Chaine, *RB* 46 [1937] 210 n. 3); the writer means that water was, in a loose sense, the instrument of creation, since it was by separating and gathering the waters that God created the world. This also provides a good parallel with the next v, which states that by means of water he afterward destroyed the world.

Creation *by the word of God* is a common idea (Gen 1:3–30; Ps 33:6; 148:5; Wis 9:1; 4 Ezra 6:38, 43; *Sib. Or.* 3:30; Heb 11:3; *1 Clem.* 27:4; Herm. *Vis.* 1:3:4; *Ker. Pet., ap.* Clem. Alex., *Strom.* 6.5.39.3). Our author is anxious to stress that the world existed only because God commanded that it should; by the same word he destroyed it (v 6) and will do so again (v 7).

6. δι' ὧν, lit. "by means of which." It is by no means obvious what the antecedent of the plural relative pronoun is. The following are the main possibilities:

(1) *οὐρανοί . . . καὶ γῆ* ("heavens and an earth") is proposed by Reicke and Marín (*EE* 50 [1975] 232 n. 44). Reicke translates "because of them," but it is unclear in what sense the Flood could be said to have occurred "because of" the heavens and the earth.

(2) *οὐρανοί* ("heavens"): James, who proposes this, translates "by means of which" (cf. Gen 7:11), but *οὐρανοί* is a remote antecedent, and why the author should have wished to say that the world was deluged "by means of the heavens" is obscure. Suggestions (1) and (2) both require that *ὁ τότε κόσμος* ("the world of that time") refer to people, not the physical universe.

(3) *ἐξ ὕδατος καὶ δι' ὕδατος* ("out of water and by means of water"), i.e. two different categories of water, the waters above and below the firmament, as in Gen 7:11 (Plumptre, Spitta, Moffatt, Chaine, Sidebottom). This suggestion depends on the view that the repetition of *ὕδατος* ("water") in v 5 refers to two different categories of water; but this is not very likely (see above). Furthermore, the use of *ὕδατι* ("with water") in v 6 becomes, on this view, wholly redundant.

(4) *ὕδατος* ("water") and *τῷ τοῦ θεοῦ λόγῳ* ("the word of God") are suggested by Bigg, Kelly, Green. This is stylistically rather awkward, but seems to give the best sense. On this view *ὕδατι* ("with water") in v 6 is still somewhat redundant, but in view of the ambiguity of δι' ὧν ("by means of which") less so than in the case of suggestion (3). The writer's argument seems to require some statement that the word of God, by which the world was created (v 5) and which has decreed its eschatological destruction by fire (v 7), also accomplished its destruction in the Flood (v 6).

If δι' ὧν refers to both water and the word of God, there is a neat parallelism in all three vv in this section: by his word and by means of water God created the world (v 5); by his word and by means of water he destroyed it (v 6); by his word and by means of fire he will destroy it in the future (v 7).

ὁ τότε κόσμος, "the world of that time." Most commentators take this phrase to refer to the whole physical universe, heavens and earth, but a few (James; Sasse in *TDNT* 3, 890; Vögtle, *Zukunft,* 134–36; cf. Green) limit it to the inhabitants of the earth, especially human beings. In favor of the former view are the references to the heavens and the earth in vv 5, 7, and especially the apparent parallelism between *ὁ τότε κόσμος* and *οἱ . . . νῦν οὐρανοὶ καὶ ἡ γῆ* ("the heavens and the earth which now exist") in v 7. Vögtle (*Zukunft,* 135) argues that the parallelism is between *οὐρανοὶ . . . ἔκπαλαι καὶ γῆ* ("heavens and an earth . . . long ago") in v 5, and *οἱ . . . νῦν οὐρανοὶ καὶ ἡ γῆ* ("the heavens and the earth which now exist") in v 7, but this parallelism itself implies that the Flood marks a break between the heavens and the earth which existed before it and those which exist now. In fact the argument of vv 5–7 requires a threefold parallelism: God created the heavens and the earth, he has destroyed them once by water, he will destroy them again by fire.

It is true that in 2:5 *ἀρχαίου κόσμου* ("the ancient world") is equivalent to *κόσμῳ ἀσεβῶν* ("the world of ungodly people"), and refers to the *people* who perished in the Flood. It is also true that, as in 2:5, the author's real concern throughout this discussion is not with cosmology but with judgment (cf. 3:7, 9, 11–14). We may therefore concede that in 3:6 his *emphasis* is on the Flood as a universal judgment on sinful men and women. But he evidently conceives this judgment as having been executed by means of a cosmic catastrophe which affected the heavens as well as the earth.

This idea is not so alien to the Genesis narrative as many commentators allege: according to Gen 7:11 the waters of chaos, confined at the creation above the firmament, poured through the windows of the firmament to inundate the earth. It is an extension of this idea when, in *1 Enoch* 83:3 (Enoch's vision of the Flood), the heaven is said to collapse onto the earth, so that the earth is swallowed up by the waters of the abyss.

ὕδατι κατακλυσθεὶς ἀπώλετο, "was deluged with water and destroyed." The verb (a NT *hapax*) is used of the Flood in Wis 10:4; Josephus, *Ant.* 5.566; *Clem. Hom.* 9.2:1 (cf. also Ezek 38:22 LXX; *Sib Or.* 3:690). The addition of *ὕδατι* ("with water") emphasizes that this destruction was by water, to make the contrast with the coming destruction by fire (*πυρί*, v 7). Perhaps there is an allusion to the Jewish tradition of a flood of fire corresponding to the flood of water in Noah's time (*Gen. Rab.* 39:6; 49:9; *Lev. Rab.* 10:1; *Mek.* Amalek 3:14; cf. 1QH 3:19–20, 29–33).

The idea of the destruction of the antediluvian world need not be taken to mean total annihilation. Rather, just as it was created by being brought out of the primeval ocean, so it was destroyed when it was once again submerged in the primeval ocean. The ordered world (*κόσμος*) reverted to chaos.

The author of 2 Peter (no doubt following his Jewish apocalyptic source) seems to envisage world history in three great periods, divided by two great cataclysms: the world before the Flood, the present world which will end in the eschatological conflagration (v 7), and the new world to come (v 13). This periodization, with the typological correspondence between the Flood and the eschatological judgment which it entails, is also presupposed in *1 Enoch* (cf. especially 10:11–11:2; 93:4) and in the Jewish Sibylline Oracles (cf. Collins, *Oracles,* 102–3). According to *Sib. Or.* 1:195; 7:11, a "second age" (*δεύτερος αἰών*) began after the Flood (cf. *παλιγγενεσία*, "regeneration," in Philo, *Mos.* 2.65; *1 Clem.* 9:4).

7. *τῷ αὐτῷ λόγῳ*, "by the same word." For a similar thought, cf. *1 Clem.* 27:4, probably dependent on the same Jewish apocalyptic source (see *Form/Structure/Setting* section) and *Ker. Pet.* (*ap.* Clem. Alex., *Strom.* 6.5.39.3): "there is one God who created the beginning of all things and has power to end them." Our author's point is that since the world was created by God's word and has already been destroyed once by God's word, we can confidently expect the future judgment which has also been decreed by his word.

τεθησαυρισμένοι εἰσὶν πυρί, "have been held in store for fire." The choice of verb is a little surprising, but may be influenced by the common use of this image, also with the sense of preservation until the Day of Judgment, with reference to the rewards of the righteous and the punishment of the ungodly "stored up" in heaven (*Pss. Sol.* 9:5: 4 Ezra 7:77, 83–84; *Frg. Tg.* Deut 32:34; Rom 2:5; *Clem. Hom.* 16:20). The Hellenistic Jewish writer Pseudo-Sophocles (*ap.* Clem. Alex., *Strom.* 5.14.121.4), writing of the eschatological conflagration, says that the air "will open the storehouse full of fire" (πυρὸς γέμοντα θησαυρόν; cf. Deut 32:34; Jer 27:25 LXX).

The idea of an eschatological world conflagration—found only in 2 Peter in the NT—has been attributed to Stoic or Iranian influence, but there can be no real doubt that its immediate background is to be found in Jewish apocalyptic. The idea of divine judgment by fire is frequent in the OT, no doubt partly because the destruction of Sodom and Gomorrah provided a paradigm (see e.g. Deut 32:22; Ps 97:3; Isa 30:30; 66:15–16; Ezek 38:22; Amos 7:4; Zeph 1:18; Mal 3:19 [EVV 4:1]; full survey and discussion in Mayer, *Weltenbrand,* 79–114). In OT texts the function of this fire is to consume the wicked, not to destroy the world, but as the idea of a universal, eschatological judgment developed (cf. already Isa 66:15–16; Mal 3:19) it is not surprising that the idea of judgment by fire should develop into the expectation of a universal conflagration, especially when the future universal judgment was envisaged by analogy with the Flood as a universal judgment in the past. The idea of an eschatological conflagration is not by any means found throughout Jewish eschatology in the postbiblical period, but it occurs in sufficient texts, both Palestinian and Hellenistic, to show that it was a fairly widespread conception (1 QH 3:19–36; *Sib. Or.* 3:54–87; 4:173–81; 5:211–13, 531; Pseudo-Sophocles, *ap.* Clem. Alex., *Strom.* 5.14.121.4; 5.14.122.1; *Adam and Eve* 49:3; Josephus, *Ant.* 1.70; *Mek.* Amalek 3:14; and see discussion in Mayer, *Weltenbrand,* 114–25). The author of 2 Peter doubtless found it in the Jewish apocalypse on which he is dependent in this chapter (see *Form/Structure/Setting* section on 3:8–10). Although it is not found in the NT outside 2 Peter, from the late first century onward it became common in Christian writings (*2 Clem.* 16:3; Herm. *Vis.* 4:3:3; *Apoc. Pet.* E 5; Justin, *1 Apol.* 20.1–2, 4; 60.8; *2 Apol.* 7.2–3; Theophilus, *Ad Autol.* 2.38; *Sib. Or.* 2:196–200; Minucius Felix, *Oct.* 11.1; 34).

An eschatological conflagration also featured in Iranian (Zoroastrian) religion (Mayer, *Weltenbrand,* 1–79; Collins, *Oracles,* 104–6), and it is probable that the Iranian ideas exercised some influences on Jewish eschatology. Such influence is perhaps especially to be found in Christian texts which depict the river of fire through which all people, good and bad, must pass to be tested and purified (cf. *Apoc. Pet.* E 5–6; *Sib. Or.* 2:196–205, 315; James, *Apocrypha,* 90–91; Lactantius, *Div. Inst.* 7.21). The Iranian eschatology was probably known in the Hellenistic world of the first century especially through the *Oracle of Hystaspes* (cf. Justin, *1 Apol.* 20:1), but the expectation of a world conflagration was even more familiar through the teaching of Stoicism. The Stoics taught that periodically the universe was dissolved and renewed by means of a conflagration (ἐκπύρωσις) in which everything returned to its most basic element, fire, before reconstituting itself (Diogenes Laertes 7.134; Cicero, *De Nat. Deorum* 2.118; cf. Collins, *Oracles,* 102; and other literature cited in Spicq). Hellenistic Jewish writers cannot have been unaware of this parallel (which Justin fully recognized: *1 Apol.* 20; *2 Apol.* 7) and it may sometimes have influenced their accounts of the eschatological conflagration. However, the essential element in most Jewish and Christian references to the eschatological conflagration is the destruction of the wicked by the fire of divine judgment; this idea, which differs from the Zoroastrian fire of purification and from the Stoic idea of a natural, deterministic cycle of destruction and renewal, is fundamentally Jewish and biblical. The author of 2 Peter, who is really interested in the conflagration as judgment on the wicked (see below), follows this Jewish tradition. If he was aware of the pagan parallels, he is unlikely to have been very concerned with them (against Fornberg, *Early Church,* 66; Neyrey, *Polemic,* 294–97).

However, a further series of parallels still requires notice. An ancient idea, found both in Plato (*Timaeus* 22C–E) and in Berossus, the Babylonian writer of the third century B.C. (*ap.* Seneca, *Quaest. Nat.* 3.29.1), envisaged the world as undergoing recurrent destructions by flood and fire alternately (cf. also Seneca, *Quaest. Nat.* 3.28; Lucretius, *De Nat. Rerum* 5; Origen, *c. Cels.* 4.11–12; see Chaine, *RB* 46 [1937] 211–14; Collins, *Oracles,* 101–2). This idea may have exercised some influence on the Jewish notion of two universal judgments, the Flood and the eschatological conflagration (Josephus, *Ant.* 1.70–71; *Adam and Eve* 49:3; *Mek.* Amalek 3:14; the same scheme is applied to the Flood and the destruction of Sodom and Gomorrah in Philo, *Mos.* 2.53; *Gen. Rab.* 27:3; 39:6; 49:9; *Lev. Rab.* 10:1; cf. also *Gos. Eg.* 63:6; cf. J. P. Lewis, *A Study of the Interpretation of Noah and the Flood in Jewish and Christian Literature* [Leiden: E. J. Brill, 1968] 169–73). Undoubtedly the pattern of destruction by flood and destruction by fire is present in 2 Pet 3:6–7, but unlike the pagan notion it is a pattern of two divine judgments in a linear, not a cyclical, scheme of world history. Its immediate antecedents are therefore Jewish.

When the author of 2 Peter writes that *by the word of God* the world "has been held in store for fire," he must mean that the expectation of the eschatological conflagration is founded on prophecy which reveals that God has decreed it. Although his immediate source is a Jewish apocalypse, the Jewish expectation was an interpretation of OT texts such as Deut 32:22 (quoted in this connection by Justin, *1 Apol.* 60.8); Isa 34:4 LXX (to which 2 Pet 3:10, 12 alludes); Mal 3:19 (EVV 4:1; cf. *2 Clem.* 16:3); Isa 66:15–16; Zeph 1:18.

τηρούμενοι εἰς ἡμέραν κρίσεως καὶ ἀπωλείας τῶν ἀσεβῶν ἀνθρώπων, "are being kept until the day of judgment and destruction of ungodly people." *τηρεῖν* ("to keep") is used as in 2:4, 9. For the phrase *ἡμέραν ἀπωλείας* ("day of destruction") cf. LXX Deut 32:35; Job 21:30. For *ἀσεβῶν* ("ungodly people," also in 2:5–6) see *Comment* on Jude 4.

This emphatic phrase makes it quite clear that the author's concern in this section is not with cosmology, for its own sake, but with judgment. It is God's coming judgment of the wicked that the scoffers deny and our author asserts. Taking up current ideas he envisages this judgment as occurring by means of a cosmic conflagration.

Explanation

The author takes up the rationalistic assumption which he has detected in the scoffers' objection. They ignore the fact that the continuance of the world as a stable habitation for mankind has always depended and continues to depend on the will of God. It was the divine decree which first brought the world into existence, separating and gathering the waters of chaos to create the sky and the earth. Nor is it true that since the creation the world has survived without major disturbance. The word of God which created the world has also once destroyed it, when in the Flood it was once again submerged beneath the waters of chaos. It is the same word of God which has decreed that the world will in the future be destroyed again, this time by fire. The observable stability of the world is therefore no guarantee of its continued stability in the future; it is being preserved in existence by God only until the time he has appointed for the judgment of the wicked. The final phrase reveals that although in this passage the author is certainly concerned with catastrophic upheavals in the physical world, which amount to the destruction and creation of worlds, he is not concerned with these for the sake of mere cosmology, but with their interpretation in a world-view which sees them as occurring by the sovereign decree of God as instruments of his judgment on humanity.

This passage is perhaps the most difficult of several passages in 2 Peter which pose serious hermeneutical difficulties for the modern reader. The author clearly uses cosmological ideas current in his time which must be regarded as mythological: creation as the emergence of the world out of a primeval ocean, the Deluge as a universal cosmic catastrophe, the idea that the world is to be subject to two universal destructions, one by water (the Flood) and the other by fire (in the future). But the religious belief which is conveyed in these mythological forms remains valid, though it is not a belief which can be detached, in a purely existential way, from any reference to the physical world. The idea of the waters of chaos held back by God's creative act to create an environment for human life, but released in the Flood to overwhelm and destroy that environment again, is not essentially alien to a modern understanding of the universe. We know very well that the continuity of an environment in which humanity can survive and flourish is not at all to be taken for granted. The forces of nature retain the appalling potential to interrupt and obliterate human history. Primitive humanity's many experiences of this destructive power of nature are perhaps summed up in the story of the Flood. Modern humanity faces the additional threat of our newly acquired power to use the forces of nature to destroy ourselves. Although the eschatological conflagration to which 2 Peter alludes is an apocalyptic image, it is an image which remains powerful today, evoking both the threat of nuclear holocaust and the eventual reabsorption of our planet into the expanding sun. The world which now permits human life to flourish is far from guaranteed against a destructive reversion to chaos. But in the biblical perspective human history is not at the mercy of chance and meaningless catastrophe. The God who created the cosmos out of chaos is in sovereign control of the forces of destruction. The threat is the threat of God's moral judgment, and even that judgment is not an end in itself, but for the sake of the new world of righteousness which he will once again create out of chaos.

Reply to Objection 4: (b) The Forbearance of the Lord (3:8–10)

Bibliography

Allmen, D. von. "L'apocalyptique juive et le retard de la parousie en II Pierre 3:1–13." *RTP* 16 (1966) 258–63. **Barnard, L. W.** "The Judgment in 2 Peter iii." *ExpTim* 68 (1956–57) 302. **Bauckham, R. J.** "The Delay of the Parousia." *TynB* 31 (1980) 3–36. **Bonus, A.** "2 Peter iii.10." *ExpTim* 32 (1920–21) 280–81. **Chaine, J.** "Cosmogonie aquatique et conflagration finale d'après la *secunda Petri.*" *RB* 46 (1937) 207–16. **Danker, F. W.** "II Peter 3:10 and Psalms of Solomon 17:10." *ZNW* 53 (1962) 82–86. **Harnisch, W.** *Eschatologische Existenz,* 105–13. **Lenhard, H.** "Ein Beitrag zur Übersetzung von II Ptr 3[10d]." *ZNW* 52 (1961) 128–29. **Lenhard, H.** "Noch einmal zu 2 Petr 3 10d." *ZNW* 69 (1978) 136. **Milligan, G.** "2 Peter iii.10." *ExpTim* 32 (1920–21) 331. **Neyrey, J. H.** "The Form and Background of the Polemic in 2 Peter." *JBL* 99 (1980) 423–27, 429–30. **Olivier, F.** "Une correction au texte du Nouveau Testament: II Pierre 3, 10." *Essais,* 129–152. **Otto, J. K. Th. von.** "Haben Barnabas, Justinus und Irenäus den zweiten Petrusbrief (3, 8) benutzt?" *ZWT* 20 (1877) 525–29. **Roberts, J. W.** "A Note on the Meaning of II Peter 3:10d." *RestQ* 6 (1962) 32–33. **Smitmans, A.** "Das Gleichnis vom Dieb." *Wort Gottes in der Zeit: Festschrift Karl Hermann Schelkle zum 65. Geburtstag,* ed. H. Feld and J. Nolte. Düsseldorf: Patmos-Verlag, 1973. 43–68. **Strobel, A.** *Untersuchungen,* 87–97. **Vansittart, A. A.** "On Two Triple Readings in the New Testament." *JP* 3 (1871) 357–59. **Vögtle, A.** *Zukunft,* 138–39. **Wilson, W. E.** "Εὑρεθήσεται in 2 Pet. iii.10." *ExpTim* 32 (1920–21) 44–45.

Translation

[8] *My dear friends, do not overlook this one fact, that with the Lord one day is as a thousand years and a thousand years are as one day.* [9] *The Lord is not late in fulfilling the promise,*[a] *according to some people's idea of lateness, but he is forbearing toward you,*[b] *because it is not his will that any should perish, but that all should come to repentance.* [10] *But the day of the Lord will come like a thief. On that day the heavens will pass away with a roar, the heavenly bodies will be dissolved in the heat, and the earth and the works in it will be found.*[c]

Notes

[a] For the genitive τῆς ἐπαγγελίας, unparalleled with βραδύνειν, "to be late": cf. BDF § 180 (5), but it is probably best explained by analogy with the genitive with ὑστερεῖν in the temporal sense, meaning "to be too late for."

[b] εἰς ὑμᾶς (P[72] B C P *al*) is preferable to δι' ὑμᾶς (א A *al*), which may arise from the unusualness of εἰς after μακροθυμεῖν, "to be forbearing," or from the desire to give v 9b a wider application, to all mankind rather than all the readers (cf. Justin, *2 Apol.* 7). εἰς ἡμᾶς (K L *al*) is poorly attested.

[c] εὑρεθήσεται, "will be found" (א B K P *al*) is undoubtedly the best reading, as the *lectio difficilior,* which allows the other readings to be explained as corrections. The other readings are: εὑρεθήσεται λυόμενα, "will be found dissolved" (P[72]); οὐχ εὑρεθήσεται, "will not be found" (sah, one MS of sy[h]; but these may well represent a *translator's* correction); ἀφανισθήσονται, "will vanish" (C); κατακαήσεται, "will be burned up" (A *al*); omission of the whole clause (ψ vg *al*).

Form/Structure/Setting

The introductory words (v 8a) correspond to v 5a and indicate that a second line of argument against the scoffers' objection in v 4 begins here. In v 5a the scoffers are accused of overlooking one important fact; in v 8a the readers are urged not to overlook one. In both cases, of course, the arguments are really addressed to the readers, so that their faith may not be shaken by the scoffers' arguments.

Verse 9, with its reference to τῆς ἐπαγγελίας ("the promise," cf. v 4), explicitly takes up the main point in v 4, and uses the οὐ . . . ἀλλά ("not . . . but") form to reject the scoffers' contention (Neyrey, *Polemic,* 18–19).

Von Allmen (*RTP* 16 [1966] 263) thinks that in 2 Peter's Jewish apocalyptic source v 10b followed immediately after v 7. He acknowledges that v 8b is a fragment of Jewish material (*RTP* 16 [1966] 261–62) and sees v 9 as the author's own formulation following Jewish ideas (*RTP* 16 [1966] 260–61), but does not derive them from the apocalyptic source which furnished vv 5–7, 10b. However, we have argued (see *Form/Structure/Setting* section on 3:1–4) that 2 Peter's Jewish apocalyptic source was explicitly concerned with the problem of eschatological delay, and since the arguments in vv 8–9 certainly derive from Jewish apocalyptic (see *Comment*), it is plausible to attribute them to the same source as the author has followed in vv 4–7. (With the allusion to Hab 2:3 in 2 Pet 3:9, cf. the composite quotation of Isa 13:22 and Mal 3:1, in a version differing from the LXX, in *1 Clem.* 23:5, immediately following *1 Clem.*'s quotation from the Jewish apocalypse. This quotation may well come from the same apocalypse.) Doubtless the author of 2 Peter has rewritten the material, and we have no hope of recovering its original form.

However, in the case of v 10, it seems likely that a fragment of 2 Peter's source survives in *2 Clem.* 16:3:

Mal. 3:19 LXX:	*2 Clem. 16:3*	*2 Pet. 3:10*
	Γινώσκετε δὲ ὅτι	
διότι ἰδοὺ ἡμέρα κυρίου ἔρχεται	ἔρχεται ἤδη ἡ ἡμέρα τῆς κρίσεως	ἥξει δὲ ἡμέρα κυρίου
καιομένη ὡς κλίβανος *Isa. 34:4 LXX* (B, Lucian): καὶ τακήσονται πᾶσαι αἱ δυνάμεις τῶν οὐρανῶν	ὡς κλίβανος καιόμενος, καὶ τακήσονταί τινες τῶν οὐρανῶν,	ὡς κλέπτης, ἐν ᾗ οἱ οὐρανοὶ ῥοιζηδὸν παρελεύσονται, στοιχεῖα δὲ καυσούμενα λυθήσεται,
	καὶ πᾶσα ἡ γῆ ὡς μόλιβος ἐπὶ πυρὶ τηκόμενος,	καὶ γῆ
	καὶ τότε φανήσεται τὰ κρύφια καὶ φανερὰ ἔργα τῶν ἀνθρώπων.	καὶ τὰ ἐν αὐτῇ ἔργα εὑρεθήσεται.
		2 Pet. 3:12
		οὐρανοὶ πυρούμενοι λυθήσονται καὶ στοιχεῖα καυσούμενα τήκεται.

Mal 3:19 LXX:	*2 Clem. 16:3*	*2 Pet 3:10*
For, behold, *the* *day of the Lord* is	But you know that *the* *day* of Judgment is now	But *the* *day* of the Lord will

coming burning *like* an oven. *Isa 34:4 LXX:* and all the powers of *the heavens* will *melt.*	*coming like* a burning oven, and some (?) of *the heavens* will *melt,*	come like a thief. On that day *the* *heavens* will pass away with a roar, the heavenly bodies will be dissolved in the
	and all *the earth* [will be] like lead *melting* in fire, *and* then *the* secret and	heat, *and the earth*
	open *works* of men will appear.	*and the works* on it will be found.
		2 Pet 3:12 . . . *the heavens* will be dissolved in flames and the heavenly bodies *melt* in the heat.

The similarity between these passages has been noticed before. Some have thought that *2 Clem.* 16:3 is dependent on 2 Pet 3:10, 12 (e.g. Salmon, *Introduction,* 521; Bigg, 209; James, 35), while Donfried (*Second Clement,* 91–92) suggests they both depend on similar traditions, but the hypothesis of a common written source seems not to have been suggested before. Yet it is fairly clear that *2 Clem.* 16:3 is a quotation, and more than a combined quotation of Mal 3:19; Isa 34:4 LXX (James, *Apocrypha,* 88, suggested the quotation came from the *Apoc. Pet.,* but it does not correspond at all closely to *Apoc. Pet.* E 5, while *2 Clem.* is probably earlier in date than the *Apoc. Pet.*) A likely source is the Jewish apocalypse already quoted in *2 Clem.* 11:2–4.

The similarity with 2 Pet 3:10, 12 is greater than can be explained by common dependence on Isa 34:4 LXX, and it should be noticed that *2 Clem.* 16:1; 17:1, in the vicinity of the quotation, express ideas similar to 2 Pet 3:9b, which may indicate that both writers found them in the original context of the quotation. The puzzling final words of 2 Pet 3:10 are illuminated if *2 Clem.* 16:3 represents their source (see *Comment*). The free adaptation of his source by the author of 2 Peter would be comparable with his adaptation of Jude in ch. 2. For the opening words of the fragment, drawn from Mal 3:19 LXX, he will have substituted a grammatically similar phrase from Christian tradition, to stress the unexpectedness of the Parousia, which his argument, following v 9, required.

The reference to the thief certainly depends ultimately on Jesus' parable of the thief (Matt 24:43 par. Luke 12:39). Against Harnisch (*Existenz,* 84–98, 110–11), who thinks 1 Thess 5:2 and, perhaps independently, 2 Pet 3:10a derive not from Gospel tradition but from Jewish apocalyptic usage, the fact that eschatological use of the thief image is found frequently but exclusively in early Christian literature shows that it derives from Jesus' parable (Smitmans, "Dieb"; R. J. Bauckham, "Synoptic Parousia Parables and the Apocalypse," *NTS* 23 [1976–77] 162–76). In 1 Thess 5:2; 2 Pet 3:10; Rev 3:3; 16:15 the image appears in "deparabolized" form (see Bauckham, "Synoptic Parousia," 167–69) as a simile: ὡς κλέπτης ("like a thief"). In Rev 3:3; 16:15 it is the Lord himself who will come ὡς κλέπτης (cf. the application of the parable in Matt 24:44 par. Luke 12:40, where the Son of Man is compared to the thief), while in 1 Thess 5:2 and 2 Pet 3:10 the simile applies to the coming of the Day of the Lord. We must assume that the simile ὡς κλέπτης, though derived from Jesus' parable, was itself a traditional element of Christian eschatological paraenesis (like other allusions to Parousia parables: see Bauckham, "Synoptic Parousia"). This observation lessens the need to suppose that 2 Pet 3:10 is dependent on 1 Thess 5:2 (as Smitmans, "Dieb," 60–61; Fornberg, *Early Church,* 25, think). The close resemblance (1 Thess 5:2: *ἡμέρα κυρίου ὡς κλέπτης ἐν νυκτὶ οὕτως ἔρχεται,* "the Day of the Lord comes like a thief in the night"; 2 Pet 3:10: *ἥξει δὲ ἡμέρα κυρίου ὡς κλέπτης,* "the Day of the Lord will come like a thief") may only reveal common dependence on paraenetic tradition. The introductory formula in 1 Thess 5:2a confirms such dependence in Paul's case, and (against Fornberg, *Early Church,* 25 n. 5) such oral traditions were certainly still current at the time when 2 Peter was written (cf. *Did.* 16:1). Although the author of 2 Peter knew a collection of Pauline letters (3:15–16), he shows so little Pauline influence (see *Comment* on 2:19; 3:15) that direct dependence on 1 Thess 5:2 seems unlikely, though not impossible.

Comment

8. *μία ἡμέρα παρὰ κυρίῳ ὡς χίλια ἔτη καὶ χίλια ἔτη ὡς ἡμέρα μία,* "with the Lord one day is as a thousand years and a thousand years are as one day." What this statement is intended to prove is disputed. All exegetes recognize that it derives from Ps 90:4 (LXX 89:4), but then they divide into two groups: (1) those who interpret the statement according to parallels in contemporary Jewish and Christian literature, and conclude that it is intended to show that "the Day of Judgment" (v 7) will last a thousand years (Spitta; Strobel, *Untersuchungen,* 93–94; von Allmen, *RTP* 16 [1966] 262); (2) the majority of commentators, who infer from the context that v 8 must be intended to meet the problem of eschatological delay, and conclude that the author has here produced an original argument which has no known precedent or parallel in the literature.

The first group point to the many Jewish and second-century Christian texts in which an eschatological chronology is based on the formula, "A day of the Lord is a thousand years." This formula seems to have been a standard exegetical rule, derived from Ps 90:4 (RSV: "For a thousand years in thy sight are but as yesterday when it is past"), but existing as a relatively independent formulation. The usual procedure is to quote a text in which the word "day" occurs; then the exegetical rule, "A day of the Lord is a thousand years," is cited, often with a further literal quotation of Ps 90:4 to support it; the conclusion is therefore that where the text says "day" it means, in human terms, a thousand years.

The exegetical rule was sometimes applied to the Genesis creation narrative, to yield the idea that the history of the world is to last six thousand years, six "days" of a thousand years each, followed by a millennial Sabbath (*Barn.* 15:4; Irenaeus, *Adv. Haer.* 5.28.3; cf. *b. Sanh.* 97a): this calculation lies behind the widespread Christian millenarianism of the second century. Similarly the rule could be applied to texts which were thought to mention the "day" or "days" of the Messiah (Ps 90:15; Isa 62:5; 65:22), yielding one, two or seven thousand years of messianic rule (Justin, *Dial.* 81; *b. Sanh.* 99a: *Midr. Ps.* 90:17; *Pesiq. R.* 1:7).

Although it is sometimes said that the rule was only applied to eschatological matters (von Allmen, *RTP* 16 [1966] 262 n. 1; cf. Strobel, *Untersuchungen,* 93), this delimitation is not in fact true. The rule was sometimes used to prove from Prov 8:30 that the Torah preceded the creation of the world by two thousand years (*Gen. Rab.* 8:2; *Lev. Rab.* 19:1; *Cant. Rab.* 5:11). Moreover, the earliest attested and the commonest use was with reference to Gen 2:17, where the "day," understood as a thousand years, could include the 930 years of Adam's life (*Jub.* 4:30; Justin, *Dial.* 81; Irenaeus, *Adv. Haer.* 5.23.2; *Midr. Ps.* 25:8; *Gen. Rab.* 19:8; 22:1; *Num. Rab.* 5:4; *Pirqe R. El.* 18). However, all these applications of the exegetical rule are strictly chronological. The point is not, as originally in Ps 90:4, to contrast God's everlasting life with the transience of human life, but simply to yield the chronological information that one of God's days, when Scripture mentions them, is equal to a thousand of our years.

If these parallels are to govern the interpretation of 2 Pet 3:8, then the v must mean that "the day of judgment," mentioned in v 7, will last a thousand years. Verse 8 is then not a contribution to the debate about the alleged delay of the Parousia, but an almost parenthetical explanation of the eschatological expectation set out in v 7.

Now it is true that 2 Pet 3:8 appears to cite the current exegetical rule in the first half of the saying ("with the Lord one day is as a thousand years": this is closer to Ps 90:4 than the usual formulation of the rule in the rabbinic writings, but for comparable forms, cf. *Barn.* 15:4; Justin, *Dial.* 81; Irenaeus, *Adv. Haer.* 5.23.2; 5.28.3), while the second half of the saying ("a thousand years are as one day") could be understood as a quotation of Ps 90:4 introduced to back up the rule. However, this distinction between the two halves of the saying is not very natural. If the two halves are taken together as complementary, they do not readily appear to be an instance of the usual exegetical rule used in chronological calculations. Moreover, the proposed exegesis of v 8 is very hard to sustain in context: (1) The introductory words of v 8 formally indicate a fresh line of thought (see *Form/Structure/Setting* section), not an explanatory footnote to v 7. (2) If v 8 means that the day of judgment will last a thousand years, it contributes nothing to the argument against the scoffers. It is hard to believe that in such a brief section the author would have allowed himself this quite redundant comment. (3) It is hard to see how a thousand-year-long day of judgment could fit into the eschatology of 2 Peter.

Neyrey (*Polemic,* 298–300; *JBL* 99 [1980] 429–300) occupies a midway position between the two groups of exegetes. He sees the application of the exegetical rule to Gen 2:17 as the relevant Jewish parallel, and points out that sometimes this was explained by the idea that God in his mercy delayed Adam's punishment for a thousand years (*Gen. Rab.* 22:1). This provides a link with 2 Pet 3:9. But, interesting though this parallel is, it cannot explain 2 Pet 3:8 satisfactorily. The application of the exegetical rule to Gen 2:17 is always a *chronological* calculation, interpreting the "day" of the text to mean a thousand years. On this analogy, 2 Pet 3:8 could only refer to the delay of the Parousia if the Parousia had been promised within "a day" or perhaps "days." Of course, it had not.

Must we then conclude, with the majority of commentators, that the author's use of Ps 90:4 in this v is entirely unprecedented? In fact there are several instances of the use of this v in Jewish literature which the commentators have not previously noticed, but which may be more relevant parallels to 2 Pet 3:8 than the material already discussed.

The first is a piece of rabbinic exegesis (*Pirqe R. El.* 28; and the same tradition in *Yal. Šimʿoni* 76) which belongs to the tradition of apocalyptic interpretation of the revelation to Abraham in Gen 15. It is ascribed to the early second-century Rabbi Eleazar b. Azariah, and although the attestation is late, the fact that it seems closely related to the traditions embodied in the *Apoc. Abr.* (chaps. 28–30; cf. Bauckham, *TynB* 31 [1980] 23 n. 42; this apocalypse dates from c. A.D. 100) may indicate its antiquity. From the text of Gen 15 it is deduced that the period during which Abraham (according to Gen 15:11) drove away the birds of prey from the sacrificial carcases was a day, from sunrise to sunset. The birds of prey are taken to represent the Gentile oppressors of Israel during the period of the four kingdoms. Therefore, R. Eleazar says, "From this incident thou mayest learn that the rule of these four kingdoms will only last one day according to the day of the Holy One" (*Pirqe R. El.* 28, tr. Friedlander). The reference to "the day of the Holy One" must be to the maxim, "A day of the Lord is a thousand years."

The relevance of this text is that, unlike the other rabbinic texts already mentioned, it does relate to the delay of the End, for in Jewish apocalyptic the period of the four kingdoms is precisely the period of eschatological delay. Moreover, the exegesis is probably not intended as a chronological calculation, at any rate primarily, again unlike the other texts. The point is that whereas for oppressed Israel the period of the rule of the four kingdoms seems very long, from God's eternal perspective it is extremely short ("only one day"). This reflection therefore has the function of consolation for Israel, in that it relativizes the importance of the period of Gentile domination. It thus provides a parallel to the thought of 2 Pet 3:8, which is surely that those who complain of the delay have got it out of perspective: in the perspective of eternity it is only a short time.

It is impossible to be quite sure that the material in *Pirqe R. El.* 28 is of sufficiently early date to be relevant to 2 Peter, but there are three other parallels which raise no problems of dating. Sir 18:9–11 is not an explicit allusion to Ps 90, but is probably inspired by it: "The number of man's days is great if he reaches a hundred years [cf. Ps 90:10]. Like a drop of water from the sea and a grain of sand so are a few years in the day of eternity [cf. Ps 90:4]. Therefore the Lord is patient (*ἐμακροθύμησεν*) with them and pours out his mercy upon them" (RSV; cf. also 18:26). The context here has no reference to eschatology, and although it is tempting to see in the reference to God's patience in v 11 a parallel to 2 Pet 3:9 (*μακροθυμεῖ*, "he is forbearing"), the thought is rather different in each case. Nevertheless, Sir 18:10 is evidence that the original idea in Ps 90:4, the contrast between the brevity of human life and God's eternity, could be well appreciated by a later Jewish writer.

A similar passage, rather more clearly derived from Ps 90:4, is *2 Apoc. Bar.* 48:12–13: "For in a little time are we born, and in a little time do we return. But with thee the hours are as the ages, and the days are as the generations." This contrast between the endless existence of God and the transience of human life is the basis for a plea for God's mercy (48:11, 14–19), a similar thought to that of Sir 18:9–11, and probably based on Ps 90:13–17. Here, however, the context is eschatological. Baruch's plea for mercy is a plea for the eschatological deliverance, and the reference to God's eternal perspective on the passage of time links up with a frequent theme in the *Apoc. Bar.:* the divine sovereignty over the times. Because, unlike man, God surveys the whole course of history and is sovereign over all events, determining their times, he alone knows the time of the End which he has appointed (48:2–3; and cf. 21:8, 10; 54:1; 56:2). Thus, although the allusion to Ps 90:4 in *2 Apoc. Bar.* 48:13 is not a precise parallel to 2 Pet 3:8, because it is not intended to explain the eschatological delay, it does provide a general parallel, in that it contrasts the transience of human life and the everlasting life of God, in the context of a concern with the time of the End which the everlasting God appoints.

Finally, *Bib. Ant.* 19:13a: "But this age [correcting *celum* to *seculum*] will be in my sight like a cloud which flies quickly by and like yesterday which passes." This clear allusion to Ps 90:4 is addressed by God to Moses at the time of his death. The period which will pass so rapidly in God's sight is the period from Moses' death to his resurrection at the End (19:12, 13b), a period which 19:15b apparently indicates will be about 1500 years (accepting the present text and reckoning with C. Perrot and P.-M. Bogaert (eds.), *Pseudo-Philon, Les Antiquités Bibliques,* vol. 2 [SC 230; Paris: Editions du Cerf, 1976] 134–35), or perhaps 4500 years (according to the emendation proposed by L. H. Feldman, in M. R. James [ed.], *The Biblical Antiquities of Philo* [2nd ed.; New York: Ktav, 1971], p. CV; and M. Wadsworth, "The Death of Moses and the Riddle of the End of Time in Pseudo-Philo," *JJS* 28 [1977] 14–15). It is therefore clear that the allusion to Ps 90:4 is not intended as a chronological reckoning, but makes the point that, although the period until the End may seem long by human standards, in God's sight it passes rapidly. (This is confirmed by 19:15a which, although textually corrupt, certainly means that the lapse of time before the End is in reality inconsiderable.) Thus in a Jewish apocalyptic passage from the late first century A.D. we find a use of Ps 90:4 very similar to the use of it in *Pirqe R. El.* 28.

These four parallels establish that in Jewish literature Ps 90:4 was used with reference to the contrast between the brevity of human life and God's eternity, that it was so used in apocalyptic contexts, and specifically that it was used with reference to the period of time up to the End, to indicate that although this period may seem long by human reckoning, in God's eternal perspective it is short. The thought of 2 Pet 3:8 may plausibly be regarded as borrowed from a Jewish apocalypse which made this point.

The essential meaning of *μία ἡμέρα παρὰ κυρίῳ ὡς χίλια ἔτη καὶ χίλια ἔτη ὡς ἡμέρα μία* ("with the Lord one day is as a thousand years and a thousand years are as one day") is therefore that in God's eyes a long period may appear short. Possibly the repetition of the statement in reverse is intended to allow also for the opposite contrast (e.g. God gives ample time for repentance [v 9], but to the unrepentant the End may come all too soon), but it may be merely for stylistic effect. The two halves of the sentence could have the same meaning ("One-day-before-the-Lord is as a thousand years, and a thousand years are as one-day-before-the-Lord": so Spitta; Harnisch, *Existenz,* 106). The fact that *2 Apoc. Bar.* 48:13 reads "with thee the hours are as the ages," when the meaning really requires "the ages are as the hours," should perhaps caution against too strict an interpretation.

The intended contrast between man's perception of time and God's is not a reference to God's eternity in the sense of atemporality (Luther, Chaine). It does not imply, as Käsemann complains, "a philosophical speculation about the being of God, to which a different conception of time is made to apply from that which applies to us" ("Apologia," 194), so that the very idea of the delay of the Parousia becomes meaningless and nothing can any longer be said about the time until the Parousia. The point is rather that God's perspective on time is not limited by a human life span. He surveys the whole of history and sets the times of events in accordance with his agelong purpose. His perspective is so much more comprehensive than that of men and women who, accustomed to short-term expectations, are impatient to see the Parousia in their own lifetime.

Nor does this v imply that the Christian should discard the imminent expectation so characteristic of primitive Christianity (against Fornberg, *Early Church,* 68). Of course, the figures used in v 8—a thousand years, one day—are borrowed from Ps 90:4 and its use in Jewish apocalyptic; they tell us nothing about the actual length of the period the author of 2 Peter expected to elapse before the Parousia (against Windisch). The author in fact continues to speak as though his readers will be alive at the Parousia (1:19; 3:14). This is not at all surprising. It was characteristic of Jewish and Christian apocalyptic to hold in tension the imminent expectation and an acknowledgment of eschatological delay (see Bauckham, *TynB* 31 [1980] 3–36). Second Peter's readers may continue to expect the Day of the Lord which will come unexpectedly like a thief, but lest they succumb to the skepticism of the scoffers, they must also consider that the delay which seems so lengthy to us may not be so significant within that total perspective on the total course of history which God commands. Because he alone has such a perspective, God retains the date of the End in his own knowledge and power, and it cannot be anticipated by any human calculation.

9. *οὐ βραδύνει κύριος τῆς ἐπαγγελίας, ὥς τινες βραδυτῆτα ἡγοῦνται,* "the Lord is not late in fulfilling the promise, according to some people's idea of lateness." The opening words of this verse are probably dependent on the last words of Hab 2:3, a verse which, as Strobel has shown in great detail (*Untersuchungen,* chaps 1–2), was the *locus classicus* for reflection on the problem of delay in Judaism (Hab 2:3 LXX, Aquila; Isa 13:22; 51:14 LXX; Sir 32:22 [Hebrew]; 35:19 LXX; 1QpHab 7:5–12; Heb 10:37; *2 Apoc. Bar.* 20:6; 48:39; *b. Sanh.* 97b). In Hab 2:3b, LXX and Aquila, the subject is not "it" (the vision), as in MT, but "he," i.e. God in his eschatological coming (Strobel, *Untersuchungen,* 53–55; cf. also *2 Apoc. Bar.* 48:39; Sir 32:22/35:19). No doubt, in 2 Peter's apocalyptic source, *κύριος* ("Lord") was God, but, following normal

early Christian practice (cf. Heb 10:37), our author may take the subject to be Christ. It is difficult to be certain (cf. 2:9, 11; 3:8, 10, 15). יאחר (RSV: "delay") in Hab 2:3 is translated *χρονίσῃ*, "he will delay" in LXX, but *βραδυνεῖ*, "he will be late," in Aquila's version, which may here represent a traditional translation already current in the time of 2 Peter (cf. Strobel, *Untersuchungen*, 68–69, 90, 146–47). Some commentators think 2 Peter is dependent, not directly on Hab 2:3, but on Sir 35:19 LXX (Schlosser, *RB* 80 [1973] 34; *contra* Strobel, *Untersuchungen*, 89–90), where certainly the combination of *βραδύνῃ* ("will be late") and *μακροθυμήσῃ* ("will be forbearing") is a striking parallel to 2 Pet 3:9. But *βραδύνῃ* there translates not יאחר but יתמהמה (cf. Strobel, *Untersuchungen*, 63), i.e. the delay which Hab 2:3 acknowledges, not the delay (lateness) which it denies, while the thought in Sir 35:19 is rather different from that of 2 Pet 3:9. Probably both texts reflect a traditional association of Hab 2:3 with the theme of God's *μακροθυμία* ("forbearance"). *τῆς ἐπαγγελίας* ("the promise") of course refers back to v 4 ("the promise of his coming").

The statement is not meant to rule out any kind of delay, for in his reference to the Lord's forbearance in the second half of this v the author clearly acknowledges a deferment of the Parousia, at any rate from the human point of view. What he here denies is that the Lord is "late," in the sense that he has failed to fulfill the promise (so Harnisch, *Existenz*, 107). The meaning is almost (see *Note*): "The Lord is not too late to fulfill the promise." The scoffers held that the promise had set a time-limit (the lifetime of the apostolic generation) which had now passed, and so the promise had not been and would not be fulfilled. Our author replies that the Lord may seem late to the scoffers—"according to some people's idea of lateness" (for the use of *τινες* see *Comment* on Jude 4)—but in v 8 he has already shown that God cannot be confined to human ideas of lateness. He does not explicitly face the issue of the alleged time-limit in the prophecy of the Parousia, but simply denies that the delay in fulfillment means that there will be no fulfillment. The Lord remains sovereign over the time of the End, and defers it in his own good purpose, as the writer will go on to explain.

As Harnisch points out (*Existenz*, 108), this rejection of the scoffers' view has something of the character of an authoritative rebuke, in that the author contradicts them in the words of the classic text on the subject from the prophetic word: Hab 2:3. However, the author does not simply counter the scoffers' argument with authority; he also produces, from the resources of the Jewish apocalyptic tradition, a theological understanding of the problem of eschatological delay (vv 8, 9b).

For this interaction between our author and the scoffers, there is an interesting parallel in later rabbinic tradition: "R. Samuel b. Nahmani [c. 260 A.D.] said in the name of R. Jonathan [c. 220]: Blasted be the bones of those who calculate the end. For they would say, since the predetermined time has arrived, and yet he has not come, he will never come" (*b. Sanh.* 97b, Soncino tr.). Like 2 Peter, R. Jonathan went on to counter this skepticism by citing Hab 2:3.

ἀλλὰ μακροθυμεῖ εἰς ὑμᾶς, μὴ βουλόμενός τινας ἀπολέσθαι, ἀλλὰ πάντας εἰς μετάνοιαν χωρῆσαι, "but he is forbearing toward you, because it is not his will that any should perish, but that all should come to repentance." The idea of God's "forbearance" ("longsuffering, patience": μακροθυμία) derives from the OT description of God as "slow to anger" in Exod 34:6, the central OT revelation of God's character, and the numerous passages which echo that text (Num 14:18; Neh 9:17; Pss 86:15 [LXX 85:15]; 103:8 [LXX 102:8]; 145:8 [LXX 144:8]; Joel 2:13; Jonah 4:2; Nah 1:3; Wis 15:1: in all these vv the LXX translation is μακρόθυμος "forbearing"; see also CD 2:4; 1QH 16:16; 4 Ezra 7:134). It is that quality by which God bears with sinners, holds back his wrath, refrains from intervening in judgment as soon as the sinner's deeds deserve it, though not indefinitely (cf. 4 Ezra 7:33; Sir 5:4–7). In Jewish theology it has a strongly chronological implication (Strobel, *Untersuchungen,* 31): God's forbearance creates an interval, a period of respite, while judgment is deferred and a last opportunity for repentance is allowed (cf. the discussion of God's forbearance in H. Küng, *Justification: The Doctrine of Karl Barth and a Catholic Reflection,* tr. T. Collins, E. E. Tolk & D. Grandskou [London: Burns & Oates, 1965] 147–54).

The divine "longsuffering" was naturally associated with the opportunity for repentance (e.g. Joel 2:12–13; Jonah 4:2, cf. 3:10; Rom 2:4; Herm. *Sim.* 8:11:1; *Clem. Hom.* 11:7:2; cf. Wis 11:23), and also with eschatology: only God's patience with sinners can account for the fact that he does not immediately intervene with eschatological judgment (*1 Enoch* 60:5; Ign. *Eph.* 11:1; Justin, *1 Apol.* 28; *Clem. Hom.* 9:19:1; 16:20). It is an especially prominent theme in the Syriac *Apoc. Bar.,* which wrestles with the problem of eschatological delay and, like 2 Peter, appeals to the notion of God's forbearance (11:3; 12:4; 21:20–21; 24:2; 48:29; 59:6; 85:8). If the author finds God's tolerance of Israel's enemies incomprehensible, God's patience with his own people, delaying the final judgment to give them the opportunity of repentance, provides at least a partial answer to the problem of eschatological delay (see Bauckham, *TynB* 31 [1980] 15–19). Evidently the idea of divine forbearance belonged to the traditional resources of Jewish apocalyptic in the face of the problem of delay (cf. also 4 Ezra 3:30; 7:33, 74; 9:21; 7:134). It permitted the appeal to God's sovereignty over the times to be filled out with some attempt to understand God's purpose in the delay, by relating it to his character as "slow to anger."

We should note that the association of repentance with the coming and the deferment of the End was also traditional. The time up to the eschatological judgment was the time for repentance; with the coming of the End opportunity for repentance would cease and forbearance give place to justice and wrath (*2 Apoc. Bar.* 89:12; 4 Ezra 7:33–34, 82; 9:11; Acts 17:30–31; *2 Clem.* 8:2–3; 16:1). Thus it was thought that the End would come only after the repentance of God's people (*T. Mos.* 1:18; *T. Jud.* 23:15; *T. Dan* 6:4; Acts 3:19–21). A famous debate between R. Eliezer b. Hyrcanus and R. Joshua b. Hananiah, which may be authentic and therefore date from the late first century A.D., concerned this issue (*Midr. Tanḥuma Beḥuqotai* 5; *y. Taʿan.* 1:1; *b. Sanh.* 97b–98a; tr. in J. Neusner, *Eliezer ben Hyrcanus: The Tradition and the Man,* vol. 1 [SJLA 3; Leiden: E. J. Brill, 1973] 477–79; on the debate, see Bauckham, *TynB* 31 [1980] 10–14). R. Joshua, maintaining the traditional apocalyptic belief in God's sovereign determination of the time of the End, held that it would come at the appointed time, whether or not Israel repented. R. Eliezer, on the other hand, made the coming redemption conditional on Israel's repentance. Probably this represents an attempt to understand the delay of redemption in the difficult times following the catastrophe of the fall of the second Temple in A.D. 70.

It is not quite clear whether Eliezer thought that the divinely appointed date for the End had actually been postponed because of Israel's sins (so Strobel, *Untersuchungen,* 23–26), as some later rabbis certainly held (*b. Sanh.* 97b; *b. ʿAbod. Zar.* 9a), or that there was no fixed date for the End (so E. E. Urbach, *The Sages: Their Concepts and Beliefs,* tr. I. Abrahams, vol. 1 [Jerusalem: Magnes Press, 1975] 669), or that Israel's repentance was itself part of God's predetermined plan (so Bauckham, *TynB* 31 [1980] 13). The same ambiguity exists in 2 Peter (cf. the controversy between Strobel, *Untersuchungen,* 91–92, and Harnisch, *Existenz,* 108–9 n. 59, about whether 2 Peter follows R. Eliezer's view). Does the author mean that lack of repentance on humanity's part can defer the Parousia (3:9), while repentance and good works can hasten its coming (3:12: see *Comment*), so that it is really not God, but humanity, that determines the date of the Parousia? He certainly does admit that, from the human point of view, there is a deferment, for the sake of human repentance, so that the Parousia comes later than was originally expected. Conversely, if there is repentance, it may come sooner than we might otherwise expect, if we take account of the divine forbearance. But this does not necessarily detract from the divine sovereignty. Not human sin, but divine forbearance, which cannot be constrained, determines the delay. It is the sovereign God who graciously grants an interval for repentance. From his eternal perspective on the course of history (cf. v 8) he can incorporate such an interval into his plan. Our author does not actually suggest that this interval can last indefinitely while Christians remain unrepentant. There can be no presuming on the Lord's patience (cf. Rom 2:4). The persistently unrepentant will find that judgment comes unexpectedly soon (v 10a).

τινας ("any") does not take up *τινες* ("some people") in v 9a, but contrasts with *πάντας* ("all"): God desires all, without exception, to repent and escape damnation. But *πάντας* ("all") is clearly limited by *ὑμᾶς* ("you"). There is no thought here of the Christian mission (against A. L. Moore, *The Parousia in the New Testament* [NovTSup 13; Leiden: E. J. Brill, 1966] 154). The author remains close to his Jewish source, for in Jewish thought it was usually for the sake of the repentance of his own people that God delayed judgment. Here it is for the sake of the repentance of 2 Peter's Christian readers. No doubt repentance from those sins into which some of them have been enticed by the false teachers (2:14, 18; 3:17) is especially in mind. We need not suppose that the author put the false teachers themselves entirely beyond possibility of repentance and salvation, but here he addresses his readers, who are distinguished from the false teachers (3:5, 8, 17).

For the idea of the present respite before the Parousia as granted for Christians to repent, cf. especially Hermas (*passim;* especially *Sim.* 9; and note 9:14:2; 10:4:4), and the emphasis on repentance before the End in *2 Clem.* (8:1–3; 13:1; 16:1; 17:1; and note that 16:1 precedes the quotation in 16:3 which corresponds to 2 Pet 3:10). For the thought that God does not desire people to perish but to repent, cf. Ezek 18:23, 32; 33:11 (echoed in the Letter of the churches of Lyons and Vienne, *ap.* Eusebius, *Hist. Eccl.* 5.1.46); 1 Tim 2:4; *1 Clem.* 8:5 ("he desires all his beloved ones to participate in repentance"). Of course, the *principle* of 2 Pet 3:9, that the Lord in his forbearance defers the End to give opportunity for repentance, can be validly extended, beyond the reference to Christians which it has in 2 Peter, to God's desire that all people should repent (cf. Acts 17:30; Justin, *1 Apol.* 28).

Some commentators (Spicq, Kelly) and especially Neyrey (*JBL* 99 [1980] 415, 425–27) point out pagan parallels to the controversy in 3:9, especially in Plutarch's *De sera numinis vindicata.* Epicurus' argument against providence appealed to the delay of divine judgment (548C, 549B: *βραδυτής*, "lateness," as in 2 Pet 3:9), and among several counter arguments, Plutarch explains that the delay demonstrates God's "gentleness and magnanimity" (*πραότης καὶ μεγαλοψυχία*: 551C) and gives opportunity for repentance (551D: *μετάνοιαν*). We have already noted (see *Comment* on 2:3b) that the false teachers may have been influenced by Epicurean polemic against the idea of divine judgment, but it is unlikely that our author's reply to them was indebted to pagan anti-Epicurean polemic. The parallels in Jewish literature are closer and, in view of the thoroughly Jewish apocalyptic character of 2 Pet 3, much more relevant.

Strobel (*Untersuchungen,* 94–96; cf. also Neyrey, *JBL* 99 [1980] 424–25) sees a Flood typology behind 3:9. Jewish tradition (*Tgs. Ps.-J.* and *Neof.* Gen 6:3; Philo, *Quaest. Gen.* 1.91; and cf. J. P. Lewis, *A Study of the Interpretation of Noah and the Flood in Jewish and Christian Literature* [Leiden; E. J. Brill, 1968] 130 n. 8) held that the Flood was delayed 120 years to give opportunity for repentance, and, following such traditions, 1 Pet 3:20 says that "God's forbearance (*μακροθυμία*) waited in the days of Noah." It would fit into the general tradition of a correspondence between the Flood and the End, which 2 Peter follows in 2:5; 3:6–7, to see the delay of the Flood as corresponding typologically to the delay of the End. But there is no hint of such a typology in 3:9, which is completely explicable by reference to Jewish traditions about the delay of the End, without reference to traditions about the delay of the Flood. The coincidence with 1 Pet 3:20 (*μακροθυμία*) probably derives from independent influence of similar Jewish ideas, about the Flood in 1 Peter, about the End in 2 Peter. There is insufficient evidence to postulate a Flood typology in 2 Pet 3:9.

10. *ἥξει δὲ ἡμέρα κυρίου ὡς κλέπτης*, "but the day of the Lord will come like a thief." *ἥξει* ("will come") placed first is emphatic. In contrast (*δέ* is adversative) to any mistaken inference from v 9b that God's forbearance cancels the day of judgment, it is made clear that it is only delayed and will certainly come (cf. *2 Apoc. Bar.* 12:4). Perhaps the allusion to Hab 2:3 (Aquila: *ἐρχόμενος ἥξει καὶ οὐ βραδυνεῖ*, "he will surely come and will not be late") in v 9a is here continued.

Thus God's forbearance is no reason for sinners to continue in sin without fear of judgment (cf. Sir 5:4–7), the more so since the coming of the End is not only certain but also unpredictable. It will come with the unexpectedness of a burglar. As with all other NT instances of this metaphor (Matt 24:43–44; Luke 12:39–40; 1 Thess 5:2; Rev 3:3; 16:15), derived from Jesus' parable (see *Form/Structure/Setting* section), it conveys both unexpectedness and threat. To those who, in spite of the opportunity which the Lord's forbearance has allowed them, remain unrepentant, the Day of the Lord should be a fearful prospect, for it marks the end of that forbearance and the arrival of judgment.

οἱ οὐρανοὶ ῥοιζηδὸν παρελεύσονται, "the heavens will pass away with a roar." *παρέρχεσθαι*, "to pass away," is used of the passing away of heaven and earth in Gospel sayings (Matt 5:18; 24:35; Mark 13:31; Luke 16:17; 21:33; cf. *Did.* 10:6), whence perhaps our author derived it. For the idea, cf. *1 Enoch* 91:16; Rev 21:1; *Clem. Rec.* 2:68:3. The more picturesque image of the sky rolled up like a scroll is used in Isa 34:4; Rev 6:14; *Apoc. Pet. ap.* Macarius Magnes, *Apocrit.* 4.7; *Sib. Or.* 3:82; 8:414; *Gos. Thom.* 111. *ῥοιζηδόν* ("with a roar") is an onomatopoeic word, used of hissing, rushing, whizzing, crackling sounds, and most commentators (following Pseudo-Oecumenius in *PG* 119. 616) refer to the crackle or roar of flames consuming the firmament. There are various parallels in passages describing the eschatological conflagration: *Sib. Or.* 4:175: *κόσμος ἅπας μύκημα καὶ ὄμβριμον ἦχον ἀκούσει*, "the whole world shall hear a rumbling [of thunder] and a mighty roar"; 1QH 3:32–36, tr. Vermes: "the deeps of the Abyss shall groan amid the roar of heaving mud. The land shall cry out because of the calamity fallen upon the world, and all its deeps shall howl . . . . For God shall sound his mighty voice, and his holy abode shall thunder with the truth of his glory. The heavenly hosts shall cry out"; *Apoc. El.* 3:82: the Lord "will command (*κελεύειν*) in a great rage, that the heaven and the earth produce fire"; cf. also *Apoc. Thom.* days 1–6. These suggest that in 2 Peter the noise may either be that of the conflagration itself, or it may be the thunder of the divine voice (*ῥοίζημα* is used of thunder in Lucian, *Jup. Trag.* 1). The latter is a standard element in theophany descriptions: God's thunderous roar announces his coming as a wrathful warrior, and nature quakes and flees before him (Pss 18:13–15 [LXX 17:14–16]; 77:18 [LXX 76:19]; 104:7 [LXX 103:7]; Amos 1:2; Joel 4:16 [EVV 3:16]; cf. 4 Ezra 13:4; 1 Thess 4:16). If this is the meaning here, then *ῥοιζηδόν* ("with a roar") contributes to a description, not simply of cosmic destruction, but of the divine Judge coming to judgment, the fire of his wrath consuming all before him.

στοιχεῖα δὲ καυσούμενα λυθήσεται, "the heavenly bodies will be dissolved in the heat." The meaning of *στοιχεῖα* here is disputed. There are three main possibilities: (1) The elements of which all physical things are composed, and of which there were normally thought to be four: water, air, fire, earth (this interpretation is adopted by Reicke; Olivier, "Correction," 150; Delling, *TDNT* 7, 686). This was a normal meaning of *στοιχεῖα* (*TDNT* 7, 672–79; Herm. *Vis.* 3:13:3; Aristides, *Apol.* 3–7). If 2 Peter's description of the conflagration is influenced by Stoic ideas, then it is relevant that the Stoics spoke of the dissolution of all the elements into the primal element, fire, in the cosmic conflagration. This interpretation might also be supported by reference to the descriptions of the conflagration in the *Sib. Or.* According to an obscure statement in *Sib. Or.* 3:80–81, "all the elements (*στοιχεῖα*) of the world will be widowed (*χηρεύσει*)"; later Sibylline writers interpreted these elements as air, earth, sea, light, heaven, days, nights (*Sib. Or.* 2:206–7; 8:337–39), a list which suggests not so much the four elements as the various constituent parts of the universe. But a reference either to the four elements or to this Sibylline list of elements is not very appropriate in 2 Pet 3:10, between a reference to the heavens and a reference to the earth. Moreover, the fact that in v 12, and probably in v 10 too, *στοιχεῖα* corresponds to *πᾶσαι αἱ δυνάμεις τῶν οὐρανῶν* ("all the powers of the heavens") in Isa 34:4 LXX (see below) is decisively against this view.

(2) The heavenly bodies (sun, moon and stars) is the interpretation favored by most commentators. This meaning of *στοιχεῖα* is well attested for the second century A.D. (*TDNT* 7, 681–82; Theophilus, *Ad Autol.* 1.4–6; 2.15, 35; Justin, *2 Apol.* 5.2; *Dial.* 23.3; Polycrates, *ap.* Eusebius, *Hist. Eccl.* 3.31.2; Tatian, *Oratio* 9–10). In view of the second mention of the *στοιχεῖα* in v 12, which says that they will "melt" (*τήκεται*), it is clear that 2 Peter's references to the *στοιχεῖα* are ultimately dependent on Isa 34:4 LXX (B, Lucian): *τακήσονται πᾶσαι αἱ δυνάμεις τῶν οὐρανῶν* ("all the powers of the heavens will melt"). In *2 Clem.* 16:3, which seems to be 2 Peter's immediate source (see *Form/Structure/Setting* section), this clause appears as: *τακήσονταί τινες τῶν οὐρανῶν* ("some of the heavens will melt"), but the text is almost certainly corrupt, and *τινες* ("some") should be corrected to *δυνάμεις* ("powers"; so J. B. Lightfoot, *The Apostolic Fathers* Part 1 vol. 2 [London; Macmillan, 1890] 250). Thus, if *στοιχεῖα* is our author's substitution for *αἱ δυνάμεις τῶν οὐρανῶν* ("the powers of the heavens"), he is most likely to have used it in the sense of "heavenly bodies." He will have made the substitution in accordance with his regular preference for Hellenistic religious vocabulary: *στοιχεῖα* in the sense of "heavenly bodies" or "zodiacal signs" was at home in the astrology of the period (*TDNT* 7, 681–82). It is worth noting that *Apoc. Pet.* E 5, following either 2 Pet 3:12 or Isa 34:4 or both, evidently took the reference to be to stars: "And the stars shall be melted by flames of fire, as if they had not been created, and the fastnesses [or, powers] of heaven shall pass away for want of water and become as though they had not been created" (tr. *NT Apoc.* 2, 671).

(3) Angelic powers presiding over nature (Spitta, Kühl, von Soden). This suggestion points to Paul's use (according to a common interpretation) of *στοιχεῖα* to refer to hostile spiritual powers (Gal 4:3; Col 2:8, 20). Second Peter's dependence on Isa 34:4 may be thought to support this meaning, for there "the host of heaven" (צבא השמים) are not simply the stars, but astral powers, and it is possible that this v in its LXX version was interpreted as a reference to angelic powers in *T. Levi* 4:1: "the invisible spirits melting away" (*τῶν ἀοράτων πνευμάτων τηκομένων*). Since, both in Jewish and in pagan circles, the stars were often thought to be—or to be controlled by—spiritual beings, this meaning cannot be ruled out in 2 Peter, though it is really additional rather than an alternative to (2) (Schrage).

καὶ γῆ καὶ τὰ ἐν αὐτῇ ἔργα εὑρεθήσεται, "and the earth and the works in it will be found." This is a *crux interpretum*. *εὑρεθήσεται* ("will be found") is undoubtedly the best reading (see *Note*), but the majority of exegetes have found it so difficult to give it an acceptable sense that they have had to reject it. Interpretations fall broadly into three categories: (1) support for variant readings; (2) emendations of the text, not supported by MS evidence; (3) attempts to make sense of the reading εὑρεθήσεται.

(*1*) *Support for variant readings.*

(a) κατακαήσεται ("will be burned up") has found little support among the commentators (von Soden), but more support than it deserves among the English translations (AV, RV, RSV, JB). It cannot be original because it would then be impossible to explain the other readings.

(b) ἀφανισθήσονται ("will vanish") is followed by one modern translation (GNB), but must be rejected for the same reason as (a).

(c) οὐχ εὑρεθήσεται ("will not be found") gives excellent sense and is therefore preferred by some (Wand, Moffatt, Schrage; Bigg, 213; Fornberg, *Early Church,* 75–77). However, it should properly be considered as an emendation rather than as a variant reading. Its two occurrences (in ancient versions, not in Greek MSS) have no chance of preserving the original reading, but they might be correct *emendations* of the text. As Mayor suggests, if οὐχ ("not") had been accidentally omitted in the autograph or in a very early copy from which all other MSS derive, then the other readings could easily be explained.

The expression "will not be found" would be a Hebraism or Septuagintalism deriving from the common Hebrew use of נמצא ("to be found") to mean virtually "to be, to exist." Thus "will not be found" (οὐχ εὑρίσκεσθαι) means "will not exist" or "will cease to exist" in Isa 35:9 LXX; Dan 11:19 Θ and LXX; *Pss. Sol.* 14:9; Rev 16:20 (cf. 18:21). All these texts are in eschatological contexts readily comparable with 2 Pet 3:10. οὐχ εὑρεθήσεται would be good apocalyptic style.

As an emendation, the addition of οὐχ is the simplest proposed, and yields such an excellent sense that it must be considered the best solution unless the reading εὑρεθήσεται can be given a satisfactory interpretation.

(d) εὑρεθήσεται λυόμενα ("will be found dissolved"), the reading of P[72], seems not to have commended itself to any scholar. In spite of our author's tendency to repeat words, the clumsy repetition of λύεσθαι three times in vv 10–11 is unlikely.

It will be observed that all the variant readings (which must be regarded as ancient emendations of εὑρεθήσεται) derive from the conviction that the context requires a word equivalent to "destroyed." The same conviction informs most of the modern emendations.

(*2*) *Emendations*

(a) πυρωθήσεται ("will be burned") (Vansittart, JP 3 [1871] 357–59).

(b) ἐκπυρωθήσεται ("will be consumed by conflagration"): the case for this emendation has been argued at length by Olivier ("Correction"; followed by Windisch). ἐκπυροῦσθαι was the technical Stoic term used in connection with the cosmic conflagration (ἐκπύρωσις).

(c) ῥυήσεται or ῥεύσεται ("will flow") was suggested by Hort, and συρρυήσεται ("will flow together") by Naber (according to Metzger, *Textual Commentary,* 706; and cf. Mayor, cc).

(d) ἀρθήσεται ("will be taken away") was tentatively suggested by Mayor.

(e) εὕσεται ("will be singed"): F. F. Bruce suggested to me that our author, with his fondness for rare words, may have been misled by the Latin *uro* into thinking this is a more general word for burning (cf. Introduction, section on *Language,* for the suggestion that the author may have been a native Latin speaker).

(f) *κριθήσεται* ("will be judged") (Nestlé, according to Metzger, *Textual Commentary,* 706).

(g) *ἰαθήσεται* or *ἐξιαθήσεται* ("will be healed") (Chase, according to Mayor, cc).

Some other emendations emend not *εὑρεθήσεται* but other parts of the clause:

(h) *γῆ καὶ ἃ ἐν αὐτῇ ἔργα εὑρεθήσεται* ("the earth and the works which are found in it") (Spitta, following Buttmann).

(i) *λῆ καὶ τὰ ἐν αὐτῇ ἔργα ἀργὰ εὑρεθήσεται* ("the earth and the works in it will be found useless") (H. Bradshaw, according to James, lv).

(j) *γῆ καὶ τὰ ἐν αὐτῇ ἀργὰ εὑρεθήσεται* ("the earth and all that is in it will be found as chaos") (Stauffer, *New Testament Theology,* 225, 320 n. 739; cf. 4 Ezra 7:30).

(k) *γῆ κατὰ τὰ ἐν αὐτῇ ἔργα εὑρεθήσεται* ("it shall be found to the earth according to the works in it," i.e. "the earth shall be judged according to the deeds done in it"). Danker (*ZNW* 53 [1962] 82–86, summarized in Danker, 90–91) proposed this emendation by analogy with *Pss. Sol.* 17:8: *κατὰ τὰ ἁμαρτήματα αὐτῶν ἀποδώσεις αὐτοῖς, ὁ θεός, εὑρεθῆναι αὐτοῖς κατὰ τὰ ἔργα αὐτῶν,* "according to their sins you will recompense them, O God, so that it may be found to them according to their works." Danker is sometimes cited in support of the reading *εὑρεθήσεται*, understood in a judicial sense (see (3)(b) below), but it should be noticed that the specialized judicial sense for which *Pss. Sol.* 17:8 seems to provide a parallel (Sir 16:14, cited by Spicq, is not a parallel, for *εὑρήσει* there probably means "obtain") really requires Danker's emendation.

Some of these proposed emendations are more plausible than others, but we should not resort to emendation unless *εὑρεθήσεται* proves incapable of a satisfactory sense.

(*3*) *The reading εὑρεθήσεται.*

(a) *εὑρεθήσεται;* ("will they be found?"). Spicq, Kelly and Marín (*EE* 50 [1975] 233) read the clause as a rhetorical question (as originally suggested by Weiss), and so get the same general sense as *οὐχ εὑρεθήσεται* ("will not be found"). But this is forced (Prov 11:31 = 1 Pet 4:18, which has *ποῦ*, "where?", is not an adequate parallel).

(b) *εὑρεθήσεται* ("will be found"). A minority of scholars (Chaine, Schelkle; Wilson, *ExpTim* 32 [1920–21] 44–45; Bonus, *ExpTim* 32 [1920–21] 280–81; Roberts, *RestQ* 6 [1962] 32–33; Lenhard, *ZNW* 52 [1961] 128–29; *ZNW* 69 [1978] 136) argue for this reading, along similar lines, giving it the general sense of "will be made manifest before God and his judgment."

The attempt to find a comparable usage of מצא ("to find") in the OT and *εὑρίσκειν* ("to find") in the LXX is not wholly successful. These verbs are certainly common in contexts concerned with moral and judicial scrutiny, but are not used in quite the same way as 2 Pet 3:10 uses *εὑρεθήσεται*. In general, there are three relevant categories of usage: (i) "sin" or "righteousness" (or synonyms) is "found" (e.g. 1 Sam 25:28; 26:18; 1 Kgs 1:52; Ps

17:3 (LXX 16:3); Jer 2:34; 50:20; Ezek 28:15; Zeph 3:13; Mal 2:6; cf. Luke 23:4; John 18:38; 19:4; Acts 13:28; 23:9; 24:20; Rev 14:5); (ii) someone is "found" righteous (or similar adjective) (e.g. Sir 44:17, 20; Dan 5:27 Θ; cf. 1 Cor 4:2; Rev 5:4; *1 Clem.* 9:3; 10:1); (iii) a criminal is said to be "found," meaning "detected, discovered" (sometimes "caught in the act") or "caught" (e.g. Exod 22:8; Deut 22:22, 28; Jer 50:24 (LXX 27:24); Ezra 10:18). None of these categories exactly fits 2 Pet 3:10. OT usage does not seem to support the absolute use of εὑρίσκειν ("to find") meaning "to subject to judgment," and although *Pss. Sol.* 17:8 (see above, (2)(k)) seems to support some such meaning, the construction is different from that in 2 Pet 3:10. (*Barn.* 21:6: ποιεῖτε ἵνα εὑρεθῆτε ἐν ἡμέρᾳ κρίσεως, "act so that you may be found on the day of judgment," is scarcely a valid parallel, for it uses "to be found" in a positive sense, presumably as the opposite of "not to be found" in the usage of (1)(c) above.)

However, although the OT usage provides no exact parallel to εὑρεθήσεται in 2 Pet 3:10, it is possible that general familiarity with that usage could have influenced the choice of words, either by the author of 2 Peter or by the author of his source. At least it could provide the word with generally judicial overtones, and when full weight is given to the passive form as a "divine" passive, meaning "will be discovered *by God,*" a plausible sense is obtained which is by no means such a weak climax to the v as the English translation suggests. εὑρεθήσεται is being used synonymously with φανήσεται ("will appear"), φανερωθήσεται ("will be made manifest") or φανερὰ γενήσεται ("will become manifest"), as used in similar contexts (Mark 4:22; Luke 18:17; John 3:21; 1 Cor 3:13; 14:25; Eph 5:13; *2 Clem.* 16:3), but with the added connotation that it is God, the Judge, who will "discover" the earth and its works.

Wilson suggests the thought is this: when the intervening heavens are burned away, the earth and its works, from the divine point of view, become visible. This provides an ironic contrast with the picture of the wicked trying to hide from God at his eschatological coming to judgment (Isa 2:19; Hos 10:8; Rev 6:15–16). Thus the author "with a fine sense of climax makes the passing away of the heavens and the destruction of the intermediate spiritual beings, while terrible in themselves, even more terrible in that they lead up to the discovery, naked and unprotected on the earth, of men and all their works by God. The Judgment is here represented not so much as a destructive act of God, as a revelation of him from which none can escape" (*ExpTim* 32 [1920–21) 44–45). Probably this view, that the manifestation of the earth is a consequence of the destruction of the heavens, is preferable to the view that καί should be given adversative meaning: everything else will be destroyed, but the world of mankind and their deeds will remain to face judgment (Roberts,*RestQ* 6 [1962] 32–33; Lenhard, *ZNW* 52 [1961] 129).

Further support for this interpretation comes from the context. The section 3:5–10 is by no means concerned solely with the Parousia as cosmic dissolution, but is primarily concerned with the Parousia as judgment of the wicked. The destruction of the universe is of interest to the author only as the means of judgment on men and women. The previous reference to the coming conflagration, in v 7, concludes on the same note of judgment as, according to the proposed interpretation, v 10 does. In v 10 itself, the introductory reference to the thief requires that which follows to describe not simply a dissolution of the physical universe, but a judgment which threatens the unrepentant (see above). Similarly the succeeding vv (11–14) focus very explicitly on the moral dimension of eschatology. In v 14 (ἄσπιλοι καὶ ἀμώμητοι αὐτῷ εὑρεθῆναι, "to be found without spot or blemish in his sight"; for this usage of εὑρίσκειν, cf. category (ii) above) there may be a deliberate contrast with εὑρεθήσεται ("will be found") in v 10. In contrast to the wicked whose evil deeds will be "found" by God to their condemnation (v 10), 2 Peter's readers are to strive to be "found" innocent (v 14).

Against this interpretation, two major objections are made: (i) The context demands a reference to the annihilation of the earth. This objection has already been largely answered: in fact, a reference to the judgment of the wicked is, in context, a more appropriate climax to v 10. For the objection that v 11a presupposes that the last words of v 10 refer to dissolution (Kelly; Fornberg, *Early Church,* 76), see *Comment* on v 11a. (ii) γῆ ("earth"), following οἱ οὐρανοί ("the heavens"), must be the physical earth, and therefore τὰ ἐν αὐτῷ ἔργα ("the works in/on it") must refer to the contents of the earth, as God's creation, not to the (evil) deeds of men and women. It is true that in this context γῆ cannot be given the sense simply of "humanity," but it can easily mean the physical earth *as the scene of human history,* the earth as the dwelling-place of humanity (cf. Matt 5:13; 10:34; Luke 12:49, 51; 18:8; John 17:4; and especially Rom 9:28). Given that the author is thinking, certainly, of a cosmic conflagration, but of a cosmic conflagration as the means of judgment on the wicked, this usage is entirely natural.

Finally, comparison with *2 Clem.* 16:3, which (as we have argued in the *Form/Structure/Setting* section) may well be a quotation from the actual source which 2 Peter here follows, supports the proposed interpretation and helps to counter objections to it: "The day of judgment is now coming like a burning oven, and some [the powers?] of the heavens will melt, and all the earth (πᾶσα ἡ γῆ) [will be] like lead melting in fire, and then the secret and open works of men will appear (καὶ τότε φανήσεται τὰ κρύφια καὶ φανερὰ ἔργα τῶν ἀνθρώπων)." Since φανήσεται ("will appear") and φανερά ("open, apparent") are here used rather awkwardly together, it is not impossible that the original text of the source quoted in *2 Clem.* had εὑρεθήσεται, which 2 Peter 3:10 reproduces, rather than φανήσεται, and that the author of *2 Clem.,* though correctly understanding εὑρεθήσεται, found it a slightly odd usage and substituted the more natural φανήσεται. If *2 Clem.* 16:3 really does represent 2 Peter's source, then it will be seen that the author of 2 Peter, by omitting the phrase describing the earth ("like lead melting in fire") has made γῆ ("the earth") as well as τὰ ἔργα ("the works") the subject of εὑρεθήσεται ("will be found"). No doubt he did this because he wished to move swiftly to the idea of judgment, and thought of the earth as the place where the deeds of the wicked were to be found, but when it is seen that he is abbreviating his source, then the slight awkwardness of his use of γῆ (see objection (ii) above), as well as the grammatical incorrectness of the singular εὑρεθήσεται ("will be found"), become intelligible (cf. 2:11, 17, where his abbreviation of Jude has produced difficulties or infelicities).

Even if the hypothesis—that *2 Clem.* 16:3 represents the source of 2 Pet

3:10—is not accepted,that v still provides an excellent parallel, which proves that a description of the eschatological conflagration which climaxes in the exposure of human deeds to judgment need not be thought surprising in 2 Pet 3:10 (against objection (i) above). Furthermore, the paraenetic context of *2 Clem.* 16:3, with its references to repentance (cf. especially 16:1; 17:1, with 2 Pet 3:9), is comparable with the context in 2 Pet 3:9, 11–14.

Explanation

To meet the problem of the delay of the Parousia, the author puts forward two arguments, both already traditional in the Jewish apocalyptic's treatment of the issue of eschatological delay. In the first place, God, who determines the time of the Parousia, does so from a different perspective on time from that of men and women. He is not limited by a human life span, but surveys the whole course of human history, so that, as the psalmist observed (Ps 90:4), periods which by human standards are of great length may be from his perspective very short. Those who complain of the delay of the Parousia, impatient to see it in their own lifetime, are limiting the divine strategy in history to the short-term expectations to which transient human beings are accustomed. But God's purpose transcends such expectations. Thus the false teachers' accusation, that it is now too late for the Parousia to be expected, is based on their own evaluation of "lateness," not necessarily on God's.

If, from the human perspective, the Parousia seems to be deferred, this delay must have its purpose in God's direction of history. So the author's second argument, again following traditional apocalyptic thinking, explains that the delay is a respite which God has graciously granted to his people before his intervention in judgment. It derives from one of the fundamental attributes of God, his forbearance, which characterizes God as "slow to anger" (Exod 34:6), mercifully deferring his judgment so that sinners may have the opportunity to repent and escape condemnation. God delays the Parousia because he is not willing that any of his Christian people should perish. From this point of view, the delay of the Parousia should not be a matter for complaint. On the contrary, 2 Peter's readers, especially those whom the false teachers have enticed into sin, should take advantage of the opportunity to repent.

Lest anyone should think that sinners can therefore presume on God's forbearance, taking advantage of the delay by *not* repenting, the author immediately stresses that God will not defer his judgment indefinitely. The day of judgment will come upon sinners with the unexpectedness of a burglar breaking in while the householder sleeps.

The apocalyptic imagery which follows depicts not simply the dissolution of the cosmos but, more importantly, the eschatological coming of the divine Judge. When the wrathful voice of God thunders out of heaven and the fire of his judgment sets the sky ablaze, the firmament and the heavenly bodies will be destroyed, and the earth, the scene of human wickedness, will be exposed to his wrath. Then it will be impossible for the wicked to hide from God's judicial scrutiny. They and their evil deeds will be discovered by him and condemned.

In this and the preceding sections there is nothing specifically Christian about the eschatology. The lack of "Christological orientation" (Käsemann) is such that it is not even possible to tell whether "the Lord" is God or Christ. With the exception of the image of the thief, derived from Jesus' parable, the whole passage could have been written by a Jewish apocalyptist, and in fact it is quite probable that the author has closely followed a Jewish apocalyptic source. This borrowing from Jewish apocalyptic is justified by the apologetic purpose of the passage. The objections of the false teachers were aimed against the expectation of eschatological *judgment,* against the hope that God will not allow wickedness to prevail in his world forever, but will intervene finally to vindicate and to establish his righteousness. For this expectation primitive Christianity was indebted to Jewish apocalyptic, which was much concerned with this theme and which had also wrestled with the theological problem posed by the apparent delay of the eschatological judgment. It was therefore appropriate that our author should draw on the resources of Jewish apocalyptic tradition to counter his opponents' objections. Both the apocalyptic hope for the triumph of God's righteousness in the world and the apocalyptic understanding of eschatological delay remain valid for Christians, even though the specifically Christian interpretation of the eschatological hope with reference to Jesus Christ can also provide new perspectives on the judgment and its delay.

Exhortation (3:11–16)

Bibliography

Conti, M. "La Sophia di 2 Petr. 3, 15." *RivB* 17 (1969) 121–38. **Klein, G.** *Die zwölf Apostel,* 103–5. **Lindemann, A.** *Paulus,* 91–97, 261–63. **Rinaldi, G.** "La 'sapienza data' a Paolo (2 Petr. 3, 15)." In *San Pietro,* Associazione Biblica Italiana. Pp. 395–411. **Strobel, A.** *Untersuchungen,* 92.

Translation

11 *Since all these things are to be dissolved* [a] *in this way,* [b] *what sort of people
ought you to be, holy and godly in all your conduct,* 12 *waiting for and hastening
the coming of the Day of God, because of which the heavens will be dissolved in
flames and the heavenly bodies melt in the heat.* 13 *But according to his promise we
are waiting for new heavens and a new earth, in which righteousness is at home.*

14 *So, my dear friends, since you are waiting for these, strive to be found without
spot or blemish in his sight, at peace,* 15 *and regard the forbearance of our Lord as
salvation, just as our dear brother Paul wrote to you in accordance with the wisdom
given to him,* 16 *as he does in all his other letters, whenever he speaks of these matters.
His letters contain some things that are hard to understand, which the uninstructed
and unstable people distort, as they do the other scriptures, so as to bring about
their own destruction.*

Notes

[a] The present participle λυομένων, lit. "being dissolved," is used with future sense: see *Comment* on 2:9 (κολαζομένους, "being punished").

[b] It is difficult to decide between οὕτως (P^{72} B C P *al*) and οὖν (א A K L *al*), but since the latter provides a more logical connection with v 10 it may be a correction.

Form/Structure/Setting

In concluding his letter with a section of eschatological paraenesis, urging the moral implications of his eschatological teaching, the author not only rounds off his apologetic argument in an appropriate way, but also fulfills the requirements of the two literary genres in which he is writing: the apostolic letter and the testament. Eschatological paraenesis is not uncommon in the concluding sections of NT letters (cf. 1 Cor 15:58; Gal 5:7–10; Eph 5:10–16; Phil 4:5; Col 4:5; 1 Tim 6:14; 2 Tim 4:1–5; 1 Pet 5:1–10), while many testaments include ethical exhortations with eschatological sanctions (*1 Enoch* 91:3–19; 94:1–5; *Jub.* 36:3–11; *2 Apoc. Bar.* 84–85; *Bib. Ant.* 33:1–3).

Clearly v 12b, but probably also vv 12a, 13, whose content is thoroughly Jewish (see *Comment;* and cf. von Allmen, *RTP* 16 [1966] 263–64), derive from the Jewish apocalypse which underlies this chapter. It may be significant that the verb προσδοκᾶν, "to wait for" (vv 12, 13, 14), which is not common with reference to eschatological expectation, occurs in the quotation in *1 Clem.* 23:5, which we suggested (see *Form/Structure/Setting* section on 3:8–10) may derive from 2 Peter's apocalyptic source.

The author's use of the present tense (instead of the future) in v 16b is his most blatant breach of the pseudepigraphal fiction, following as it does immediately after his reference, in Peter's *persona,* to "our dear brother Paul," and preceding immediately his resumption of the idea of prediction in v 17a (*προγινώσκοντες*, "knowing in advance").

Comment

11. *τούτων οὕτως πάντων λυομένων*, "since all these things are to be dissolved in this way." This opening phrase may seem to contradict our interpretation of the last clause in v 10, according to which that clause refers not to the dissolution of the earth but to the judgment of humanity. It is true that v 10 does not then refer explicitly to the dissolution of "all these things" (i.e. the heavens and the earth, cf. v 13), but only to the dissolution of the heavens. But this is probably because the author has abbreviated a source which made the dissolution of the earth explicit (see *Comment* on v 10), rather than because he wished to exclude the dissolution of the earth, which is implied in v 7 as well as in v 13. But why does v 11 not take up the thought of the judgment of human works with which, according to our interpretation, v 10 ends? The reason is that in vv 11–14 the author wishes to base his exhortation to his readers not only on the threat of judgment, but more broadly on the eschatological expectation of a new world of righteousness (v 13). Since the present world, the scene of human wickedness, is to disappear and be replaced by a new world, the home of righteousness, his readers should be the kind of people who will be able to live in that new world. Then when they face the judgment of God they will be found to be fit, not to perish with the old world, but to enter the new (v 14). Though the author's eschatological paraenesis, like that of the NT generally, contains a negative warning (the unrepentant will perish), its emphasis is positive (the hope for the triumph of God's righteousness demands righteous living now).

ἐν ἁγίαις ἀναστροφαῖς καὶ εὐσεβείαις, lit. "in holy forms of behavior and godly acts": the force of the plurals, indicating many different forms of holy and godly behavior (cf. *ἀσελγείαις*, "dissolute practices," 2:2, 18), can only be conveyed in English by paraphrase ("holy and godly in all your conduct"); cf. 1 Pet 1:15. For *εὐσεβείαις*, "godly acts," see *Comment* on 1:3; it is probably our author's vocabulary, rather than that of his source.

12. *προσδοκῶντας*, "waiting for." On eschatological "waiting" in the NT, see *Comment* on Jude 21. The verb *προσδοκᾶν* (also used of eschatological expectation in 2 Macc 7:14; 12:44; Matt 11:3; Luke 7:19–20; *1 Clem.* 23:5; Ign. *Pol.* 3:2; Justin, *Dial.* 120.3; cf. Ign. *Magn.* 9:3) is used three times in vv 12–14. In view of the allusion to Hab 2:3 in v 9, it is probable that the emphasis on waiting in these vv also derives from that text, whose demand for action, in the face of the eschatological delay, is "wait for it/him" (LXX: *ὑπομεῖνον αὐτόν*; Aquila: *προσδέχου αὐτόν*; cf. *1 Clem.* 23:5; *2 Apoc. Bar.* 83:4; *b. Sanh.* 97b).

σπεύδοντας, "hastening," could perhaps mean "striving for" (Reicke), but the Jewish background is decisive in favor of "hastening." Isa 60:22b (RSV: "in its time I will hasten it"; LXX does not give this meaning) was the basis for a whole series of Jewish texts which speak of God hastening the time of the End (Sir 33:8[36:7] LXX: *σπεῦσον καιρόν*, "hasten the time"; *2 Apoc. Bar.* 20:1–2; 54:1; 83:1; *Bib. Ant.* 19:13; *Barn.* 4:3; cf. also Isa 10:23 LXX). It featured in the debate between R. Eliezer and R. Joshua (see *Comment* on v 9). R. Joshua interpreted it to mean that redemption would come at the appointed time, irrespective of repentance, but (in one version of the debate: *y. Taᶜan.* 1:1) R. Eliezer taught that it meant that the Lord would hasten the coming of redemption in response to Israel's repentance. A similar interpretation is attributed to R. Joshua b. Levi (c. A.D. 250): "If you have merit, I will hasten it; if not, [it comes] in its time" (*y. Taᶜan.* 1:1; *b. Sanh.* 98a; *Cant. Rab.* 8:14). Usually, as in Isa 60:22, it is God who is said to hasten the coming of the End, but R. Eliezer's view implies that, since God hastens in response to repentance, repentance itself might be said to hasten the End. Later rabbinic texts actually say that repentance (*b. Yoma* 86b, attributed to the early second-century R. Jose the Galilean; cf. also *y. Taᶜan.* 1:1; *b. Sanh.* 97b; Acts 3:19) or charity (*b. B. Bat.* 10a, attributed to R. Judah, c. A.D. 150) brings repentance nearer. An important parallel which demonstrates the influence of these Jewish ideas in the Christian milieu from which 2 Peter derives is *2 Clem.* 12:6: "When you do these things [good works, especially sexual purity], he [Jesus] says, the kingdom of my Father will come" (and cf. the exhortation to immediate repentance in 13:1; on this text, see Strobel, *Untersuchungen,* 126–27). Cf. also Herm. *Sim.* 10:4:4.

Clearly this idea of hastening the End is the corollary of the explanation (v 9) that God defers the Parousia because he desires Christians to repent. Their repentance and holy living may therefore, from the human standpoint, hasten its coming. This does not detract from God's sovereignty in determining the time of the End (cf. *Comment* on v 9), but means only that his sovereign determination graciously takes human affairs into account.

τὴν παρουσίαν τῆς τοῦ θεοῦ ἡμέρας, "the coming of the Day of God." Elsewhere in early Christian literature *παρουσία* always has a personal subject, and with eschatological reference the subject is always Christ (as in 2 Pet 1:16; 3:4). Also very unusual is the expression "the Day of God," in place of the normal "the Day of the Lord" (*Apoc. Pet.* E4 has "the day of God," but is probably dependent on this passage; Rev 16:14 has *τῆς μεγάλης ἡμέρας τοῦ θεοῦ τοῦ παντοκράτορος*, "the great Day of God the Almighty"; cf. *2 Apoc. Bar.* 55:6: "the Day of the Mighty One"). Whether 2 Peter intends a distinction between "the Day of the Lord" (= Christ?) in v 10, and "the Day of God" (= the Father) here, is very uncertain.

δι' ἥν, "because of which," indicates that the coming of the day of God is the cause of the destruction, which will therefore "not be the result of any natural cyclic process, like the periodical conflagration envisaged in Stoic thought, but the direct effect of God's all-sovereign will" (Kelly).

στοιχεῖα καυσούμενα τήκεται, "the heavenly bodies melt in the heat." This clause derives from Isa 34:4 LXX (B, Lucian): *τακήσονται πᾶσαι αἱ δυνάμεις τῶν οὐρανῶν* ("all the powers of the heavens will melt"): see *Comment* on v

10. (The verb τήκεσθαι, "to melt," here a NT *hapax,* is also used of the melting of the mountains at the eschatological coming of God: LXX Isa 63:19–64:1; Mic 1:4; *1 Enoch* 1:6). The description of the conflagration is repeated, with slight variations from v 10, in order to prepare for v 13.

13. καινοὺς δὲ οὐρανοὺς καὶ γῆν καινὴν κατὰ τὸ ἐπάγγελμα αὐτοῦ προσδοκῶμεν, "but according to his promise we are waiting for new heavens and a new earth." The hope for a new heaven and a new earth is based on Isa 65:17; 66:22, which must be the "promise" to which this v refers, and is found throughout Jewish apocalyptic (*Jub.* 1:29; *1 Enoch* 45:4–5; 72:1; 91:16; *Sib. Or.* 5:212; *2 Apoc. Bar.* 32:6; 44:12; 57:2; 4 Ezra 7:75; *Bib. Ant.* 3:10; Pseudo-Sophocles, *ap.* Clem. Alex., *Strom.* 5.14.122.1; *Apoc. El.* 3:98) and was taken up in early Christianity (Matt 19:28; Rom 8:21; Rev 21:1). The cosmic dissolution described in vv 10, 12, was a return to the primeval chaos, as in the Flood (3:6), so that a new creation may emerge (cf. 4 Ezra 7:30–31). Such passages emphasize the radical discontinuity between the old and the new, but it is nevertheless clear that they intend to describe a renewal, not an abolition, of creation (cf. *1 Enoch* 54:4–5; Rom 8:21).

ἐν οἷς δικαιοσύνη κατοικεῖ, "in which righteousness is at home." "Righteousness" is personified, as in Isa 32:16 (LXX: δικαιοσύνη ἐν τῷ Καρμήλῳ κατοικήσει, "righteousness will dwell in Carmel"). The only feature of the new world which the writer considers relevant is that it will be a world in which God's will will be done. In this he is in the mainstream of Jewish and Christian eschatology. For the righteousness of the new age, cf. Isa 9:7; 11:4–5; *Pss. Sol.* 17:40; *1 Enoch* 5:8–9; 10:16, 20–21; 91:17; *2 Enoch* 65:8; 4 Ezra 7:114; Rom 14:17.

14. ταῦτα προσδοκῶντες, "since you are waiting for these." "These" are the new heavens and the new earth. Because a new world of righteousness is coming, which only the righteous can enter, Christians must live righteously now to be fit to enter it. By abandoning the hope for the triumph of righteousness, the false teachers had removed this motive for holiness.

σπουδάσατε, "strive": see *Comment* on 1:10.

ἄσπιλοι καὶ ἀμώμητοι αὐτῷ εὑρεθῆναι, "to be found without spot or blemish in his sight." ἄσπιλοι καὶ ἀμώμητοι ("without spot or blemish") is an example of our author's predilection for pairs of synonyms, but in this case he probably follows a traditional phrase. The combination ἀμώμου καὶ ἀσπίλου occurs in 1 Pet 1:19, and similar phrases including either ἄμωμος or ἀσπίλος are common in early Christian literature (ἄμωμος with a synonym: Eph 1:4; 5:27; Col 1:22; *1 Clem.* 1:3; 45:1; Herm. *Vis.* 4:2:5; ἀσπίλος with a synonym: 1 Tim 6:14; Herm. *Vis.* 4:3:5; *Sim.* 5:6:7; ἄμωμος alone in a comparable context: Jude 24, where *v. l.* adds ἀσπιλους; *1 Clem.* 50:2; Ign. *Trall.* 13:3; cf. *1 Clem.* 63:1; and comparable pairs of synonyms: Phil 1:10; 2:15; Jas 1:27; *1 Clem.* 29:1; *2 Clem.* 6:9; Herm. *Mand.* 2:7; cf. 1 Thess 3:13; 5:23). The majority of these parallels are in an eschatological context, and many of them refer to the state in which Christians or the church ought to be at the Parousia (Eph 1:4; 5:27; Col 1:22; Herm. *Vis.* 4:3:5; *Sim.* 5:6:7; Jude 24; Ign. *Trall.* 13:3; *1 Clem.* 63:1; Phil 1:10; 2:15; 1 Thess 3:13; 5:23; perhaps *1 Clem.* 50:2; cf. also 1 Cor 1:8). Of these, three use the verb εὑρίσκειν ("to find") as in 2 Peter (*1 Clem.* 50:2; Herm. *Sim.* 5:6:7; Ign. *Trall.* 13:3; cf. also Sir 31:8).

Clearly the author of 2 Peter here draws on standard terminology from liturgical or paraenetic tradition (cf. *Comment* on 2:13 and Jude 24). It is unlikely that he is dependent on Paul (who does not provide the closest parallels; against Fornberg, *Early Church,* 24–25) or on 1 Pet 1:19 (where the context is quite different; against Kelly) or on Jude 24.

ἀσπίλος, "without spot," describes sacrificial animals (1 Pet 1:19; pagan usage in *TDNT* 1, 502), though it also came to denote moral purity (Job 15:15 Symmachus; Jas 1:27). Instead of ἄμωμος ("without blemish"), which is the usual LXX term, used of sacrifical victims (e.g. Exod 29:38; Lev 1:3; 3:1; Heb 9:14), 2 Peter uses the rarer word ἀμώμητος ("without blemish"), a biblical *hapax* (except Phil 2:15 *v.l.*, following LXX Deut 32:5: μωμητά), although the LXX once uses μωμητός to mean "blemished" (Deut 32:5). In combination with ἀσπίλος it is probably intended to continue the sacrificial metaphor, although (like ἄμωμος, which derives its sacrificial meaning solely from LXX usage) in normal Greek usage it referred to moral blamelessness (*TDNT* 4, 831). The two words describe Christians as morally pure, metaphorically an unblemished sacrifice to God.

Christians are to be so "found" by the Lord at his coming to judgment (cf. Phil 3:9; *1 Clem.* 35:4; 57:2; *2 Clem.* 6:9; Herm. *Sim.* 5:6:7; 9:13:2; Ign. *Trall* 2:2; 13:3; *Magn.* 9:2). Probably there is an echo of 3:10 (see *Comment* on that v). αὐτῷ probably means "in his sight," rather than "found *by him*" (or "at peace *with him*"), and probably has a judicial sense ("in the eyes of the judge") rather than cultic overtones (as in Jude 24).

ἐν εἰρήνῃ, "at peace", i.e. "at peace *with God,*" in the state of reconciliation with God which is Christian salvation. Our author, like most early Christian writers, expects his readers to be alive when the Lord comes.

15. τὴν τοῦ κυρίου ἡμῶν μακροθυμίαν σωτηρίαν ἡγεῖσθε, "regard the forbearance of our Lord as salvation." In contrast to the false teachers, who interpret the delay of the Parousia as "lateness" (3:9), 2 Peter's readers can give it a positive interpretation, as an opportunity to secure, through repentance, the salvation which they might have missed if the Parousia had come sooner (cf. *2 Clem.* 16:1).

ὁ ἀγαπητὸς ἡμῶν ἀδελφὸς Παῦλος, "our dear brother Paul." The term ἀδελφός ("brother") is regularly used by Paul as a term for his fellow-workers, his colleagues in the service of the gospel (e.g. 2 Cor 2:13; Phil 2:25; 1 Thess 3:2), and 1 Pet 5:12 shows that this usage was not confined to Paul but was familiar among the leaders of the church in Rome. The term was by no means confined to apostles. Paul uses ἀγαπητὸς ἀδελφός ("dear brother") in Eph 6:21; Col 4:7, 9 (cf. Col 1:7; Phlm 1; and for ἀγαπητός, "beloved," alone, cf. Acts 15:25; Rom 16:12; 3 John 1), probably indicating that ἀγαπητός is not merely conventional, but conveys affection.

ἡμῶν ("our") is not likely to mean simply "my," though many commentators assume this. True epistolary plurals occur rarely, if at all, in the NT. Apparent examples in Paul always (or almost always) include Paul's colleagues, Timothy and others. When Paul says "our brother" rather than "my brother," it is probable that he means the plural literally (notice the careful alternation of first person singular and plural in 2 Cor 8:22–23; even in 1 Thess 3:2 "our" is probably "Paul's and Silvanus' "). In 2 Peter, the first person plural in

1:1, 16–19 means "we apostles," and the first person singular is used for Peter himself in 1:12–15; 3:1. Probably, therefore, the first person plural in 3:15 means, not "we Christians" (Mayor), but "we apostles" (Schrage). This need not imply that the author excluded Paul from the ranks of the apostles, which would be very surprising (cf. *1 Clem.* 5:3–5), but simply means that Paul is considered a fellow-worker with the rest of the apostles. Another possibility (less likely because the first person plural would then have a different reference from the first person plural in 1:16–18) is that "we" are Peter and his immediate colleagues, the Petrine "circle" of Christian leaders in Rome.

Most commentators remark that this phrase could not have been used by the historical Peter, because of the tension between him and Paul (Gal 2:11–14), and that it indicates the view of the postapostolic age, which looked back to Peter and Paul as the two great leaders of the apostolic church (Acts; *1 Clem.* 5; Ign. *Rom.* 4:3; cf. *Ep. Apost.* 31–33). In fact Gal 1:18; 2:7–9 show that Peter recognized Paul as a fellow-apostle, and it is naïve to suppose that their disagreement at Antioch need have prevented Peter from writing of Paul in the terms used here. It was only one incident in a long relationship of which we otherwise know next to nothing. If Peter had a critical view of Paul, it is odd to find Silvanus in the Petrine circle in Rome (1 Pet 5:12). As far as our evidence goes, there is nothing implausible in the attitude to Paul here attributed to Peter (so also Mayor, Green; Robinson, *Redating,* 181). Our author, who had probably been a colleague of Peter's, may in fact be reflecting accurately the historical Peter's cordial regard for Paul.

On the other hand, the fact that postapostolic authors generally refer to Paul in more reverential terms (*1 Clem.* 47:1; Ign. *Eph.* 12:2; Pol. *Phil.* 3:2; *Act. Verc.* 3) does not show that only Peter himself could have written 2 Pet 3:15 (against Green). In adopting a phrase which would be plausible on the lips of the historical Peter, our author follows the practice of most pseudepigraphal writers, who were easily able to avoid crass anachronisms like "the blessed apostle Paul" on the lips of a fellow-apostle (cf. the *Ep. Pet. Phil.* [CG 8,2] 132:13–14: "Philip our beloved brother and our fellow apostle").

Some think the reference to Paul is an only too obvious attempt to bolster the author's claim to speak as the apostle Peter, but this is a misunderstanding of the pseudepigraphal device. The literary fiction of Petrine authorship is carried through with verisimilitude, and the *manner* of referring to Paul is an instance of this, but the fiction is not intended to deceive. The need for verisimilitude cannot therefore explain *why* the author introduced the reference to Paul. As in the rather similar case of 1:16–18, the reference to Paul has an apologetic purpose. The author wishes to point out that his own teaching (specifically in 3:14–15a) is in harmony with Paul's because Paul was an important authority for his readers. The reason for this is clear: the churches to which he writes (or at least some of them) had been founded in the Pauline mission and naturally held in high regard the Pauline letters which they preserved and read. The author's appeal to Paul's letters is precisely parallel to the appeal which *1 Clem.* 47:1 makes to 1 Corinthians. Clement, a contemporary of our author, also writing from Rome to a church founded by Paul (Corinth), similarly supports his own teaching by referring to the letter Paul had written to his readers.

κατὰ τὴν δοθεῖσαν αὐτῷ σοφίαν, "in accordance with the wisdom given to him," is equivalent to *πνευματικῶς* ("under the inspiration of the Spirit") in *1 Clem.* 47:1. In both cases the appeal to Paul's teaching in his letters is reinforced by reference to the fact that the apostle wrote under divine inspiration. *δοθεῖσαν* ("given") is a "divine" passive, with God as the implied agent, and Paul's "wisdom" is therefore a charismatic gift of God (cf. "the utterance of wisdom," *λόγος σοφίας*: 1 Cor 12:8; and for wisdom as the gift of God, cf. Ezra 7:25; Dan 1:19; Wis 7:7; 9:17; Eph 1:17; Col 1:9; Mark 6:2; Jas 1:5; and for wisdom associated with the Spirit: Acts 6:3, 10; 1 Cor 2:13).

Paul himself frequently refers to the "grace (*χάρις*) given to" him (Rom 12:3; 15:15; Gal 2:9; 1 Cor 3:10; Eph 3:2, 7; cf. Col 1:25), i.e. his apostolic commission, the divine enabling by which he receives and understands the revelation of God's purpose in the gospel (Eph 3:2–10), and by which he speaks and writes with the authority of one who conveys God's message (Rom 12:3; 15:15–16). Second Peter's reference to his charismatic wisdom implies no more and no less than this. The choice of the word *σοφία* ("wisdom"), rather than the general term *χάρις* ("grace"), is appropriate in a reference to Paul's teaching in his letters (cf. 1 Cor 2:6–13). It was with God-given insight into the truth of the gospel, the charisma of wisdom, that Paul wrote his letters. (For wisdom as the gift of an inspired writer, cf. *Prot. Jas.* 25: "the Lord who gave me wisdom to write this history"; Pol. *Phil.* 3:2: "the wisdom of the blessed and glorious Paul," with reference both to his preaching and to his writing Philippians.)

It is possible that the author of 2 Peter deliberately echoes the Pauline "slogan," "the grace given to me" (Conti, *RivB* 17 [1969] 129, 131–34; Fornberg, *Early Church,* 26), and it may be significant that two of the most appropriate parallels occur in Romans (12:3; 15:15; for our author's possible familiarity with Romans, see *Comment* on 2:19). But the phrase is too natural for dependence on Paul to be demonstrable. At any rate, the idea of the inspiration of Paul's letters expressed in this v cannot be branded "the later ecclesiastical idea" (Knoch, "Vermächtnis," 154). It faithfully reflects the apostle's own consciousness of apostolic authority and charismatic inspiration.

Conti rightly points out the parallel between this description of Paul's inspiration and the account of the inspiration of the OT prophets (1:20–21). Like them, Paul did not speak out of his own wisdom, but in accordance with the wisdom given him by God. It is this that accounts for the treatment of Paul's letters, alongside the OT writings, as "scriptures" (v 16). Their inspiration gives them normative authority, though not yet canonical status (see below).

ἔγραψεν ὑμῖν, "wrote to you." Some think "you" are all Christians (Moffatt, Spicq, Kelly, Sidebottom, Schrage, Senior; Lindemann, *Paulus,* 92), but this makes the comparison between what Paul wrote "to you" and what he wrote in "all his letters" (v 16) meaningless. These two verses are only intelligible if "you" are a specific church or specific churches which had been the recipients of one or more Pauline letters, and the claim that 2 Peter is a "catholic" letter, addressed to all Christians indiscriminately, comes to grief especially in the exegesis of these verses. (The idea that Paul's letters were intentionally written for the whole church, which would be presupposed if "you" were all Christians, is not in evidence in this period; cf. *1 Clem.* 47:1; Pol. *Phil.* 3:2.)

To which letter(s) of Paul does this v refer? Most of the letters in the Pauline corpus have been suggested: e.g. Romans (Mayor; Selwyn, *Christian Prophets,* 157–58), Ephesians (von Soden), the Thessalonian letters (Plumptre, Reicke), Hebrews (R. P. C. Hanson, *Tradition in the Early Church* [London: SCM Press, 1962] 189; already suggested by Bengel), or a lost letter (Spitta; Zahn, *Introduction,* 198–99). The grounds on which these choices have been made are basically two: (1) Destination. If 3:1 indicates that the churches addressed are those of 1 Pet 1:1, then Galatians, Colossians and Ephesians are possibilities. (2) Subject-matter. If the *καθὼς καί* ("just as") clause relates only to v 15a, the letter must be one which treats of divine forbearance (Mayor), and among extant letters Romans is then the only plausible candidate (see especially Rom 2:4; cf. also 3:25; 9:22–23; 11:22–23). But there is no need to limit the subject-matter so narrowly. The *καθὼς καί* clause is naturally taken to relate to the whole of vv 14–15a. In that case the subject-matter is the much more general one of eschatological paraenesis, ethical exhortation in view of the coming Parousia, a theme which is found in nearly all Paul's letters (e.g. Rom 13:11–14; 1 Cor 7:27–35; 15:58; 2 Cor 7:1; 9:6; Gal 5:21; 6:7–8; Phil 2:15–16; 3:20; 4:5; Col 3:4–6, 23–25; 1 Thess 5:4–11), though unfortunately it is not easy to find in Ephesians (cf. 4:30; 5:5, 16, 27; 6:13), which might otherwise be a very suitable candidate. Some take the subject-matter to be, more broadly, the eschatological discussion of chap 3, and therefore suggest the Thessalonian letters as the most appropriate, but it is doubtful whether this is justified.

The attempt to select a letter on grounds of subject-matter is, however, misguided, since according to v 16 (where *περὶ τουτῶν*, "of these matters," cannot, as Mayor thinks, refer to a broader subject, but continues the reference to vv 14–15a) the same subject is treated throughout Paul's correspondence. The reason why the letter to 2 Peter's readers is singled out for special mention in v 15b is not that it treated the subject more explicitly or more fully, but simply that it was written to 2 Peter's readers.

The destination of 2 Peter must be decided on other grounds, principally the indication in 3:1 that the churches addressed are those (or some of those) addressed in 1 Pet 1:1. If the reference is to an extant Pauline letter, it must therefore have been Galatians, Colossians or Ephesians. There is no way of deciding between these, and perhaps even the author of 2 Peter did not decide. Since he shows no great familiarity with the Pauline letters, we need not suppose that he had in mind much more than that Paul frequently included eschatological paraenesis in his letters and that Paul had written letters to some of the churches to which his own letter was addressed.

16. *ἐν πάσαις ἐπιστολαῖς*, "in all his letters," must imply that the author had some acquaintance with a number of Pauline letters, and so probably with some kind of collection of Pauline letters, however small and informal, in use in his church. But of course he refers only to those Pauline letters he

knew, and we have no means of knowing how many they were. His own work contains no certain allusions to Pauline material, and the only possible allusions which are at all plausible are to Romans (in 2:19; 3:15), which if he wrote from Rome is not surprising, and to 1 Thessalonians (in 3:10).

Thus, although this phrase is rather unlikely in a letter written from Rome before Peter's death, it gives little further help in determining the date of 2 Peter. Pauline letters may have begun to circulate to churches other than those to which they were written even before Paul's death, and small local collections probably preceded the formation of the corpus of ten letters (cf. L. Mowry, "The Early Circulation of Paul's Letters," *JBL* 63 [1944] 73–86). Clement certainly knew, not only Romans, but also 1 Corinthians (*1 Clem.* 47:1), and perhaps other Pauline letters. The author of *2 Clem.* seems to have known a collection of Pauline letters (Donfried, *Second Clement,* 93–95, 108, 160–65), as Ignatius (*Eph.* 12:2) and Polycarp certainly did.

δυσνόητά τινα ἃ οἱ ἀμαθεῖς καὶ ἀστήρικτοι στρεβλοῦσιν, "some things that are hard to understand, which the uninstructed and unstable people distort." *δυσνόητος* ("hard to understand") is a rare word, used of texts which are difficult to interpret (Diogenes Laertes, *Vit. Phil.* 9.13) and by Hermas of his symbolic visions (Herm. *Sim.* 9:14:4). It is no qualification of Paul's "wisdom" (v 15) to admit that Paul's writings contain difficult passages, since it is only the *ἀμαθεῖς καὶ ἀστήρικτοι* ("uninstructed and unstable people") who will be liable to misinterpret them, and they also misinterpret the "other scriptures" (see below; cf. Lindemann, *Paulus,* 94). The reference is probably therefore to passages which are liable to be misunderstood unless they are interpreted in the light of the rest of Paul's teaching and of the apostolic teaching generally, rather than to passages which are simply obscure. (The point is therefore different from that made by Origen, *Comm. in Rom.* 6, who attributes the variety of interpretations of Paul to the fact that he was unable to express himself clearly.) For the correct interpretation of such passages some instruction in Christian teaching is required.

ἀμαθεῖς (a fairly common word which happens not to be used elsewhere in early Christian literature) means not simply "ignorant" but "uninstructed." These people have not received sufficient instruction in the faith to be able to interpret difficult passages in the Scriptures correctly. *ἀστήρικτοι* ("unstable") has a similar connotation (cf. *Comment* on 1:12; 2:14): they are easily misled because their understanding and experience of Christianity are relatively superficial. There may be an element of condemnation in the description: these people are ignorant because they are *unwilling* to learn, and unstable because they *allow themselves* to be misled.

The description "uninstructed and unstable" might seem to suit the followers of the false teachers, rather than the false teachers themselves. *ἀστήρικτοι* ("unstable") is used of those who are "ensnared" by the false teachers in 2:14 (*ψυχὰς ἀστηρίκτους*, "unstable people"), while 2:18 characterizes their victims as recent converts. Yet it is unlikely that misuse of the Scriptures would be attributed to the false teachers' followers and not to the false teachers themselves. Probably we should assume that the author speaks here of both (so Zahn, *Introduction,* 228–29). The false teachers themselves he regards as incompetent exegetes because they have never taken the trouble to understand

Christian teaching thoroughly (for their ignorance, cf. 2:12; 3:5). They and their followers are a case of the blind leading the blind.

στρεβλοῦν, "to twist, torture," is interpreted by Neyrey (*Polemic,* 56–58) to mean that they reject Paul's teaching (as they did OT prophecies: 1:20–21), but in combination with *δυσνόητα* ("hard to understand") it must mean "distort," in the sense of "misinterpret." This could imply either that they give Paul's teaching an unacceptable sense and reject it, or that they misinterpret it in such a way as to make it support their own misguided views. In the first case, it could be that they interpreted Paul's statements about the imminence of the Parousia (e.g. Rom 13:11–12; 16:20; 1 Cor 7:29; Phil 4:5; 1 Thess 4:15) in such a way as to imply that his expectations were not fulfilled and therefore that his future eschatology must be rejected. In the second case, the most likely texts (as most commentators argue) would be those which could be held to support antinomianism (e.g. Rom 4:15; 5:20; 8:1; 1 Cor 6:12; and the doctrine of justification by faith as a whole) and the false teachers' offer of "freedom" (2:19; cf. Rom 8:2; 2 Cor 3:17). Such Pauline texts were so used by second-century Gnostics (E. H. Pagels, *The Gnostic Paul: Gnostic Exegesis of the Pauline Letters* [Philadelphia: Fortress Press, 1975] 66–67). Some commentators think that 2 Peter's opponents used Pauline texts in the interests of a wholly realized eschatology, excluding the future expectation of the Parousia, but this is unlikely, both because such texts are much more difficult to find (second-century Gnostics used Pauline texts to support a spiritual, rather than a physical, resurrection, but that is an issue to which 2 Peter makes no reference), and because 2 Peter offers no evidence that the opponents taught a realized eschatology.

It is difficult to decide between the two possibilities. The first fits well into 2 Peter's portrait of the false teachers as skeptical about future eschatology. The second could correspond to 2:19, and is perhaps a more obvious misuse of Paul, based on a misunderstanding of him which he himself had to counter (Rom 3:8; 6:15; Gal 5:13).

Even if the second possibility is the correct interpretation, it does not really offer much support for the common opinion that the opponents were radical Paulinists and that the author of 2 Peter refers to Paul because Paul was the major authority for his opponents. He refers to Paul primarily because Paul was an important authority for the *churches* to which he writes (see above), and this will also be the reason why the false teachers referred to Paul. It was not necessarily because Paul's letters were their major inspiration, but because Paul's letters were a major theological authority in their churches, that the false teachers discussed Paul's teaching, whether in order to reject it or in order to use it in support of their own views.

Still less justified is the opinion that 2 Pet 3:15–16 is an attempt to rehabilitate Paul in "orthodox" circles, which had viewed the Pauline letters with suspicion because of the gnostic heretics' use of them. Lindemann (*Paulus,* 95–96) points out that there is no evidence for a negative attitude to Paul in "orthodox" church circles. Second Peter's positive picture of Paul as a witness to the authentic apostolic teaching fits into the general trend of early Christian attitudes to Paul (Acts, *1 Clem.*, Ignatius, Polycarp, as well as the deutero-Pauline letters if they are pseudepigraphal).

For heretical misuse of early Christian writings, cf. Pol. *Phil.* 7:1, which condemns anyone who "perverts (μεθοδευη) the sayings of the Lord to his own lusts (πρὸς τὰς ἰδίας ἐπιθυμίας)"; and the Pseudo-Clementine *Ep. Pet. James* 2:4, where Peter complains that some have tried to distort (μετασχηματίζειν) his words to support the abolition of the Law.

τὰς λοιπὰς γραφάς, "the other scriptures." It would make no sense to take γραφάς in the nontechnical sense of "writings"; the definite article requires us to give it its technical sense (as always in the NT) of "inspired, authoritative writings," i.e. "scriptures." λοιπάς (lit. "remaining") must (against Green) imply that Paul's letters are included in the category of γραφαί.

To determine the precise implication of this, we should first note that the term γραφή ("scripture") was not limited to the books of the OT canon, but could be used for apocryphal writings (Jas 4:5; *Barn.* 16:5; *1 Clem.* 23:3; cf. Herm. *Vis.* 2:3:4: ὡς γέγραπται, "as it is written"). It need not therefore imply a *canon* of Scripture at all. The inclusion of Paul's letters in this category certainly means they are regarded as inspired, authoritative writings (as v 15 in fact says), ranked alongside the OT and probably various other books, including other apostolic writings. Probably the implication is that they are suitable for reading in Christian worship. But this does not at all require the conclusion that the author of 2 Peter knows a NT *canon.* Apostolic writings must have ranked as authoritative writings, suitable for reading in Christian worship, long before there was any fixed NT canon.

It is hard to tell at what date Paul's letters could have begun to be called γραφαί ("scriptures"), but there is no real difficulty in dating 2 Pet 3:16 in the late first century. In *2 Clem.* 14:2 apostolic writings are ranked alongside the OT: "the books (τὰ βιβλία, i.e. the OT) and the apostles declare" (see Donfried, *Second Clement,* 93–95). Possible early instances of NT texts being called γραφαί ("scriptures") are 1 Tim 5:18 (perhaps a quotation of Matt 10:10, called γραφή along with an OT text); *2 Clem.* 2:4 (a Gospel saying is called ἑτέρα γραφή, "another scripture," following an OT quotation); *Barn.* 4:14 (ὡς γέγραπται, "as it is written," introduces a quotaton from Matt 22:14); Pol. *Phil.* 12:1 (Ps 4:5 and Eph 4:26 are called *his scripturis,* "these scriptures"). The fact that in four of these instances a NT quotation is placed alongside an OT text is not insignificant. It shows that Gospels and apostolic writings were coming to be ranked with the OT Scriptures. There is nothing at all surprising in this development. Apostolic writings were regarded as inspired and authoritative from the beginning (see above). Once they were being read along with the OT in Christian worship, it was quite natural that the term γραφή ("scripture") should come to be used for them.

"The other scriptures" could have included Gospels, whose predictions of the imminent Parousia the false teachers would have interpreted as false prophecy and rejected, as perhaps they did Paul's. We know (from 1:20–21) that they misinterpreted OT prophecies, in that they interpreted them as only the human ideas of the prophets and therefore dismissed them. Whether it is also implied that there were OT and non-Pauline apostolic writings in which the false teachers claimed to find *support* for their views it is impossible to tell.

πρὸς τὴν ἰδίαν αὐτῶν ἀπώλειαν, "so as to bring about their own destruction."

The misuse of the Scriptures by the false teachers and their followers was serious enough to imperil their salvation. It was therefore not a question of minor doctrinal errors, but of using their misinterpretations to justify immorality, for it is 2 Peter's consistent teaching that eschatological judgment (*ἀπώλεια*, "destruction") is coming on the false teachers because of their ungodly lives. In relation to their misinterpretation of Paul, this is clearly the case if they appeal to Paul's teaching about Christian freedom to justify libertinism. If they misinterpret Paul in order to reject his eschatological expectation, this too is in the interests of immorality, since it removes the eschatological motive from Christian ethics. The false teachers' rejection of eschatology will therefore lead to their judgment, just as 2 Peter's readers' proper understanding of eschatology should lead to their salvation (vv 14–15a).

The emphatic *ἰδίαν* ("own") recalls 1:20, and perhaps suggests an irony concealed in this phrase. Perhaps the author was going to say that they twist the Scriptures "to their own interpretation" (*πρὸς τὴν ἰδίαν ἐπιλύσιν*, cf. 1:20), turning back on them their own accusation against the prophets. Instead he states what this amounts to: "their own destruction" (cf. Pol. *Phil.* 7:1: *πρὸς τὰς ἰδίας ἐπιθυμίας*, "to their own lusts").

Explanation

The false teachers' denial of future eschatology was the corollary of their libertine behavior. In this section of exhortation the author shows how, by contrast, his readers' eschatological expectation should have as its corollary a life of active Christian righteousness in the present. Eschatology supplies a motive for ethical conduct, not only as a negative warning of judgment, but also as a positive hope for a new world in which God's righteous will shall entirely prevail. The present world in which evil is all too dominant is coming to an end and will be replaced by a world in which righteousness is at home. Christians, waiting in hope for this new world, should aim to be the sort of people who can enter it, rather than the sort of people who must perish with the old world. By repentance and righteousness, fulfilling God's purpose in his deferment of the Parousia, they can even "hasten" its arrival.

The false teachers, who interpreted the Lord's forbearance in delaying the Parousia as "lateness," made this an excuse for moral laxity which puts them in danger of condemnation when the day of judgment does come. By contrast, 2 Peter's readers, who interpret the Lord's forbearance as an opportunity to repent and so be sure of salvation, should aim to be, when the Lord does come, reconciled to him and innocent before his judgment seat.

That the expectation of the Parousia should be a motive for Christian righteousness and the period up to the Parousia an opportunity for repentance and righteousness had also been Paul's teaching in his letters. The author makes this point to support his argument with the additional authority of Paul, who, as founder of some of the churches to which 2 Peter was addressed, was a major theological authority for the readers. Because of the location of these churches in Asia Minor (1 Pet 1:1; 2 Pet 3:1), the reference to what Paul had written to the readers of 2 Peter is presumably to Galatians, Colossians or Ephesians, or to more than one of these letters. Since, as the author himself says, eschatological paraenesis occurs throughout Paul's extant correspondence, it is impossible to be more specific.

Paul is said to have written under divine inspiration. The reference to his endowment with the gift of wisdom faithfully reflects Paul's own consciousness of charismatic inspiration and apostolic authority. As inspired, authoritative writings, Paul's letters rank alongside "the other scriptures," i.e. the OT and (probably) other apostolic literature. This does not imply that the author knows a NT canon, but probably means that some kind of collection of Paul's letters—we cannot tell how many—was known to the author, and that they were read in Christian worship along with the OT Scriptures. This passage belongs to a fairly early stage in the process which led to the formal recognition of a canon of apostolic writings.

His reference to Paul gives the author the opportunity for a final attack on the false teachers. Since Paul was a theological authority in their churches, the false teachers were also obliged to refer to his teaching in his letters, but in the author's view their exegesis amounted to a serious misinterpretation of passages which were too difficult for the "uninstructed and unstable" to understand. The correct interpretation of such passages required a broad and sound knowledge of apostolic teaching. The author does not intend to imply that exegesis of Paul should therefore be limited to the church's official teachers: his opponents may in fact have held office as teachers in their churches. His argument is that, for all their pretensions to be teachers, they have never bothered to acquire sufficient knowledge of Christian teaching to be able to understand either Paul or the other Scriptures which they also misinterpret. Consequently they easily go astray. But 2 Peter's readers, whether teachers or not, are evidently expected to be well enough instructed (partly by 2 Peter) to understand Paul correctly.

It is impossible to be sure how the false teachers misinterpreted Paul. They may have used his teaching about justification by faith and Christian freedom to support their antinomian attitude to morality and their offer of "freedom" (2:19). Alternatively, they may have taken his statements about the imminence of the Parousia to be prophecies which the delay of the Parousia had disproved, with the result that Paul's teaching on future eschatology could be discarded. Whatever their misinterpretations of Paul and of the "other scriptures" were, they used them to justify immorality and so they would lead to their destruction on the Day of Judgment.

Conclusion (*3:17–18*)

Translation

[17] *So you, my dear friends, since you know this in advance, be on your guard so that you may not be carried away by the error of these lawless people and fall from your stable position.* [18] *But grow in grace and in the knowledge of our Lord and Savior Jesus Christ.*

To him belongs [a] *the glory both now and on the day of eternity.* [b]

Notes

[a] The verb "to be" is understood, and most translations supply "be," making the doxology a prayer. But for the indicative meaning as normal in doxologies, see the commentary on Jude 24–25.

[b] Most MSS add *αμην*, "amen," but this is omitted in a few MSS (including B 1739). Since most doxologies conclude with "Amen" and all other NT doxologies do so, it is more likely to have been added than to have been omitted here.

Form/Structure/Setting

The concluding exhortation (vv 17–18a), while it connects immediately with v 16 (note especially *ἀστήρικτοι*, "unstable," v 16; *στηριγμοῦ*, "stable position," v 17), also serves to conclude the whole letter, since it summarizes the overall message of the letter. *προγινώσκοντες* ("since you know this in advance") evokes the central idea in the author's use of the testament genre: Peter's prediction of the false teachers. The rest of the exhortation recalls themes from earlier parts of the letter (*πλάνῃ*, "error": cf. 2:15; *στηριγμοῦ*, "stable position," cf. 1:12; v 18a, cf. 1:5–7).

For the form of doxologies, see the commentary on Jude 24–25. Second Peter's follows simply the most basic form, with the exception of the indication of time and the omission of "Amen" (see *Note*). The indication of time is a twofold form referring to present and future (as in *1 Clem.* 64; *Mart. Pol.* 14:3; cf. *1 Clem.* 61:3) and is therefore not modeled on Jude 25, which has a (unique) threefold form (against Fornberg, *Early Church,* 92). The use of *εἰς ἡμέραν αἰῶνος* ("on the day of eternity") in place of the usual *εἰς τοὺς αἰῶνας* ("for ever"; and expansions of this) is unique and probably a modification of the usual formula originated by the author of 2 Peter.

Doxologies addressed to Christ are unusual in early Christian literature (2 Tim 4:18; Rev 1:5–6 are the only other certain examples; less certain examples are Heb 13:21; 1 Pet 4:11; *1 Clem.* 20:12; 50:7).

For doxologies concluding letters, see the commentary on Jude 24–25. Like Jude, but unlike most early Christian letters, 2 Peter has no specifically epistolary conclusion and no personal greetings. The latter would have involved elaborating the pseudepigraphal fiction for its own sake, whereas our author uses it purely functionally, as a device to convey what he has to say.

Comment

17. *ὑμεῖς οὖν, ἀγαπητοί, προγινώσκοντες*, "so you, my dear friends, since you know this in advance." *ὑμεῖς* ("you") is emphatic, in contrast to the false teachers and their followers who were the subject of the preceding v. *προγινώσκοντες* is not, *pace* Bigg, equivalent to *ταῦτα πρῶτον γινώσκοντες* ("above all understanding": 1:20; 3:3), but means "knowing beforehand." The fiction of Peter's prophecy is resumed from 2:1–3; 3:3–4. Peter is represented as having predicted the rise of the false teachers after his death, so that his readers, who according to the fiction are supposed to receive the letter before his death (1:13), will be forewarned even before they encounter the false teachers. Of course, in reality the readers received the letter when the false teachers were already active in their churches (hence the present tense even in v 16), but the author wishes to remind them that the expectation of such "scoffers" did in fact form part of common apostolic teaching about the last days (cf. Jude 17–18). His letter informs them that these eschatological figures about whom they had been warned are the very people now teaching in their churches!

ἵνα μὴ τῇ τῶν ἀθέσμων πλάνῃ συναπαχθέντες, "so that you may not be carried away by the error of these lawless people." *πλάνῃ* ("error") may combine passive and active senses (see *Comment* on Jude 11): their going astray (cf. 2:15) and their leading others astray. *ἀθέσμων* ("lawless") was used in 2:7 of the Sodomites: it characterizes the false teachers as people who ignore all moral constraints. *συναπάγειν* ("to carry away") is similarly used in Gal 2:13.

ἐκπέσητε τοῦ ἰδίου στηριγμοῦ, "fall from your stable position." *στηριγμοῦ* (contrast *ἀστήρικτοι*, "unstable" in v 16; and for this word-group in 2 Peter, see *Comment* on 1:12) is not to be taken as an abstraction ("steadfastness") but as a fixed position (used of the "stations" of the planets by Plutarch, *Mor.* 76D; cf. the quotation from Pseudo-Longinus, *De Sub.* 40, in Bigg). The author thinks of experienced and well-instructed Christians as firmly established in a fixed position from which they ought not to be swayed. No doubt the verb is chosen because of the common use of *πίπτειν*, "to fall" (*T. Gad* 4:3; Rom 11:11, 22; 14:4; 1 Cor 10:12; Heb 4:11; Rev 2:5; *1 Clem.* 59:4; *2 Clem.* 2:6) and compounds (*ἐκπίπτειν*, "to fall from," Gal 5:4; *ἀποπίπτειν*: "to fall from": *2 Clem.* 5:7) for moral declension and apostasy.

18. *αὐξάνετε δὲ ἐν χάριτι καὶ γνώσει τοῦ κυρίου ἡμῶν καὶ σωτῆρος Ἰησοῦ Χριστοῦ*, "but grow in grace and in the knowledge of our Lord and Savior Jesus Christ," takes up the theme of 1:5–10: the need for progress in the Christian life. The phrase "of our Lord and Savior Jesus Christ" could be taken with both *χάριτι* and *γνώσει* ("in the grace and knowledge of our Lord and Savior Jesus Christ"), but with *χάριτι* it would have to be a subjective genitive ("grace given by Jesus Christ"), whereas with *γνώσει* it is most natural to take it as an objective genitive ("knowledge of Jesus Christ"). That the same phrase should be taken in both ways is not impossible, but it is awkward (Mayor, Kelly). Some do take *γνώσει τοῦ κυρίου ἡμῶν* to be knowledge *given by* Jesus Christ, on the grounds that our author preserves a distinction between *γνῶσις* and *ἐπίγνωσις*, and reserves the latter for knowledge of Jesus Christ (so Bigg, Green). However, the distinction between the two terms, as used in 2 Peter,

is that ἐπίγνωσις designates the fundamental Christian knowledge received in conversion, whereas γνῶσις is knowledge which can be acquired and developed in the course of Christian life (see *Comment* on 1:2, 6). Both can be knowledge of Jesus Christ. Here γνῶσις is that deepening experience of Christ and understanding of the truth of Christ which should continue to increase until the Parousia brings a full revelation of him (cf 1 Cor 13:8–9, 12). There is no allusion to heretical γνῶσις, of which 2 Peter is not aware. For the title "our Lord and Savior," see *Comment* on 1:11.

αὐτῷ ἡ δόξα, "to him belongs the glory." Although doxologies to Christ are rare in early Christian literature (see *Form/Structure/Setting* section), there is at least one unquestionable example from the first century (Rev 1:5–6) and so there is no need to date 2 Peter's in the second century. Their occasional appearance is in line with other evidence of a Christian attitude of worship toward Christ, which corresponded to his function in early Christianity (cf. Matt 28:9, 17; John 5:23; Phil 2:10; Heb 1:6; Pliny, *Ep.* 10.96; and on the material in Revelation and the *Asc. Isa.*, see R. J. Bauckham, "The Worship of Jesus in Apocalyptic Christianity," *NTS* 27 [1980–81] 322–41). For 2 Peter's high Christology see *Comment* on 1:1.

εἰς ἡμέραν αἰῶνος, "on the day of eternity." This unique substitution for the phrase εἰς τοὺς αἰῶνας ("forever"), which is usual in doxologies, probably refers to the eschatological age as a day which will dawn at the Parousia (1:19) and last forever. The notion of the eternal day may derive from Isa 60:19–20: "Your sun shall no more go down, nor your moon withdraw itself; for the Lord will be your everlasting light" (RSV; note the proximity to 60:22, echoed in 2 Pet 3:12). The actual phrase ἡμέρα αἰῶνος ("the day of eternity") occurs elsewhere only in Sir 18:10: "Like a drop of water from the sea and a grain of sand so are a few years in the day of eternity" (RSV). Since that passage is based on Ps 90:4 (see *Comment* on 3:8), it is possible that our author connected the phrase ἡμέρα αἰῶνος ("the day of eternity") with his reflection of Ps 90:4: the age to come is a day in the Lord's timescale which cannot be measured in the timescale of this world.

Explanation

The message of the letter is summed up in a concluding exhortation. According to the fiction of Peter's testament, the readers have been forewarned of the false teachers who will arise after Paul's death, so that they can recognize them as the danger they are, and avoid the perils of error and apostasy which they represent. This negative advice to beware of the false teachers has as its positive counterpart the theme taken up from 1:3–11: the need for progress in the Christian life.

The concluding doxology addressed to Christ corresponds to the high Christology of 1:1 ("our God and Savior Jesus Christ"), and shows the importance which the Christian attitude of praise and worship toward Christ had for the recognition of his divine status. The author's own modification of the standard formula of the doxology reflects the eschatological theme of his letter; glory belongs to Christ not simply "forever" (the usual word), but throughout the endless day which will dawn when he comes in glory (cf. 1:19).

2 Peter

Bibliography

A. Commentaries

These are referred to throughout the commentary by authors' names only.

Barnett, A. E. "The Second Epistle of Peter." *The Interpreter's Bible.* vol. 12. New York/Nashville: Abingdon Press, 1957. **Bigg, C.** *A Critical and Exegetical Commentary on the Epistles of St. Peter and St. Jude.* ICC. Edinburgh: T. & T. Clark, 1901. **Boobyer, G. H.** "II Peter." *Peake's Commentary on the Bible,* ed. M. Black and H. H. Rowley. London: Thomas Nelson, 1962. **Bowman, J. W.** *Hebrews, James, I & II Peter.* LBC. London: SCM Press/Richmond, Virginia: John Knox Press, 1963. **Calvin, John.** *Commentaries on the Catholic Epistles.* Tr. J. Owen. Edinburgh: Calvin Translation Society, 1855. **Chaine, J.** *Les épîtres catholiques: La seconde épître de saint Pierre, les épîtres de saint Jean, l'épître de saint Jude.* EBib. 2nd ed. Paris: Gabalda, 1939. **Cranfield, C. E. B.** *I & II Peter and Jude.* TBC. London: SCM Press, 1960. **Danker, F. W.** "The Second Letter of Peter." *Hebrews, James, 1 and 2 Peter, Jude, Revelation,* by R. H. Fuller, G. S. Sloyan, G. Krodel, F. W. Danker, E. S. Fiorenza. PC. Philadelphia: Fortress Press, 1977. **Green, M.** *The Second Epistle General of Peter and the General Epistle of Jude.* TNTC. Leicester: Inter-Varsity Press, 1968. **Grundmann, W.** *Der Brief des Judas und der zweite Brief des Petrus.* THKNT 15. Berlin: Evangelische Verlagsanstalt, 1974. **Hauck, F.** *Die katholischen Briefe.* NTD 10. 3rd ed. Göttingen: Vandenhoeck & Ruprecht, 1937. **James, M. R.** *The Second Epistle General of Peter and the General Epistle of Jude.* CGTSC. Cambridge: Cambridge University Press, 1912. **Kelly, J. N. D.** *A Commentary on the Epistles of Peter and Jude.* BNTC. London: A. & C. Black, 1969. **Knopf, R.** *Die Briefe Petri und Judä.* MeyerK 12. 7th ed. Göttingen: Vandenhoeck & Ruprecht, 1912. **Kühl, E.** *Die Briefe Petri und Judae.* MeyerK 12. 6th ed. Göttingen: Vandenhoeck & Ruprecht, 1897. **Leaney, A. R. C.** *The Letters of Peter and Jude.* CBC. Cambridge: Cambridge University Press, 1967. **Lumby, J. R.** *The Epistles of St. Peter.* ExpB. 2nd ed. London: Hodder & Stoughton, 1908. **Luther, Martin.** "Sermons on the Second Epistle of St. Peter." Tr. M. H. Bertram. *The Catholic Epistles,* ed. J. Pelikan and W. A. Hansen. Luther's Works 30. St Louis, Missouri: Concordia Publishing House, 1967. **Mayor, J. B.** *The Epistle of St. Jude and the Second Epistle of St. Peter.* London: Macmillan, 1907. **Michl, J.** *Die katholischen Briefe.* RNT 8. 2nd ed. Regensburg: Verlag Friedrich Pustet, 1968. **Moffatt, J.** *The General Epistles: James, Peter, and Judas.* MNTC. London: Hodder & Stoughton, 1928. **Plumptre, E. H.** *The General Epistles of St Peter and St Jude.* CBSC. Cambridge: Cambridge University Press, 1892. **Reicke, B.** *The Epistles of James, Peter, and Jude.* AB. New York: Doubleday, 1964. **Schelkle, K. H.** *Die Petrusbriefe, der Judasbrief.* HTKNT 13/2. Freiburg/Basel/Vienna: Herder, 1961. **Schlatter, A.** *Die Briefe des Petrus, Judas, Jakobus, der Brief an die Hebräer.* Stuttgart: Calwer Verlag, 1964. **Schneider, J.** *Die Briefe des Jakobus, Petrus, Judas und Johannes: Die katholischen Briefe.* NTD 10. 9th ed. Göttingen: Vandenhoeck & Ruprecht, 1961. **Schrage, W.** *Die "katholischen" Briefe: Die Briefe des Jakobus, Petrus, Johannes und Judas,* by H. Balz and W. Schrage. NTD 10. 11th ed. Göttingen: Vandenhoeck & Ruprecht, 1973. **Senior, D.** *1 & 2 Peter,* NTM 20. Dublin: Veritas Publications, 1980. **Sidebottom, E. M.** *James, Jude and 2 Peter.* NCB. London: Thomas Nelson, 1967. **Soden, H. von.** *Hebräerbrief, Briefe des Petrus, Jakobus, Judas.* HKNT 3/2. Freiburg i. B.: J. C. B. Mohr, 1899. **Spicq, C.** *Les Epîtres de Saint Pierre.* SB. Paris: Gabalda, 1966. **Spitta, F.** *Die zweite Brief des Petrus und der Brief des Judas.* Halle a. S.: Verlag der Buchhandlung des Waisenhauses, 1885. **Stöger, A.** *The Second Epistle of*

Peter. Tr. W. Jerman. (One vol. with The First Epistle of Peter, by B. Schwank.) NTSR. London: Burns and Oates, 1969. **Wand, J. W. C.** *The General Epistles of St. Peter and St. Jude.* WC. London: Methuen, 1934. **Wettstein, J. J.** *H KAINH ΔIAΘHKH, Novum Testamentum Graece editionis receptae cum lectionibus variantibus codicum MSS, editionum aliarum, versionum et Patrum, nec non commentario pleniore ex scriptoribus veteribus Hebraeis, Graecis et Latinis Historiam et vim verborum illustrante opera et studio Joannis Jacobi Wetstenii.* Vol. 2. Amsterdam, 1752. **Windisch, H.** *Die katholischen Briefe.* HNT 15. 3rd ed., ed. H. Preisker, Tübingen: J. C. B. Mohr, 1951.

B. Other Works

Abbott, E. A. *Contrast or a prophet and a forger.* London: A. & C. Black, 1903. **Abbott, E. A.** "On the Second Epistle of St. Peter. I. Had the Author Read Josephus? II. Had the Author read St. Jude? III. Was the Author St. Peter?" *Exp* 2/3 (1882) 49–63, 139–53, 204–19. **Allmen, D. von.** "L'apocalyptique juive et le retard de la parousie en II Pierre 3:1–13." *RTP* 61 (1966) 255–74. **Associazione Biblica Italiana.** *San Pietro: Atti della XIX Settimana Biblica.* Brescia: Paideia, 1967. **Barnett, A. E.** *Paul becomes a literary influence.* Chicago: University of Chicago Press, 1941. **Bauckham, R. J.** "The Delay of the Parousia." *TynB* 31 (1980) 3–36. **Bauer, W., Arndt, W. F.,** and **Gingrich, F. W.** *A Greek-English Lexicon of the New Testament and Other Early Christian Literature.* 2nd ed., ed. F. W. Gingrich and F. W. Danker. Chicago/London: University of Chicago Press, 1979. **Bishop, E. F. F.** *Apostles of Palestine.* London: Lutterworth Press, 1958. **Blass, F., Debrunner, A.,** and **Funk, R. W.** *A Greek Grammar of the New Testament and Other Early Christian Literature.* Chicago/London: University of Chicago Press, 1961. **Boobyer, G. H.** "The indebtedness of 2 Peter to 1 Peter." *New Testament Essays: Studies in Memory of Thomas Walter Manson,* ed. A. J. B. Higgins. Manchester: Manchester University Press, 1959. 34–53. **Cavallin, H. C. C.** "The False Teachers of 2 Pt as Pseudo-Prophets." *NovT* 21 (1979) 263–70. **Charles, R. H.** ed. *The Apocrypha and Pseudepigrapha of the Old Testament.* 2 vols. Oxford: Clarendon Press, 1913. **Charles, R. H.** ed. *The Apocalypse of Baruch.* London: 1896. **Chase, F. H.** "Peter, Second Epistle of." *DB*(*H*) 3, 796–813. **Collins, J. J.** *The Sibylline Oracles of Egyptian Judaism.* SBLDS 13. Missoula, Montana: Scholars Press, 1974. **Deissmann, G. A.** *Bible Studies.* Tr. A. Grieve. Edinburgh: T. & T. Clark, 1901. **Dillenseger, P. J.** "L'authenticité de la II[a] Petri." *MFOB* 2 (1907) 173–212. **Donfried, K. P.** *The setting of Second Clement in early Christianity.* NovTSup 38. Leiden: E. J. Brill, 1974. **Dupont, J.** *Gnosis: La connaissance religieuse dans les épîtres de Saint Paul.* Louvain: Nauwelaerts/Paris: Gabalda, 1949. **Edmundson, G.** *The Church of Rome in the First Century.* BaL 1913. London: Longmans, Green, 1913. **Elliott, J. H.** "Peter, Silvanus and Mark in 1 Peter and Acts: Sociological-Exegetical Perspectives on a Petrine Group in Rome." *Wort in der Zeit: Neutestamentliche Studien.* K. H. Rengstorf Festschrift. Ed. W. Haubeck and M. Bachmann. Leiden: E. J. Brill, 1980. 250–67. **Falconer, R. A.** "Is Second Peter a Genuine Epistle to the Churches of Samaria?" *Exp* 6/5 (1902) 459–72; 6/6 (1902) 47–56, 117–27, 218–27. **Farrar, F. W.** "Dr. Abbott on the Second Epistle of St. Peter." *Exp* 2/3 (1882) 401–23. **Farrar, F. W.** "The Second Epistle of St. Peter and Josephus." *Exp* 3/8 (1888) 58–69. **Fillion, L.** "Pierre (Deuxième Epître de Saint)." *DB*(*V*) 5, cols. 398–413. **Fornberg, T.** *An Early Church in a Pluralistic Society: A Study of 2 Peter.* ConB.NT 9. Lund: C. W. K. Gleerup, 1977. **Friedlander, G.** tr. *Pirḳê de Rabbi Eliezer.* 2nd ed. New York: Hermon Press, 1965. **Green, E. M. B.** *2 Peter Reconsidered.* TynNTL 1960. London: Tyndale Press, 1961. **Guthrie, D.** *New Testament Introduction.* 3rd ed. London: Inter-Varsity Press, 1970. **Harnisch, W.** *Eschatologische Existenz: Ein exegetische Beitrag zum Sachanliegen von 1. Thessalonicher 4, 13–5, 11.* FRLANT 110. Göttingen: Vandenhoeck & Ruprecht, 1973. **Hastings, J.** ed. *Dictionary of the Apostolic Church.* 2 vols. Edinburgh: T. & T. Clark, 1915, 1918. **Hastings, J.** ed. *A Dictionary of the Bible.* 5 vols. Edinburgh:

T. & T. Clark, 1898–1904. **Hennecke, E., Schneemelcher, W.,** and **Wilson, R. McL.** *New Testament Apocrypha.* 2 vols. London: Lutterworth Press, 1963, 1965. **Holzmeister, U.** "Vocabularium secundae Epistolae S. Petri erroresque quidam de eo divulgati." *Bib* 30 (1949) 339–55. **James, M. R.** *The Lost Apocrypha of the Old Testament.* London: S. P. C. K./New York: Macmillan, 1920. **Käsemann, E.** "An Apologia for Primitive Christian Eschatology." *Essays on New Testament Themes.* SBT 41. Tr. W. J. Montague. London: SCM Press, 1964. 169–95. **Kittel, G.** *Theological Dictionary of the New Testament.* Tr. G. W. Bromiley. 10 vols. Grand Rapids, Michigan: Eerdmans, 1964–76. **Klein, G.** *Die zwölf Apostel: Ursprung und Gehalt einer Idee.* FRLANT 59. Göttingen: Vandenhoeck & Ruprecht, 1961. **Klinger, J.** "The Second Epistle of Peter: An Essay in Understanding." *SVTQ* 17 (1973) 152–69. **Knoch, O.** "Das Vermächtnis des Petrus: Der zweite Petrusbrief." *Wort Gottes in der Zeit.* K. H. Schelkle Festschrift. Ed. H. Feld and J. Nolte. Düsseldorf: Patmos-Verlag, 1973. 149–65. (= Knoch, O. *Die "Testamente" des Petrus und Paulus.* SBS 62. Stuttgart: KBW Verlag, 1973. 65–81.) **Kolenkow, A. B.** "The Genre Testament and Forecasts of the Future in the Hellenistic Jewish Milieu." *JSJ* 6 (1975) 57–71. **Kümmel, W. G.** *Introduction to the New Testament.* Tr. H. C. Kee. 2nd ed. London: SCM Press, 1975. **Lightfoot, J. B.** *The Apostolic Fathers.* Ed. and completed J. R. Harmer. London: Macmillan, 1891. **Lindemann, A.** *Paulus im ältesten Christentum: Das Bild des Apostels und die Rezeption der paulinischen Theologie in der frühchristlichen Literatur bis Marcion.* BHT 58. Tübingen: J. C. B. Mohr, 1979. **McNamara, M.** "The Unity of Second Peter: A Reconsideration." *Scr* 12 (1960) 13–19. **Malan, S. C.** *The Book of Adam and Eve, also called The Conflict of Adam and Eve with Satan.* London: Williams & Norgate, 1882. **Marín, F.** "Apostolicidad de los escritos neotestamentarios." *EE* 50 (1975) 211–39. **Mayer, R.** *Die biblische Vorstellung vom Weltenbrand: Eine Untersuchung über die Beziehungen zwischen Parsismus und Judentum.* BOS 4. Bonn: Selbstverlag des Orientalischen Seminars der Universität Bonn, 1956. **Metzger, B. M.** *A Textual Commentary on the Greek New Testament.* London/New York: United Bible Societies, 1971. **Migne, J. P.** *Patrologiae Cursus Completus. Series Graeca.* 167 vols. Paris: J. P. Migne, 1857–66. **Migne, J. P.** *Patrologiae Cursus Completus. Series Latina.* 217 vols. Paris: J. P. Migne, 1841–55. **Moulton, J. H.** *A Grammar of New Testament Greek. Vol. II. Accidence and Word-Formation,* by J. H. Moulton and W. F. Howard. Edinburgh: T. & T. Clark, 1929. *Vol. III. Syntax,* by N. Turner. Edinburgh: T. & T. Clark, 1963. *Vol. IV. Style,* by N. Turner. Edinburgh: T. & T. Clark, 1976. **Moulton, J. H.** and **Milligan, G.** *The Vocabulary of the Greek Testament illustrated from the papyri and other non-literary sources.* London: Hodder & Stoughton, 1929. **Neyrey, J. H.** "The Apologetic Use of the Transfiguration in 2 Peter 1:16–21." *CBQ* 42 (1980) 504–19. **Neyrey, J. H.** "The Form and Background of the Polemic in 2 Peter." *JBL* 99 (1980) 407–31. **Neyrey, J. H.** *The Form and Background of the Polemic in 2 Peter.* Unpublished doctoral dissertation, Yale University, 1977. **Olivier, F.** "Une correction au texte du Nouveau Testament: II Pierre 3, 10." *Essais dans le domaine du monde gréco-romain antique et dans celui du Nouveau Testament.* Geneva: Librairie Droz, 1963. 129–152. (= *RTP* 8 (1920) 237–78.) **Pirot, L., Cazelles, H.,** and **Feuillet, A.** ed. *Supplément au Dictionnaire de la Bible.* Paris: Letouzey & Ané, 1928–. **Repo, E.** *Der "Weg" als Sebstbezeichnung des Urchristentums: Eine traditionsgeschichtliche und semasiologische Untersuchung.* STAT B.132,2. Helsinki: Suomalainen Tiedeakatemia, 1964. **Robinson, J. A. T.** *Redating the New Testament.* London: SCM Press, 1976. **Robson, E. I.** *Studies in the Second Epistle of St Peter.* Cambridge: Cambridge University Press, 1915. **Salmon, G.** *A Historical Introduction to the Study of the Books of the New Testament.* 1st ed. London: John Murray, 1885. **Schelkle, K. H.** "Spätapostolische Briefe als frühkatholisches Zeugnis." *Neutestamentliche Aufsätze für J. Schmid.,* ed. J. Blinzler, O. Kuss, F. Mussner. Regensburg: Verlag Friedrich Pustet, 1963. 225–32. **Schlosser, J.** "Les jours de Noé et de Lot: A propos de Luc, XVII, 26–30." *RB* 80 (1973) 13–36. **Schmitt, J.** "Pierre (Seconde épître de)." *DBSup*

7, cols. 1455–63. **Selwyn, E. C.** *The Christian Prophets and the Prophetic Apocalypse.* London: Macmillan, 1900. **Smith, T. V.** *Petrine Controversies in Early Christianity: Attitudes Towards Peter in Christian Writings of the First Two Centuries.* Unpublished doctoral dissertation, King's College, University of London, 1981. **Spicq, C.** *Notes de Lexicographie Néo-Testamentaire.* 2 vols. OBO 22. Fribourg: Editions Universitaires/Göttingen: Vandenhoeck & Ruprecht, 1978. **Stauffer, E.** *New Testament Theology.* Tr. J. Marsh. London: SCM Press, 1955. **Strobel, A.** *Untersuchungen zum eschatologischen Verzögerungsproblem auf Grund der spätjüdisch-urchristlichen Geschichte von Habakuk 2, 2 ff.* NovTSup 2. Leiden: E. J. Brill, 1961. (Talmud) **Epstein, I.** ed. *The Babylonian Talmud.* 35 vols. London: Soncino Press, 1935–52. **Vermes, G.** *The Dead Sea Scrolls in English.* 3rd ed. Harmondsworth, Middx.: Penguin Books, 1968. **Vermes, G.** *Scripture and Tradition in Judaism: Haggadic studies.* SPB 4. Leiden: E. J. Brill, 1961. **Vigoroux, F.** and **Pirot, L.** ed. *Dictionnaire de la Bible.* 5 vols. Paris: Letouzey & Ané, 1895–1912. **Vögtle, A.** *Das Neue Testament und die Zukunft des Kosmos.* Düsseldorf: Patmos-Verlag, 1970. **Werdermann, H.** *Die Irrlehrer des Judas- und 2. Petrusbriefes.* BFCT 17/6. Gütersloh: C. Bertelsmann, 1913. **Zahn, T.** *Introduction to the New Testament.* vol. 2. Tr. M. W. Jacobus and others. Edinburgh: T. & T. Clark, 1909. **Zmijewski, J.** "Apostolische Paradosis und Pseudepigraphie im Neuen Testament. 'Durch Erinnerung wachhalten' (2 Petr 1, 13; 3, 1)." *BZ* 23 (1979) 161–71.

Index of Ancient Authors

Index of Modern Authors

Index of Principal Subjects

Index of Principal Passages Cited

Old Testament

Apocrypha

New Testament

Old Testament Pseudepigrapha

Dead Sea Scrolls

Targums

Rabbinic Literature

New Testament Apocrypha and Other Early Christian Literature

Apostolic Fathers